My Dearest

My Dearest,

A war story, a love story, a true story of WWI by those who lived it

Publisher: Property People JV Ltd

Published by Property People JV Ltd, company registration no. 5732761 (England and Wales)
A Member of the Publishers Licensing Society

© Copyright: all material in this book is copyright of Property People JV Ltd 2014
This book is sold subject to the condition that is shall not, by way of trade or otherwise, be lent, resold, hired out, or otherwise circulated without the publisher's prior consent in any form of binding or cover other than that in which it is published and without a similar condition including this condition being imposed on the subsequent purchaser.

Compiled and edited by Aura Kate Hargreaves
Editorial Design by Dave Radley
www.printechnique.co.uk, printed by Henry Ling Limited in England

ISBN: 978-0-9929965-0-5

Contents

Who's Who   p.4
London 1914-16   p.6-35
France & Belgium 1917   p.36-152
Missing 1917   p.153-165
Prisoner of War 1917-18   p.166-500
Sheerness 1919   p.501-525
Epilogue   p.526-528

Who's who

David Henry Taylor = brother to Ethel (Ginger), son to Fanny

Ginger = Ethel Linn (nee Taylor), David's sister, married to John, living in New Jersey, mother to Erl and Jack, old school friend of May's

Fanny Taylor = mother to David and Ethel (Ginger), nee Christmas

Peter = David's dog

May (Mabel) Muggridge = David's "Dearest", sister to Bert and Ern and Ethel

Bert = Albert, May's younger brother

Ethel Muggridge = May's sister

Ern = Ernest, May's older brother

Polly Day = "poor relation" of Fanny Taylor

Aunt Anne = one of Fanny Taylor's sisters (she had several)

Auntie Bessie = younger sister of Fanny Taylor

Beatie Bulford = a relative on David's father side

Webbers = David had a quantity surveyor pupilship with WH Webber 1907-1910

Aunt Sophia = one of Fanny Taylor's sisters, married Alfred Pratt who had his own business in Watford

Aunt Maria = a sister of Fanny Taylor

Mrs Stanley = a relative of Fanny's

Mrs Capel = nee Christmas, a relative of Fanny's

W Rushbrooke = David's old headmaster at St Olave's

Edward Campbell 'B' Coy 2nd KRRC = David's senior officer

Miss Willsher, a piano playing friend of May's

Maud = an old school friend of May's

Mr & Mrs Sandys = May's aunt and uncle (May's mother nee Sandys)

Vi = cousin of May's

Miss Rudge = a old teacher of whom May was very fond

and where

56 Ramsden Rd, Balham = home to David and Fanny

18 Manor Rd, Beckenham = home to May and her family

246 Aycrigg Ave, Passaic, New Jersey = home to Ethel (Ginger) and family

5 Moorgate St, 5th Floor, London EC1 = May's office Northern Assurance

Watford = family home of Christmas family

Upcot Street = Fanny Taylor owned several houses on this street

Glen Roy = name of house where uncle & aunt of David's lived

WWI

From 28th July 1914 until 11th November 1918 a global war was fought, centred in Europe, known as the World War or the Great War. In America it was initially called the European War. On the approach to the Second World War, the Great War became known as the First World War, World War I (WWI or WW1).

The war cost nearly 9 million lives and nearly 30 million casualties or missing on both sides.

Key dates in this compilation:
Battle of Ypres Oct/Nov 1914
David joined up December 1915
Battle of Somme July/Nov 1916
David to France 6th Feb 1917
Battle of Arras April/May 1917
Battle of Nieuport Bains 10th July 1917
David is PoW 10th July 1917 til 11th Nov 1918
David home 19th Dec 1918
David demobilised 28th March 1919

14. MEMBERS.

The Surveyors' Institution
(INCORPORATED BY ROYAL CHARTER).

12, GREAT GEORGE STREET,
WESTMINSTER, S.W.

May, 1914

FINAL EXAMINATION.

DEAR SIR,

I have the pleasure to inform you that you have passed the Final Examination of the Institution.

I am directed to call your special attention to the following conditions governing transfer to the Fellowship :—

That the Candidate shall have had five years' experience as a Surveyor in circumstances satisfactory to the Council, either

- (*a*) As a Principal in an established business as defined by the By-Laws ;
- (*b*) As responsible Manager of an established business as defined by the By-Laws ;
- (*c*) As Head of a Department in the office of a public body ; reporting direct to his Board or Council.

Yours faithfully,

A. GODDARD,
Secretary.

D. H. Taylor, Esq.

NOTE.—Owing to the large amount of correspondence entailed by the examinations, no particulars of the marks obtained can be given to successful Candidates.

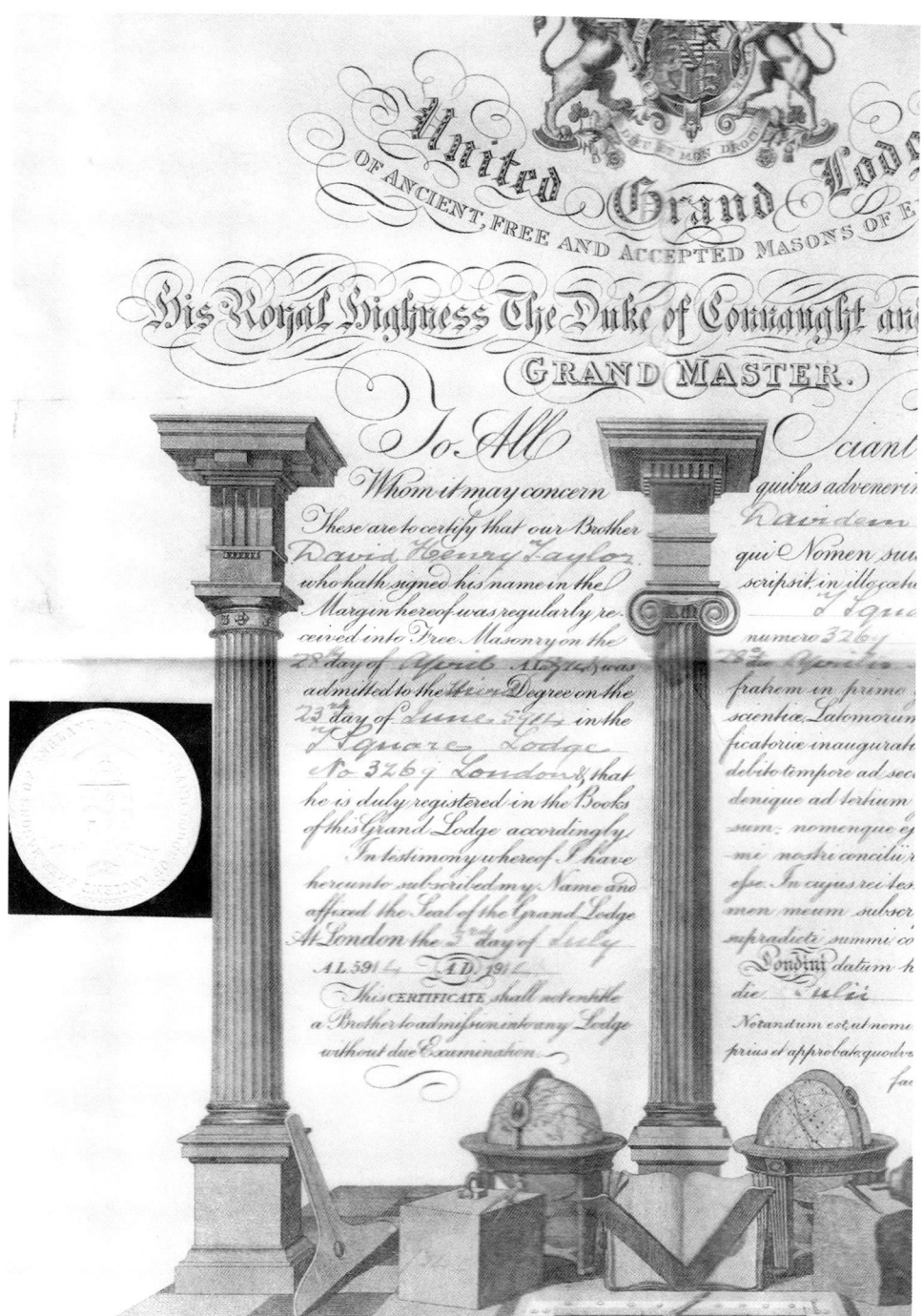

3rd July 1914

my dearest 7

Ypres

10 cartes vues phototon   Série 2.

YPRES
RUE STEURS.

18.

The Surveyors' Institution.
(INCORPORATED BY ROYAL CHARTER.)

12, Great George Street,
Westminster, S.W.,
April 27th 1915

Dear Sir,

I have the pleasure to inform you that you have been transferred from the class of "Professional Associates" to that of "Fellows" of the Institution, and a fresh Diploma will be forwarded to you in due course.

The amount due from you on the transfer is stated below, and I shall be obliged if you will forward me a cheque.

David H. Taylor Esq
56 Ramsden Road
Balham S.W.

I am, dear Sir,

Yours faithfully,

A. GODDARD,
Secretary.

Amount due:
Difference of Entrance Fee between the two classes ... £ 2 : 2 : 0
Difference of Subscription for year 1915 ... ... 1 : 1 : 0
3 . 3 . 0

P

my dearest 11

David to Ginger (Ethel Linn)   56 Ramsden Rd, Balham SW   15th Sept 1915

Dear Ginger,

I have just returned from a holiday at Brighton and have had a glorious time there.

Mum went to Chesham and afterwards to Watford and Polly to Broadstairs.

Mum stayed with Aunt Annie and took Peter with her and from her account I should think the whole of the dogs at Chesham and Watford were itching to fight and Peter most kindly obliged them. One particular dog went for him and then of course the dog's owner went for Peter upon which Mum joined the battle and went for the dog's owner (a sort of four sided duel a la Midshipman Easy) but the most upset of the whole lot was Aunt Bessie who really had nothing to do with it except look on.

Again, at Chesham, Peter found a convenient opening in the garden hedge and went off for a picnic on his lonesome. On missing him Mum went one way and Aunt Bessie the other but found no Peter although they went for some distance. In the meantime a thunder storm came and they both got wet through. About two hours afterwards Peter turned up also wet through and I think was gently reproved with the whip.

I have just returned from viewing the damage done by the Zeppelins last week.

It is bad, but not so bad as I expected from the reports I heard from various people, but reports get so exaggerated.

I was very glad that Mum was out of London when they came as they were pretty close to us all.

Just around the corner from Upcot Street a house was smashed, and some of our people were out in the street in their night clothes, but luckily nothing was done to our places.

Alberta Street people also seem to have been out and they are most upset of the lot.

I first went to Farringdon Road, opposite the Goods Station one house had been gutted, the front wall of the two top stories blown into the street, and the two houses on either side considerably damaged of of course the windows for some distance either way and opposite were smashed.

In Leather Lane, the L.C.C. buildings in which Beatie Bulford lives (only a block at the back of hers) a bomb stripped the roof, blew part of the front wall into the street, tore out the windows bodily, the bedding is hanging down the front of the building, (some of it in the street) and of course the windows and shop fronts up and down the street are all gone. In this case the explosion had a most curious effect, the two windows immediately below the damaged wall are still perfect the glass not being even cracked whilst those opposite and on either side are smashed to atoms.

A Public House in Red Lion Street, (just at the back of Bedford Road) looks for all the world as though somebody has lifted it bodily and dropped it again, it has that crumpled appearance and the Penny Bank next door has no windows left and the shop fronts all round are gone.

Wood Street (which you remember was burnt a few years back) and Aldermanbury the darlings sprinkled with incendiary bombs setting fire to several large buildings. It was here that the most damage was done as 5 or 6 large blocks of offices and warehouses were gutted.

They played the giddy ox with Liverpool Street Station, wrecking a signal box so that no trains could get in and had to stop for some time at Bethnal Green.

One bomb fell on a bus outside Liverpool Street and the bus and passengers (about 8 in number I think) went to heaven suddenly.

Some damage was done in Lombard Street and Moorgate Street, and a corner of a roof was knocked off in Cheapside opposite the G.P.O.

All this seems a great deal, but when one considers the size of London and the number of people there, it is very small indeed (with all the damage about 100 were killed and injured) and people taking little notice of it and already in most cases they are rebuilding as fast as possible, new shop fronts are being put in and in the meantime the shops display large notices "Business as usual".

Very few people were looking at the damage and those chiefly ladies out for amusement from the suburbs.

The streets are barricaded round the damaged parts and as an extra attraction a recruiting meeting was in full swing against one of the barricades.

In Leather Lane the Cheap Jacks attracted far more attention and larger crowds than did the damaged buildings but then you see it happened 4 days ago and so much goes on now that it must be something big to attract attention at all.

One result is, that the Insurance Companies have a crowd 3 deep in their offices.

I insured everything back in the spring at Lloyds before the Government Insurance scheme came along and in consequence had to pay 6% (that is 2/6%) more, but never mind it set Mums more or less at rest when previous raids came.

Immediately after I insured there was a raid and Harry insured and he had to pay ¾% so I considered at the time that I scored.

There is another raid just reported "somewhere", this makes 5 in 7 days, pretty good going, however I don't know whether they all got back as there are stories on one being brought down in Kent and another in Essex.

Whilst at Brighton there were airships or aeroplanes along practically every day, and one day we saw about 30 aeroplanes flying towards Shoreham.

With regard to the hinges they were £1-7-9, and I sent 5/6 to Kleo for that cable to you, making £1-13-3. I don't know of anything else.

We are in a lively state at the office as we have just moved and everything is lost and will never be found again from the look of things.

Our new address is Furnival Street, Holborn E.C., telegrams Morseby, Fleet, London A.B.C. code.

The Kennington folks shut up this week, but I don't know when they move, their new address is Ambleside Avenue, Streatham.

Many thanks for the newspapers and cuttings, I was very amused at the Hudson River battle. That magazine part of the New York Times is particularly interesting. You might send some more and also any important news, as you get much more news than we do. The photos are better than we get too as you get both sides.

I see that I have written 8 pages so that as my fountain pen is exhausted I will now go and get my hair cut.

Yours

David

Lord Derby's Scheme

In the spring of 1915 voluntary enlistments had averaged 100,000 men per month, but this was unsustainable. The upper age limit was raised but it became clear that voluntary recruitment was insufficient

On 15th July 1915 the government passed the National Registration Act to stimulate recruitment and to discover how many men aged between 15 and 65 were engaged in each trade. The results of this census showed there were nearly 5 million males of military age who were not in the forces, if which 1.6 million were in the protected, high or scarce skills jobs.

Edward Stanley, Lord Derby played a major part in raising volunteers and was appointed Director-General of Recruiting in October 1915. Within 5 days of his appointment he brought forward a programme, often called the Derby Scheme although its official title was the Group Scheme, for raising the numbers. The scheme informed men aged 18 to 40 that they could continue to enlist voluntarily or attest with an obligation to come if called up later on.

The War Office notified the public that the last day for voluntary enlistment would be 15 December 1915.

David to Ginger   Balham   4th Nov 1915

Dear Ginger,

Again we have had the Zeppelins, this time I was fortunate enough to have a very good view of the whole thing, (a great many people did not see them but only heard them).

It happened about 9.30. Earlier in the evening a passing man said to me, "Another Zep raid tonight" – I did not take much notice, thinking that another had been reported in the papers "somewhere". I happened to be on the common, when I heard boom, boom, boom, and thought that some guns were being tested, or something of the sort, as we often hear them now and also we have a practice ground for bomb throwing on Clapham Common – then almost immediately two more booms – it struck me that it might be Zeps and I looked round the sky but saw nothing – then there was a burst of firing and I saw my beauty just coming from behind some trees. It was really a beautiful sight, a large cigar shaped bar of silver, floating along, shining in the light of the search lights. It was a fine clear evening, with the stars shining but no moon and so of course pretty dark, which threw the Zep up more. The guns were going now for all they were worth and I could see the shells bursting all round, for all the world like stars popping in and out, but they did not seem to hit, and I stood and watched it out of sight going South East.

Later in the evening about 12 o'clock, having thoroughly enjoyed their stay amongst us I suppose, they returned and again I had a good view, but this time it was so far off (over Aldgate) that it only looked like a large elongated star, and the shells looked like little flashes of light round it. One or two shells seemed to get very near, but it was too far away to tell definitely. It seemed to remain still for some minutes and then turned and made off. I may say that they only appear to keep two search lights on it with another just hovering around outside, nearly all the others are out!

Again they have done comparatively little damage, although the loss of life is greater. They dropped bombs all round our new office again (within about 100 yards) in Chancery Lane and Grays Inn. Harry was in the thick of it as he was in the office at the time. This is his tale. He heard an explosion, and then a second. He put on his hat and rushed down and as he opened the front door he saw a bomb falling, he closed the door and the bomb exploded, he opened the door again, and saw another bomb falling, closed the door again, and that one exploded. He then went out and could see the Zep just going away. By this time the street was full of sulphur fumes. He went down the street, turned the corner, when another bomb fell close enough to blow back the tails of his coat. He then went into Chancery Lane where by this time there was a young river flowing, one bomb having burst a water main. He afterwards came back to the office and got some brandy, which he took out into Holborn and gave to some women, bringing several back to the office.

I have been round to look at some of the damage. The bomb in Chancery Lane fell in the road just outside Stone Buildings, by the Safe Deposit, smashed all the glass around, knocked lumps of the stonework off, and burst the water main. The water got under the wood block paving and lifted it for about 100 yards, leaving it in graceful waves. An incendiary bomb fell on

Stone Buildings, causing a small fire. The bomb which fell in Gary's Inn, fell in that big grass ground close to the houses, and has blown out the windows so that you can see through from front to back of the ground floor offices and books fittings furniture etc etc all mixed up together, just as though "the devil with his pitch fork" had been stirring things up.

We are doing some work to a block of offices backing on to Grays Inn, about 100 yards away from the spot where the bomb fell.

It has blown out all the glass on two sides of the building, a great many of the internal fanlights are gone, it cracked two of the walls, and on the far side of the building it blew open the casement windows, wrenching the fastenings off and in two cases snapping the cast iron stays. They were certainly cheap things but they were cut clear in two, although the glass of the windows was sound.

One bomb fell in the court yard of the Law Courts, knocking lumps of the masonry off and smashing all the windows around, and if that isn't cheek tell me.

Another fell in the old skating rink in Aldwych, and it has made a mess of it – of course being a light temporary sort of building, the explosion ripped the whole thing from end to end, leaving just the roof trusses bare.

Another fell in the road in Aldwych, opposite the Gaid, bursting a gas main which took fire and burnt for some considerable time, but of course did not spread.

Another fell on the building next door to the Lyceum, doing a good deal of damage but the building is still standing.

In Algate I believe a bank at the corner of the Minories was smashed and the various windows and shop fronts all round were pretty well smashed up.

Croydon was visited, and some damage done, but on the whole it is chiefly glass that has suffered most, as usual.

Various reports get about, one that there was a panic in the Lyceum, but two women told Harry that they were at the theatre when the bomb fell, and that the entrance doors were knocked down and burnt, but were quickly put out, and that the audience walked out quietly over them.

Another tale is that George Grosswith was singing when the bombs fell outside, he stopped, and said "Well we are as safe here as outside, let us go on with the performance" and he went on singing.

Of course one hears the usual "why don't they do this and why don't they do that" from the enquire-within-upon-everything gentlemen who are ever ready to give advice about anything to anybody, but when one sees the shells bursting round the Zeps, one realises how difficult it is to hit them, especially when they are moving quickly (the first one I saw came and was out of sight within ten minutes).

I have sent your punching ball to Kleo and she has written to saying that the men are highly delighted with it. It was £1-1-0 and there was some delay at first owing to the fact that they had none in stock and the only excuse one hears on all sides today to account for delay is "on account of the war".

We have been over to Bessie's at Pendle Road – Archie has got a two to three years job at

Huddersfield and has already gone. Bessie is now letting the house and is following as soon as possible.

Yours

David

David to Ginger   Balham   28th Dec 1915

Dear Ginger,

Many thanks for the coat hangers, they will be most useful when I get my commission, that is if I do get one.

I don't know if Mum has told you that I have joined the Army. I have joined under Lord Derby's scheme and shall be called up with my class.

I had also joined previously The London University Officers Training Corps Engineers Unit and I am now down at Kensington being instructed in the gentle art of "strafing" Germans.

I shall of course apply for a commission in the Engineers as soon as possible, that is if the powers that be will allow me to continue with the O.T.C. and do not shove me into anything they think fit when my class is called up under Derby's scheme.

I have not been to camp yet but that will come later I expect.

Some while ago I thought of applying for a commission direct and after much trial and tribulation I gave it up on Mr Rushbrooke's advice. I got the signatures of two magistrates as to my good moral character and then went to Rushie to get his as to my education and he strongly advised me not to send the application in as I had no military training, but to join an O.T.C. He pointed out that I should be responsible for the lives of the men under me and that we had already lost large numbers through young officers being incompetent. I have since heard that the War Office are now not giving commissions to men without previous military training.

Mum wants you to buy the boy something for his birthday and has asked me to send you £1-1-0 for this. I am enclosing cheque made up as follows:

Dr Constable's bill	£3-5-6	Cheque for	£5-2-0
Hunby's	7-6	Boy's present	1-1-0
Cable	5-6	Cheque	26-8-9
Hangers	1-7-9		32-11-9
Punch Ball	1-1-0		6-17-0
Cake	6-9		
Pipe	3-0		
	£6-17-0		£25-14-9

I sent the pipe on to Uncle John so that he got it before Christmas day.

I am sorry I was unable to send a cable to Billy Mason but Jean wrote saying that they had not got his address and he has received no letters since he has been away. I hope you received yours safely.

I am sorry Jack did not get his present but I sent him a rag book enclosed with Erl's dolls, so I suppose this got lost in the post.

Yours

David

David to Ginger   Cadet DH Taylor No 7137   Artists Rifles O.T.C.
28th County of London   Hare Hall Camp, Gidea Park, Romford Essex
Date Unknown, Year Doubtful

Dear Ginger,
It is your birthday within a fortnight I think and I am enclosing a small brooch to replace that other you had.
I tried to get one at Christmas at Christmas but was unable to do so.
The above is my present address, but if you write to me, address the letter to Ramsden Rd as the Angels in heaven above know where I may be by the time you write, such is the indefinite state of life at the present moment.
I have not written before as I really have had no time.
I transferred to the Artists as I seemed to be getting no further forward in the University O.T.C. This regiment as you probably know is an ordinary Territorial Regiment but was made an O.T.C. by French out at the front.
I was at Headquarters in London for several weeks drilling in Regents Park and at Hampstead, and have now been sent down here.
I have missed several things, as several fellows out of the 11 who joined the same day as I did, have already been sent to France to get their training there.
We are fairly hard worked, as not only do we have the ordinary Tommy's work to do, but we have the officers part to do as well.
We are up about 5.45, wash etc and have tea and biscuits (this sounds better than it is, as the tea has no sugar in it, and sometimes no milk and the biscuits are like those on the Viking, only stale).
At 6.30 physical drill until 7. We then go back and make our beds, clean buttons, belts and equipment generally. Breakfast 7.45 consisting of porridge (made with water and served in an enamelled bowl, from which you dip it on to an enamelled plate, with a mug), boiled bacon (in slices ½ inch thick, put on the same plate after you have eaten your porridge), bread and margarine (if you are lucky) and marmalade (if there is any left), and all this eaten from the one plate with the same knife, fork and spoon. You dip your tea in a mug from a pail placed on the floor, and stir it with the spoon used for the porridge.
At 8.30 parade for the days work, which may be squad drill, platoon drill, company drill, or forty other kinds of drill, with two or three lectures in between times.
You have to take lunch rations with you, consisting of bully beef (a very close course pressed beef in tins) and bread. Lunch from 1 to 2 o'clock. Parade at 2 for work again, which may be trench digging, map reading and drawing etc etc until about 4 or a little after.
Dinner at 5 pm – stew (served in the same way as the porridge) and bread, and on alternate days, pudding, usually plum duff, of course eaten from the same plate.
The whole of the above for 1/- a day inclusive, paid weekly.
At 6 o'clock parade again for a lecture until 7, when we are free for the remainder of the evening in order to write up lectures etc.

We have to be in at 9.15 and all lights out at 10, and generally speaking, you don't want to go on after 10.

The camp being full I have been put into en empty house with 15 others.

There are 4 in my room (size 12' x 12') and we have three planks 9" wide placed on two trestles raised about 6" off the floor for beds. These of course we put up and take down each day.

Beside this we have four blankets and I have "borrowed" a fifth.

I don't know when these blankets were new or whether they are ever washed, but they are a discreet dark brown colour, so that one takes them as they come, and does not wonder what they would be like had they once been white.

I could not sleep much the first night, but I have now got quite used to the hard bed, and can sleep as long as possible.

I was inoculated against typhoid in London, this you get in two doses, the stuff being injected into your arm and of course it makes your arm swell and ache a bit, and you feel as though you have got influenza for two or three days.

You get a variety of jobs to do – for instance the first day I became an Artist I was sent with about 16 others with a pantechnican to Liverpool Street.

Imagine one clothed in purple and fine linen riding in state through the City of London seated on top of a pantechnican and on arrival at Liverpool Street unloading boxes and other stores from a train, into the state coach and then driving back to Headquarters.

Another day I was Hall Porter at headquarters, yesterday I was house orderly, which means that I had had to clean the house from top to bottom, scrubbing the floor and being general housemaid. Its a gay life.

I get Saturday afternoon and Sunday fairly free unless they happen to take us for a route march or some such country excursion, but all leave has been stopped, so that I am bound down to a 2 mile radius of the camp.

However, being close to London is better than being a long way off, and Mum came down yesterday.

I am sending some photos (as demanded) but they have not yet turned up although I had them taken weeks ago.

Yours

David

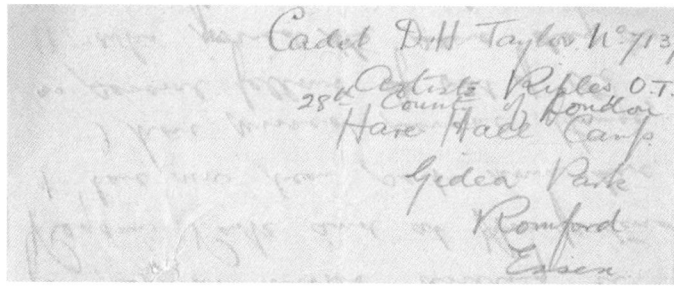

Somewhere in the U.S.A.   Sometime in June (1916)
(see post-mark for more definite information!)

Ginger to David

Dear Kid,

The order re not quoting your address etc is a real brainy one, seeing the powers that be did not order the post office to leave the post-mark off, but it is training for the Front presumably. I am enclosing a programme of a fine show we saw on Saturday – maybe it is being shown in England. Our national anthem was played three times and the crowd stood up each time, cheered King George's picture etc. I really think there must have been a few British there. I comment on the rising for our national anthem, as when the American was played with the Flag (oh! Those flags!) on the sheet there was considerable hesitation. However, they did finally stand up.

This is the land of flags. I don't know if I told you the story (a newspaper report of a few weeks ago) of a carter who saw a Stars and Stripes in the gutter. Having no red flag to hang on the end of the girder he was carting, he picked up The flag, it having red in it, and tied it to the end of the girder. He was hauled up and fined for disrespect to The Flag. From the manner of the explanation it was obvious the man meant nothing, especially as he found it in the gutter, but he was not let off.

Another instance occurred last week. We hear about the International Brotherhood, and apparently brothers of all nationalities met in a backyard in Brooklyn and burnt their respective flags, to signify that there should be no nationality. The American "got lock up and put in the clink" for desecrating the flag. How much he will be fined I know not. Personally I think the bunch of them must have been graduating for a lunatic asylum, but you will note that in a free country you may not burn flags if you want to. Still they know our national anthem.

I am sending some pictures today. Next week I hope to send you a "Current History" – a lot of excellent articles in it which I am sure you will enjoy.

We are thinking of purchasing the set, as it will be a valuable history to have, quoting, as it does, so many viewpoints.

I wonder how Dick Taylor has managed to escape the Army. It does not seem fair to me that he should escape while Walter Writer (with his small children) should be called up – nor economy either. If I were over there I should be very tempted to write to the Tribunal at Clapham Junction pointing out our slacker. I cannot help wondering at some of the healthy young Britishers over here. Cane who visits here is under no misapprehension as to what I think of him, or if so, he must be as dense as a turnip.

We went to Lord Kitchener's Memorial Service at Trinity Church, Wall St., on Wednesday morning. The church was packed to the pavement, and we were part of the crowd in the vestibule. The service was spoilt for me by a small man who tried to shuffle – by means of pushing – to the front. He succeeded apparently until he got to the back of me. Unfortunately, to be purposely arouses my temper to a higher pitch than most things, and I had fully

determined if I had to take him by the scruff of his neck and gently lead him out that he was not going to push in front of me. He was not having a nice time when suddenly John discovered what was going on, and before he had time to realise what had happened, the pusher found himself behind a much taller man than himself. By the gradual movements of the crowd the three of us found ourselves nearer the interior between a comparatively narrow door way. There is beautiful panelling with well raised ridges, and presumably the gentleman had the time of his life between John and those ridges. Every time anyone struggled out, the gentleman had the ridges well moulded into his form, not to mention John's elbow on the other side, and he was not allowed to move from that position til the service was over.
The war news generally makes pretty good reading at present.
Your letters make good reading too, so please send more.

Yours ever,

Ethel.

LYCEUM THEATRE

LYCEUM THEATRE COMPANY .... PROPRIETOR
DANIEL FROHMAN .... PRESIDENT

THIS THEATRE, UNDER NORMAL CONDITIONS, WITH EVERY SEAT OCCUPIED, CAN BE EMPTIED IN LESS THAN THREE MINUTES. LOOK AROUND NOW, CHOOSE THE NEAREST EXIT TO YOUR SEAT, AND IN CASE OF DISTURBANCE OF ANY KIND, TO AVOID THE DANGERS OF PANIC, WALK (DO-NOT RUN) TO THAT EXIT.

WEEK BEGINNING MONDAY, JUNE 5, 1916.
Twice Daily, 2:15 and 8:15 P. M.

How Britain Prepared

A MOTION PICTURE MESSAGE TO AMERICA
OFFICAL FILMS OF THE BRITISH EMPIRE
Produced under the auspices of
Earl Kitchener, Minister of War; Hon. Arthur Balfour, First Lord of the Admiralty; Hon. Lloyd George, Minister of Munitions.
Made under the direction of CHARLES URBAN.
The Patriot Film Corporation, New York, Lessees and Distributors.
Al. Lichtman, General Manager.

Overture...................... Edward J. Howe, Musical Director

BRITAIN'S NEW ARMY IN THE MAKING
Showing how four million civilians were turned into a highly efficient army within fifteen months

PART I.

(a) Recruiting and Drilling of Volunteers
Liberal response to the Recruiting Officers' appeal—Volunteers receiving their papers and marching to barracks—Emerging khaki-clad—The first drill—Drill of Army Instructors,—Who, in turn, drill the Recruits—Bayonet charge practice—Cavalry sword drill—Wagon drill—Games to keep the men supple—Route marching.

(b) Making Munition (Manufacturing Shrapnel Shells)
Steel rods being cut into lengths for forging—Carting the rough shell case stampings to machine shops—Turning a shell—Women and girls working lathes—"Drop stamp"—Making fuses—Assembling and filling shells—Packing the finished shells for transport—Armored lorries convey same to destination.

(c) Trench Work
The "spade" brigade—Sappers—Digging trenches—Roofing a dug-out—Erecting barbed wire entanglements—Manning the trenches—Rushing a trench—Bombing during the charge—New trench weapons; the Lewis gun and types of catapults—Disguising trench from aeroplane—A communication tunnel—Throwing hand grenades and exploding bombs—Sapping and blowing up mines—Warfare in the chalk trenches—Using portable steel shields—Enfilading trenches, etc., etc.

(d) Cavalry, Artillery, and Mounted Infantry
Cavalry in training—Jumping obstacles—Charging a hill—Lance and sabre practice—Reconnoitring—Field Artillery on road—Mounted Infantry Advance—Dismount—Approach—Retreat—To horse and away.

(e) Field Telegraph and Signalling Corps
The Engineer Corps—The "reel" Mule and Driver—Preparing a station—Laying the wire—Tapping wire and sending message—Another station—Protecting a wire crossing a road—The Operator—Despatching messages—Flag and Heliograph signals.

(f) Royal Flying Corps
Ascent of Air Fleet—Chasing a "hostile" Aeroplane (photographed from a pursuing aeroplane at a height of over 5,000 feet)—Bomb dropping—The descent and landing—An aerial messenger.

(g) Motor-Cycle Machine-Gun Section (four batteries) **at Work**

Artists Rifles

The Volunteer Corps was formed in 1859 in response to patriotic fervour generated by the threat of invasion from Napoleon III of France. The Artists Rifles was formed in 1860, the idea for a special corps for artists, coming from Edward Sterling, an art student.

This 'Corps of Artists' consisted of painters, sculptors, engravers, musician, architects and actors. As the years went by the composition of the regiment was broadened to include lawyers, doctors and civil engineers.

The Artists' Rifles mobilised on 4th Aug 1914 and became part of London Division Army Troops in the St Albans area.

A stream of officers provided by the Artists grew to reach a total of over 10,000 before the war was over.

Visé Paris n° 838
GUERRE EUROPÉENNE — Bataille de la Somme
Curlu-Hem. — Vue d'ensemble d'une ancienne ligne de défense
allemandes. — A view of german defences. — LL.

27 GUERRE EUROPÉENNE. — Bataille de la Somme. — Hem. — Le Château et la Ferme après le bombardement — The Castle and the bombardment. — LL.
Visé Paris n° 827

my dearest 25

David to Ginger   Hut   2 Sept 28th 1916

Dear Ginger,

Thanks very much for the socks. They fit splendidly and are altogether just all that I want.

I am due to go into the school next Monday and shall in all probability be put into an empty house again.

It is rather remarkable that I discovered quite by chance that my Captain is a member of the T Square Lodge and that there is another man in the next hut who is also a member there.

Here in camp they have just instituted two new ideas.

One is that 120 men are served out with rifles and ammunition and have to be ready with equipment and food to be sent anywhere to guard any Zepps that may be brought down.

The second is that another 90 men have to be ready to go off to hold down any Zepp that may come down in a damaged condition.

We have just had one or two raids.

One, last Saturday, came across South London.

They dropped bombs within about 200 yards of Glen Roy but luckily Uncle and Aunty were at Brghton and only Aunt Martha and Harry were there.

I was at home and heard some of the firing, but Mum was also at Brighton. Polly was at home with me and said "she wasn't frightened although she didn't like it."

They did some damage at Streatham and Kennington but I don't think it was serious.

Later:

I have just had your letter.

Please thank Jean for helping with the socks.

I will write later on and give you all the 'orrible details of the school.

Yours

David

PS I have found the photo of the hut and am enclosing it. My bed is just off the photo in the bottom left hand corner.

Of course the hut is not by any means dressed in its Sunday best but it gives you some idea of things.

David to Ginger   Hare   Sunday (probably Oct) 1916

Sunday being a day of rest, I am writing to you. You ought to think yourself highly honoured – I expect you do.

They are putting us through our paces thoroughly here and get little or no time to ourselves. I have got quite used to undressing in the dark after lights out, but I have made it a rule now not to work after 9.45 and then I read until 10.15.

Friday is our busiest day usually, being up at 5.30 as usual, and after physical drill and breakfast etc, we spend the day on the entertaining sport called "open fighting".

This usually takes the form of "belly flopping", that is you are loaded with all the things they can find for you to carry and you are then marched somewhere or other and then set out across country, running 50 yards or so, and then flopping down full length.

If you are lucky you don't flop into a mud puddle, or a bed of gorse, or thistles, or a ploughed field, but you find a lovely smooth patch of grass – but then you are not often lucky. You then get up, run another 50 yards and flop again and so on, and then to vary the monotony of this, scramble through a hedge or two, leaving most of your skin, hair, clothes etc behind, and taking most of the hedge with you, or else you fall into a ditch.

It's a grand game.

After all this you come back just after 4 o'clock and get paid your princely salary, which a grateful government allows you.

Then a lecture from 4.50 until just after 6 o'clock.

Dinner at 6.20 and then an exam from 7.50 till 9, when you are allowed to go to your room and clean your things for the morning.

There is no means of letting things slide in the way of writing notes, as they collect the note books to see that they are written up.

There is one very good thing, practically the only fatigue which we get is on Saturday mornings, when we have to scrub our rooms and generally get everything especially spick and span, not that things can get left in the ordinary way, as our rooms are liable to be inspected at any time.

I have just read through the above and it looks as though I am grumbling – I am not – I merely keeping up the reputation of the British Army.

Really the school is miles in front of the battalion and very much more interesting and for all the work I would not go back.

You see there is such a terrific lot to get through in a short time, that everyone must work to get it done.

I have a different uniform now (that is when I am "Walking out") being clothed in purple and fine linen, or at least if not in that, in exceeding splendour. It is practically an officers uniform except for one or two small details and you occasionally get saluted by "poor ignorant Tommies" and of course feel a fool in not being entitled to it and not being able to acknowledge it.

By the way Harry Webber is called up for Nov 1st and I hear he has employed Lidiard to intercede for him with the powers that be.

Write to me when you can even if I don't reply – I don't get many letters.

Yours

David

PS If there is a glut of field glasses in America and people are throwing them away, don't hestitate to pick a pair up and send to me.

PPS Had a fine view of the last Zepp that got "straffed".

I was in bed in camp and awoke to find that someone had fallen on my chest.

I lay awake for a time, whilst some of the others hung out of the window (we were not allowed to leave the huts) in their endeavours to see something.

Presently the whole camp began to cheer (although we were ordered to keep quiet etc etc) and I shot out of the window just in time to see the whole sky alight with the red glare of the flaming Zepp.

I did not see the Zepp itself, but a few of the fellows did, although it was at Potters Bar.

D.

1916 July/Nov note by David on back of Somme post card
Some time ago I lived in the cellar of this house for about a week. I shared it with 3 others & a young nation of rats. The grand facade & front entrance (through which you had to double to get in & then fell down some steps) is round the corner

Architects' War (Selection) Committee

ROYAL INSTITUTE OF BRITISH ARCHITECTS,

9 CONDUIT STREET, LONDON, W.

Decr 20th 1916.

DEAR SIR,

Since the issue of the War Service Form, in addition to giving individual help to applicants—naturally a matter of increasing difficulty under conscription—my Committee has constantly kept in view the general recognition of the qualifications of Architects and others with allied knowledge who are serving, and I have now much pleasure in enclosing a card signed by my Chairman giving an epitome of your professional qualifications designed for insertion in the pocket of your Army Pay Book No. 64.

This card, as indicated at the foot thereof, is issued with the approval of the War Office, which has brought my Committee's scheme to the notice of the Commanders-in-Chief by the circulation of similar blank cards with a covering letter. You will therefore be in order in adding your regimental number and other service designations to the first line of the card and in producing it as occasion offers, it being understood that the circumstances leading to the desirability for its production should originate with your Officer Commanding.

Hoping that this official recognition of my Committee's efforts on your behalf may prove to be of service.

I am, yours faithfully,

Alan E. Brumby

Hon. Secretary.

ARTISTS' RIFLES CADET UNIT,

GIDEA PARK,
ROMFORD.

No. **92**

The Bearer of this Pass has leave of absence from Quarters.

For Name and dates see last entry on inside of card. The entry must bear the initials of Coy. Commander.

_____ Cadet
O/C 2 Coy.

No.	Name	Period	Initials O/C Coy.	No.	Name	Period	In...
211	Dixon J.G.	1 pm 20/4/16 — 11 pm 24/4/16					
554	Morgan J.	Dis. 29/4/16 9.30pm 30/4/16					
556	Reynolds C.W.	Dis. 13/5/16					
556	Reynolds C.W.	Dis. 27/5/16					
556	Reynolds C.W.	Dis. 31/5/16 10pm 31/5/16					
556	Reynolds C.W.	Dis 10/6/16					
556	Reynolds	10pm 17/6/16					
556	Reynolds	Dis 24/6/16					
~~556~~	~~Reynolds~~						
811	Stanford G.	9.45pm 13/7/16					
811	Stanford G.	Dis 15/7/16 12 noon 16/7/16					
811	Stanford G.	Dis 29/7/16 11.30pm 30/7/16					
811	Stanford G.	4pm 18/8/16 — 11.30pm 20/8/16					
811	Stanford G.	10.30pm 3/9/16					
1137	Taylor D.H.	Dis 29/11/16 9.30pm 29/11/16					

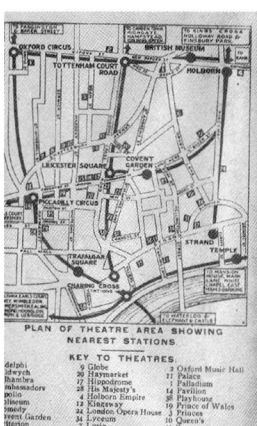
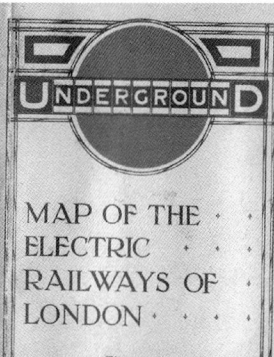

DIRECTORY OF USEFUL INFORMATION.

ADVERTISEMENTS.
Picture Posters issued by the Companies may be obtained from the Advertising Department, Electric Railway House, Broadway, Westminster, at prices from 6d. upwards.

BICYCLE STORES.
At nearly all District Railway Booking Offices bicycles can be left daily, or as often as required, at a charge of 1s. per week, 1s. 9d. per fortnight, 3s. per month, and 7s. 6d. per quarter. At Golders Green (free for the first 24 hours, 1d. per day afterwards). Apply at Booking Offices.

CATHEDRALS.

	Nearest Station	
Westminster Cathedral	Victoria	Free to visitors Daily, 9 a.m. to dusk. Tower and Crypt 6d. each daily, from 10 a.m.
Southwark Cathedral	London Bridge or Monument	Free Daily, 7.30 a.m. to 5 p.m.
St. Paul's Cathedral	Mansion House or Post Office	Free Daily, 9 a.m. to 5 p.m. Library, Whispering and Stone Galleries, Crypt 6d.; Golden Gallery, Ball, 1/-.
Westminster Abbey	Westminster	Free Weekdays, 9 a.m. till dusk. Services at 10 a.m. and 3 p.m. Sunday, Services at 8 a.m., 10 a.m., 3 p.m., and 7 p.m. Royal Chapels, Free Mondays, Tuesdays; 6d.Wednesdays, Thursdays, Fridays and Saturdays. Closed during hours of Service.

CHEAP TICKET FACILITIES.
The Cheap Return Tickets to the country resorts of Middlesex, such as Sudbury, Harrow, Ruislip and Uxbridge and to Southend are withdrawn in accordance with the instructions of the Railway Executive Committee of the Board of Trade. The ordinary return fares to these places are some of the cheapest round London. Southend is the nearest seaside resort to London.
Cheap Return Tickets are still issued on the L.E. Ry., C. & S.L., and C.L.R. to Hampstead and Golders Green (Thursdays and Saturdays after 1.0 p.m., Sundays all day). Season Tickets at reduced rates are issued to Scholars. For particulars apply to Passenger Agent.
Children under 3 years of age are carried free; over 3 and under 12 at half rates.

COMPLAINTS.
To be addressed to the Operating Manager, Electric Railway House, Broadway, Westminster, S.W., who is *never* pleased to get them, but is *always* pleased to cure them when he can.

CRICKET GROUNDS, Etc.
Oval.—Oval Station. Lords.—St. John's Wood Station.
All England Tennis Club —Wimbledon.
Queen's Club.—West Kensington or Barons Court.
Mostly in the hands of the Military Authorities.

CURRENT.
This is generated at Lot's Road Power House. It takes 500 tons of coal a day. It is the largest power station in England, and has the largest turbine in this country, viz., 15,000 K.W.

DOGS AND FOLDING MAILCARTS.
Dogs and Folding Mailcarts (when accompanied by passengers) are carried at the same rates as for passengers, with a maximum of 3d., at owners' risk only. Dogs must be on leads and under proper control; they must not occupy seats.

EXTENSIONS (MOTOR BUS).

		Journey Time mins.	Fare.	Intervals mins. (Approx.)
BOW ROAD STATION.				
Route No.				
10a	to Loughton	67	5½d.	15
A25a	Chadwell Heath	48	4d.	6-7
25	Seven Kings	39	3d.	2-3
10, 10a, 25	Stratford	10	1d.	2-3
10 & 10a	Wanstead	28	2½d.	5
A10	Woodford Bridge	47	4d.	8-9
CLAPHAM COMMON STATION.				
Route No.				
A178	to Lower Kingswood	84	9d.	9-10
A107	Dorking	125	1/-	8-9
88	Mitcham ("Cricketers")	29	3d.	8-9
37 & 37a	Wandsworth	20	2d.	4-5
FINSBURY PARK STATION.				
Route No.				
106	to Stoke Newington Station	10	1d.	8
42	Stamford Hill	11	1d.	8-9
111	Muswell Hill ("Victoria")	15	2d.	3-4
A157	High Beech	72	7d.	7-8
GOLDERS GREEN STATION.				
Route No.				
13	to Hendon ("Bell")	9	1d.	10
83	Hendon (Station Road)	23	2d.	16
84	St. Albans	86	9d.	30
A155	Hatfield	88	9d.	13

my dearest 33

David to Ginger   [location not known]   24th Jan 1917

Dear Ginger

Until last Monday I was on leave, now I am not – alas.

I went for my final exam on Dec 19th and managed to get through it and am now a full blown officer or as they put it in the gazette a temporary second lieutenant (on probation).

My name has not yet been actually put into the gazette, but I expect it will be within a day or so when I will send it on to you.

Two days after the exam I left G.P. for good so that I was home for Christmas.

Mum seemed to think I was ill and for a considerable time my chief diet was Dutch Drops, Lung healers, and any other similar dainty that I would submit to.

The exam was not easy, there being only 3 or 4 questions out of the whole 3 papers that one could answer from knowledge that could be got from books or that was really taught in the school.

On the other hand I think it was a very good exam from the point of view of choosing officers. Nobody got very high marks, the top man only getting 183 out of a possible 220. I was 25th with 159.

I reported here on Monday last and am already well at work.

Today, Wednesday, I am orderly officer which means that I have to inspect practically everything that can be inspected, rations, rooms, kitchens, prisoners, etc etc, look after the men's meals, in order to see if they have sufficient and that the food is good etc.

Mount the guards on duty and inspect them. Altogether a fairly long day as I started soon after 6 this morning and I shall not finish until about 11.30 this evening.

Thursday:

This morning I got nothing to do as the men I should have were taken off for gas practice by another lieutenant, so I went on a voyage of discovery around the town here.

This place is a pretty dreary sort of show.

It consists of two main streets chiefly filled with small shops which do not sell anything in particular or at least anything that one really wants.

When you come to the end of the main streets you find yourself out in some low lying flat fields, so that it is not an ideal place for a walk.

It is also a prohibited area and everyone has to have a pass to get into or out of the town, which means I expect that Mum will be unable to come down to see me even if it were worth while her doing so.

There are only 3 of us here who have not been out to the front so that we feel somewhat out of it.

The other two are from the Inns of Court and went through the same exam as I did and joined here the same time.

I have got rather friendly with one of these two but unfortunately I am not sharing the same room.

This afternoon my men did physical and bayonet fighting and I, with the other officers, joined them and drilled under the physical instructors. I was rather glad as it was very cold indeed and doing physical kept us warm, otherwise we should have been standing around doing nothing.

By the way did I ever write and thank you for that last pair of socks you sent. They are splendid and I have them on now.

I am sharing a room with two other men (a Captain and a Lieutenant) in barracks, and we sleep on camp beds and even with a sleeping bag and 3 blankets it is none too warm

At present things are rather slow as I know nobody here and have to get at everything by asking questions and at times this is rather slow work as of course everyone has got their own job to do and doesn't care about anyone else.

However I expect things will improve as I get on a bit.

Write to me as often as you can.

Yours ever

David

Fanny to Ethel   Balham   6th Feb 1917

My darling Ethel,

Just a line to tell you David started for France, he went off bright and early and it's a beautiful sunny morning, he is very well. Hoping you are all well and will be kept from harm.

With fondest love from your loving Mamma

I have sent little Erl a lock for her bracelet in a letter Feb 3. Hope you will get it. Mamma

FIELD
9 APR 1917
3rd CORPS

Army Form W. 3241F.

OFFICER'S ADVANCE BOOK. No. A 34426 to A 34450

Only to be used by *Lt. D.H. Taylor,*
2nd K.R.R.C.

(C 8479) Wt. 5873/8735. 20,000 bks. 8/16. J. P. & Co., Ltd. (E. 337.)

No. A 34426

No. A 34426   Army Form W. 3241F.
ADVANCE OF PAY.
Agents :— Messrs. Cox & Co.

Rank and Name _____
(In BLOCK letters)
Unit _____
RECEIVED from Cashier _____
Francs _____ the sum of _____ francs.
(Figures)

Date _____   Date _____   _____
Signature.

INSTRUCTIONS.

1. The receipt will be detached from the book by the Cashier, who will affix his office stamp to, or endorse the counterfoil.

2. If the payment is to be made to a brother officer, the form on the back of the receipt must be completed, and the book presented to the Cashier.

3. Officers must state the Unit to which they belong, and not that to which they are attached.

N.B.—This authority is only valid when in favour of an officer.

I authorise

_____

_____

to receive _____ francs

on my behalf.

_____
(Signature.)

285. ARRAS. — Effet d'un obus sur une maison rue St-Nicolas.
La Guerre 1914-15
L. C. H. Paris

David Henry Taylor

my dearest 39

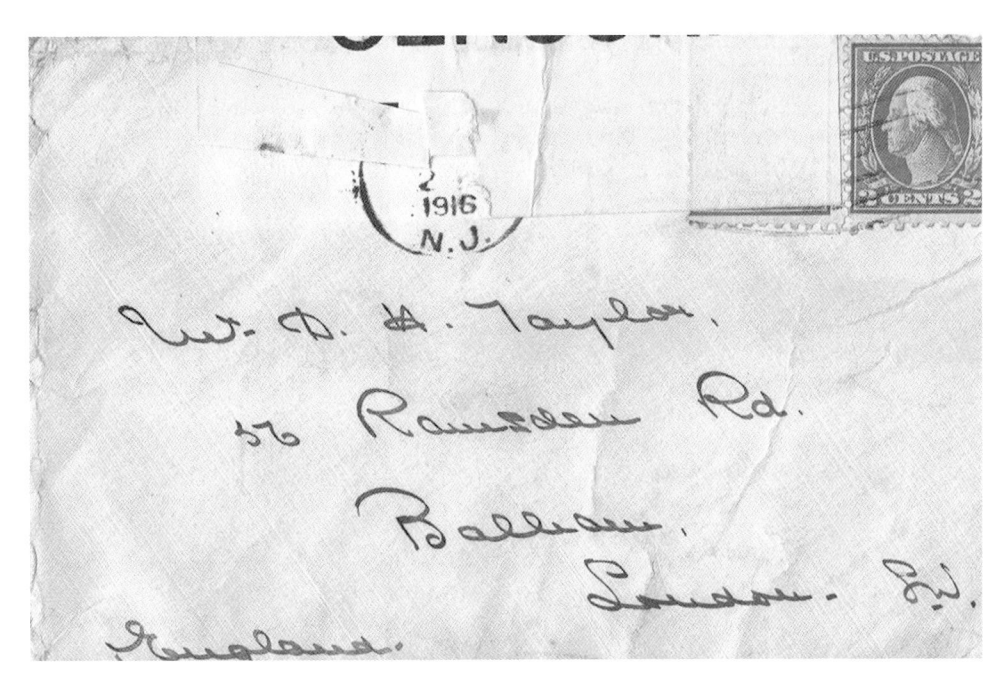

Ethel (Ginger) Linn, nee Taylor

Fanny Taylor

The Muggridge Family.
Left to right: Bert, Ethel, Mamma, May and Ern

May Muggridge

Northern Assurance

Northern Assurance

The Northern Assurance Company was established in Aberdeen in 1836 as the North of Scotland Fire and Life Assurance Company and renamed Northern Assurance Company in 1848. The company initially had two departments: fire assurance and life assurance. In 1837 a new prospectus stated that "the company insures houses, manufactories, furniture, goods, and merchandise, farming stock, shipping in Port and Dock, and while Building, Repairing, or used on Navigable Canals, and all other Property, from Loss or Damage by fire". The business also included "endowments of children, the purchase and sale of annuities, insurance on joint lives and survivorships, and every Transaction dependent on the Contingency of Life." It is now part of Aviva.

At the outbreak of WWI, between 50 and 60 of the 361 male staff in the UK were already in the territorial forces or naval reserve. By the end of 1914, 105 staff had joined up. By the end of the war, 335 men were serving in the forces, 61 were known to have died: 18% of those who served.

David to Fanny   [address censored]   Sat Feb 10th 1917

Dear Mum,

Today has been glorious. Quite warm in fact.

We had drill all the morning which I quite enjoyed, as I had charge of a platoon.

This afternoon I went with west into the port and bought several things, some woollen gloves and some biscuits etc etc.

Things are fairly dear. I had to pay 2/6 a pound for the biscuits and they were something like "Osborne".

While there I saw some German prisoners, clearing the snow from the roads. They are a low looking crowd, much worse than any of the other soldiers one sees anywhere.

I have asked the [censored] people to send my field boots to you. Please keep them for me.

This place is much better than [censored] as far as the other officers are concerned, as they are much more sociable, in fact I have got on with everybody very well so far.

Will you please send me some more socks, and also the tin of metal polish and some brown nugget and rags for cleaning purposes.

There is no difficulty about passing English notes out here and I got 27 francs in exchange for a pound, which is quite good.

I can also travel at about quarter fare on the railway and this makes first class much cheaper even than the trams. The only difficulty is however that there are only about 4 or 5 trains a day to the port.

I have to go on parade now, so must stop.

Dave

May to David   18 Manor Road, Beckenham.   19.2.17 Monday, 11.0.

My dear David,

Now for a long letter - if the Fates will permit. I left the Office at 1. 0. on Saturday and went and had dinner -yes.,. I own it was coffee and ham sandwiches at an A.B.C. , and I enjoyed them. The girl who sat in my seat just before I entered came back and said she had left an oilskin on the seat, so the whole staff and -a few others came and watched me eat my lunch all the time I was there, and looked hard at my music case which was suspiciously bulky and my attache case. I had stuck my shoes in the music case at the last moment, and it certainly looked as if I had hastily pushed In an oilskin. I did not hurry over my lunch, but as I said before, thoroughly enjoyed it.

Really I felt sorry for the girl, she seemed so very put out about it. After awhile she went out a fetched an elderly lady to join her. 0, it was lovely. Eventually I walked to St. Pauls. I might have been followed, but did not trouble to look back, and caught the 1. 57. to Herne Hill and then a bus to the Plough. Next I walked the back way up to Maud's to make tender enquiries. It was barely 2.30.I had not been there long when a ring came, and a Sunday School teacher (a real male) called. I was in the Drawing room, while the male (by the bye I suppose Sunday School male teachers can be men, but I don't know any, so please excuse my ignorance) was taken into the dining room. From the sounds which eminated it, seemed that he was an ordinary rational being, and I think Maud enjoyed his call, of course I teased her when she came in to me after disposing of him, mentioning that I should certainly have to tell you of her carryings on.

Mrs A is worse and Maud is really very down, though I tried to cheer her up. She was very shocked at her cousin who has just lost her mother. They live rather close by, and I went to their house one day at a Jews' sale of work and muffin scramble to play an accompaniment for Maud -I daresay you remember the circumstance. Well, this aforesaid cousin called on Maud a day or so ago and actually was wearing a dark blue and black blouse under her black coat, whereas Maud has discarded the dark blue jersey she has been wearing Indoors and has bought a black one. I tried to make seasonable remarks, and as Maud did not gasp out "May!" I think I must have succeeded tolerably.

1.30. I left as quickly as I could and went on to No. 56 where Mrs Taylor was watching for me in the window, and I got a most hearty welcome from her and Peter. I have never seen Mrs. Taylor look better, and have never known her in a more cheerful mood. She kept jolly and was making jokes during the whole of my stay. One of the first things she said was "I have sent my boy 3 parcels, and am having such cheerful letters from him each day. I had copied out portions of your letters, and showed her, and she came to the conclusion she was getting all the same news, at which she seemed very pleased. Maud was also highly delighted at hearing from you and had sent by me her letter to Mrs Taylor. Your ears did ought to burn ferociously. Mrs Day had gone off for the weekend before I arrived, so Mrs T & I had the place to ourselves. (Peter, I beg your pardon.) We knitted Saturday evening and talked. Your mother would wait on me that she was taking your place as well as hers, except that there was no hugging. I don't believe she learnt that art as we know it.

Sunday morning when I was sitting over the fire reading a book Maud had lent me, "Windyridge", of which she thinks a lot, but don't waste time reading it, Peter noticed a vacant lap and not approving of the vacancy came and put his head there. I was supposed to be making the bed but I didn't do it. I did not do anything except wipe a few knives and forks and cups, and consequently feel ashamed of myself. On Sunday morning Mrs Taylor got up at 7.5 and went down for tea. She returned at 7.15 with the tray. Then we drank tea and talked until 9.30. I reminded her that it was not David that was keeping us in bed, and added "Did David tell you he wanted me to be engaged to him before he went away?" She said "No" in a distinctly interested tone, so I added "I said No, as he has quite enough responsibility just now as it is", to which she replied "O, well, it will come to the same thing in the end" (how people will jump to conclusions!) No wonder he is so cheerful". She did not say whether she was pleased or otherwise but she sounded pleased, and 10 minutes later when she was dressing she put her skirt on twice on the wrong side, and the 3rd time back in front, so I called her to order, said she must be in love and that it was my duty as a Christian to inform you. She promptly cheeked me, danced about, and skipped higher than I believe I could, while holding on to the bedpost. And she has been cheeky ever since, but nothing more has been said on that subject. I felt I ought to let her know, and have been pleased ever since. Please, however, don't think my conscience has given way. I simply am not thinking about that pest of a nuisance. You hear of different things dying a natural death; perhaps my conscience will if I ignore it.

As I aforesaid I read in the morning, it being rather misty out, but after dinner the sun came out and it was lovely, so we both went to see Miss Massey.

4.30 We arrived soon after 3.0 at the Hospital (Kings College) and saw Mrs Marks who had been there since 2.0 and was just coming away. Miss Massy's first question was about you. Yes, you are growing positively important; I shall have a job with you when you come back. It was a tumor she had. She looks very well indeed and seemed jolly; but of course she was excited. She is getting on well and will be sent on Wednesday to Hemel Hempstead for 3 weeks; after that she is going to stay at Balham. We were turned out at 4.0 and found a grand fire in the drawing room awaiting us. After tea I played hymns (very good practice for sight reading) which I think Mrs Taylor enjoyed. Of course I picked out all the lovely ones and made them sound more or less

[rest of letter missing]

Soldier to Ethel Linn   B.E.F. France   Thursday 4th April [1917]

Dear Friend,

Just a few lines to let you know that I have received a issue of cigarettes from the Over Seas Club Tobacco Fund of which you have been subscribing to and got your address out of the cigarette case and I thought it was my duty to write and thank you for the way you are helping us lads through this Great Campaign so I hope you will not be offended for me taking this liberty in writing to you. I send my address

Stretcher Bearer Groves 11466, 16 Platoon, D Coy, 2nd KRR, British Ex. Force, France, hoping I am not asking too much I would like you to write me a few lines in answer to this letter so that I know you have received it safe, so close with Best Respect and every success in the future.

Believe Me

Yours Sincerely

S.B. Groves

David to May   B.E.F. France   28.3.17

Thanks for your letter of 19th which came today. I am glad you and Mrs. M. find my letters interesting. You ask about signalling. This is rather interesting work, as there are various sorts of signalling, and it includes laying telephone wires and keeping them connected up when they get broken or go wrong, and ours, at all events, are always going wrong. They are just laid down on the ground or through a trench, and naturally they get broken and disconnected in all sorts of ways, so the signallers are kept fairly busy in this way.

With your letter there was the one from Cox & Co. containing my pass book. I find I have a balance there of nearly £30, and as I am entitled to about another £10 for field allowance &c. which has never been credited to me, I have about £40 there. Not so bad, is it? Of course I am spending as little as possible and beyond my mess bills which I can't control I have not drawn any other money since I have been here.

We are still at work on the roads and appear as though we shall for some time to come.

I was up at 5.30 this morning to take a party to a village about 3 miles away. The village was the usual heap of bricks and rubbish and my job was to see that poles about 10 feet long were loaded into A.S.C. wagons to be taken up to our bit of the road. I had been at work for about an hour when I had a message asking me to go back. I had to see about some bricks in a village a mile the other way. As soon as 2 or 3 wagons were loaded I got up on one and rode back in style so as to direct operations the other end. So I have spent the greater part of the day rising backwards and forwards on these wagons.

The wind has been very cold, but apart from that it has been a glorious day. At lunch the horses were given an hour's rest and I got into a shell hole out of the wind, ate bully beef and sandwiches and afterwards lay down and nearly went to sleep, the sun was so warm.

Those "Fragments from France" are not exaggerated in the least, and one sees similar things out here all the time. You remember that one of the colonel who was asked for some details of some jam when the shells were flying around. Well, you get exactly that sort of thing here. When you are especially busy and have some particular thing on or perhaps the Germans are giving some trouble you will suddenly get a message asking how many rounds of ammunition you have, or how many picks and shovels, and even here where we are quite quiet and go to bed at night we get orders sent round about 1.0. and in this case the orderly has to walk over to me to deliver his message to the captain.

The leggings have just arrived by parcel post altho' you paid letter post. They do splendidly.

An interfering old general, the chief of our little lot of generals, came along and found the captain of another company without his belt and promptly went for him right and left, and we have since had a special order sent from headquarters that all officers are to wear belts. It is so important you see, even though you cant get a decent wash. I have just had a wash and shave in water taken from a shell hole. This water is always somewhat muddy, but a wash is a wash, and as clean water can only be used for drinking you just use the other. You are quite right about the name of that place. All our football is stopped for the time being, and I don't know when we shall finish that competition. You can't play football on ground that is pitted with shell holes, so that there is little or no room between them. Goodbye once again.

David to May   B.E.F. France   25 April 1917

I haven't much news today.

This morning we were out on the range soon after 6.0. until 8.0. I think my platoon did rather better than last time, but still even now they are not by any means good.

We got back at 8.15, had breakfast and then went out over the same ground as yesterday in order to do the whole of yesterday's work over again.

Before starting, however, we did a little company drill and then went across country the same as yesterday but over somewhat different ground.

Everything went alright for a time, and then the colonel appeared on the scene and put all sorts of new things into the scheme that nobody knew anything about at the start, with the result that most of us got gloriously muddled and then the colonel came along and said everything was wrong. Luckily I was right away from his neighbourhood so did not come in contact with him until the final wind up, when he told us all that had happened and all the mistakes that had been made.

We got back about 2.0 and had lunch.

Just before going in, Taylor, my bright and shining light, came to me and said he wanted to go before the colonel with a complaint that my platoon sergeant had kicked him.

Now I know that the sergeant is somewhat of a bully, but on the other hand Taylor is like a naughty child and wants a spanking at times, so I guessed it was 6 of one and half a dozen of the other, and told Taylor to go and get dinner and think over his complaint and come to me again. I have heard nothing of it since.

This afternoon I took the platoon out and played football just between the platoon only, not against anyone else.

This evening a good many of the men are running races in order to decide which will run on Saturday in the brigade sports.

Today I had a letter from a girl asking to give her news of her "young man" as he hadn't written for six weeks. I have interviewed the young man and have an idea that he will write tonight. Most of the married men are very good at writing and send letters as often as possible, but some of the others don't write at all and then we get these sort of letters which means of course that we have to talk pretty straight to the particular man concerned.

Last night soon after I laid down a couple of rats started an awful row with some paper under the bed and kept me awake for some time.

26h April

No mail in today.

We have not had a specially hard day. This morning we started at 7.30 and marched out about 5 or 6 miles. We then went off the road, and had a short rest and did company drill for about an hour. I thoroughly enjoyed this. I find that the others know no more about Company drill than I do so that if I make a mistake it is not so noticeable as it would be if they were perfect. I had the leading platoon this morning and managed to get through fairly well.

After company drill we had some platoon drill to teach the men heads up. It felt almost like being in Gidea Park again, except for the fact that I was yelling at the men to hold themselves up instead of being yelled at myself.

After this the colonel gave us a short lecture on scouting while the whole battalion sat round him in a ring.

According to the latest rumour we are to have at least 3 more weeks at special training and probably more, not necessarily here, but probably somewhere further along the line.

Of course all this drill is to smarten us up to show the Guards what we can do as we are going to join them.

We have been given instruction that we are to salute in the one and only proper manner and any poor beggar of a rifleman whom we meet in the street in this way, or who isn't dressed just so is to be hauled up before the colonel and shot at dawn. I expect I shall be looking at something very interesting in the opposite direction when there are any men who don't salute properly.

Yesterday I wrote and bought 15 Malayalam Rubber Shares. I believe the Company is a pretty sound one and is likely to increase its dividend (the shares at present pay about 10% on the present price of 38/- and so the shares will probably also rise in price too. I found I had something like £40 at Cox's and as there is an allowance of about £10 which should have been paid to my account by now, and then there is my pay at the end of the month, I thought I had too much money lying idle and might as well invest some of it.

Now off to bed, so Goodbye.

27th April

No mail in again today.

We have had a sort of mixed day today. We marched out about 3 miles, had a rest and then each company went off separately. We had platoon drill then for about ¾ hour. My platoon started off pretty badly, but after being shouted at first by myself (until my throat was sore) and then by my platoon sergeant they improved considerably.

Then we had a march past for practice. I suppose there is an inspection by some general or other looming in the distance. I have marched past many times before but always in the ranks, this being the first time I have had to march past at the head of my own platoon, and you feel awful lonesome out in front there by yourself with everybody watching you as you go by.

We then had a small attack all on our own, my platoon and two others attacking another. I was the leading platoon and had to do all the scouting, but we didn't have time to do much as it was getting past 1.0 and we were due back. This afternoon I have been playing football with the men. We played No.6 platoon and beat them – the second time within a week. The weather is much better and it was pretty hot playing. The latest addition to the battalion is a set of bagpipes, and we marched back this morning with a piper at the head of the company but one man piping doesn't sound anything great; still it helps the men along a good deal. There have been some races this evening and a tug-of-war in preparation for tomorrow, but I am not very interested in them. I had another kit inspection after tea, and altho' I only inspected the men's kit about a fortnight ago yet most of them had something missing. They would loose themselves if they had half a chance.

Goodbye.

David to May   B.E.F. France   April 28.1917

This should reach you on your birthday. Many, many happy returns.

I have just got your letter (Monday 22nd).

I wish I could be more cheerful over that twelve months business, but it seems such an awful time to be away from everyone. Still, I have not got the job yet.

So you have had measles in the office. We have had a few cases here and also one of spotted fever. This last was when we were or the road but the men who were in the same dugout as the patient were isolated, and luckily it didn't spread.

This morning we marched out about 3 miles again. We were to do a new scheme of scouting. Another man & I were sent off with our platoons to carry out a scheme each, and from the very start I came under the colonel's eye and seemed to stay there, in fact I couldn't get rid of him. We had no sooner started than he rode up and altered the whole original idea (as I understood it) and sent us off on quite a different plan. Again we hadn't started very long before we were stopped, but this time I was allowed to go on while the other man had to alter the positions of his men.

Finally the colonel called me out and told me to carry out a small attack with my platoon down a valley while the whole of the remainder of the battalion sat round on the hills surrounding it and looked on.

The scheme of course brought in this new scouting idea, and I was shivering in my shoes all the time and wondering how much of it I was doing wrong.

Anyhow, we got down the valley and attacked and wiped out the imaginary enemy and that ended the morning's work.

I marched the platoon off and met the battalion as they came along and soon afterwards the colonel waited till I came up and said that we had carried out the whole thing quite well, and that there was only one criticism and that was that I might have ordered my Lewis gun into a somewhat different position. So I suppose it wasn't so bad. But its an awful thing for a poor inexperienced subaltern like myself to be sent out before all these captains and a brigade staff major (no less) who was sent to watch the battalions work, to say nothing of all the other veterans in the battalion.

This afternoon the brigade sports have been held, all four regiments in the brigade taking part of course.

Our own General was there and also our own particular General of Generals. This last gentleman is known throughout the division as Frosty Face, and is noted for "strafing" anybody and everybody about everything.

I have only come in contact with him once and that was on the road. Three of us were discussing the work and how a certain drain should be dug. He arrived on the scene suddenly, told us that we should not be talking together and ordered us back to our men. He's a darling.

I am afraid we have not done so well as we might in the races, but we won a few things.

During the sports one of the battalions, the Lancashires, were "At Home". They had a marquee put up, brought their band, and supplied the officers with tea. One might have been at home almost and somebody said there is a war on.

I am very glad you had a good weekend. It is good of you to go to see Mum as often as you do.
Goodbye,
David.

David to May   B.E.F. France   April 29 1917

To-day there is no church service, no parades, no nothing except that we are playing football against the Black Watch this afternoon, so I have most of the day to myself.

I am on the top of a hill (it is more like a cliff as it breaks off suddenly and goes down very steeply) overlooking the river. At the bottom there is a road, then the flat bed of the river which is perhaps 1/2 mile across, and opposite another hill more gradual than this one and laid out in a patchwork pattern of crops.

Unless you knew it was a river you wouldn't recognize it as one, for it looks like so many large and small lakes stretching off in all directions with flat reedy grass islands in between and a few trees dotted about here and there, while down the centre runs a straight canal with the usual two straight lines of poplars.

Away to the left there is another steep wooded hill with a village at the foot and on the right the valley takes a huge bend and disappears behind the hills.

We have had a very good report on our work out on the road. It said we had done the work very well under very bad weather conditions and by doing so had helped forward the advance far more rapidly than would otherwise have been the case.

As a matter of fact the weather was so bad at times that the men simply couldn't do much, although we were out on the road all the time, so I suppose we really could have done the work even quicker than we did.

Yesterday and to-day are the first two really warm days we have had and certainly to-day it is piping hot, and I expect I will have to play football this afternoon too.

2. 30.

I have got to play for the officers against the Black Match this afternoon as I expected, so must go now.

6. 30.

We have played and won the game and B Company also beat B Company of the Black Watch.

Afterwards we brought the officers back to tea while our men gave their people tea in the garden.

They have now gone back.

9. 30.

As I have said before nothing is certain in the army. We are moving to-morrow about 12 miles further up the line, this time to make railways.

Goodbye.
David.

David to May   B.E.F. France   May 2, 1917

On Monday we had had a very long day and were lumped down in the fields with practically nothing and had had very little to eat, and I was just turning in when the post came. I had a letter, and that cheered me up. We were told that we were going about 12 miles up the line. That 12 miles turned out to be 24. We started at 8a.m. and marched about 8 miles. It was awfully hot and we were all loaded pretty well, in consequence some of the men began to look as tho' they might fall out, so that by the time we got to the end of the march most of the officers were carrying rifles and sundry other parts of the men's kit as well as their own. However, none of my men fell out altho' I was very doubtful of two of them.

We ended up at the place where I first stopped on coming up from the base. You remember perhaps the "rest house" I slept in. We had lunch here, seated in what was once the station yard. We (the officers) had had no breakfast as we had been too busy, and we didn't get much lunch for the servants hadn't put much in the mess box, and even that was gloriously mixed up. Candles, cheese, bread, tinned fruit, knives, plates &c. &c. all just thrown in and in a filthy condition at that. You see they hadn't reckoned on us going to the box ourselves.

After lunch we got into a train of the French military pattern, that is goods trucks and cattle trucks. Then we started to do the remaining 16 miles. First of all we went back practically to where we started in the morning. I dont mean that we did this all at once. Not by no means. We rattled, & bumped & jerked & shunted and then went off for a tour of the South of France and the Red Sea (at least it seemed like it) & finally landed at our new stopping place just before midnight, having done 16 miles in 10 hours.

At one place during the afternoon we got off the train and played football and at another the commanding officer got off, left the train for a minute or two, cameback and found it gone. However, he turned up again a bit further down the line, and as he climbed into the truck we all cheered.

Can you imagine about 20 or 25 of us all sitting, lying or standing in a cattle truck which had just been emptied of straw and not swept out, or all of us sitting on the floor or on our packs having dinner and afterwards most of the noisy ones yelling the latest revue songs at the top of their voices.

As soon as we arrived the Germans greeted us with a shell which whistled overhead. The line is not very far off, and each evening they send a few shells over by way of reminding us that they are there, but they always fall some distance off and do no damage.

They had managed to get some tents up for us, but the transport did not arrive until next day so that we had to sleep just in what we had with us, which in my case was a waterproof sheet and my rain-coat.

Next day we started repairing the railway or rather re-making it for the Germans have destroyed it very thoroughly.

They have carefully blown bits out of each length of rail and at junctions and level crossings blown the whole lot up bodily. At present our chief work is unloading and levelling.

Goodbye.

David to May   B.E.F. France   May 3 1917

My Dearest,

Again, this will be a short letter as I haven't had a moment to spare all day.

This morning we went out onto the line at 8.0. and have been there all day..

We are working on what was once a level crossing, but the Germans just put a mine under the middle and blew the whole thing up with the consequence that there is a huge hole: to be filled up and the railway track relaid over it.

The explosion buried large pieces of the track and these have to be dug out and as some of them are pretty big, (at one time I had about 40 men trying to move one piece and not succeeding) they have to be taken apart.

The weather is glorious and my face is as sore as it can be with the sun and wind, and of course has its usual brilliant hue.

I am very sorry to hear Bert has moved up again, but this may not necessarily mean that they are going into the fighting line. Anyway try not to worry Dear, he will be fairly safe now that he is signalling.

Must stop to catch the post,

Goodbye.

May 4.

I woke up this morning to hear one of our Lewis guns which is just at the back of my tent rattling away at an aeroplace. Presently there was a whistle of something and I afterwards heard that one of our anti-aircraft shells had fallen into the camp. Isn't that the limit, to have one's own shells thrown at one.

Again we have been out on the railway. We have got one siding laid. We are working under some Canadian Engineers, and they never set any of the work out, never mark out any levels & only roughly indicate where they want the sidings laid. Consequently quite a lot of work has to be done twice, especially digging.

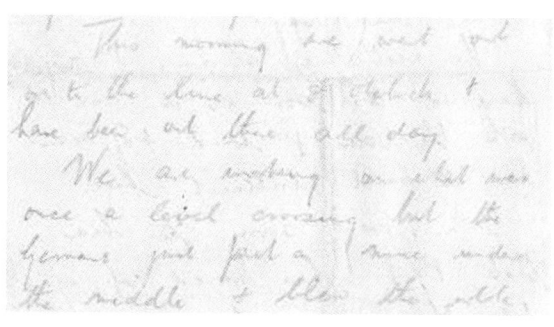

Yesterday I took out several large lengths of rails with sleepers, bolted to them, pieces which had been half buried. Today they have all had to be moved a second time, keeping about 10

men at work practically all day.

This siding that is finished has been moved backwards and forwards with levers all the afternoon because they had it laid in the wrong place to start with.

We have a rough shelter put up for our meals with some tables and forms which makes it very pleasant.

This is the end of the rly. here, that is as far as it is repaired and we were the first troops to come up by train.

Just round about the Germans have most carefully destroyed everything. There is a factory close by, pretty badly knocked about by shells but the machinery was not all touched so they have destroyed it with hammers, knocked holes in the boilers & have done as much damage as possible. One of our fellows went into the small village cemetery & found that a large vault had been broken open & the coffins smashed.

The country is similar to the Downs but not so fine.

Goodbye.

Ruines d'Ypres 1914-18 Ruines de la Gare.

Ginger to David   Passaic, N.J.   May 4th 1917

Dear Kid,

Last week I sent you some chocolate direct to France, but as I have no address, it is a toss-up whether it will reach you. I think it perfectly absurd to pay two postages besides wasting time, unless letters and packages from England go to the B.E.F. free or at a reduced rate. Anyway I want your address, as I want to send cigarettes either from here or England. I expect to send four more pairs of socks next week.

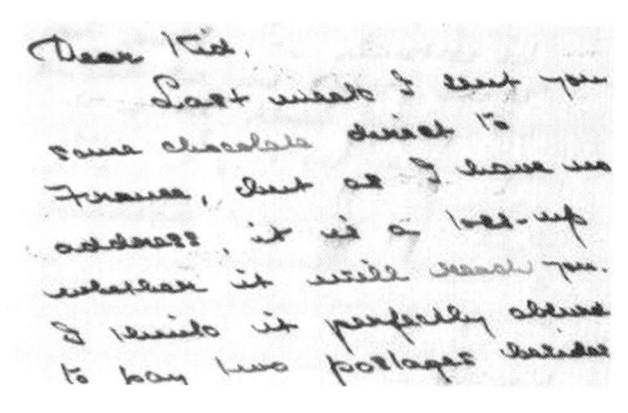

John went to Cleveland last night, so J.F. Junior came in to my bed this morning. He is so fat, not fat but solid flesh, that the only bone he can feel or see in himself is his ankle, so when he put his arms round my neck, he felt a bone and asked "Have 'oo got an ankle in your neck?". The other day he announced that "boys have 'atch-keys and pipes", and that "they sit in front of the fi'(re) and smoke". When he gets a little bigger I anticipate inquiries about the cigarettes left in the smoke-room from their owner. He certainly is "some" boy, If he keeps on as he is doing he will be a splendid fellow for the British Navy.

Erl has to have adenoids and tonsils removed. I am expecting this the week after next. She has been improving in health and weight ever since I took her to a specialist, but, nevertheless, I wish I could take the operation for her.

I wish these Americans would buck up and get some ships afloat. There is a mighty lot of discussion about it.

I think many people are growing some vegetables this year in order to help, including, of course, ourselves. But there have been heaps of foolish suggestions from responsible bodies of war, such as digging up the ivy in the Park and planting vegetables (the ground would not be fit for a year) when there are acres and acres of used ground a quarter of a mile away. I want four times as much ground as we have. I am beginning to want to get out in the country, so that we could grow everything, including chickens, pigeons, geese etc, only then there is the question of the children's schooling. Erl might go soon.

Everything is getting frightfully dear.

Did I tell you John had a presentation on his 25th anniversary with Dicks from the American branch, including not only the branches scattered about the U.S.A. and Marseilles but the factory hands too? I chose it – a canteen of silver – 1 doz. spoons, forks and knives in solid silver, with 30 service pieces and four meat dishes – at Tiffany's.

It was suggested it should be exhibited at the Factory for the men, but I preferred their seeing it here, and, consequently, we had about 60 here last Friday night.

The silver is plain in design of an old English shape with "J.F.L." monogram on every piece. The promoter of the scheme asked me to choose. I thought there would be $200 to $300, so had intended choosing a tray, but when I heard the sum they had reached I was flabbergasted and had to alter my ideas. I had to keep that secret from Feb. 9 til March 1st and nearly "busted", especially after the gorgeous afternoon I spent at Tiffany's. I almost felt like a millionaire during that time only there were plenty of other things I should have purchased at the same time, if I were. And sometimes I hate having these nice things when I read about the starving youngsters over there. As far as this country and England go, I think having to economise will do both countries good, although I see little sign of economy here yet, except in this house, but I am told that people are economising.

Certainly, prices will make them economise.

We went to see "Peter Ibbotson" on Wed. I really think the most wonderful staging I have ever seen – it gave such a correct impression of the book.

I am wondering if you will think all this piffle, but the only thing one ever thinks about is the war and you are in it and have enough of it without our making remarks about it – only I wish I knew where you are.

Best of luck.

Yours,

Ethel.

David to May   B.E.F. France   May 6. 1917

To-day is Sunday and we all started off to the railway this morning but found that the Canadian Engineers don't work on a Sunday so we were all sent back again, and in consequence the men have a day off.
I am going riding at 10. 30, or rather I am going for a riding lesson.

I had my riding lesson this morning and didn't fall off.
The transport officer and sergeant were there and gave us the lesson. It is rather good being taught by these fellows, especially the sergeant, as I think he knows a horse inside and out, and moreover has been a riding instructor.
This afternoon my platoon played another at football, but I didn't play, but went out and watched them.
The band is playing outside the tent, or as one of my men wrote in a letter "we are having tea while the band is playing on the lawn".
That reminds me of a funny remark Taylor made on that march here. Somebody asked if he were singing. He said "No, I'm not singing; that's my back creaking."
This evening I have been doing some revolver firing.
They have started leave again out here (there has been none all the time I have been out), and that of two kinds. You can go home, and also leave is given for 4 or 5 days but you have to stay in France, and this does not interfere with your home leave when your turn comes. Also Officer's wives are allowed to come across and spend 4 or 5 days with their husbands. Now why, 0 why, am I not married? Of course those who have gone are at the top of the list, and I am very near the bottom, but still it does raise one's hopes of seeing England.
There are several observation balloons just round here (one within a few hundred yards of the camp). They seem to have a particular attraction for German aeroplanes and yesterday they had three attempts at burning them.
The first two failed altho' the observers had to jump out and come down on parachutes; the third time (late in the evening) the German made for our balloon; and again the observer jumped, and the balloon was hauled down in time. Then he made straight for the next, our guns firing at him all the time. The second observer jumped but the German circled round the balloon and a moment or two after it burst into flames.
It looked from where we were as though some of the wreckage would fall on the observer as he slowly floated down, but we heard to-day that each time the men got away alright.
No post in to-day.
I must write to Mum as I have not written for 3 or 4 days.

Goodbye.

David to May   B.E.F. France   May 7th 1917

My Dearest,

I was up at 5 o'clock this morning and took the men to the river to wash. We are not actually on the main river itself but there is a small stream about a mile away which runs into it. It is only a few inches deep but makes the most of itself, in the way streams have about here, by spreading out and forming shallow lakes and marshes.

There must be millions of frogs there I think for at night their croaking sounds like a shrill whistle.

My mess bill for April was brought in last night, it was £5-18-0, which is lighter than last month but is still I think too much. However I don't expect it will be reduced much.

We hear out here how you are going short of certain things at home such as potatoes etc.

I do hope things are not as bad as the papers and rumours would have us believe.

I expect things are of course always getting dearer.

While we were at work today I saw one of our own airmen flying up and down over the German lines being fired at all the time. I watched him for a little while and suddenly he turned up on end and dived straight down turning round and round as he came. I thought he had been hit although more of the shells seemed to burst very near him, but after falling some considerable distance he suddenly righted himself, flew on a little way, looped the loop, and then flew back over our lines and out of sight. I suppose it was his way of putting his fingers to his nose at the Germans.

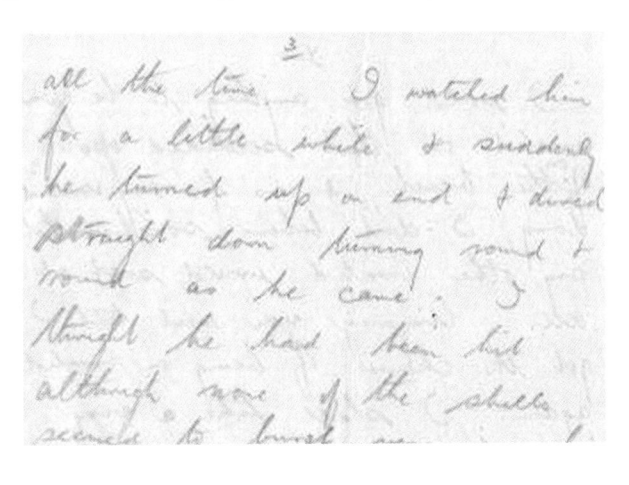

5pm

Just got your letter May 1st. I would give anything to be your invalid in that secluded spot on the beach, and as for any invalid doing, I don't believe somehow that any other invalid would suit at all. Anyway you wait till I get the chance of being an invalid again. I shall take a very, very long time getting well.

I thought Tullie Thomson was much too delicate to have another youngster.

As you say the Ansteys are indeed strange over that nurse. I don't think I should want her about my place.

I see no reason why Mum shouldn't read "The Great Scourge", but I leave it entirely to you as to whether take it to her. Just do as you think fit.

During the morning my platoon had to do drill (we take it in turns to do this) as being in with people like the Guards we are to be as smart as smart can be. Everything has to be done "just so" according to the book. As a matter of fact I don't believe anyone here (at all events amongst the senior officers) knows a great deal about drill so that I feel rather more sure of myself over it than I do of most other things, my Artists training coming in very well in this direction.

After drill we or rather another company did an attack which we followed up and criticised. I am awfully good at finding faults with other peoples things.

This afternoon I was on the railway, cleaning the track and putting down sleepers.

This evening I am going for another riding lesson.

Goodbye

David

David to May   B.E.F. France   May 12th 1917

My Dearest,

I haven't much news at all today.

We went out as usual on to the railway this morning. There was no train to take us, so we had to march. We were sent to work on the same bridge as we were on the other day, filling in the hole with chalk which we got from a quarry close by loaded it into wagons and unloaded it afterwards.

It was a glorious day and on such days as this I simply long for you, to be away from everybody else, right away in the country, with just ourselves. Wouldn't it be lovely? Generally speaking while we are at work a German aeroplane will sail across every now and then and get turned back again by our guns and we always take our own Lewis gun with us in case they get close enough to take a shot at them. Two of them yesterday at different times did, and our gun had a go at them, but it is awfully difficult to hit a machine high up like they are.

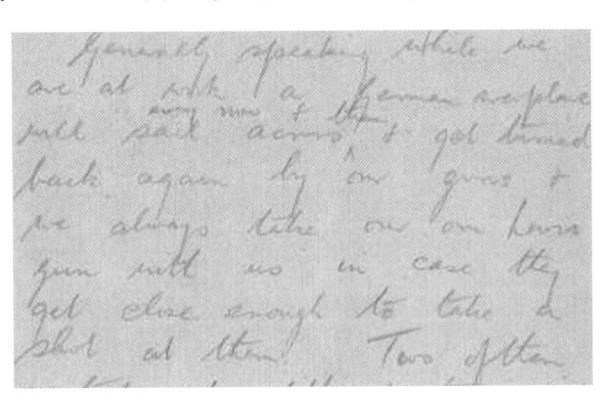

In the afternoon all those who could be spared were sent back to watch an outpost scheme done by the company whose turn it was for training. So that I spent the whole afternoon wandering about with three others, making the riflemen who were acting as sentries etc. uncomfortable, by asking them questions to see if they knew their work in much the same way as I was questioned and made uncomfortable when I was in the A [censored] When we got back to camp the colonel gave us his idea of how the thing should have been done (of course it was different to the way it had been done), and whilst talking he mentioned that he thought we should probably be doing some night training shortly.

After tea I got a horse and went with two others for a ride. We were out for some time and had several races across the fields. I was on the fastest horse (none of them were very fast), and he usually kept in front whilst one of the other fellows who can ride very well was coming up behind yelling hunting calls and calling to his horse to go faster, which simply made my own horse go for all he was worth. However, I managed to keep on him and really thoroughly enjoyed it.

When I can ride decently I must teach you and then we can go out together. I know you will like it.

I got back just in time to inspect my men's rifles and then found your letter waiting for me (7th). Yes sometimes it does seem only a short time since we were together, at others I have such a longing to have you just all to myself again, that it seems years, and still more years until I am likely to get you again.

You don't understand my relations. It is the thing to quote scripture in your letters. It doesn't matter if it makes sense or not, it must be done to show how very perfect you are. I mean the writer of the letter. The stranger of course referred to is Miss Capel, not you.

I did laugh over your description of the chapel service and Mum's remarks.

We have just gone to bed, I mean we two (the tent is empty and the others are playing cards)) and you have just asked me to put my head in its nest. You are a dear.

Goodbye.

David

David to May   B.E.F. France   14th May 1917

I expect this will be the last letter you will get for perhaps 3 days, as tomorrow's post goes out before we shall be bank in camp from the railway and Wednesday & Thursday we shall be on the road back to our old quarters, and I shall not be able to post letters.

To-morrow we shall be at work as usual but the next day we start at 5. 30. a.m. which means of course that we shall have to be up about 3. o'clock.

Last night I woke up to find a terrific thunder storm going on. There was a gale blowing with it and the lightning was almost continuous lighting up the inside of the tent, although of course we were completely shut in. I expected the tent to be lifted and blown away every second or to find myself suddenly floating down the valley on a sort of tidal wave.

However, the tent held although sheets and other things were being blown about outside and we really got very little water in but a great many of the other tents were flooded. It lasted about 20 minutes perhaps, and then I tucked myself up and went to sleep.

I had to be up just after 5 this morning as I was orderly officer and had to dismiss one of the guards.

I then got ready to take the company to wash at the stream, but found that all the orders had been suddenly altered.

We spent most of the morning on the range and at drill (this being our day for training) and this afternoon we did another outpost scheme.

As usual I got cornered by the colonel who asked me all sorts of questions which I wasn't prepared for. He ought to give me fair warning of this sort of thing and then I might answer his puzzles better.

He went off after a bit (in disgust I expect) and left me to myself much relieved that he had cleared out.

I got back to camp about 5 saw that the men's teas were alright, had my own, then inspected and mounted the guard, dismissed the old guard, inspected my own platoon's rifles and then had dinner.

In the middle of dinner I had to go out to have the orderly sergeants report their companies present and then go to the colonel to report the battalion present and now I am waiting for

10.15. when I can turn out the guard, visit the prisoners and sentries and go to bed.
I got a parcel from Mum to-day with your socks in it. You are a dear to make them for me. I really wanted them too as I was running rather short.
Must go out to the guard now.

Goodbye.

15th day
I have got the morning free so shall be able to catch the post.
People here are still going on leave. They go at the rate of about two a fortnight, so in the course of a few months it will work down to my turn, that is if all leave isn't stopped again.
I got up this morning thinking I was going on to the rly, as usual, but it was found that two of us were not actually required so I am having the morning off and going down to relieve the others this afternoon.
According to the present plan we not only march back, to our old village, but we do all sorts of attacks and other training on the way, and then when we get there we are to do a whole lot of night operations.
We are going to enjoy ourselves,
Later:
I have wandered out of camp and am now lying on a hillside having lovely daydream. I have been thinking of the time at Rottingdean, but this sort of thing only makes our longing for home worse.

Goodbye

Bert Muggridge

David to May   B.E.F. France   May 15th 1917

I have just got your news, your terrible news. My Dear, I wish I could be with you or in some way do something to lighten your grief, but I seem so absolutely helpless.

I think you have done the best thing in writing to Bert's Platoon Commander (the address you gave should find him at once) as he is more likely to have particulars than anyone else.

You might also write to the Adjutant but his reply is more likely to be of a formal nature as he deals with the whole battalion.

If you could write to a man of his platoon or better still his section (a man that perhaps Bert has mentioned in his letters) you might get particulars which would be better even than the platoon commander as he may not have been on the spot at the time.

As Hepplethwaite was a friend of Bert's perhaps he could get more news.

Poor Mrs Muggridge and poor you. Don't make yourself ill with worry and work and of course don't worry about writing to me.

Goodbye

David

David to May   B.E.F. France   May 21st 1917

There is no mail in today and therefore no letter from you. I didn't expect one really, but still I am always anxious to get your letters.

We have had rather a busy day today. We started at 7.30 for a route march of about 8 or 9 miles. This was of course because the men marched so badly the other day. The country round here is not so fine as that we have just left. It is simply undulating agricultural country with patches of wood here and there. In the middle of a wood we halted for about ¾ hour, took our packs off and then went out into a field outside the wood and did some musketry. It rained pretty heavily off and on most of the morning but I was dry again by the time I got back. We got back to lunch and afterward a number of the officers (myself amongst them) had to go out to work out an outpost scheme for practices.

We did a whole lot of walking about but it was not bad as the weather had cleared up and the whole thing was simply a discussion on various points.

These outpost schemes of course vary with every different piece of ground and as no two men's opinions are the same you can always reckon that whatever scheme you have it won't meet with the approval of the officer who happens to be in command of the whole thing.

We got back to tea and afterwards had to go out and learn how to salute. Our own particular general says that none of the officers in the division salute properly, wherefore we are hauled out and taught how the forefinger should come one inch and no more or less above the right eye. I regret to say that one of the fellows whilst undergoing this instruction did not treat it as seriously as the occasion demanded and pulled out a protractor in order to measure the exact error in his own case.

I am sending a few postcards. Assevillers was one of the villages we went to soon after coming out of the trenches and the two views give you a very good idea of what these ruined villages look like.

When you are billeted in one of these places you live in the cellar of one of these wrecked cottages or perhaps in a dugout under one of the heaps of rubbish.

We went through Peronne on our way up to the railway. Of course I haven't been near Combles but the view gives you an excellent idea of the landscape anywhere near the front line trenches.

Campbell has gone to Paris with another man, Warner, for 4 days leave. I could get this French leave too, but I shall not do so, as I don't want a holiday unless you can be with me. Goodbye.

David

David to May   B.E.F. France   May 22nd 1917

Yesterday we heard from the billeting officer that there were several billets in the town empty, so another fellow and myself went to see them.

We went to several and it was rather fun interviewing the various ladies whose rooms they were. The other man would ask if she had a billet for officers and she would reply, and he would ask another question (I think he must speak French perfectly for sometimes he could get a whole sentence out without even pausing to think and even I could understand most of what he said) and she would reply more energetically and so they would go on, she beginning to throw her arms and head about more and more until she was fairly dancing about, with a stream of words flowing faster and faster, but I don't think any of these ladies could really speak French well for I could scarcely understand a word they said.

The 3 or 4 houses we visited were rather small and I was not keen on going there, as although they certainly had beds in them, I don't know how long those beds had been slept in and I preferred my valise in the hut, and as they were scattered about we decided to stay where we were.

At one place we had been told to go to No 15. We found the usual archway and in the courtyard inside there were five small houses. After much enquiry and much waving of hands on the part of five ladies, who all talked at once, we found that four out of the five houses were numbered 15 and the fifth one 15BIS and that each one had a room for officers but that they were all occupied.

At another place another lady, having shown us the room, brought out a very bad photo of Sir Douglas Haig in a weekly paper, and another of the Prince of Wales, and went into raptures over both.

We were to have gone for a route march again this morning but it was raining hard so they let us off. Instead we spent the morning fitting the men's equipment on to them. A good many of them won't take the trouble to tighten the straps or let them out and so carry an uncomfortable pack, which makes all the difference on the march.

After that we did some musketry and then physical drill.

This afternoon there are some brigade sports in preparation for the divisional sports but I have gone in the opposite direction and am now sitting in a wood. I like to get away from the army as often as possible.

The hut we are in is in the drive up to that chateau I sent. At one time it must have been a fine place. It is built in the middle of a wood with a double avenue of trees leading from the front gates up to the house. These huts have been built in this drive and of course the whole place is very neglected.

The stables close to us are built round a big courtyard but at present they are occupied by the men of another battalion.

I hope you get those postcards and that the censor doesn't stop them.

David

Français souvenons-nous!

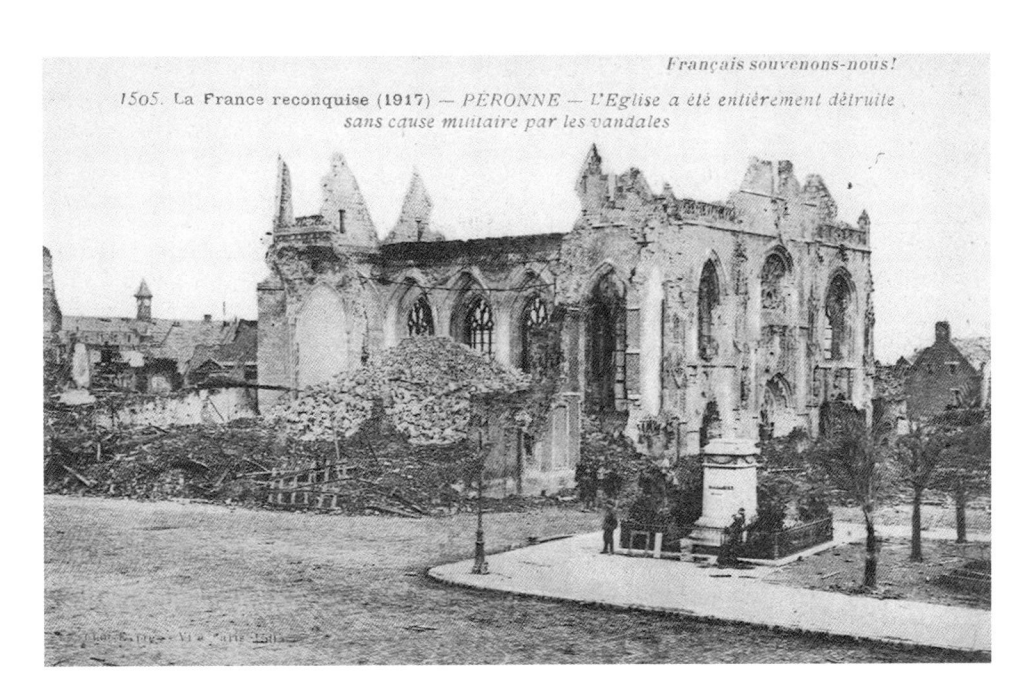

1505. La France reconquise (1917) — PERONNE — L'Eglise a été entièrement détruite sans cause militaire par les vandales

VILLERS-BRETONNEUX — Place des Halles

1263 LA GRANDE GUERRE 1914-17 — Offensive Franco-Anglaise de la Somme
French and English offensive de la Somme — *ASSEVILLERS* - Ruines de la Mairie

70 my dearest

VILLERS-BRETONNEUX — Le Château (Propriété E. D.)

VILLERS-BRETONNEUX — Place des Halles

my dearest 71

David to May   B.E.F. France   May 23rd 1917

Today we have had a picnic, they told us it was a route march, but they really meant a picnic. We started off at 8 o'clock this morning and marched over the hills and far away along a dead straight road. Any number of these French roads are perfectly straight and of course lined each side with trees, so that you can nearly always pick up a road for you see these long lines of trees and know at once that they are lining a road. I think they were originally made by Napoleon for moving his troops about and now they are being used again for the same purpose and are kept in repair by little groups of German prisoners. Generally speaking they have about 20 or 30 in a group with a Tommy with a fixed bayonet in charge and they look quite tame and to be having quite a good time. As we pass the NCO (they have their own NCO) in charge of the party stands up and salutes.

They wear their old German uniforms, but have a dark blue patch on the leg of their trousers which gives them a somewhat dilapidated appearance and if they happen to have their overcoats on and to be working under the French, they have a huge yellow P.G. on their tracks.

We went on for a few miles and finally marched through a tiny village and halted in a small wood just outside and in front of a fairly big chateau. This chateau is where the divisional school lives and as the man in command there belongs to the regiment we sort of paid a call. The river ran through part of the grounds as usual forming large lakes and we split the men into two parties, one of those who could swim and one of those who couldn't and then we took them to bathe.

I went with the swimmers, and the lake was quite deep, in fact you couldn't touch bottom anywhere.

One of the party that I was looking after got cramp and hung round another fellow's neck and then of course they both went under, but they were not very far out and I yelled to three other men to get hold of them and so got them out fairly easily.

After the men had finished, the officers had their swim. It was lovely - you simply dived in from the bank and the water was quite warm.

After that we took the men back to the wood for dinner. We had the cookers with us. These are really splendid things as they cook whilst on the move, so that when the men halt there is a hot meal ready for them at once.

After dinner we did some practice in getting the men's gas masks on quickly and firing with them on and then marched back, getting in about 4,30.

Since then I have gone for a walk and am now sitting in a wood writing this.

David

David to May   B.E.F. France   May 24th 1917

I have had a lazy day today. All the other officers had to go out to do an outpost scheme and as I had been one of the small party [censored]. I had to take the company out for a route march.

I marched them down to the river about 2 or 3 miles away. Instead of marching in the ordinary way I divided up the company as an advanced guard.

Down near the river I found a small wood or rather a large group of trees, so I took the men in there, sat them down in a circle round me and then read out a letter of congratulation from the General of the Army Corps that we were in until we were [censored]. Then I read some-points on the recent fighting and then afterwards gave them some practice in getting their gas masks on and off.

All this took about ¾ hour which really gave them a fair rest. Then I moved on taking a road which was marked on the map as a second class road. After a little while this second class road began to get worse and worse until it became merely two cart ruts and then finally ended in a field.

We went on for a bit and got on to another second class road and after a while struck the main road and got back in time for the men's dinners.

This afternoon there have been divisional sports. The battalion got five prizes and the brigade did fairly well, but I don't know whether we were top or not.

David

David to May   B.E.F. France   May 24th 1917

I am enclosing Hepplethwaite's reply to my letter. He gives no further information and doesn't appear to have been near Bert at the time.
Bert must have done awfully well to get as far as he did.
I am sorry I am able to get no more than this.
I do wish I were near you and able to do things for you.
Goodbye.

David

Hepplethwaite to David   B.E.F. France   20th May 1917

Dear Sir,
I am in receipt of your letter of the 15th instant re Pte H.G. Muggridge and am afraid I can only repeat my statement to his mother viz - that he was killed in the German Lines and three or four men in his platoon say that they saw him lying dead. As you probably know he was a personal friend of mine and therefore you can imagine I have made all possible enquiries and am afraid I cannot tell you anything further.
Yours sincerely
(Sgd.) R S Hepplethwaite
2 Lt.

B.E.F.
France
20th May 1917

Dear Sir,

I am in receipt of your letter of the 15th inst re Pte H.G. Muggridge and am afraid I can only repeat my statement to his brother viz — that he was killed in the German lines and three or four men in his platoon say that they saw him lying dead. As you probably know he was a personal friend of mine and therefore you can imagine I have made all possible enquiries and am afraid I cannot tell you anything further.

Yours sincerely,
R. A. Hellawaite
2/Lt.

David to May **B.E.F. France** **May 25th 1917**

If you can get hold of one of the privates in Bert's platoon there is no reason why he shouldn't give you a full account of what happened.

I certainly do tell you more than the men here write about, (they usually talk about the weather and the health of themselves and the people at home and very little else, which is really a good thing, as there is then no doubt about crossing things out) but if you wrote to one of the men he could probably give you a better account of it than Hepplethwaite can.

I will write myself if you can get the name of a man, but I think that you yourself would probably get more information than I should. I am sorry Mrs. Muggridge seems so bad, but you can scarcely wonder at it. I do hope you are getting as much sleep as possible at night as otherwise you will be ill yourself.

I may not be able to write for the next two days or perhaps three as we are moving again and there will be no post tomorrow.

I believe we are going right up north into Belgium this time and once you get on a train here you never quite know when you are getting off again.

My Dear, I would give anything to have you in my arms again.

Goodbye.

David

David to May   B.E.F. France   May 25th 1917

We were threatened with an early parade this morning in order to take the men to the baths, but this was cancelled at the last moment and they were sent to refit with new clothing,
In consequence we didn't parade until 9 o'clock and then marched over the same ground and in the same way as I did yesterday.
We halted where I did yesterday and had lunch there. There was a disused hut close by and the servants went in and found a table and a couple of wire beds so we had lunch in style.
After lunch we took the company a bit further on to a canal. We again picked out the swimmers and non swimmers, fixed two points as a limit for the men to go and put several swimmers to swim about and keep their eye on the men.
The non swimmers were to bathe along the bank.
After the men had nearly finished we started, had a fine swim and we nearly dressed again when the report came along that there was a suit of clothes with no owner. We made enquiries, called the roll and sure enough there was a man missing.
We looked everywhere for him and went up and down the canal but could find no trace of him. He was a non swimmer and had been bathing in the middle of the river and there were several sergeants who were not bathing watching the men from the bank apart from the picquet who was swimming in the water and yet nobody saw him at all.
We can only conclude that he slipped off without a sound into deep water and was carried down under the water by the current.
We then marched back again while three of the officers stayed behind to make further enquiries but they found no trace of him.

David

David to May   B.E.F. France   May 26th 1917

We were up at 5 o'clock this morning and started off at 6.30.

We were to be Germans for the time being and were to be attacked by the remainder of the battalion!

The idea was that we were being driven through a big wood. Two platoons waited just inside the wood and retired slowly to a position, but my platoon and another were in further back.

We had quite a good position with machine guns (represented by a man with a tin can which he banged with a stick)) to wipe out anybody who came near.

We also put up a barricade with brushwood (there had been a number of trees cut down) and made quite a strong place of it.

After a long wait the enemy appeared (they had all been shot several times before this) close to us and advanced in a most heroic way against a tremendous imaginary machine gun and rifle fire, and had got close up to our barricade and were just making up their minds to rush it, (I am sure they were all dead long before this)) when the bugle sounded the cease fire and also said that the war was over, at least for the morning.

Then the officers were collected round the commanding officer (the colonel by the way is on leave in England)) and had to give their explanation of what happened and each pointed out where the other side had all been wiped out and then the C.O. gave his idea of the thing and then we all went back to lunch.

This afternoon we had nothing much to do (I suppose because we are moving in the middle of the night) but I had to have another last inspection and also inspected the men's boots.

I was just coming away when one of my sergeants asked if he might speak to me so with boundless generosity and goodness of heart I permitted him to.

It appeared that about 2 months ago his wife had written to him saying that she didn't want anything more to do with him and although he had written several times since, he could get no reply. Could I do anything for him? The troubles and trials of being a platoon commander!!!

He also said that he didn't trouble much about his wife, but there was a youngster about 2 years old and the thing that troubled him most of all seemed to be that he was making an allowance of 1/10 a day to her out of his pay.

I questioned him and suggested that he should write to one or two people in order to see if his wife were living in the same place and see what this would do.

Am just off to bed.

David

BAILLEUL — Rue des Foulons
Ficheroulle-Beheydt, édit., Bailleul

731. La Grande Guerre 1914-15. - Un des portails de la Cathédral d'Arras après les derniers bombardements.
Visé Paris 731

my dearest 79

David to May   B.E.F.   May 27th 1917

We were up at 3 o'clock this morning, got everything packed and loaded on to the wagons and marched off at 6.30.

This time we got breakfast, in fact we did everything pretty comfortably.

We marched to the station got the men into the train, loaded the wagons and baggage and found that, wonder of wonders, the officers were to travel in 2nd class carriages.

Certainly most of the windows were missing and in one compartment they afterwards found some livestock walking about, but still there they were, a whole coach of 2nd class carriages.

Whilst waiting for the train to start we amused ourselves by playing cricket alongside the train. The bat consisted of a piece of wood, the ball of the knob of a brass bed post and the wicket of an old oil keg with a pair of old boots on top. When the match had gone on some time, the train suddenly decided to start and we all had to scramble in. There were six in our compartment and four of them began to play cards and I started to read and dropped off to sleep.

I woke up about 11 o'clock and found we were still travelling and we continued to do so until about l o'clock when we stopped for something or other and we all went into the next truck where the food was and had lunch.

We went on with a stop or two occasionally all the afternoon with no special incident except that at one time B company servants made some tea in a jug (without milk or sugar) and brought to us and hearing of it, some of the other officers tried to raid the compartment, and we had to beat them off. About 5 o'clock we came in sight of the sea. It looked lovely and it seemed almost as though we were on the way home and it was awfully tantalizing to know that home was only just across that strip of sea and yet so far off.

We ran along by the sea for a time and then turned inland again and finally stopped about 8 o'clock.

After leaving the train we had to march about 2 to 3 miles to a village - a fairly big one.

On the way we passed a number of Australians. They are a lot and seem to go out of their way to get a bad name for themselves.

Any number of them were drunk and rolling along the streets. The roads here are cobble stones (pave) and although it was only a short march we noticed the difference at once.

I expect marching will play us up a bit until we get used to it. We saw the men into their billets (they have all got wire beds and should be fairly comfortable) and then I went to find mine.

An old lady opened the door and evidently expected me, for she didn't say anything, but merely bowed and led me to my room and went straight away.

It was a small room but there was a BED. A BED with a deep spring mattress and some sort of a bed on top and clean SHEETS and an EIDER-DOWN.

This is the first bed I have seen out here and I wanted to get in then at once so as to waste no time but I had to find the mess and, then had supper and am now off to bed, it being about 12 o'clock.

David

David to May   B.E.F. France   May 27th 1917

My Dearest,

I found two letters waiting for me here today (20th, 21st and 22nd combined) and two such lovely long letters too. You say you don't think you will be able to write and then you snatch every opportunity to do so. You really are the dearest little girl that ever was, but you know that, don't you?

Well perhaps I have been a bit down-hearted lately, but it was simply because I was thinking about you and wondering how you were and you don't know how I have wanted to comfort you. Thanks very much for the cuttings.

I am sitting up in bed writing this and all the time you keep pulling me down. Well I suppose you must have your own way as usual.

There you are is that nice?

David

David to May   B.E.F. France   May 28th 1917

Three letters from you this morning (Wed, Thurs and Fri), and such loving letters. You are a darling.

Last night was lovely.

You had your new vest on but there were no buttons on it and after I laid down as you wanted me to you insisted on cuddling my head and pressing it close into its nest. Then we got too hot so I threw the blankets etc. off and you turned your back to me and I had both arms round you that way, like we used to and you went to sleep like this. But later on you woke up and said you wanted your cheek against mine and wanted to be held quite close against me and then you dropped off to sleep again.

This morning I woke up at 7 but you were still asleep in my arms and didn't wake up until 8.30. Then I had to get up in a hurry.

I am glad Mrs. Muggridge is better but I wish she could get over those trembling fits.

Looks here from your letter lot of heavy work. Don't do too much and knock yourself up there's a dear.

Goodbye.

David

P.S. I walked out into the fields this morning with the intention of reading a whole collection of your letters and then burning them (I have a pocket full and there is not much room for any more and I must always carry them for fear of other people seeing them which I couldn't stand) but I read them and then I found I simply couldn't burn them (they are all I have of you at present except your photo) so there they are still.

David to May   B.E.F. France   May 28th 1917

That bed last night was good and I tried to sleep with the sheets, blankets and eider-down all on top so as to get the full benefit of it and not waste any, but the heat was so terrible that I couldn't stand it long and had to throw it all off except the sheet.
But still it did seem like throwing away a good thing.
We haven't done much today. There was a rifle inspection this morning and this afternoon we did some drill from 2 o'clock until 4.20 but that was all.
I haven't been able to get any postcards of Arras except the one I am enclosing but I will try again.
Please thank Em for Printers Pie and it is good of you to send it.

David

David to May   B.E.F. France   May 29th 1917

We were up at 4 o'clock this morning.
I was company orderly officer and had to see the men's breakfasts.
We went for a route march starting at 5.15. We marched out with the band playing and bugles blowing and I guess the good people blessed us for waking them up.
The people in my billet can only speak a few English words so that it took some time and many repetitions to make them understand that I should be moving around about 4 o'clock and that my servant would be coming in about that time.
We only marched about 7 or 8 miles. The country around is pretty flat everywhere and I should imagine in winter time pretty dreary, with plenty of mud, for there are ditches dug everywhere to drain the land. At present however it isn't so bad as there are a number of trees and everything is green.
We got back about 9 o'clock, had a short rest and then had to parade again for bayonet fighting and drill.
Then I saw that dinner was good and this afternoon being orderly officer I had to take the company to the baths.
The baths are about 1 1/2 miles away and we started at four o'clock and after they had all washed it was near 7 before we got back, so you see we have had a fair day.
Since then I have read through and censored about 30 letters and am now off to bed.

David

David to May   B.E.F. France   May 29th 1917 second

My Dearest,

No letters from you today but of course I didn't really expect one and have had to read through again the three that came yesterday instead.

You re a darling aren't you, and I wish I could kiss you goodnight as you say.

One of our fellows in B Company went off on leave this evening and he landed at the end of December so perhaps with a certain amount of luck my turn will come in about a couple of months, and then and then…well come here and be hugged, just to see if we can image what it will really be like.

I am writing this in bed as usual and…Oh alright if I must get in I must.

Goodbye

David

David to May   B.E.F. France   May 30th 1917

My Dearest,

I have just got your letter (27th), a lovely long one too and written from home on Sunday. You are a darling.

I like your daydream while you were polishing the hall, but I guess I didn't give you the day off – a partner in a business just has the day whenever she wants it.

I guess I must see that small dress you are making in case our order for boys is misunderstood and we get girls.

I do hope you persuade Mrs Muggridge to go to West Wickham (you really ought to look about for a spot, in case we manage to live there) and I hope you have a good day. Its an awful pity she doesn't sleep well as that is probably causing half the trouble.

I missed the post yesterday so am sending the letter today.

I must write to Mum now, so

Goodbye

David

David to May   B.E.F. France   May 30th 1917

My servant came along and woke me up at 6.30 this morning and then brought in coffee and excellent coffee too, made of course by the people I am billeted with. I have had this two mornings now. Isn't it good of them. They seem to be doing all they can to make me comfortable, although I have hardly seen them but they told my servant he could put my clothes etc. into a sort of bureau which acts as a chest of drawers and they sent in this coffee quite of their own accord.

The mess is a few hundred yards away and here too (although they are not quite such good class people as my people) we are made quite welcome and practically have the run of the place.

My billet is beautifully clean too.

I think the people here generally seem to welcome the troops and this I think speaks rather well for the British, as of course they have been here about $2\frac{1}{2}$ years now, long enough in fact that they, as usual, have taught nearly all the inhabitants to speak some English.

I haven't yet seen any post cards but please tell Ethel I will get some as soon as I can.

This morning we did some bayonet fighting first on some sacks that there are here then some musketry and then practiced one small part of an attack.

This afternoon we are to parade at 2.30 to go shooting on a range some distance away and which is supposed to take until 7 o'clock but I don't think we shall finish by then.

We marched about 3 miles to the range and then one platoon started firing.

The colonel by the way has returned from his leave and as usual this afternoon he (figuratively speaking) took me by the scruff of my neck and held me up before all mankind as a specimen of what an officer should not be.

He started off by calling me on one side and pointing out, very emphatically and distinctly, that my men looked as though they had had no drill whatever and that unless I pulled them up the whole platoon would go to blazes, and seeing that they were walking on some boards across the middle of a ploughed field perhaps he was right about their appearance. Anyhow I didn't argue with him.

The next thing that happened was that he told me to suppose that they were a lot of recruits and I was to teach them fire control.

Now you never quite know where to begin with the colonel, so I always question him as to just exactly what he does want and he doesn't like being questioned and gets more and more snappy as each question is asked. However I started and went on for a short while, when he took the whole thing out of my hands and did it himself for which I was truly thankful.

He went on for some time giving each of my section commanders a bad time in turn and when he had finished he turned to me and said I must (he is very fond of the word must) give my platoon practice in fire control and then said I was to carry on with judging distance.

It took much too long for the other platoons to fire so that my platoon and another didn't get their chance and I expect we shall have to go again, probably tomorrow.

I marched these two platoons back again leaving the others still on the range.

David

David to May   B.E.F. France   May 31st 1917

My Dearest,
No letter from you today so I suppose you managed to get Mrs Muggridge to go to West Wickham.
I do hope you had a splendid day and thoroughly enjoyed yourselves.
Goodbye

David

David to May   B.E.F. France   May 31st 1917

I have just had a new corporal sent to my platoon.
There was some bother between him, the sergeant and the platoon commander of No.6 platoon so he has been passed on to me.
He has been given a Russian Order for doing something or other.
It always strikes me as being awfully humourous that I, who know so little of army work, should be put in charge of men who have been in the army all their lives and who have seen much more of the war than I have and that I should tell them what to do, or what not to do and how to do it. And what is most funny still, they take me seriously and do as I tell them. Really the army is a funny place.
This morning or rather last night there was a route march ordered, starting very early again, but just before we went to bed this was cancelled as far as the officers were concerned and all except one of us had to go out with the colonel for what is called a "staff ride". Why it is called a "ride" nobody can tell because everyone walked, including the colonel.
We walked out a little way, found a windmill and sat down and discussed an outpost position in front of us.
From that we drifted on to the use of the prismatic compass, the colonel asking all sorts of questions on it.
Then we walked round to see the actual ground that we had discussed for the outpost and then had another discussion on it and came back for lunch.
I have to parade at 4 o'clock for a General's inspection so must cut my hair and powder my nose.
Later
The General has inspected us and I suppose everything was alright as nothing was said.
I have to be up at 4 o'clock again tomorrow to go shooting so I suppose I had better go to bed.

David

David to May   B.E.F. France   June 1st 1917

My Dearest,

What does Lxxxxxn mean like the enclosed? I can't possibly guess. Don't you think you might write it in full?

I am awfully sorry Mrs Muggridge is still so unwell and worst of all unable to sleep, for of course that does not help to make things better.

The letters came in two batches today and there was nothing from you at first and I thought it was going to be another day without a letter, but it came about 2 hours later and I was glad. But look here you mustn't write to me if it makes a rush for you (and I know you are awfully busy) I'll just have to go without.

After I had written that letter to Mrs Muggridge, I was sorry I had sent it as I guess that letters only upset her and it would have been better if I hadn't written at all.

I think its like the Base Censor's impudence to read our letters, or rather my letter (I have never had any of yours opened).

The Generals congratulations was on the good work the division had done – they had been in a good many of the big fights before I got here.

Now just cuddle up close and then you'll get to sleep quickly.

Goodbye

David

Northern Assurance

David to May   Western Front   June 1st 1917

When we went bathing the other day we had towels but strange to relate they don't provide bathing machines along that canal, and in the middle of our bathe two ladies came walking along the tow path and we had to get the men into the water quickly.

I am sending some postcards but unfortunately I could only get two of Arras. Postcards are scarce as none are being printed and so the selection is very poor but please tell Ethel I will try again elsewhere.

We have had a very short day today.

This morning we did some bayonet fighting for about 1 1/2 hours and I took my fellows with some Lewis gun work.

Afterwards there was to be an inspection by the colonel but that didn't come off and we went for a short march instead. This afternoon the men were paid and we had a last inspection and I looked at their boots and that finished the day.

I then went into the town to get those postcards but didn't succeed unfortunately.

I went in an ambulance and came back in a lorry.

That is one thing out here, you can nearly always get a lift or at least if you are near any of the main roads some distance behind the line you just simply stop any motor and ask for a lift as far as you are going, climb in and away you go.

One of our fellows had a funny experience yesterday.

Apparently last night the Germans dropped a few long range shells just outside the village (I didn't hear them as I was asleep) and the old lady that he is billeted with came into his room for a few minutes while he was in bed because she was frightened.

The people in the house where our mess is have stayed there since the war started and had German officers billeted on them and saw the Germans driven out by the British.

David

David to May   Western Front   June 2nd 1917

We were up at 5 o'clock this morning and did bayonet fighting.
There is to be a competition in this and I am hoping that one of my sections will win it.
One of them is rather good but the others are not, but perhaps they will improve.
After that we did some musketry for about an hour and then went for a route march until lunch time.
At lunch it was discovered that we are shooting tomorrow and that it was doubtful whether there would be any targets to fire at so I said I would go to the range to find out.
I got a horse (the range being about 3 miles away) and went off.
I hadn't had this horse before and he shied at every gate leading into a field or anything that had the least suggestion of white about it. Then at every road junction he would stop and read the finger posts and if he thought the side road would eventually lead in the direction of home he would promptly try to go in that direction. However after a little trouble I persuaded him to go as far as the range, arranged about the targets and started back.
The horse knew at once that we were on the road back but I disappointed him rather by turning off and taking a longer way round. He went along fairly and we were trotting fairly well down a road (you can't go across country here because every inch is cultivated) when he came to a white canvas horse trough by the side of the road, planted his fore feet and stopped dead.
I myself didn't stop quite so suddenly but rolled over his head and landed in the road. He no sooner got me off his back then he turned round with a sigh of relief and began quietly grazing by the side of the road.
If that wasn't adding insult to injury tell me.
I got up knocked off some of the dust and came back, managing to sit on him for the rest of the way.
I have since found that two other people had the same trouble with this horse. I don't mind so much now, but they didn't come off of course, I have to be up at 5 o'clock again tomorrow to go shooting and on a Sunday too. Isn't it disgraceful? I think I shall ask Maud to write to the colonel about it giving her opinion. I am certain that that ought to have the effect of stopping the war on Sundays.

David
P.S. I have just heard that the early shooting is all off and we go to church instead, so it won't be necessary for Maud to write after all.

David to May   Western Front   June 2nd 1917

My Dearest,

Or perhaps you would like it written My Dxxxxxt – as you do to me.

Just got your letter of 30th.

I am sorry about your hair, but I guess its the worry you've had and also the fact that you haven't had a holiday. Wish I could take you away somewhere.

About Bert – I should think the corporal is right and Hepplethwaite wrong, as the corporal was on the spot at the time.

I went to bed immediately after dinner yesterday, for now I have a room to myself and I am always anxious to get there, because you are always waiting for me there and always say and do such nice things, cheeky things sometimes, but I always know thats because you can't help it.

Goodbye

David

I am enclosing a letter from Ethel. Don't want it back. The chocolate she mentions turned up today having been about 6 weeks on the road.

David to May   Western Front   June 3rd 1917

We got up this morning with the idea of going to church, but while I was dressing an orderly came along to say that the church parade was off, (you never can tell what you are doing from one minute to the next, its a little way they have in the army) and that the colonel wanted to see all officers and NCOs at 10 o'clock. I was glad in a way, because I was pretty late and this gave me more time.

When he turned up he gave us a lecture on musketry for about an hour. The General has sent along an order that the musketry is not all as it should be, so that everything has to give way to musketry for the moment.

After that we had to give the NCOs belonging to our own platoons some practice in giving firing orders. This lasted until lunch time. After lunch having nothing to do I thought I would have a bath, (I haven't had one since I have been here) and was just in the middle of it when somebody else wanted to see me this time a sergeant who called through the key hole that the General was coming to inspect billets this afternoon.

I said I was delighted to hear it, but that it didn't concern me as I was not orderly officer or any other sort of officer at the moment (not having any clothes on) and he had better go away and find out who it was he really wanted. He went.

I have just got your letter (31st).

It is good of Mrs Muggridge to ask you to write about my bathing and to warn me about the Germans putting wire in the canals (which is quite likely). Please tell her I'll be very careful and certainly don't intend to be fished up from the bottom with a hook, and there are no mines or canals etc. about here, so that we cannot bathe now.

There are always numbers of areoplanes about and at the moment (I am sitting in a field having strolled out away from the village) I can count a dozen from where I am.

Later

The Germans have just sent over 3 or 4 shells (I suppose they were incendiary) and have set fire to some farm buildings about a mile out of the village and they are blazing away like anything. The beggars (the Germans I mean).

David

David to May   Western Front   June 3rd 1917

My Dearest,

I woke up this morning, looked at my watch and then knew that I had about 2 hours before I had to get up.

You were still asleep in my arms, with your back to me and you looked so nice that I just wanted to squeeze you and kiss you, but couldn't do it because of waking you.

You see up to that time you hadn't kicked me out as you usually do (that is, according to your letters) and in fact when you did wake up you insisted on cuddling my head. It was lovely.

I finally got up at 8.30 and then had tea as I was due on parade at 9.30.

I am glad my letters are some good to Mrs Muggridge (I feel quite important) but I really don't think they are all that interesting to anyone except perhaps you.

Yes I feel that I have heaps of hours in your arms owing to me (I have been away from you nearly 5 months) and I mean to get them with compound interest as soon as I get home.

Goodbye

David

David to Ginger   Western Front   June 3rd 1917

Dear Ginger,

Now to thank you for all sorts of good things.

First of all another Buzzard cake, which I got some days ago and which disappeared very quickly indeed. Buzzard cakes I think go even more quicker than others out here.

Then yesterday both the chocolate and a box of cigarettes arrived at the same time, although of course the chocolate had been on the road longer but having been to the base was naturally delayed. However, everything came splendidly, although the boxes were a good deal knocked about.

This morning the papers came. Thanks ever so much for them all and everything.

I passed the cigarettes on to the platoon and I think they were very quickly shared out. Its jolly good of you to send them, and the men like cigarettes better than anything I think, in fact I know, for they constantly ask the folks at home to send them out.

We have moved again and are right away up the other end of the line. It was quite a long train journey and we took all day over it, but this time we really travelled pretty fast at times.

We are in proper billets here and I have a room to myself with actually a BED – a proper bed with clean sheets, blankets and an eiderdown all complete.

It is the first bed I have seen since I have been out here and the first night I tried to get full value out of it and had the sheets, blankets and eiderdown all on top, but the heat was so terrific that I couldn't stand it and simply had to throw them off. It was very sad.

Next morning I had another shock – my servant brought me coffee in bed, made by the people in the house and served up quite nicely with sugar, milk etc and moreover a spoon to stir it with.

I may say that this last is somewhat of a luxury as in the mess we usually can only raise 2 or 3 spoons between 7 of us.

I don't know whether I told you about our bathing at the last place we were at.

The weather has been very hot and we took the company several times bathing.

The day before we moved we went swimming in a canal about 2 or 3 miles from where we were, but unfortunately one of the men got drowned.

He couldn't swim and was bathing along the edge of the canal and must have slipped off into deep water and disappeared.

We didn't find it out until everybody was nearly dressed and nobody claimed his clothes.

We had a guard of 8 men swimming in the canal and several sergeants watching from the bank and yet nobody saw or heard him go.

I expect Mum has told you that Bert Muggridge has been killed. He apparently was in an attack and had got into the German lines when he was hit by a shell.

Yesterday I had to go out to a rifle range about 3 miles away, so I got a horse and rode out. I had never had this horse before and he shied at every mortal thing.

Then at every road junction he would stop, read the finger post and if he thought the side road went in the direction of home he promptly tried to turn up that road.

However, I persuaded him to go as far as I wanted and then turned back.
He knew he was going home and went along very well for a bit and then I disappointed him by turning off and going a longer way round. But he had his revenge.
We were trotting along quite well down a road (you can't ride across country here as every inch is cultivated) when he saw a white canvas horse trough and promptly planted his fore feet and stopped dead.
I couldn't stop quite so suddenly and rolled over his head and landed in the road.
Then with a sigh of relief he turned round and began quietly grazing by the side of the road. If that wasn't adding insult to injury tell me.
The Germans have just sent over 3 or 4 large shells just outside the village and have set fire to something I should think by the smoke, probably a farm building. The beggars!
Yours ever

David

P.S. My platoon sergeant has just thanked me on behalf of the platoon for the cigarettes.

Soldier to Ethel Linn   Western Front   [June 1917]

Dear Miss Linn,
Many thanks for the smokes sent by you.
They were appreciated very much. The card is quite unfit to send, more so its America, as it has been in my pocket for some time. Hence this epistle. I suppose you wonder who on earth this can be from. In that case, Lcpl O.W. Geary 2nd K.R.R., B.E/F. Was the fellow that enjoyed your cigarettes and please accept the best thanks and wishes.
I am

Sincerely Yours

O.W. Geary

David to May   Western Front   June 4th 1917

Just got your letter. Please tell Mrs Muggridge that my present surroundings are not so very awful, in fact they are quite good. This is a fair sized place and hasn't been knocked about by shells. Please thank her also for the cuttings.

Don't ever trouble to weigh your letters to me as I have never had one overweight.

We are constantly getting orders as to censoring letters. We are not allowed to mention anything at all it seems, either when we move or have moved or any other sort of news, so in future I shall write "hoping this finds you in the best of health as it etc. etc." then mention that the sun is shining and that it rained a fortnight ago, but this last will have to be done in such a way that it conveys no information to you.

We were up just after 4 o'clock this morning and marched to the rifle range and spent the whole of the morning firing there. We had the bugles and band going out and they did their best to wake the whole of Northern France I think and probably succeeded.

Last night the brigade padre called into the mess and when he heard that we were going out marching he asked to come too and sure enough there he was this morning although we paraded at 5 o'clock. We took breakfast with us and got it as best we could. Can't you see me with a ham sandwich in one hand and checking a man's shots with the other.

There is to be a brigade shooting competition this week and the officers are to shoot; so after the men had finished, several of us fired, to see which should be sent to fire for the battalion. Now I am not a good shot by any means but I was sent with another fellow to shoot for the company and then did very badly even for me, so that I am not firing in the competition.

While we were shooting apparently two of the companies were being put through their paces in musketry by our General of Generals and made a mess of things, in consequence of which we had to take all the NCOs out for special instruction this evening and now I expect we shall do musketry, musketry, musketry for ever and ever, world without end.

David

David to May Western Front June 4th 1917

My Dearest,

Two letters from you today 1st and 2nd the last one only taking two days to get here.

Now you are a dear naughty little girl to go buying things for me and spending your money on me and I know that tongues must be particularly expensive.

Really you shouldn't. We feed really very well in the mess and we ought to, seeing the amount that my mess bills are and I personally don't see why I should give things to the mess especially expensive things like tongues.

So I wouldn't send any more if I were you. You don't mind me telling you, do you? But I know you don't.

Look here if you tease me any more about that coat I'll – I'll – but there you know that when I threaten things, you only look more hugable than usual and I can't resist you.

Come along and I'll show you what I'll do.

Goodbye

David

P.S. I have torn off the bottom as perhaps I put something down as I "didn't oughter"

David to May   Western Front   June 5th 1917

We started a route march this morning at 7 o'clock, marched away several miles and then halted and gave our platoons some practice in giving firing orders.

It was awfully hot and dusty, but I managed to get into a field where there was some shade and got the men along under a hedge and got their equipment off.

They really do want a good deal of practice and it seems that we are to have it. Really though one cannot expect too much, seeing what little training they get before being sent out here, added to which some of them are conscripts and the great majority would never had been soldiers but for the war and therefore cannot be expected to be as keen as the man who is spending his life in the army.

We marched back about 11 o'clock, had a short break and then went for some bayonet fighting in preparation for the competition this week.

Did I ever tell you about our mascot or perhaps I should say mascots for apart from the battalion mascot there are innumerable dogs always around of weird and wonderful breeds (I saw one even in the trenches).

The battalion mascot is a small black pony about the size of a Newfoundland dog and as he is petted by all and sundry and fed on all sorts of things by the men he is about as round as he is high and as touchy as a spoilt child. He delights in the name of Coal Box and whenever there is a competition or match of any sort on, he is taken along to assist.

Our own Company mascot is the ugliest yellow kitten you ever saw. She was found in some trenches miles from anywhere when we were training away down South and now when we move she is carried by one of my platoon, in a box with her head hanging out of a hole.

That reminds me, my own special nickname with the other officers is Sandy.

The Germans sent over a number of big shells this morning and afternoon into, or just outside, another village some way off and in consequence a number of people from there have cleared out and have been coming through here with the idea of getting out of harms way.

I am afraid they set fire to something as there was a good deal of smoke at one time.

However their artillery dosen't compare with ours and we have guns and guns and still more guns.

This afternoon we had the NCOs out for a lecture or rather a lesson in musketry again.

As I go on out here, I realise that the training I got in the school at G.P was very good and I only wish I had had more of it.

David

David to May**Western Front****June 5th 1917**

My Dearest,

The tongue arrived today.

You had to have an extra special hug for it last night and now it has arrived you must be hugged again, because you ought to be and well – because I can't help it.

No letter from you today, but I suppose I had today's letter yesterday and perhaps I'll have to go without again tomorrow, which will be Sunday's letter. Lets hope you managed to write one.

I do hope Mrs Muggridge is getting better and that you yourself – oh I do want to have you again.

Goodbye

David

David to May**Western Front****June 6th 1917**

We had to be up pretty early again this morning as we were on parade at 6.15.

We marched about 8 miles and finally halted by a canal with a sort of wood on the banks.

It was not exactly a wood but there were a number of trees with a lot of undergrowth. Quite an ideal place to lie about in for an hour or so.

The canal was shallow enough for anyone to walk across so it was possible for everyone to bathe. I bathed too (I knew as it was so shallow Mrs Muggridge didn't consider this the sort of place that she warned me against), but it was not so good as before as the bottom was very muddy and the men soon stirred this up and the water was not clear, to say the least of it.

Afterwards we had lunch and then had about 2 hours lying about in the shade, most of us asleep.

They had brought the cookers out, so that just before we fell in to march back some tea was served out to the men and we begged some too.

After about the first hour's march it had been awfully hot all day, but we hadn't started on the way back very long before a thunderstorm began to come up behind and made things somewhat cooler.

It rained slightly practically all the way back, but this made marching rather more pleasant than otherwise. We got back about half past six.

Our guns have been thudding away for the last 2 or 3 days like anything. The Germans must be quite enjoying themselves.

David

David to May   Western Front   June 6th 1917

My Dearest,

No letter again today but I expect Monday's letter is taking 3 days so I'll get it tomorrow.

While we were out today we had about 2 hours rest under some trees and most of us went to sleep but I enjoyed myself by having day dreams of some of the wonderful times we have had, Switzerland, Rottingdean, Bramber, that bunker at G.P. which turned into a little bit of heaven, Hayes and then we were together in that small castle of ours and all sorts of wonderful things happened to us there and of course it will all happen and will come true. I know it must.
Goodbye

David

David to May   Western Front   June 7th 1917

We spent the first part of the morning drilling, and then the sergeants took over the men while the officers went out into some fields and worked out various imaginary problems which might come about at different times.

There were 4 of us doing this in one group when the colonel came along and asked for our ideas of the thing. When it came to my turn I gave him my idea and he at once remarked that I seemed to be commanding a division instead of a platoon.

Somehow the colonel's ideas and mine never seem to exactly agree. Perhaps it is because he's only a colonel.

Anyhow after some discussion Campbell agreed with most of my scheme.

After this we went back to the men and practiced marching past. I expect somebody or other is coming to inspect us so we are to show off our paces.

Its somewhat different marching past in front of your platoon than in the ranks and you feel a bit lonesome out there all by yourself.

There has been splendid news coming in all day and the guns are still thumping away so I expect the Germans are still enjoying themselves.

We had to parade again this afternoon to check the organization of our platoons and afterwards we had a lecture by the colonel.

Just before that however he had two men out and punished them. He caught them drinking yesterday from a dirty stream. Of course it was awfully hot and they had used all the water they had with them and then had gone to the stream.

We have to be very careful of water here always, as so much of it is bad, so the two caught it pretty hot.

He then read out some of the good news and then began to talk of the traditions of the regiment and how they had got to be carried on etc. etc.

We had a pretty heavy thunderstorm this evening which has made things much cooler.

David

David to May   Western Front   June 7th 1917

My Dearest,

I have got Monday's letter 4th, a nice long one. Look here don't you go having any more nightmares. I hardly know what a trench is now and in any case am not going to do any acrobatic feats like you saw.
I am glad you have been obedient and got your coat but now I want to see you in it.
Goodbye

David

David to May   Western Front   June 8th 1917

Had a very easy day today.
We paraded at 7.30 and did drill, bayonet fighting, and musketry during the morning.
Then we had to practice marching past again and saluting. This afternoon the company was out again practicing bayonet fighting for the competition that is coming off. I have got two sections that are pretty good and I am hoping that one of them will come out top of the company, if not of the battalion.
My platoon is I think the strongest in the company at present (I have got 240 men) but the numbers are constantly changing as you get men taken away for all sorts and conditions of things.
Headquarters send along and say they want 4+ men to train as stretcher bearers, or scouts, or pioneers, or snipers, or some fancy business of their own and they always add that they must be good men and in consequence you always send the men you can most easily part with. But this sort of thing is an awful nuisance and some times you have to let men go that are doing their own particular jobs very well indeed and this splits your sections up. Only today, a man who is in my platoon but has been doing one of these special jobs, got punished for something and is returned to the platoon and Campbell (without saying anything to me) promptly put one of my best rifle grendiers in his place. Of course I objected to it and I am getting him back again, but still thats the sort of thing that goes on.
I have just censored my platoon's letters. Its rather astonishing how these fellows spend their money (they have just been been paid) on gorgeous, but very useless, handkerchiefs and wonderful works of art in the shape of postcards, costing anything up to a franc, I suppose, and then send them home by registered post and you know perfectly well that their wives must have all their work cut out to keep the kids fed.
More and more good news today, which I expect by this time you will have heard.
The guns have been pretty silent all day but started again a little while back. The Germans have caught it with avengeance this time.

David

David to May   Western Front   June 8th 1917

My Dearest,
Another letter from you today (5th).
I am glad Mrs Muggridge is getting better.
I do wish your girls wouldn't catch things like mumps and measles and I wish still more that it wasn't near you.
I hope you get them back quickly, because of the work and also that you get Miss Hebblethwaite. Of course you are going to accept the chief's offer to let the men write some of the policies. Do them good and make them appreciate some of the things you do for them.
Fancy you ever dreaming of making grimaces. Can't image you being so unlady-like as to put your tongue out even. Now I come to think of it I really believe I do remember your doing it – and didn't you get kissed by way of punishment?
I don't know whether I got any bruises from the horse because I didn't look, but there are all sorts of places that want kissing awfully badly.
"Alright, I'll lie down" – "No, you can't have my head there tonight " – "I must cuddle you occasionally."
Goodbye

David

> I am orderly officer today & so had to be up to see the mens breakfast.
> Then we went on parade & did some drill & bayonet fighting.
> Then by way of giving the men a change we started them relay racing half a platoon against the other half.
> Then we had two men on the back of two others & each

David to May   Western Front   June 9th 1917

There was a tremendous bombardment again yesterday evening and two or three of us went and watched the flashes of the shells bursting.

Today has been quite quiet so I expect we have done all we wanted and have stopped.

I am orderly officer today and so had to be up to see the men's breakfasts.

Then we went on parade and did some drill and bayonet fighting. Then by way of giving the men a change we started them relay racing half a platoon against the other half.

Then we had two men on the back of two others and each pair trying to get the other down. After a good many pairs had had a go Campbell got on my back and we went for a pair of the men and pulled them over easily. Just at that moment the Adjutant and the Regimental Sergeant Major walked up (two of the biggest men in the regiment) and had the impudence to challenge us.

We had three turns. The first one we went for them and got them down and the second and third ended in all four of us landing in a seething heap on the ground, the men all the time standing round in a circle and yelling delight at our struggles.

I came out of the fray minus two buttons and a collar stud.

After that I left the platoon to the tender care of my sergeant and went to inspect billets, cook houses and the officers servants quarters. These last are noted always for being especially dirty, I don't know why but they are, and you invariably have to do more "Strafing" there than anywhere.

This afternoon there was a shooting competition but being orderly officer I couldn't go, but had to attend "office" afterwards when the miserable offenders of the day came up for judgment.

I am just going to a concert for the men and given by them.

David

David to May   Western Front   June 9th 1917

My Dearest,

No letter from you today, 'specks I'll get two tomorrow, hope so anyway.

Today has been glorious just the sort of Saturday which you ought to have taken me up the river.

Wouldn't it be lovely but then – wouldn't it be lovely to be anywhere with you again.

Goodbye

David

David to May   Western Front   June 10th 1917

Last night I went to the concert in a Y.M.C.A. hut and got there very late. The place was packed and I had to sit on the floor between the knees of another officer and with my nose flattened against the big drum (more or less).
It was not at all bad, seeing that none of the men had had any training and of course most of the songs were of the music hall type, but then this pleased the audience more than anything else would have done.
One of the officers imitated a parson (his father was a parson so perhaps he copied it from life) which was very good especially as he introduced several references to recent events, particularly one or two things when we were road-making.
Another man did some ventriloquism, using a home-made doll for the purpose.
In the middle of it all, the form I was leaning against collapsed, sending everyone into a heap on the floor. I was underneath as usual.
It was over about 10.15 and about 10.45 I had to go to the staff parade to receive the orderly sergeants reports that the battalion was present.
After that I turned out the guard looked at the prisoners in the guard room and then went to bed.
Today we have done nothing except go to church, I first of all had to go and report that everything was alright with the battalion yesterday, and then we marched to a field just outside the village where the service was held.
Our officers are playing cricket against the remainder of the brigade this afternoon but I haven't gone as I wanted to write letters, the post being collected especially early today.
Don't expect a letter tomorrow as I shall probably not be able to post one until the next day.

David

David to May   Western Front   June 10th 1917

My Dearest,

I like your letters written in the train because when I read them I feel as though I am close to you when you are writing them.

With your letter dated 6th came one from Mum. Anyone can tell she has been to Watford from the way she writes. I guess those pious relatives of mine have been sitting round with long faces, sighing and condoling with her, until she imagines that I am already half dead and buried – the idiots.

She said that dividends for just over £11 had arrived – what shall we do with it?

That book sounds alright, but why Doreen should bolt from Reg when she knew that he loved her I don't understand. I can't see what good it could do for him or her except make them both mighty miserable.

This afternoon I have been out into the fields and burnt your letters, a beastly job, but my pocket was so full of them that it has busted so that there was nothing for it but to burn them.

Goodbye

David

David to May   Western Front   June 11th 1917

I am no longer in my comfy billet, but in another not quite so good, but still not so bad - but to start at the beginning.

This morning we were up very early and cleared out of the billet or rather I went to breakfast while my servant packed up.

Afterwards I went back to hand in my key (I had been given a front door key). The old lady wouldn't hear of my paying for the coffee etc. and seemed only to pleased to have been able to do it.

We are now in different billets. Three of us were to sleep in one house and the mess was to be there too. Two of the rooms were awfully small (smaller than my bedroom at home) and the beds were of the Norwegian pattern about 4' 6" long and the third bed was in the room where we were to have our mess.

After we had been there a little while we suddenly heard that 2 or 3 rooms were to be had a little way off so we trotted round there.

Then we went back to the old lady and tried to explain things to her (none of us could speak French) and when she found that we were not going to sleep there she got fearfully excited flung her arms about and shrieked at us.

It was awfully funny and I doubled up with laughter. There were four us all talking at once but the old lady beat us all easily and of course nobody could understand the other. At last we gave it up and came away leaving it to be explained by the only one of us who could speak any French. Some time after he calmed her down and when she found that she would not lose by the new arrangement she allowed the servants to use the fire (which up to this time she had refused) and so eventually we had dinner (about 9 o'clock).

This last push has, from accounts here, been splendidly managed and was quite different to the previous pushes. The Germans lost very heavily indeed whereas our men went forward in many places without finding any Germans left - they had all been wiped out by our guns.

I will write more about my present billet tomorrow.

David

David to May   Western Front   June 11th 1917

My Dearest,

Just got your letter 7th.

I think your idea of getting Mrs Muggridge a dog is a fine one and although she will of course make objections, just on principal, she will I expect really be pleased.

I think your chiefs are mad – how do they expect you to get girls when they will only pay half the amount they can get elsewhere. I am sorry you have so many away – but don't work late if you can help.

I don't wonder that you kick that hubby out of bed, but it will be altogether different when....
Goodbye

David

David to May   Western Front   June 12th 1917

My present billet has I think been a girl's school at one time. Anyhow there is a long dormitory with several rooms leading off it, all having small windows in the roof.

There are 3 of us, each having a room. My bed is beautifully soft. I think it must be feathers but I haven't investigated that far, as I am somewhat afraid of stirring it up too much, as it is none too clean, the whole place isn't for that matter, but out here a bed is a bed and you take it and thank your lucky stars you've got it.

However this morning I had enough warm water for a bath (in my canvas bath, which requires much practice before you can really get a bath in it, as it is something like balancing oneself in a teacup) and coffee, so that really I am living in the lap of luxury.

The old lady at the mess has quieted down a good deal, but I think she looks upon me as a mortal enemy as she scowls at me every time I go in and out. Really I am mortally afraid of her as she has such a powerful stream of language when she gets going, that I dread doing anything that may upset her, in case she turns it on me, when I know I should be helpless and completely at her mercy.

We have had quite an easy day today only doing musketry this morning and practicing fire orders, during which time the colonel came round and asked the platoon questions to see how they were getting on.

Did I tell you about the brigade shooting competition last Saturday? We won several things and finally came out top of the brigade which shows that the musketry has improved seeing that the colonel told us a few weeks ago that we were the bottom of the brigade.

Those mines in that last big attack fairly shook the ground. From accounts of prisoners the Germans are afraid of their own men. They of course in this particular case could see what was coming and withdrew a number of their guns, but in order not to let the infantry know this fact, they sent the artillery observing officers up to the front line as usual. This is the reason why we captured comparatively few guns and the reason why we didn't get more prisoners was because they weren't there to take having already been wiped out by our guns.

When our men went over, their trenches had been so smashed that they didn't exist, whilst ours were still practically intact.

This evening we started playing rounders, my platoon against the Rhodesians, we are always rivals as the two platoons always seem to be about equal at most things) and we all thoroughly enjoyed it at least the men seemed to and I know we two officers did.

After dinner we again went out and found them playing cricket. The wicket consisted of two old petrol tins, the bats of two pieces of wood nailed together, a tennis ball and we played in grass anything up to 9 inches high.

We played on until suddenly a big voice bawled at the men telling them to get to their billets at once. It was the regimental sergeant major. We hadn't noticed the time and it was after tattoo 9.15 the time that all men have to be in their billets. However when he saw us he calmed down and we explained that it was our fault so that everything was alright. After that we two went for a stroll and then back to bed.

We walked down a lane and across some fields and got some fine yellow irises growing on the edge of a small pond. I have never seen them growing wild before.

The names of 10 more officers have been sent in for leave, so that it is getting near my turn for my name to go in. I should think that in the ordinary course of events I ought to get home in about 7 or 8 weeks time.

David

David to May   Western Front   June 12th 1917

Just got your letter (8th).

Thanks very much for the birthday wishes. Like you I do hope we spend our future birthdays together. They must be holidays too.

I did laugh over your letter to the post office. I couldn't have written a letter like that. The Liverpool man has evidently got tired of it and has passed it off on to somebody else. It is good of you though to take all this trouble.

I am sorry about your girls being away like they are and I wish they wouldn't get infectious things.

Round about this neighbourhood they make a good deal of lace (on pillows) so I have bought a length. It is rather narrow and coarse, but the girl hadn't anything better, except some collar arrangements which I didn't think would be much good to you and perhaps you will be able to use this piece for something or other. I am sending it by registered post and you must let me know whether you have to pay duty on it and if so how much.

If only I do get leave – just fancy 10 whole days with you, it would be ....but I suppose I mustn't count too much on it.

Goodbye

David

David to May   Western Front   June 13th 1917

They have altered the time for posting letters again and are collecting them in the middle of the afternoon so you will get todays news tomorrow.

Getting up this morning and being in my usual bright and cheery 5 o'clock-in-the-morning mood I broke out into song (the mood you see got the better of me), wherefore at breakfast afterwards I was subjected to a great many rude and unseemly remarks from the others. Moreover they were still more rude, when I threatened not to sing any more. A prophet is not without honour etc.!

We had to parade at 6.30 and take the men for a walk and a run for 2 or 3 miles and then come back to breakfast.

After that there was bayonet fighting.

One of my men in jumping a trench and sticking a German twisted his knee and has had to go to hospital.

Then we marched out a little way and did some musketry and fire orders again.

And that ended the day's work taking up to lunch time.

This evening we are to have more rounders and cricket.

This afternoon we are moving the mess, leaving the old lady's house and moving to the house where I sleep, which has a much better room.

Now I have discovered that I am not the only one who is afraid of the old lady, but that all the others are too and this being so we each and all of us considered that somebody else ought to break the news of our departure to her. After much discussion we decided that as Campbell was the only one who could speak French at all, and as he was Captain of the Company, it was his bounden duty to tell her. Having decided that we came away and left him to it.

He was last seen dragging the battalion billeting officer in forcibly and whether they both escaped alive we don't know.

We hope so.

David

David to May   Western Front   June 14th 1917

My Dearest,

I have just got two letters 9th and 10th.

You poor little girl, what a horrible time you are having. I have longed to comfort you.

I am not at all near the war at present, but all the same I shall have to be taken to the quietest of quiet places when I come home.

I do like getting letters from you written "on a Sunday too" as then there are no blank days without a letter at all.

Must stop.

Goodbye

David

David to May   Western Front   June 14th 1917

I have just received your letter enclosing copies of those others about Bert. Thanks very much for sending them. I haven't the least doubt at all that Cp Yeoman's account is the correct one. Hebblethwaite you see, being a Captain, was not even in charge of Bert's platoon, and could only get his information secondhand.

Obviously the private and L/Corporal sat down side by side and wrote practically the same letter and probably got others to help them, as their letters might almost have been dictated by the way they are written.

Obviously too, they saw Hebblethwaite before writing their letters and very likely showed them to him afterwards before sending them off.

The corporal on the other hand writes his in his own way and seems to have his wits about him being very definite over everything. Moreover he and he only would be responsible for knowing what happened to the men in his section and would have to give an account of them and he naturally would know whether Bert was buried or not.

In these affairs the various sections get scattered over such a wide front that it is impossible even for the platoon commander to be in touch all the time with the whole lot and the corporals are the only people who really know what happens to individual men.

This morning we went for a walk and run for about 2 or 3 miles and then went to a rifle range for the remainder of the morning.

The post corporal has just come for the letters so I must stop. Will write more tomorrow.

David

David to May   Western Front   June 15th 1917

Yesterday after posting your letter I went out to play rounders with the men. We played against No.6 platoon and got beaten by one point.

We had just finished the game when our General of Generals walked into the field. There were several tents in the field which some of the men are using and they had their kits packed outside.

They had just had a meal and there were a good many pieces of paper lying about and also he found a half finished pot of jam tucked away in one of the tents. This is a fearful crime as all food has to be most carefully kept under cover because of flies.

I was rather quaking at these things as I was company orderly officer and had been round only two hours before and found everything quite alright but he only pointed out that it should be cleared up and then went away. The other day he stopped the leave of all the officers of one battalion over something like this.

After this one of the other fellows and myself went for a ride. He is a very good rider and I picked up quite a number of things from him. The country about here is not nearly so good for riding as that near our railway, as it is all cultivated, so that you can't ride across country and unless you get on a track running across a farm it is impossible to gallop, as you have to keep to the roads.

I had a different horse this time and he allowed me to stay on his back the whole time and I thoroughly enjoyed it.

While we were out we went to an areodrome and watched the areoplanes coming in. There were a number of them and as the other man said it seemed just like a swarm of bees.

This morning we went out for our usual walk and run before breakfast.

Came back had a cold bath in my canvas tea cup (I believe I got wet all over) had breakfast and then spent the rest of the morning at musketry.

We had men out in the country in front of us hidden in hedges etc. who occasionally fired blank shots at us and we had to pick them out and fire at them.

Afterwards the colonel came along and we had some criticism on what we were doing and I got mixed up in an argument with him. I always seem to be doing this.

This afternoon there is an inspection by the colonel so I expect he will find something wrong somewhere.

Then this evening we are practicing bayonet fighting for a competition which comes off on Sunday.

David

David to May   Western Front   June 15th 1917

My Dearest,

I have got your letter 12th.

Yes I know I had my birthday kiss or kisses and then you hugged me ever so nicely and then you turned round slightly and caressed me. You are a darling aren't you.

I am glad you are getting extra help from the temporary girls but doesn't this make a lot of work for you teaching them. That new girl sounds as though she is going to be alright but I notice that your chiefs have had to raise the salary. I suppose that was your doings.

Must go out and parade now.

Goodbye

David

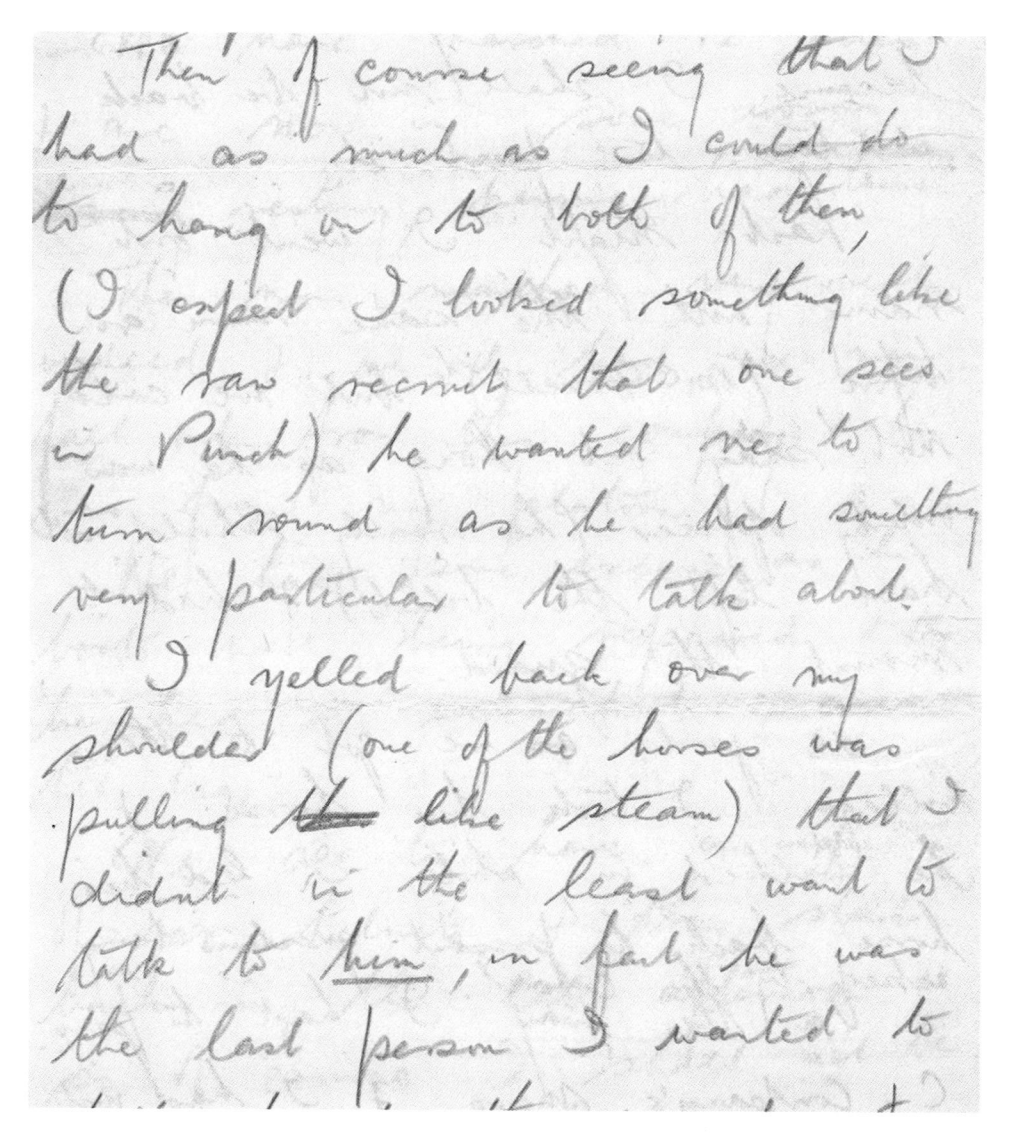

Then of course seeing that I had as much as I could do to hang on to both of them, (I expect I looked something like the raw recruit that one sees in Punch) he wanted me to turn round as he had something very particular to talk about. I yelled back over my shoulder (one of the horses was pulling like steam) that I didn't in the least want to talk to him, in fact he was the last person I wanted to

David to May   Western Front   June 16th 1917

Don't expect you will get this letter when you should, because I shall not be back in time to post it.

Last night I went out riding with the same man as before, (McDowell) but we could not stay out long as he was orderly officer (he really should not have left the billets) and had to mount the guard.

So just as we got to the village I took his horse and he walked in while I led his horse back to prevent questions being asked by the colonel.

On the way I had to pass C Company's mess and I had just gone by when Hill (who is now Captain of C Company) rushed out and yelled "I say Sandy what are you doing with two horses when you cant manage one".

Then of course seeing that I had as much as I could do to hang on to both of them, (I expect I looked something like the raw recruit that one sees in Punch) he wanted me to turn round as he had something very particular to talk about.

I yelled back over my shoulder (one of the horses was pulling like steam) that I didn't in the least want to talk to him, in fact he was the last person I wanted to talk to, at the moment, and went on or rather was taken on. However, I got them back to the transport lines handed over McDowell's horse and then went out again by myself. I took all the side roads and lanes I could find with the idea of keeping the horse on soft ground and then I lost myself or rather got further away than I intended and had to take a wide circle to get back. On the way I came across some tractors pulling some heavy guns and my horse didn't like the look of them a bit and I thought I was going to have some trouble, but I managed to get it past them alright and finally got back - very late for dinner.

This morning we were up at 4.30 and started marching at 6 o'clock. We have marched 12 miles and are now in some woods resting, having had lunch.

The men marched very well indeed and we only had one man fall out from this company and he was from my platoon. He had some excuse as his boots were being repaired and those he had on were about 4 sizes too big.

We are to have an inspection of gas helmets and then start back in the later afternoon and so of course I shall not be able to post this.

Whether we shall get the men back as well, remains to be seen.

Later

We got back about 9.30. They came back a bit shorter way, knocking off a couple of miles or so. I only had two men fall out on the way back which was good as others had more. Two others told me they would have to, but I managed to get them along and they both came in, one of them however dropped just before we got in and had to be carried the last few yards.

David

David to May   Western Front   June 16th 1917

My Dearest,

We are resting in some woods and whenever I get into these sort of places I think of Hayes and want you more than ever.

It is tremendously hot and marching in full kit doesn't help one to keep cool, but still beyond the fact that I have got pretty wet with perspiration I haven't felt the march a great deal.

Later

I have just had a cold bath, supper, and am now lying or rather sitting in bed.

Come on then, if I must, I must – there, is that how you want me – O yes, you know I want to be there!

Goodbye

David

P.S. There was no mail today and I am enclosing a cutting from Punch which rather illustrates the feeling one has when there is no letter from you.

David to Ginger   Western Front   June 17th 1917

Dear Ginger,

Mum sent another Buzzard cake from you on my birthday, such a fine one too. Thanks very much indeed.

I also got another lot of papers from you.

I have been unable to write before as we get very little time for letter writing and have been moving about from place to place a good deal which makes things worse.

In your last letter you asked my idea about a sleeveless jacket you are making.

I wouldn't trouble to make them as the troops are served out with woollen cardigans by the army and also leather waistcoats so that they are pretty well provided that way.

We can however always do with socks as they are always wearing out and sometimes we can't get them a fresh pair for 3 or 4 weeks together and of course they want a change pretty frequently and sometimes they don't get a chance to wash them. You ask too about home leave – this is a very doubtful thing out here. My turn should come round in about a couple of months but whether I shall get it is quite a different matter.

Another thing you ask is how long parcels take to reach me. The last one got here in just over a fortnight.

I am afraid this letter will only be short as the post is just going.

Yours

David

David to May   Western Front   June 17th 1917

Had a lazy day today.

I went or rather the whole lot of us went to church this morning. The church being the middle of a field.

Our own particular general came too. Generals it seems go to church sometimes as well as the ordinary Tommy.

After that I had to go to see an addition fitted to our gas helmets which stops anything and everything in the way of gas getting into your lungs so now I suppose when the Germans send over some gas you just ask for some more.

These helmets are not the acme of comfort though as they are made with elastic bands which fit tight round under your chin and over your head. You have a rubber tube stuffed between your teeth, a wire clip on your nose, and you look like a member of the Spanish Inquisition and feel worse.

The men have gone to the baths today but I didn't have to take them.

Today is a Saints day I believe (most days are here) and I have just seen a wonderful procession but I can't describe it as the post is just going.

David

David to May   Western Front   June 17th 1917

My Dearest,

I have just got your letters 13th and 14th.

Look here, when these blessed German air raids are on, please don't go up on to the roof or any place like that. I know it's very nice to see things, but what should I do if you got hurt. What made you wake up wondering if life were worth living – was it anything in particular or did you feel humpy? Well, come here – there is that nice – feel humpy now?

I am awfully glad to get your letter because I heard that the raid was in London and wondered if you were safe.

Yes I get all your letters, as I check all the dates but sometimes they come irregularly. I am awfully sorry that letter went to No. 5 Manor Rd. I am usually very careful about checking the address, in case they should go astray.

Look here, you mustn't worry about things in my letters and image I am going into action, and so on. As a matter of fact we were only in reserve and miles away from the show and weren't wanted and so didn't go near it.

And if you write shorter letters or tease me any more, Ill – I'll – well I'll hug you hard next time I get the chance.

I do hope you get your war bonus and I hope it was be as much as you deserve (only they never give you enough) and I think we must buy a daughter – and a son.

Goodbye

David

David to May   Western Front   June 18th 1917

I think I had got as far as the procession yesterday. Certainly it was a gorgeous affair.

First of all I walked down the road sometime before the thing was due to start and found that they had erected a sort of temporary altar just outside the village by the side of the road. Three steps led up to it and then there was a small table with candles burning and flowers and so on.

About 3 o'clock the procession came along (I had gone inside but I saw it from my window). First of all came four girls dressed in white with gilt crowns and a sort of bridal veil over the whole lot. Then a number of small children also in white, then a girl in a wonderful costume of red, white and blue then more small children in white, then four girls in white carrying a figure of the Virgin on their shoulders, more children, four more girls carrying another figure on their shoulders, then girls with banners and following these an old fat priest in a wonderful cloth of gold dress and walking under a golden canopy held over him by four more girls in white.

Then followed a number of old men in black and behind these a number of the village people and bringing up the rear of the whole thing were several of our ammunition wagons who were in a hurry to get by and couldn't.

You rather wondered that a small village such as this could produce such a show and how they managed to get money enough to provide the costumes etc.

The church bell had been banging at intervals for about 2 hours so I suppose it all stood for a good deal but I couldn't make out what.

Being Sunday and a day of rest there was a boxing competition for the men in the late afternoon and I went and watched it for a little while but boxing isn't to my taste so I didn't stay long.

Instead I went off with McDowell for a ride. We rode into a town close by, or rather perhaps a larger village. This place is on the top of a steep conical hill and just as we got to the top I saw the flat country beyond with a slight mist over it looking for all the world like the sea.

McDowell wanted to see a man he knew, so after going about from place to place for half an hour we eventually found him. He was on the staff and as we arrived about dinner time he asked us to dinner so that I found myself sitting beside all sorts of gorgeous people with red tabs and blue tabs all over them.

Before going into the mess we had to do something with our horses so not being able to find a better place we took their saddles off and tied them up to some trees in the front garden. This staff man was an Engineer (in civil life a surveyor) and his job was preparing maps of the front showing the German trenches. He took us round his offices and we saw these maps being printed.

The post corporal has just turned up so I must stop.

David

David to May   Western Front   June 19th 1917

I only got as far as the printing of the maps. They had a regular printing works, the maps being turned out by the thousand.

We then went back and then came the question of saddling the horses again. Never having saddled a horse in my life before of course I knew all about it. However I managed to put the saddle on the right way up, but whether it was on the right part of the horse's back I didn't know, but I strapped it on, said goodbye and mounted the horse and then immediately the saddle slipped round under the horses tummy.

I had pulled the girths up as tight as they would go but I think he must have gone into a rapid consumption whilst we were having dinner because I pulled the straps up as far as they would go and still the saddle slipped, so that finally McDowell had to hang on to one side whilst I climbed up the other.

We then rode back. Most of these villages are paved with cobbles and the horses were slipping and sliding at every step but he didn't throw me off so I got back alright.

Today we went out for a run first thing this morning and afterwards spent the whole morning on the range. It was baking hot but we had no coats on so that made things somewhat better.

In the afternoon there was a bayonet fighting competition. I had some men in for it but none of them won anything, although they were fairly near the top.

I left out a page of yesterday's letter and am enclosing it today.

David

David to May   Western Front   June 19th 1917

I have just heard that our letters (that is the officers letters) are to be censored by the colonel. Isn't it perfectly – well there aren't no words. I shall be reduced to writing field cards soon. Don't expect a letter for a couple of days as we are going for a long march and I don't expect I shall be able to post one.

I am enclosing a letter from Ethel to Mum. Don't want it back. As you will see Ethel is economising in every possible direction.

That reminds me. I see that there are still Exchequer Bonds for sale through the post office and as I have about £25 in the County Bank lying idle I may as well buy some more.

Would you mind getting me £20 of the 1919 Exchequer Bonds. I am enclosing a cheque for £20.

Goodbye

David
PS I have crossed the cheque but the P.O. should take it.

David to May (card)   Western Front   21 June 1917

Haven't had a chance to write today.
As our letters have now to be sent in to be censored they may be delayed a day.

D.

David to May   Western Front   June 22nd 1917

The last day or two we have been getting up about 2 o'clock or soon after having breakfast and then going for a route march with the idea of getting it over before the sun got up and made things too hot.
It so happened though that the sun didn't get up but the rain descended and the floods came and having no umbrellas we got wet.
Just lately we have been billeted at a farmhouse. The French farms beat anything you ever saw for filth. I don't think they ever clear anything up and in fact seem to go out of their way to collect it.
The farm buildings are usually built round a square courtyard and in the centre there is sort of a pool hollowed out and into this all the refuse is thrown and allowed to rot. You can just imagine the state the place gets into and the way it smells.
Added to all this they usually have their wells within a few feet of this heap of filth. How it is that they haven't all died of typhoid years ago I can't tell, but it seems to agree with them somehow.
At one of these farms there were a number of tiny ducklings evidently been hatched by a hen, and she was fussing around them and telling them what they should do arid what they shouldn't, but they simply took no notice but put their fingers to their noses and went into a pond where of course she couldn't follow and had to stand on the edge and tell them what would happen if they didn't do as they were told.
My present bed is a wonderful affair. It looks something like a large rustic basket on legs. It is just a shallow basket made with thin branches of trees woven together and the whole thing propped up on some thicker stumps. It originally had a mattress on top (a large sack filled with straw) but I have removed that thinking I should probably spend a quieter night without it and so have simply got my valise which makes quite a comfortable bed.
It has rained practically all day today but we have had very little to do, so that it has made very little difference, except make the place look somewhat desolate. This must be a dismal sort of country in winter!

David

David to May   Western Front   June 22nd 1917

My Dearest,
I can't write – I am in much too bad a temper for that and I feel like swearing.
All our letters in future are possibly to be censored by the colonel.
Apparently an officer can be trusted to censor other people's letters but can't be allowed to censor his own.
How can one write as one feels knowing it is liable to be read before it leaves here.
I have your two letters 18th and 19th.
I do think you might tell me what it was I whispered on Sunday morning. You tell me everything else and then leave that out. You will let me know won't you?
I thought your holiday started on the 16th? Why aren't you taking it, you know you need it badly.
I can't understand that lace not turning up before. I sent it off with the letter I wrote telling you it was coming. Still I am glad you have got it.
There is no letter from you today but possibly it will come later this evening.
Goodbye

David

David to May   Western Front   June 24 th 1917

I have been cast away (with my platoon) on a desert island as it were.
I was just settling down in my billet when I was told to take my platoon and myself and go off and take over job which meant that I was to be away entirely on my own and that the platoon was to do its own cooking etc. etc. and in fact that we were to be entirely self contained,
So off I went.
I found that we were to live in two empty houses, or parts of them about half a mile apart. Having found the first one I settled half the platoon with a sergeant and went on to the next. I made all the necessary arrangements here and then went back.
I am afraid I then upset the sergeant for when I got there I found that he and two corporals had put all their belongings into my room, evidently with the idea of sharing it.
Now this particular sergeant is one of those people who always seem to be hanging round and on the slightest encouragement tries to become a bosom friend, so that I am constantly having to keep him at arms length. He was therefore very upset when I told him to take everything out and go elsewhere.
I was in and out all through the night (the job we were doing had to be done at night). It was a glorious night but rather cold and I could have done with your woolly waistcoat but I had left it in my valise and so of course couldn't have it.
I got the cook to make some tea for the men about 12 o'clock. This was some extra tea over and above their rations, but the cook always seems, in some mysterious fashion, to be able to produce extra tea.
This morning (Sunday) I had a rifle inspection and got a whole lot of litter and mess left by previous people cleared up and then I took the men bathing.
The water was quite shallow and they went in whilst I stood on the edge and looked at them (something like the old hen and the ducklings the other day).
I have had visits from various people during the day, the colonel amongst others, just to see how things were.
My spell of duty ends this evening when I return to my normal state again.
Later
Thanks for the copy of Cpl Yeoman's letter. It confirms my idea that this man is right and the others wrong.

David

David to May   Western Front   June 24th 1917

My Dearest,

You haven't had a letter for days and I expect by this time you are beginning to imagine all sorts of things.

As a matter of fact I haven't been able to get the letters off or you would have had them. I did however manage to send a post card which I hope you got.

During the next week or two I may not be able to write regularly so if several days go by without a letter, don't worry. Of course I shall write if I can.

I too have had nothing from you for 3 days so I am hoping for a whole bunch when they do come.

Later

I have just got back and found a letter Thurs 21st, Wednesday's hasn't come yet. Wonder what they are doing with it.

I am sorry you are so busy. Have you still a number of girls away.

You do make our train journeys real. When I read them I am "there" – both sides.

Goodbye

David

David to May   Western Front   June 25 th 1917

We have been out this morning doing battle, murder and sudden death, or in other words, training.

We marched out some distance, not a very great way, but marching here takes time and is pretty tiring as even where there is loose dusty sand, ankle deep, which makes it pretty hard going.

The roads, where there are any, consist of a strip of pave or cobbles with a stretch of this loose sand on either side so that you have the choice of marching on the cobbles, which is not by any means comfortable, or in the sand and in any case you frequently have to get off the road for the traffic.

Having got to our starting point, I was told to carry out an attack with my platoon across country on a strong position, bristling with machine guns and Germans, (represented by an officer sitting on the top of a mound taking notes of the way we did it).

We advanced, killed all the Germans, captured all the machine guns and generally wiped the whole thing off the face of the earth.

Of course I am not at all sure that we weren't all killed before we got there, but in these things you have to have such a tremendous imagination and in any case both sides always win – or say they do.

You remember what a dilapidated, heart-broken, and forlorn appearance Seaford had - well this place reminds me of that, only this is far more scattered and more forlorn.

David

We have been out this morning doing battle, murder & sudden death, or in other words training.

We marched out some distance, not a very great way, but marching here takes time & is pretty trying as everywhere there is loose dusty sand, ankle deep, which makes it pretty hard (an officer sitting on the top of a mound taking notes of the way we did it)

We advanced, killed all the Germans, captured all the machine guns & generally wiped the whole thing off the face of the earth.

Of course I am not at all sure that we weren't all killed

David to May   Western Front   June 26th 1917

Last evening after sending your letter off I went for a bathe. I thought it was going to be rather cold but it wasn't, the water being fairly warm and the wind only was somewhat chilly. Afterwards McDowell and I went for a ride. We rode out a little way and then got down on to the beach and went for a gallop. McDowell's horse was very nervous of the water and previous to starting he had made a bet that he would ride in so we both went. My horse (much to my relief) didn't mind it in the least and went in quite quietly, but McDowell's didn't like it a bit and jumped around and wanted to go anywhere but straight on, but finally he did get her right in.

We rode on again and after a while tried the same thing again and this time he didn't have as much difficulty. Coming back we were flying along, when we suddenly came across a stream running right across in front and for a second I thought my horse was going to pull up short, but luckily for me it didn't but went on beautifully.

A bit further on we came across the colonel who was playing polo, but his horse didn't take kindly to the game, so he borrowed McDowell's which turned out to be much better.

Today we have been out training again, doing much about the same sort of work as yesterday. At first I took up a position and was attacked by one of the other platoons and afterwards we reversed, the order of things and attacked them. As usual in both cases both sides won.

This afternoon we all went bathing again and I, and I think everyone thoroughly enjoyed it. Must stop now as the post is going.

David

David to May   Western Front   June 26th 1917

My Dearest,

There is no mail today and in consequence I am thirsting for somebody's blood. However it may come later so I haven't yet given up all hope.

I haven't much to write about today and besides as the post goes early in the afternoon now, there is very little time to write.

Goodbye

David

David to May   Western Front   June 27th 1917

We are billeted in huts again, but such huts that with a small stretch of imagination you might think you were in a most fashionable hotel in the heart of London. They are divided off into rooms, mine being about 6 feet by 8. It is furnished in the most costly, not to say luxurious style, the furniture consisting of a small table covered with a piece of brown paper by way of a doyley, (isn't that the word) a cane chair, (it stands or rather reclines on three legs so that you have to sit against the wall to make up for the fourth) a handsome and charming set of bookshelves, (made out of ration boxes) two other small shelves and about two dozen nails driven in in a beautiful pattern all round the room.

There is no carpet on the floor, but it is most smoothly [censored] the cracks in the walls and everywhere else it can and doesn't by any means confine itself to the floor.

The partitions are decorated with sundry pairs of breeches, coats, haversacks, towels etc. etc. and my valise is stretched down the centre of the floor, so that you can fall over it at any moment.

This morning we were to have gone out to do some shooting but somebody else had got the range so that we couldn't. Instead we did physical drill for a while, and then I started my platoon playing various things.

We first of all had a relay race, half the platoon against the other half. Then I started them on each other's backs one against the other the idea being for each pair to pull the other down. After that we had. "Sergeant Major Murphy says" which is a game in which you drill the men, prefacing each command with "Sergeant Major Murphy says __ " upon which the men act on the command, but if you give a command without this they stand still. Of course you catch a number both ways and they fall out until you only have about 2 or 3 remaining.

It is all rather good fun and the men thoroughly enjoy it. After that we had bayonet fighting and then some practice in fire control. Must stop now.

David

David to May   Western Front   June 27th 1917

My Dearest,

I have been obedient again, (obedience is so ingrained now that I can't help myself) and have carried out your instructions to the letter and written to Maud.

I offered her my heartfelt congratulations, telling her at the same time that you had told me to do so. You did, didn't you?

Later

Just got your letter (23rd). I am glad you didn't go up on Saturday, but you don't seem to take a holiday for all that.

Thanks very much for buying those things for me. I wish you would keep the receipt for me. It doesn't matter about the dividends going to Balham as I have asked Mum to open all letters for me and she pays all these things into my London County Bank account.

It is good of you to take all the trouble you do with those socks and to allow for the Belgian method of washing them. You will have to be thanked very thoroughly tonight.

Goodbye

David

David to May   Western Front   June 28th 1917

Letter writing in these times is an awful thing, or perhaps, looking at it the other way on, has to be reduced to a fine art and its no ordinary person who can write a letter (unless it be one ordering a pair of boots or a cap) without much thought and consideration.

Yesterday, in the innocence of my heart I apparently mentioned things as I didn't oughter and in consequence have had the letter returned and have had to scratch out the offending words, so that now instead of a letter you have a missing word puzzle.

It doesn't make sense so that you will have to use your imagination and fill in the scratchings as you think fit.

Till now I have been writing just the first thing that came into my head, but now I must think over each sentence three times before sticking it down and then having done so, find that it tells you some military secret, or that I have mentioned [censored] course I shouldn't like others to read, and so have to tear the whole thing up and start all over again.

It's an awful strain - no wonder I am going grey.

We were up just after 5 this morning and went out to do some shooting but it was raining fairly hard and seemed as though it would continue so that before e we got to the range we turned tail and came back.

I believe we are doing it this afternoon instead and there are night operations of some sort tonight.

Yesterday we all went bathing again and afterwards I went for a ride. It wasn't much of a success though, as I had a most uncomfortable horse. It was the learned one, the one that always carries a map with it and reads the finger posts to see the nearest road home and then when you don't turn back just when it thinks you should, takes it out of you by shying at every mortal thing.

David to May   Western Front   June 28th 1917

My Dearest,

Such a nice letter (25th) from you today, especially the first part, (the train journey and the reason it's a good thing you are not tall).

I wish I could write like that but I can't.

You seem to have your doubts as to whether Mrs. Anstey allowed herself to be buried, or whether she suddenly woke up at the last minute and came back to be "very kind and patient" to Maud.

The socks haven't come yet but there were no parcels today so perhaps they will come tomorrow.

Now I am going to get you to do something more for me.

You remember I bought some Malayalam Rubber Shares some time ago (to be exact on April 30th). At the end of May I asked Read & Brigstock, 5 Lothbury, to buy 10 more at 38/6 or under, sending them a cheque for £19. They acknowledged the cheque on May 29th and said they couldn't buy them at the price. Since then I have written twice asking them to buy them at 40/- or under but have heard nothing further.

Since then also I have seen the shares quoted below 38/-. I wish you would ring them up and find out what they are doing. Probably, the order being small they haven't worried their heads about it.

The "narrative" has been held up, but I may be able to send it tomorrow.

Goodbye.

David

David to May   Western Front   June 29th 1917

My Dearest,

No letter from you today and I expected one. Wonder what the delay is this time.

I had a letter from Miss Willsher giving a time and exact account of the money she spent. She seems to have some change left and wants to know what she shall do with it. Don't you think you might get tickets for a concert or something of the sort, or the two of you go out and spend it in some way you like best (there is about 19/-).

And, 0 yes, she also says that she "thinks you will never again tease or torment me". What's happened? Are you ill, or has some extraordinary change come over you?

I also had a letter from Read & Brigstock. Of course, just as I have worried you with the thing. They seem to have mixed things up. From what I can make out they seem to have bought 10 shares on June 6th, but they did not tell me of this or perhaps their letter went astray. Then they received my letter asking them to buy the shares at anything under 40/- and mistook this for a further order for another 10 and bought these on the 25th.

So now I am asking them what it is all about.

I am enclosing my letter of 27th which was stopped.

Goodbye.

David

David to May   Western Front   June 30th 1917

Yesterday morning after doing some drill in getting gas masks on quickly and having them inspected, we went out and did some more training.

I had to do another attack on a German position and of course I and the whole of the platoon were killed many times before we got there, or at least so I was told but when you are attacking a man with a pair of field glasses, or a blue flag, it is difficult to imagine that that same blue flag is simply pouring bullets into you with machine guns.

And then again everybody imagines something different so that no two people's ideas are alike and each one is certain that his own particular idea is the correct one. Always after these sort of affairs there are tremendous arguments, in which nobody is ever converted to the other's opinion but is still more firmly convinced that his own scheme was right.

In the afternoon we went bathing again. We are remarkably lucky here, as the men can bathe practically every day and besides this there is a very good bath in the camp itself with plenty of hot water.

In the evening there was a battalion concert. The first portion of the programme was not bad but was very similar to the last on. The second half was done by five of the officers dressed as pierrots, the costumes consisting of their pyjamas with small black pieces of fluff stuck on here and there. All except me, who was got up as a girl with the usual short dress on, but you never saw such a funny girl. He had got a weird and wonderful headdress on and he had been padded out and after a bit his stuffing slipped down, greatly adding to his charming appearance. They sang and did various other things including one or two skits on things in the battalion and then they took a number of the officers and made up a small rhyme on some characteristic of each.

Finally they wound up with a comic sketch called "Chu Chin Chow of China". This time they were got up in some wonderful costumes with steel helmets on, which made quite good Chinese hats. They fooled about a good deal and finally Chu Chin Chow (whose costume consisted of a bathing suit in red and black rings with a sort of red overall over it) was stabbed by the girl and he fell dead with the words "She's done me in". Then they did a war dance over his body in which after a minute or so he got up and joined in too.

Today I am orderly officer so have had the usual round of inspections. We haven't done much in the way of work this morning (it has been raining pretty hard) except some gas drill and inspections of kit and equipment and so on, but we are going out this afternoon and there are night operations this evening.

Dave

David to May   Western Front   June 30th 1917

My Dearest,

Just got your letter 26th which by the way you say was Wed and if was so I haven't yet had Tuesday's letter. I think perhaps though you made a mistake on the day but the date is correct.

I don't in the least mind missing the "scenery" and when we are etc etc of course we shall do exactly the same, only you mustn't pitch me on the floor without due notice.

As for "getting your own back" by writing in that way – I call it hitting a fellow when he can't help himself. I'm an awful martyr.

With regard to Bert's affairs: I don't think you are liable for death duties as he was killed out here.

Goodbye

David

David to May   Western Front   July 1st 1917

Yesterday we were to have done all sorts of things, but it blew and blew and rained and rained practically all day, so that we did very little.

I spent most of the afternoon and evening tracing a map, but didn't get it finished because it was taken away from me before I had time.

We were to have night operations last night but it was still raining, so that was cancelled.

This morning we went to church, the service being held in the same hall as the concert the other evening.

Since then there has been nothing to do except this afternoon when the men went for a bath. The night operations which have been put off twice are to come off tonight.

I have just lost one of my best men again. That's the worst of the army. You get your men together just as you want them and sorted out and working together and then suddenly one goes into hospital for something or other (one man the other day put his knee out whilst bayonet fighting and is now in England) and you probably don't see him again and then they want a man for working on the roads, or for the tunnelling company, or to guard prisoners of war, or to pray for the General's soul or some other equally unimportant thing, (I am not in the least interested in any of these things and am therefore perfectly certain they are not important) and they must take your men and they must take your best men too. In this case I am sorry to lose the man, but he has gone to a job which will give him more money and I know he wants it as his father has just died and I know he sends the greater part of his money to his mother, so for that I am rather glad he has got the job.

Must go now.

Goodbye.

David

David to May   Western Front   July 1st 1917

My Dearest,

Just got your two letters 27th and 28th so evidently I got Tuesdays alright.

Your socks have come and as usual are splendid. I haven't put them on yet, but they look alright. By the way a day or so ago you asked if I would like them with shorter legs for the summer. I like them just as you make them, with the leg pretty long as they are most comfortable like that. It is good of you to do them.

I woke up about 6 this morning but as there was only church parade I didn't get up until after 8 and even then I kept putting it off and putting it off until I simply had to drag myself away.

I know that you are perfectly capable of writing "in a sensible manner" but if you dare.....

Goodbye

David

Now don't go and do it just because I have written that.

May to David   On Penge Station   Sunday 1 July 1917 1.10pm

My dear David,

Like a blooming ejjut I stuck your envelope down and now discover I have 12 mins to spare. Never mind. This must go tomorrow.

I must tell you about our painters. They have not done yet. There are 5 of them, old and daft, who spend the day getting at one another. They are awfully slow and independent. On the day of "The Fete" a lot of well dressed ladies went down the road to Kelsey Park. In spite of the threatening sky, distant thunder and occasional rain drops they were bedecked in the daintiest of muslins. There was a man up a ladder painting my bedroom window and another up a ladder painting Ethel's. Mama was down in the diningroom and this is what she heard the old fools say: "Seems a lot of females about this afternoon. Where do they all come from." "O, there's a munition factory close by, tho' I don't rightly knows exactly where." "Ah." "Look at that in the grey. She don't look so bad now. I rather likes the looks of them flounces. Yes, she'll do." The female in question was an important looking matron with a lovely pale grey dress with 3 flounces; quite a creation, and she must have heard the remarks unless she was stone deaf, as the men spoke loudly and slowly.

Here's the train. Goodbye for awhile again. Give me a kiss quick as I must go up the other end of the platform. We are at present hidden by the waiting room. O I am hungry. Give me a bite of your nose. What, too tender? Spose I must go into the garden and eat worms then.

Monday. In 8.30 train with 5 females (no good – you'll have to behave yourself. Yes I know it is extremely hard on you). I caught the 3.19 yesterday and reached Maud's at 4.0. Lor, she does look thin and worn out but seemed excited at seeing me. She said she had not had time to write to you, so I told her I had done it and no doubt she would hear from you when you had time to write. She has found room in the Abberville Rd, 3 rooms and a bathroom, the house is owned by a widow who has the downstairs, rent 10/6 a week. She expects to move in by Friday fortnight. The nurse leaves tomorrow and then Maud will feel lonely. This nurse is a brick and saw about funeral etc, told Maud about money matters and took her rooms. Brother John wants to buy some furniture, which is all left to Maud, and he is having all the rubbish for which he is paying £6.10/- not cash down as he has already been trying to borrow from Maud, who flared up at him and refused. The Dr has told Maud she ought to go to seaside for 6 weeks but as prices are so exorbitant she says she can't afford it. I have suggested she goes to a farm for a month, and winds up with a fortnight in Sept at the sea, and she likes the idea. I have an address of a place in Northampton where they take paying guests so will write today. John is sending for furniture on Wednesday. Maud is going to sleep next door then. She has bought herself a new bedstead, hat rack and bookcase and a lot of clothes, and has discovered she loves spending.

11.0 Your letter of 26th was waiting for me at office. So you are now on the coast. You dodge about so much that I can't trace you. Can you see our coast on a clear day? When you grow rich you will have to have a horse and I will have a donkey chaise. Another case of mumps, one of my hopefuls worse luck. That letter that came from you this mg: I ought to have had that last Friday so I stand a chance of getting 3 more from you today! That's the best of missing a day or two.

Look here, I've just seen Tom Gayford; came home yesterday for 10 days leave. It isn't fair, as I believe he went out after you. I must write to the Govt about it.

I have just taken £19-19-0. Now what shall we buy?

4.30 A grand budget of letters from you this afternoon, 27,28 & 29. I must puzzle out those missing words. Sounds as tho' you are in Belgium now. The colonel must grin over yr letters. Have just written to War Office asking them to look in Bert's paybook for a will. They won't let us have it without probate or Letters of Administration. Awfully busy so Goodbye

May

David to May   Western Front   July 2nd 1917

Yesterday a number of the officers started playing Ruby football just outside and of course I joined in too. It was quite good fun although a bit strenuous. I don't know which side won, the net result as far as I personally was concerned being the skin taken off one of my shins and a sprained finger.

An awful game is Rugby!

After that we had dinner and then went out for night operations. The night ops were rather a failure. Two platoons of which mine was one were to take up a position and two other platoons were to send out patrols to find, out all about us and then to attack us.

We got there, took up our position and made ready to catch as many of them as possible and then waited. And waited and waited and nothing happened except that after a time we captured two of their men and then a third. After waiting about 2 hours we discovered that the other two platoons had lost themselves or rather had never found us so then we packed up and went back to bed getting there about 1.30.

This morning we did physical jerks and after played games again, "Sergeant Major Murphy" being played by special request of the men.

This afternoon we were out training again. I had to chase the enemy across country for a while and then to attack them. I did the chasing alright, but they got into such a strong place, that although I attacked them it would have been hopeless to have got at them in reality and we should have all been wiped out long before we got there.

There are night ops again tonight. We are enjoying ourselves.

David

David to May   Western Front   July 2nd 1917

My Dearest,

No letter from you today but I rather expected that, although I looked out for one.

I tried on the socks and they are just right with enough room to allow for shrinkage.

I went out last night again and had a small bonfire all to myself.

Have you anything to do with the Marine business or is this to be entirely separate?

I am very glad you have got your girls back again and that no more have got bad.

You don't say anything about holidays. When are you going?

I may not be able to get a letter off to you for the next week or so perhaps 10 days, so if you don't get one, don't get worried. Of course I shall write if I can. I shall get yours alright.

Goodbye

David

May to David   In waiting room, Beckenham   Sunday 10.0 [2 July 1917]

My dear David,

This is the first opportunity I have had of writing to you. Am now off to cemetery and have 5 mins to wait.

On Thursday I caught our 6.0 train, but something went wrong with the works as it stopped on the wrong line at Loughboro' and the porter called out "change for Herne Hill"; so I changed and so did nearly everyone else. The station master was on the main platform and he said there was a breakdown in Penge tunnel and it may be hours before a train got thro', so that those who could walk had better do so. I then went back to the loop line platform and took the next train to Ravensbourne. It was very slow and finally turned me out at Nunhead. However another train came along and I reached home 1 hour late. Mama of course was worried. It was drizzling with rain, but you held the umbrella right over me so that I did not get wet. Of course I was cross with you, for which I got some cheek. That day was the day of the fete. The local paper said that Princess Patricia made the people understand why she was so popular, and then went on to say she arrived late, stayed a very short time, and announced that she wanted the affair to be as quiet as possible and no fuss!!!

Here is the train. No empty compt. This will do. Only a boy in it and I have brought the magic dust with me. Gently you are smashing the breath out of my body.

Kent House. He's got out. Stand in the window and scowl. O too late. Here come 3 youths in flannels and a picnic basket. You can't be full length now. What, you don't mind? That's right. Been aching for you.

Now how far had I got? O yes. Thursday night Mama did not sleep a wink and on Friday we had to give her brandy before we started off to Somerset House. We caught the 9.30 fast to Victoria. Twice at Somerset House she almost broke down and could not speak, and while waiting in one room she almost fainted. Then as a climax, the last man we saw told her that as there was no Will all four of us would have to share equally. Thought Mama would collapse that time so promptly told the man that Mama should have everything and that I didn't care 2d for the law when it went against my brother's wish. There's nothing like a temper for overcoming hysteria, and I quietly worked up Mama's temper about the law. The man (who really was a decent sort and rather young) had the gumption to see how upset and ill Mama was, said to me "I think you and your sister had better be sureties and then your mother need only to be troubled once more; will you all three come here at 12.15 next Friday. You will not be kept waiting then." We had waited 1½ hours in one room to have our name called out. I fancy after next Friday Ethel and I can manage everything tho' the man warned me it will be no easy job. We just caught the 12.23 home, and then gave Mama some brandy and port mixed. In the evening Ern got 6 bottles of champagne. Friday afternoon Mama who was a bit hysterical said we must all make wills, and not leave her anything as she could not go thro' this again.

(In the cemetery). So as Ethel went to work on Saturday and I didn't, I asked her to bring home will forms which she did. I am going to leave everything to Ethel and write a note and attach to will, saying it is my express wish that all I leave goes to benefit Mama during her life time and Ethel will spend the dividends on her. Ethel is leaving everything nominally to me with a similar note. Ethel said "I guess your money will be spent on port and champagne as we both like them, and Mama would never buy them herself." Of course if I get married my will is "null and void".

During Friday evening Mama brightened up considerably, and slept a little that night. On Saturday too she seemed alright. We had a busy day. I wanted to go to cemetery but it was too windy so I have come today and planted geraniums. Ten more to come up. Did a lot of needlework yesterday and did some more of your lace. It is lovely. Mama slept up to 3.0 this morning, and would have slept longer but last night's lobster woke her up. She seems very well this morning. Am going to Maud's this afternoon. Mustn't stop longer now, or will lose my train.

Goodbye

May
Band is playing lovely on Rye.

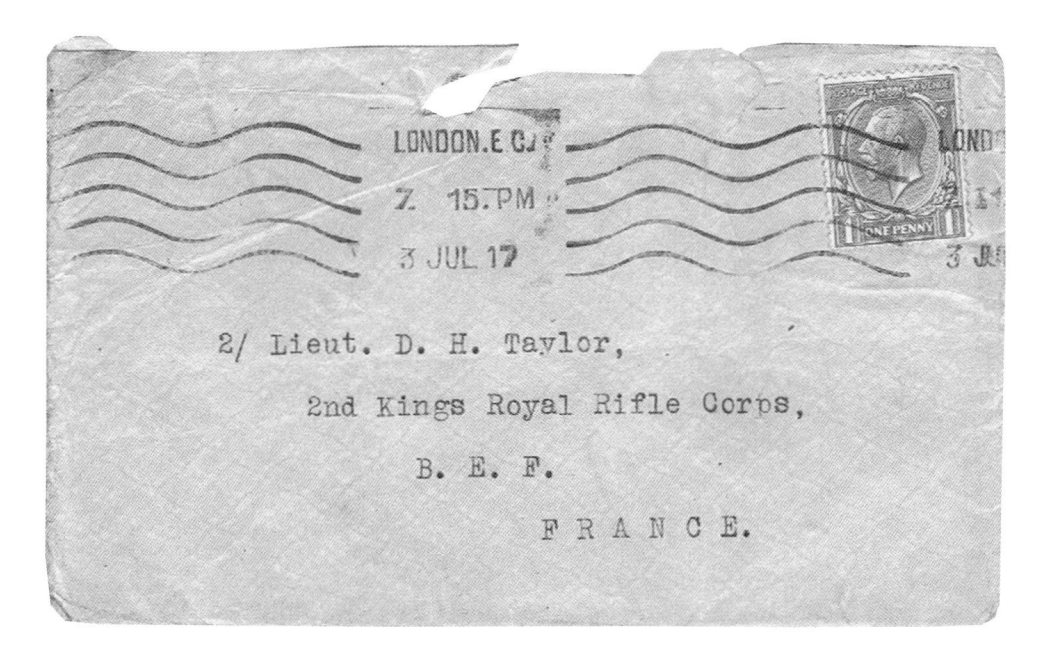

May to David   Beckenham   Tuesday 3 July 1917

My dear David,

Very sorry but we are the 8.30 again. It can't be helped as I want to call in at Stores a day this week if possible as next week is their sale, and I can only get 7 lb sugar at a time. It will be impossible to get served next week. There are only 2 old codgers in this compt, but they have their noses buried in papers, no doubt interested in its being Baby week, so you are lying full length. You'll have to get up at Dulwich. Make yourself comfy; I'll tell you when we get there. Tunnel. I have to hug you extra much going thro' that as you are frightened. You see you are my baby, so you can't help it. Your wanting a kiss between each half sentence is rather a hindrance to writing, but I suppose I had better give way to you.

I think yr letters to me are deliciously cheeky (Out of tunnel now, so I needn't hold you so tightly. No you are not frightened now, it is all bunkum. O, you want a slapping). If the colonel doesn't enjoy yr letters he is silly and has no bump of humour.

Dulwich. Quick. Gently, don't kick his eyes out. Now here come 2 girls. All sitting on the other side. Thank goodness. I have made you invisible, but you mustn't cheek me as I can't stop them from hearing you. Don't know that I would if I could, must have some peace and quietness some times.

The weather has turned glorious again. Uncle wrote to Ethel and me this morning. Fortunately Mama didn't hear the letter come, so we did not show her. He mentions that he is glad Mama is a little better. That will upset her if she knew as she says she is never going to get better, only worse.

I didn't have time to ring those people yesterday as the letter came too late but will do so today.

Herne Hill. Lots of folks waiting on platform. You had better get up. Make yourself small and sit on my lap. No one getting in! Perhaps they think the compt is spooky. Wish the others did also and get out. Off. No one got in so you can lie full length. If you squeeze me so hard I shall call out and then what will the folks think? No, I know you don't care. Aren't you the worry of my life? Do you know, the night before last I almost gouged your eyes out? It was when you were turning me over on the other side. One of my wavers touched your face close to your right eye, so now I have "acquired" one of Ern's large handkerchiefs and fit it over my head, fastening back my 3 wavers. Mama thinks it is because I am putting cocoanut oil on my hair, and don't want to grease the sheets. I let her think it.

It is going to be hot today. Hadn't you better get out of my arms and sit up properly? Incorrigible! What would the sergeant say, and the General of Generals?

You ask me about my holidays. Well. I ought to have been at home last week and week before really, but we were busy at office and shorthanded, and then perhaps you might get leave and I would like to get time off then if poss. So thought I would be a martyr and go to work. At any rate I shall have a fortnight in Sept. Must put this away now.

By the Bye, did I scrunch you too much last night? If so it was your fault, because it was too good of you to send Miss Wiltshire so much for me. I will now write to her and tell her what

you say about going out together. She does deserve a treat – a good soul not appreciated. We could not make out the missing words yesterday. Possibly they refer to livestock.
4.30 Nothing from you and no time to write more.
Lunch time I wrote to Maud, who wants me at 37 for the whole day next Sunday, and asked her to come out for a picnic on Shirley Hills instead. Picnic on a Sunday too! What will she say? I also suggested going to 56 to tea (unasked).
At 1.30. I wrote to Miss Willsher and told her what you said about going out together
Goodbye

May

3.7.17   Messrs Read & Brigstock 5, Lothbury, E.C.5 Moorgate St, EC

Dear Sirs,
I am writing on behalf of Lt. D.H. Taylor, 2nd Kings Royal Rifle Corps, B.E.F. France, who writes me as under:-
"I bought some Malayalam Rubber Shares on 30th April. At the end of May I asked Messrs. Read & Brigstock, 5 Lothbury, to buy 10 more at 38/6 or under, sending them a cheque for £19.
"They acknowledged the cheque on 29th May and said they could buy them at the price. Since then I have written twice asking them to buy at 40/- or under, but have heard nothing further.
"Since then I have also seen the shares quoted below 38/-.
"Please find out what they are doing, and let me know by return."
As I am writing to this gentleman today, I shall be pleased if you will let me have a reply per bearer.
Yours faithfully,

David to May   Western Front   July 4th 1917

I have just found that there is a possibility of this getting posted to you and I have about 2 minutes to scribble it.
Haven't done anything very exciting the last two days.
Yesterday we had a parade in the morning and then a night march.
Today we haven't done anything in particular.
I will write more tomorrow if possible but don't expect a letter and I may not be able to write.
Had no letter yet but may get it tonight.
Goodbye

David

Fanny to Ethel   Balham   4 July 1917

My darling Ethel,
I expect you are all out enjoying the lovely sunshine with your dear children. Have you anyone to help you. For seaside is work with children, and their many wants. Yet I do hope you will all have an enjoyable time.
We have had some grand weather this last week, real seaside sort, made me think of old times.
On Monday after finishing at Kent House I went up West, and ordered another cake to be sent to David from you. So I hope he will get it by Sunday.
I heard from him on Monday, he is still in the same place and well.
We are getting plenty of potatoes now $3^{1}/_{2}$ d per lb. And very good. Fruit is dear, but fruit without the sugar is not much and sugar is scarce $^{1}/_{2}$ lb at a time, when we can get it, but we manage alright.
I heard that Tommy Archer was improving, his wife went to Glasgow to see him a week ago. Walter Writer is unfit for active service.
They were all well at Glen Roy yesterday, just returned home from the draper's and dressmaker.
I have just heard that the Flying Devils have visited the City E and N. We heard the guns, but said to each other it was practicing on the Common, but it was not so, it was this morning between 11-12 am. Mary Stanley was here, she had been to the Doctor, and it came on to rain. She said, that sounds like bombs. I said no, it's practice on the Common. She is very well. I think I told you she went to see Mattie, she and Mattie did not get on very well so she packed up and came away, and left Mattie to it. She said it was a lovely baby, and had beautiful presents sent him, in wearing apparel. I asked Mary, what did she give him (Nothing). Mary is coming to Holdons sale tomorrow early, something she is wanting.

I hope all of you are well. My love to all, and yourself,
From your Loving

Mama

David to May   Western Front   July 5th 1917

My Dearest,
Just got your letter (Sunday) all about your journey to Somerset House. You poor little girl, what an awful time you are having. I am sorry to hear Mrs Muggridge is still so slowly recovering.
Look here don't worry too much yourself. You are watching Mrs Muggridge all the time, and you know when she sleeps and when she doesn't, but it seems to me that you are getting no sleep yourself. You'll be ill if you go on like that.
I have just heard about the Russians getting their haul of prisoners. Isn't it splendid.
One of the fellows here had an idea this morning. He said the Allies should push on each front alternatively, then the Germans would begin to take troops from one front to the other alternatively, until at last they would have them coming and going so quickly that they would have an army stuck half way between the two and not know which way to turn, which would give us our chance. We still have some brains in the army!
I wish I could take all that worry business off your hands and do it all for you.
Goodbye

David

May to David   Office   5 July 1917

My dear David,

1.30 and this is the first opportunity I have had of writing to you.

I had to go with Ern this morning as he was taking up our deed box, and wanted someone to see he did not forget it or drop it in the river, or something else of that sort, so I had to sit opposite him in a first class compt and watch. It was such a smooth journey that had I written I am sure you could have read it! Perhaps that would have been tame, though. Guess you prefer the puzzles you get; or can't you make them out?

The deed box is being deposited in our strong room in the basement for a few days, as Mama will have to leave the house to itself at least once.

I told you, didn't I, that I had written to War Office to look in Bart's pay book to see if he had filled in the will form that I hear is in each book, and to let me know by tomorrow. Also wrote the same thing to Hounslow, Record Office for R.W.K., but so far have had no reply; so in case we do not hear in time for tomorrow, not wanting to give Mama a journey for nothing, I this morning called in at Somerset House, and asked them if necessary could we postpone our visit for the Administration Letters till Friday week or fortnight, and told him the reason, that I had written to War Office, and had received no reply as yet. The man said "Come when you like", and spoke so courteously. Before I thought he was a bear. Perhaps I smiled at him, either this time or last, and didn't on the other occasion.

Had a nice letter from Mrs. Taylor this morning asking me for the weekend. Have replied that as I sleep with Mama I had better not stay over the night, but would see her some time Sunday, and told her about Maud.

Time is up.

Last night I knitted. Have almost finished a pair of socks for the Corporal, only he hasn't written to say he wants them yet. If he doesn't write I shall have to pass them on to you to get rid of them, but I haven't made them quite so long in the leg. Perhaps if you don't want them they might do for one of your men.

We did laugh over your letters yesterday.

4.30 Nothing from you yet.

Saw Lutt this morning. He transferred one of the supers to our Marine Dept in Old Broad St. She did not approve and came in yesterday and gave Lutt a bit of her mind about it. Said he wasn't going to risk transferring another girl. So suppose he had better get another in. I said "I knew the very girl you want" (I was thinking of Maud) "but she won't be ready till 2 months time." He said "We must have someone at once, but speak to me when your friend is ready to come." I think it would be a good thing for Maud to go to the Marine Indemnity.

May

David to May   Western Front   July 6th 1917

My Dearest,

Just got your Sunday and Monday letters combined. You read my letters just as I intended you to read them. I am sorry you have another girl away with the same old thing and in your own department too.

Tom Gayford probably got leave sooner than me. Leave comes so very slowly here, ever so much too slowly. I want to be with you again and I have been thinking what we shall do and what it will be like. I am always at it. Still it is getting gradually nearer.

Your description of the painters was awfully funny and your picture of Maud standing up to her brother and making him pay up, fills me with amazement and awe.

Sorry I can't write much.

Goodbye.

David

May to David   Beckenham   Friday 6 July 1917

My dear David,

We are on the 8.30 but there is no room for you to lie in your favourite position. There is no word from War Office so we are postponing our visit to Somerset House.

Heard from Maud last night. She is evidently shocked at thoughts of the picnic. Moreover, an old Datchelor girl, Kate Foale, has booked rooms for fortnight from 25 July at Watchet, Somerset, after that she is going to Winchester for 10 days; then in Sept would like to go with me to Goring, near Worthing. Had a p.c. from Mrs Taylor this morning asking me to bring Maud over next Sunday as early as possible. Good soul. We'll go.

I see by the papers you are in the fighting. How I wished I was with you, and how you are glad I'm not.

Dulwich.

11.0 We filled up at Dulwich, so I had to take you on my lap and then I got out First Aid. I think we are going to have some practice under the chief's scrutiny. He will be quite as bad as army colonel.

I also had a letter from that farm in Northampton. The lady can't take anyone in August as she has her relations, so it as well Maud is going to Somerset.

Found a letter up here from you this morning. You say I shall not get a letter from you for perhaps 10 days. Specks I'll imagine you send me one each day, and I specks I'll get them in the train, and will read them with you in my arms. Very busy, must stop.

1.30 It has turned out a lovely day. I have been thinking. On Sunday morning I'll go to cemetery, and then on from there to Maud's with my trowel, basket and pots. Won't she be charmed! I shall not get to her till dinner time and immediately after we will be off to 56. Maud says she has had a letter from you and is very pleased. She moves on the 15th. I think she is feeling very consequential.

Helen and her children came yesterday to tea, and left at 7.5. They were noisy. It made a change for Mama, but I think she was glad when they had gone. She said so. She tried to persuade Mama to go away with Auntie, but didn't succeed. Auntie gets on everyone's nerves, as she will talk about her imaginary complaints. She always was a martyr. Your occasional martyrdom is nothing compared with hers.

Yesterday one of the temporary girls called in, a Mrs Rogers, whom all like. Her hubby had a post (in the army) up in Edinburgh so she went there after a while in our Edinburgh Branch. He has now been passed as A.1. so she has come to her mother's home. I asked her if she were going back to Edinburgh; she said No, so I said "Mrs Rogers, you went away looking happy, but you have come back looking even happier." That did it. I thought she was going to embrace me, but she didn't. She beamed away and said "I am. I couldn't be happier; and what has helped me be so happy is that my husband is so pleased. You have no idea how delighted he is" (I think perhaps he must be something like you, only of course not so nearly as good). "So now when he goes across I shall not mind so much as he has left me something to live for. Strange to say my health is much better than it ever was before. Its going to be the making of me." She was the girl who was the Bank of England clerk before she was married. She finished by saying she had had this extra happiness for 4 months.

By the bye, I don't think you ought to read the above, so please consider it censored off the face of the globe.

5.30 Had a very busy day.

Now look. I know you'll want to write if you only get a chance. But don't go without sleep or rest on that account. I shan't have blue canary fits for nothing.

Goodbye

May

David to May   Western Front   July 7th 1917

I got your letter. (3rd) just as I came off duty about 2 A.M. this morning, so that I almost had two letters in one day. I crawled into my bunk, stuck a candle up just behind my head and then went over two or three times all you described.

So you are having a holiday in September. Well I may be able to get home by then - don't expect it will be before then, but I ought to be going about that time I should think. Where shall we go and what shall we do - I guess I know the answer to the last or at least I know the greater part of it.

I am glad you are going out with Miss Willsher and I want you to have as good a time as you can. Wish I could be there and finish up by going down to Beckenham with you.

Goodbye.

David

Fanny to Ethel   Balham   9 July 1917

My darling Ethel,

I was glad to get your letter on Friday last. It was 18 days coming, I shall send it on to David, and he will be able to answer about the jacket.

He is moving again, and he told me he might not be able to write for several days, but I was not to worry. He was well and had been playing football.

No doubt you will know before this reaches you that we had another visit of the Air Devils. Yes and close home, but no damage was done here. It is a trying time for all. If all is well I am going to spend a weekend with Frances Bruming at Chesham, going on Wednesday and returning Monday morning. Polly will be here and Nelly and her baby until I come back. I cannot say if Auntie and Uncle worry very much about Minnie, you see it's been years coming, and they did not heed what her Doctor told them. So now there is no cure, although she is under another specialist. I don't know how many that makes since they moved. I am sorry for her. But I do not think she would have been so bad if she had done what Dr Constable order he to do. Go out in the mornings all weathers come in and rest and out again, to keep out in the air. She took his medicine, and never went outside the door more than she could help, and now she cannot go out alone. I don't go over there very often, I find plenty to do. Auntie is looking very well, she still goes to hospital for the light and massage. The rest are well. Cousin Charles is back from Plymouth, I have not seen him. I hear he is well. I heard this morning the damage was bad up his way.

I am pleased to say Auntie Bessie is quite her old self again. And in her letter to me, I was to be sure to give her love and a kiss to the dear children. Sophia nerves are bad through these raids, her nerves have not been good since her operation, otherwise she and Alf are well.

Your dear children will sleep better when the winter comes, so don't trouble, as long as they are well. But you seem run down. The lovely sea and country will do you all good. Nellie's is a good baby girl, she cannot walk alone, yet, she can talk a little.

I am well and Polly likewise.

I do hope you have got some help. Hoping you all will enjoy yourselves, my love to all.

From your Loving

Mama

Potatoes are 2d per lb.

1   will

56. Ramsdell Road.
Balham.
London. S.W.12
9 July. 1917

My darling Ethel

I was glad to get your letter on Friday last, It was 10 days coming, I shall send it on to David, And he will be able to answer about the jacket. He is moving again, And he told me he might not be able to write for several days, but I was not to worry, he was well, And had been playing football. No doubt you know before this reaches you, That we have had another visit of the Air Devils. "Yes" And close home, but no damage was done here. It is a trying time for all. If all is well I am going to spend a week end with Frances Browning at Chesham, going on Wednesday And return Monday morning. Polly will be here And Nelly & her baby untill I come back. I cannot say Auntie & Uncle worry very much about Connie, You see it's been years coming, And they did not heed what the Doctors told them. So now there is no cure, although she is under another Specialist, I don't know how many that makes, since they moved. I am sorry for her. But I do not think she would have been so bad. If she had done what Dr Constable ordered her to do. Go out in the mornings all weathers Come in and rest and out again. To keep out in the Air. She took his medicine, And never went outside the door more than she could help, And now she cannot go out alone. I don't go over there very often, I find plenty to do. Auntie is looking very well she still goes to Hospital for the light and massage the rest are well. Cousin Charles is back from Plymouth, I have not seen him. I hear he is well. I heard this morning the damage was bad up his way.

I am pleased to say Auntie Bessie is quite herself again, And in her letter to me, I was to be sure to give her love and a kiss to the dear Children. Sophia nerves are bad through these raids. her nerves have not been good since her operation other wise she & her self are well. Your dear Children will sleep better when the winter comes, So don't trouble. As long as they are well But you seem run down. The lovely sea And Country will do you all good. Nellis is a good baby girl, she cannot walk alone, Yet she can talk a little.
I am well & Polly likewise.
I do hope you have got some help, Hopeing you all will enjoy your selves, my love to all.
From Your Loveing
Potatoes ar 2d pett,   Mamma

Copy of British Report July 11th 1917

After a heavy bombardment lasting 24 hours the enemy yesterday made a strong attack against our positions on the Nieuport front. The violent concentrated fire of the German Artillery succeeded in completely destroying our defensive works in the Dune Sector of the Coast which were cut off by the destruction of the bridges across the Yser. The enemy was able to break through our defences on a 1300 metre front & a width of 600 metres which enabled him to reach the bank of the Yser close to the sea. The German artillery fire which had developed intense violence on the Nieuport Front is now slackening. Our guns continue active. The weather interfered with our flying activity.

Copy of British Report   July 11th 1917

After a heavy bombardment lasting 24 hours the enemy yesterday made a strong attack against our positions on the Nieuport front. The violent concentrated fire of the German Artillery succeeded in completely destroying our defensive works in the Dune Sector of the Coast which were cut off by the destruction of the bridges across the Yser. The enemy was able to break through our defences on a 1300 metre front & a width of 600 metres which enabled him to reach the bank of the Yser close to the sea. The German Artillery fire which had developed intense violence on the Nieuport Front is now slackening. Our guns continue active. The weather interfered with our flying activity.

Jack and Erl Linn

Kings Royal Rifles

The Kings Royal Rifle Corps raised 22 battalions in total during the course of WWI and saw action on the Western Front, Macedonia and Italy. The regiment lost 12,840 men who were killed during the course of the war.

The 2nd Battalion was stationed at Blackdown, Aldershot at the outbreak of war as part of the 2nd Brigade of the 1st Division. In August 1914 it was mobilised for war and landed at Havre and engaged in various action on the Western Front.

On 10th July 1917 the 1st Division had relieved the French in the narrow bridge-head over the River Yser. Two battalions were across the river: the 2nd Battalion KRR and the 1st Northamptonshires. A heavy bombardment commenced in the early evening and then the German infantry attacked. German aeroplanes machined gunned the breastworks. The KRR recorded losses of officers as 7 killed, 4 wounded, 6 missing, and the loss of 481 other ranks.

May to David   Beckenham   Monday 9 July 1917
[returned marked Missing 10/7/17]

My dear David,

At last we are in the 8.46, well up front, all to our two little selves, and I don't think anyone would want to come in, as it is pouring with rain and we are beyond the station cover. O you are wet. Take off your waterproof in readiness.

On Saturday I left at 12.30 and caught the 12.44 which went off to time and got home at 1.15. Mama was alright, tho she had watched the planes over London for some time, and saw 17 of them break away and come direct towards her. For a while she could not move and her knees were shaking. Then she remembered Bert's letters. That broke the spell and she rushed downstairs with them into the cellar. Our shrapnel has broken the glass in Cannon Street Station.

We're off. Quick....what! your finger still bad! And after I had nursed it all night again! I think it is a most ungrateful finger. O, a <u>little</u> better, is it? Well, I suppose you had better continue the treatment. Is that nice? I think you had better go to sleep. With your eyes shut I mean...... Quite asleep yet? Alright, then I can go on writing.

On Saturday afternoon we had a lovely washing day. The guns were going all the afternoon down the river, the raiders trying to get back again, but they did not succeed. Owing to the workman we had not had a washing day for a fortnight. The men haven't finished yet, but have gone on another job, which is a little way they have out of the army.

Saturday night I had a lovely sleep, and slept on till 8.45 without a break. I lost my train to Maud's, but managed to catch the 12.28, arriving at 37 at 1.10.

Catford. Quick. No, I didn't kick you on the floor. It's your own fault entirely. I shall put this away now and get out first aid. Have miniaturized you, and have tucked you in my coat with your finger still getting better – slowly, very slowly.

1.30 Had your letter of 4th given me when I arrived here. So desperately glad to get it.

Well, I had dinner at Maud's. The place is upside down. Maud looks brighter tho' awfully thin and white. She says she is enjoying being her own mistress at last! Aren't you shocked at her? After dinner we washed up and then went to 56 for tea, which we both enjoyed very much, in fact, I think all three of us did. We talked and talked and talked. Maud left at 6.15 to go to church. We left at 7.50 and Mrs Taylor came to Herne Hill with me. Caught the 8.43 home. We both had a glass of wine before we left. The tip of my nose is red! I know I have a bit of a cold and there is a small rough place on my tip, but of course you might have caused both. Mrs Taylor is off to Chesham on Wednesday till following Monday, and the folks there have invited Mrs Capel. So Mrs Taylor is feeling highly delighted. She has been bargain hunting lately. She has a hat which she trimmed herself, some stuff for a dress, mauve, which she is going to make up, and some lovely back broad trimming for a dress. She doesn't seem to realise you are near danger at all, leave alone being in it. Its a good thing too; I'm sure I'm not going to enlighten her. Fortunately she doesn't read the papers. Mars Way does that for her.

4.30 Had two more letters from you. You are a dear to write. You are not 'training' now, but doing the real thing, I know.

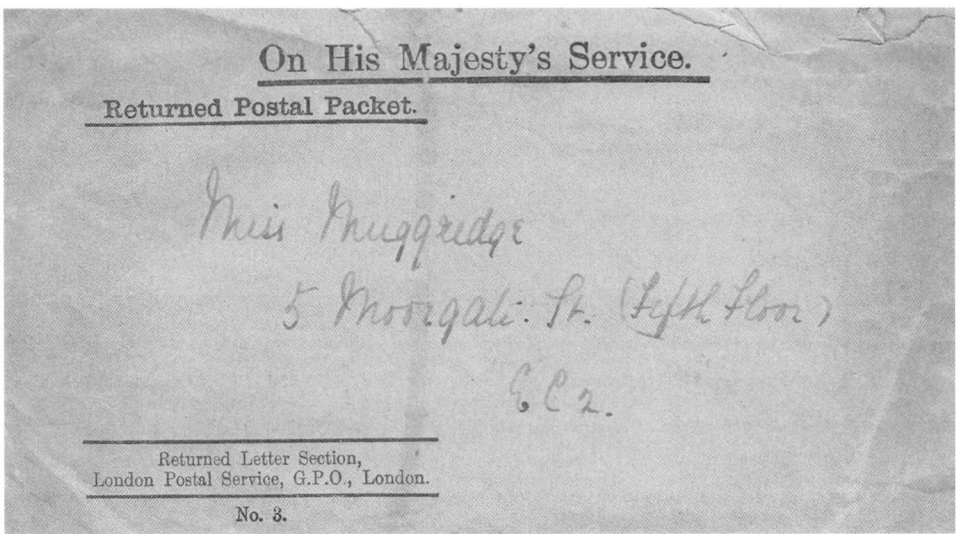

Your special pastime is imagining grand things of me, but as I told you before, you see me thro' rose coloured glass. I am very ordinary really, and not doing anything out of the way, like you are. How disappointed you'll be in me one of these fine days!

Mr Gayford sent for me this morning and asked how the girls got on on Saturday. I told him they kept quite calm and I felt proud of them. He asked if any fainted and seemed surprised when I said no. Mrs Gayford came up about 12.45 to see us. She said Tom's turn came extra quickly for leave as several before him were transferred, but it will be ages before he gets home again.

Very busy. Can't stop any longer, so Goodbye till tomorrow.

May

P.S. I got Maud's insurance for fire, burglary and domestic labour – discussed it on a Sunday too! Might get her personal accident by aircraft too.

P.S. I told Maud I could not make any promises about going away with her in September. What do you think about that for obedience. Am staying at home for a week from 28 July most likely.

May to David   Tuesday 10 July 1917
[returned marked Wounded and Missing]

My dear David,

Such a shame. The compartment filled up at Beckenham this morning. I caught the 8. 30. because we are so busy and I asked all the girls to start work at 9 0. this morning rather than stay late. Still, we did enjoy ourselves last night, didn't we? I have borrowed a more recent First Aid book than my own, so read that in the train. The Germans see they are so busted up all round that their only chance is, they think, to frighten the women workers in London.   Silly fools; it only makes us think that that is what our men folks are going through, so take it calmly and philosophically, only of course you have the concentrated essence of it, and we are only getting a flavouring.

Caught my early train home last night as usual, and knitted as usual. The workmen have not yet come back so we cannot transplant our vegetables yet as they will only tramp on them.

We are getting or with our work very nicely indeed, though raids are a hindrance. We are only 5 days behindhand. Of course these raids make us extra busy; they are very good for business.

I slept very well last night; only wish you could sleep as well. I know you are having a hard time. Never mind; you shall have a rest one day, and shan't we both enjoy it?

Cannot stop any longer just now.

1. 30. Last Saturday morning one of the girl supers gave me a piece of white heather that had come up from Scotland. White heather is supposed to stand for good luck, so I am told. I gave it to Mama when I got home, but she said "Send it to David. It will bring him home safely." But I have forgotten it each day; I must send it to-morrow, or a bit of it.

No raid today so far, and it is just an ideal day for one. Bright with white clouds for the devils to hide behind. It is rather chilly. The brilliant hue of my nose is disappearing, I am glad to say, but it looks swollen. Yes, I evidently have taken to drink.

Can't think of anything else to say just now.

Did I tell you we are going to send our old office cleaner away this year? She knows someone at Brighton who will board and lodge her for 14/- for the week. The fare will be 12/7, and she will have 11/- of her own to spare. We have already collected £1., so she will be able to be a real lady again for a whole week. The thoughts of it are keeping her going. Poor old soul, these last two raids were very bad round her neighbourhood, and she was too bad after each to come to work.

4.30 Connie is coming this afternoon to see Mama, who by the bye is not anxious to see her. She will be gone before we get home. We have not told Ern. No raiders here yet.

5.30 Goodnight. See you later.

May

Campbell to Fanny   In the Field   12th July 1917

Dear Mrs Taylor,
I am afraid that I cannot get any news of your son.
The last seen of him was in Bn.H.G. in the line, wounded in the head. The rest of my company was blown to bits except a few men who swam back across the river the following day.
The whole of the 2nd Battn K.R.R. except the few who managed to get away (about 3 officers and 30 men) were either killed, buried or wounded. I have hopes that your son was taken prisoner, but I can lay out no hope.
He was a most gallant officer and one where friendship was worth having. He first thought was duty and this was noticeable in the trenches up to the time he was wounded. This was on 10th July about midday.
My 2nd in command and other platoon commanders were both killed. I deeply regret his loss (if it is so) and sympathise with you, for as a brother officer there was none better, so as a son he must have meant everything to you.
His cheery presence will be missed greatly, however I have great hopes that you will get good news. It is hard to say.
Yours sincerely

Edward Campbell
'B' Coy 2nd K.R.R.C.

Fanny to Ethel   Balham   17 July 1917

My darling Ethel,

I know you feel like I do, sad at heart, of the news of our David. I cabled as soon as I know it, which was Monday morning. It was in that dreadful battle of the 10th where the Kings R Rifle and Northampton fought in the death. I received another Telegram from the War office, saying wounded and missing. Further reports will be sent immediately. And I will let you know. If you can dear Ethel don't look on the dark side but hope for the best. It a cross we have got to bear. But not as heavy as our King Jesus bore for us.

Pray don't try to come home here, everything is too unsafe. And John and the dear children need you where safer than home.

I went to spend the week end with Frances Bruming and the change was good and returned home before eleven on Monday where the first Telegram awaited. That was missing. The one in the afternoon was wounded and missing. He got your cake a few days before. On his field card he said well, and received parcel. My last parcel he could not have received which was fruit, dear boy. Everyone is very kind to me.

Auntie and Uncle came over at once. They were here when I cable you. Oh dear Ethel try and keep bright. We are not alone in this sad trial. You are ever in my thoughts.

I am keeping fairly well. I want to try and keep so for your sake and David's.

Kiss the dear children for Grannie. Polly is very good to me. Nellie returns home tomorrow and they send their love.

My fond love to you all. And I trust your maid turned up and of use to you. You mentioned her in your last letter which I received on Friday.

From your Loving Mamma

F Taylor

Fanny to May   Balham   18 July 1917

My dear May,

Many thanks for letter shall be pleased to see you. Come to dinner.

The enclose is a copy of a letter I had this morning. I know you would like. The returned letter came yesterday.

Remember me very kindly to your mother. And much love to yourself.

From Yours affectionately

Fanny Taylor

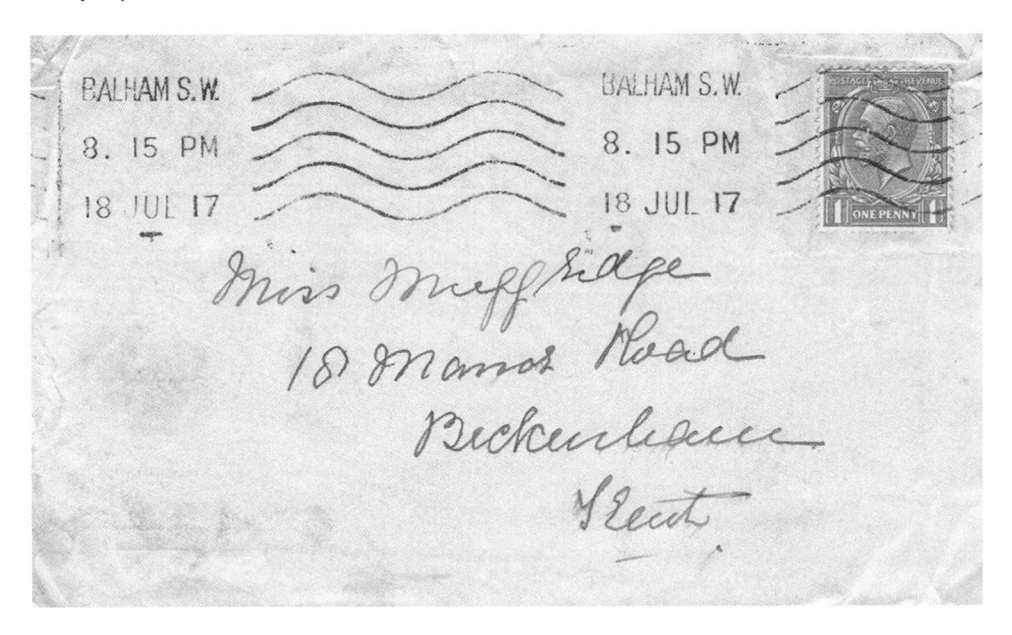

Fanny to Ethel   Balham   18 July 1917

My darling Ethel

The enclosed is a copy of a letter I received this morning. I know you will like to know all. And that I will try to do. I feel I have nothing more to write about.

Do hope you are all well with fondest love

From your Loving

Mamma

[copy of letter is the one from Campbell dated 12th July].

Fanny to Ethel   Balham   23 July 1917

My darling Ethel

I was so pleased to get your letter, and to know the air is better for you just now. I was not surprised to hear about the maid. At present girls are much of a muchness here. I know you must have heard the sad news of David and that your heart is aching like mine. At present I have not any more news of him. I shall try and find out if he is alive. I fear not, for it was a dreadful battle, one of the worse. I read it on the Saturday morning, while on a visit to Mrs Brunings, and said to them My boy is in that. And how many more dear ones. We cannot tell. As soon as I get any more news I will send on to you. It is not fighting, it is murder.

Mr Bomier that lived in next door, that let the little boy cry so, while the mother was out. Was only out there a few weeks was killed, leaves wife and 4 children.

I do hope if David is alive they will treat him kindly.

I know your thoughts (I would like to go home to Mamma) but dear Ethel don't attempt it, for it is not safe to come. And to live here is not. One never knows when a raid is coming.

And it would just kill me to loose you. I am trying my best to keep well, and every body is very kind, and willing to do anything for me.

Polly is very kind, she loved him dearly. And all those who knew him liked him (he was a dear).

My dear don't you bother to buy me anything for my birthday. I have your love and that is the best of things.

Everything is going on alright with the property, I manage it myself.

We saw Auntie Jane and the others yesterday, Hilda and children was there, Walter still at Sittingborne. They all send their love.

Kiss the dear children for Grannie and love to Jean. Hope they will enjoy the changes.

With fond love to you both

From Your Loving

Mamma

F Taylor

Fanny to Ethel   Balham   July 26 1917

My darling Ethel

I feel I have not much to write about. Yesterday I went to the War Office, to see if I could get any news of David. Not any. I went then to the Red Cross. I was told they would do all they could. And told me to write to The Director, International Red Cross, Geneva Switzerland and enclose cost of a telegram, which I did at once. And if I heard anything to let them know. And if they heard they would send to me.

I have a list of all his clothing sent to me. And just now while writing to you, the post has just brought a parcel of chocolate I sent him on the sixth, he never received. This is a blow to one. Although I might have expected it. For it is not war. I hope you will try and stay your time at the Lake. It will do you all good. Every body is very kind and the weather likewise.

Auntie Jane and Uncle send their love. I am told Walter Writer is looking ill. I have not seen him since he joined. Now dear Ethel excuse this, I am feeling tired.

Kiss the dear children for Grannie and love to dear Jean, Polly sends her love.

Much love to you both
From
Your Loving Mamma

F Taylor

Fanny to Ethel   Balham   27 July 1917

My darling Ethel

I see in this week's Weekly Times (this morning) that David is a prisoner in German hands.
I do hope they will be kind to all of them.
I am fairly well. Polly likewise. Hoping all is well with you all.
My fond love to all.
From Your Loving
Mamma

F Taylor

Fanny to Ethel   Balham   30 July 1917

My darling Ethel

I feel so sorry, we had the paragraph in the Weekly Times wrong. It belonged to some others, below his paragraph. So as far as we know he is still wounded and missing. I have done all I can to know. So I must wait. But in my own thoughts he is killed. The fighting was dreadful.
I met old Doctor Constable last Thursday he had just returned from a visit to his wounded son, who was in hospital when you was here. He is at the sea near Brighton, just able to get about a little. He has two more in the war.
When I told him about my boy, he said, I am sorry it was his head. He wished to be kindly remembered.
Cousin Charles came to me last week, he had a cold which caused him to stay in, he wished to be remembered. All at Glen Roy are as usual, and greaved at the news of David, every one is. I told Doctor you wanted to come home, and he said tell her not to come, it is too dangerous.
I do hope you are all well and enjoying the change. The Bulfords have shut up their home in Broadstairs, and gone to Nottingham to Auntie Dolly. They could not stand it any longer, so often layed down at nights half dressed. The last raid decided it. Bettie came to dinner on Sunday, she is looking just the same.
The box of chocolates I sent to David on the 6 of July has been returned marked Missing. I know I am not the only Mother who son is gone. As soon as I hear any thing more, I will write to you at once.
I am keeping fairly well.
Polly sends her love.
Give the dear children a loving kiss, and my love to Jean and much to your dear selves.
From your Loving

Mamma

Fanny to Ethel   Balham   Aug 5 1917

My darling Ethel,

Last evening I received a telegram from Geneva Switzerland saying Lieut David Taylor reported prisoner Karlsruhe. Red Cross.

I cabled you at once. So that tells us he is alive. I shall go up to the Red Cross (on Tuesday) if I don't hear any more before. To know if I can ascertain if he is wounded, and I will let you know all. Cousin Charles called this afternoon to know if I had heard any more news of my boy, and he was glad to hear, although he would rather have heard better news (but he was alive). He said he could quite understand how you felt, and you have his sympathy. He is looking better. Miss Massy is here for a few days, she is improving, but slowly, she sends her love.

Now dearie we must try and look on the bright side, and pray that all will be kind to David.

I am keeping fairly well, and I do hope that John and the dear three children are well, likewise yourself.

With fond love
From your loving

Mamma

Edward Campbell to May   B.E.F.   6 Aug 1917

Dear Miss Muggridge,

Thank you for your letter. I got such a nice strong letter from Mrs Taylor about her son. Her view of the loss was so brave and one that other people might do well to copy. How bravely she is taking it. I must sympathise with you most sincerely on the loss of such a friend. However, there is quite a good chance of his being a wounded prisoner, and I think you would be perfectly right to rely on that for a time first, as news will take a long time to come come through and the Germans admit 27 officer prisoners. Otherwise I have no news alas to give you about him. I should of course let you know immediately I heard anything.
Yours Sincerely

Edward Campbell

Fanny to Ethel   Balham   Aug 8 1917

My darling Ethel
This morning I went to the War Office and they had not any more news of David. I took my telegram, that I had received from Geneva Switzerland Red Cross, which they was very pleased to see, and told me they might not heard for a month or two, but I might hear from my son before. And if I did would I kindly let them know at once. I also went to the Red Cross, and showed them the telegram, which they asked me to do, and they was pleased. And told me it was a large camp. I am now sending another per paid telegram to the Red Cross Geneva Switzerland asking if he is wounded badly. The Red Cross said I had heard quickly. I have done all that can be done, and I am the first one that will receive all news.
I received a post card yesterday, which I have enclosed. Am answering it by this post, telling him David is a prisoner of war at Karlsruhe camp.
I will let you know as soon as I receive any news. I quite know how anxious you are feeling. Every one is very kind to me, and all who knew him are sorry.
I do hope you are all well and still enjoying the change. I am fairly well. Polly sends her love.
Fond love
From Mamma

F Taylor

Fanny to Ethel   Balham   Aug 10 1917

My darling Ethel,
Just received your letter.
Now I have good news of David. The enclosed will explain a lot. I went to 84 Queen St and saw the cheque. It was David's hand writing, and signed well. They told me he could not have been wounded, if so only slight, or he would not be in that camp. He said I could write to him as many letters as I like, but be careful what I put in. I came home and wrote to him at once. I had to go up there again today. And they are going to send him a parcel of eatable, which I paid them for £1-4-0, the 4/- is for the telegram. They send the parcel through Holland. He told he had money enough to buy things in the Camp. Now I am sending him a change of underclothes, and when I get his things I shall send them. Cox's Bank will send them on to me. I have the list sent me. So now we know David is alive, and many of his officers are in the same Camp. They told me he would only be allowed to write 4 cards a month, but we could write as many as we liked. No newspapers.
So now darling, we must hope and trust that all will be well. I will let you know all I hear of him, as soon as I get any news. I am keeping well. I hope John has returned safely, and the dear children enjoying themselves. I often think of them. Kiss them all for me, and I can see Jean quite grown up. Give the dear child my love. And now dearie try and enjoy the end of your stay. My love to you both
From your loving
Mamma

F Taylor

Campbell to May   B.E.F.   16 Aug 1917

Dear Miss Muggridge
I am delighted to hear that Mr Taylor is safe. How excellent. I am so glad for you and Mrs Taylor. Please convey to her my best congratulations. I will not write to him as I have only the same thing to say as to you. I am very busy so perhaps she will excuse me. I can, if you have had no letter from him, prove he is a prisoner by a photograph of him walking through Bruge, amongst several other of the B'll. He has his head bandaged but otherwise looks alright. Best congratulations.
Yours sincerely,

Edward Campbell

Fanny to Ethel   Balham   18 Aug 1917

My darling Ethel,

Good News. God has spared our David, received a card last night, written on the 25th July. This is what is on the card - I am quite alright my head and ear going on well. Will you please send me such things as tinned meat, tin butter, milk, tea, Quaker oats, ginger biscuits I expect he is longing for them and Vaseline, please send parcels of food frequently. The best way to send them is through the International Red Cross, 4 Thurslow Place, London S.W.. Some of these things I have asked for before, and are doing so again, in case you didn't get my letter I did not get the letter. I will write more fully later. I believe parcels take about 10 weeks from the date of the post card to get here.

I wrote and told you I had sent him some food. And I also sent him last Monday some under cloths. So they are on their way.

Now I shall go to the War Office with his card. Then to Cox's Bank and get his cloths sent and all he asks for. I wrote and told him I had sent him food and clean cloths. Polly's gone over to Auntie Jane to tell them the news. I am expecting Miss Massy to tea, she does not get strong, she sends her love. All who knew David are rejoicing to know he is alive. The suspense has been great to one, but today I am feeling bright and fairly well. My veg are doing well in the garden. Now I hope you all are still enjoying yourselves.

I will send all the news of David as soon as I get them.

Kiss the dear children for Grannie, give my fond love to Jean, hoping John and Yourself are well.

With much love from your loving Mamma

F Taylor
Prisoner of War
2/Lt D H Taylor
2nd Kings Royal Rifle Corps Officer
Krilgsgefangenenlager
Karlsruhe
Germany

David to May   Absendung [= Post]   July 14 1917

I hope I was not reported as "missing" as I know you would worry as to what had happened to me and by now Mum should have received my card and should know that I am a prisoner. I was taken on the 10 July. We were sent into an impossible position with a river behind us crossed by 3 small bridges which of course were very soon smashed cutting us off completely. The whole of the battalion were lost, either killed or taken prisoners.

On the morning of the 10th they woke me up (I had had 3 or 4 hours sleep having been at work the day and night before) as it was my turn for duty. I had not time for anything to eat but went straight up to the front line. We were being shelled heavily by then. I could not find Heberden the man I wanted to relieve, but was told he was some distance up the trench. I went along to him and then found that a shell had burst and had blown in the trench, burying 4 or 5 men. Heberden had apparently been trying to dig them out, when another shell had blown his leg off. I crawled up to him having to cross another man who was stripped naked, with a hole in his chest and of course dead. Heberden had all his wits about him and indeed had got his own field bandage out and was trying to unfasten it. It was hopeless for me to try to do anything for him as not only was his leg off but he was hit in the chest as well. I told him I had better not touch him but get the doctor as soon as I could and he agreed that that would be best. So rushed back to headquarters and telephoned for the doctor. They got him into a dugout but although the doctor operated on him he died soon after.

After this I got the men who were left into two dugouts, one in the front line and one just behind. I stayed up in the front line with 5 of the men in a small dugout; as by keeping just outside the entrance I could see the German line and thought I might be able to see if they were attacking but after a time the shelling became so heavy that I had to give it up. This dugout was very little protection really and after a little while the men asked if they could chance getting further back. As it meant practically certain death to remain there I agreed and we went a little way back to the dugout where Heberden was. By this time he was dead, and another man wounded there. He had been dressed by the doctor. We stayed there for some time the shelling by this time being terrific and really we were awfully lucky not to had had the dugout hit and have all been sent up together. After a time two sergeants and myself went out to try and do something to the trench to help matters. We couldn't do a great deal and had to go back.

I was just getting into the dugout when a shell burst behind me and forceably assisted in. I landed in a heap and after I had collected myself I found that I had been hit with some fragments round the left ear and the back of the head. It was nothing very much and I soon got one of the other men to bind me up. There were about 10 of us there and I could see very little hope for us so I decided to go back to see if I could get some further men sent up. The trench going back in was in an awful state having been blown in all over the place so that I had to get out and climb over the top every few yards or so. When I got to the headquarter dugout it had been blown to pieces and those in it evidently went with it. I then went on to the battalion headquarters, this part of the journey being no better than the first half and I got knocked down one and shaken up pretty much, although I was not otherwise touched. Finally I got there and found the colonel and asked if he could get anybody up to the men I had left. I told him all I knew and answered his questions but it was rather difficult as by this time I was in a pretty bad state and had been deafened by the explosion so that I couldn't hear very well. I told them various things and lay there a little while and then I suppose I went to sleep or fainted or something as I don't remember anything for a while, and then woke up to find a number of men standing about but none of the officers, and very soon after the place was surrounded by the Germans and we had to march out and give ourselves up. We were sent to the rear immediately. Having gone some distance I was separated from the rest as I was an officer and sent to another group where I found several more of our officers who had been captured. I think it must have been a German naval mess as there were a number of naval officers standing about. They treated us very decently, offered us mineral waters, and several who could speak English talked to us. We stayed here a little while and were then taken further back, finally being taken into the cellar of a large hotel, I think, in the middle of a town some distance behind the line. Here we had to give up all our papers but were told we should get them back again. We stayed the night here and early next morning were marched to another town where we stopped for several hours and had our first meal, bread and coffee, after which we went on further and finally were taken to a large barracks outside another town.

We had another meal and then a most glorious bath and it was whilst having this bath that I discovered that several other small splinters had been driven into me by the shell. There were 3 or 4 in my back, one or two in my left arm and one just at the back of my knee, but as I hadn't felt them before you can guess that they were practically only scratches. I seem to have been filled up with splinters something like a rabbit is when it is hit with a shot gun. We stopped here the night being made fairly comfortable and next morning were marched into the town, taken to the Town Hall and kept there for some time. After this we were taken by train to another town where we are at present. I cannot give you any address yet as we have not yet reached our final destination.

I am allowed to send one letter of 6 pages a fortnight and one post card a week, so I shall write to you and Mum in the one letter and you must read Mum's portion and then read out your portion to her or such of it as you think fit, but I wouldn't give her all the 'orrible details I have told you as she would only worry probably. By the way will you write to Read & Brigstock telling them I will settle their account of £20 as soon as I can but they have taken my cheque book so that I cannot send it at present. Heberden's people would probably like to know what became of him. They live at Cheltenham but I don't know the address but if you wrote to there it would find them, I think.

We are all a pretty looking lot at present as of course none of us have anything except just what we stand up in and added to this most of us are pretty ragged, myself especially so, as I got my clothes pretty much torn by the barbed wire in getting back from the front line and then add to this that I have yards and yards of bandage wound around my head and neck, no collar, or tie and about 5 days growth on my chin (or had until this morning) and there you have my portrait at present.

I forgot to say that I was taken to a hospital yesterday and had my head dressed and the doctor there also took a piece of wood out of my ear and then as I told him I was a bit deaf he poured some stuff into my ear with the idea of cleaning it I suppose. Anyway it all feels very much better now. He also patched up the small places in my back.

At the place where we had the bath they took our clothes and put them into a steam fumigator. This seems to have given the clothes a dirty appearance as the dirt seems to have gone right into them although of course the idea was alright as I expect it really cleaned them in other ways. So far as I can gather a number of my own men are prisoners but the dugout where they were was blown in burying several of them although several managed to get out and several more were hit on the previous days.

I left your photo in my valise in case anything happened, so when this arrives home will you ask Mum for them and keep them for me please. Now don't worry — I am quite alright and only longing for you. When I do come home we shall have to make up for all this lost time. Goodbye.

July 14th 1.

I hope ....ed at "missing" as I kn..
you would worry as to ...... had happened to me &
now Mum ...... have received my card & you should ..
that I am ...... prisoner. I was taken on the 10th. We ..
sent into an impossible position with a river behind ..
crossed by 3 small bridges which of course were ..
soon smashed, cutting us off completely. The whole of ..
battalion were lost, either killed or taken prisone..
On the morning of the 10th they woke me up (I had had ..
hours sleep having been at work the day & night before).
was my turn for duty. I had no time for anything to ..
but went straight up to the front line. We were bei..
shelled heavily then. I could not find Heberden the man I wan..
to relieve but was told he was some distance further ..
the trench. I went along to him & then found that a she..
had burst & had blown in the trench, burying 4 or ..
men. Heberden had apparently been trying to dig them out..
another shell had blown his leg off. I crawled ..
to him having to cross another man who was stripped
naked with a hole in his chest & of course dea..
Heberden had all his wits about him & indeed had g..
his own field bandage out & was trying to unfast..
it. It was hopeless for me to try to do anything for ..
as not only was his leg off but he was hit in t..
chest as well. I told him I had better not touch..
but get the doctor as soon as I could & he a..
that that would be best. So I rushed back to hea..
& telephoned for the doctor. They got him into a dug..
but although the doctor operated on him there he di..
soon after. After this I got the men who were le..
into two dugouts, one in the front line & one just be..
I stayed up in the front line with 5 of the men in ..
small dugout as by keeping just outside the entrance ..
could see the German line & thought I might ..
able to see if they were attacking but after a ..
the shelling became so heavy that I had to ..
it up. This dugout was very little protection really t..
a little while the men asked if they could chan..
getting further back. As it meant practically certain ..
to remain there I agreed & we went a little way ..
to the dugout where Heberden was. By this time he ..
dead, & another man wounded there. He had bee..

my dearest 169

David to May   Karlsruhe   July 19th 1917

2/ Lieut D.H. Taylor
2nd Kings Royal Rifle Corps
Offiziergefangenenlager
Karlsruhe i. B.

The above is my address. I don't think there are any restrictions against my receiving letters, but I shall not be able to write as I did before. The days went awfully slowly at the place I wrote from before, one day being practically like another. Of course we were not allowed out and were allowed to take exercise in a yard. The fellows used to walk round and round, but I couldn't even do this as I had a blistered heel which I had got from marching. They had a number of English novels there and lent these to us and indeed they all treated us quite well. We were able to send out for a few things and luckily I had about 30 francs with me and so was able to buy a few absolutely necessary things like a tooth brush, razor, soap etc. but everything was pretty dear, so that 30 francs didn't go far especially as we only got about 1/5th value for them in German money. Most of us used to spend the greater part of the day reading or asleep and watching the time for the next meal.

I went again to the hospital and this time saw another doctor who shaved some of my hair off and dressed my head and ear again. He was much more gentle with me than the first man and took a good deal of trouble. My head and ear seem to be going on quite well and give me no trouble except that there is a small discharge from my ear which makes me somewhat deaf still (and I think my clothes must have rubbed one or two of the small places on my back as they are somewhat inflamed). However it is nothing very much.

The others went to some swimming baths twice, but again I could not go on account of my blessed bandages. Seeing that we had nothing to do and all day to do it of course we didn't trouble to get up especially early so that on Monday morning we were still in bed (there were three of us in one room) when they came in and told us that we were to start for Germany in a quarter of an hour.

We scrambled into our things and were taken to the station. We had, by the way, been separated from the men before going to this last place and they were evidently taken elsewhere. At each of these towns that we came through we seemed to cause a little excitement, the people rushing down to look at us as we passed. At one or two places we seem to have been expected, for it seemed as though half the town turned out to look at us. One of the last things I ever expected to do was to take part in a procession, a sort of Lord Mayor's Show without the gilding, but still you never can tell. But I am getting off the track. We got into a train 2nd class and travelled for about an hour when we were all told to get out again, this at another fairly large town. We were all taken down below the station here and locked in a sort of cellar for a time and then afterwards were taken to some barracks a short distance away. We were kept here the remainder of the day. It looked as though we were going to get nothing to eat this day but we asked for something and after a while we got some soup. I had got hold of a book from one of the others and read most of the time and a few of the others played cards.

About 10 o'clock that night we were again taken to the station and put into 3rd class carriages. These carriages were about the same as the Walthamstow Line at home and as the compartment was full it was none too comfy. We travelled all night this way until about 10 o'clock next day going right up through Belgium and finally stopping at Cologne in Germany. After it got light I was naturally curious to see what the country looked like but the whole of Belgium or at all events that part that we went through is very flat and uninteresting and I don't think we will go there later on. When we got near the frontier and were going through the Ardennes the scenery was quite different and this part isn't at all bad, but unfortunately I couldn't see a great deal from the train. At Coln we were again taken into a sort of store room below the station and had to wait there several hours until about 3 o'clock. We were all pretty hungry again and were allowed to have lunch sent down from a restaurant, consisting of soup and some fish for which we each paid 3- marks.

About 3 o'clock we got into another train, this time 2nd class which was quite comfortable and then began a really fine train journey. You remember some years ago Ethel had a holiday in Germany and went up the Rhine, well I think I must have gone over a good deal of the same ground only I believe she did some part of it by boat and of course we went by train. Anyway we went all along the Rhine (the railway practically follows the river for the greater part of the way) past Assmanhausen (where I think Ethel stopped) through Coblence and finally stopped at a little place about 20 miles, I should think, before getting to Mainz.

We got there about 8 o'clock and really it was fine. Nearly all the way the river runs between a chain of fairly high hills which go up steeply from the waters edge except here and there where there is a small break.

Every few miles there is a small village dumped down where there happens to be a flat piece between the river and the hillside. Each of these villages is similar to the last, with a church in the centre with a square steeple and the rest consisting of a small cluster of hotels (I should think) for these villages I imagine are used as summer resorts. Then again every mile or so on the top of the hills (or every few hundred yards in places) there would be the ruins of an old castle. The railway itself is in a great many places cut out of the side of the hills and they go up practically straight. In lots of places the hills are cut down in terraces and cultivated somewhat like they did in Norway only of course you could scarcely compare it with Norway. We had a meal at this stop about the best we had had so far with some coffee. I have by the way become practically a vegetarian. About 10 o'clock our carriage was put on to a goods train and we again travelled all night getting here about 10 o'clock next morning.

I am enclosing a letter to Mum and wish you would read parts of this to her. I am longing for a letter from you but expect it will be about 3 weeks before I get one. Goodbye.

David

David to Mum   Karlsruhe   Aug 1st 1917

Dear Mum,

I hope everything is alright at home but of course it will be 7 or 8 weeks at least before I can hear from you. I am quite comfortable and my head and neck are getting along very well, although my ear is still somewhat troublesome.

I have been in the camp nearly a fortnight now and was here, and was sent here rather earlier than some of the others, as I had to see the Doctor here. If you haven't sent an overcoat, I should like my British warm overcoat, the one I sent home you remember, but of course I shall not need two. Although I expect I shall want pretty warm clothing later on beside things to eat, some soap and Vaseline, tin meats, fish, biscuits and such like. I have asked for these things before. Please send me some gloves. Will you please by the Weekly Times each week for me and keep at home so that I shall know of what is going on. Will you also get the Telegraph of July 5 to 12 inclusive and also the paper in which my name appeared with casualty list, as I shall possibly need all these when I return. My letter to you seems to be begging letter entirely, but at present I can't help myself. You might give my address to Ethel as I cannot write to her.

Dave

May to David   Beckenham   9. 8. 17.

My dear David.,

Mrs Taylor and Miss Massey called at the Office this morning, the former looking very bright and pretty, and she gave me your address saying that I was only to write about domestic affairs. She added that you would only be allowed to send four post cards a month, so that I shall not expect any from you. I go to Balham each week and can see what you write there, as no doubt you will write them all to your mother. How often can I write to you, and would you like me to send you a German Dictionary?

You can imagine how pleased I am to be able to write again.
I felt very miserable for a day or two when your letters ceased, but one night I distinctly felt your cheek against mine, so of course took heart, and knew everything would come right in the end. I still enjoy the same train journeys up in the morning, and have the same evenings. Last Saturday I went to Balham and stayed there till Tuesday morning. Miss Massey was there too, and we all three enjoyed ourselves. On Monday (August Bank Holiday) we went to Richmond; started about midday and went by bus. It was a glorious day and everywhere was packed. We spent most of the time in the Terrace Gardens. It was a job to get a seat. I took knitting with me, but used my tongue more than my fingers, of course talking about the times we have had on the river. The sun made the River look most enticing. You remember that meadow we walked through near the river edge. It was partly under water. The recent rains have made the Thames rise over 6 feet. We thought we would have tea in the Park, but the place was so packed that we came back to the Terrace. As it was impossible to get into a bus we returned by train, getting home soon after 8. 0. Miss Massey has had one week's holiday and is going away again soon. She seems jolly but is not very strong yet. Mrs. Taylor is a marvel and surprises everyone by her excellent spirits. I think I am going away with her in Sept. for a fortnight most likely to Worthing; everywhere is so packed just now.
Maud is in Watchet in Somerset, a quaint old-fashioned seaside place, close to Minehead. She has gone with an old school-girl who apparently somewhat annoys Maud because shill will go to church everyday for an hour or so for meditation, and Maud does not approve! She would rather they were both out of doors walking. Moreover, the girl is high church, and Maud is not. Maud cannot sleep yet, but otherwise she is getting better. Brother Charlie has gone across. Maud moved into new flat before she went away, in the Abbeville Road.
There is a big Bazaar coming off in the Autumn for 3 days in aid of St. Dunstan's Hostel for Blinded Soldiers and Sailors, and the Northern have been asked to supply a stall. We have been working hard now for the last 2 weeks. Mrs Taylor is also helping and has asked others. I wrote to all the branch offices and have had nice replies. Have already made a pair of reins with 5 bells in front, and am now trying my luck at knitting a white woolly coat for a child of two and a cap to match. Ethel has started an afternoon tea cloth, with plenty of crotchet in it. Have the promise of some articles from the School of Art Needlework. Of course I am plaguing all my friends, Maud included. She wrote back to say she would be very pleased to

make me something, and that she was having her church bazaar in November!

Ethel knocked her arm a little over a week ago and it gave her bursitis, which is housemaid's knee in the elbow. It was very painful for a few days and swollen, and she had her arm in a sling, but it is just about alright now. It stopped her crotchet work for a few days. She stayed at home last week, though the Doctor said she could have gone up, but her chief told her to have the week off. Mama was very pleased, and so was Ethel.

We are very busy at the Office, but not staying late, I had better leave off now as it is nearly 5.0. and I have several more letters to write, so Goodbye, will write next week, and each week until I hear I must not.

May

Sept 8th 1917

18 Manor Road,
Beckenham, Kent.
9. 8. 17.

My dear David,

Mrs. Taylor and Miss Massey called at the Office this morning, the former looking very bright and pretty, and she gave me your address saying that I was only to write about domestic affairs. She added that you would only be allowed to send four post cards a month, so that I shall not expect any from you; I go to Balham each week and can see what you write there, as no doubt you will write them all to your mother. How often can I write to you, and would you like me to send you a German Dictionary?

You can imagine how pleased I am to be able to write again.

I felt very miserable for a day or two when your letters ceased, but one night I distinctly felt your cheek against mine, so of course took heart, and knew everything would come right in the end

I still enjoy the same train journeys up in the morning, and have the same evenings.

Last Saturday I went to Balham and stayed there till Tuesday morning. Miss Massey was there too, and we all three enjoyed ourselves. On Monday (August Bank Holiday) we went to Richmond; started about midday and went by bus. It was a glorious day and everywhere was packed. We spent most of the time in the Terrace Gardens. It was a job to get a seat. I took knitting with me, but used my tongue more than my fingers, of course talking about the times we have had on the River.

May to David   Beckenham   13.8.17

My dear David,

I last wrote to you on the 9th instant. In future I shall be writing each Monday. My last contained an account of the August Bank Holiday weekend which I spent at Balham, and also mentioned the Bazaar we are going to help with.

There is nothing much to relate this week. Ethel's arm is alright again. Mama is as usual – not very bright, but not ill. She still sleeps badly. I have had two letters from Maud asking me to go down to her at Watchet, but I am not going; one letter from Muriel asking if I have news of you; two letters from Esther giving an account of Mary's and Madeleine's adenoids and tonsils being removed. The children were very ill afterwards and in Madeleine's case blood poisoning set in and she was not able to swallow for four days. They thought it was all up with her, but she is recovering. They want me to go to Bognor with them in September, and if David can get off on Saturday or Sunday next he is going down to get rooms. David is still at the Palace, but has been expecting to get drafted off every day for several weeks past. The children are now going out again for their daily walks. Also had a nice though short letter from Campbell. We are still very busy at the office. When not there I am living in the Land of Day Dreams, not my old Dream World, though, but more Dreams of the Future. They are very happy ones. Hope you are feeling as happy as I am. Doubt it, though.

I have caught my early train each evening, and have spent the evenings gardening and knitting. Ethel's cucumber plant is hardly a success. There are eight cucumbers on it, but the biggest one is barely $1\frac{1}{2}$ inches long and has been 3 weeks growing! Something must be wrong with its works. She has now tied the plant up with pale blue tape to encourage it to grow!

Sunday afternoon I went to see Mrs Taylor. She was busy getting a parcel of clothing together and was looking so happy about it. Miss Massey was with her. We all three talked our hardest till 8.0 when I left, the two seeing me into a bus at the Plough. I brought away with me a huge bouquet of white and red phlox, I never saw so much in a garden before, or such huge blooms. It is just a sheet of dazzling white.

I shall type my letters to you as it will be easier for the censors to read, and they must be hard worked.

Looking forward to seeing your writing on a postcard,

Yours as ever,

May

David to May   Karlsruhle   August 19th 1917

My Dearest,

I have been a prisoner now a thousand years and even in that short time the life in France seems to have faded into the dim distant past. Things at home seem to be much nearer and this only makes me long all the more to be with you again and to be doing things. Although I know it will be 6 or 7 weeks before I can hope to hear from you, yet already I look for letters every day. There is a small library in the camp, which of course is a great boon, but of course there are no technical books in it, but I can have books sent to me, provided they do not deal with the war, politics etc. etc., so would you mind getting me a few. I want a book or books on Civil Engineering, dealing more particularly with works in and under water, such as foundations of wharves, docks, bridges, tunnels, sewers, dams and breakwaters, but I want one illustrated and showing works of a fairly small type, as this sort of book has a way of only describing things on the scale of the Panama Canal etc. Also a book on builder's bookkeeping and office routine, (if you can't get a better one Corse & Co., Theobald's Road opposite Bedford Row, W.C. publish one)) the duties of a builder's foreman, and also the duties of a clerk of works. I want to read up things from their point of view. Unfortunately I can't give you the titles or publishers of any of the above, but I expect Batsford & Co. (opposite Holborn Music Hall) can give you what I want. Please get the money from Mum and I will settle with her.

My head and neck etc. have practically healed and the discharge from my ear has eased up somewhat but the doctor after examining it yesterday said it had not improved much otherwise, but still it is bound to be a long business.

My French has been cut off in its youth (at all events for the present), as the Frenchman that I used to converse with has been sent to another camp. I have heard that some of the papers had an account of how we were captured at Nieuport and if you can get hold of it, I wish you would and keep it for me as I should like to see their idea of it. It would be published I imagine about July 12th or 13th. If you happen to see my name in the casualty list, I wish you would keep those papers too, as they will probably be useful to me because of the dates. The other day I suddenly heard somebody playing the Morning Song (we have a piano in camp) and although he played it without a scrap of feeling, it was good to hear music again, other than the usual ragtime and revue jingles, so that I sat down and listened for some tune. Since then however I have discovered a Frenchman who plays awfully well and as he plays pretty frequently I sit and listen while he plays Beethoven, Grieg etc. The other evening there were about 6 of us there and after he had played for some time, he and an Englishman played 2 or 3 duets and then another Frenchman sang several songs - altogether we had a small concert.

There is no regard paid here as to what costume you shall wear, as of course there can't be, for men turn up in all sorts of weird uniforms, having lost part, or all of their own and had it made up with oddments of English, French and German things, so we dress as we please and on hot days some go about in a shirt and a pair of shorts (made out of a towel or something similar) and nobody puts on a collar and tie, which is lucky as I lost mine. I arrived too, minus a cap, but have been given one by a Frenchman, so that now I appear in all the glories of a French Tommy's cap, which to be quite correct, has to be worn over one ear and gives me a decided rakish appearance.

I am enclosing a letter to Mum and I wish you would pass on any news in this to her. Will you ask her to send my address to Ethel. I am also enclosing a letter to my cherub Taylor's Mother, which I wish you would forward. He poor kid, was killed the night before we were taken.

There is no limit to the number of letters I may receive, although I can only write 2 a month and 4 post cards and only 6 sides per letter.

I do hope Mrs Muggridge is quite alright again and that you yourself are having as easy a time as you can. What would I give to have you again? Well, the war will soon end and then – and then----

Goodbye

David

May to David   Beckenham   20.8.17

My dear David,

Now for my third weekly despatch.

Things are going on as usual, business all day, gardening, mending and bazaar work each evening.

Business: We are taking over another company which makes the fifth within the last few years. It has made us very busy but we have not stayed late, which is all we trouble about. On Saturday I heard of a chance of getting Maud in here, so I have written to her making an appointment for 3rd Sept. She is not coming back till 31st August from Watchet. She is much better and thinks she is growing fat again (she had got very thin), so I addressed her as Dear Vanishing Snowflake. I wonder how she will take it! She cannot sleep much yet.

Gardening: Our potatoes are a grand success. Mrs Taylor gave us seed potatoes. As we dig them up we transplant cauliflowers and parsnips.

Bazaar: In my first letter I told you we had been asked to take a stall at the bazaar to be held in the autumn in aid of St Dunstan's Hostel for Blinded Soldiers and Sailors. We are working very hard for it, and one day last week one of our Acquired Companies sent me £2.5/- towards it with an apology for its smallness. As they are working for a similar institute (in Edinburgh) I thought it was very generous of them.

Mending: There is nothing to write about over mending; you groan about it under your breath and murmur dreadful things.

Yesterday afternoon (Sunday) I went to see Mrs Taylor and found her most excited. She had received a postcard from you dated 25th July, the first thing she had had since you have been in Germany. You refer to a letter you had written, so apparently postcards travel quicker than letters. I am glad you sent it to her, and as you are not allowed to write often hope you will send everything to her. She has promised to let me see what you write. I could not sleep last night for feeling pleased. Now I want to know which ear is hurt, how bad it is, also your head, how you are otherwise, and if you are at all deaf. Don't forget to say which side is hurt. Mrs Taylor cannot think of holidays now; she is so full of sending parcels. Already she has despatched two, one food and one clothing. She would not let me take your postcard away with me so I learnt it by heart.

Would you like me to send a German dictionary?

I expect the censors think this letter is long enough, so goodbye till next week.

May

P.S. Since writing above I have received a letter from Campbell, short, saying he has just heard you are alive and can prove it if we have not heard from you. Also he is fearfully busy. That man is a brick.

Red Cross to David   Geneva   Aug 20th 1917

D.H. Taylor
Kings Royal Rifles

Dear Sir,
We shall be glad if you can give some news of yourself, as to your health, etc. If wounded, how are you progressing. If you are not well enough to write yourself, perhaps a fellow prisoner would do so for you.

We are, Sir,
Yours faithfully
Comite International de la Croix- Rouge
Geneve
Agence Internationale des Prisonniers de Guerre
British Section

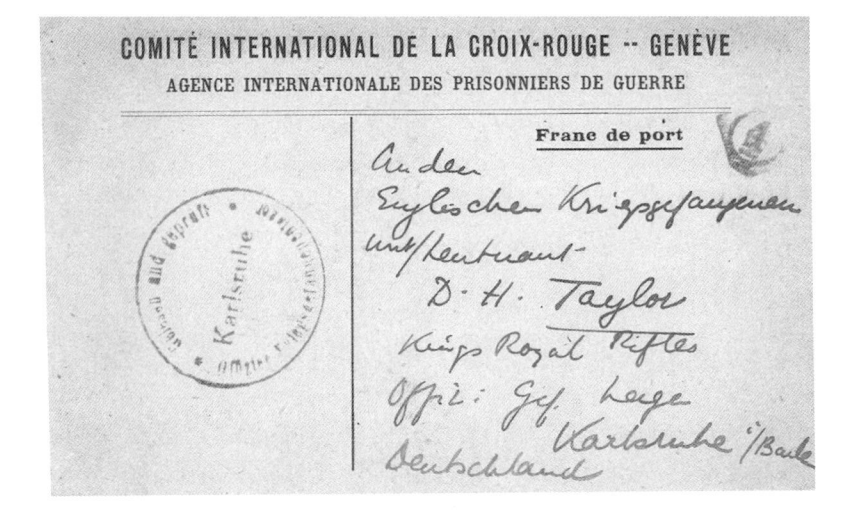

Fanny to Ethel   Balham   Aug 27 1917

My darling Ethel,

I am pleased to enclose you more good news.

I have sent two parcels of food through the American Express Agents through Holland so he will have got one by now and another shortly. And I sent at once some underclothes and socks etc. And I am sending a parcel through the Prisoner of War Committee weekly, and I can send two. Now I do truly hope you are quite well and rested. I was pleased to know Nanna was back.

I have just received David's things from the front, every thing alright. Now dearie we will hope all will be well with him, and that we have him home once again. I loss no time in sending to him a week before I had his card, and before they could tell me at the War Office where he was. Now try and be happy again. I am feeling the reaction this last two or three days. They are all rejoicing at GlenRoy, and all keeping about the same. I shall try and have a few days away from home, now I know what to do.

Miss Massey sends her love. Polly came over to see Nelly just for the week and they are well. We are having stormy weather. My veg garden is doing well, only it makes me very tired and Peter helps sometimes.

Kiss the dear children for Grannie and love to Jean, hoping she has had a good time, and fond love to you both.

From your loving Mamma

F Taylor

May to David   Beckenham   27.8.17

My dear David,

This is my fourth weekly letter. Hope you do not mind their being typed, but this way it is easier for the censors to read. Maud has written you a letter and postcard but both have been returned. Her writing is not too plain. My letters have not contained much news, only account of my weekly visit to Balham, how busy we are at office, the work we are doing for the bazaar to be held in aid of blinded soldiers and sailors (Northern have been asked to supply a stall, and the girls agreed), and the post I have received each week. I usually get 2 letters a week from Maud at Watchet. Her last letter sounded positively frivolous – for Maud – so evidently she is much better. She returns next Friday, and has an interview with Lutt next Monday with a view to taking a temporary post there. Since you have been in Germany I have had 2 nice though short letters from Campbell which I am saving for you. To-night I expect to finish the little white woolly coat I am making for bazaar. It is looking dainty. I wonder what you would say if you saw it! I like to surmise as I work. Have already made some reins with gorgeous bells on them. We are taking over another Company, the fifth within the last few years. It has made us busy, but we are not working late, which I am afraid is all we trouble about. Esther has had her two eldest children bad, tonsils and adenoids removed, blood poisoning following in Madeleine's case. They are well again, but Esther is trying to take them to the seaside. So far every place she has written to is full up, and she has asked me to try my luck. She wants me to go with her. Unless I can persuade Mrs Taylor to spend a fortnight with me I think I will go. By the bye, I have already had about 4 weeks' holiday, but expect I deserve another two. Guess I would enjoy a romp with the kiddies. Can you imagine me building sand castles? Esther wants to commence holidays on 8th Sept, and so do I.

On Saturday morning your letter of 19th July reached me. O, the joy we all felt! You had evidently written before, but that letter has not come yet. The one I got gave me a grand account of your journey through Belgium and Germany. It certainly does sound pretty along the Rhine and well worth a visit. No, we will not go to Belgium; I do not like flat scenery. Miss Bradford tried hard to persuade me to go up the Rhine in a steamer. She likes it. She cannot speak German, but said the purser knew English, and helper to make her holiday most enjoyable. She stayed at one of those villages, and the boat picked her up on its return journey. I believe they are cargo boats that carry a few passengers. The trip was not at all expensive.

I could not go to Balham on Saturday as Ethel did not get home till evening, but went yesterday. More excitement in which Miss Massey joined! (She has been a brick, and went with Mrs Taylor each time she went to the War Office, Red Cross Office and other places). We each had a glass of wine before we came away, and drank to your health. Mrs Taylor saw me to the tram, and then I took Underground to Elephant & Castle where I joined the main line. The buses are so full now. Mrs Taylor had got your clothes back, and we both looked at them – I should say gazed and gazed at them. Have you got your woolly waistcoat with you? Shall I make you another? Would you like me to send you some books or anything else? A German dictionary for instance?

You do not say which ear is bad, and I do want to know. What is wrong with your back? I did not read that part out to Mrs Taylor as you did not mention it in your postcard to her of 25th July which by the way arrived a week sooner than your letter of 19th July.

Mrs Taylor is still as bright and cheerful as ever. She is a marvel to everyone.

I have just finished reading Lord Lytton's "Strange Story" which I enjoyed. Shall I send it on to you? It is Mrs Taylor's book. Perhaps you have read it. It is deliciously spooky, and proves that mind and soul are two distinct things.

I had better not write any more now. Will write again next Monday.

Goodbye. Best wishes from everyone, including

May

P.S. I have taken to dreaming about you, quite nice dreams.

Campbell to David   BEF Field Post Office   1.9.17

Dear Taylor,

I am so very glad to hear you are o.k. though badly wounded. What an awful time you must have had, but its an ill wind etc! I have had a most awfully nice letter from your Mother, which I shall always keep. Also have had two letters, to which I replied, from Miss Muggridge. I am so glad you are o.k. You know I suppose that Smith Butler and Gracie got away. Poor old Heb was killed. Can you tell me anything of Jumbo Munro? Shaw is safe, but we heard that the Batt. is in very good condition. B Company dug out was blown in. However if Shaw is safe there is no reason why Jumbo should not be safe. Jarman and Plum are very well. Cub has gone to the T.M.'s. I have left the Company temporarily as a G [?] to the Bgde – I think it is the best thing to do as my health would not hold out the winter and I don't suppose there would be much work to do. The weather has been vile but is improving slightly now.

I have had a very nice 10 days leave since I last saw you so I am as pleased as punch! Goodbye and best of luck

Yours ever

E Campbell

David to May   Karlsruhe   Sept 1st 1917

My Dearest,

We have been tremendously busy. We have designed a house for ourselves, written the specification, built it. We have started a business, carried out innumerable large and varied contracts, turned the thing into a company, started a profit sharing scheme for the employees, with a sort of pension fund, etc etc, combined several allied businesses and are now negotiating for several more. All castles in the air – and now I had better start the letter.

Of course I have had no word from you yet and shall not for 3 or 4 weeks yet, but still I am hoping. There is no limit to the number or length of letters we may receive, so please write often and please send a photo of yourself. I left mine in my valise in order not to lose it and I do want another.

Two days ago I had a post card from the Red Cross at Geneva enquiring after my health, so presume you have put an enquiry through them. My ear seems much about the same. The doctor said a few days ago, that as the discharge had continued so long, there was a possibility of the hole in the drum remaining open instead of healing, so now you know what to expect. When you ask some question like "Will you have some more tea", I shall put my hand to my ear, with my head on one side and reply "Eh? What? Oh yes we'll do up the river shall we?" But still it isn't quite as bad that, as since then, he has examined it and said it was a little better and of course I have the other ear, which is in splendid working order.

Yesterday a parcel came for me from Rotterdam, with nothing to say who sent it. There was butter, jam, coffee, cocoa, bacon and 12 eggs, so I immediately dashed off to the canteen and bought a saucepan and frying pan. Behold me cooking! I rise up early in the morning, as the French exercise says, light the fire, (the fire consists of a few pieces of charcoal in a tinned pineapple tin, with some holes in it) fry the bacon, upset the whole lot, burn my fingers, gather up the pieces and finally fry two of the eggs. Still eggs and bacon and coffee and bread and butter and jam for breakfast are worth it. I shall do it again, even down to burning my fingers. Could you send me a book or books on Civil Engineering. I want one showing work in and under water such as foundations of buildings, docks, bridges, dams, breakwaters etc. I would like one illustrated and showing fairly small works. Also a book on builder's bookkeeping and office routine (if you can't get a better one Corse & Co. Theobolds Road opposite Bedford Row sell one), one on the duties of a builder's foreman, and one on the duties of a clerk of works. I can't give you any particulars of any of them, but Batsford & Co. (opposite Holborn Music Hall) will give you what I want. Please get the money from Mum.

I have got another Frenchman to "converse" with, so now I walk about each day waggling my head and waving my arms about like a semaphore at a naval review. It takes the place of physical jerks, thus killing two birds with one stone.

I believe there was an account of how we were captured at Nienport in the Daily Mail or one of the papers and I should like you to keep it for me if you can get hold of it. It was published I imagine about July 12th and 13th and will you please keep those papers in which my name appeared in the casualty list if you happen to see it. They may be useful.

I am enclosing a letter to Mum. Will you read what little news is in it and then pass it on and you might tell her the news in this.

Your socks are splendid. Of course I only have the one pair with me, but I must have worn them for 3 months and they have only just got a hole in them and that I have darned so that they are still quite alright.

Yesterday we had another concert. One man sang rather well and at the end there was a sketch, which was absolute fooling, but still rather funny and the fellows acted spendidly.

I hope Mrs Muggridge is quite well again. I hope too, that you yourself have had a holiday and thoroughly enjoyed it. I am longing to hear how everything is with you. Write as often as you can.

At present I can only dream dreams. (I expect you are doing the same). How I could whisper them to you.

Goodbye

David

May to David   Beckenham   3. 9. 17.

My dear David,

This is my fifth weekly letter, and this time I really have got some news to tell you.

Nothing happened during the week; life flowed on as usual - business all day, bazaar work and mending each evening. Maud returned from Watchet Friday evening, so on Saturday afternoon I called on her, saw her flat which isn't at all bad, and then took her off to Ramsden Road to tea. Maud looks, splendid and says she hasn't felt so well for years. A coastguard used to take her out rowing each morning and evening, and Mrs Taylor and I teased her about it. We had a very lively few hours at Balham, and then I went home laden with flowers as usual. Mrs Taylor's garden is packed with things. She has done very well this year. It was very showery the whole of last week, but it hasn't spoilt her flowers at all, and she has a good many roses still.

Sunday (yesterday) was a glorious day, and so is to-day. Helen and the two children came. Billy was two a few days ago. He is a monster for his age, but too lazy to talk. This rather worried his mother. However, now he is two he has commenced to talk. He only says three words, but says them persistently and with a broad Irish accent, though he has been in England 6 months now. The three words he says, though Helen does not know where he heard them, are "Damn and begorra", and when his mother says "That is silly talk; daddy does not say that", he simply says "Damndamndamndamn". Isn't it awful? We had a very lively day. During the morning we were playing ball, while in the afternoon I was kept hard at work by Georgie making paper boats. He had a big basin of water on the lawn, his sleeves rolled up and a towel in front of him. I am afraid the boats went to the bottom quicker than I could replace them, as the little imp would fill them with stones.

This morning Maud came to the Northern at 10. 30. to have an interview with Lutt. She was feeling very nervous, so I took her down myself, and told him she was a friend of mine, and then left them together. She return a few minutes later to say she quite enjoyed the interview, that she was engaged as a temporary clerk, to commence next Monday and that he, at the close of the interview, had shaken hands with her and said "Goodbye". She is struck with him. He certainly can make himself nice when he likes. Most folks can.

One more item of news. On Saturday Esther wrote me that she and the kiddies are off to Littlehampton on the 9th for 4 weeks. They tried to get in at Bognor and Worthing, but both places are full up. David would be going for the first week with them, and would I go for the 2nd and 3rd. I asked Mrs. Taylor about it, as I wanted to go with her, but she said she did not want to go away now she knows you are alright, but would rather send you parcels, so I have written to Esther to say I would go and have a romp with them for the 2 weeks. I am in hopes of being able to persuade your mother to come down too, if only for a week. I believe she is going to Watford soon for a few days as she hears your favourite Aunt Anne is not very well. Our rush is over at last; in fact some of the girls have been doing bazaar work in the next room quite unknown to me (?). The coat is finished. It looks lovely and just fits Helen's baby. I told her I should want 15/- for it. She did not offer to buy it, but said it was worth more. Shall be finishing the cap to-night, and then I am going to make another vest as before.

We did not hear from you last Saturday, but I hope a post card will come through saying you are getting on alright. We talk about you every day, and think about you continuously.

Goodbye, for the present,

May.

P.S. I forgot to mention before that we managed to send our old office cleaner away to Brighton for a week. She bought me a poem on a card, which had a little piece of ribbon to hang it up by. I asked her to write her name on the back, and she wrote "From a grateful Heart to dear Miss Muggridge who has been a dear Friend to one who is friendless. My God reward her and watch over her and all those who are dear to her is the sincere wish of Mary Matthews."

I did think it was good of the poor old soul. Her gratitude, and sincerity puts a good many educated folks to shame.

May to David   Beckenham   5. 9. 17.

My dear David,

Just a line to say that yesterday morning I received an envelope from you containing your pay book, a letter addressed to Cox's and one addressed to "Dear Mum". I took them over to Balham and Mrs Taylor asked me to read her letter to her. From that it appears you wrote to me also, but the letter evidently has been dropped out. At any rate, I know you are getting on alright, are comfortable, and that your wounds are progressing. You mentioned your neck for the first time. What is wrong with it, and I don't know yet which side of your head is damaged. Is your back alright, and what was wrong with it?

I stayed the night with Mrs Taylor, and had a very enjoyable evening, finishing two pairs of socks which Mrs Taylor says I can have for the bazaar. We have arranged to go to-morrow morning to Cox's bank together. By the bye yesterday's letter was dated 1st Aug. and is the second we have received. The first one you wrote has not yet turned up.

You are having lots of parcels sent you by your mother which you ought to be receiving by now.

I hear only educational books can be sent you. Would you like any on building? or anything else?

Goodbye for the present,

May

May to David   Letter No. 7.   Beckenham   10. 9. 17.

My dear David,

Last Thursday Mrs Taylor called for me at the office at 11. 0. and we both went out and enjoyed ourselves. We called at the American Express Co, Carey St., Cox's, Prisoners of War Committee, and also had dinner out, all of which we enjoyed. Cox's are going to write you direct. Your pay goes on the same, but they will keep your book, we had dinner at a place close by where you once took me to tea on a Sunday. It was full of officers and their girls, the band was playing merrily, and we had a very good feed. I did not get back till 3.0. On Friday Maud called to see Mama, and we had a lively couple of hours, Maud making Mama laugh very much at her terror of going to business. On Saturday Ethel went to Florrie Bullocks and came back laden with garden produce, while I stayed at home, re-trimmed a hat, did up front garden, darned stockings (in more ways than one) and started making a child's vest for the bazaar. I have not finished the other I was making yet, but that can wait. On Sunday I went to Balham, armed with two letters which came that morning, one from you dated 19th Aug. giving a graphic account of the dress as found in the camp which we enjoyed immensely. I would like to see you look rakish. Can't possibly imagine it. Fancy having a piano! I am glad. This afternoon I am going after the books. Shall feel quite learned in getting such technical works. Shall have to go to a publisher that has a permit for sending to Germany. I don't know now which side of your head is bad, and it is tantalizing. I believe you are keeping me in ignorance purposely to tease me.

(G.M. just sent for me. Gave me a basket of large pears! Had to hold on to table leg for support, while his typist murmured "Why! the man's actually getting human! ") Mama is getting much brighter when we are about, but still indulges in tears when alone. That was a nice letter you wrote to the cherub's mother. I also added one saying you had written home mentioning her son, telling how he had helped with the range unasked. Hope you don't mind, but I thought it might please her.

The other letter in yesterday's post was from Esther at Littlehampton. She went down sooner than she was going as the kiddies didn't seem well, and then couldn't get in anywhere and missed the last train back. Eventually she found one small bedroom far away. The rooms she has booked for this and the next 3 weeks are dirty and the house smelly. She says she can't stay there. Don't know what is going to happen. David was to have gone down yesterday. I got her nice rooms at Worthing, £3. 15/- inclusive, but a friend of David's recommended much cheaper ones at Littlehampton, terms not inclusive, and this is the result. I am not going to a dirty place, and if they can't get something better Mrs Taylor has again promised to go away with me, then we shall most likely visit Hastings. First she was coming with me, then when she heard from you she said she would rather stay at home and send you parcels. I don't know what we shall do finally. All go to a nice place, I hope.

I understand I can only write two pages, so shall have to write more frequently. Maud turned up at business this morning.

Goodbye

May

May to David   Beckenham   11. 9. 17

My dear David,
Just a short letter to tell you I have sent some books off this morning to you:-
The Builders Foreman (-/6)
Clerk of the Works (2/6) by G. Metson.
River & Canal Engineering (6/6) by Bellasis.

I took over half an hour chasing these at Batsfords who have a permit for sending them, and promised to despatch them at once. The man seemed to understand building books, but knew very little about engineering works. We looked through piles, but they are mostly about 30/- per volume, and I did not know whether you wanted to pay as much just now. I can't find any engineering bock there giving wharves, docks, bridges, tunnels, sewers, dams &

breakwaters all in one book; they seem mostly in separate volumes. When you get these books will you write and let me know the next subject you would like, and the price you will go to.

Last night the following letter came from David Smith:-

21 York Rd. Littlehampton.
Dear Mabel,
Don't address any letters here as Esther & I have found a better place to stay, on the sea front in such a charming portion of the town. I came down to-day and found them all in trouble; the rooms are filthy. We go to the new apartments Wed. night. I return to London Thursday night. Esther will expect you on Saturday. The address is Mrs Street 17, South Terrace, Littlehampton.
Love from
Esther

I have been looking up trains and expect to go by the 1. 50. pm from London Bridge, due Littlehampton at 3. 42.

Just as I started this letter Maud came in (at 11. 0). She is radiantly happy. Heavens, she is funny! I went with her as far as Blackfriars yesterday, and it was a job to keep from laughing. She is a Tom Pinch with a vengeance. She works for a man named Bishop. He is alright; I haven't had a quarrel with him yet. Maud seems to think he is perfection, and was worried all the way home because she had not said Goodnight to him. She wanted to, but didn't know whether she ought, and now she wishes she had. She was highly amused this morning. Two of the supers on the ground floor where she works have taken her under their wing. Both these girls are well under 5.0. high, and one is as fat as butter. They said when Maud heard any of the supers talking about "Mummy" they meant Miss Muggridge and that she was a [deleted: perfect dear]. Maud thinks she kept a straight face. She won't hear that from the men. By the bye, my girls nicknamed me "Mum" years ago. Is it a coincidence, or do I look so old and motherly? Guess it is the latter. I made one of the men apologise this morning. He actually said one of my girls ought to have finished her work 1/2 hour before she had. He did not mean me to know it, but a new boy told me, so ---------

Must get on with my work now. 0, Ethel took Maud out to lunch yesterday at a restaurant run by a girl who was housekeeper at the Enterprise. It is remarkably cheap and yet good.

Goodbye.

May.

Miss Muggridge. LONDON, Sept 11th 1917

BOUGHT OF B. T. BATSFORD, LTD
BOOKSELLERS AND PUBLISHERS.
94, HIGH HOLBORN, W.C.1.

ARCHITECTURE
DECORATION
FINE ARTS
ENGINEERING
APPLIED SCIENCE

LIBRARIES OF
ARCHITECTURAL
ENGINEERING
AND
SCIENTIFIC
BOOKS PURCHASED.

CHEQUES SHOULD BE CROSSED LONDON AND COUNTY AND WESTMINSTER BANK LTD;
AND MADE PAYABLE TO B.T. BATSFORD, LIMITED.
NO REMITTANCE UNDER 5/- ACKNOWLEDGED UNLESS ACCOMPANIED BY STAMP.

1	Nelson: Clerk of the Works	2 6
1	Bellasis: River & Canal Engineering	8 6
1	Builders Foreman	6
		11 6

Received Sept. 11th. 1917.
for B. T. Batsford.

May to David   Beckenham   12. 9. 17.

My dear David,

I did not intend to write you to-day but I must tell you this. One of the earliest temporary girls here I got through the Enterprise Club and she has turned out trumps. After a few months she was put on to work the "Accident" Dept. men never thought could be done by a woman, and strange to say she has beaten record over it. Yesterday the G.M. sent for me, made various inquiries about the girls, and finally said he did not think I should get my transferred girls back again as they found the girls could do certain work "alright", and that after the war I should have to have a larger department - instead of 18, about 30, but that they would all have to be under me, whether working in my room or not. He finished by saying he would bring us up some more pears!

I walked as far as Queen St. yesterday with Maud. She is so excited, and told me she was getting on splendidly, as yesterday afternoon she was allowed to sit up by the side of Bishop and call back some work with him, instead of addressing envelopes and putting rubber stamps on papers. Although she said all along she was not going to let anyone know she knew me yet she told Bishop she was at school with me, and that she had lost her mother. He told her she was capable of doing higher work, and he told me this morning he thought Maud was going to be a great asset. Maud almost worships him. He is rather tall, well covered, sleek black hair that waves at the ends, the length of which would give the military Authorities half a dozen blue-canary-fits straight off, and he has a curate-ish appearance with colourless moist face, but he is really alright and quite a decent sort.

I brought up the little coat and cap this morning to show the girls. They think it ought to sell for £1.1.0 and declare they are in love with it. It cost me 8/- to make.

Shall be busy for the rest of this week as I am going away Saturday, so expect the next time I write will be from Littlehampton.

Maud has made you such a nice pair of socks, but Mrs Taylor is not going to send them yet, as you have got to finish off your old ones first.

Goodbye, and hope you are getting on alright,

May

David to May   Holzminden   September 12th 1917

My Dearest,

On Sunday a great and glorious thing happened - your first letter arrived and next day your second came, together with one from Mum and Godwin,

You can imagine how excited I was and how glad to get your letter. I had been worrying as to how long it would be before you heard of me. They have been telling you a lot of rubbish at home. You can write as often and as much as you like and anything you like. Of course everything is censored both ends. So write as often as you can as letters are the one joy of life. Its awfully good of you to go to Balham as you do and I know it must cheer Mum up a lot. I am sorry Mrs Muggridge doesn't seem to be as well as she should be -- I hope she will get better soon as I know it falls back on you. I am very glad to know that you are at last going for a holiday and I hope you are away now.

Could you send me a book on books on Civil Engineering, one illustrated and dealing with fairly small works particularly works under water such as foundations of wharves, docks, bridges, dams, breakwaters etc. also one on builder's office routine, (Corse & Co. Theobalds Road, opposite Bedford Row, sell one if you can't get a better), one on the duties of a clerk of works, and one on the duties of a builder's foreman. I can't give you the titles, but Batsford & Co. opposite Holborn Music Hall will give you what I want. Please get the money from Mum. I am repeating all the above.

Thanks very much for the offer of a German Dictionary, but I think I can get that here. As you will see by the address I have moved, but luckily, letters etc. sent to Karlsruhe will be forwarded.

When your letter came I took it away and read it and re-read it until I knew it practically by heart. You see I had looked forward to it so much and then to get it some time before I expected to hear was grand. I think I know about the time when you felt my cheek for I tried for a long time to do it and once it seemed as though I did. Anyway I am glad you have heard of me even if you haven't had my first letter yet.

I left Karlsruhe on Monday and after a train journey of 21 hours arrived here. The camp is in rather a fine position being practically surrounded by hills at a distance of 2 or 3 miles and there are some really fine views. Unfortunately this is an absolutely new camp and we are the first in it and things are not yet running as no doubt they will later.

My ear is just about the same. The discharge from it is still going on, but I think it is slightly better, I have not yet seen a doctor here but I think I am tomorrow.

Like you I have many dreams of the future and they are very very happy ones and I know they will come true.

I am writing to Mum as usual, will you please forward it.

There was I believe an account of our capture in one of the papers, probably The Daily Mail, I wish you would save it for me, it would probably be published about July 12th or 13th.

It is nearly time for "lights out" so I must get to bed and - well, you know. I am glad to have had your letters but now I want a photo.

Goodbye.

David

> Holzminden prisoner-of-war (PoW) camp was a WWI camp for British and British Empire Officers (Offizier Gefangenenlager) located in Holzminden, Lower Saxony, Germany. It operated between September 1917 and December 1918 occupying the premises of calvary barracks erected in 1913. The two four storey blocks were known as Kaserne. Wooden single storey buildings in front of the the barrack blocks incorporated cookhouses, woodshed, bath-house and parcel-room. The two main barrack blocks of the camp survive to this day and are still in military use as barracks for the German Army.

May to David   17 South Terrace, Littlehampton   Sunday 16th Sept 8.0pm

My dear David,

I have just put back Father Time one hour, and not knowing what to do with it I thought I had better write to you. Sounds as tho' I am making a makeshift of you, doesn't it?

Well, I got away on Saturday at 1.20, and Maud saw me to the station, in fact, watched me go. The train was only ¾ hour late. Esther and the children were walking up and down the front waiting for me. Our house is on the front, the east end of Littlehampton which is better than the River end. The weather is fine and fresh, and I guess I shall be all the better for the change. In my bedroom are 2 beds, Mary in one, and myself in the other. Mary woke up early this morning and spent some time trying to climb up the wall by means of the pattern on the wall paper. The pattern was gaudy somewhat, but as it was not raised Mary did not succeed. Esther is picking up, while the children already look bonny, except perhaps Madeleine, but she doesn't look bad. David came down last night and went back tonight. He looks remarkably well, and as brown as a berry. He is supposed to have taken two snapshots of me, but I don't know when he did it. He says he has taken them for you as unmounted photos of people can be sent to Germany. He and Esther say very nice things about you, but I shall not say what for fear of your getting a swelled head.

How are your poor wounds getting on, and how did you get hurt? But perhaps you cannot tell me. Is there any shot in your ear? I do want to nurse you.

Ern went to Worthing on Saturday, I wish he had not gone at the same time as me, but it seems you can't get everything you want in this world.

Have you received those three educational books yet? And do they suit your lordship?

Bishop told Maud he thought she was going to be transferred to the Foreign Fire Dept, so she is wondering whether she is being "kicked out". She feels she is quite a business woman now, she told me on Saturday, and is very glad her first week is over. She had dreams and headaches over her work, which as far as I can make out chiefly consisted of addressing envelopes and stamping circulars!

We will not have the bungalow at Littlehampton. The beach consists of stretches of sand, and the sand is only surface. After tea today I walked to Rustington – about a mile and a half away. There is going to be a garden city there one day. They already have an artistic board notifying the fact, which I should think must have been put up several years ago, and there is also a huge roof with most probably a house underneath it, but I did not investigate.

Esther is going to finish this letter. She is trying to make me believe it is my duty to marry you. Poor you.

Goodbye

May

My Dear David, It is lovely having Mabel here, and I shall look after her for you. She looks a bonny girl today, she might have been here a week to see her rosy cheeks. We have had a bit of difficulty in getting her to eat today, but she can't get over my David. I hope you are feeing better, we all looking forward to your safe return and making a home for this little girl, and "live happily ever after".

Kind remembrances from us both,

Yours Esther

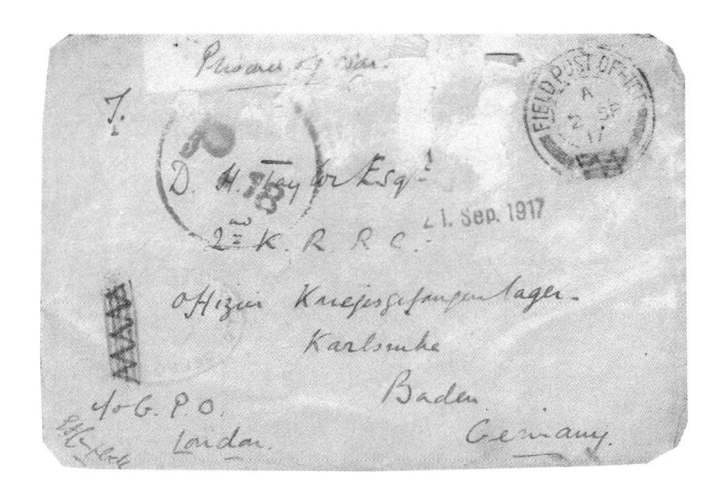

David to May   Holzminden   September 22nd 1917

My Dearest,

I got your 3rd letter (Aug. 20th) on the 15th and mighty glad I was to get it. The people at home have evidently told you a lot of rubbish, you can write as often as you like and as much as you like. I am glad Campbell wrote to you and I am also glad you saw my post card.

In my letter on July 14th I gave you some sort of description of what happened to me. I had been out with two sergeants and was just getting back into a dugout when a shell burst behind me and assisted me in forcibly. The three of us landed considerably tangled. After we had sorted ourselves out, I found that I was bleeding from one or two places on the left side of my head and neck and also that I was deaf. Later I got knocked over, but not hit, by another shell, but this shook me up considerably. I managed to reach the dugout I was making for, but I don't remember much after, until a few minutes before the place was surrounded and we had to give ourselves up.

Two days after, whilst having a bath, I found my clothes stuck to my shoulder and the back of my knee and a fellow pointed out 2 or 3 more small places on my back, none of which I had felt before. I seem to have been filled up with bits, like a rabbit full of shot. Two days after a piece of wood was taken out of the top of my ear and another piece of something out of my neck. I don't know whether I was hit by the bits of shell or by the bits of stuff that it threw around. Anyway it was nothing very much.

With regard to my ear (its the left one) I am glad to say that today the doctor said the discharge had stopped. He and an English doctor here have examined it and both said that the drum was pretty thoroughly smashed and that I shall be deaf that side always. This is the 6th doctor who has said this, but I know better - they are all wrong and it will get alright in time. Luckily enough, although the bit of wood went right through the lobe of my ear, it has healed up and left no noticeable mark.

Would you mind sending me Macaulay's History of England and Essays, Lambs Essays of Elia, and Froude's Historical Essays, all from the "Everyman Library". These may have to be sent by the publisher. Will you also please send lists of the "Everyman" and "Wayfarers" libraries. This being a new camp there is no library yet and so books are very scarce and I am looking forward to your sending those technical books I asked for.

My French too has suffered another check, as there are to be no Frenchmen here. However we are now allowed out for walks, on giving our parole, and I have been out twice for two hours each time. Its simply glorious to get out like this and go for a country walk and the country around about is very good, not unlike the Sussex Downs but rather more wooded. The camp is in the middle of a sort of basin surrounded with hills at a distance of 2 or 3 miles. I got Mum's first letter today (I have had two before) and also a letter from Ethel dated August 15th and sent through Berne. I am enclosing one to her which I wish you would forward. Whilst at Karlsruhe I found that one of my teeth was going so that as there was a dentist available I had it stopped and then he found that 3 others wanted doing so we spent quite a pleasant time together and finally my plate cracked in the old place again and he took an impression and put that right. Its a splendid way of passing the time. I have had one or two good times with the doctor here too. He gets me to swallow some water, (after syringing my ear) at the same time holding my nose and puffing air up one nostrel. It feels as though my head is being turned into a balloon and is just ready to be pricked and busted, but I think this won't have to be done again. This letter seems to be full of doctors and diseases, I had better shut up.

I hope Mrs. Muggridge is better. In your last letter you said she was not very bright. Do write as often as you can - you don't know how I look forward to your letters and what a long time it seems between each one. You see I have to imagine things more than ever now and your letters help tremendously. I have saved a few that I got in France although they have been taken away several times, but each time I have managed to get them back. They are getting rather worn now.

Goodbye.

David

Note new address

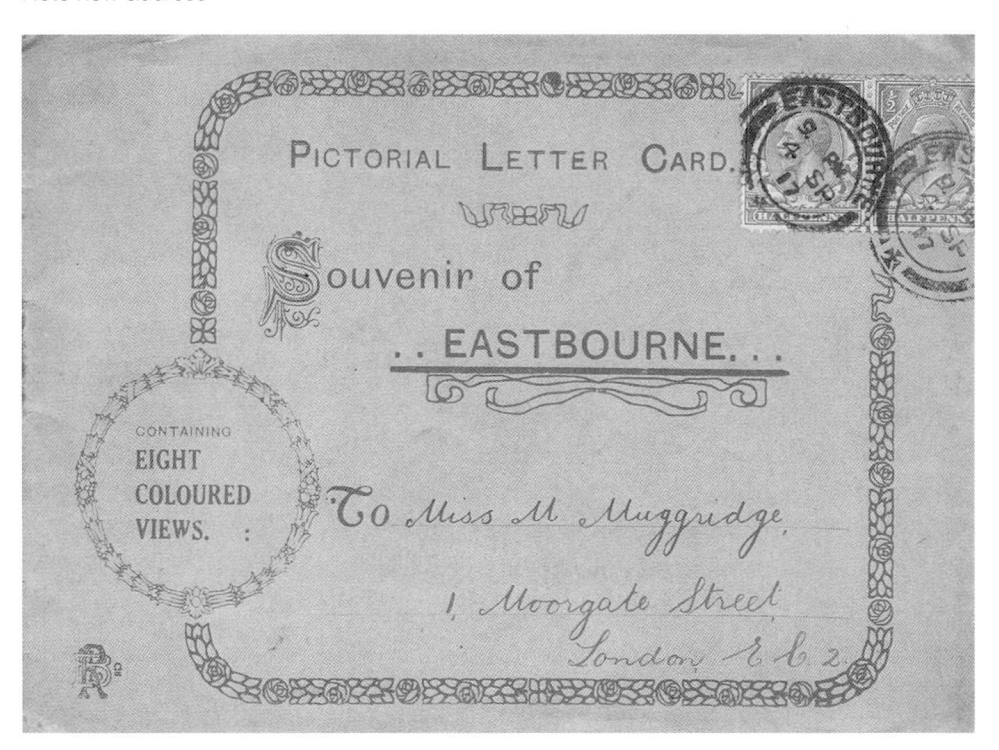

David to Ginger   Holzminden   Sept 22nd 1917

Dear Ginger,

I got your letter of Aug 15th today as quickly as those from home. I have been moved here your letter being forwarded from Karlsruhe. I was not badly hit. I had been out in the trench with two sergeants and was just getting back into a dugout when a shell burst behind me and assisted me in forcibly. The three of us landed pretty well mixed and after we had sorted ourselves out, I found that I was bleeding from one or two places on the left side of my head and neck and also that I was deaf. Later I got knocked over, but not hit, by another shell, and this one shook me up considerably. However I managed to get to the dugout I was making for, but I don't remember much after, until a few minutes before the place was surrounded and we had to give ourselves up. Two days after, whilst having a bath, I found my clothes stuck to my shoulder and back of my knee and a fellow pointed out 2 or 3 more small places on my back, none of which I had felt before. I don't know if I was hit by the bits of shell or by the stuff that it threw up, but two days after a small piece of wood was taken out of the lobe of my ear and something else from my neck. None of these things were very much however. The doctors tell me that the drum of my ear is pretty thoroughly smashed and I shall be deaf that side, but of course the other side is still working alright. Thanks very much for your offer to send things and I shall be awfully glad to have them. Tinned meat, fish, milk, biscuits, tinned fruit, jam, Quaker Oats and such like, are the things I would like most. Be sure to pack them in wooden or stout cardboard as they get knocked about a good deal. If you can send saccharine or sugar too it is most welcome. I hope you have had a good time at the lake. I should like to hear as often as possible.

David

Sept. 22nd 1917

2/Lt. D. H. Taylor
2nd Kings Royal Rifles
Offizier Kriegsgefangenenlager
1 Kaserne
Holzminden
Hanover

Dear Ginger,

I got your letter of Aug 15th today as quickly as those from home. I have been moved here your letter being forwarded from Karlsruhe. I was not badly hit. I had been out in the trench with two sergeants & was just getting back into a dugout when a shell burst behind me & assisted me in forcibly. The three of us landed pretty well mixed & after we had sorted ourselves out, I found that I was bleeding from one or two places on the left side of my head & neck & also that I was deaf. Later I got knocked over, but not hit, by another shell, & this one shook me up considerably. However I managed to get to the dugout I was making for, but I don't remember much after, until a few minutes before the place was surrounded & we had to give ourselves up. Two days after, whilst having a bath, I found my clothes stuck to my

Nov 2nd

17, South Terrace
Littlehampton.
23.9.17
Sunday

My dear David,

What a week I have had! I expected to write to you each day but these three children keep "Auntie" well employed, & then in the evening there is a good deal of mending &c. to do. Esther & I have our supper at 8.30, & are off to bed at 9.30. We have breakfast at 8.30, getting up at 7.30, & then a strenuous day commences. One day we had the biggest castle on the sands. The children are so funny, & it is difficult to keep a straight face often. For instance in the middle of a meal the youngest suddenly remembers grace, & putting her hands together jumbles out something. The other two soon get tired of it, so say "Ah-men", & then they commence & finish with "O Lord stop the war quick & send father down here." The other day one said "O Lord I dot me mouth full wait a minute", but the other two wouldn't wait & saved time by saying their prayers at the table while the youngest emptied the contents of her mouth on the plate. David came down today with his officer chief, a bachelor who was highly amused at the children. The weather is very fresh & bracing & I feel all the better for the change, which is such a big change, as I am living in baby world. We had two wet afternoons during the week, so I set the two eldest to do a

200 my dearest

page of the alphabet, & then when the quicker writer, who was Mary, had finished told her to feel in my magic coat pocket. She found a beautiful green bead necklace. That buck-ed up Madeleine, then she found a yellow bead necklace. Of course after that Nathalie had to find one. They have also found hair ribbons & small looking glasses, & although I am watched very closely, often feeling in my pockets, they have never detected me putting anything in. I am supposed to be very friendly with a fairy godmother who rewards good children.

I had a letter from Mrs Taylor this morning, she is not coming down. She wrote from Watford where she is enjoying herself. Your favourite aunt is better.

The other day I heard from Maud. She is put in another section of the ---- ---- dept, & I do hope she is afraid her business capabilities are not so ---- as she thought they would be. She is not near Mr Bishop now as she is working in the Committee room with 2 or 3 more girls.

I am enclosing one of the old snapshots I wrote to you about & will send you another next week if I can.

I must now write to Maud as I have not done so since I have been here, & I promised her I would. Believe she has the hump. Longing to hear how you are. Goodbye May

May to David   17 South Terrace, Littlehampton   23.9.17 Sunday

My dear David,

What a week I have had! I expected to write to you each day but these three children keep "Auntie" well employed, and then in the evening there is a good deal of mending etc to do. Esther and I have our supper at 8.30 and are off to bed at 9.30. We have breakfast at 8.30, getting up at 7.30, then a strenuous day commences. One day we had the biggest castle on the sands. The children are so funny, and it is difficult to keep a straight face often. For instance in the middle of a meal the youngest suddenly remembers grace, and putting her hands together jumbles out something. Then the other two soon get tired of it, so say "A-h-men" and then they commence and finish with "O Lord stop the war quick and send father down here." The other day one said "O Lord I dot me mouth full wait a minute", but the other two wouldn't wait and saved time by saying their prayers at the table while the youngest emptied the contents of her mouth on the plate. David came down today with his officer chief, a bachelor, who was highly amused at the children. The weather is very fresh and bracing and I feel all the better for the change which is such a big change, as I am living in a baby world. We had two wet afternoons during the week, so I set the two eldest to do a page of the alphabet, and then when the quicker writer, who was Mary, had finished told her to feel in my magic coat pocket. She found a beautiful green bead necklace. That bucked up Madeleine and then she found a yellow bead necklace. Of course after that Nathalie had to find one. They have also found hair ribbons and small looking glasses, and although I am watched very closely, often feeling in my pocket, they have never detected me putting anything in. I am supposed to be very friendly with a fairy godmother who rewards good children.

I had a letter from Mrs Taylor this morning. She is not coming down. She wrote from Watford where she is enjoying herself. Your favourite aunt is better.

The other day I heard from Maud. She is put in another section of the Marine Fire Dept and says she is afraid her business capabilities are not so good as she thought they would be. She is not near Mr Bishop now as she is working in the Committee room with 2 or 3 more girls.

I am enclosing one of the old snapshots I wrote to you about and will send another next week if I can.

I must now write to Maud as I have not done so since I have been here and I promised her I would. Believe she has the hump. Longing to hear how you are.

Goodbye

May

Dear David,

This is a pleasure to be able to drop you a line, I hope you are feeling better and that we shall be having you home soon. Well this has been a most enjoyable week having Mabel with us getting her hand in. She is absolutely splendid with the children. She might have been used to them all her life. I only wish you were here to enjoy her company as well. She is going to make an ideal wife. When I get the time, I'm going to give her a few lessons in cooking and then she will be perfect, of course I've only her word for it. I expect she can cook really but you know how she understates her capabilities. However I can talk for her propensities in the care of children she is wonderful!!!! I'd like to tell you all, but space is limited. Good luck warm remembrances,

Esther

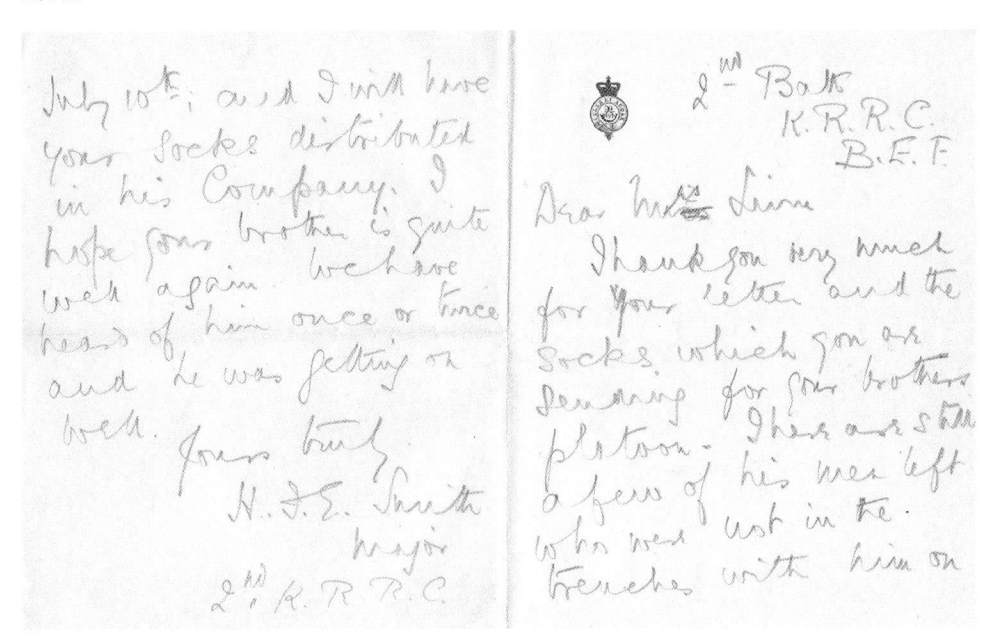

2nd Batt, K.R.R.,   B.E.F.

Dear Mrs Linn,
Thank you very much for your letter and the socks which you are sending for your brother's platoon. There are still a few of his men left who were not in the trenches with him on July 10th, and I will have your socks distributed in his Company. I hope your brother is quite well again. We have heard of him once or twice and he was getting on well.
Yours truly

H.F.E. Smith
Major
2nd K.R.R.C.

May to David   Office.   1. 10. 17.

My dear David,

Back again in a desperately busy world which you know I like. I surprised everyone by returning home from Littlehampton on Wednesday. Nothing was wrong, but I got fed up, so, as my bedroom was let (Esther had moved in the previous Wednesday week), and they wanted me to turn into a smaller one I made Mama an excuse for spending my last few days with her. Besides, I was feeling quite well again, the place and the cold weather agreed with me. The real reason was that as time got on I missed you more & more, and also Mrs. Taylor. It does not seem right to be on holidays without you. I would rather be at work. Those children are dear little souls and well behaved, but they took to me so much, and deserted their mother for me, so that Esther felt I was ousting her. She was awfully sorry, though, when I came away, and has written a very nice letter to me. David S. made me wild. Esther had a letter from him on the second Tuesday which she read out to us, and in it he said "Give my love to Mabel". She paused a moment after reading it, so I guess she felt a bit hurt. I ignored it, but if ever I get him to myself I will say things to him that are not complimentary. The silly fool does not mean anything, but mischief is made that way, and Esther is jealously fond of him and the children.

On Thursday morning I had your letter from your new address in which you say you have received my first to you. I am glad you are hearing from me now. I sent you three books several weeks ago. Have you got them? Mama has saved an account of the battle, and Mrs Taylor has got a lot of back newspapers. She is sending you parcels galore. I think they help to keep her spirits up. She is certainly full of life. Of course directly after dinner on Thursday I went to see her, taking your letter with me. She had been to Watford for a holiday, but said she missed me very much and wished I was with her. We promised each other not to spend another holiday apart again, and had a good hug. Then we had a good time together. Beatie Bulford has made a lot of things for the bazaar - covered boxes with pretty wall papers. She has done them beautifully. Also given some charms and other things she says she does not want. I have not written to thank her yet but will do so today. I could not carry all her gifts away at one go. One of Ethel's men has painted a table centre on white satin; price £2.2.0. An elderly lady has painted a picture, and it looks very well. I found 6 small pictures in my desk this morning. Mrs Taylor and Mrs. Day are knitting 6 pairs of socks.

Maud has just popped in. She felt so miserable about her work last week that she thought she would leave! I think the chief clerk frightens her, just because he barks a bit! We work for him, and I thoroughly enjoy talking to him like a mother. He crumples up at once. However, she is feeling better now. I am afraid she is rather faint-hearted.

Ern has been to Worthing. He does not like the place as a seaside resort, but the country is lovely at the back, so we are talking about retiring there after the war. We could not think of leaving before. Mrs Capel is much better again, and has sent a few gifts for the bazaar also. It is quite exciting seeing the things pour in.

Must stop now, as I have a fortnight's back work to do. Will write again in a day or two. Hope your ear does not hurt too much.

May.
I enclose another of those photos.

May to David   Office.   2. 10. 17.

My dear David,
I did not have time to finish yesterday's letter, so will to do so now - if hindrances will permit. I enclose another of those rough snapshots. I am promised better ones later on.   I was blinking at the time. I have not got a bit thinner, have I?
Your letter was marked No. 6, but it is only the 3rd, or 4th, I have received. The first and third went astray I know, as you referred to them in the 2nd and 4th. This is my 13th or 14th to you.
Tullie Thomson has another son, and is going to try to go to the south coast for a holiday, most likely Hastings or Bexhill, if she can get in, but most places are full up till Christmas as far as I can make out. It seems a lot of the lower class are having the time of their lives, receiving such excellent wages, and so are going about galore and buying most expensive clothes.
Maud's spirits are sky-high again. She has been helping Mr. Bishop turn up policy numbers etc., and is so happy over it, and feels she is learning a tremendous lot of business. Her simple-mindedness is so refreshing. She reminds me of a book I am reading and enjoying.   I will tell you about it when I have finished.
Can't stop any longer now, so Goodbye; will write in a day or two.

May

Fanny to Ethel   Balham   Oct 3. 1917

My darling Ethel,

I received your letter in the morning, as Polly received hers at night. I received a card from David saying he had just received my first letter, his card is dated the 4 September, he says his ear is about the same, otherwise he is well, pleased send parcels of food frequently. I ordered through the American Express Agent, on 10 Aug, and they told me he would get it in about fortnight time. Thinking he would get it so soon I went and order another 4 parcels in all. Then I went to the Red Cross Prisoner of War on the 18 of Aug. They ordered one to be sent at once, he has just got that one. They will continue to send him every week. And I have sent him some from home, two last week. And as soon as Aunt Bessie heard of him, she sent him a good parcel of food, so he will get them frequently.

I went up to the American Express and told them he had not received a parcel, and they assured me he had got the first and told me what was sent. If he got it, it was a good parcel. And if he gets what as been sent from home, and what Auntie Bessie has sent he will get on. It is all done in tins, I have sent his cloths, and he asked on his last card for a sleeping bag, a blanket sewn up so he gets into it. I have sent that.

I have done all I can do, and spared nothing. I was not satisfied about his wounds. So I wrote to the Red Cross Switzerland and asked them to let me know. I had the reply on Monday evening. It was David's own card that he sent to them with a letter to me. This is what is on the card.

I was wounded by a shell in the head neck and back, but not seriously, my left ear is also injured causing me to be deaf that side.

Every card I have had he complained of his ear. They have moved him to another Camp. It was 21 hours journey. This is the address.

2/ Lieut D H Taylor
2nd Kings Royal Rifle Corps
Offizier. Kriegsgefangenenlager
Kaserne Holzminder
Hanover

He tells me all his letters and parcels will be forwarded to him. I shall continue to send parcels, he said it was a grand day to him when he received my letter and one from the young man that was at his office. It was Sunday. It's a new Camp and not quite finished and he thinks they will be very...

[rest of letter missing]

May to David   Office, 1 Moorgate St, E.C.   3.10.17

My dear David,

I have a nice little item of news. Hearing that some of the Insurance Companies, or rather one, were going back to their original short hours, I tackled Mr Lutt yesterday on the subject. He could not do anything on his own in the matter but said he would put it before the General Manager, who promptly said he would not give way, that we should have to keep to the long hours. However, an hour later we had a notice to say we could leave at 5.0. until further notice, a compromise which we appreciate. This only applies to the girls who form a good proportion of the staff. I guess the Secretary had a tough job to get that much for us. Of course we shall have to get through the same amount of work, hence my not being able to write you long letters. However, I expect short and frequent will suit you just as well.
Nothing else to tell you just now, so Goodbye.

May.

P.S. I enclose another of the snapshots. My face not being visible I think this is the best one of me. Those that are visible are Esther, Nathalie and Mary.

May to David   Beckenham   4.10.17

My dear David,

Yesterday afternoon we had a little bit of excitement at the Office. An old temporary gentleman in the Accountant's Dept had a fit. Two temporary girls who were handy knew first aid. They did their best, and then came in and asked me for my First Aid book. They went outside my room and read up treatment. By the time they had studied it and gone back, the poor old soul had got well again – fortunately for him.

One of the office clerks put me up to a good thing for the bazaar. He said his sister held a stall one year and sold a lot of second hand novels, chiefly 7d editions, that had been given her, and she got more money from them than the rest of the stall. So yesterday we put up a notice on the notice boards with the result that already I have several books, good ones too, and more promised. This particular clerk has a son who is a schoolboy, and he has made us a model of an aeroplane, about a foot long. It looks alright as far as I can tell.

On Saturday I am going out shopping with Maud. She is going to buy a hat, boots and I forget the rest. I shall be buying a dress, and will then take it to her dressmakers. She wants me to stay the night with her, but I shall not do that.

I had a nice letter from Mrs Taylor this morning, who also wants me for the weekend, but I am not going as I shall be too busy. What do you think? Maud slips off before time of an evening! I asked her where her conscience was. Moreover, she is getting frivolous over the dress. She came in to me this morning during the 11.0 break and said one of her relations had written asking her how she was getting on at playing at business. She wrote back indignantly saying how hard she was working, living in a most busy world, and that she was getting on very well, and had learnt a lot. She then told me she had got on to folding up policies and putting them into envelopes! I gathered from her tone that that is very advanced work. Bless her heart.

A son of one of the general managers (not Gayford) was married last Tuesday afternoon. Gayford and Foot were to go to the ceremony which was at 2.0 at Hampstead. At 5. to 2.0 a clerk came up to him (he was talking to me at the time) and asked him if he weren't going? He calmly answered "O, I suppose I am", but then he never budged. Perhaps he thought the ceremony would wait for him. It couldn't wait long as the bridegroom only had a few days' leave.

Helen and the children have gone to Southsea to stay with a relation of Uncle's. Helen has not heard from Jack for nearly two months and is getting worried.

I must leave off now, so Goodbye for a day or so.

May.

David to May   Holzminden   October 6th 1917

My Dearest,

I have got all your letters to September 12th, the last today. Please write more often. Your letters are everything. I also want a photo, I left mine in my valise, so that it shouldn't get lost and now I want another here. I should be delighted to have another woolley waistcoat. I left mine in the dugout and it went up and all my other things with it.

I am enclosing letters to Campbell, Lady Shippard (Mum has her address) and Mrs Walker, 25 Kidmore Road, Caversham, Reading. Will you please forward them. They give you a few details, so read them if you care to, but they are rather gruesome.

Thanks for going with Mum to Cox's etc. It is good of you and thanks too for sending the books. I expect I shall get them soon. Could you get me Laxton's Builders Price Book (Batsford), and Estimating (this last in my bookcase), and also the following from the "Everyman" library:- Carlyles French Revolution, Lockharts Life of Napoleon, Irvings Life of Mahomet, Macaulays History of England, and his Essays. Will you send a list of Batsfords, "Everyman" and "Wayfarers" libraries.

My ear (its the left one) is better, the discharge having stopped, in fact the doctor has stopped dressing it, and is merely keeping it under observation, in case I suppose it has a relapse and gets hydrophobia or something. Anyway its alright now except that its no good for hearing purposes.

The arrangements about your holiday seem to have been unsatisfactory. I am sorry. Never mind we'll have a good time when I get home. Anyway I do hope you had a good holiday eventually. I am glad the chief is so pleased with you and your girls.

Had a letter from Maud, and today a very nice one from Muriel Maconachie. Please thank them both and ask them to write again, although I cannot reply to them. Muriel says "it is so nice being strong enough to do something again" and also "that she is taking a man's place" in an office. I must remind her of this later. Please congratulate Maud on having started business although I know it is all your doing.

I have come across 6 or 7 officers of my regiment here, who were captured in 1914 and they have been awfully good to me. I am still dreaming dreams, one the other night was awfully real, but I will tell you all about that later. Goodbye.

David

May to David   Office   6. 10. 17.

My dear David,

I have changed my plans for this afternoon. Maud's dressmaker can't see me as she is off to a funeral. There is no moon next week, so as it means waiting till next Saturday afternoon. I am going to my own dressmaker at Sydenham this afternoon instead. I am looking too shabby for words. Maud will have to do her own shopping by herself. After seeing the dressmaker I shall have to hurry home, to be busy. Mama has had the blues this week, and has scarcely done any work, and we suddenly hear that Mac (Miss Bradfield) is coming tomorrow, so we shall have to buck up. Thank goodness; it will do Mama good. I had a letter from Muriel this morning asking for news of you. She says she wrote you a long letter recently. Ethel is buying a lot of flannelette today and is asking Mama to make it up into nighties for a poor woman she knows. This, too, will do Mama good. Nothing like work. I wonder every night if you have had the blues during the day. Guess you have. Then I wonder if your wound is any better, and conclude it is never going to be well any more, at any rate, not when I get you to myself.

Did I tell you the Office is divided into sections so that when a raid warning comes we each go to our special place of safety. The Actuary is the head of our section, and during the whole time we are downstairs he chats most affably to all, making no distinction; but wait till the all-clear whistle goes. He never assumes airs, but somehow he wraps a different atmosphere round him and walks off. No one would dare speak to him then, and he would not think of speaking to anyone. Isn't it strange how folks can alter without actually looking any different. You could understand it in the case of uniforms, especially very good ones. That reminds me, I hope you have received some clothes by now. You must be looking delapidated, especially with your bandaged head and French Tommy's cap; what you might call "the limit".

I cannot stop any longer now as I want to leave early, so Goodbye, will write next week.

May.

May to David   Beckenham   Monday. 6.10.17.

My dear David,

On Saturday I called at the dressmaker's as arranged and she is actually going to get the dress finished by Thursday! Record.

Then I went home and was busy for the rest of the day. Mama is heaps better, and is busy now making up that flanelette. There is nothing like work if you are down in the dumps. Have you got those three books yet. Hope so, as they will make you feel better when you study them. I am very anxious to know if that engineering book on rivers and canals suits you. Yesterday turned out very wet, cold, with passing thunderstorms! Miss Bradfield did not turn up. We sat over the fire and read and talked. It seemed wintry enough for Christmas. I wondered what sort of as Christmas you would have. Hope you can get a little bit of cheer. Last year I had a very quiet Christmas, but most enjoyable. Should like this year's to be the same. There certainly seems a possibility of it being repeated.

I must tell you about a wonderful piece of surgery I have heard of. It was performed by a German doctor on one of our Tommies in Germany. His jaw, or part of it, had been blown away, and this doctor took out a rib and made him a new jaw with it. He is getting on alright. Mrs. Day told me about it. I expect she got the news from the Hospital. She often goes down there to spend an enjoyable afternoon listening to all the dreadful cases there are. She says the German surgeons are very clever. Well, I hope the doctors are too and that they will heal you alright. When I can't sleep I always imagine your head is bad and aching dreadfully.

We had some fun this morning. Ethel had made a tea cloth for the bazaar and valued it at two guineas. I raffled it and it brought in 62/-. It went to a temporary girl.

I cannot stop any longer. This is our busy month, so don't expect another letter for a week. Goodbye.

May.

May to David   Beckenham   10.10.17 (Wednesday)

My dear David,

Last night I had your letter dated 22nd Sept. Wasn't that quick work, and wasn't I glad to get it? It gave me an a/c of your capture. You do make light of your wounds; it just sounds as though you didn't feel bad at all, [censored]. So it is your left side that is hurt. I thought so all along. Can you lie on that side now? Of course I mean on something soft? I am sorry for your sake that you are deaf on one side. Does it sound horribly selfish, but the fact is I think it would be a good thing for me if you were always a bit deaf, because then I should have to speak a little louder which would be so good for my throat. My speaking quietly and badly is sheer laziness, and it would be doing me a good turn to make me speak louder. Sometimes I say a few words to that dismal deaf old post, Eccles, for the sake of exercising my voice.

I copied out a good deal, almost all, of your letter yesterday and sent to Mrs Taylor. She wrote to me and our letters crossed. She is so pleased because you have asked for your football clothes, and also because the parcels are reaching you. I expect to see her Saturday.

This morning I called at Batsfords. They had not the books or lists with them, but will get them today and post them on.

Last night I called at the dressmaker's. It was rather dark coming away, but I imagined you were with me, so was not nervous – not that I ever have felt nervous. Don't think we are built that way, except a few selfish old crocks, like my esteemed Aunt and her hubby. No word from Jack yet.

I have been thinking a good deal about the bungalow lately. You remember I said the back room would be the kitchen and scullery combined. Well, couldn't we have the small middle room made into a kitchen and scullery combined (we should only want a place big enough for cooking and washing up), and have the back room made into a meal room. Your camp bedstead arrangement could be rolled up and stood in one corner, so that if we wanted to make up a bed for anyone extra we could do so easily. That would leave us three bedrooms upstairs. What do you think?

I must not stop any longer now; too busy; so goodbye.

May

P.S. Miss Willsher came in yesterday and brought me a miniature rock garden with Alpine plants on it. It is a grand novelty, and so minute. She bought it with the money you sent her for me, so thanks.

David to Ginger   Holzminden   Oct 12th 1917 postcard

I have your letters of Aug 8th and 15th, the 15th as quickly as those from home. Also on Oct 9th I received a very welcome parcel from Harrods and I suppose it was from Mr Charrington. The Red Cross at Berne are sending me your bread. Thanks very much indeed for them all, it is good of you. With regard to what I want, tinned meats with and without vegetables and packed foods generally, sugar or saccharine, tinned butter and similar things are the best, as we cook these things ourselves. Everything must be packed in strong cardboard or wooden boxes. I believe the American Express Co. will make up and forward parcels. I got hit round about the head and shoulder but not seriously, but the same shell broke my left ear drum and they tell me my left ear will be useless, otherwise I are now quite alright. You will note I have moved, but everything is forwarded. Write often.

David

May to David   Beckenham   12.10.17 and 13th

My dear David,

As arranged I called at the dressmaker's last night, and came away with my new garment, and this morning I am dressed in all the glories of it. Really, it does alright; a soft grey trimmed with black velvet. If it is a bright day tomorrow, and Maud helps to drag me along, I might be tempted to be photographed in it; and if the photo turns out tolerably well for me I might then be tempted to send you a copy.

We are very busy this morning, extra busy, as we are trying to scrimmage in time to price some of the bazaar goods and stow them in the strong room. This morning I brought up a water colour, the Thames past Richmond, done by an uncle of one of Ethel's girls. He has given it to us which was good of him as the picture was hung in 1914. I don't know the price of it yet, but I expect we will raffle it. We are raffling another table cloth on Monday. It is not such a beauty as Ethel's, and so far we have only 29 names given in.

After spending Saturday afternoon with Maud I am going on to Balham to stay the weekend with Mrs Taylor, as Mama is so much better again.

13.10.17

I didn't have time to finish my letter to you yesterday so will try to now, tho' we are desperately busy this morning. The bazaar things we stowed in the strong room yesterday were priced at £4.11.3. It turned out awfully wet, and I got a bit drenched going home – too bad with my best coat on and in all the glories of a new frock! When I reached home I found a parcel from Connie containing two dresses for children, priced 15/- and 4/6, and a dressing jacket priced 10/6. Arriving here this morning I saw Mr Maconachie who gave me a parcel containing several baby's bonnets, one in particular a perfect gem worked in white silk, and is about guaranteed to set one longing, and various other things; also 5/- from Mrs English. People are good. The help we are getting is tremendous, and everyone is so delighted to do things for us, or rather, for the Blinded Soldiers and Sailors.

I must not stop any longer, as I want to get finished by 1.0. By the bye, it is a dismal day, and rains occasionally. Unless it changes considerably it will be no good to think of the photographer's shop.

Will write again on Monday, so Goodbye.

May

1 Moorgate St, E.C.2   15th Oct 1917

Messrs. Read & Brigstock
5, Lothbury. E.C.

Dear Sirs,
I am writing on behalf of Mrs Taylor of 56, Ramsden Road, Balham, S.W.
Last June her son, 2/ Lieut. D.H.Taylor, K.R.R., B.E.F. France, asked you to buy for him ten Malayalam shares. As he was taken prisoner in July Mrs Taylor said she would have the shares put in her name. You obtained them for her from the Rev. Leslie Baron, but she says she has not yet received the share certificate.
Will you kindly look into the matter and let me hear from you?

Yours faithfully,
[M Muggridge]

READ & BRIGSTOCK.

ERNEST A. READ.
ARNOLD H. READ.
WALTER H. LANE.

TELEGRAMS: "SPECIE, STOCK, LONDON."
TELEPHONE: LONDON WALL 6120 (2 LINES)

CODES,
A.B.C. 5TH EDITION.
LIEBER'S.
WESTERN UNION.

5, LOTHBURY,
AND STOCK EXCHANGE
LONDON, E.C.2.

15th October, 1917.

M. Muggridge, Esq.,
   1, Moorgate Street,
      E.C. 2.

Dear Sir,

    We beg to thank you for your letter of even date regarding Mrs. Taylor's certificate for her son's Malayalam Shares. The certificate will not be ready to be handed to us by the Company until about ten days time. As soon as we receive it we shall forward same to Mrs. Taylor direct.

          Yours faithfully,

          Read & Brigstock

May to David   5 Moorgate St E.C.   15.10.17 (Monday) & 16th

My dear David,

Maud and I left here at 1.0 last Saturday and went to lunch at Aldermanbury. Then we walked to London Bridge and took the train to Denmark Hill. While at London Bridge it came over dark and rained, so I felt disappointed. However, it brightened up when we arrived at D. Hill so we went to the photographers and I went thro' that wretched performance again. He seemed a gloomy sort of photographer and almost greeted me with the words "Your eyes are very dark, and they are difficult to take", so I don't feel very hopeful about the result. Then we went shopping at Clapham, and finally arrived at Balham to tea at 5.0. Maud looks younger than she has done for years. We had a lively tea time, and Maud left at 6.30. It is awfully funny how Mrs T and Mrs Day get at one another; I don't mean in an irritable way, because they are both laughing. The winks Mrs Day gives me are enough to make me split with suppressed laughter. I got on nicely, i.e. when laughter would permit me, with the jersey I am making for the bazaar. It is quite half finished now. This morning I came away with a huge bundle of goods from 56, including 6 pairs of socks that Mrs Taylor and Mrs Day had made, and various mats, table centre, and table cloth; also some things from Mrs Capel! We went to chapel yesterday morning and saw the choir master do his physical jerks. The minister made me laugh several times. He was actually making jokes from the pulpit! He was smiling himself, so he plainly meant them for jokes, and they were very good ones too. He at any rate takes on a cheerful, and, as I think, a correct view, of religion.

Censor or no censor, I must tell you this –

Sunday morning; both dressing; Mrs T had been chatting for over an hour, and suddenly starts a fresh subject thus:-

"Grandfather Christmas. Sounds funny. But that is what he is. I'm talking about Brother Alf. But they've made a mistake. It's a girl. They should have had a boy first. Just you bear that in mind. A boy should be the eldest. Then if you like, you can have a girl. But don't stop there. Only two in the family is a mistake. They both get spoilt. You must go on and have some more."

So I told her we would go to her about our orders.

She finally finished her talk by saying "I don't know that I am coming to live with you; but at any rate I would like to live next door." She was quite serious the whole time!

Altogether, it was a very enjoyable and humorous weekend. I came away this morning at 9 something, and Mrs Taylor saw me into the tram.

We have just had the second raffle, and one of the men supers is the winner. We are all pleased, as he is a decent sort, and very much worried by one of my pet abominations – Humphries.

Can't stop any longer; will write again as soon as I can.

May

16.10.17

P.S. I had such a rush at the end of the day that I went off without this. There is nothing to add except that the proof of the photo came this morning. I think it flatters me, so have written to the man to proceed.

May to David   Beckenham   17.10.17

My dear David,

Not much news this time. Spent last night in getting on with the red jersey and hope to finish it tonight. Then I want to make a cap to match, and that will finish my contributions to the bazaar. Things are pouring in now. We have already priced articles to the amount of over £11, and have had £19 given us, mostly in half-crowns, so we feel we are getting on. We would like to reach £100, but shall really be pleased if we reach £50.

I think I told you Helen and the boys are down at Southsea. A cousin of her father's has a house there. She has gone away on a visit to London, or rather Sanderstead, till the beginning of December, and has lent Helen the house in the meantime. She wrote to Mama and said her folks' nerves, i.e. Auntie's and Uncle's, were very bad, and that they considered it was the fault of the children. The letter was a miserable one, and no wonder when she is not hearing from her hubby. She added that no one seemed to want them. That did it. Mama wrote back to say she could have Bert's bedroom with a couple of beds in it, and the morning room, and that the children would not upset her. Helen is delighted, and says if the "nerves" are no better when she gets back again, she will come round. We think it will be a good thing for Mama, as she will have to have her dinner in middle of day, and the boys will keep her lively.

I have been thinking. I cannot see any chance of building that bungalow this coming spring, and very likely the spring after we shall be too busy with other business, so I am drawing out some of the money I had saved for that purpose and investing it, and will so get a few pounds extra. I shall be able to sell out when I want to. Mama is now investing Bert's money which will be the finish of his affairs.

Cannot stop any longer. Am longing to hear how you are getting on. Only wish you felt as well as I do. Goodbye.

May

P.S. I had a letter from Esther this morning. She is back home again and has just got 3 tons of coal in for the winter. As per usual Passmore is worrying them by saying he will close the shop. David was to see him last night about it, and she will write me again. She has sent me 4 d'oyleys which she received from India as part of her wedding present. They are to be sold on our stall.

B T Batsford, 94 High Holborn W.C.1   Oct 19th 1917

To Miss M Muggridge

Dear Madam,

With reference to the books you ordered here last week, we regret the delay, owing to some of them being out of stock at the publishers. We have now been able to procure Macaulay's History of England 3 Vols, Macaulay's Essays, and Lambs Essays of Elia, which we will forward to Lieut Taylor without delay. Froudes Historical Essays are now binding. Shall we keep these on order and advise you when ready?

Yrs faithfully
Pp B T Batsford Ltd

Miss. M. Muggeridge   LONDON, Oct 19. 1917.

BOUGHT OF **B. T. BATSFORD, LTD**

ARCHITECTURE · DECORATION · FINE ARTS · ENGINEERING · APPLIED SCIENCE

BOOKSELLERS AND PUBLISHERS.
94, HIGH HOLBORN, W. C. 1.

LIBRARIES OF ARCHITECTURAL, ENGINEERING AND SCIENTIFIC BOOKS PURCHASED.

CHEQUES SHOULD BE CROSSED LONDON AND COUNTY AND WESTMINSTER BANK LTD, AND MADE PAYABLE TO B.T. BATSFORD, LIMITED.
NO REMITTANCE UNDER 5/- ACKNOWLEDGED UNLESS ACCOMPANIED BY STAMP.

Macaulay. History of England 3 Vols. @ 1-3	3.	9.
Lambs. Essays of Elia	1.	3.
Macaulay. Historical Essays. 2 Vols @ 1-3	2.	6.
	7.	6.
Paid 23/10/17 pp B T Batsford Ltd	8.	0.

MEMORANDUM

From
B.T. Batsford, Ltd
BOOKSELLERS & PUBLISHERS
ARCHITECTURE
DECORATION
FINE ARTS
ENGINEERING
APPLIED SCIENCE
Telephone: Central 7693

94 High Holborn W.C.1

London Oct 19th 1917

Miss M. Muggridge.

Dear Madam,

With reference to the books you ordered here last week, we regret the delay, owing to some of them being out of stock at the publishers. We have now been able to procure, Macaulay's History of England 3 Vols, Macaulay's Essays, & Lambs Essays of Elia, which we will forward to Lieut Taylor without delay. Froudes Historical Essays are now binding, Shall we keep these on order & advise you when ready?

Yrs faithfully,
pp. B. T. Batsford Ltd.
WW

May to David   Beckenham   19.10.17

My dear David,

This letter No.21, though I don't think some of them could be called letters, being so short. The only item of news this time is that I have had my palm read by one of the temporary girls. She is splendid. I had heard about her, so thought I would test her with a view of offering her services at the Bazaar. She works for Mr Maconachie, and told him about a love affair of his that no one knows about, not even Mrs Mac. He is struck with her. She told me about you, said a truer man did not live, that you were on the continent, in difficulties, though if you were not where you were it would be worse for you; that you were very clever, figures being your speciality; that we would be married, not quite as soon as we expected, on account of business; that it is quite likely we would be married quietly one morning and that I should come on to business afterwards; that we should have an elderly lady living with us for a few years, when she would die quite happily; that we should always work together, shoulder to shoulder, and would be thoroughly well matched; that you would have a good post offered you abroad, something scientific, like the head of large aeroplane works for instance; that there would be half dressed blacks around us; we might have one youngster, and might not; that after a long and extremely happy married life I should die abroad. She also mentioned that someone else wanted to marry me; that he is now married and has a baby daughter; that he sees his mistake and is now longing for me, but that he is a perfect gentleman, though when he gets a chance he will be telling me; that I do not like men (with one exception over whom I have fairly lost my head) because men will confide in me, especially the married ones, but they cannot help it because I have a man's mind and that attracts them. Though I am a born organiser I am not in my right place, as I ought to have been a detective or a nurse. I shall have another post offered me soon, but it will be best not to take it as I shall be getting a large increase here, though I shall be willing to give it up when I can help you. At present I am the only one who can help you, though it is little I can do. (I should think so indeed – she did not know of your existence, or of course where you are).

That is enough rubbish for you to get on with this week.

Tomorrow I shall be paying the bills, doing gardening, and seeing about a hat for the winter. I have not heard from Mrs Taylor for a day or two, so she is probably at Watford for the weekend. Terribly busy, so Goodbye.

May.

P.S. The girl also said that in five years' time we should be thoroughly settled down to our work, and that something is going to happen (don't know what) in six months' time that could not happen if the war were still going on. Hope that will be true. By the bye, this girl sees spiritual things. She looks quite normal herself; in fact good looking, and works well. A girl who can spins yarns like this ought to fetch in a lot of money. She talked hard for 20 min for 1/- !!!

David to May   Holzminden   October 22nd 1917

My Dearest,

I have been reading over your letters again. Please tell me some of the other nice things that the chief said beside the fact that your department is to be practically doubled. I suppose it didn't strike him to double your salary as well as your responsibility? You will have almost forgotten your holiday, but I am longing to hear all about it and about yourself generally. <u>Please</u> write more often.

By the way thanks very much for writing yourself to Taylor's mother, I expect your letter would please her a great deal more than anything.

I am enclosing that official Receiver form, a letter to Mum and one to Cox & Co. I am asking Cox's to send a cheque for £10 to Mum every month. When she has taken what she wants from it, will you please add the remainder to that other money, but first of all take a few pounds and get a Christmas present for yourself. Now do, please, because I can't get it myself so I know you won't mind.

In my last letter I asked you to get me some books. Would you mind getting me Laxtons Builders Price Book (Batsford) "Estimating" (this last in my bookcase) and the following from the "Everyman" Library, Carlyles French Revolution, Lockharts Life of Napoleon, Irvings Life of Mahomet, Macaulays History of England and Essays. Will you also send a list of the Everyman and Wayfarers Libraries.

By the way there are no less than six Taylor's in the camp and four of us have either D or H for our initials, so when writing be careful to put both initials and the regiment.

Please ask Mum to send the Builder and the Builders Journal once a month alternately. I expect the publishers will have to send them. I would send the book by post as it is more reliable than American Express and quicker.

Ethel, in one of her letters said that she read the report of our affair on July 14th. I wonder if you could get it and save it for me. Since I have been here I have come across several officers of my regiment, who, as soon as they heard of me, came and found me and who have been very good to me since. They have all been prisoners since the early part of the war. By the way, Mum asked me if I know anything of the Colonel. I only heard that one of the men saw him lying dead, but of course it was only a report and one can't count too much on it.

Will you please thank Muriel Maconachie and Maud for their letters and ask them both to write again, although I can't reply to them. In one or two of your letters you ask which side of my head is damaged. I am sorry I didn't say before, but I believe I gave you an account of what happened to me in my first letter. Anyhow its the left side, but its all quite alright now, except of course that I am still deaf and my ear rings a bit at times.

In another letter you ask if I would like another waistcoat - I would, most muchly. Your other one went up with the dugout and all my other things with it. I am just off to bed now - the time just before going to sleep and that before getting up are always by far the best times to me. You know why. Goodbye.

David

May to David   Beckenham   22.10.17   No.22

My dear David,

I was hoping to hear from you this weekend, but I have not so far. I know I am greedy where your letters are concerned and want a lot. Last week I finished the red jersey and cap, and on Saturday night I made a little wool gaiter. Hope to make the second tonight. Every day I have at least one large parcel of things. This morning I heard from the Bazaar people, and they would be delighted to have our palmist.

Saturday afternoon I did shopping and wound wool. On Sunday I walked to cemetery, and brought away some of the geraniums, leaving 9 still up there. It was a lovely day, like summer. During the afternoon and evening we all sat over the fire and talked. I got a good deal of teasing about living amongst blacks. On the way home from the cemetery I called at Auntie's. She was a martyr. I don't quite know why, as I did not go in, not having time. She said "Helen is coming up from Southsea on Monday to get her allowance. She wants to stay the night I fancy, but I have written to tell her not to. She seems to think I don't want her, but it is nothing of the sort." Helen evidently hasn't told her mother about Mama's offer, or I think I should have heard about it.

I invested £100 this morning, and the time it took me has helped to make me busy and behind. It is our busy month really.

My photo hasn't come yet. Now that I have been taken I am in a hurry to despatch it to you. A few days ago I wrote to Batsfords asking if the books had been despatched, and they replied that they had sent:-

Macauley, History of England, 3 vols @1/3	3/9
Lambs Essays of Elia	1/3
Macaulay, Historical Essays, 2 vols @ 1/3	2/6
	7/6

But that Frouds Historical Essays were then being bound. The books seem very cheap. Hope they are good enough. They did not say anything about the lists I asked them to send. I will see them tomorrow and ask.

Can't stop any longer. Hope I shall find a letter saying how you are. Every night I fancy you are ill and want nursing. Do you feel bad, or is it my imagination?

May.

P.S. I have heard from Mrs Taylor. She has been down to Watford since Wednesday. Coming up today. Having a nice time. Mrs Capel quite well and bonny again, and wished to be remembered to me!

May to David   Beckenham   24.10.17

My dear David,

Last Monday I wrote to you. On Tuesday morning I called at Batsfords who assured me they had sent you a list of the two "libraries", and that Froude's book was not yet ready but would be sent on immediately they had it. We had a fearfully busy day, but I managed to leave at 5.5 and caught the 5.15 from Cannon St arriving home in time to get your letter of the 1st Sept, which gave a most amusing account of your first parcel, or rather, the cooking of it; and also your daydreams. You have more time for daydreams than I have just now, so I have to get mine in at night. I had previously had your letters of 12th and 22nd Sept.

This morning your letter of the 14th July came. I read it in the train, when tears permitted me, not having had time to open it before I left. You darling. No, my darling.

We are very busy today again, and as I must write to Mrs Taylor and copy out parts of your two letters I cannot stop any longer now, but will finish later, or rather, continue.

Uncle and Auntie from Ireland sent you nice messages the other day, but I have forgotten what they are.

Goodbye for the present.

May

May to David   Beckenham   25.10.17

My dear David,

I am trying to snatch five seconds to continue yesterday's letter which was short and (?) sweet.

Answering your letter of 14th July which came yesterday I have written to the Town Clerk at Cheltenham for the address of the family of Heberden who lost a member on 19th July as I wanted to write to them about the said lost member. Sounds as though I was a spiritualist, but I did not put it like that. When I hear from the family I shall say how you went to relieve Heberden, found him stunned by a shell which exploded close by while he was evidently trying to dig some buried people out of a dugout; that you immediately phoned for the doctor who came at once; that he was carried into the nearest dugout, and that when you returned shortly after he was dead. I shall not say anything about the leg being blown off or the wound on his chest. News like that might kill an elderly lady with a weak heart, or if he is married his wife would probably have a horrid picture in her mind for the rest of her life. I shall also say that I have asked you if the doctor is taken prisoner, and if so, could you ask him if the man recovered consciousness and gave a message. I think it is better generally if there are no messages.

As regards Read and Brigstock, no doubt Mrs Taylor has told you she has cancelled the second order and is having the first put in her name. She consulted H. Webber about this matter.

I have had a letter from Mrs Taylor this morning, and have written saying I shall be over to dinner on Saturday. Maud is coming to stay the weekend with us the week after.

It was too windy to sleep last night, so I dreamt instead, which was nicer. I imagined I put a necklace of V.C's round your neck, and then something else. The V.C's were as thick as beads, but you calmly said you preferred the something else. When I called you to order you said "Bosh" and -   . No, I won't say the rest. Think of the censors!

We have had heaps of things in today for the bazaar, and a couple of cheques. Goods priced and money received now amount to over £60, and more to come! Haven't I been plaguing folks? Thank your lucky stars you are in Germany and so safely away from it all!

Goodbye.

May

May to David   Office   29.10.17   No.25.

My dear David,

I am so excited. If this letter is a hopeless jumble you will know the reason. It is all because of our Sale. We hoped in our wildest moments to reach £50. Behold, we have priced goods and received donations to the tune of £100, and more to come! We are off our heads with delight! Let me think; I wrote you last on Thursday. I have not heard from you since, but did not expect to. We are frightfully busy at the Office, and of course in the evenings I am still at Bazaar work. On Saturday afternoon I left at 12.30 and went to dinner with Mrs Taylor, and as usual had a very enjoyable time, finally taking away with me another huge parcel! Everyone is turning up trumps. Miss Massey worked a lovely table centre in green silk, Mrs T supplying the material. Mrs Day gave me several sets of d'oyleys to go over butter and milk jugs and sugar basins to keep off the flies; very pretty ones; also pin cushion beautifully worked, and her daughter had worked some towels. There were several other things, hair tidies &c., and I also brought away with me the remainder of Beatie's boxes, 16 in all; some were wooden and some stout cardboard, all covered with very good wall paper. They will fetch 6d. 1/- and 1/6d. each. But the crowning point of the afternoon was having your photograph. Now you never told me you had it taken with your platoon last June. However, Mr Campbell sent over 3 copies of "Sandy's Platoon" and Mrs Taylor let me have my choice. You have come out splendidly; but aren't you thin, and shan't I have to feed you when I get you? Guess you are thinner now if possible. Are you? Do let me know exactly how you are, as at present I imagine your bones rattle as you walk, that you are feeling a bit miserable in spite of your cheerful letters, and that your wound aches. And that reminds me; I do hope you will have a scar to show me.

Mama asked me this morning if I sent you nice messages from her. I said "No". She said "that was too bad of you. I am as pleased as his mother is that he is safe and getting on" !!!!!!!!!!

Yesterday I went to the cemetery in the morning and brought back the remainder of the geraniums, and the rest of the day sat over the fire, except when I was writing to Heberden's mother, whose address is The Grange, Charlton Kings, near Cheltenham. I told her you found her son stunned, but not dead, so phoned to the doctor who came immediately and took him to the dugout; that you left the two together and continued your work; that when you returned he was dead; that he was rescuing some men in a blown-in trench when he met his fate; that I had written asking you if the doctor is also a prisoner, and if so could you find out from him whether he regained consciousness and sent any message.

It has turned fearfully cold, and there are several inches of snow in the Midlands and up North. We are so anxious to hear if you have received your clothes yet. I am keeping you awfully warm in imagination, but am afraid you are not benefitting really.

Can't stop any longer; very busy; Goodbye.

May

P.S. I forgot to mention what is most important to you, viz. that your mother is still in very good health and spirits. She planted a lot of cabbages during the week, and was none the worse for the work. I tell her I let you know how she is, so I don't think she would let herself mope on any account, not that she is the mopy sort. She came with me as far as the Plough. She usually does, unless she comes to Herne Hill. I asked her if she let you know about those Malayalam shares. She said "No; you can write about business. I don't like doing so." I think I told you what happened. H. Webber told her to stop the 3 blank cheques which she did. She cancelled the order for the second lot of shares, so there is no need for you to pay for them, and ordered the first lot to be put into her name for the time being, as she did not know then if you were living. As regards the winding up of Strattons; we went together to Carey St., told the man we could get into communication with you, so Mrs T sent you a paper to sign. He would not let Mrs T do it for you without first writing to you. If the paper goes astray then I shall be calling at Carey St. in December to tell them so. That is all so far.

```
Platoon" and Mrs. T. let me have my choice.  You have come out
splendidly; but aren't you thin, and sha'n't I have to feed you
when I get you?   Guess you are thinner now if possible.  Are
you?   Do let me know exactly how you are, as at present  I imagine
your bones rattle as you walk, that you are feeling a bit miserable
in spite of your cheerful letters, and that your wound aches.  And
that reminds me;   I do hope you will have a scar to show me.
       Mama asked me this morning if I sent you nice messages from
her.  I said "No".   She said "that is too bad of you.  I am as
pleased as his mother is that he is safe and getting on"!!!!!!!!!!
       Yesterday I went to the cemetery in the morning and brought
back the remainder of the geraniums, and the rest of the day sat
over the fire, except when I was writing to Heberden's mother,
```

Mrs Heberden to May **The Grange, Charlton Kings, Cheltenham** **Oct 30. 17**

Dear Miss Muggridge,

I think it is so very kind of you to have written me so fully about my dear son's end and I am so glad to have the sad particulars you are able to give. Thank you very much. Will you please thank Mr Taylor too so much for thinking of me in this way and if he could find out where the Dr is now in Germany. I should so like to write to him. Col. Brom..[?] the commander of the 6th Reserve Corps K.R.R. at Sheerness in his letter on July 17, says "The 2nd Bat, fought magnificently all day on the 10th against all possible odds. Your son was killed by a shell in the morning. I saw a letter from the Adj. when in London yesterday. The Batt went into the line about 520 men and 20 officers and have lost about 450 men and 15 officers, we do not know how many killed or wounded. Some officers and men ...the lines and escaped on the nights of the 10th and 11th. I am afraid most of the men and officers are killed but I gather the Drs Ward and Gott were seen going away as prisoners. The Dr had been wounded while attending to your Son." Since then he told me 8 of the officers had cleared cheques to Germany so are prisoners of war.

I have heard several times from Capt Campbell too and he most kindly sent me the 2 nice photos of the officers and NCO of B Company and the one of my Son and his platoon and says he believes nearly all his men have gone with him. I tell you these details thinking it may interest you. Mr Taylor has mentioned as being wounded in the letter we were allowed to see by the kindness of Col. Denis Butler [?] from his Son (who ...saw the ...at night) giving particulars of that terrible Battle. I do hope he will receive proper treatment at the hands of the Huns but I know how very anxious all his friends must be.

In the midst of all the sorrow and anxiety we can indeed give thanks for the noble self sacrificing lives and deaths of our splendid men and one longs so to be worthy of them. As a friend has written to me "When I read the details of the fighting – the splendid stand made by our officers and men in the face of hopeless odds ones heart thrilled with pride and admiration of their deeds and that they are ours and in spite of your deep grief. You must feel proud that your Son – and such a son - was one of that glorious band." Forgive me if I have said too much but as a friend of those splendid men, I think you will appreciate these words.

Believe me

Sincerely
Mary Heberden

THE GRANGE,
CHARLTON KINGS,
CHELTENHAM.

Dear Miss Muggridge,

I think it is so very good of you to have written me so fully about my dear Son's end, & I am so glad to have the sad particulars you are able to give. Thank you very much. Will you please thank Mr Taylor too so much for thinking of me in this way, & if he could find out where the R. is now in Germany, I should so like to

(who swam the river at night)
from his Son. Every particular of that terrible battle. I do hope he will receive proper treatment at the hands of the Huns but I know how very anxious all his friends must be.

In the midst of all the sorrow & anxiety we can indeed give thanks for the noble self sacrificing lives & deaths of our splendid men, & one longs so to be worthy of them. As a friend has written "one" when I read the details of the fighting — the splendid stand made by our Officers & men. In the face of hopeless odds, one's heart thrilled with pride & admiration of their deeds — & that they were ours. And in spite of, & deep grief, you must feel proud that your Son — & such a Son, was one of that glorious band — — For me one of a thousand

Miss Muggridge
18. Manor Road
Beckenham
Kent.

CHELTENHAM 6.30 PM OCT 30 17
CHELTENHAM 6.30 PM OCT 30 17

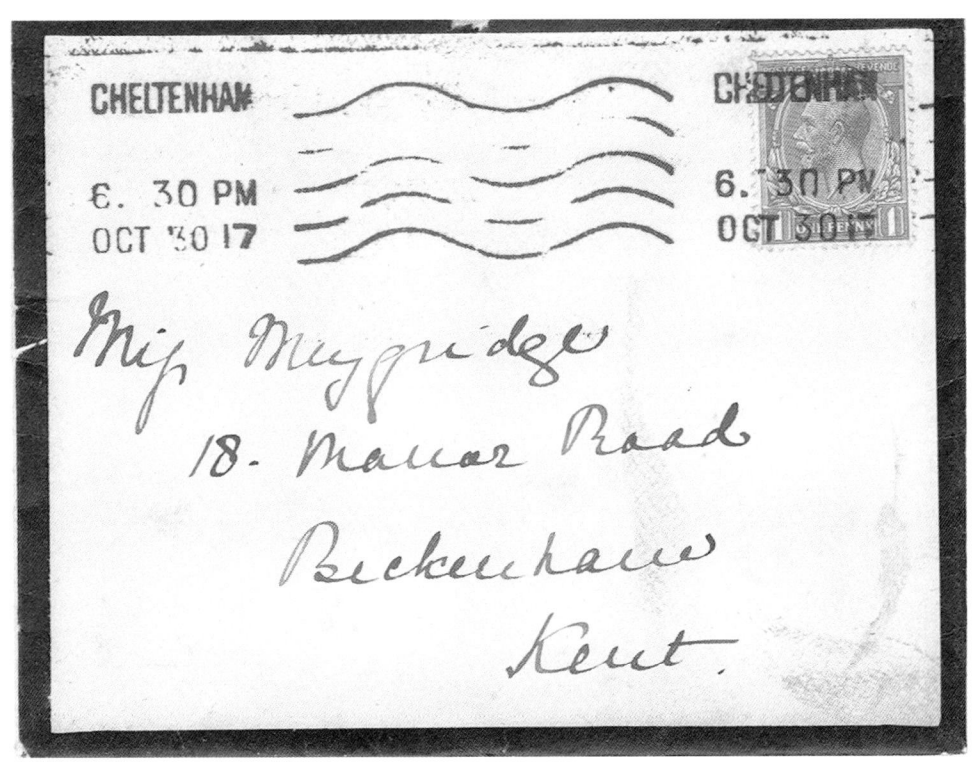

May to David   Office   31.10.17   No.26.

My dear David,

I have put by £8 this month (this is pay day), and that is all the news I have for you.

No, it isn't. Last night a letter came from David Smith saying he is laid up with concussion of the brain owing to an accident, and that Esther and the children are away in Northants at a farm; he took them there last Sunday week, and was to have gone down last Sunday, only couldn't on account of the accident, so he wrote and told Esther he was working on Sunday instead as he did not want her to worry about him; in fact, she would only come straight back with the children, and she is not due home till next Sunday, I think. I wrote him a short note this morning saying I was sorry he was queer, hoped it was nothing serious, that I would not tell Esther who was the most devoted wife and mother in existence, and that I would write and tell her how the Sale was going on. I wrote to her this morning, just mentioning that David had let me have her address, and told her I had made a red jersey and cap for a boy, and was now making a green jersey and tam o'shanter for boy, and that Mama was much better, also that our efforts in the Sale line exceeded £100.

Maud has just popped in. She is going to spend the next weekend with us, and is just like a child for excitement. She is the greatest oddity out, and you have no idea how amusing. She is so desperately earnest over everything, especially trivials, and is always changing her mind. I do wish I could hear whether you have received any of the books that have been sent you; also clothing.

Yesterday for a change I lost my early mainline train, so came up by the 8.46 Mid Kent. It was pouring with rain, so did not do my usual Alpine climb along the end of the platform. It was rather exciting in a way. The train was in the station, and ourselves too, for a quarter of an hour before it started, and we got quite excited in case anyone else should get in. However, our scowls were efficacious. At last the train whistled, and slowly crawled out. No sooner had it cleared the platform than –

(To be continued in our next.)

Goodbye

May

P.S. Our Palmist told me I ought to be an author, as I should be very good at writing tales. What do you think? She said I had an inventive brain. Sounds as though I ought to be an excellent fibber.

May to David   Office   2.11.17

My dear David,

Yesterday we raffled the picture and got 75/- for it. It was won by one of the staff girls I am glad to say. Goods are still pouring in. I have finished the boy's jersey in green and a tam o'shanter. Next Friday is Lord Mayor's Show Day, and the chief wants to celebrate it by letting the girls show their goods up here to their friends, and to the wives of the chiefs if they care to come. The General Manager said he would not have anyone up to the Office, but the chief may overrule him, as he has before for us.

I had a letter from Mrs Heberden the other night. I meant to have brought it up and quoted pieces from it, but forgot so will try Monday.

There is no news. Very busy. Things are going on as usual. They are very busy indeed, or think they are, on the ground floor, so that last evening, at closing time, Maud popped in and said she was fearfully worried and was sure she would be dismissed, so I conclude she has made some trivial fault or omission that does not matter at all.

If ever I take to journalism (which I ought to do according to "our palmist") I shall write a book on temporary clerks. This is what happened yesterday:-

There is a man, named Threadgold, who spends his day running about for other people, though he is called a clerk. By the bye, the supers spend half their time looking for others, and the other half quarrelling with them when found. The said Threadgold came up to me for the seventieth time about 4.0. Then came half an hours lull. Then a pompous creature of huge dimensions without any sideways sailed slowly and magistically in. On reaching my desk he bowed very carefully. I was expecting an accident but it didn't come. Then in a ridiculous small voice he asked "Is Mr Threadgold up here?" Now my room is not large enough to stow away men. I said "No; I have not seen him for $1/2$ hour." Slowly but surely he girated, after giving another bow. In course of time he disappeared out of the doorway. Fortunately it is a good sized doorway. Ten minutes later Threadgold came in. He is the man with the strawberry nose. I said to him, "Someone has been enquiring after you", to which he replied while handing me a drafted letter, "yes, Miss, it was to tell me to take this letter up to you", and he slowly and sadly wandered off.

It was almost an hour ago when I started this letter. In the meantime we have priced another big packet of goods (are you not tired of hearing about the Sale?) and now the salaries have arrived, so I must leave off and dole out.

Goodbye; shall be glad to hear from you.

May

Dec 19th 1917

18 Manor Rd.
Beckenham.
2. 11. 17

My dear David

At last I enclose you a photo. Miss Willsher has just brought them in.

Excuse more; in haste

May.

David to May   Holzminden   November 3rd 1917   Letter No.10

My Dearest,

I have just had your two first letters while you were away.

Now for a grumble. Please write more often, you see your letters are all I have got now, and don't let other people write notes on the end of them. Its very nice hearing from Esther, but your letters are - well, your letters. I also got a picture of a groin, a small kiddie and a blurr, which you say David had the cheek to suggest was a snapshot of you. Please send me a photo, the one that was in my valise will do if you haven't a better one. I put it there in case it was destroyed. I hope you had a good holiday, though your letters sound as though it was good hard work.

The 3 books have not yet turned up, but they are probably in the offing (the nautical term is the consequence of having a naval officer amongst my room companions).

By the way in one of Mum's letters she says "May has been a great comfort to me" and in another (while you were away) "I am longing to see May, I seem to miss her." It is good of you to go and see her so often and do as much as you do for her. In one of your letters you asked if I would like another waistcoat. I would just. Your other went up with the dugout.

Another grumble - your letters are full of other people and devil a bit about yourself. Esther says you couldn't eat, so I guess you were pretty much run down. Don't overwork - you know I can't get at you to bullying you, or punish you in other ways. In my last letter I asked you to get a Christmas present for yourself. Now do be a good little girl (for once only) and do it. You will won't you? What would I give to spend Christmas together as we did last year.

I have had a letter from Taylor's relatives in which his mother seems to have been very pleased with your letter. Two letters ago I enclosed a letter to Mrs Walker. I hope you got it as she has written to me again and seems to be heart-broken.

There are six Taylors in the camp here so when writing put always both my initials and my regiment. Four of us have one of the same initials too.

I have been longing to hear you play again. I miss music. When I get home we'll go to the Queens Hall and we'll - oh well, we'll do lots of things, wont we? A few days ago we had quite a heavy fall of snow and ice on the puddles, so I expect it will be rather cool later on. Would you mind buying a Christmas present for Mum for me. Ask her what she would like. The other day we were innoculated but it didn't make me queer in the least.

I am enclosing a letter to Mum and Aunt Bessie and Ethel. She, Aunt Bessie, and the cousin who lives with Aunt Sophie have sent me parcels. Isn't it good of them, the more so as I know that neither of them can possibly afford to do this sort of thing. I am quite alright now, but I know I shall get awfully bad all over the moment I get you to myself.

Goodbye.

David

David to Ginger   Holzminden   Nov 3rd 1917

Dear Ginger,
Thank both John and yourself for your offer to keep my bank balance going, but I believe my pay etc goes on as before, so that I can get along quite well. Your bread is coming regularly now and is very good, thanks most muchly. I think I told you that your letters arrive as quickly as those from home, especially that via Berne. Will you please thank Mr Charrington for me for all he did. As you can see I am in another camp and have met about 6 or 7 other officers of my regiment who were taken in the early days of the war. They were most good to me when I first arrived. My head and all the rest have now quite healed and my ear apart from the deafness is alright again. It will be Xmas when you get this and I hope you will all have a very good time.

David

May to David   Office   Monday 5.11.17   No. 28

My dear David,
On Saturday afternoon Maud and I went to lunch at Seatons in Aldermanbury, and then took the tram to Brixton. It was a wretched grey day and at times rained. I bought a small coney hat which is most comfy. We also did some other shopping, not so interesting though, and then went home to tea. Every few minutes during the weekend Maud exclaimed how she was enjoying herself, and I think she did. On arriving she told Mama she was going to let herself go and gave me a good cheeking as she had to behave herself so much at the Office. However, Ethel took good care she did not get a chance of cheeking anyone, and she was busy the whole time receiving shocks from Ethel. For instance, during Saturday evening Maud remarked that she had not washed her hair this week. I immediately turned to Ethel and said seriously "We have a small tooth comb, haven't we?" to which Ethel replied in a tragic stage whisper "No, we wore it out you know; but we have a good supply of Keatings." Can you imagine Maud's horror? She almost choked several times. On Sunday morning we went to Christ Church to hear Harrington Lees. He is a fine preacher and a very clever man. He has written several books, and his fame has reached even that remote district called Clapham. Maud was charmed. After Church we walked through Kelsey Park then home. In the afternoon, being a glorious day, we again went out for a walk round about Kelsey Park. Of course directly the others saw my new hat they called it "Fido", and both Mama (who has been quite lively and jocular the whole time, teasing us as much as the rest) and Ethel teased me about it for quite half an hour, saying the most atrocious things. When off to Church Mama said very solemnly "I think you had better take a lead for Fido" (I had got my new hat on), which made Maud gasp out "O, and on a Sunday too". Just what Auntie said in Switzerland! Do you remember? Wasn't that a grand holiday?
I had a p.c. from Mrs Taylor on Saturday morning asking me to dinner that day. I have not

replied, so had better write to her now. I had told her Maud was coming for the weekend. I guess I will spend next weekend with her, unless she is off to Watford.

I wish I had a letter from you that I could copy out for her; perhaps one will come tonight. Hope you are hearing from us.

Maud's immediate chief, Bishop, has been away for a fortnight, during which time his 3 or 4 girls got at sixes and sevens. He has returned this morning, and actually shook hands with Maud. She is now in her seventh of delight. Really we would not think of saying the awful things to her that we do if she were not so desperately genteel. She has her wits about her after all. She said to Mama "I let people know I know May apart from business, as I quickly found out it would pay me". And she was the one to say she wanted to get on on her own merits only!

Last Friday I posted my photo to you. Do you like it?

May

May to David   Office   9.11.17

My dear David,

The Show is now going by, and by the noise of cheering and usual conglomeration of other sounds, called bands, I should think it was a huge success. I have sent my girls downstairs. No one offered them seats, so when the music started I phoned to the ground floor and asked if the supers were gazing. On hearing Yes I told the man what I thought of him and his want of loyalty to the staff girls and gave him $1/2$ minute to find places for them all while they were on their way down. I wonder what is happening. For my own part I have been out on the parapet and thoroughly enjoyed seeing two tanks try to get round the corner in front of No. 1. You know it is a sharp corner, and Moorgate St is narrow, evidently not built for tanks. Well, they got round eventually, and nobody was hurt, but you can trace those tanks unmistakeably. They have left big marks on the roadway, quite cuts, and some of the curb has gone. The climax was when a trap door opened out of the top and a red face popped up, then some tacking was done, and away they went amid fearsome cheers. It is a lovely day, and I do wish you could have heard the bands. Some were splendid, and the fanfare of trumpets (or some other instruments, I am not sure what) just before "the" coach came along was ripping, the best I have heard. The girl landworkers looked splendid. Later on when some girls in khaki with skirts and long coats came along they looked out of place in skirts. Girls look heaps better in knickers. Now you know what to expect to see me wear when you come back! This morning I received your letter of 6th Oct and was highly delighted to hear from you. I immediately posted on Mrs Taylor's portion, and will copy out mine and take her tomorrow. I sent you a professional photo of myself a week or so ago. The waistcoat I will start next week. This week I shall finish off my second vest. I am making Ern socks in the train. Mrs Taylor has enough to keep you going for awhile, she says. I am awfully glad you want a waistcoat. Hope the dimensions will be alright. Before, I used to try it on Bert. Expect I shall spend the weekend at No. 56. You see, dear, I have a new hat to show off, so that, as you know, is every inducement to go to see someone. I have given Maud your message, and will write a short note to Muriel.

If I don't leave off and get on with the work we shall have to stay late. The Show is over and the girls had very good seats on the ground floor. All's well that ends well. I have since received many semi-apologies from the Cashier's Dept. They all saved the best seats for the staff girls, and then when the Show started and our girls did come down they let the temporary girls have them. Perhaps!

There are three girls away queer from this department, hence we are behindhand, and the Chief wants us to take on more work. However, he has given us a week to pull up. Goodbye.

May

P.S. When I told Mama this morning you wanted another waistcoat, she said "Bless his heart" !!!!!

May to David   Beckenham   12.11.17

My dear David,

I am feeling absolutely bewildered. Well, it won't last much longer, and I think I shall be glad when it is all over. Of course I am referring to the Sale. Another raffle this morning – a painting of Gladys Cooper signed by herself. Fetched 50/-. I did not win it; wasn't anxious to. There is a lovely etching of Marlborough House to be raffled next, and I would like that. It is the only one of its kind, and Queen Alexandra gave the artist permission to do it. Goods still pouring in. The letters of thanks I have to write each day! Still three girls away ill, and fearfully behindhand with the work. O well, it can't be helped. I am not going to worry. Will get the Bazaar off my chest first. Royalty will be there, so you can guess we are a bit flustered!

I am not beginning this letter at the beginning. On Saturday I went to Balham, and had a lovely dinner. How you would have enjoyed it. We despatched the various letters you enclosed, and Mrs Taylor told me to send you the enclosed cutting from the Sketch Supplement. It is a photo of Captain Campbell's girl, and we think she looks lovely. She has beautiful neck and arms. Apparently they are getting married soon. I reckon he is to be congratulated. Miss Massey saw the picture and sent it to Mrs Taylor for you. I did not stay over the weekend after all, because Ern said he was going away as he had Saturday off. He was not up when I left home, and directly after breakfast he said he would mend his bike and then go off. He mended it, and then found another place and so on. Twice he had to go out to buy more solutions etc. When I reached home at 6.30 he was then washing his hands, having completed his work. I think he patched more than was necessary, as it was not until teatime that Ethel discovered the air was leaking at the valve, and not from the holes as he thought. He said – No, I won't say what he said. It certainly would not pass the censor. In the evening I finished the second vest, and now I am going to start the waistcoat. On Sunday morning I planted the bulbs at the cemetery, and spent the afternoon and evening sitting over the fire. Went to bed early and had nightmares over the Bazaar.

Mrs Taylor was very pleased at receiving your letter. She had started to worry over you as she had not had any postcards or letters from you for 2 or 3 weeks. I believe she thought you were at least dead. I am wondering whether I have upset Ethel, your Ethel. You remember you wrote her a letter which I forwarded. At the same time as I thought she would wonder at my writing on the envelope I enclosed a note to say you were only allowed to send one letter of 6 pages a fortnight. I also mentioned that I had had from you a very interesting narrative of your doings while in the Army which I would be pleased to let her see; and that when I had time I wanted to type it all out, and would give her a copy if she liked. She wrote back to Mrs Day asking if it were true you could only write so little? It is a strange thing, but that palmist of ours told me to beware of a redheaded man or woman all my life; I was to have nothing at all to do with him, as mischief would only follow. I wish I had not told her you wrote me; I did not think at the time it might make her jealous. I ought to have thought of it as I know how very fond of you she is. I forgot to write you about Mrs Heberden's letter last week. This is what she said:- "I think it is so very good of you to have written me so fully about our dear son's end, and I am glad to have the sad particulars you are able to give. Thank you very much. Will you please thank Mr Taylor too so much for thinking of me in this way, and if he could find out where the Dr is now in Germany I should so like to write to him." etc etc. I am saving the letter for you. I do hope if she write to the Dr that he won't say his leg was blown off, though I expect he will. At any rate I hope he won't mention that he was conscious.

Can't stop any longer. Will write again Wednesday. Goodbye,

May

P.S. I don't think you can be feeling well; or, why were those officers good to you?
P.P.S. So you indulge in day dreams. So do I each night, and always in the train. We have grand conversations, but they always end in one way, - not Lieder ohne Worte, but Conversations without words.

May to David   Office   14.11.17

My dear David,

I am still living in a whirl, and shall not be able to write to you again until Monday, as tomorrow at 8.0 am I start on this Bazaar, and it will not be over till 10.0 pm on Saty. We have taken about £70 in cash, - donations, raffles and goods sold in advance. It is desperately hard work, but grand fun. Princess Beatrice is coming tomorrow. Lady Jellicoe the day after, and Lady Macready the day after. In the chair will be the Duchess of Somerset, the Marquis de Ruvigny and Major Studd – not altogether though. Already I am feeling weary, as though I would like to sleep with Someone's arms round me, not that I could thus indulge even if that Someone were in England. Now, I didn't say I meant you, did I?

Yesterday morning I ordered the following books from Batsford's, to be sent with "Estimating" which I found in your bookcase, as you said, and also a catalogue of Architects &c books also in your bookcase, as it might give you ideas:-

Laxton's Builders Price Book, Carlyle's French Revolution, Lockhart's Life of Napoleon, Irvings Life of Mahomet & Froudes Historical Essays; also The Builder & Builders Journal every month alternatively.

They were not in stock, but would be sent immediately.

Mrs Taylor called this morning to show me the certificate she had received from Brigstock's for 10 shares. It is put into her name for the time being, but she is going to write on a slip of paper and attach that is your property. The second lot you know she cancelled as they were not paid for.

I have started your waistcoat, and am enjoying my evenings accordingly.

We had some grand fun just now. As I told you we have had several raffles. One of the Accountant's men thought he would play a trick, so pasted a coloured picture of Maud Allan on to a large piece of thick brown paper, sent it round by a girl to Mrs Daffarn we could raffle it. The girl thought he meant it. We did not let on that we could see the joke, and Mrs Daffarn told her to say it would be raffled very soon. After lunch I sent for him. At first he thought I was angry with him for playing about (I do not send for people unless something serious is up) and did not want to come. Others said he must, so he did his hair and came round. I said very seriously "Thank you, Mr Young, for the picture. It was a 6d raffle, and I am pleased to say you are the winner. Please pay your 6d to Miss Daffarn", and I handed him back the picture. He paid the 6d!

We are a week behind with our work, and will of course get worse, as I shall scarcely be here for the rest of the week. Ern is going to help us tomorrow morning to decorate the stall. He has been collecting nails for several evenings!

Can't stop longer, so Goodbye

David to May   Holzminden   November 16th 1917

My Dearest,

I have your letters from October 1st to 10th. Although you didn't say anything in your letters while you were away, I got the idea somehow that the holiday was not the success that your holiday should be. I am awfully sorry and wish I could have been with you. Never mind we'll have some splendid holidays later on. I have now got 5 blurs (said to be snapshots), but if that is the best David Smith can do, its time he gave up caricature and took to photography. Now do please send me a photo. I want one badly. In the one where you are somewhat discernible you seem to have got thinner. I hope it isn't so. I am very glad indeed that you are leaving half an hour earlier but don't spoil it by staying late. Can't you get Lutt to reduce it still further. Thanks very much for writing more often - I look forward to your letters more than to anything else.

Thanks very much too for going about those books, it is good of you. Please get the money from Mum and by the bye will you please add any other money Mum has of mine to that other amount. As you know Mum always has some forms to fill up at the beginning of the year, would you mind helping her with them. I am enclosing a letter to her as usual and also a form asking for some books from the Board of Education. Will you please forward it to them. Your first three books haven't come yet, but I live in hopes.

My football things have arrived and will be most useful for although we don't play football, I intend to go for a run round the enclosure every morning by way of keeping fit.

I was inoculated again yesterday. They do it in one's chest here, instead of the arm which I think is better, as it doesn't make one's arm stiff.

Within the last few days two of the officers who were taken at the same time a myself have turned up here. They left Karlsruhe for another camp before I did and have now come here.

I hope Mrs Muggridge is better and please thank her for saving that paper for me. In one of your letters you mention a Frenchman's cap. That same Frenchman (he was a servant in the camp) was awfully good to me in other ways. My ear was giving me a good deal of trouble at the time and I wasn't very well generally and was lying about most of the day and he used to bring me small offerings, such as some dried fruit, a piece of chocolate etc. etc.

Your suggestion with regard to the bungalow is quite alright. The kitchen could be in the centre and the front entrance at the side, with the staircase going up close to it. I haven't yet drawn it out, but will do so. I think it should work alright. The aspect need not make a great deal of difference, as if necessary, the whole arrangement could be reversed, without any alteration to the general idea of the arrangement of the rooms. I have long ago drawn out another house with more rooms, having 5 bedrooms, a good big hall (which I know you like) and the other rooms to correspond. It all seemed to work fairly well, (certainly one or two things seemed to be suspended from the clouds, but that of course is a detail) except that the cost might be somewhat high.

I have sketched a charming old oak half timbered front with stone round the front entrance. Don't expect we can run to it in the bungalow and moreover I hardly think it will be suitable.

By the way have you thought anything about the internal fittings? A good many might be put in in building. The book on Specifications ought to be of some assistance with these, from what I remember of it. Another thing that I managed to put in, was a covered sort of lobby at the back overlooking the garden, which, if it faced south, ought to be an ideal place for tea in warm weather and this without making the room behind dark, as it had a large window in the other end which would be quite sufficient to light the whole room. The only thing now is that I want you to see it and improve on it.

Thanks very much for going to see Mum so often and especially for spending weekends with her. I know how she looks forward to your coming by her letters. So you do at least know that it was my left ear which got damaged, I am awfully sorry you didn't find out before, but I really did write you some sort of an account of it in two letters. You ask "Can I lie on that side now?" I can, for of course it is quite alright now and from all appearances has never been wrong but it will never be really comfortable again until it is resting on the softest of all soft places. I have made myself a small soft pillow which is fine - it makes day dreams much more real. I do hope you have a good time at Christmas. Goodbye.

David

P.S. I want a full description of the bazaar.

May to David   Office.   19.11.17.

My dear David,
At last I have a little breathing time, though not much owing to work having got fearfully behindhand.
The Bazaar which was held at the Polytechnic Headquarters was a great success. We have taken £130, including money from the Palmist (£15) and donations. As we have about 10 boxes of goods unsold we brought them away with us rather than sell by auction, which is almost giving things away, and I told Lutt about it this morning. He said he and his wife were on the way up on Saturday to the sale, but as she was taken bad he had to get her home, and now she has a trained nurse in attendance. I guess your sister could sympathise with her. He added that the baby who is 7 months old and long for her age is in want of some things, and that if I brought them up he would take a selection home; also that we might have a private sale on Saturday week at the Office. What we cannot sell then we will pass on to Mrs Maconachie and anyone else who has a Bazaar for the Wounded.
Before the first morning was up my feet were aching. It was hard work decorating the stall. It was about midnight when I reached home on Thursday night, (and then I was too tired to sleep,) a little earlier on Friday, and 1. 30. Saturday night. Ern came all three nights, I am glad to say. It was announced on Saturday night that the Bazaar had then reached £1700. I expect the total will be £2000. All stalls but one were run by Insurance Offices, and all but ourselves were helped by the Heads and Directors. Our Palmist was the hit of the evening, and many

were turned away. The other Palmist was a fraud, though gorgeously arrayed.

The first day I think I told you Princess Beatrice came, with the Marquis de Ruvigny in the Chair. The Marquis spotted our Palmist and promptly had his palm read. He was delighted and gave a guinea. The Princess made straight for some socks on our Stall, after of course being introduced to me (!), turned them well over and then selected 3 made by Mrs Taylor. Mine she snubbed, but I afterwards sold them to a Northern Johnny. The Marquis paid. The second day the opening was far livelier - Lady Jellicoe, with the Duchess of Somerset in the Chair. The latter made a good long speech which made everyone laugh, and Lady Jellicoe spoke very well, but not for so long. They bought a lot. The third day Lady Macready opened the Bazaar, with a Major in the chair. The Major spoke best of all and was very interesting. Lady Macready shook hands with me when introduced. Being on the Committee I had to be introduced formally. Altogether it was hard work with plenty of fun.

I thought I would stay in bed on Sunday, but got up to breakfast after all.

Mrs Taylor came on Saturday afternoon and was with Ethel. Maud had arranged to meet Mrs Taylor at the entrance at 2. 30, but turned up with a Sunday school teacher, or something of that sort, and so did not trouble about your mother or Ethel. She has gone down in everyone's estimation. She might have waited for the two ladies and then gone with the gentleman.

Can't stop longer. Will finish Wednesday.

May

David to Ginger   Holzminden   Nov 19th 1917   Post Card No. 3

I have had your letter of Sept 13th via home, this being the third, also a long epistle "with love and kisses from Erl Linn" and the two photos. Please thank Erl for her letter and ask her to write again. Today I had the third parcel from Harrods. It is awfully good of both of you and John to send these things and also for your offer with regard to my bank balance. I believe my pay goes on as before, so that I can get along quite well that far. I am also getting your bread from Berne, which I shall be very glad if you would continue. I am quite alright, my ear giving me now no trouble, beyond the fact that it rings a good deal, but this will probably wear off in time. Thanks very much indeed for everything. The photos are excellent.

David

Mrs Heberden to May   The Grange, Charlton Kings, Cheltenham   Nov.19.17

Dear Miss Muggridge,

You were so very kind in letting me know all Mr Taylor was able to tell me about my son's death on July 10 that I should like you to know a week ago I received a letter from a Sergt. Taylor (now a prisoner of War in Germany at Leinburg-am-Lahn) of the 2nd K.R.R. who was with my dear son when he died. We had hoped from what you told us that he had not regained consciousness, but Sergt. Taylor said he was hit in the leg and badly wounded while digging out 4 or 5 of his men who were buried in the trench. He had to have his leg off and died shortly afterwards leaving a message for us at home. He could not hear the right address, but though his letter was directed The Manor, Cheltenham, it came through. He added "I must say he was a brave soldier and died a hero".

It was very nice of him to write and I am thankful to know that a shell fell afterwards and buried the dugout with the body so that no Germans touched it.

I think it is so very nice of these brave soldiers to think of me in my sorrow and I hope you will tell Mr Taylor so, and he may like to know that the Sergt. was with him to the very last. I do hope you have good accounts of him and that his wounds are doing well, and that he is in a good camp, as we hear such different accounts any how. I know how very anxious all his friends must be and I sympathise so much with them. Again thanking you for so kindly writing. Believe me

Yours sincerely,
Mary Heberden

1944
Jan. 17th

18 Manor Road,
Beckenham.
20.11.17.

My dear David,
    Yesterday's letter ended rather abruptly, and so I expect will this.   I can't catch up with the work.
    The Insurance Institute is now opened to women, so as there was a lecture last night on Marine Insurance I went with one of my girls.   The lecture was most interesting.   I think I told you Lutt wanted me to take over the Marine business, and I would like to, only I know nothing about it and it is very complicated, and moreover I cannot get straight with the work.   The speaker was Sir Douglas Owen, and he was very amusing.
    I had a nice long letter from Mrs. Taylor this morning. She enjoyed the Bazaar, and was very pleased about her socks being bought by the Princess.   She wrote "Go up one, Mrs. Taylor". She had just received a postcard from you which had delighted her. I expect I shall be spending the next weekend with her.

May to David   Office   21.11.17

My dear David,

5.15, and this is the first moment I have had to spare. Being Wednesday I must write to you, if only a line.

Had a letter from Mrs Heberden this morning, in which she says that she has received a letter from a Sergt. Taylor now a prisoner to say he was with her her son when he died, that he was wounded in the leg and that he sent her a message before he died. Don't know what the message was. She also inquires after your health. Both the letters she has written me are very nice. I am saving them for you to see.

I sold some of the bazaar good to Lutt. Sent them home to his wife yesterday, and he has just paid me 16/3. He says his wife never recovered. Wouldn't you think he would have taken her away before now. It is 7 months since she was ill.

Have written to Mrs Taylor to say I am going for weekend, and have fixed up with Miss Willsher for the 3 of us to go on a tour with a clergyman (true – no bunkum) to visit a couple of interesting churches next Sunday morning, meeting at Mansion House Station at 10.30. He is taking round a party, 2/- each. There have been several of these excursions, and I think this is the last. They are very interesting. By the bye, you are paying for this outing with some of the money you sent Miss Willsher. Will write you about it next week.

More urgent work just come in, so I must leave off.

Goodbye, hope you are keeping alright and cheerful.

May.

May to David   Beckenham   21.11.17

My dear David,

I did not have time to finish my last three letters to you, so as I have arrived at the office early will make another attempt.

This is part of Mrs Heberden's letter which I received yesterday:-

"Dear Miss Muggridge,

You were so very kind in letting me know all Mr Taylor was able to tell me about my son's death on July 10 that I should like you to know a week ago I received a letter from a Sergt. Taylor (now a prisoner of War in Germany at Leinburg-am-Lahn) (?) K.R.R. who was with my dear son when he died. We had hoped from what you told us that he had not regained consciousness, but Sergt. Taylor said he was hit in the leg and badly wounded while digging out 4 or 5 of his men who were buried in the trench. He had to have his leg off and died shortly afterwards leaving a message for us at home. He could not hear the right address, but though his letter was directed The Manor, Cheltenham, it came through. He added "I must say he was a brave soldier and died a hero".

It was very nice of him to write and I am thankful to know that a shell fell afterwards and buried the dugout with his body in it... ...

I think it is so very nice of these brave soldiers to think of me in my sorrow and I hope you will tell Mr Taylor so, and he may like to know that the Sergt. was with him to the very last. I do hope you have good accounts of him and that his wounds are doing well, and that he is in a good camp." Etc etc.

Now why did the Sergt. want to tell her about her son's leg being amputated? Some folks, especially the lower class, glory in horrors. I had particularly left that part out, and it read so nicely without it.

There is no news of Helen's hubby. Fortunately he is a mason, so the children will be educated well free. Is that not so?

Did I tell you Esther's shop is closed; that they have to be out of the place by end of year or pay £40 a year rent? Esther is highly indignant, but I don't see why she should be.

Has your wound interfered with your singing? I have heard that deafness sometimes affect the voice. You don't know how I have been longing to hear you sing again.

Can't stop any longer, so Goodbye pro tem.

May

94 High Holborn, London WC1   Nov 24th 1917

Miss Muggridge

Dear Madam,
With reference to your esteemed order of the 13th we have to inform you that as we have no copies left of Laxton's Price Book we shall send Lockwood's Price Book which is much the same as regards information contained therein. We regret that we are unable to send any technical journals to Prisoners of War of Germany owing to restrictions of the Censor.
We are Madam

Yours faithfully
For B.T. Batsford Ltd.

Riflemen

✓ R 17004 Sgt. Lewis — Left out
✓ R. 34446 L/C Turvey — L.G. 1st Div Sch. P. Mar 1917
✓ R 22671 Rfn Higgins F. — Bomb 1st Div Sch Sept 1916
✓ R 19698 — Haines A
✓ R 9946 — Shoter G.T. P.
  R 31572 — George Y. P. Scout Reg Apr 1917
  C 3408 — Stephenson G.
✓ R 33367 — Slaney F. — Left out
✓ R 22577 — Driscoll J. P.
  R 21026 — Miller C
✓ 5966 L/C Lowther J. K

Bombers.

✓? 33947 ~~Rfn Colling G.B.~~ P.? W

✓? 5599   Cp McGuire E.

✓? R15459 Cp Bloor E.   P? Bomb 1st Div Sch Nov 1916
                         Training Do.   Jan 1916
                         1st Cl Sig   1911

✓ 6/1335   Rfn Brown W. W. Bombg 1st Div Sch Jan 1916
                         P.T. & B.F. Reg Mar 1917

✓ R33910   - Alleway F. P Bombg 1st Div Sch Jan 1917

✓ R2856   - Hewish J.   P Bombg 1st Div Sch Dec 1916
                         P.T. Reg Oct 1916

✓ 5/4781   - Taylor C.   K Bombg 1st Div Sch Mar 1916

✓ R22562   - Harris W.J. Bombg Left out. Do. Sept 1916

✓ R22938   - Enerton F. P Bombg Do. Sept 19..
                         Scouts Reg Apr. 1917

Bombers. Cont'd

✓ R 33947 Rfn Collie G Bombg 1st Div Sch Dec 1916
Batt England Mar 1916

Rifle Grenadiers

11623 Sgt Austin H Mus Hythe Course Left out.
P.T. & BF Reg Mar 1917
Scout Apr 1917

R 35278 C/p Hewitt J Bomb 1st Div Sch Feb 1917
Sig Ldn Dist Sch May 1916

R 22705 Rfm Hitching J Stokes Mortar 1st Div Sch Feb 1917

A 696 — Bradstreet Bomb 1st Div Sch Mar 1917

Y 877 — James Do.

R 31522 — Hersey J Bomb. 1st Div Sch May 1917

A 1670 — Rothery W Do Apr 1917

R 31669 — Penfold T.

R 20289 — Gregory Bomb 1st Div Sch Oct 1916

Abadie	Lindsey
Lees	Golding
Ward	Madeley
Robinson	Clinton
Gott	Sheepshanks
Gracie	Dawson
Butler	Simpson
Campbell	Baucher
Monro	Chevis
Aberdein	Pinnock
McDowell	
Warner	
Farran	
Taylor	
Cull	
Smith	
Barnes	
Anson	
Mills	
McCabe	
Forrest	
Cherry	
Hill	
Blackett	

Lewis Gunners

? 8748 Cp Pemberton 1st Div Sch L.G. May 1917
                              Reg L.G.   P?
                              Reg P.T. Feb 1917

~~R~~ 9510 L/C Bennell A Reg L.G. Aug 1916

R 9346 Rfn Hill J. L.G. 3rd Army Sch Jan 1917

203045 — Hancock W L.G. 1st Div Sch Mar 1917
                    Bomb. Do. Oct 1917
                              P

R 20403 — Fountain P. L.G. 3rd Army Sch Jan 1917

R 14160 — Mullis H L.G. Reg
                    L.G. 1st Div Sch May 1917

R 22679 — Hardington G. L.G. Reg Oct 1916

12952 — Evans AV L.G. England 1915

R 16977 — Greenwood W. L.G. 3rd Army Corps

Platoon Headquarters.

✓ C 779   Sgt Morton J.   P.
✓ R 20645 Rfn Mugford   K?
✓ R 20289 —   Walker   K?

Company Headquarters.

9176   Rfn Smith T.W.   L.G. Reg.
✓ 018 —   Hughes F.   P.
  1650 —   Buller R.   Bomb. 1st Div Sch. Feb 1917
                         Sig.

Please read carefully before filling in.

BRITISH PRISONERS OF WAR BOOK SCHEME
(EDUCATIONAL).   *(A war-time organisation dependent on voluntary contributions).*
Victoria and Albert Museum, S. Kensington, London, S.W.7.
Founder and Hon. Director: Sir ALFRED T. DAVIES, K.B.E., C.B.

(Registered under the War Charities Act, 1916).

Registrar.	Number of Requests previously	
Register Number.		Last Request
Form Received.		
Despatched.	Packer.	

SPECIAL REQUEST

by, or on behalf of, a BRITISH PRISONER OF WAR for Educational Books (not light literature*) for private or class study during internment.

Name and Rank ....

Regiment, &c. ....

Full Camp Address ....

    Gef. Lager ....

Previous Occupation ....

Home Address...

Books are forwarded post free. Not more than one parcel can ordinarily be sent to any one prisoner.
The Books should be stated in the list in the order in which they are most wanted.
A separate Form (or a sheet of paper with the same details) should be used by each applicant, and be filled in by himself. If possible, avoid using Postcards.
Applications for expensive, advanced or unusual, works should be supported by a statement of qualifications, standard of attainment, examination aimed at, etc

Subject.	Name, or kind, of Book required.	Grade (Elem., Intermed. or Advanced).	No. of probable readers.	Remarks.

SPECIAL INSTRUCTIONS (if any):

Please show this Form to your companions, and if further copies of it are required in the Camp, kindly state here to whom they should be sent. (The address will be assumed to be as entered above unless otherwise stated) Copies are sent, in any case, with the despatch notes of parcels.

(a) Please do not send Requests both direct to us and also through other persons; this leads to delay and unnecessary labour.
(b) In view of the large demands for educational books, you are asked to limit your request as far as possible and to your immediate needs.
(c) Delays in despatch or inability to supply are often unavoidable. A book may be untraced, out of stock, out of print, too costly, prohibited for export, etc., and the Committee cannot undertake always to supply specific books or all the works asked for. In some cases substitutes are sent.
(d) The Books, when done with, should be placed at the disposal of other men (*e.g.,* in a Camp Library), and all except those of small value should be made available for ultimate return to us, for the use of other students later.
(e) Books that have belonged to a prisoner or been in the hands of his friends cannot be forwarded to him. They can, however, be sent to us for our stock with a request to forward to him equivalents. Or we can be authorised to purchase books and collect the cost from a representative in Great Britain. Books to be supplied "by Purchase or in Exchange" should be entered on the red Form so headed and will be marked accordingly before despatch.
(f) Copies of the "Form of Record" for recording and authenticating any regular course of study pursued by a Prisoner during internment can be had on application.

* Requests for light literature, fiction, &c., should be addressed to "The Camps Library, 45, Horseferry Road, London, S.W.1."
NOTE.—This Form, being "printed matter," must not be sent out to a Prisoner except by Mr. A. T. DAVIES. It may be returned to Mr. Davies from abroad either direct or through friends, who should forward it immediately.

my dearest   251

May to David   Beckenham   24.11.17

My dear David,

I was too busy to write yesterday, and so I am today really.

Last night after leaving office I went to Polytechnic to get some more programmes to send to those who helped us, and today I have sent them off. I have already handed in to Treasurer £132, and there will be more to come! In the evening I continued with your waistcoat, but have not finished the back yet! Very slow this time.

Am leaving in a few minutes to go to spend the weekend with Mrs Taylor. Of course I am taking my knitting with me. Thank goodness it is extremely mild. Hope you have warm weather too, or you will be cold without a woolly.

I was in hopes of having a letter from you this morning, but alas, it did not come.

Will write you Monday. Goodbye, just off to enjoy myself. Wish you were enjoying yourself too, but still you are out of the fighting, and that feeling is a great relief to us.

May

May to David   5 Moorgate St, London EC2   26.11.17

My dear David,

I was in hopes of writing you a nice long letter today, but alas, it will be short again, unless I stay late, which I don't want to do as I wish to get on with the waistcoat. How I would have liked it done for you for Xmas, instead of which I expect it will be Xmas when you get this. I know what you will do during that time – think of me, and that is what I shall do of you, and we shall both enjoy the thoughts.

I left office at 12.40 on Saturday and went straight to Balham. After an enjoyable dinner, during which time the three of us talked of you – as per usual – Mrs Taylor and I rested over the fire and knitted, while Mrs Day went off to her daughter's for the weekend. After a while Mrs T and I went for a walk, taken by Peter. Then we looked at the shops, and finally came back to tea about 6.0. We had thoroughly enjoyed ourselves. After tea I finished the back of the waistcoat. On Sunday we were at Mansion House Stn at 10.10! We met Miss Willshire and Mr Blake of the Historical Research Society and some other folks, and then went off to see St Alphage and I think the other place was St Mary, Aldermanbury. At any rate, we had a most interesting time, and it was almost 2.0 when we reached the Bank again. While in one church listening to some lovely singing and music generally there was a blizzard, but the sun was shining again when we came out. During the afternoon and evening we sat over the fire and talked and read. There were two Artists Mags which I have taken away with me. In the Nov number you were reported as wounded and missing, so I have written to Major Higham to put the matter right. Can't stop any longer, so Goodbye for the present.

May

P.S. I think this is letter No. 39 at least.

May to David   5 Moorgate St. EC2   27.11.17

My dear David,

I left the office at 5.15 last night and bought some shoes on the way home. For years I had promised myself some velvet ones, but have always forgotten them when buying, and so had the leather time after time. I forgot yesterday, but the man mentioned he had some nice velvet ones, good sensible shape, so I got them – 4/11, and they are comfortable. In the evening I got on with the waistcoat, now doing the front. At 9.30 just as we were going to have supper I remembered the front was too narrow, so after supper I ripped it all undone, and away went my evening's work. Have started it again this morning in the train.

I called at Batsfords this morning on the way up and paid the bill. They have sent you:-

    Life of Mahomet

    French Revolution, Vol. I & II

    History of Napoleon

    Froundes Essays 2 Vols, and

    Lockwoods Price Book (They had not Laxtons, and said Lockwoods contained same information) with Stephenson's Estimating.

The Censor won't let them send technical periodicals.

A funny thing happened Sunday. Ern thought that a box of matches which he had kept in his bedroom must be damp, so he brought them down and put in front of fire to dry. Finding he had several boxes up in his room he brought them all down, about 16 in all. (He always was good at hoarding them). They were drying in front of a scorching fire all afternoon and evening. About 8.0 he thought they might be dry and opened a box to see. He opened all the boxes – to find they were, or rather had been, wax matches! The result was not distinguishable.

If it keeps fine I am going with Ethel to Brixton to buy her a hat. She wants a fur hat like mine! And that after the teasing I got about Fido!

Goodbye.

May

May to David   Beckenham   28.11.17

My dear David,

After waiting for Ethel 3 quarters of an hour I gave up, and went home. Just as she was coming away her chief sent for her and gave her more work. Chiefs ought not to be allowed to do these things. So I went home and knitted.

This is letter No. 41 at least, while I have only had 6 from you! Your last was dated 6th October. You very nicely said that my letters were the only joy of life you had now. I can return that compliment. It seems to me you are having a good deal more joy than I am, i.e. if you are getting all I write.

Ethel amused us the other night. One of their men clerks sold his piano the other day. It was not an expensive one to start with. The children had learnt music on it. It had been moved to Manchester and back, which moving did not agree with it. It had had the damp in, and had to go back to makers two or three times. The last time, the makers said the piano was not even worth tuning again; so when nothing more could be done with it he sold it, and got £1 less for it than he originally paid! The piano dealer said if he had 50 more like it he would be pleased to take them all at the same price. The piano dealer belongs to Fulham or somewhere in that district, and they are, I believe, several factories around there. The lower classes are earning tremendous money, and their great idea is to buy a "pianner". The clerk asked the dealer what he would do to the inside to make it workable and listenable. The man promptly answered "Why, nothing, Sir. Only give the outside a big polish, and it will sell at once!" Isn't too awful for words?

Must now get on with my work, which is still behindhand, but not so bad as it has been. In fact, we are now on that which came up on 20th.

Goodbye.

May

May to David   Beckenham   30.11.17 Friday

My dear David,

This is payday, and I expect to put by £8 – as usual, or rather, I try to put by £8 each month, but do not always succeed.

We are getting on nicely with the work; in fact we are on that which came up on the 27th, instead of being 2 or 3 weeks behind.

Tomorrow we are selling off the remaining bazaar goods. The sale will take place in my large room between 1 and 3, and of course we are all getting excited. Mrs Kingston is coming. I think we shall supply teas one end of the room.

I have ordered some more photos of myself, including one unmounted one which I will send you in case the previous one went astray. Have not heard from you yet. Your last letter was dated 6th Oct, and I believe I am getting impatient in my old age.

After leaving office tomorrow afternoon Ethel and I are going to Brixton to get her hat. After that I expect I shall pop in at Balham. Maud has asked either Ethel or me to stay with her the following weekend, and we neither want to go. Isn't it awful? Guess I'll go to Balham instead. I try to spend every other weekend there if possible.

I have done the back and one front of your waistcoat. Afraid I am very slow. Thank goodness the weather is very mild; but perhaps you are not getting it so warm as we are.

We are having 3 more raffles today. They are fun, but an awful hindrance. Of course I go in for them all, but win nothing.

Cannot stop any longer as I want to write to Mrs Taylor.

By the bye, I have had several letters from Connie Hughes, or rather Mrs Stuart Ringham, lately. She is staying at Dorking with her hubby, except when she was in a nursing home at Reigate. She has had another cyst cut out. She seems to deal in them, poor thing, but keeps awfully cheerful, and is always pitying other people and looking after them.

Really I must leave off now, so Goodbye.

May

David to May   Holzminden   December 2nd 1917   Letter No 12

My Dearest,

I have your letters up to No 23 October 25th, the last three being especially nice ones. Hurrah, you are actually getting your photo taken, now I am itching to get it. I think I mentioned in my last letter that I have got those five snapshots, but they only make me want the decent photo more. How I do wish I could see you yourself.

I hope your sleeplessness is not a usual thing as you will be bad if it is. Don't get worrying. And look here, if Helen comes to stay, don't get doing any more work in consequence, you will get thoroughly fagged out and it isn't fair to yourself. I hope it will do Mrs Muggridge good if it isn't too hard work.

That girl palmist seems to be rather remarkable, I hope some of the things she said come true. Anyway she ought to be a success for the Bazaar. I am glad it is going so well but it sounds as though you are living in a fearful rush all the time. By the bye I thought I should be too late or otherwise I would have offered a contribution. Anyhow if it is any good now, please take what you like.

Thanks very much for writing to Mrs Heberden and for taking the trouble you did. Of course the way you wrote was by far the best, Heberden wasn't married but naturally his mother would be upset if she knew he was badly injured. I really only thought she would like to know what became of him. The Doctor was taken prisoner, but is not at this camp.

It is good of you to send on those books to me. I have received the first three, but they have now gone to be censored. It is usually somewhat difficult to do any serious reading as being one of ten in the room (the majority of the other nine are usually whistling, singing or groaning some music hall ditty or revue jig) does not tend to assist much. However I manage to do some. In my last letter I enclosed a form to the Board of Education which I asked you to forward. I hope you got it.

In one of your letters you tell me all about Mum's talk with regard to my cousins' mistake over their youngster, which is rather amusing (the talk I mean) and then you say "She finished her talk by saying she would like to live next to us", but you don't tell me what you talked about in between. I want to know. I do feel injured in not being able to see that new dress and not being able to go with you to the dressmaker. Somehow we always managed to lose that train and didn't succeed in catching the next. Didn't we?

Thanks very much for finding out how things stood with Read & Brigstock. I am very glad to know that that matter is settled. Mum hadn't mentioned it in her letters.

By the way I have discovered that I can hear a little with my game ear, so perhaps after all you won't have to yell down an ear trumpet in order to talk to me. It still whistles a good deal, but one gets used to that.

A few days ago I got hold of a book called "Women & Labour", by Olive Schreiner, the author of "The Dop Doctor'. You ought to read it. A number of the things it mentions you have already told me, but still it is well worth reading.

I have had a letter from Ethel Barnet. She starts "Dear David (I ought to say Mr Taylor, I know, but it sounds so formal, and even if you raise your eyebrows and look shocked, I'm not there to see, so it doesn't matter)." and is looking forward to a "rheumatickky" old age in order to be wheeled to dancing in a bath chair and then appear in the illustrated papers as a "fine example of English grit and spirit". Please thank her for writing, though I can't reply and it is good of you to get people to write. Next time you are writing, please remember me to Mr & Mrs Sandys.

I have been sketching out the bungalow again. I think I can make your suggestion work. The front entrance is at the side as I told you end I have got the two living rooms back and front with the kitchen in the centre, and up above three bedrooms and I think I can get in a tiny bathroom and downstairs too there could be a fair sized place for coals etc. and this without squeezing into the front door edgeways on. There is no waste room except for a short passage on each floor, which obviates the rooms leading out of each other. It all looks alright and even the stairs don't seem to go out through the roof, or a chimney stack come up casually through the centre of a room but still these things have been known to happen.

7/12/17 I have been indulging in one of my "old pain in the side" attacks, hence the reason that this was not posted before. However I think I have scored over it, as there has been thick snow and frost outside and I have been tucked up warm in bed. Two days ago I was down on a list of a number of officers to be moved to another camp, but being "krank" I could not be sent and yesterday my clothes got here. So its an ill wind etc.

Today your second lot of books came and have gone to be censored. They were all "Everyman" volumes, so I suppose Batsfords are sending "Estimating" and Laxtons Builders Price Book separately. Thanks very much indeed for getting them all for me.

According to the latest bulletins "After a peaceful night, I am progressing favourably". I may say that the peaceful night was very much added to by some awfully nice day dreams (arising from that palmist's talk) this morning.

Goodbye.

David

P.S. I am enclosing a letter to Mum which please give to her.

May to David   Beckenham   3.12.17

My dear David,

Now for a long letter, I hope. Friday evening, knitting as usual.

Saturday, a tremendous day. By 12.30 we had the room prepared for the Sale. Before 1.0 buyers came in. I sold a guinea's worth in a few seconds to a Scotchman, and both he and his wife were delighted! I did not give the things away either. Guess after that I cannot be such a bad saleswoman. At 1.0 people poured in, and we had a hard and most enjoyable time til 3.0. We had teas at one end of the room. We possess a small kettle, a smaller teapot, and five cups and saucers, with one spoon. So people had to wait their turns. We gave them a cup of tea and two wafer biscuits for 3d., and they were very pleased. I brought up some artificial flowers for the table, for which we did not charge extra. Altogether we took over £8, making the total about £160. We have just a few things over, amongst them an overall that Mrs Capel made, but nothing of Mrs Taylor's or Mrs Day's. My own red jersey and cap did not sell, but I was not anxious for it to, and did not reduce it, as I am going to give it to Helen for her baby boy. We have made up a parcel for Mrs Kingston who came Saturday and told us she would be having a bazaar this week for wounded horses at the front. We have given her about £2 worth of articles, and there will be about double that quantity for Mrs Maconachie. Out of the 40 boxes of goods, mostly large ones, we only have 2 rather small boxes left! Have we not done well? We left at 3.0 after having a hurried clear up, and Ethel and I caught the 3.22 from St Paul's to Herne Hill, and a tram on to Brixton, where she bought a little fur hat like my own, and some other things. Altogether we went into four departments. The shop was packed, and it was a job to get served. However, we were out by 4.40 and as a bus was coming along for Herne Hill I bundled Ethel into it, packages and all, and she caught the 5.0 fast train home, while I jumped into one bound for Clapham, and then a tram on to Balham, reaching there a few minutes after 5.0 – just in time for a nice cup of tea. I told Mrs Taylor I should be calling for a few minutes. Miss Willsher had come in to the Office on Friday with another ticket for a ramble round the Tower and to service at the interesting old church there, and I asked Mrs Taylor if she would like to come too. She had spent all Saturday afternoon gardening, putting in bulbs etc, and was feeling tired. As it meant getting up early Sunday to be at Mark Lane Station by 10.15 she thought she had better not promise, which was as well, as on Sunday, although it was a glorious sun shining day, the wind was terribly cutting, and we had to stand about. I was glad of those woollies I had made. They kept me in a glow all the while, and they do help my imagination, as they seem to hug me. Mrs Taylor as usual saw me into the tram on Saturday and then it started to rain, so I kept in till Clapham Rd Stn and went Underground to the Elephant where I had 35 mins to wait. Guess what I did. You'll never guess, so I had better tell you – knitted! Half way through the second front now.

I did enjoy Sunday. Had to catch the 9.4 from Beckenham. Met Miss Willsher on Embankment at 9.50 and then took Underground to Mark Lane. I ordered some photos like the one I sent you, and she had got them with her. I enclose you another unmounted one in case the previous went astray. I have now one mounted waiting for you when you return, and I have given one each to my four seniors.

In the afternoon and evening I sat over the fire reading "The Definite Object", a first class novel.

Today it is beautifully fine again and cold, though not as cold as yesterday. I hope you are not frozen. No letter from you this weekend. Hope you are getting all mine. This is No. 43 at least. Must not stop any longer now, so Goodbye for a few days.

May

May to David   Beckenham   5.12.17 Wednesday

My dear David,

Since I last wrote to you nothing of any importance has happened with the exception that I had a postcard from Mrs Taylor this morning saying she had just received a p.c. from you dated I think 5th Nov or thereabouts. This has bucked me up as I had not had a letter since that dated 6th Oct. So long as we get post cards I don't mind the letters taking a long time. I am going to Balham for the weekend, going in time for dinner on Saturday.

I have finished the two fronts of the waistcoat, and am now on the sleeves. Must get it off this week. The weather is very cold, so I know you want extra woollies.

We have sent a box of Bazaar goods to Mrs Kingston and have such a nice letter from her this morning. Two packets have gone to Mrs Maconachie, and a small parcel to one of the temporary girls who helped us considerably. That leaves half a dozen things at the outside. We have to find the donors and ask them if they will have them back before we dispose of them, and it is not very easy to find the donors, considering about 200 people must have worked for us. Hope to get everything settled this week.

Did I tell you once, or perhaps it was more than once, that I was going to turn over a new leaf? Well! You can guess what has happened.

One of my pet abominations is the chief clerk of the Accident Dept. He is an A 1 man, well under 40, and yet still out of the army! This to start with does not please me. And then the bumptious little man irritates me, by his conceit. He has 7 temporary girls in his dept. And whenever I go for a report he smiles his hardest and sings their praises tremendously. That has always pleased me, as you know how glad I am to hear of any girls getting on. By the bye, several of these excellent girls have told me that the man is not fit to be a chief clerk, but of course I keep that to myself. A few days ago he was praising them again to me, and then it dawned on me that he was trying to make me jealous, as at the same time he growled at one of the staff girls, at least he thought she was staff, but she isn't. Then the devil entered into me – as usual – (I had forgotten my new leaf) and I helped him to say the nicest things possible about his temporaries. When he was exhausted I said "It certainly is nicer dealing with these girls than the Accident men who have gone; there are not the quarrels; apparently the work is done better and quicker as well as smoother, so as my girls approve of your girls we will take them on to the staff, and you shall always have them." The man almost dropped, as he is dead against girls replacing the men. He gasped and could not speak for awhile. Finally he said "What about when the men come back?" I said "I don't think they will stay long". "Neither do I" said he. "In the meantime we shall be losing these exceptional girls and they will be snapped up elsewhere. No, we won't risk that, but I will take them on. The chief told me to look around with that idea, and you are the only man who has sung the praises of temporary girls." Then I left him.

Lutt is back. He and his wife have been to Bournemouth a week. She was better while away but bad again now. He has applied to go back to Navy but GO won't let him go. He says it is easier in Navy than doing his present work.

Goodbye

May

P.S. Last Monday I sent you another photo of myself. Did you get it?

May to David   Beckenham   7.12.17

My dear David,

This morning your much longer-for letter of 22nd Oct came marked No.9, although it is No.8 that I have received; it contained Cox's letter, the Stratton's form, a letter for Mrs Taylor, and most important of all, one for me. Thanks very much for the Xmas present, but I cannot think of anything that I want, except you, and I shall have to wait till after Xmas. I was thinking yesterday morning, being such a glorious sun-shiny frosty day, how I would like to be off for a long walk with you (not that we should get far), and then I thought that the war will not last for ever while our souls will, unless we act the fool with them which we are neither likely to do, so what is a few months compared to eternity?

You want me to write more often, but I do write as often as I can. You see nothing much happens to write about; one day being like the next. Hard work all day long, and knitting in the evening which is a nice recreation. War news or politics I must not mention. The latter I cannot understand, and as for the former, I have given up reading papers since you are out of the fighting, only looking at the headlines which are as usual. We are told every now and then we must be careful and not waste food, or there will be a shortage etc etc, but all I actually know is that I still give in our usual weekly grocery list at the Stores, and they are sent to us – as usual. We have never gone short of anything, but live in the same old style, except that I am taking to eat a little porridge before my usual breakfast, with Golden Syrup, and am getting quite used to it. My digestion is very much better than it used to be, and so are my inside nerves – in fact, I am keeping remarkably well. We never in this dept. work after 6.0, though a good many offices are working on Sunday. I pointed out to the chief that it is to no advantage to work late – it would only mean slower work all day, and he agreed, but the men stay.

You ask in your letter all the General Manager said to me. I really forget. He is very subdued now, poor thing; he has lost his eldest son, the pride of the family. He was in the R.E's and making a profession of the Army.

I have sent you three lots of books – all you have asked for, and have told Batsford they are very slow in reaching you, but they say it is not their fault. I hope you will get them in time. Yesterday Mrs Taylor called at the Office, and together we went to the American Express. They can't send you any of the things you want, but suggested that your dressing gown should go, so of course you will get that in time. Your mother is sending all she can for you, and does not leave a stone unturned. She is indefatigable in going about and making inquiries. I shall be spending this weekend with her, and know we shall enjoy ourselves, when I hope to finish the waistcoat. May you get it before the warm weather sets in!

You are only allowed to have sent 100 lbs food per month, and this quantity is sent. This is letter 45 at least. Do you get them all, and have you received my photos? Have sent about 7.

May

5.45 Just had a glorious row with my pet abomination. He has apologised!

May to David   Beckenham   10.12.17

My dear David,
Now for my regular Monday's letter.
Left the Office at 12.40 on Saturday, and went off to Balham, arriving there at 1.30 just as dinner was ready. Mrs Day had gone to Glenroy for the weekend to keep Aunt Martha company who is not very well, but not ill enough to have a doctor. So the two of us were together, and I think thoroughly enjoyed each other's company. Eventually we finished dinner and then sat over a roaring fire and knitted. I did want to finish that waistcoat, but didn't after all succeed. After tea we went out to get a bottle of port. We wanted to drink your health, which we did. You can guess the topic of conversation the whole of the weekend. I had made a copy of your letter to me, except the last paragraph which was essentially for me only, and Mrs Taylor was very pleased. We came to the conclusion that you were as well off as circs. would allow. I never let her think I worry over you. It would only start her off, and mothers are so good at worrying; they don't want any encouraging. In the evening I did knitting as well as drink port, and then we had supper – both drinking Ovaltine, and then to bed at about 11.30. Mrs Taylor puts her arm over me to cuddle, so it is cuddled, while I indulge in lovely fancies. After good night's sleep we awoke to find a dismal rainy day, but it did not damp our spirits. We had tea in bed, and talked about you. (It appears there never was such a lovely and saintly baby and youngster generally as you were). After breakfast we went to chapel, and had a very good sermon. The anthem, by the bye, was sung quietly – the first quiet singing I have ever heard there, and it was good. The choir master is a very nice man I should think. He gave a lecture a little while back on geology, and showed his collection of fossils. Mrs Taylor went to the lecture which was free, and enjoyed it very much.
I forgot to mention further back that when I read out that bit about buying myself a Xmas

present with your money Mrs Taylor said "Quite right, and I'll keep you up to it. I think I had better come with you."

After dinner Mrs Taylor lay down on the sofa, but of course did not sleep, though it sounded remarkably like it, while I finished reading a book that one of the girls had lent me. It is called The Definite Object, and is a splendid novel. I did like it. Just before tea we went out to give Peter a run. We followed him very well, and he brought us safely home again. Then we had tea. Then we talked. I forgot to mention we had breakfast and all meals in the drawing room which so cheerful with its blazing fire. Bed at 11.0. How I slept! Off in a few minutes; woke at 5.30 and soon sleep again till 7.15. Tea in bed again, and then I hugged myself till 7.45 when I positively had to get up. It was not quite 10.0, though awfully near it, when I arrived at the Office. Also, we drank port for dinner and during the evening yesterday. You must expect to find me with a red nose when you return!

Goodbye

May

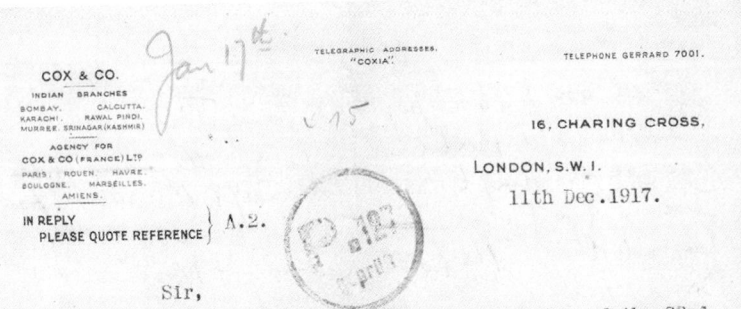

COX & CO.

INDIAN BRANCHES
BOMBAY. CALCUTTA.
KARACHI. RAWAL PINDI.
MURREE. SRINAGAR (KASHMIR).

AGENCY FOR
COX & CO (FRANCE) L.TD
PARIS. ROUEN. HAVRE.
BOULOGNE. MARSEILLES.
AMIENS.

IN REPLY
PLEASE QUOTE REFERENCE } A.2.

TELEGRAPHIC ADDRESSES.
"COXIA".

TELEPHONE GERRARD 7001.

16, CHARING CROSS,

LONDON, S.W.I.

11th Dec. 1917.

Sir,

    We are in receipt of your letter of the 22nd October, and as requested, we will remit the sum of £10. monthly to Mrs. F. Taylor.

    As you wish this to be negotiated through the London County & Westminster Bank, Newington, future monthly payments will be made by us direct to that Bank for the credit of Mrs. Taylor. After deduction of this amount, there is a balance of £77.14.0. to your credit, less any cheques that you may have cashed through the American Express Company.

          We are, Sir,

          Your obedient Servants,

          COX & CO.

          For the Manager.

D.H. Taylor, Esq.,
  Kings Royal Rifles,
    Holzminden, Germany.

May to David   Beckenham   11.12.17

My dear David,

Just got half a minute to spare (while I am having tea and answering phone) so will try to write you.

I do want to know exactly how you are, what you do all day, what the camp is like, what sort of bed you have, if you have enough to keep yourself fit, and what sort of companions you have. We are all of us quite alright and desperately busy. The weather has been glorious today, and I hope it will be tomorrow as Mrs Taylor is most likely coming up for me, and then we are going off to the Liquidator for that money.

I have sent you all three lots of books that you asked for. Have you got them yet? Also sent about 7 photos of myself, two being real proper ones, and the others snapshots, very amateurish.

Campbell I believe was married last Saturday. I think Mama said there was a photo of him in the paper. At any rate she has saved paper, only I have not had time to look at it. I will save it for you. We have saved papers giving an account of your capture.

I hope to finish the waistcoat tonight. To make it look tempting it out to be ironed down the front, only it won't get it till you come back. Also it will want the two wedges let in either side as last, but these I am leaving out purposely. They shall go in on your return.

Can't stop any longer, so Goodbye once again.

May

David to Ginger   Holzminden   Dec 12th 1917   Post Card 4

In all I have had 10 parcels from Mr Charrington via Harrods up to date. Thanks most muchly, it is good of you. I told you in my last post card that I had your letter with the two photos. I am also getting your bread from Berne regularly, which is excellent. Thanks very much for that too. Please keep those books and magazines for me, I should like to see them later on. If you happen to have got that account of our show, I wish you would keep that too. I should like to see their idea of it. I am getting along quite well and I have discovered that I can hear a little with my game ear so all is well in the land. I intend to send you one card each month and other news you must get from Mum. Best wishes for all the good things to you all in the New Year.

David

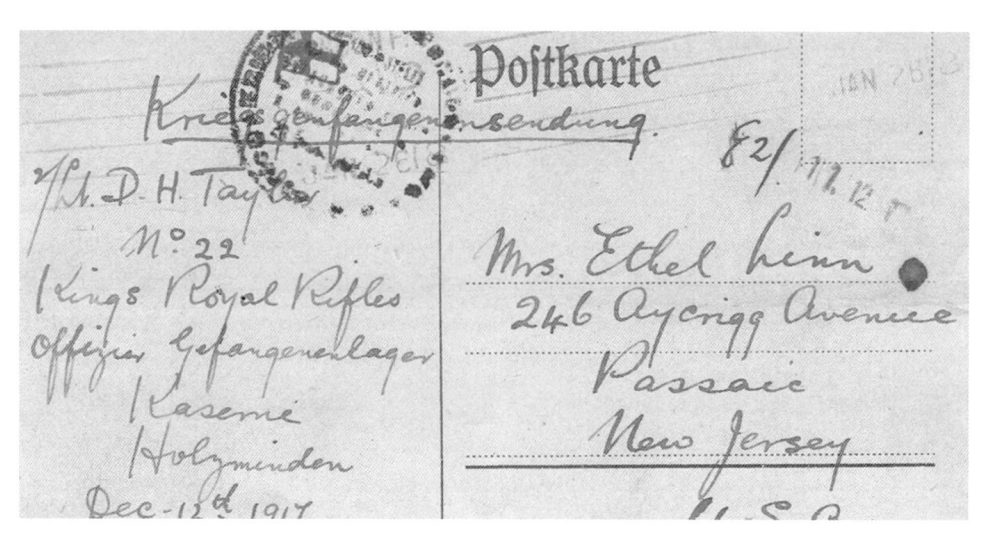

May to David   Beckenham   12.12.17

My dear David,

Last night I finished the waistcoat, and packed it up in a box that Mrs Taylor made. I wore the waistcoat before packing it. Then I went to bed and had an excellent night's rest. Woke too late for my physical jerks this morning and lost my train, which did not matter as I caught the 8.46 travelling in the front part of the train, which we had to ourselves as far as Catford. How we did enjoy the journey! Of course instead of getting up directly I said the words my companion got down, as per usual.

During the morning Mrs Taylor called in and together we went to Carey St with Strattons papers. The cheque will now have to be made out in Mrs Taylor's name, and she will receive it some time next week. There will be another payment to come, a small one, so as far as I recollect you have not done badly with those shares. While out we invested £10 of your money, and will add some more to it next week. You are going to grow rich. Then we had dinner. After dinner Mrs Taylor said we were to get married as soon as you come home; we were not to wait to settle in business or anything else. She had everything out and dried, so that I dare not even suggest that perhaps when you returned you might not want me. I showed her the picture of Capt Campbell and his wife with their bridesmaid (Lady Cynthia North, looking about 8 years old) and page (Master John de la Rue). Mrs C. Is almost as tall as her hubby in the picture, and they both look awfully nice, especially the bride with her long train. They were married at St Paul's, Knightsbridge. I am saving the picture for you. Had better not send it on as it has some printing on the back, (Sunday Pictorial) which i don't expect would pass the censor.

Must not stop any longer, busy, so Goodbye.

May

P.S. the waistcoat was posted at the G.P.O. today when I went out with Mrs Taylor.

May to David   Beckenham   14.12.17   Letter No. 49

My dear David,

I wrote and told you the waistcoat had been sent off last Wednesday, and that Mrs Taylor and I had been up to the Liquidator about Stratton's Independence, and afterwards invested some money of yours. Since then Miss Willsher called in at the office and gave me a lovely enlargement of your best photo. You have no idea how nice you look! Now get vain! But I warn you, if you come back conceited I will take it out of you. I had given Miss Willsher a photo of you, had a few extra copies taken and gave one each to Mrs Day and her daughter, though I have not told Mrs Taylor so in case she would not like it; but they did want one of you so badly. You don't mind, do you? Guess it is all the same if you do now. I would like after Xmas to get an enlargement done for Mrs Taylor. Even Mama remarked "He does look handsome." I am going to Balham on Sunday and will stay till Monday morning. I must do some work at home on Saturday, and besides Ethel is going to Florrie Bulloch's then.

Maud has her rise. She finds that the younger girls are much quicker than she is, and that she is very slow at picking up anything and her memory is bad. Poor Maud! She is having the conceit taken out of her. As a matter of fact Mr Bishop spoke very well of her, but I have not told her so. If she gets too cocksure of herself she will come a fall.

I had a letter from Mrs Taylor this morning enclosing a p.c. from you dated 2nd Oct in which you say you have received 6 letters from me. That should bring you up to 5th Sept. We don't get your letters and post cards in the right order, but so long as we do get them we don't mind the order. The letter from Mrs Taylor said that Miss Massey was not so well. I think her heart is getting weak, no doubt the result of her two operations. Poor old soul. I do feel sorry for her. I have not seen her since August. Just manage to miss her each time. She was splendid while we did not know your fate, and took Mrs Taylor up to the War Office and to Red Cross etc making enquiries. She saved your mother from breaking down, it is my belief. I shall never forget those four weeks. They were the longest on record.

What do you think? Mt new chief has found me two shorthand typists, and says I can have both, one of whom will have to be paid over £2 a week! I did not ask him for a girl. Isn't he different to my old chief? I said we had no machines for them, and he promptly said I could buy two new ones, and did not mind when I said how much the price of them had gone up. I shall have nothing to do but walk round and look important, or try to.

Now I have finished the waistcoat I am not idle in the evening, but have started a little white woollen cap for Miss Carter's nephew. I had some wool left over from my vests, and I think it will be enough for the cap. The money she pays for it will be handed over to the War Depot where she and some more of Northern girls go in the evenings to do war work, i.e. making bandages, bed garments and heaps of other things for the hospitals. There are 2000 girls working there during the week, on different nights, a lot of them being west end shop girls, and besides making the garments they have a collection each evening, a few coppers each, to pay for the material. I expect Miss Carter will pay 2/6 for the cap, and that will do for the depot. I think they are bricks working like that after a good day's work in the city. They enjoy themselves very much, though, and on one evening a week usually some well known artiste goes and sings or plays to them.

We have just had a lively lunch time. The girls have been asking each other conundrums taken from their local papers – the usual dreadful jokes. I think the best (though pretty poor) was What is the difference between the Pope's barber and a demented circus man? One is a shaving Roman and the other a raving showman.

We have just had a nice surprise. The cashier sent for us and gave us each a bonus. Mine came to £9.7.6. and is the second I have had this year. What shall we do with it?

Cannot stop any longer, so Goodbye.

May

May to David   Beckenham   19.12.17   Letter No. 51

My dear David,

Just a week ago today I posted your waistcoat at the G.P.O. I wonder if it has left England yet. Hope so; you must want it. We are having very cold weather.

Nothing of importance to relate since I last wrote to you, except that your letter of the 3rd Nov. came yesterday. How I did enjoy it; and I did like the two grumbles. It sounds as though you are alright when you grumble. I have made a copy of your letter to me, more or less, and sent it on to Mrs Taylor with the other letters. I also mentioned that I would go with her to get her present. She made me buy one from you, my furs, and am I not delighted to have them? I should be frozen without them. I did send your letter to Mrs Walker about a month ago. In the evenings I am now making socks for Ern.

We are going to lose some more men most likely from the Office, and the General Manager wants me to part with at least another girl. So we are haggling. Honestly I don't mind if I do let another go, but of course I shall be a martyr over it. You know the cold weather always did agree with me and make me fell full of life. Already I have had three go's at my new chief, and his chief clerk. The only girl I suggested could be sent would be his chief clerk's, and then he, the new chief and the General Manager would have to share 2 between them instead of having one each, and the assistance of 2 other girls. I am afraid I am still a little divil. Of course I have to be as you call me one, otherwise you would be telling stories. I am taking four girls I have had over a year on to the staff next year, and one new girl expert. There were two coming, but one has written to say she has a better job elsewhere. Again I am a martyr, though I don't know what I should do with her when I got her. We are slack now.

We are having an extra day's holiday at Xmas, half staff the day before and half staff the day after. I shall not get either, as there is sure to be trouble if I do stay away leaving so few to cope with the work, but of course I shall take that day later on when the weather is better, and when you come home. I will treat myself and you to one days outing to celebrate your return! Won't that be magnanimous of me?

Last Monday I went to that lecture on Some Effects of the War on Life Assurance, and enjoyed it very much. The lecturer was 70 years old, and seemed a young 50. He was awfully funny and spoke so hopefully about everything. His anecdotes were very good too, but I cannot stop any longer now, as I have let one of my head girls go off shopping, so Goodbye for the present.

May

P.S. I have sent you 2 real photos.

May to David   Beckenham   17.12.17   No. 50.

My dear David,

Now for my weekly weekend budget.

Friday night I finished the white woolly cap for Miss Carter's nephew which by the bye does very well for the little man. She is handing 2/- over to the War Depot for it. It cost about 1/8 for the wool.

Saturday: Shopped on the way up. Such nice shopping. Bought myself a seal coney and muff, and charged you for it! Yes, it is my Xmas present from you, and came to £2 all but a few coppers. Mrs Taylor said I was to spend that amount, and that she would make me and give me no peace till I had done it. Behold, the weather has promptly turned fearfully cold, so I feel my virtue has been rewarded; but it did seem a shame taking the money belonging to you. However, I thank you very much for them. The collar is the warmest I have ever had, and comes up to my ears, keeping them beautifully warm. How I wish you were as warm. I know you are not. In the afternoon I shopped again – not interesting shopping this time, though, and then made fish paste, darned my stockings etc and Ern's things, and then converted, or perverted, my old golf skirt, the pale blue and fawn mixture one which I had washed and shrunk, into another and more useful article. It took me till well after 11.0, and then I had supper and went to bed.

Sunday: Got up pretty early. After breakfast sallied forth in all the glories of my new furs which by the bye match my hat, and went to Auntie's. Found Helen and the children returned. There is no word yet from Jack, so it looks as though he is killed. Helen wrote to her old chief a few weeks back, and he advised her to go back to business. He is in a few place himself, and there is a vacancy which he would like her to fill, somewhere in Chiswick, so I believe she is going in the new year, but in the meantime is trying to get a nursemaid to look after the children, so I suppose if this works we shall not be having them living with us. I took the red jersey and cap and it fitted the younger one to perfection. Helen is delighted with it. I also took Auntie a photo of myself, but I don't think she cared much for it. Said it made me looked older than I did, but I thought it was flattering. Went home to dinner, and in afternoon caught the 3.19 and went to Balham where I stayed the night. Mrs Taylor was so pleased with the furs. After tea we went to chapel in spite of the drizzling rain which turned to sleet when we came out and then froze during the night, covering the place with a sheet of ice this morning. The sermon was most interesting. Mr Brown is a fine man and improves upon acquaintance when you are once used to his excited style at times. On the whole he talked quietly last night. His subject was the Jews, and I only wish I could tell you all he said, but as he touched on the war in connection with the Jews as foretold in the Bible I am afraid it would not pass the Censor. However, it is safe to say that he thinks this is not the Armageddon, and that we shall not live to see that fortunately, as it will be heaps worse than the present war. He says Jerusalem is to be besieged 28 times in all according to the Bible. The last siege was No. 27. The effect of the present war would be to unite 10 nations. These between them would put the Jews back in Palestine. After a while, however, there would be another scrap of paper business and then these 10 nations would turn on the Jews. Jerusalem would be besieged for the last time, and Christ would come and raise the siege, and the Jews at last be converted. Then Christ would reign as a King, the King of the Jews, and other kings would go to Jerusalem there to pay Him homage. I do wish you would have heard it all. It was so interesting.

This morning the Artists Journal came, and I have got it with me.

This evening I am going to a lecture at the Insurance Institute on Some Effects of the War on Life Assurance. Sounds rather dry, but it may be interesting.

I am sending the final cheque to the Bazaar folks. £160 in all. Isn't that good?

Must stop now, so Goodbye for a little while.

May

P.S. You would have laughed at Peter last night. He would insist on being nursed by Mrs Taylor and me at the same time. Mrs Taylor had to have his head, while I had his tail half.

May to David   Beckenham   21.12.17

My dear David,

For days lately we have had the most lovely white frost you have ever seen. People can improve the land, and make gardens look beautiful, but nothing comes up to a thick hoar-frost. The glass is going back considerable, so I expect it will now give over. Every morning I have longed to go for a long walk with you, but then think if you were here I should have to be off to work instead.

There is not much news; in fact, no news. Each evening I have been knitting Ern's socks. The girls have asked to frame your enlarged photo. They saw me undo it, or rather peep in the paper the day Miss Willsher brought it up to me, and I mentioned it was a large photo. I do think it is nice of them to want to frame it, and I have said they might.

Yesterday afternoon a large parcel came addressed to me from Harrod's Stores. It contained the loveliest carnations you ever saw, and were sent by Mrs Wilson. It was good of her to think of us like that. Last year she was nearly dead; had a sudden collapse, and the doctors say she will never be quite well again; heart trouble. She wrote a note and enclosed it in the parcel.

A few letters back I mentioned that the Daily Mail warned people that they must not waste, or there would be a shortage. I thought that referred to England. Now I find it refers to the whole world and not to any country in particular. You see the Daily Mail is now a 1d. Paper, so has to deal in big things. As far as I can make out there is always a shortage of something somewhere, so in future each time there is a drought, storm, or anything else the other side of the world having a devastating effect we shall read in the D.M. "As we foretold etc."

I wrote to Batsford yesterday telling them you had not yet received the first parcel, leave alone the second or third, and couldn't they do something to expedite matters. If they don't hurry up the war will be over before you get the books and then most likely you would not get them at all, which would be a pity.

I am still acting the little 'divil' with the powers-that-be, and have got my new chief in a nice corner. He doesn't seem at all pleased, so I smile at him. He occasionally tries to talk as though he is chief, which of course he is, whereas in the past I used to sometimes to slightly domineer over him, I am afraid. Guess I am too old to alter. Honestly I am sorry for him; he doesn't have a nice time.

Can't stop any longer; this is pay day for the supers, so Goodbye.

May

P.S.1. Some of the supers have given me such a lovely silver trinket. My rings will very nice in it by and bye.

P.S.2. I am going to turn over a new leaf in the new year and not be such a little 'divil' anymore.

David to May   Holzminden   December 22nd 1917   Letter No.13

My Dearest,

At last I have your photo, but even now it isn't you as I want you. One of these days I shall have to have your portrait painted and see whether it is possible to get you as you really are, that way. Still it is good to have it again, but, oh my dear, it sets me longing more than ever. I have your letters up to November 12th. It's a good idea of yours to type them all, as I think I get them quicker.

I have just received the Engineering book and the Clerk of Works book back from the censor, so now I can do some serious reading. They are just what I wanted, I also have three of the other books back. Thanks very much indeed for taking all the trouble you have over them, you must have had to catch a very early train in order to call at Batsfords in the morning. It is good of you. By the way they haven't sent Laxtons "Builders Price Book" nor "Estimating" and I haven't got their own list nor the Wayfarers Library list. Perhaps I asked for these in a later letter.

So Campbell sent that photo did he? It was taken about last June. I didn't tell you as I intended to send the completed thing to you, and then we got moved, and although the photographer promised to send the proofs on to us, he never did so. However it has an additional interest now although a good many of the poor fellows are dead and the others prisoners.

Thanks very much for writing to Mrs. Heberden as you did. I think I told you in my last letter that the doctor was taken prisoner, but he is not with me here.

I have had another letter from Maud, please thank her for me. (Its very good of Mrs Muggridge to say such nice things about me. I am glad she seems better.)

I look for your letters more than anything, but I don't want you to get missing things just for the sake of writing to me. You shouldn't have been writing when everyone else was enjoying the passing show. Reading your description of the girl land-workers, made the other fellows in the room ask what was making me blush. Really I am surprised, not to say shocked. By the way, most of the lady railway servants in Germany have much the same costume.

Thanks for sending that photo of Campbell's girl. I had seen it before. He had a large copy of it with him in France.

You ask about scars - sorry I can't rake up any. Certainly there is a tiny blemish on the delicate bloom of my cheek, which might easily be taken for a ring-worm and when my hair is short, there is a bare patch on the back of my neck, as though you had pulled my hair somewhat harder than usual, and a small tuft had come away - and that is all. Sad isn't it?

I shall be glad to hear that that bazaar is over - you seem to be killing yourself between that and the office work, and naturally, as it doesn't effect them, the men would want you to do more, without any sort of consideration for you. (It was beastly of Ethel, not to reply to your letter and then to write to Polly Day in that way, but she is awfully jealous of you and has been for years, so that makes her do petty things at times. I am very sorry she was so rude to you, but please make allowances for her, I shall not write to her in a letter again but shall send a post card occasionally instead.)

One of the officers here called Bernard, gave an exhibition of some water colours that he had done since he has been a prisoner. He does a number of those funny pictures in the Sketch etc, those that he showed were very good indeed. There was one called "Prisoners of War at work and play" and showed three officers lounging in deck chairs outside a hut, with books which they weren't reading, as they were all asleep or wearing the most bored expressions you ever saw. I have got one picture. It is an illustration to "Rip Van Winkle" and shows two Brownies coming out of the depths of a wood. In the foreground are four or five trees with the light catching a pool just behind them and the depth of the wood behind forms a dark background. I think you will like it.

Its Christmas Day in 3 days. One is apt to forget it, as it seems any time rather than Christmas, except that it is Christmasy outside, everything being frozen, with snow on the hilltops all round. I have had a letter from the T. Square Lodge, asking if they can send me any parcels. Wasn't it good of them? I enclose a reply, which I wish you would send on and also my usual letter to Mum. I have been inoculated again. I am now proof against all things and feel like a man who has just insured his life - I couldn't catch anything now if I tried.

How I wish we could really do one of those train journeys together, or better still, spend a day together in our bunker. Do you remember our great day there?

Goodbye.

David

> Artist CEB Bernard was active between 1914 and 1929. His works have been sold at Christie's (South Kensington and Scotland) and Illustration House. He worked with pen and ink and watercolour.

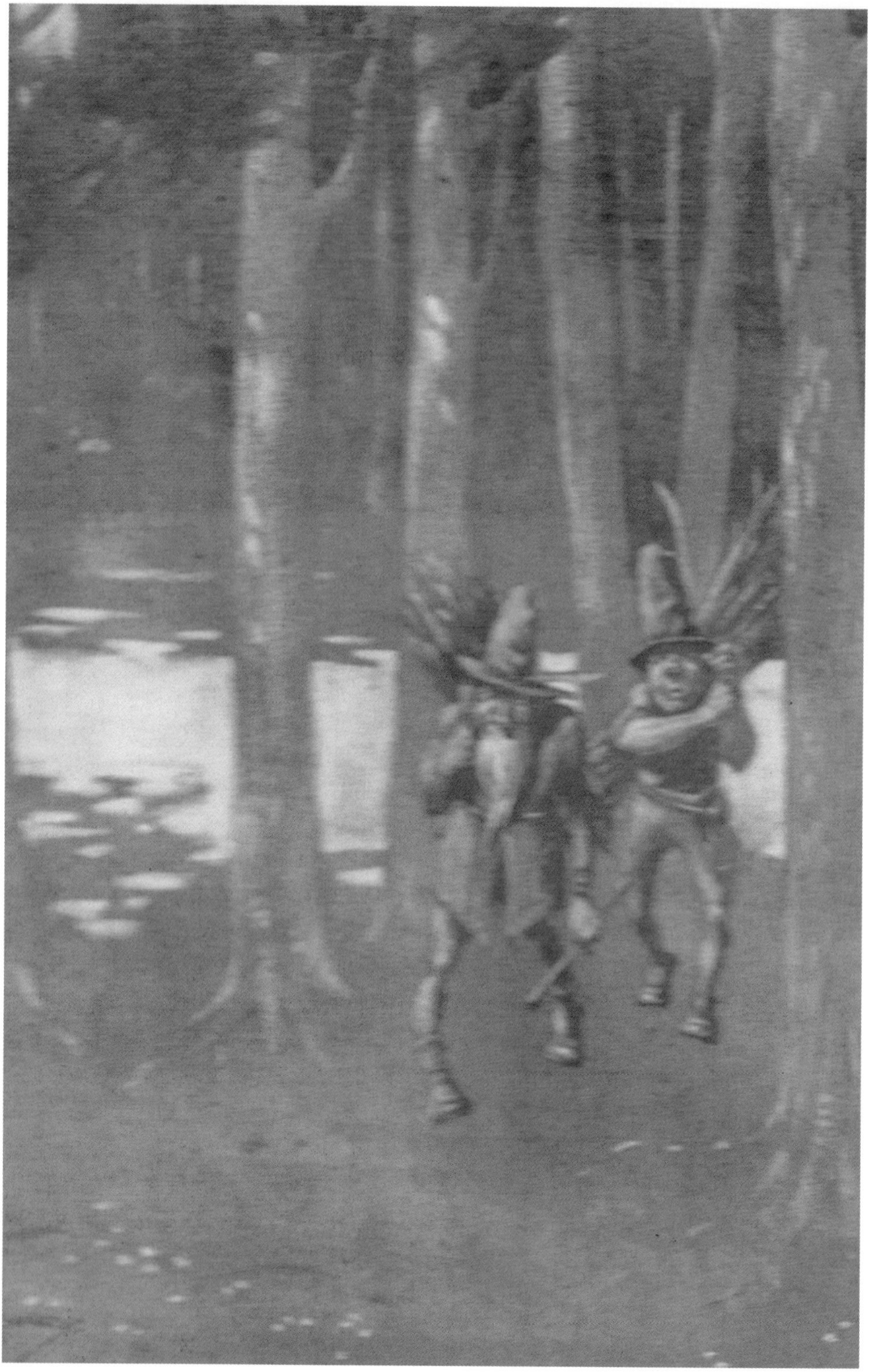

Illustration to Rip Van Winkle
C.E.B. Barnard
POW Camp, Holzminden
1917

May to David   Beckenham   22.12.17   Letter No. 53

My dear David,

Last night I found two letters waiting for me – one from Mrs Taylor containing a lovely pair of grey suede gloves and an invitation to go over this afternoon, and the other from you dated 16th Nov. Two in one week from you! Scrumptious.

At last you admit you were not feeling up to the mark for about 3 months. Of course I knew it, and acted in imagination accordingly. Hope you felt the benefit! I shall not tell Mrs Taylor so; she would only worry, and it seems to me that she is always looking out for something to worry about over you.

I must read all about that bungalow again, and think about it. I don't suppose we shall be able to afford one directly you come back. There will be too much to do; but I can see I must save more than ever this coming year, which I shall do.

That lovely hoar frost is about over now, and although it is bright there is no sun – a day too good to sit over the fire this afternoon, yet hardly enjoyable enough for walking. I specks if you were here we would go to the theatre this aft. Strange to say I feel no inclination to go to any theatre, concert or other place of amusement without you – not even the pictures! Nor have I practiced the piano since you've gone, but my daydreams are more vivid than ever, and they are so lovely.

I know I got a bit thin during July and the first part of August (I thought I might have lost you), but am as fat as ever now, in spite of my morning physical jerks.

Have just finished reading the Money Moon, a really absurd tale, but very well written. It is about an American millionaire who is jilted by an American girl for the sake of a real live Duke, and the same day he sets out on foot and reaches a farm in Kent run by a girl, whom he violently falls in love with on the spot, and marries in about a month, the girl all the time not knowing who he is!

As I want to leave early I must leave off; so Goodbye once again,

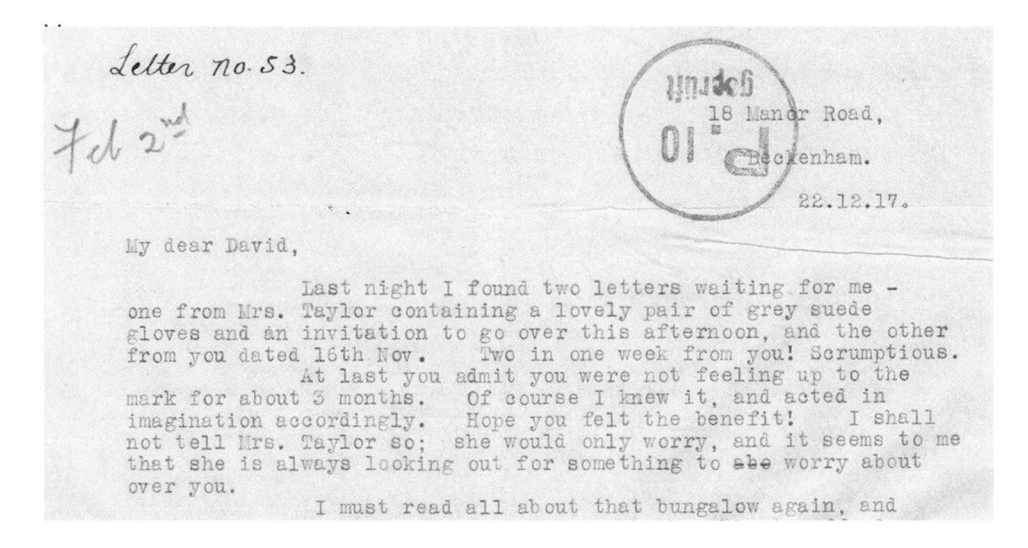

May to David   Beckenham   24.12.17

My dear David,

Christmas Eve; dull, slightly foggy, and cold. Just the day for a blazing fire. I am working with half staff; the other half will be up Thursday. I am coming in both days, but as I believe I before told you I will take the extra day when the weather is better.

Saturday. Left early, and went to Balham to dinner. Found Mrs Day lying on the sofa. She was feeling cold at breakfast, so as Mrs Taylor thought she might have taken a cold through going backwards and forwards to Glenroy to look after your Aunt Martha, who, by the way, is much better now, she told Mrs Day to take a couple of Seidlitz powders, which she did, and then lie down on the sofa wrapped in a blanket with a hot water bottle. By tea-time she was alright, and drank two cups of tea. She must be strong. I reckon one of those powders would almost kill me if I had taken a cold; but two! And she was looking quite alright when I came away, and said she felt well again.

They were both so pleased with your letters. Mrs Taylor was going away to Watford for Christmas to stay with Mrs Capel, but as the weather is so cold she thought she would not risk the journey but wait till it was warmer. This is as well, as Mrs Capel is not very well, and stays in bed a good deal I fancy. Mrs Taylor would only be waiting on her, and then get tired herself, though she says she will not do such a thing as get over tired, as she must keep well on account of looking after the property. Instead, she is going to Glenroy on Christmas Day, leaving early, and I am going for Boxing Day to No. 56, and will stay the night. I wonder what you will be doing.

I left soon after tea, though it was a bright night, and did a little knitting, and then to bed early. Slept beautifully and woke up feeling awfully well at 6.0. Then followed two glorious hours. We talked about the bungalow; at least we intended to, but I doubt whether we finished a single sentence on account of interruptions. At 8.15 I got up, and when passing Ethel's door saw her getting up too. This was the conversation:-

"Don't get up, Ethel; do be my invalid and get into my bed while I get your breakfast." "But I'm alright." "That doesn't matter. Pretend you are not." "But I'm awfully hungry." "Then I'll cook you a big breakfast." "Right", and she ran into my room. Lovely day dreams while I cooked porridge, eggs, bacon and toast. She enjoyed her breakfast. At 12.0 I took her up some port. After drinking it she jumped up and refused to be an invalid any longer! She declared the port had not got into her head. Ern had bought it, and it certainly was glorious. Sat over the fire in afternoon and evening and read "The Lure of a Soul" lent me by one of the gentlemen at the Office, a very nice Scotchman who gave me 10/- towards the Bazaar! Last week I sent him an account of the Sale and a statement of the £.s.d., and on it he noticed £15 from the Palmist. Now that worried him, although it was good money, but the man is really religious, and in his mind palmistry and spiritism (usually called spiritualism in error) are abominations and belong to the devil, so that those who go in for such nonsense lose their souls. In order to save me he has lent me this book. I have read almost half of it and don't think much of the way in which it is written. It seems so babyish somehow. To me spiritism seems tommyrot, as spirits never seem to do or say anything sensible, and therefore are not worth thinking about. This book declares that all these sorts of spirits are wicked demons. Poor things, I suppose all they are allowed to do is to rap and make strange noises. Now palmistry seems so different. The past is written on your hands, the present we know about, so don't want telling, while we have a free will for the future, so that it does not follow that we shall carry our what is supposed to be written on our palms to do. Now that woman at St Leonards (you remember, we went together) told me there were three openings for me, - one was single blessedness which I should find most awfully lonely, another, marry a man I had not known for very long, and so gain a good social position, and the other, marry a man I had known for a long time, and be very happy with him, only he would have some drawback. Guess that is your deafness.

Really I ought to get on with my work, so I will close.

Goodbye till Thursday.

May

P.S. I hear you have now received the first three books; I had better write to Batsford's and forgive them. Is that Engineering book alright, and shall I send you another? If so, what price will you go up to?

P.P.S. We have heard from Uncle. Cousin Bert has applied for leave to get married. They were then expecting him home; the wedding day was fixed for Boxing Day, and I fancy he has to go back to Aldershot the day after.

XMAS MENU.

1917.

Purée de Légumes

Saumon en Casserole

Dinde au Jambon
à la Diable

Pommes de Terre Beurrées
Haricots
Petits Pois

Macaroni à la Française

Compote de Fruits

Bonbons

Café

Vins de Rhin

Pouding de Noël — Sauce à la Crème

HOLZMINDEN

Kriegsgefangenensendung.

R. Richards Lieut
60th Rifles
U. Rose Sub-Lt. R.N.R
Hy Townsend
  2Lt.
  R.F.A.
R. L. Cowley 2nd Lt Northamptonshire Regt
H S Toogood 5th Bedfordshire Regt
D. W. Taylor 2/Lieut 60th Rifles
H Barker 2/Lt. Rifle Brigade
R. Bird Lieut 5th Norfolks R.E.
F Lucas Lieut K.R.R.C.

May to David   Beckenham   28.12.17

My dear David,

Being Friday I am writing to you, but unfortunately there is no news. The weather is still cold, with occasional snow showers. Musn't boast, but I have not had a cold this winter yet, and you know I usually have a terror during the autumn and another in the winter.

Had a letter from Connie this morning. She is still at Dorking. Is alright again after her operation. They had to come up during Christmas on account of burst pipes!

The chief made the telephone girl laugh. He wanted a number on the phone, made a mess of it and then said "As you were". Did I tell you about David Smith's yarn? The chaplain was away, so one of the officers took the service. He always was a muddler, and did not surprise anyone when he said "We have done those things which we ought to do and have left undone those things which we ought not to do – as you were".

Must stop now, so Goodbye. By the bye, I am sure you have a dreadful cold and are wanting a lot of looking after.

May

May to David   Beckenham   31.12.17   letter No. 57.

My dear David,

The last day of the old year. I wonder what the new year will bring us? I think happiness. After all I am only going to make one resolution for 1918, and that is to save £100. I have made that resolution before, several times in fact, but alas, I have fallen decidedly short hitherto. Don't know what I have saved this year; nor can I find out as I did not keep an account of the dates on which I paid Ethel off. There have been heaps of charities, so I don't think I have done very well. I would like to put by £1000 before I finish business. Must.

Now for my doings over the weekend. Left business early, and walked from Penge Station to Sydenham, taking your enlarged photo with me. It will be ready next Thursday. Miss Carter is going to fetch it and pay the bill which will be about 8/6. I saw Uncle at Penge Station and walked with him as far as his house. He is growing a disagreeable old thing. Says the children get on his nerves! I told him he should play with them, and so grow young again. He declares they are making him older. Silly old idiot. And Auntie is just as bad, according to Uncle. Guess she hasn't got over being called "a giddy aunt". Did I tell you Helen had been asked by her old chief to go back to business? She was going, but as the place where she would have to work is at Chiswick, it would be very awkward to get to, so she has declined the post, and is waiting for something else to turn up.

Saturday evening I sat over the fire and darned stockings and got on with my knitting. Have finished one stocking and am now on the second. They will be warm. The wool is about as thick as the heather mixture, but not as good; in fact it is rather uneven. Went to bed soon after 10.0, and slept beautifully. Awoke at 6.0 as usual, but did not get up till after 8.0. We managed to discuss a little about the bungalow, but not much. We were thinking about having glass let in over the fireplaces in each room. That makes the rooms look larger, I think. Also, we would have cupboards in the bedrooms, instead of wardrobes, and two glass panels let in the doors. Could that be done? Also a closed-in dresser with coloured glass in top half. It was a dismal wet cold day Sunday, and we spent the afternoon and evening over the fire, as usual. Went to bed at 10.0 sharp. I read 'Captains Courageous' during the day. I prefer Kiplings soldier stories, don't you?

Here comes my Income Tax paper. Must say Goodbye for the time being, and check the wretched thing.

May

P.S. The "wretched thing" isn't so bad after all. I had saved £2 to pay it and it doesn't come to £1. Hurrah. They have evidently allowed all my deductions, as I only have to pay 9/10 for the half year!

Mrs Taylor called in this afternoon as she was up this way. She looks very well, and is going to Watford tomorrow for a few days.

egiment? With regard to the kiddies very common [...] for the youngsters to go into the Mason's Orphan Home, but they usually have to get a number [of] votes for this, or perhaps the lodge might make Helen a grant. She should, however, get in [tou]ch with the lodge to which he belonged & the Secretary will probably tell her what to do. [I a]m telling you this in case it should be of any use. It is rather a nuisance that Sgt. Taylor should have written to Mrs Heberden. He was Heberden's platoon sergeant, so I suppose he thought he ought to write & of course gave a number of lurid details in doing so. I suppose he was in the dugout when the operation was going on, as I found him there afterwards. I have had today another letter from Muriel Maconachie "hoping that I shall get it about Christmas & just to let me know that they will be thinking of me". Please thank her & tell her that curiosity is one of the deadly sins against which she should be warned in time & which she should endeavour to resist, lest it consume & overcome her. Please thank Mrs Maconachie for her good wishes. In one of your letters you ask if in getting my [...]

& I am beginning to hear quite well again, although it still whistles a good deal. On Xmas Day we had dinner, nine of us, — a great & mighty feast — with a table cloth, Chairman, Vice Chairman, toasts (I made a speech) & a menu & all & all — but to start at the beginning. We drew lots as to who should do what & another fellow & I had to make out the menu. The two cooks were cooking nearly all day & I think about five of the others laid the table. You should have seen that table — it was a sight for the gods. A blanket served for a table cloth & set off the silver (save the mark) & cutlery (all sparkling & winking in the light) splendidly. But the central ornament was the thing. As a doily there was a smooth cotton towel (it hadn't been used more than a week) & then a gorgeous epergne made up of the base of a metal shaving mirror & filled with some silver covered chocolates & some imitation Christmas greenery. Then the menu was sketched on some post cards & showed a big bursting butler ringing a bell for dinner. Then there was the [...]

to do for the lot of us) "Dinde en jambon à la Diable", (or as one of the fellows said "a d—n of a mess") "Pommes de Terre Beurrées, Haricots, Petits Pois" (all tinned of course, but turned out quite well) "Macaroni à la Française" (macaroni & cheese put into a saucepan together & boiled & guaranteed if you weren't already ill to make you so) "Pouding de Noël & Sauce à la Crème (Mum's Christmas pudding & Bird's custard powder jolly good, "Compote de Fruits", (tinned pineapple & apricots) "Bonbons" (the aforesaid epergne was dismantled) "Café". And even then I have survived. The toasts were "The King", "Reunion" (which accounted for my speech) & "The Ladies", (there being none within five hundred miles of course) Afterwards we all sang songs collectively & as noisily as possible until lights out & bed time. But all this is all very well, but after I had gone to bed I lay there thinking how much better it would have been if we two could have spent it together in the way we did last year, so I had to go all over last year again & try to imagine you were there. Never mind next year [...]

David to May   Holzminden   January 2nd 1918

My Dearest,

I woke up on Christmas morning wishing and wishing that I were with you and that we could spend the holiday together - just ourselves. Since my last letter on December 22nd I have had four of yours ranging from November 14th to December 15th. The second photo hasn't come yet. I am hoping for it soon.

Thanks very much indeed for ordering those books and for sending on the list of Architects books. It will be exactly what I wanted. Could you send me "The Builders Clerk" by T. Bales, published by Spon Ltd. (Batsford should have it).

I am glad to know that the Bazaar is over - I know you would fag yourself out over it and I would give anything to have you sleep like you say. You have done awfully well though with the Bazaar and I am anxious to know the total result (I haven't got your letter yet), and I want a full description of it all. When I asked for that waistcoat I didn't intend you to slave away at it when you were so busy with everything else.

It is rather curious that nothing has been heard of Helen's husband. Can she get no news from the War Office, or from his regiment? With regard to the kiddies being educated by the Masons. It is usual in these cases for the youngsters to go into the Mason's Orphan Home, but they usually have to get a number of votes for this, or perhaps the Lodge might make Helen a grant. She should, however, get in touch with the Lodge to which he belonged and the Secretary will probably tell her what, to do. I am telling you this in case it should be of any use.

It is rather a nuisance that Sgt. Taylor should have written to Mrs Heberden. He was Heberden's platoon sergeant, so I suppose he thought he ought to write and of course gave a number of lurid details in doing so. I suppose he was in the dugout when the operation was going on, as I found him there afterwards.

I have had today another letter from Muriel Maconachie "hoping that I shall get it about Christmas and just to let me know that they will be thinking of me". Please thank her and tell her that curiosity is one of the deadly sins, against which she should be warned in time and which she should endeavour to resist, lest it consume and overcome her. Please thank Mrs Maconachie for her good wishes.

In one of your letters you ask if in getting my ear knocked about I got my voice cracked too. I don't think so, but I haven't sung anything since I sang to you last. By the way my deafness seems to be gradually going and I am beginning to hear quite well again, although it still whistles a good deal.

On Xmas Day we had dinner, nine of us, a great and mighty feast - with a table cloth, Chairman, Vice Chairman, toasts (I made a speech), and a menu and all and all - but to start at the beginning. We drew lots as to who should do what and another fellow and I had to make out the menu. The two cooks were cooking nearly all day and I think about five of the others laid the table. You should have seen that table - it was a sight for the gods. A blanket served for a table cloth and set off the silver (save the mark) and cutlery (all sparkling and winking in the light) splendidly. But the central ornament was the thing. As a doily there was a smooth cotton towel (it hadn't been used more than a week) and then a gorgeous epergne made up of the base of a metal shaving mirror and filled with some silver covered chocolates and some imitation Christmas greenery. Then the menu was sketched on some post cards and showed a big busting butler ringing a bell for dinner. Then there was the menu itself - "Puree de Legumes" (half a dozen packet soup powders all mixed together indiscriminately and regardless of flavour, but the result wasn't at all bad) "Saumon en Casserole" (as a matter of fact it was cooked in a frying pan and one tin of salmon had to do for the lot of us) "Dinde au Jambon a la Diable", (or as one of the fellows said "a devil of a mesa") "Pommes de Terre Beurrees, Haricots, Petits Poise" (all tinned of course, but turned out quite well), "Macaroni a la Francaise" (macaroni and cheese put into a saucepan together and boiled and guaranteed if you weren't already ill to make you so), "Pouding de Noel and Sauce a la Creme (Mum's Christmas pudding and Birds custard powder) jolly good, "Compote de Fruits", (tinned pineapple and apricots) "Boubons" (the aforesaid epergne was dismantled) "Cafe". And even then I have survived. The toasts were "The King", "Reunion" (which accounted for my speech) and "The Ladies", (there being one within five hundred miles of course). Afterwards we all sang songs collectively and as noisily as possible until lights out and bed time.

But all this is all very well, but after I had gone to bed I lay there thinking how much better it would have been if we two could have spent it together in the way we did last year, so I had to go all over last year again and try to imagine you were there. Never mind next year perhaps we shall be together again. I think you did for Mr Young splendidly over that picture, only you should have made the price considerably higher.

Talking about turning over new leaves - I think you turn over your new leaves alright, but somehow you generally turn them back again, don't you - but perhaps I have told you this before. Are these temporary girls which you are selecting for the staff to be in your own department and form part of the increase you told me about? Its rather amusing if the Accident girls and girls in other departments are to be under you, for you will then have control of parts of all these departments. The only thing against that is, that it seems to me that it will increase your work and make it heavier than it already is, and that I don't like.

Thanks very much for telling me about Brigstock. By the way, have they sent Mum a certificate for a previous 15 shares bought on April 30th making 25 in all? I am enclosing another letter to Mum as usual. A number of officers have gone to Holland from here, those that have been captured over 18 months. I envy them, but I don't want to go to Holland - I want to get back to you.

Goodbye.

David

May to David   Beckenham   2.1.18.

My dear David,

This year has come in cold. You must be frozen. How do you manage? I do want to know what you do all day, and if you can keep warm enough at night. I am sure you have a bad cold and cough. How are you off for food? What do your Red Cross and Harrod's parcels contain, and is it sufficient, to keep you strong? Do you get that pain in your side again? You want to know everything about me, and all my letters are about myself, but you do not say anything about yourself. What books can I send you now? Don't guess you have your woolly waistcoat yet, and you must want it dreadfully badly.

There is no news. I am still on my first pair of stockings, which I hope to finish to-night, and in the train I am reading the "Lure of a Soul". It is beautifully creepy. I ought to be able to raise demons by the time I have finished the book; not that I am going to attempt anything so absurd and time-wasting. As I belong to the visible world I don't think it is right to interfere with the invisible world. Like Brer Tarrapin I say "You go your way and you go yours, and don't you interfere."

My constant companion and I have had our first quarrel. We have quite forgotten what it is about, but we are still making it up. Lost my early train purposely this morning so that we could continue the making up all to ourselves as far as Catford, which we did. By the time we have finished we shall be thoroughly reconciled, but like that complaint of yours it will take 50 years of the present treatment to be a cure.

We have had a very busy day. I have been getting out my last year's records, and comparing them with the previous year. They do not compare well, and yet we seem to have worked harder. If I could only get all my own girls back we should get through more work in much less time. The supers' idea is to do as little as possible for the money, it is, my belief, - but it is not my idea. I have my most expensive super (£2. 4/- a week) sitting by the side of me, and she thinks I am killing her. I told her today we are about to have a busy month, and that she would then have some work to do. You should have seen her look at me.

It is now 5.20, and everyone has gone, so I think I will go too.

By the bye, now that we have started a new card for your investments there is no more filling in to do, so Mrs Taylor is going by herself to put in your monthly cheque. She is so pleased to do it.

Goodbye.

May.

B.T. BATSFORD, LTD
BOOKSELLERS & PUBLISHERS
ARCHITECTURE
DECORATION
FINE ARTS
ENGINEERING
APPLIED SCIENCE
Telephone Central 7893

94 High Holborn W.C.1.

London 2nd January 19 18.

Miss M. Muggridge.

Dear Madam,

With regard to the parcel of books sent to Lieut. Taylor on the 2nd October last, we have received the enclosed letter from the War Prisoners Aid Association, and you will see that they state that it usually takes two or three months for books to reach the prisoner, so that it is possible that they may yet arrive. We fear that nothing further can be done to expedite them. We can only hope that the later consignments will be more fortunate.

We remain,

Yours faithfully,

B.T. BATSFORD, LTD.

LONDON.W.C.
8.15 PM
JAN 2 18

BUY NATIONAL WAR BONDS NOW

Miss M. Muggridge,
   18, Manor Road,
      Beckenham.

BT Batsford   High Holborn   2nd January 1918

Miss M Muggridge

Dear Madam,

With regard to the parcel of books sent to Lieut. Taylor on 2nd October last, we have received the enclosed letter from the War Prisoners Aid Association, and you will see that they state that it usually takes two or three months for books to reach the prisoner, so that it is possible that they may yet arrive. We fear that nothing further can be done to expedite them. We can only hope that the later consignments will be more fortunate.

We remain,

Yours faithfully,

B.T.Batsford, Ltd

Campbell to Ethel Lynn   3.1.18

Dear Mrs Linn,

I have instructed the Quarter Master of the Rifles Depot to forward the photos you require to Mrs Taylor. There is no charge for them. I don't know what the regulations about photos are so I thought it best to send them to your Mother.

I am glad your brother is well. I have had one letter from him. With best wishes for the New Year.

Yours sincerely,

L F Campbell

> **BRITISH PRISONERS DIG OUT**
> Twenty-nine Officers Escape by Tunnel from Holzminden.
> AMSTERDAM, Aug. 6.—Twenty-nine British officers recently escaped from a prisoners' camp at Holsminden, according to the Osnabrueck Tageblatt, and they are still at large. They made their escape through a subterranean passage which it took the officers nine months to dig.
> A big reward has been offered by the commanding General in Hanover for their recapture.

3/1/18

Dear Mrs Lunn.

I have instructed the Quarter Master of Rifle Depôt to forward the photos you require to Mrs Taylor. There is no charge for them. I don't know what the regulations about photos are so I thought it best to send them to your mother.

I am glad your brother is well. I have had one letter from him. With best wishes for the New Year.

Yours sincerely
P.F. Campbell

May to David   Beckenham   4. 1. 18.   11.0

My dear David,
This will be a short letter as we are so busy. Our rush has started, and I have four girls away to-day, two being seniors! Won't the men be pleased?
I finished my first pair of stockings last night, and this morning started another pair. Almost finished the "Lure of a Soul" last night.
It is still very cold, and every now and then we get a sprinkle of snow which freezes away.
Can't stop longer now; will write more later on I hope.
1. 30. Yesterday I caught my late train again. We like that train. To-day I had to leave earlier because of paying the supers.
I am longing for a letter from you. As I had two the week before last I must expect to have to wait a month, but waiting is hard. I don't mind if Mrs Taylor gets a postcard, but she has not dad one since the last letter. Directly she has one she writes to me. Doesn't it make you feel important?
5.40 Just finished, and tired out. How I long to fling myself down full length.
Goodbye.

May

May to David   Beckenham   5.1.18

My dear David,
Sorry I could not finish yesterday's letter, but we were so busy. Last night I was asleep in a few seconds and slept heavily right on to nearly 6.0. Feel full of work today. This is supposed to be my Saturday off, but we are too busy for holidays though I want to leave at 12.0 sharp to go to Whiteley's to get Ethel some dress material. They close at 1.0, and Ethel cannot get off.
Had a letter from Mrs Taylor this morning from Watford. She is staying over the weekend as they want her so. Your beloved Aunt is much better; the weather has been very cold there, and she has had no word from you, and have I heard? No, I haven't heard. Will I write to her at Balham? Yes, I will do so now. When shall she see me again? I have told her she shall have my day off as she likes, and we will go to Brixton about that business of hers, but she has not got all the charges in yet. She has promised to let me know directly she has them, and we will go at once then and get the matter settled up.
I must get on now with the work, so Goodbye for a short time.

May.

P.S. Your photo that has been enlarged has now been framed, and Miss Carter brought it up this morning. There are at present 19 girls gazing at it, and saying such nice things – about you, not the frame. Thank goodness you can't hear them. You might get conceited. Guess the tale will go round the Office now that I am engaged, and speculations will be made as to who will take my place, and what fine times they will have etc etc.

May to David   Letter No. 61.   Beckenham   7. 1. 18.

My dear David,

I left Office at 12. 0. Saturday as I said, and went to Whiteley's and bought Ethel's dress. Did more shopping locally in the afternoon and mending and knitting in the evening. Have now started on my second pair of stockings.

Sunday I woke up just before 7. 0. having slept almost 8 hours at straight away off. I sleep much better than I used. How do you sleep? I believe you are too cold. Do you have fires? From 7.0. till after 9. 0. I had lovely dreams. We had you home again, nursed you back to health which took several months, and then went to Devonshire, don't know what place, but it was awfully pretty, and there we had our honeymoon. Mrs Taylor came with us. At first she said she wouldn't, but we pointed out that she helped us in our courting, and must now help in the honey mooning. She was wanting a change by then, and so we took her away with us. Sometimes we were left to ourselves, but we generally had her with us, and the three of us had such fun that several times I almost laughed aloud and woke myself and others up! After breakfast I walked to the cemetery, of course having my constant companion with me. On the way back it started to rain. Not having an umbrella I got into a bus, and so missed calling in at Auntie's which disappointed Mama--who wanted to-know-If - our "Giddy Aunt" had recovered. In the afternoon I finished "The Lure of a Soul". You must read it when you return. It is all about the perfidiousness of the occult.

In the evening I read several newspapers. They read the same as ever. According to one article it seems as though the war will be over in six months, another gives one the impression that it will be a five years' war, while according to some articles on how to be self-supporting it is apparent the war is going to last for ever! However, all the articles sound quite cheerful, even those that talk as though the war will never end!

Last week's Cassell's contained several very good drawings and jokes. Sorry I can't send it on. There has been a lot of talk about Government controlled food of late. One of the drawings was a provision shop with three-fourths of a large cheese on the counter evidently of the "racing gorgonzola" type. A huge woman was pointing to it, saying "Young man, is that cheese controlled?" Another drawing was a lake, a notice saying 40/- for bathing, and a dirty tramp who was saying "Forty bob! Why I should want twice that before I would get into the water."

Cannot stop any longer, very busy.   Goodbye,

May.

May to David   Beckenham   9.1.18

My dear David,

Yesterday morning your 12th letter came – a grand long letter. You don't know how I look forward to them. Suppose you had to wait 3 weeks for my next letter; wouldn't you long for it? Perhaps you do have to wait though.

You were queer a long time, quite five days for that attack. It must have been more than an ordinary 'side' attack. Did you take a chill as well? I expect you did.

I have quite forgotten all that Mrs Taylor and I talked about when she was discussing 'Grandfather Christmas'. I believe I had told her she had better arrange all our affairs, and boss the household generally, that made her say she did not think it right to manage other folks' affairs, but might live next door.

Thanks very much indeed for offering a donation towards the Bazaar, but you must not do it. I am wondering if you have sufficient left at Cox's for your own wants after having that cheque sent to Balham each month. Now, don't go short; there is no need.

We woke up yesterday to find ourselves in a white world. The cold is intense, and we are feeling very pleased to know you have received your parcel of warm clothes. Guess even now you are none too warm.

Last night I knitted as usual.

This morning I called at Balham, leaving home at the usual time, and Mrs Taylor and I went to Brixton Hill, where we got on much better than expected; in fact, I think everything is alright now. Then your mother came with me by tram to Kennington where we took the Underground, Mrs Taylor home, and myself to work. Your mother wanted me to go to a theatre tomorrow afternoon with her (and this was after spending nearly a week at Watford!) but unfortunately we are too busy. However, we are going to have a day's holiday together when the weather is warmer, evenings brighter, and work slacker.

Cannot stop any longer now, so Goodbye.

May

P.S. I know you have a wretched cough.

You say my last 3 letters were especially nice. I've forgotten what they were about, so don't know what you consider nice. I think they are all full of piffle and not worth reading, but then I am not allowed to put news.

Please arrange the bungalow so that we don't get any burst pipes.

About that whistling; please imagine me doing it. You know I have always longed to whistle, but never yet succeeded.

May to David   Beckenham   11.1.18.

My dear David,

It is now 4. 30. having tea, and is my first chance of writing. Fearfully busy but enjoying it.

Wednesday evening; got home in time to find half the kitchen ceiling raining beautifully. Couldn't turn the water off. Something wrong with the tank on top floor. 2 or 3 hours later Ern came home and succeeded in shutting of the water at the main. By bedtime we were able to dispense with punts and punt poles. No casualties.

Thursday morning; saw a pretty violet velvet blouse in shop window in Churchyard. Thought Mama would like it; bought it. Gave it her. She said she felt too dismal to go into colours yet. At the time she was speaking she was wearing dark blue dress and brown overall. So am wearing it myself.

To-morrow Ethel is going to Croydon about a new dress, so I must go home. Have written to tell Mrs Taylor I will go to see her Sunday and stay the night.

Must not stop any longer, so Goodbye. May.

P.S. I have just heard I have a £10 rise plus $12\frac{1}{2}$ % which makes £30. Does that suit your lordship? I have had my Thrift Society interest made up. It comes to £2. 4. 2. What shall we do with it?

May to David   Beckenham   14. 1. 18.

My dear David,

On the way up to business on Saturday I called in at the Churchyard and found the shop where I bought the blouse had some material to match for a skirt, so got some. On the way home I took it to the dressmakers. The dressmaker, by the way, inquired about you. It appears she, or one of the household, used to see you waiting for me. Aren't folks inquisitive?

In the afternoon I did other shopping locally, and in the evening needlework.

Sunday morning I put on a pair of the stockings I had made. They are comfy and warm, though I don't yet like the look of them being used to fine ones. Must now buck up and finish the second pair. In the afternoon I went over to Balham and stayed the night. Mrs Taylor and I sat on the floor in front of the fire and talked and talked all the afternoon and evening, till nearly midnight. She said she did enjoy herself. I know I did. Really she did all the talking. She is a wonder. As a matter of fact I have not actually done any business for her, but she likes to have someone to talk to about it and do the writing, though she always says what she wants put. She had an idea she could not do business, but I made her see yesterday that she was doing everything, and so far things have been very satisfactory.

Here come the girls, so I must leave off. Give me a kiss; quick. I didn't say put your moustache in my mouth. What, I shouldn't have such a big mouth! You cheeky beggar! I won't write to you any more - today.

Goodbye,

May

P.S. Very surprised to find myself in a white world again this morning. Although freezing it did not seem cold.

May to David   Letter No. 64.   Beckenham   15.1.18.

My dear David,

I did not finish my letter yesterday owing to somebody's sauce, as far as I can recollect, or else it was that we were too busy. I will try again.

Yesterday morning it was freezing; to-day it is quite mild. And yet there are some folks who think they can prophesy weather.

I read in the paper the other day that people's brains are at their best in the fifties. There is, therefore, some hope for me.

No one has been to see about our tank going wrong yet. Ethel says "Tell David when he builds the bungalow to put a stand pipe at the bottom of the garden instead of having any water laid on in the house." The tank will hold some water, so we are not so badly off as we might be, but we have to keep the water turned off at the main, or we are swamped.

Really there isn't any news. We are very busy; got two seniors away queer. Expect we shall have to work overtime on Saturday afternoon. Rather do that than stay in the evening. Of course if you were here I should (or else you would) object to staying on Saturday. Overtime, 2/- an hour for me, less for the others. Lunch time is up. Just see If you can't kiss me better this time. The fact of the matter is that you are out of practice. You will have to make up for lost time later on.

How are you feeling now? Of course I know you are "alright"; you always are according to you, but I know better.

It is 5 weeks ago to-morrow when I sent off your waistcoat. I do hope you have got it, though I have my doubts. It was the only thing in the parcel, so would not take long to examine.

Wednesday 16.1.18.

It was pouring last night, and inches deep in slush. Coming up this morning it was snowing; now left off, but the place looks dreary. We only just caught our late train this morning, the 8.46. which we had to ourselves as far as Catford. We talked about Ethel's dream which was that she saw you and me get into a carriage and drive off to be married. I told her she ought not to dream such things, as dreams are supposed to go by contrary.

The men called to mend the tank, or rather to look at it and talk about it, just as I was coming away this morning. Last night I got on with my second stocking. I am taking longer to knit the second pair.

I am reading "Where Love is"' by Wm. Locke. It is not at all bad, but I haven't found out where love is yet. At any rate, no officers' camps are mentioned so far.

It is now 5.15. and we have had another busy day. Rather amusing day too. This morning a man from our Marine Dept. came over (that Dept. is in Broad St., and they have 2 of my girls there) in a bad temper and complained to Lutt about one of the girls. She was no good etc etc, so he sent for me. I promptly said "Very well, then; when you send her over here to lunch I will keep her and send you someone else. She suits me alright." The man thanked me and I came away. Lunch time I asked the girl if she would like to give up Marine business, to which she said "No; as that would mean failure"; so I sent her back. Later on in the afternoon I called on the article myself, and a quarter of an hour after entering his room he was shaking hands with me, bowing, smiling and saying "I am very pleased you sent her back to me, and should be very sorry to part with her." I wonder if the man has the Influenza coming on, or if he is in love, or merely overworked. Aren't men funny things? Really they ought not to be left to their own devices.

Must stop now, as I have not any news to tell you. Goodbye.

May.

David to May   Holzminden   January 16th 1918

My Dearest,

I have your letters of November 21st and 28th and now today one of the 19th which gives me the first short account of the Bazaar. You poor little girl - how thoroughly fagged out you must have been. I know there is nothing more tiring than standing about all day when you are not used to it, and you certainly would not have stayed there until 1.30 in the morning if I had been with you, even if I had to carry you home. Surely somebody could have relieved you. What is this that you tell me - that you have been hobnobbing with Princesses, Duchesses, Ladies, Emperors, etc. etc. to say nothing of such small fry as a Marquis, and then on the top of all, this that you have actually (wonder of wonders) been to church (and this on a Sunday too) chaperoned by a clergyman, no less. That Princess of yours was either blind or didn't know what was good, or she would have bought your socks. I have a pair here which are miles ahead of any others. (Mum only sent me one pair of yours). Certainly as far as the feet are concerned there is not much left of the original, as most of it consists of darn. Truly artistic is this darning too, (you didn't know I could darn did you) more especially as no two holes are darned with the same coloured wool. At present there is a fierce contest raging between another officer of my regiment and myself over our darning, but of course his can't compare with mine (although he is of the opposite opinion naturally). Anyhow I am very glad that Bazaar is over for your sake. You did do splendidly and I am awfully glad that your Palmist, being your discovery, was such a success. I want a much fuller account of it all than I have at present. Your second photo hasn't yet come, nor has the waistcoat and I do wish they would. Still the anticipation is a great thing. About that visit to church - I am delighted that you should have, at last, turned over that long threatened new leaf of yours. I expect even Maud has hopes of you now. As for me I have wept tears of joy that you have at last listened to the entreaties and supplications, which you know I have continually made to you and now see the error of your ways. Being at a perfectly safe distance I know you can't reply in your usual way and therefore I am safe.

Talking about church - sometimes on a Sunday afternoon somebody or other gives a lecture and some of them have been very good. One was by the commander of our destroyers in the Jutland fight. He led the attack by the destroyers on the German battle cruisers and I believe got the V.C. for his work during this fight. His boat and another were both disabled and afterwards sunk within a short distance of one another and afterwards he and his men were picked up and made prisoners. He described how previously to this, while he was in command of a destroyer he had taken the crew off a stranded cruiser. The cruiser had run ashore on a rock and it was impossible to get the boats out owing to the rough sea. He therefore run the destroyer alongside and managed to keep it there while the men on the cruiser jumped on to the deck of the destroyer. He was also in the Falkland Islands fight and described this to us too. Its most interesting to hear of these fights from a man who has taken a leading part in them and although he was out of the latter part of the Jutland fight, that portion that he did see was fine.

Last Sunday we had a lecture on big game shooting in Africa by a Major here. He described how he watched two elands fighting for about a quarter of an hour until one was beaten and went off. Apparently they had not injured one another at all, but afterwards he shot one and then found that it had been cut badly by the other's horns and was bleeding considerably internally. At another time he was following the tracks of a buffalo through the jungle and suddenly found himself surrounded by a large herd which he had not seen owing to the jungle being so thick, although some of them were only about five yards away. Luckily for him they did not attack as they sometimes do and he got back alright. He told another tale of a buffalo, which had been shot three times, standing at bay until the whole of the remainder of the herd had passed and got away and then fell dead.

In my last letter I asked you to send me "The Builders Clerk" by T. Bales, published by Spon & Co. (Batsfords ought to have it). There is a report here that the decimal system for weights and measures etc. is to be introduced at home. If this is so could you send me a book on arithmetic on the new system as soon as there is one published.

I have been skating. You ought to have seen me. It must have been a glorious sight. As one of the fellows said "Its only a matter of balance" and of course that's all it is, only I find that I can keep my balance infinitely better sitting down or lying on my back. As it has been freezing here for some time we applied for and got permission to flood part of the enclosure and so formed quite a fair rink, of, I should say, 40 yards by 20. I managed to borrow a pair of skates and so went out to learn how to fall down. Seriously though, it was only when I was inveigled into trying to turn somersaults on one foot and to stand on my head and such like antics that I took a seat somewhat abruptly and even now I haven't broken my neck. But its grand exercise (I mean skating not breaking your neck). Since then I have bought the borrowed skates and now a thaw has come and there is no more skating. Such is life.

You remember I told you about some relations of the Webbers named Madge - well I had a letter from Charles Webber today and he says "Grandniece Norah Madge" (its a little peculiarity of his to call people Nephew, Cousin, Widow etc etc) told me in the office where she is now engaged, was Miss Muggridge whom she knew very well, and I said so do I, and another in the family knows hers". I don't know the girl, but it is rather funny she should be in your office.

I have been reading a book about gardens by Dean Hole. It makes one want a garden. Have you ever tried to imagine the sort of garden you would like, and thought of some of the things

we will plant in it? I have, only I doubt whether the real thing, when it comes will be like the castle (or garden) in the air, as it will probably not be big enough to hold it all. By the way, Mum tells me that she bought a babes bonnet from you at the Bazaar. Was it the one which you said set you longing?
Goodbye.

David

May to David   Beckenham   17.1.18 (Thursday)

My dear David,
The workmen finished mending our water works yesterday. The tank was alright, but the pipe that ran into it wasn't. The landlord is highly indignant. He has a burst pipe. Being the landlord, and a builder, and having a son a plummer, he considers he ought to have exemption from bursts. One of the men told Mama "The guvnor ain't arf laying us all out jest because he's treated like the rest of us by the frost." It was freezing again going home last night. This morning there are 2 inches of snow everywhere, and was snowing hard up to the time I left home. However, it has turned to rain in London, the slush being choice, though I expect after Belgium you would think it positively dry.
I have only got one girl away ill now, and we are coping with the work beautifully.
Last night I got halfway through the second stocking of the second pair. Guess I had better make thinner stockings next for spring wear. Mrs Taylor says' she has sufficient socks for you for awhile. To-night I go to the dressmakers. There will be a piece of a moon, so it will not be too dark. You preferred it dark though, didn't you?
I regularly wake up before 6.0. each morning, and then have beautiful daydreams till 7.0. Strange to say you are always mixed up in them. Then I do my physical jerks, but alas, am not any slenderer. Last time I slept with Mrs Taylor she called me "Little Fatty". Isn't it too bad? I deserve a medal for my efforts to become genteel & willowy.
18. 1. 18.
Called at dressmakers last night, and got back home remarkably early compared with the time it used to take me. Finished reading "Where Love Is" in the train. A rather queer tale. Will tell you about when I have time. This is my day of hindrances. Found a letter from Mrs Taylor enclosing your card of 12th Dec. She says your Aunt Martha is dead. Really I think it is a good thing for the old lady. She had grown dreadfully obstinate, and I believe fell downstairs. Ethel is away with a bad cold; at least I go to business with colds heaps worse, but Ethel is sensible and believes in taking care of herself. I prefer someone else to take care of me. Did knitting last, night and hope to finish, my second pair of stockings to-night. If Ethel is alright on Sunday I will go to Balham again and stay the night.
What do you think of this idea for a honeymoon? Go for a tramp through counties near the sea, perhaps staying a day or so at a village if we like the look of it, of course carrying knapsacks. The month of May ought to be grand for that sort of thing.

Can't stop longer, must now write to Mrs Taylor. Goodbye.

May.

P.S. Weather awfully mild again, and the streams overflowing their banks. Is it as changeable in Germany? or do you know what to expect? One of our boys from the Front, the first to go from here, has just returned from France. He is most cheerful and says war will soon be over. According to the Bible I hear it will be over next month. Won't it be grand to have you again!

David to May   Holzminden   Post card   January 17th 1918

I have just had your letter of November 20th today. Re your learning Marine work, I have gleaned the following and hope it may be of some use. The Insurance Institute, 11 Queen Street, E.C. hold classes in insurance subjects and have a very good library of books on insurance and charge only a small fee for same. Also the London School of Law, Lincolns Inn, give instruction by correspondence on various insurance subjects. You did not tell me about this Marine Insurance before. Does it mean that you may get control of the Marine Department and if so, shall you be able to run your present department and the Marine as well? You seem to be fearfully busy. Whatever you do, don't work too hard and overdo it. Your second photo hasn't come yet. Will you please tell Mum that you have got this post card as she will be another one short this month, one having already gone to Ethel. Goodbye.

David

May to David   Beckenham   21.1.18

My dear David,

This is, I believe, Letter No. 66. Isn't grand being able to write to each other, even if we can't say much?

On Saturday afternoon we worked till 4.30, and then I was tired. In fact I did not get out of the train at Penge and go for my dress. Don't imagine I was feeling ill; it was sheer laziness. In the evening I finished my stockings, i.e. the second pair.

Sunday was horribly wet. I had told Mrs Taylor I might be calling on Sunday afternoon, but as it was wet, and I was still feeling tired I stayed at home and went to bed soon after 9. 0.

I knew if I went to Balham I should sit up and talk till nearly midnight. We always do. We did get on so well with the work Saturday, and it has made me feel clear for this week, as we are up to date with the policies. We shall most likely stay next Saturday afternoon. I get 6/- an afternoon of 3 hours. Not bad, is it?

And that is all the news!

I have written to Mrs Taylor and told her I hoped to spend next weekend with her. She might call in this afternoon. It is a lovely sunshiney warm, spring like day, and she might be tempted to come in after seeing about her business.

I was hoping to have a letter from you this morning, but it has not come yet.

Yesterday morning I had some lovely dreams. We had taken the train to Lyme Regis in Dorset, stayed there a week, and then tramped to Penzance, and back from there by train, only we did not leave the place in my dreams. It took us weeks.

Must stop now.

May

May to David   Beckenham   22.1.18

My dear David,

After leaving business last night I called at Mudie's and got out a new book – "The Amateur Gentleman" by Farnol. Started to read it in the train, and think I shall like it. Called at the dressmakers, and have now got my new dress on. Don't know yet that I altogether like the way the skirt is made, but I do like the colour – violet.

In the evening I did some needlework – alterations and repairs, nothing interesting. And that is all the news.

Your letter is overdue. I do wish it would hurry up. I am sure you are feeling bad and look white and thin, with your skin going into folds. I have put your photo up in the morning room facing the window where I can see you all the evening. On the wall facing the fire is Papa's photo. The tale of that book I have just finished reading, "Where Love Is", is not much of a tale, though well written. The hero is an artist, poor, unsuccessful, but a perfect model of a character. His great chum is a wealthy rising member of Parliament, but is not so good as he ought to be, and is engaged to be married to the heroine – at least I suppose she is the heroine. She is divinely beautiful but has a bitter cynical tongue. She moves in grand society but has contempt for it and shows it. However, everyone seeks her. One day the artist goes to some grand dinner party given by his cousin who is a widow and a friend of the heroine's, and she is very wealthy. The artist not knowing the heroine is the sweetheart of his great chum falls in love with her or her looks, though she is rather sneering to him. He does not say much, but what he does say wakes her up to the fact that she has no soul. Next a bit of scandal is coming to light, the villain being the Artist's chum, now engaged to the heroine. To shield him and save the heroine's feelings the artist takes all the blame, and he then goes tramping in France with Italy. In the meantime the heroine breaks off her engagement. When the hero returns she engages herself to him though he will not clear his character. He points out the difference in the life he leads and his sordid surroundings. At first she is blind to it all, but suddenly she feels aversion to the poverty, and rushes off to another man, an American widower who told her some time back he was looking for a "decorative wife". The next day they go off to America, and that is the end of them, while the hero marries his widowed cousin.

1.0

Mrs Taylor has called in. I have promised to spend next weekend with her. She missed me last week, though I had not promised to go. Mr Charrington has again written for more coupons for your parcels. Mrs T had already written that they would not be sent her till 24th, so I advised her to go and see him. She said she would, and then go to New Cross to pay a bill and on to Miss Massey.

P.S. I had a lovely dream early this morning, but cannot tell you about it. Had a similar one before you left England which I told you about then.

May to David   Beckenham   23. 1. 18.

My dear David,

It is a glorious day, so warm and bright, and I had a grand sleep last night and did not wake till passed 7. 0. I dreamt I was going to a ball, and just at the last moment almost one of my front teeth dropped out. I did not have time to dream about you as I usually do from 6.0. to 7.0. Don't you feel neglected?

Last night I knitted mittens with some fine wool the dressmaker gave me, asking if I could do something for a soldier. She only had 22 oz. so could only make mittens with that quantity. Being fine wool I am putting in half thumbs.

I was called over the coals this morning. One of my girls was 22 times late last year. Fog and trains being held up are no excuse. Three other girls were 11 times late. By the way they are all laughing in the next room they are evidently enjoying the reprimanding I have given them. And I did try to look serious.

To-night I shall be calling at the dressmaker again. I want her to see my new skirt on. I think it

ought to be altered. I admit I am no skeleton, but I make a barrel look slender in this.
Time is up, and I must get back to work.
According to the meaning of dreams, I am going to lose a friend. I shall not believe in that dream. By the bye, it was an artificial tooth I dreamt about, so I suppose I am going to lose a false friend. That's alright.
I was reading The Amateur Gentleman in the train this morning, and think it will be worth reading.
I am longing to hear whether you have got those two missing books. I have not taken the matter up with Batsfords yet, thinking I would wait for your next letter.
Goodbye.

May.

May to David   Beckenham   24.1.18 Thursday

My dear David,
Last night I called at the dressmakers on the way home, and during the evening finished the first mitten.
Caught the 8.30. this morning as usual and shopped at the Stores. And that is all the news. Yesterday Miss Daffarn gave me a photo of herself. She does look lovely. If you only saw her you would not want me. What! I am shocked at you.
Still no word from you, but I remember there was a notice in the paper that for a fortnight before Xmas no letters or parcels would be transmitted in Germany, so guess I must wait another week, and then get two. It is very nice to think two are on the way.

25. 1. 18.
This morning Mrs Taylor called looking so happy. She had a card from you with her, the one about the Xmas dinner and her pudding. She fairly wanted to dance for joy. She had been round to Mr Charrington and had a good talk with him, and she was then going on to Harrod's to do some ordering. I shall be working till 4.30. to-morrow and then will go on the Balham till Monday. The weather is keeping glorious, and what with the sunshine and your postcard we can't help feeling lighthearted.
There was a letter from Ethel L telling her mother she could do the ordering direct instead of asking Mr Charrington, who had to get permission and a permit from Mrs Taylor. I am very glad Mr C is being left out of it. He must think Ethel a queer sort to snub her mother as she was doing. She asked him to try and trace you when you were missing, but he could not find out anything, while Mrs T was most prompt and found out I think in record time, not leaving a stone unturned, and not being put off by anyone. I am so glad Mrs Taylor keeps fit. When I mentioned it she said proudly "I must, for who is going to look after my boy if I get ill? You know he never writes without asking for something, so I am taking great care of myself."
Aren't you two wrapped up in each other?

This morning I received from my esteemed General Manager the following note.

"Following the digest of the Late Attendance Book for 1915, 16 & 17

It is gratifying to note that on the whole the Dept. shows a good record though there is a distinct falling off as compared with previous years, even after deducting Miss Eagles' late attendance which is by permission. Miss Chubb's record is the one bad feature and this your lady should be reprimanded. Three others with double figures will also doubtless notice they are above the average.

The great increases seem in number of days absent from illness. This is very disappointing when it is borne in mind that compared with the male staff the ladies are not asked to put in late work, and it will be well if Miss Muggridge made a brief report, giving her opinion as to the causes of this increase."

Miss M promptly replied as under:-

"The year 1917 was the worst on record for attendance owing chiefly to epidemics being spread through overcrowding, there have been four cases of mumps, two cases of measles, and two or 3 cases of influenza.

There were also one case each of rheumatism (18 days absence), pleurisy (13 days) and nervous breakdown (45 days).

The remaining absentees were 5 girls who were away a few days with colds.

Though not asked to stay late the typists have been very willing to give 228 hours overtime between them, in addition to the extra hour each day.

As the dressing room accommodation has recently been improved a better attendance record is expected for 1918."

Pip. Pip.

Nothing more to relate just now, so goodbye for a few days.

May

Lt Col Kelly to Mrs Linn   24.1.18

To Mrs Linn
Dear Madam,
I beg to acknowledge receipt of the socks (30 prs) you have so kindly sent for the Battalion. They are very welcome, and I have arranged that they should go to what was your brother's platoon. With many thanks
Believe me
Yours truly

Kelly (Lt Col) 2/KRR

May to David   Beckenham   28.1.18   Letter No. 70.

My dear David,

Friday evening I called for my dress on the home, and did needlework (an uninteresting alteration) in the evening. Bed about midnight.

Saturday, caught the 8.46. and had a nice journey as far as Catford, and an ordinary one after that. Worked in the afternoon from 1.20 to 4.20 for which I shall be paid 6/-, and then took the underground to Clapham Rd, and tram on. Mrs Taylor had tea waiting. Mrs Day had already gone to her daughter. So we talked and talked and talked till 10.0. when we went to bed. Woke about 6.0, and talked and talked and talked (at least it was Mrs Taylor who did practically all the talking really) till 10.0 when we went to bed again and slept till 6.0, and then talked and talked and talked till 8.45 when Mrs Taylor said goodbye to me at Balham Station. (I tried via Victoria and Underground to Mansion House and found it quicker and not quite so crowded.) We did other things besides talking. For instance, being up too late for chapel and it being a most glorious day, we went for a walk, taken by Peter across the Common and up and down roads. Maud called unexpectedly during the morning. She had not been to Church! We were horrified. During the afternoon Mrs Taylor had a short doze while I went on reading "The Amateur Gentleman", and in the evening we went to Chapel arriving there just as the second hymn was finished. The sermon was good, as usual.

I can't get Mrs Taylor to say what she would like for her Christmas present, so have got her to promise to come to Selfridges with me in about a fortnight's time as I want to buy something for myself, and hope then to get something for her.

During Saturday evening the postie brought a paper for Mrs Taylor. Strattons are paying up the final payment – 1/4d. per share, making your sum the magnificent amount of 4/2! We promptly discussed what we should advise you to do with it, but do not think we came to any definite decision. You might like to buy land in Africa, or Canada, or possibly house property in England. You may decide for yourself. In the meantime I expect it will go into the Bank. This morning Ern telephoned to say there was a letter from you at home waiting for me. Fancy not bringing it up to me! I of course asked him why he did not, and he said Mama told him to leave it where it was as he would only lose it. So of course he feels a martyr. It is now 2.0. I wish it time to go home. Guess I will catch my early train - I do want that letter. Goodbye.

May

P.S. The 6/- have just arrived. That makes 10/2 between us. Lets go and enjoy ourselves.

May to David   Beckenham   29.1.18.

My dear David,

I caught my earl train last night and then pounced on your letter. It was a nice one. I know it just about by heart, and have made a copy of it, more or less, for Mrs Taylor and now it is being posted.

Ethel L. does not upset me at all. I only feel sorry for her and wish I could avoid making her jealous. She suffers, I don't. I do hope I shall never experience that feeling. It must be a horrible disease. From her letter to her mother last weekend she is evidently jealous of Jean, too. She will end in sickening her hubby if she is not careful. Why can't a drug or herb be found to cure it? The world would be a far better place if the malady could only be cured.

Those lists of books ought to have been sent with the second batch of books. I will drop a line to Batsfords. No, it is not a trouble. You know it is a pleasure, and it doesn't take so long as you think. I get out at Holborn, and come back by tube to the Bank.

I read out parts of your letter to Mama. It did make her laugh.

No photo or even portrait of me would suit you. You see I can't look at other folks as I can you. As a matter of fact that that photo you have is highly flattering.

You say you blushed at the description of the Show. Now I don't believe you can blush, even if you try ever so hard.

I have sent off that letter to Mr Rowell. Yes, it was good of them to write you, and I hope they will again.

It must be nice to be able to sketch. Glad you have a picture. I believe you have one or two others at No. 56, haven't you? I have about 7 pictures, half dozen tea knives and silver spoons, and two candlesticks, an ink stand and a cruet - almost enough to set up housekeeping!

I am making a green wool knitted coat with some green wool I bought cheap off a girl at business, for the daughter of one of the men at the Office, age about 6, and the money he pays for it will be handed over to a war comforts depot of which he is a member. I expect it will take about a month to make.

Must leave off now, so Goodbye.

May

May to David   Beckenham   30.1.18.

My dear David,

Being Wednesday I am writing to you, but I have nothing to say.

It is very foggy this morning, so like the great majority I was late. However, I got on nicely with the little coat I am making in the train. I think it will be the prettiest pattern one I have done, but not the colour. I would like to do it in white. If it were being made for someone for you to take out it would be in white. It is payday to-day, and I have put £5 in the Thrift Society and will put £5 in something else on my way home. Am I not wealthy? I don't expect to keep up £10 each month.

I am going to Maud's next Saturday afternoon when we stall be giving each other music lessons. Then we are off to No. 56 to tea, but I don't expect to stay the night. I rather fancy some-one feels hurt if I spend each weekend away.

Maud has just come in and says I am to remember her to you, and that she is struggling along at business with little success.

I wrote to Batsford's yesterday.

What do you do with yourself all day long, and how are you getting, on with cooking? Do you have plenty of fires?

It is a dismal looking day. I would just like to be in your drawing room sitting over a blazing fire, with you lying full length on the sofa saying cheeky things to me -as usual. Must leave off now, so Goodbye.

May.

P.S. May I give you a hint in the cooking line, though I guess you know more about that art than I do. If the oatmeal you get sent you is not rolled, but coarse oats, the only way to cook them is by making the water boil first, and while boiling sprinkle the oats in gently, as that is the only way to burst the cells, otherwise you might simmer them for ages but the cells would not burst or get soft. A Scotchman told me this two days ago. Mama had the night before (though I did not know it then being away at Balham) tried to cook coarse oatmeal in a porringer as usual, but it was scrunchy.

May to David   Beckenham   31.1.18

My dear David,

Another month come to an end; thank goodness, as I feel it brings you nearer, though I cannot help thinking that there are a good many people who do not want this war to come to a close; they seem to like it. No wonder John Bull is always drawn with a bulldog beside him. You know bulldogs don't start fighting quickly, like Airedales and most other dogs, but when once they start they don't want to leave off. We haven't had our last year's holiday together, and there are oceans of weekends due to us. It is most selfish of others to want to keep us apart. Never mind, we will make up for lost time, and I bet we will start making it up this year. We might do that holiday in the Channel Isles that we were going to when war broke out. I would like it, only instead of having a fortnight we must make it four weeks!

On the way home last night I invested the other £5, and in the evening knitted that coat. It was awfully foggy this morning, and of course the train took a long time, but I sat and knitted and so did not mind. Not halfway through the first front yet. It is rather a slow pattern; besides which the wool had been used before, and that makes it slower to work.

Having arrived late at St Paul's station I thought I might as well be later still, so called in at the Churchyard and bought a little bit more of the violet serge, enough to make a complete dress, and then as luck would have it I noticed a remnant of silk that matched perfectly, and of course I bought that. Then I saw a straw hat that I believe would match, but did not stop for that. I might see some prettier ones later on.

We are back in winter again now, and have had frosts for the last two mornings.

This morning I had a p.c. from Mrs Taylor thanking me for sending on your letter and copy of mine. She thought it was bright.

Do you get my letters singly, or do they arrive in batches?

Friday.

It was not foggy on our line last night, so we got home alright, but some of the girls took 3 and 4 hours to reach their homes. Knitted last night as usual. Slightly foggy and very cold this morning. I woke up at 5.0 and thought it was striking 6.0. After enjoying an hour's daydreams behold it struck 6.0. I was so pleased. Of course I was not dreaming of you!

We are getting quite slack for us. I shall be at home tomorrow morning – at least, I am going out to the dressmaker's and shopping in the morning; over to Maud's in the afternoon, and on to 56 to tea. If I have time in the morning I shall call on my "Giddy" Aunt. We have not seen or heard from her since she called before Xmas and was called "Giddy Aunt" by Ethel! Mama had a letter from Uncle Fred yesterday. Cousin Bert is in Aldershot, and his wife gone back to her home. I wish they would send him across to France.

No more news.

Miss Willsher called this aft. and enquired after you. The old lady who lives with Miss Rudge will be 92 next June, but is not expected to last til then. She is always in bed now.

Goodbye

May

B. T. BATSFORD, LTD
BOOKSELLERS & PUBLISHERS
ARCHITECTURE
DECORATION
FINE ARTS
ENGINEERING
APPLIED SCIENCE

Telephone: Central 7693

94 HIGH HOLBORN W.C.1.

LONDON February 1st. 1918.

Miss M. Muggridge.

Dear Madam,

    We are obliged by your favour of the 29th ult. with regard to your order of the 17th of November last, but we are utterly unable to understand how it is that Mr. Taylor has only received a part of the consignment, since we are positive that all the books were despatched by us, (in one parcel), on the 17th of December. We are certain that Lockwood's "Price Book", Stephenson's "Estimating" and the Catalogues were included, and we can only surmise that the authorities of the prison camp opened the parcel and for some reason or other took out these particular books. Had they been removed by our own Censorship officials, we should have been advised of the fact.

    We are glad to hear that the previous consignment has now come to hand safely; there is, of course, just a chance that the missing items from the last consignment may yet find their way to him.

                    We remain,

                          Yours faithfully,

                            for. B. T. BATSFORD, LTD.

308   my dearest

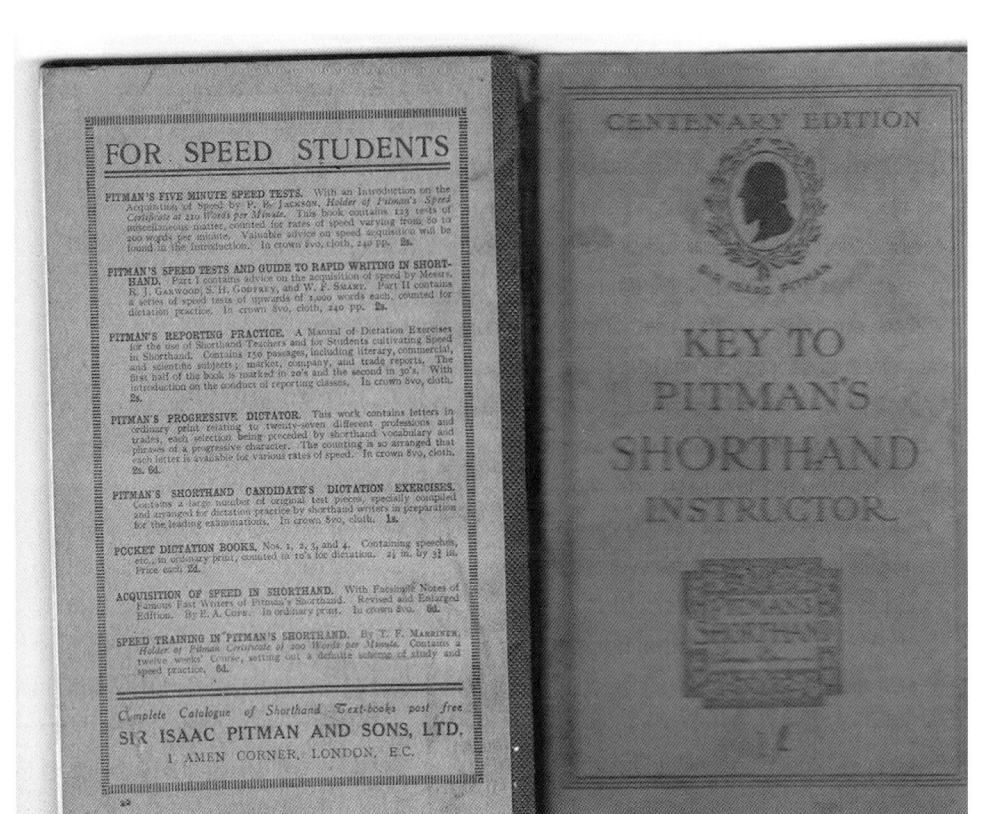

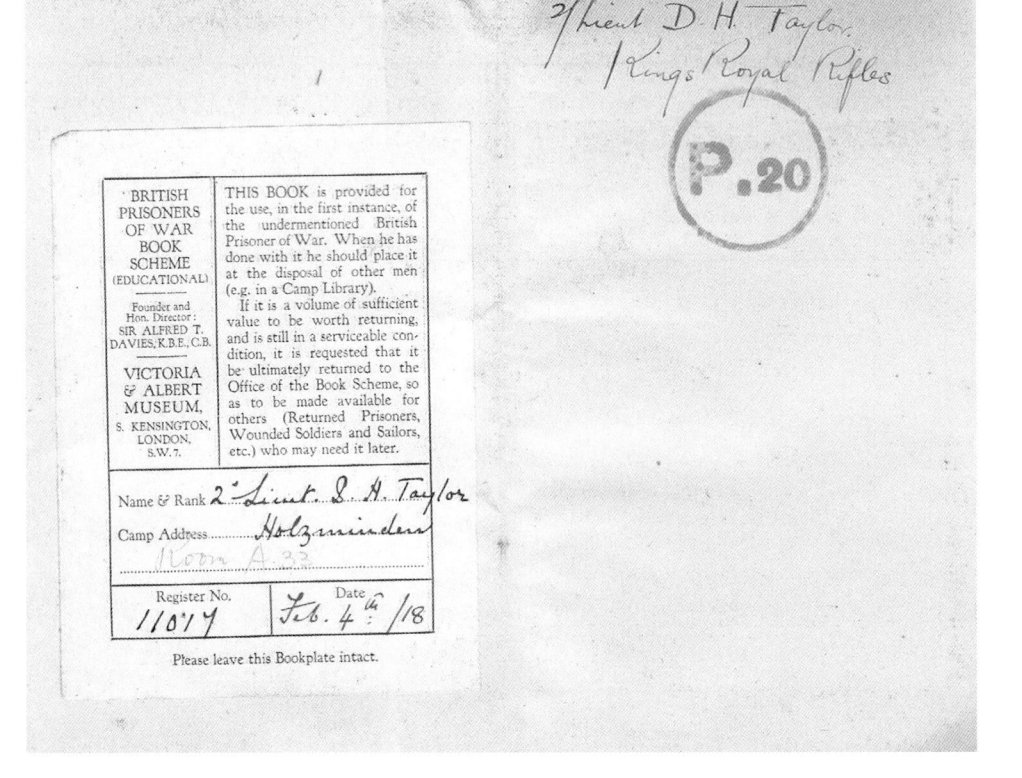

David to Ginger   Feb 4th 1918   Post card No. 6

I was awfully sorry to hear from Mum of Mrs Linn's death. Please give John my deepest sympathy. She also says that John is alright again, which is great good news. I have your letters of Nov 15th and 24th and glad to get them, as they contain some news which we don't get much of here. Thanks ever so much for sending the socks to the battalion. A few of my own men were not with me that day, so doubtless they got some of your good things. Can you send me some of Dicks belting for boot repairs together with plenty of brads and hob nails. I can't get these from home and in consequence am having to go very carefully with my boots. Berne have written saying they are continuing the bread, but it hasn't turned up for the last 3 or 4 weeks. I think there has been some stoppage in the transport somewhere. A number of officers are going to Holland from here, those captured early in the war. I envy them, but I don't want to go to Holland I want to get home. I have had 4 photos of the kiddies and can do with some more.
Yours

David

May to David   Letter No. 74.   Beckenham   Monday 4. 2. 18.

My dear David,

I quite forget last Friday evening, but expect I was knitting. Saturday I had off; went shopping in the morning, to the dressmakers and to see my "Giddy" Aunt. She was not giddy but said she was absolutely dazed. Helen has gone to business, went the Monday after Christmas, and Auntie cannot get anyone to look after the children, so she is acting nurse herself! I think it is really funny, though I am sorry for the children. Georgie was in bed. I went up to see him. He seemed very happy with his toys on his bed, playing all by himself, but I don't think myself there was any need for him to be in bed. Naturally when he and Billy are together they are noisy and mischievous, so it is my belief Auntie was only too glad to keep him upstairs for the sake of quietness. He certainly looks a bit pale for a youngster, and wouldn't eat his breakfast. I got back in time to cook the dinner, though poor little Georgie held me very tightly to keep me there.

The afternoon I enjoyed thoroughly. Maud told me to be over at her place very early to give her a lesson, and then we were to go to No. 56 at 4.0. I reached Maud's before 3.0. to find her out. That is the third time I have been to her house and found her out. I was glad. I knew she was over at Beckenham to see her sister-in-law. She lost her train owing to a clock being slow (most clocks are awful now the males are away) and it was a long wait for the next train.

It was getting on for 5.0. when she arrived, I believe. In the meantime I looked at a photo of you close to the piano and that gave me an inspiration and a longing. For the first time since you left I practised! Fortunately I had that book with me, one of those you gave me containing the Prelude and the Cradle piece. I practiced hard, and you seemed to encourage me. It seemed as though you were in the room, and after I had finished I felt I was walking on air.

Directly Maud came in I said we would start then and there. It was 5.0. when we reached Balham. We had a lively tea, and I left about 6.30. as I had some work to do at home. It was about 8.0. when I got home, and then I did my sewing.

Sunday morning I cleaned the front of my grey dress with benzine - at least I tried to, but the last state of that dress was worse than the first. I don't think I can be very successful in the use of benzine.

In the afternoon Ethel went out for a walk with Percy Wraight. How far do you think they walked? As far as the Wraight's drawing room, where they laughed and talked all the afternoon and evening. She left home at 2.20. so as to get a good long walk. I know of two others who used to set out for long walks and suddenly stop when they came to a convenient bunker.

The weather has turned wet and warm, though it hasn't rained much. I heard from Batsfords on Saturday. The missing books and lists passed our censor, so I suppose you will get them sooner or later,

Hadn't I better order you some more books now as they take so long to reach you?

No more news, so Goodbye for the present.

Mrs T's affairs are now all settled, and I believe they came to less than last time. I only wrote 2 letters about them and paid one visit. Mrs T really did everything herself.

David Henry Taylor

May to David   Beckenham   Wednesday 6.2.18

My dear David,

Monday. Left at 5.30. (our hours have gone back to that time, as it is now light when we leave), went straight home and knitted. I would like to know how many miles of knitting I have done during my life time. Finished the first front of the coat. It looks a remarkable shape on the shoulder, but perhaps when the back is done it may be alright. The shoulders usually worry me. The knitting books generally make them too clumsy.

Tuesday. Nothing of importance happened. At the office the work is now going on very smoothly. Got my senior girl back again now. Came back Monday. She has been away a month, breakdown through overwork. She would slave at her work in the office (being an old Datchelor girl I suppose she cannot help it) and then during the weekends she used to work at a hospital. Now it is a mistake to have definite work you feel you must do during weekends if you work hard all the week. In the evening I knitted.

This morning your postcard arrived dated 17th January. Really you are a dear to write like that. I think I have mentioned that the Insurance Institute is now opened to women, so I promptly joined. The lectures are one a month at the Gresham. Next Monday there will be one on Motor Insurance. Having taken over the "White Cross" which I believe is the best paying Motor Insce. Co. I shall be going to the lecture, though I do not know that I shall benefit from any extra knowledge; but I may as well have it. It was thought that we should have the Marine Dept. in our building, but was found impracticable, so the Co. have taken an extra room over at the Indemnity Mutual Marine which we have bought up, and I have sent two of my girls there, and they work with two of our men, one of them (who looks after the girls) being a bad tempered (somewhat) man named Taylor. The work is increasing so much that when there are some straightforward copy-policies wanted one of these girls beings them over to us and I give them to a super to do. Now, you need not worry about my working too hard. I don't do the work, I do the martyr, while the others do the work.

I have sent your postcard on to Mrs Taylor with instructions to keep it till the weekend when I expect to come over. I have ordered some slack lime for the garden. If it arrives today expect I shall be busy on Saturday putting it on the ground, and in that case will go to 56 on Sunday afternoon and stay the night.

Cannot stop any longer now, as I have given my head girl the day off. It was owing to her. Perhaps I shall have a day off next week, in which case Mrs Taylor and I shall be shopping, I hope. Goodbye for the present.

May

P.S. Mrs Taylor just called. She bought 2 pieces of yours, 17th Dec and about 7th Jan. Last Saturday I took over to Balham an enlargement of you done by Wykehams. They could not get it done before Xmas – in fact it was only finished last week. It is excellent. She came to say how pleased she is with it. She is off to Watford tomorrow for a few days.

May to David   Beckenham   8. 2. 18.

My dear David,

I usually like to start Friday's letter on Thursday, but I did not get a ghost of a chance yesterday, and as this is my busy day (it is now 1.45. and I have not done a stroke of my own work) I guess you won't get much of an epistle, which perhaps is as well as I have no news. The last two evenings I got on with knitting that coat. About halfway through the second front. Here come a few hindrances, so I had better give up.

It is rather a nuisance, but the final meeting re the Bazaar total figures is to be held at Langham Place next Monday. Tea at 5.30. Now we have a lecture on Motor Insce. at the Institute on Monday at 5.30. Which shall I attend? Guess I shall be putting duty first - as usual. Really I deserve to be put in a stained glass window with a halo round my head and unsightly seams all over me. What glory!

Don't know what I am doing this weekend. Mrs Taylor said she would write me, but I have not got the letter yet. If she comes back from Watford I am going to her for the weekend, but they may keep her there till Monday. The weather is so warm, though wet underfoot. It has almost seemed like summer to-day owing to a brilliant sun. O, for a walk (?) across Hayes Common. I didn't say with you, now, did I?

That slack lime I ordered hasn't arrived. Must hurry it up to-night.

This letter looks drunk owing to having to take the paper out every now and then, and not having time to put it in properly.

5. 15. I am so glad you are getting better parcels. Mrs Taylor is sending you the best she possibly can. It is a great joy to her.

This is the weekend that I expect a letter from you, tho' I don't always get them during the weekend. Expect it will come Monday.

We have almost finished our work. It will be done by 5.30, and so another day got through, and another day nearer you.

Goodbye

May.

May to David   Beckenham   11.2.18.

My dear David,

Friday: caught usual train home, and got on with the coat in the evening. Just a usual day.
Saturday: glorious morning. Went to catch my late train so that we could have a good talk etc, and found a man in my seat! There was no time to turn him out - even if he would go, which was doubtful, so got into another compartment with the result that someone got in at the next station. We were martyrs. Got on very nicely with the work, and left soon after 12. 30.
Had a favourite Saturday's dinner for me - coffee, tongue and bread & butter. Next made kipper paste while I was digesting my dinner, and then Mama and I went out into the garden. The slack lime had arrived, so I dug up the garden leaving it very rough, while Mama came behind and dug in the lime, leaving some on top. During the afternoon a gale got up, but it did not interfere with us as we were stooping down. We worked until it was dark, and my back has felt like breaking ever since. Did not know I had so many muscles. In the evening I finished the second front of the woolly coat. I did enjoy the afternoon and evening, and then slept hard.
Sunday: Not so much sun, but plenty of wind. After breakfast (which was a hearty one) my constant companion and I went up to the cemetery to see if the bulbs were alright. I forgot to mention that on Saturday morning there was a letter from Mrs Taylor saying she would be staying at Watford till Monday, and that she was enjoying herself very much. She had been to a lecture on the war with her brother Alfred the previous evening and liked it immensely and wished I had been there to enjoy it as well. Mrs Capel is better.
We took the train to Penge, and then I went in to Auntie's to see how Georgie was. He was very lively, and I wore him round my neck the whole time I was there. His mother tried to make him get down, but he simply wouldn't go. Then the baby got jealous, and Helen had to have him round her neck. Auntie, who was a tremendous martyr, was in bed resting. She has not got anyone to help her with the children yet. All the time we were there we were up in her bedroom. I told her with these lively youngsters about she would have no time to get old. But even that did not cheer her. She did look funny; she had not got her teeth in. Georgie had been in bed 3 days. I would have taken him up to the cemetery with me, but it was too far for him to walk, and my back was aching too much to push the car. He cried a bit to come with me, but finally decided to eat a lot of pudding to make his legs grow when he would take me out for long walks then. From the house to the cemetery I walked, and found the grave looking very well, the crocuses, snowdrops and hyacinths coming up thick. We walked back to Penge Station and then caught a train home.
In the afternoon I looked through the papers for jokes, and this time found a few worth repeating. Each week Mama sends to the Royal West Kents the following papers - John Bull, Bystander, Cassell's weekly, London Opinion, Answers & Titbits, and if I am at home for the weekend of course I look through. Last week there was not a joke worth repeating, though the pictures were good. These were the best this time:-
Little girl (interrupting 2 officers who were frequently using the word camouflage) "My Mama

wears pink ribbons in her camouflage."

Young Man. Don't tell anyone I kissed your sister, Bobby. Bobby (wearily) That's what they all say.

A sailor just returned from sea rambled into a restaurant. After glancing at the bill of fare he looked around for the waiter. "Yessir" said the waiter sliding over in response.
"Tell me, waiter, have you frogs legs."
"No sir, its rhumatism that makes me walk like this."

Sergeant "Can't you form 4's? What's your number?
Elderly Rookie (slightly confused) 190139
Sergeant "I didn't ask yer bloomin' age. What's yer number in the ranks?"

Waiter (to elderly spinster) "Are you 'a little duck'"?

Sentry "Halt whogoesthere?"
Absentminded one "Season".

Caller (looking at oil painting) Is this an old master? Butler. No sir, that's the old missus.

"Did you go to Bill Smith's blowout at the New year?"
"Yus, and it was success. I 'ear his missus got 3/- on the empties the next day."

Doctor "I am extremely sorry to tell you your wife has completely lost her mind"
Husband (wearily) "I am not surprised. She has given me a bit of it every day for the last 15 years."

The illustrations to the above were all very good.
After looking at the papers I finished my book, "The Amateur Gentleman". A very good tale, but full of duels and suchlike. I have now lent the book to Maud. Went' to bed at 10.0 and slept like a top till 7.0 this morning. No letter from you but it may come during the day. Goodbye.

May.
5.40 Am now waiting for lecture to start. It is 'Motor Insurance in theory and practice.'

May to David   Beckenham   13. 2. 18.

My dear David,

Last Monday's lecture was not worth listening to. Half the words could not be heard, and the remaining half were not at all interesting. Caught the 7. 3. home and then knitted.

Tuesday: Having been a perfect little cherub for several weeks straight off, and got my pet abomination, Cave, reduced to the state he should be in, I got tired of the tameness of things, so when my two chiefs sent for me, to discuss a matter which I cannot mention, as I don't think the Censor would approve, I disagreed with all that was said, on principle, and argued and argued, of course keeping my temper, until the General Manager got positively rude, when I naturally felt I had a right to talk to him like a mother. In the end I said for my own part unless they gave way to me they could get someone else in my place. The Secretary came out, into the corridor to tame me as I was going off, but I walked away. The G. M. this morning again sent for me. He has come down a bit - but I haven't, so I don't know what is going to happen, nor do I care. When you come home I hope to learn your business, and in the meantime I could easily get a good temporary place. Now, you need not think I am in the right and the others in the wrong. From their point of view they are doing the best they can for us - only it is not my point of view, and I said I thought they were dictatorial to which I objected very much. O that poor Secretary. Of course the General Manager turned on him when he was only doing his best to smooth things between us. How I did enjoy myself yesterday. I came out with a few home truths without any flattery. Don't you think you had better place your affections elsewhere while there is time? Really, I am a little divvil at times.

Mrs Taylor came in yesterday morning. I think she is rather worried about Mrs Capel not being stronger than she is. Also, as regards those papers she had to fill up, the people noticed they had undercharged, and had sent in another charge which puts the matter right now - as last year.

Yesterday I had a letter from Ethel Barnett. She and her sister want to send you a book to read, and asked how to set about it, and what you could have. I have had no time to reply yet. How would you like "Harvey's Meditations amongst the Tombs"? I have not read the book yet, in spite of its enticing title, but I believe Ethel did and enjoyed it, though she could not say what it was about, but fancied it was amusing. She likes doleful music.

No letter from you yet. On Saturday afternoon I think I shall be gardening until teatime and then be going to Balham for the weekend. I am longing to know how you are, though I know you will say you are alright. I take that with a grain of salt.

Goodbye.

May.

David to May   Holzminden   February 14th 1918

My Dearest,
The last letter of yours which I have is January 9th. When I asked you to help Mum with her affairs I didn't expect you would let it interfere with your going to the office as usual. It was awfully good of you to go to Brixton with her as you did. And again its awfully good of you to spend your weekends with her. She does appreciate it, as her letters to me are full of how you spend these times together. Fancy getting my photo enlarged and fancy your girls asking to frame it. The picture of nineteen girls gazing at it is most embarrassing. By the way, which photo is it? Have the speculations as to your engagement gone to any great length yet? Look here, you mustn't give up going to theatres and things just because I'm not there and for goodness sake don't let your music drop. I am constantly longing to hear you play again. Its awfully good of you to take so much trouble over those books - they haven't arrived yet, nor has the waistcoat, nor those books which were on that form which you forwarded to the Board of Education, but I expect all these will turn up soon. Hope so anyhow, So Cousin Bert has married. Is it the girl he was engaged to before? I have had another letter from Maud. Will you please thank her for me.

I have been reading some notes (such as they were) on gardening-vegetable gardening (and as a consequence doing more "dreaming"). Also I have been talking to the two men of my regiment who are in my room. One of them said that his father-in-law grew more than enough vegetables for six, on a piece of ground of about 30 yards by 50 yards. I have been wondering whether we might not try growing our own vegetables some day. Have you any sort of idea how much you spend in vegetables in a year, or say some shorter time, because if you have we could perhaps tell whether it would be worth while trying. With regard to the fittings in the house. I like your idea of cupboards with glass in the doors instead of wardrobes, and I have been trying to think of some arrangement of double glasses so that you would be able to see both sides of yourself at once, but haven't yet hit on one, except by having a separate glass on a stand, which is not very satisfactory. What do you think of fitted wash basins in the bedrooms? Also I have been thinking about a shoot with a sieve leading from the ground floor fires into the cellar (supposing there is one), so that cinders etc. could be cleared away once a month instead of daily. What sort of windows do you want, casements or sliding, and have you any idea of some place for cold storage other than a cellar, as I am not sure that a cellar would be worth the extra cost. Would a covered brick pit outside do for this? The above reads something like notes on a specification, but still, let me know what you think and also give me any other ideas you have. I have heard here that the metric system of measures is to be introduced at home. If this is so, could you send me an arithmetic book giving this system as soon as one is published. I think I have asked for this either in my last letter or the one before. You want to know what I do all day! Well its very much like Mark Twains Diary - "First Day - Get up, dressed, went to bed". 2nd Day - "Got up, washed, went to bed". 3rd Day - "Got up, dressed, went to bed", and so and so on. Its something like this. I get up about 7.30, do physical jerks and have breakfast. At 9 o'clock there is roll call. Afterwards do any small things that have to be done such as get parcels, letters etc. Then I walk round the enclosure for exercise (and usually dream about the things we'll do when I get back) for about an hour until 11.30, when the cooking of lunch puts and end to the walk. Lunch between 12 and 1. After lunch I usually read most of the afternoon or do any odd jobs such as darning (and there is much darning in more ways than one), sewing, etc. that wont be put off any longer. About 4 o'clock I usually go out for another walk round the enclosure for an hour. Roll call at 5 and afterwards I have tea. I read again during the evening until roll call at 9.30 and then bed and "lights out" at 10 o'clock and that my usual day. It seems like so much of one's life practically useless, but still it won't last much longer I suppose, and then we'll make up for it all won't we?

Goodbye.

I am enclosing letters to Mum and Charles Webber. He gave Mum some money to send me a Christmas present. Don't know whats taken him, he never did this before. Still it was good of him wasn't it?

2/Lt. D.H. Taylor　　　　Letter No. 17.　　　Miss M. Muggridge
No. 22　　　　　　　　　　　　　　　　　　18 Manor Road
Kings Royal Rifles　　　　　　　　　　　　　Beckenham
Offizier Gefangenenlager　Feb. 14th 1918　　Kent
Kaserne
Holzminden

My Dearest,

The last letter of yours which I have is Jan 9th. When I asked you to help Mum with her affairs I didn't expect you would let it interfere with your going to the office as usual. It was awfully good of you to go to Brixton with her as you did. And again its awfully good of you to spend your weekends with her. She does appreciate it, as her letters to me are full of how you spend these times together. Fancy getting my photo enlarged & fancy your girls asking to frame it. The picture of nineteen girls gazing at it is most embarrassing. By the way, which photo is it? (Have the speculations as to your engagement gone to any great length yet?) Look here, you mustn't give up going to theatres & things (just because I'm not there) & for goodness sake don't let your music drop. I am constantly longing to hear you play again. Its awfully good of you to take so much trouble over those books – they haven't arrived yet, nor

May to David   15.2.18   Letter No.79

My dear David,

11.0. Everything is deadly dull again, and I have not a scrap of news. My telephone girl, who before she was married was a supervisor at the Telephone Co., is away because her little girl has the whooping cough, and is likely to remain away for several weeks. That has made us busy, just when a slack time was coming on, too. We are keeping the place open for her, firstly, because we can't get anyone else, and secondly, because we like her very much and she is no trouble.

This morning Maud brought me in a letter from Miss Rigg with a photo. Miss Rigg retired last Christmas and doesn't like it. Being unemployed gives her fits of depression. I suppose she is too old to take up some hobby. Now, I don't guess I shall have time to have fits of depression, as for one thing I shall make you sufficient handful to keep me going. Don't forget you have promised to be ill at least every Sunday morning, and of course you will have to be bad on holidays so as I can fuss you up. Now I don't suppose Miss Rigg has thought about fussing anybody up; at any rate, she never fussed me up at school.

I have not seen either of the chiefs since Wednesday, but they are speaking very nicely on the telephone, what little they do say. The General Manager has practically told me that as I am so old he will allow me to know my own mind with regard to myself, only of course he did not put it that way. Most folks don't shine at giving way.

Here come the salaries, so I must put this away.

1.50. Your letter which I expected last week has not yet arrived. Still, it must be on its way, and the next one too.

Tomorrow I shall be leaving early, doing shopping on the way home, gardening in the afternoon, tea early, and then to Balham for the weekend.

I have told you about our two old cronies of policy examiners, Watkins and Harding, whom I will call by the wrong names, and thus insulting both intensely - so they say. Well, Watkins has just this moment come in to show me a photo of himself, a proof, and says when he gets the rest home he is going to give me one!

Now about 2/3rds through the knitted coat.

Must not stop any longer, so Goodbye,

May.

P.S. During the afternoon L. paid us his first visit as CHIEF of the London Office. He intended entering and walking across the room to Miss Carter in his most magisterial manner; but - . One of my young hopefuls (but a hopeless at present) reached the door at the same time as he opened it. She was holding out well in front a smoky steaming kettle, and yelling out "Its boiling". He recovered to bow and smile at me and collide with a chair at the same time. The chair certainly was out of its place, and slap in the gangway. To reach Miss Carter he had to get between two desks, only he was too large, so he had to recline forward at a great angle, -

and on to the gum, which I admit was also in the wrong place. By that time the girls could not keep their twitters in. He quickly told his girl what he wanted done, and went out still quicker. We do not expect to see him again for a while.

Prisoner Undertaking

I herewith give my word of honour that I shall not, in case of my taking part in a walk, make an attempt of escape during such walk, i.e. from the time of leaving the camp until having returned to it, and not to commit any acts that are directed against the safety of the German Empire.

I give also my word of honour to use this card only myself and not to give it to any other prisoner of war.

Holzminden, den 16.2.18
Name: DH Taylor

May to David   Beckenham   18.2.8.

My dear David,

Saturday: Lost even my late train in the morning, but left early to make up for it. Called at butchers and dressmakers on the way home, had dinner, did more shopping, then needlework, and by that time there was no chance of gardening, so had tea and went to Balham by the 6. 5. Arrived there at 7.0. There was a glorious smell of cooking. Mrs Taylor had been very busy making a cake (am eating a big chunk now), cooking meat; making several loaves of bread which looked most tempting, and a pie of those raspberries (or blackberries, I forget which) that you brought home from Gidea Park; and also an apple turnover. Isn't it too bad of me to write about such lovely things when you can't get them? You must imagine you had them. At 7.30. we started supper, and took a long time over it. Then we sat over the fire doing knitting and talking until about midnight. Was soon asleep. It has turned frosty, and is beautifully bright. The result is we are feeling frisky. It is a good thing you are not here, as I am afraid. I should sauce you. And fancy saucing a real live officer!

Sunday: Got up in time to be 20 minutes late for chapel. Very good sermon by Mr Brown. Maud was waiting for us outside. She had not been to church. As we had we were naturally extra horrified that she had not been. Then Mrs Taylor went in to cook the dinner, sirloin of beef and 3 vegetables, while Peter took Maud and me across the Common. In the afternoon in spite of being heavily laden inwardly we went to see Miss Massey. She is in St. Thomas's Hospital to be under observation. Her doctor thinks the two operations have been rather trying for her heart, so she is resting in bed, and she is told that very likely she will have to give up housework. I can't imagine her ever doing any, but I suppose she has done some in her time. She looked very well and was joking away, and sent you her love. Her lips look a bit blue which I know is a sign of heart trouble. We reached home about 5.15, and were just finishing tea when Mrs Day came home. She had been to her daughter's. She looks very well, but cannot make out how it is you have not had her letters. In the evening we again went to chapel, late as usual, then home to supper. Mrs Taylor said we should have some port. She poured it out in tumblers instead of wine glasses. Almost full! The result was that it went straight to my head. We turned round to the fire to have a final warm before retiring early, and all talked and laughed at once, goodness knows what about. Then I noticed Mrs Day had fallen asleep suddenly, and Mrs Taylor was nodding; so I curled myself up in your chair, and got drowsey. Suddenly I looked at the clock to find it was 12.30. We all had fits, and hurried ourselves for the first time that day. At 12.40. we were either in bed, or just stepping in. This morning I was late for business. Not surprised. I found an Old Moore's Almanac at No. 56, so we tried to make out all that was foretold for this year. January predicted the commencement of peace negociations and the passing of the Women's Suffrage Bill, both events having come to pass, but as far as I can make out, which isn't much I'll admit, the peace negociations have fallen through. By June apparently the peace negociations are completed, but in Sept. there is a big council in Paris as some of the negociations do not work well and certain things will be resettled. In December the women are actually voting wisely and well, which of course they would.

I hear, but of course take it with a grain of salt, that Germany has practically no soap. How do you manage? Is it a case of "Pass me the chisel and sandpaper when you have finished." We have plenty of that commodity, and as the price has not gone up it looks as if we are likely to have as much as we want. I do not think the Daily Mail's wonderful "World Shortage" can have commenced yet, as we are still getting all we want, which must be disappointing to that paper. Must get on with my work now, so Goodbye.

May

Fanny to Ethel   Balham   Feb 20th 1918

My darling Ethel,
I told you I would let you know when I got a letter from David. Well I received one last night dated Jan 2. This is part of it.
"On Xmas day we had dinner, nine of us, - a great and mighty feast. And a menu and all and all, - but to start at the beginning. We drew lots as to who should do what, and another fellow and I had to make out the menu. The two cooks were cooking nearly all day. And I think about 5 of the others laid the table. You should have seen that table, It was a sight for the gods. A blanket served for a table cloth, and set off the silver (save the mark) and cutlery (all sparkling and winking in the light) splendidly.
But the central ornament was the thing. As a d'oyley there was a smooth cotton towel (it had not been used more than a week) and then a gorgeous spergne made up of the base of a metal shaving mirror and filled with some silver covered chocolates and some imitation Christmas greenery. Then the menu was sketched on some post cards and showed a big busting butler ringing a bell for dinner. Then there was the menu itself – 'Puree de legumes' (half a doz packets soup powder all mixed together indiscriminately and regardless of flavour, but the result was not at all bad), 'Saumon en Casserole' as a matter of fact it was cooked in a frying pan and one tin of salmon and to do for the lot of us; 'Dinde au Jambon a la Diable', for as one of the fellows said, a divil of a mess; 'Pommes de Terr Beurrees, Harricots, Petit Pois' (all tinned of course, but turned out quite well); 'Macaroni a la Francaise' (macaroni and cheese put into a saucepan together and boiled and guaranteed if you weren't already ill to make you so; 'Pouding de Noel and Sauce a la Creme' (Mum's Christmas pudding and Birds Custard powder, jolly good; 'Compote de Fruite' (tinned pineapple and apricots); 'Bonbons' (the aforesaid espergne was dismantled); 'cafe', and even then I have survived. The toasts were 'The King', 'Reunion' (which accounted for my speech) 'The Ladies' (there being none within five hundred miles). Afterwards we all sang songs collectively and as noisily as possible until lights out and bed time.
My deafness seems to be gradually going and I am beginning to hear quite well again, although it still whistles. A number of Officers have gone to Holland from here, those that have

been captured over 18 months. I envy them, I don't want to go to Holland, but come back to you all. Dave"

I do hope Nanna is back again. And that the Doctor may only have to tell John he must rest in bed, it is a trying time for you both, but we must hope for the best. Yesterday I went for our ration in butter, I asked for ¼ lb. I wanted 2 – ¼ lb for Polly. You cannot have a ¼ lb only 2 oz and 6 oz of marg. This morning I went for a ¼ bacon, that is the quantity per week (no bacon Madam, but the rations are not in working order yet, but it is a treat to go shop now.

I have done a little of the garden this afternoon. Hoping to hear better news.

With much love

From Your Loving Mamma

London S.W.12
Feb 28 1918

My darling Ethel

I told you I would let you know when I got a letter from David, well I received one last night, dated Jan 2. This is part of it. On Xmas day we had dinner, nine of us, — a great & mighty feast, And a menu And all And all, — but to start at the beginning, We drew lots as to who should do what, And another fellow and I had to make out the menu. The two cooks were cooking nearly all day. And I think about 5 of the others laid the table. You should have seen that table, It was a sight for the folks. A blanket served for a table cloth, And set off the silver (save working in the light) and cutlery (all sparkling and But the ~~~~ Central) splendidly. thing. As a d'oyley ornament was the cotton towel, (it had a smooth there was a than a week) And then a gorgeous sperque made up of the base of a metal shaving mirror And filled with some silver covered chocolates and some

324 my dearest

May to David   Beckenham   20.2.18.

My dear David,

Our glorious bright cold frosty weather has changed. It changed last night. Now it is misty, drizzling and not nearly so cold.

Nothing has happened since I last wrote you. We are very busy, but not staying late. We are all keeping in good health, I should say the "Best of Health" with capital letters, and Mama is much chirpier again. Ern had a letter from Goodchild. You remember him and his wife at Ramsgate where Ern used to stay, but they would not put him up that year we went to Broadstairs. His father was a builder and owned several houses in Ramsgate, while he learnt bricklaying, and the property came to him at his father's death. Now he is 79 and his wife 77. Several of his houses are empty, and scarcely any visitors go to Ramsgate now as the guns can be heard too distinctly there, so they are feeling very worried. Ern wrote them a long letter last night and sent them some cash to carry on with.

Yesterday I wrote to Ethel Barnett and told her you were fond of reading, and what books you have had sent. I am longing to hear if you have them all. Not had a letter from you for 3 1/2 weeks, but I am not worrying as you have perhaps been moved to another camp, or perhaps the censors have been too busy to read prisoners' letters. We have had to wait before now, and then get two together.

Still knitting the coat in the evenings. I expect to finish it this week.

Maud has just been in. She wants me to go with her and Maud Dunstan (nee Harding) to a Queens Hall Concert on Saturday week in the afternoon. Don't want to go without you.

Must leave off now, as I want to copy out a recipe for Mrs Taylor. Give me a kiss, quick; here come the girls.

May.

P.S. I forgot to mention in my last letter that Mrs Taylor has bought Mrs Day some material for a dress, black, and Mrs Day has had it made up. The dress looks very nice, and she is delighted with it. I mention this to let you know how well the two are getting on together. Yesterday Eccles was taken bad soon after reaching business. He had had some fish for breakfast, and the doctor thinks it has poisoned him. I guess he is likely to be very bad as the poor silly duffer has been under eating ever since the war commenced in case there would be a shortage. He was the gloomy soul who told me none of our men at business would come back. Now, if he were only married his better half would not have let him half starved himself, then he would not have been so miserable. A few months ago he lost his brother, a doctor in the R.A.M.C.

I am still doing physical jerks to try to get thin.

May to David   Beckenham   22. 2. 18.

My dear David,

This is letter No. 82 I believe.

Wednesday evening I finished knitting the body of the woolly coat, and now I only have the collar to do, buttons to make, and sewing together, and then it is done! And I shall be ready to start my next piece of work.

Wednesday evening I said to Mama "I think the damp has got in my throat". (It was pouring with rain). I believe she had the feeling for fussing over someone, so said to me "Don't get up tomorrow morning til I come in to you". She sleeps with Ethel and me alternately. To please her I said "Alright". Soon after 7.0 next morning in she came and asked me how it was. I could see she wanted to fuss me up, knowing the symptoms myself, so I said "it feels as though I have a cold in it. One of my girls has a bad cold cold; guess I have taken it from her, and it will spread all over me in time." She seemed quite pleased at the prospect of having a case, and said "You had better stay in bed to-day and I will bring up your meals". Now I didn't bargain for that, and I have been to the office with really bad colds before now, aching all over, so it did seem ridiculous to stay at home because my voice sounded a bit thick. However, she looked so pleading, and I remembered there was a day owing me, that I agreed, sending a message by Ern that I was having that day off. Well, I did enjoy myself. Instead of fussing up-my companion, I let my companion fuss me up all day long, at least until after teatime, when I felt I could not act the humbug any longer. Really, I have got a slight cold in my head, and staying in bed and keeping hot (I was fearfully hot) might have prevented a cough. I was boasting one day this week that I had not had a cold or cough the whole of this winter, nor last autumn either, I believe the first autumn and winter on record. Working hard suits me evidently. The rest was nice yesterday, but I must make up for lost time now.

Last evening a letter came from Mrs Taylor. She is down at Watford, having heard that Mrs Capel is not so well. I guess she is thoroughly enjoying fussing up Mrs Capel the same as Mama enjoyed fussing over me. Mama wanted me to stay at home to-day, but my conscience would not let me, but I compromised matters by saying perhaps I would leave at 4.30.

Now, don't imagine I am bad. I have told you that whole facts of the case, as I promised to let you know everything. I only wish you would let me know how bad you are at times. You don't, you know. Perhaps you have been bad again, and that is why I am not hearing from you. Here come the salaries, so I must say goodbye. May

P.S. If fine to-morrow I hope to do some gardening.

May to David   Beckenham   26. 2. 18.

My dear David,

Friday afternoon I left a little early, and so pleased Mama. Before leaving Miss Carter asked me if she could come up the next day (it was her Saturday off) instead of the one after (which was mine) as she wanted to go to Ascot for the weekend which should be mine. I willingly changed, and intended to do some gardening on Saturday morning and afternoon. The front wanted doing up badly, and some more lime wanted digging in in the back. It was a beautiful bright day with plenty of sunshine but as the wind was cold Mama said I had better stay indoors. So I wasted the day practically, except that I finished that coat and it looks alright. Sunday Mac came. She looks awfully well and brought us a photo of her. She was as chatty as ever, but had not any news. On Sunday I read a book called "Love and a Cottage"; nothing in it, but well written. It did make me laugh.

Monday was wet and cold, and Mama asserted herself. She said she was not going to let me turn out in that weather, so I sat over a blazing fire and made a tam o'shanter, and enjoyed myself generally. Of course I was imagining you were with me the whole time, so was not at all lonely. Mama came in every half hour or so (it was her busy day) and brought me in either something to eat or drink. I did some physical exercises this morning to try to counteract the stuffing.

To-day being fine I am allowed back at work. And it is quite time I came too. Just had a complaint of looting. Had a similar complaint some time ago, found the delinquent who was promptly turned out. Now I must look into this, so Goodbye for a while.

It seems to me the girls' own faults for losing money. They left it in their coat pockets, the dressing room door unlocked, and wide open, and the electric light on, and this room is close to the side entrance. It was asking for trouble.

Mama was reading out of the newspaper some very interesting remarks about Jericho the other night. It appears a lot of the Old Testament Kings had palaces there; Anthony & Cleopatra patronised the place, and excavators have found traces of the old wall. I forget dimensions, but it was a most impregnable wall then. If I were profane I would be thinking awful things of the Jews' rendering of music when by their mere blasts the walls fell flat. Must not stop any longer, very busy. Goodbye once again.

May.

May to David   Beckenham   27. 2. 18.

My dear David,

This morning your letter of 2nd Jan. arrived, and you did succeed in making it sound jolly. It contained an account of your Xmas dinner. I should like to have seen that feast and particularly to have heard your speech. As it was 4½ weeks since I had your last letter this one was particularly welcome. So you only had 4 letters from 14th Nov to 5th Dec. As a matter of fact I wrote 12. I expect the Xmas traffic had upset them and that you will get them all in time. Guess one contained an account of the Bazaar, and how Princess Beatrice bought 6 pairs of socks made by Mrs Taylor, ignoring mine.

I will write to Muriel and give her your message. I have forgotten about Brigstock, but will ask Mrs Taylor next time I go over. I have copied out most of your letter and sent her this morning.

So you hope to be home next Xmas. We expect you home long before then.

Having a ball of your waistcoat wool left over, I last night commenced to make a teapot cosy with it. It will have a pale blue ribbon run round the top.

I read a good yarn out Lord Milner. He was at a friend's wedding, but had never seen the bride before. To make himself affable he told her he knew all about her as Jack so often read out pieces of the letters "dear Nellie" wrote to him, whereupon the bride froze, saying "My name is Joan".

No more just now, so Goodbye.

P.S. Those temporary girls I have taken on had been working for me all along. Two I still have, and the third I have sent over to the "Indemnity".

May to Batsford   Beckenham   28.2.18

Messrs B T Batsford Ltd
94 High Holborn, WC1

Dear Sirs,
Please send at your earliest convenience to
2/ Lieut D H Taylor, No. 22,
Kings Royal Rifles,
Offizier Gefangenenlager,
Kaserne, Holzminden, Germany
The following:-
"The Builders Clerk" by T Bales (published by Spon Ld.)
"In the Twinkling of an Eye" by Sydney Watson
Lists of "Everyman" and "Wayfarers" Libraries, and
Catalogue of Engineering Books,
Sending the invoice to me.

Yours truly

David to May   Holzminden   March 1st 1918   Letter No. 18

My Dearest,
The waistcoat has come and is just splendid, even better than the first one. It is so nice and long and fits like a glove (how did you manage to get it to fit like this) and seems to hug me. I nearly went to bed in it the first night, but didn't after all as I thought I should pull it out of shape.
The third lot of books has also come. Thanks awfully for getting them, it is good of you. The Estimating and Lockwoods books are going to be most useful, Batsfords however did not send their list and the Surveyors Institution Library list of Architectural books was not included. In my letter of November 16th I enclosed a form to the Board of Education. As you have made no mention of it and the books haven't come I am enclosing another. Will you please forward it.
I am also enclosing a letter to Cox, asking them to increase the monthly amounts to £15. I find I can manage this amount. Also there is Mum's letter as usual. I have most of your letters up to January 16th. You do say some nice things in some of them - things which have to be read over many more times even than the letters themselves. I do wish I were home and able to carry you off somewhere, instead of your having to stay working on Saturday afternoons or any other time. Can't you possibly do without this sort of thing. I an awfully glad you have managed to go so long without a cold. Hope you manage to go through the winter in the same way. You ask how I am - I am "quite well thank you" but still I am longing to be looked

after in the way you mean and want it badly.

It is awfully good of you to spend so many weekends with Mum and to look after her business matters in the way you do, but don't let her keep you talking until midnight when you have to go to the office next morning. I have had "a second epistle to the Lieutenant" from Ethel Barnett for which she hopes the censor won't excommunicate her and in which she offers to send me a book. Isn't good of her? Please thank her both for the letter and the book, but tell her that we now have a small library here, from which we can get novels, so that I only really want technical books and the few that you send me.

The last few days we have been out for some walks on parade and it is good to get out again. We go out in parties of about forty. The Weser runs close by and the other morning we walked down to it and went for some distance along the bank, (on the opposite side the hills go up practically from the water's edge for about 600 or 700 feet and are very well wooded) for some distance, then crossed some fields and came back through two villages which are close to the camp. One of these villages is rather picturesque, as nearly all the houses are half timbered, the panels between the timbers generally being filled in with rough cast and whitened, giving a very clean appearance to the whole place. Our party going through caused a small stir, numbers of the people coming to their windows to see us. I have never had so much notice taken of me in my life. Another day we went a somewhat different route through a piece of pine wood, about two miles from the camp. Nearly all the hills round the camp have these pine woods growing round their upper slopes and they really are fine, both the woods themselves and from the point of view of scenery. As we came out of the wood we got a very good view over part of the Weser and down a valley between two ranges of hills with 2 or 3 villages in the distance. All this will, of course, be even better when things begin to get green later on.

It will be your birthday within a few days after you get this, so be a dear little girl again and buy yourself something for me. I know you will. I wish I could be with you, to wish you many happy returns in the way I would like most.

Goodbye.

David

May to David   Beckenham   1. 3. 18.

My dear David,

Just a line to say we are alright, very busy, but not working late. I have no news to tell you. I have finished that tea-pot cosy, and as it does very nicely am now making another.

March has come in like a lion as it is supposed to do.

I have ordered "The Builders Clerk" from Batsford, to be sent with lists of Everyman & Wayfarers Libraries and catalogue of engineering books, and also a copy of a book I am now reading, "In the twinkling of an eye". I expect you will think it is's goody goody book, but it contains some very interesting facts about the Jews.

To-morrow afternoon I am spending with Mrs Taylor as Mama thinks it will be too cold for me to do gardening again, while on Sunday I particularly want to go to the cemetery to look at those bulbs. The birds have a nasty way of pecking at the bulbs, so I have to go and cover them up every now and then.

Must stop now as it is payday for the temporaries. By the bye I was paid Wednesday and have again invested £10. Looks like beating record this year.

Goodbye,

May.

David to Ginger   Post Card No. 7   Mar 2nd 1918

The last letter I had from you was dated Nov 24th since when I have had no other and I am wanting letters, so you might write as often as possible. By the way I hope you get these cards. I write once a month. Yesterday I had a parcel from Harrods. They had stopped for a time, the two previous ones getting here on Dec 18th and Jan 6th. You probably know too that the Berne bread has also stopped. Your letters always have news in them that I don't get in others. Life here resolves itself into something like Mark Twains Diary "1st day – Got up, washed, went to bed 2nd day – got up, washed, went to bed" – and so on and so on. We however do a good deal of reading, as I get books out from home sent by publishers and there is also a small library of novels here. Can you send me some of Dicks belting stuff for boot repairs, with heaps of hob nails. I can't get these from home. Hope you are all well.

David

May to David   Beckenham   4. 3. 18.

My dear David,

Saturday was an intensely cold and boisterous but bright day. Went to Office in the morning, and to Balham in the afternoon. Was greeted with a lovely smell of home made sausages and apple tarts just taken out of the oven. They tasted as nice as they smelt. I left in time to catch the 6. 8. from Brixton, Mrs Taylor coming with me as far as the Plough. Just as I was leaving I had a fit of coughing which lasted quite 10 seconds, when Mrs Taylor promptly put into my bag a pot of honey and several lemons. I mixed them when I got home, and they quickly cured me. Isn't she a dear?

Soon after arriving home the postie brought your letter of the 16th Jan. making two in one week! It contained an account of your lectures. I read most of the letter out to them at home, and we laughed ourselves hoarse. It was awfully well written, and at a glance sounds as though you have some comparatively happy times though a prisoner.

I also brought away with me some fine black yarny wool which I have bought from one of your aunts (though I have not paid for it), and have now started to make myself some thinner stockings for the summer. They will take ages to make as the wool is so fine.

Fancy you darning. You poor dear! When I get you home I shall not want you to do a stroke of work any more.

I had a letter from Muriel Saturday asking if you would like books sent to you. I said Yes. Fancy Norah Madge being a relation of yours! Yes, she is, or rather was, one of the temporaries, but left a week ago on account of her chest being delicate. Now, I consider myself strong, but if I went about dressed about as scantily as she does I should expect to be dead in a fortnight. She used to go to boarding school with Muriel, and when here worked with Miss Andrews (the palmist) for Mr Maconachie. Small world.

I did not go to the cemetery Sunday as I anticipated. The clerk of the weather said No most emphatically. It was blowing as hard as possible, raining as hard as possible, and awfully cold. I had a lazy day instead, and read the newspapers, but could not find any news.

I have asked Mrs Taylor how many Malayalam Shares she has a certificate for, and she is going to look. She put that matter in Mr H Webber's hands, asking me all I knew about them. I copied out from your letters all reference to them, and then some weeks after asked what had happened. She said Mr Webber had seen about them, had cancelled your last order as she did not want the shares, and those due were put in her name pro tem, but that she has not paid any money to Read & Brigstock. I asked her then if she had told you, and she said No, she felt she could not, but said I might. The bald headed fossil, Watkins, has brought up his photo to-day duly signed by himself. It is splendid of him. On Friday he was standing by me when one of the temporary girls, Miss Watkins, aged about 18, came in for her money. I asked Watkins if he were any relation (I knew he wasn't) and he calmly looked at her and said "No, I have no sisters." And then looked injured innocence when all flew at him.

Goodbye

May

MEMORANDUM

FROM

B.T. BATSFORD, LTD
BOOKSELLERS & PUBLISHERS
ARCHITECTURE
DECORATION
FINE ARTS
ENGINEERING
APPLIED SCIENCE
Telephone: Central 7693

94 HIGH HOLBORN W.C.1

LONDON   6th March,   1918

Dear Madam,

We are obliged for your favour of the 28th ulto., and shall be happy to despatch the books mentioned therein to 2/Lt. D. H. Taylor at the address given, as soon as the necessary permit is forthcoming.

We will duly advise you of despatch, and will then forward the invoice to you

Yours faithfully,

B. T. BATSFORD. LTD.

Miss M. Muggridge.

May to David   Beckenham   6. 3. 18.

My dear David,

The weather has improved tremendously. Maples have sent me my dividend with a bonus of nearly £3. The country seems full of money, and there is more work than folks to do it. I have done about 5 inches of my stockings. The knitting is awfully fine. We are behindhand with our policy work, now, on the 27th ult. instead of the 4th inst. which is the utmost allowed! Humphries is dreadfully excited about it, so I have told him to go to Lutt (I didn't like to say "Go to blazes", so did the next best thing). I don't guess I shall hear anything further, as I would like to. We are not staying late, by the bye.

It has been funny lately. You know we own a company in this building. Well, the General Manager is chairman of the directors, and the other blustering chief, The Accident Supt., is one of the directors of this company. Apparently the new company does not particularly like being taken over, and things are not working smoothly. It used to be a good paying concern. It might be now for all I know, but there is something wrong. Chiefs are born, not made. You know I have lately had a difference of opinion with the General Manager, and would not give way. The other day the Accident Supt. sent for me, and started asking me silly questions about how to manage girls. I politely asked him what he was driving at, so he owned up to the bother about this acquired company, and practically said the management was beyond them, and was sending the G.M. into an early grave. Finally the G.M. had passed the matter over to the Ace. Supt. to make a report on the details, and to get ideas from me! I gave the Supt. my last years figures to go on, so that he should know what amount of work to expect from the girls, and he is going to have another go at managing; but, he added, it might be necessary to ask me to go down into the company and manage it personally for a while. Nice job that! Imagine me dealing out the sack all round.

Must now get on with my work, so Goodbye for a few days.

May.

May to David   Beckenham   8. 3. 18.

My dear David,

As usual I have not any news.

I had a letter from Mrs. Taylor yesterday asking me there for the weekend, but I have written to say I would be over on Sunday and stay the night. We really must work tomorrow afternoon, and in the evening I want to go to the dressmakers. On Sunday morning I want go up to the cemetery, weather permitting, as it did not permit last Sunday.

The stockings I am knitting are progressing very slowly - like your health when I have got you, - only done six inches of the first one; but I have a new book out of the library which is awfully funny, called "Sally on the Rocks".

On the way home yesterday I called on Vi as it was her birthday, and wished her "A happy new year". She grinned and said "I know what you mean". Mama sent her a silk bag which she bought from the bazaar, and which has pleased Vi immensely. Georgie is in bed with a cold again; otherwise there is no news, except that Auntie has at last got a woman to help her, and so far she is a treasure. She won't be for long, though.

I saw an awfully good drawing the other day. A majestic "Special" and a ragged urchin pushing a homemade barrow on the path. The words were "You must wheel that in the road, my boy." "Garn; I passed a real cop down the road just now, and 'e never said nuffink. See."

Got four girls away, so guess I had better get on with my work. Eccles is back again at work - has been the whole week, but he does not at all well.

Goodbye.

May.

P.S. I am always wondering what you are doing all day, but suppose you are not allowed to say.

May to David   Beckenham   13.3.18

My dear David,

There is nothing to relate since my last letter. Mrs Taylor posted me on your p.c. dated 28th Jan. So you have my second photo, but say nothing about the waistcoat. Hope you have that too.

We have been deciding about the Easter and Whitsun Saty. holiday this morning. I am having Whitsun as Ethel will be away at Easter at Huntingdon, so I must be at home, though Mrs Taylor did want me to spend the time with her. However, I might spend Whitsun with her. Maud, who is always thinking and talking about her health, has decided she must have a week's holiday, so she went to her Dr. who has given her a medical certificate to say she must have a change. She has written to a cousin at Sutton, and is going there next Saturday for a week. A staff girl would have pulled herself together and held over till Easter. These duration creatures are the limit, and sometimes I almost feel sorry I got Maud here. Of course she is not healthy, and that is not her fault, but I can't help fancying she thinks too much about herself, and is somewhat conceited, or at any rate, self-important.

I am reading the sequel to that book I have ordered for you, (In the twinkling of an eye), viz. "The mark of the beast". This is an account of the time of the Great Tribulation, 7 years, mentioned in the bible following the Second Coming of Christ into the air when He takes away the saints who are dead and those who are living, leaving behind, alas, according to the author, even bishops and such like, and all people who go to theatres. Then the Holy Spirit leaves the earth and the devil comes, and all but a very few get dreadfully depraved. From the texts the author quotes this apparently is going to happen, and also after 42 months of the universal war during the Great Tribulation when the Anti-Christ is reigning at Jerusalem Christ will come as a King to reign for 1000 years on earth. The whole theme is very interesting, but the author, humanlike, puts in his own prejudices. For instance, the woman's movement worries him, so that the awful time to come is a good deal due to the equality of the sexes, as then the emancipated women will promptly do away with the marriage service and live in wickedness! Poor man, how he must have worried himself for nothing. In spite of his wonderful knowledge of the bible he has overlooked that during the Christian era there was to be "neither male nor female" thereby denoting equality of the sexes. Well, the book is worth reading. I suppose the poor soul preferred being apparently toadied to by the women folk, but in reality fooled, as I guess his better half had her own way if she thought it was for his good. That reminds me, Ethel has two tickets given to her by her chief for the Albert Hall, Mrs Pankhurst in the chair. This is, I believe, the first mass meeting since women have had the vote extended to them.

Last night I went to a lecture on "Exceptions in Policies", i.e. Policies of all sorts, given by a very learned barrister. I listened for quite a long time, and then my thoughts, as usual, wandered to you, our past and future, which reminds me: I dreamt the other night that we had another dwelling as well as the bungalow. This was a beach hut somewhere on the south coast, and consisted of a sort of barn divided into 3. The part nearest the sea, i.e. actually on the beach, was the sitting room, and the whole front seemed somehow to open. Behind that was a small division containing shelves, a small cupboard, a range, and a sink. The furthest part was divided by match boarding into two slips of rooms, and each of these contained two sort of benches which had a mattress on each with some blankets, and were meant for beds, so that this barn would sleep 4. I don't know what possessed me to dream of this, as I had not been thinking of anything of the sort.

Nothing more to say just now, and no time to say it in either, so Goodbye for the present.

May.

May to David   Beckenham   15.3.18

My dear David,

Excuse the red type, but I am filling in headings this morning, having about completed the first portion of the classifications of Investments. Have got on with the work better this year than usual.

Nothing has happened to write about since I last wrote you. We are very busy but I am leaving sharp at 5.30 each evening.

(Maud has just come in and taken up all my ten minutes. But, never mind, she is going to write to you while away at Sutton where she goes tomorrow for a week, and has asked me for an addressed envelope for you. She has her rise to-day which makes her salary £1.12.6.)

I read something rather funny the other day. A resigned husband was saying to his wife "You must be an angel; you are always harping on something, and never seem to have much to wear." I wonder if you will ever call me an angel. If you do I shall know what you mean.

I have finished reading "Mark of the Beast". It is the most awful book I have ever read. The author died a few months back. I don't know what of, but should think gloomy vivid awful imaginations must have something to do with his death. I shall not send the book on to you, but the previous one "In the Twinkling of an Eye" is alright. I lent it to Maud, but after a day or two she returned it unread. I believe she is frightened of reading any books on religion in case her own pet theories are upset. She would not read that book of Russell's though she had it in her house for several weeks.

It is a lovely day, so bright and cold. I would like to go for a long walk, only if you were here it would be no good going with you, as you would not get far.

Can't think of anything more to say, so Goodbye for the present.

May

OFFICERS' SECTION.

Invalid Comforts Fund for Prisoners of War
19 SECOND AVENUE, HOVE.

Date 16.3.18

Despatched to 2/Lt S H Taylor No 22
King's Royal Rifles
Holzminden

Apr. 23rd

18 Manor Road,
Beckenham.
18.3.18.

My dear David.

...Saturday evening I did some needlework, and then to bed where I had some lovely dreams about you. In one of the dreams you were in civilian clothes again, and teasing me in such a realistic manner. I was sorry to wake up.

Sunday morning I called on Mac. I had been going to see her for ages. She is going away Wednesday for her Easter holiday. Nothing like starting in good time. She has not altered in the slightest, and looks so well in spite of hard work. In the afternoon and evening I read newspapers, but could not find any news.

We are having beautiful weather, though the wind is rather cold.

Having three girls away owing to illness makes us rather busy; therefore I guess I had better leave off and "get on with it!"
Goodbye.

May.

P.S. Since writing above I have had £5 bonus given to me. What shall we do with it? Let me think (I am now having tea so have time to think). Yes, we will spend a few days wandering over the Surrey Hills; not directly though, as the leaves are not yet out.

May to David   Beckenham   18.3.18

My dear David

[half of page cut by censor]

Saturday evening I did some needlework, and then to bed where I had some lovely dreams about you. In one of the dreams you were in civilian clothes again, and teasing me in such a realistic manner. I was sorry to wake up.

Sunday morning I called on Mac. I had been going to see her for ages. She is going away Wednesday for her Easter holiday. Nothing like starting in good time. She has not altered in the slightest, and looks so well in spite of hard work. In the afternoon and evening I read newspapers, but could not find any news.

We are having beautiful weather, though the wind is rather cold.

Having three girls away owing to illness makes us rather busy; therefore I guess I had better leave off and "get on with it".

Goodbye.

May

P.S. Since writing above had had £5 bonus given to me. What shall we do with it? Let me think (I am now having tea so have time to think). Yes, we will spend a few days wandering over the Surrey Hills; not directly though, as the leaves are not yet out.

May to David   Beckenham   20.3.18

My dear David,

Last Monday evening I spent looking through the papers for jokes. All the best were topical ones, hence I had better not repeat, but there was one picture which makes me laugh each time I think of it. Of course you do not know that in Ladies papers there are illustrations of golf corsets, especially in the sporting papers. Well, this picture was an illustration of an advertisement. Right in the middle was a lady swinging her club, dressed in corsets and a couple of lace frills below. The caddy was holding his cap over his face. Two men coming up behind were evidently overcome, and one had his club fairly in the other's eye, while a wicked old bounder was peeping over a bunker. Isn't it shocking? Now, I wonder if the censor will pass this. Still, the picture was far more shocking to look at.

Yesterday was grey and drizzling all day. I made kipper paste in the evening and did some knitting. Not yet finished the first stocking! I prefer making socks; they are much quicker. Today it is glorious. I lost my early train purposely this morning so as to enjoy my companion's company, which we did immensely. We came to the conclusion that it did not seem as if you had been gone over a year, no doubt because we are always talking to each other. It is a blessing we can write although we cannot give each other any important news.

Monday night Mama dreamt about you for the first time; dreamt you and Ethel were getting married! Now that is a very dreadful sign, meaning a death. Ethel is going strong. Have you been and gone and died? If you have, I shall die too, as I don't want to live without you. I do not mind your being miles away as I feel you are still "doing your bit", though I guess you do not like the inaction, but that cannot be helped. Hope you have plenty to read. I know your thoughts are happy ones.

I have given up hopes of ever becoming thin, willowy and graceful, and you will come back to find me a barrel. I am having no exercise, while I am eating more than ever! You remember my breakfasts used to consist of one thin piece of bread & butter and a small cup of tea. Well now, Mama read in the paper several months back an article written about the value of oats, and apparently if everyone eat oatmeal and less wheat there would be no trouble about the food question and the whole world would be saved etc etc – you know the style. Then another food crank wrote saying all people living in England should eat fat bacon. Now as a duty to my nation I start with a large plateful of porridge with golden syrup, then bacon and bread & butter, and then I have another slice with marmalade on in case I feel bilious. And still I eat my usual amount during the day!

One of the invalids has returned today, and another expected tomorrow.

Goodbye.

May

May to David   Beckenham   22.3.18

My dear David,

Friday, and a lovely day too. It is good thing you are not here, as I should only be grumbling to myself for having to stay in and work instead of going out with you. As it is it is no good grumbling.

I had a letter card from Maud the other day. Usual wording, plus the fact that she is better. Another girl who used to work in the same room with her has taken it into her head to be away this week, too. I would like to turn a few out.

Tomorrow Mrs Taylor and I are going out shopping. I am going to buy a new hat to go with my violet dress. There's vanity. On Sunday I am going over again and staying the night.

I have no news. Did a little more knitting and some darning last night, but have not finished the first stocking yet.

I have invested the bonus I had the other day, and hope to add more to it next Wednesday. Cannot stop any longer now; must see to the salaries.

Thank goodness I've got the money off my chest. It would not come right at first, having a short quantity sent up.

Tonight I shall be calling at the dressmaker's for my skirt which I have had altered again. May it do alright this time. Then I have the bils to pay at the butcher; after that, home, and knitting. We are now getting news in the newspapers. Thank goodness, as I shall not be sorry to have normal times again. One of Ethel's men called in her office the other day, and Ethel asked him how soon he thought the war would be over, thinking of course of her holidays. He said [rest of letter cut by censor]

May to David   Beckenham   25.3.18

My dear David,
Now for my weekend diary.
Friday night. Called at dressmaker's on way home from business accompanied by my companion, with whom I quarrelled because he would carry the parcel, and then on to the butcher's to pay the bills. Arrived home late, though not so late as I used when you used to come with me personally. Then knitting, supper and to bed.
Saturday, glorious; went to work in my new dress which does alright at last. Left early, at 12.30 sharp, (very sharp), and went to Balham, getting there shortly after one. Had a lovely dinner. (what was that you called me? A little beast? Just because you can't get lovely dinners. Never mind; you shall make up for lost time by and bye, and grow a corporation. Hope I shan't poison you with my attempts at cooking.) After dinner we went shopping , and after turning out thoroughly the contents of four large shops selected a hat. I was so glad Mrs Taylor came with me. I don't know what I should have done without her. You know I never think any hat suits me, which is vanity. Of course I ought to have a new face. These hats suit other people alright. Then we went back to tea, and afterwards Mrs Taylor came with me as far as the Plough. Went home to knit, but did not do much as I had just reached an interesting part in the book I am reading. I don't think I ought to tell you about it; doubt whether you are old enough to know, as it is shocking in places. After supper we put on the clocks to summer time and went to bed. I was soon asleep and slept well. I nearly always do now. Is it an excellent conscience, or is it that my imagination is so vivid that I can almost feel I am being fondled to sleep? Perhaps after all it is only because I am so tired at the end of the day! Well, I woke up in good time, ie 8.0 summer time, but remembering that the clock was put on I stayed in bed an extra long time to make up for it and to enjoy some lovely dreams. Eventually got up at 9.30! It was another glorious day. I meant to have walked to the cemetery in the morning, but alas, I didn't. I just muddled about til dinner time, and then caught the 3.19. We had mint sauce for dinner, which reminded us of summer. It was warmer out than in. Of course I wore my new hat, and of course I went to chapel in it. I did not like it on Saturday but I did on Sunday, and it is quite comfortable. I am sure you will like it because it has a wide brim, and you could not possibly walk too closely to me.
The chapel was packed again, people sitting on the steps and even standing. It was the anniversary of the Sunday School, and the singing was very good. The choir master flourished his baton in grand style, standing on the edge of the gallery instead of his usual place, and once or twice he spoke to the people. It was all most hearty, and I quite enjoyed it, in spite of the fact that Mr Brown did not continue the sermon I wanted him to. He preached on "The

fear of the Lord is the beginning of wisdom", and a very good sermon it was; but I wanted to hear the continuation of the Second Coming of Christ, which is in the air for His saints, and it seems to me that it might take place any time now. After chapel Peter took us out for a walk, and then we had supper and bed.

This morning I reached the office at 9.30, and is the second time I have done that since I have been spending weekends at Balham. Mrs Taylor gets up early enough, but I will stop and talk and eat and enjoy myself generally.

I was pleased to see a post card from you Saturday, dated I think Feb 6 mentioning your letter of 1 Feb in which you enclose one for Cox's, but that has not come yet. Don't run yourself too short of money. You might want some.

The newspapers are full of news now. So glad they are getting on with the war. Of course both sides are winning – as usual. Apparently people are being despatched to glory 'en masse'. We shall all grow callous in time, at this rate.

Must not stop longer, hoping you are really alright as you say you are.

May

May to David   Beckenham   27.3.18

My dear David,

We are now back in winter again, and yesterday it snowed in north London. The wind is not so cutting today, but it is horribly grey. Never mind, they are getting on with the war, and better times are ahead. In the meantime we have heaps to do. You don't know how thankful I am feeling to know you are out of the present scrap, though I guess you would rather be in it.

Mrs Grayford has just called in to see us. Whenever she comes up she always pops into our room and seems so motherly to us all. She looks very queer, though talks cheerfully.

Maud has also looked in and taken up almost all my 10 minutes. She feels cross with herself because she does not feel better. I brutally told her she was alright really, but thought too much about herself, and that she was to give up being selfish. She took it very well, and admitted perhaps she did think about herself more than she ought.

I believe Ethel's holiday is all off, as Percy phoned her yesterday that he heard he was to go to work Saturday and Easter Monday. Ethel does not seem to mind a bit, but she was put out about a new blouse she bought yesterday, a grey silk, only 9/11d, and looks good value. When she tried it on last night she found it was a little too small. She has grown fatter, and will be huge before long.

Ern is going to grow tomatoes, or try to, and Ethel is again attempting cucumbers. You remember she did succeed in growing one (alas one only) last year and that it was a beauty. Now she and Ern will be having a competition. Mama and I hope to grow the rest of the produce. I do wish our grass was cut up, but it isn't.

We have been paid this morning, and I am going to invest another £10, which will make £35 this year already!

I have finished reading the Sale of Lady Daventry, and yesterday got out another book, The Smiths of Surbiton which I have almost finished, but I do not think much of it. It is awfully tame, especially after the previous book which contained two terrible scandals which caused two deaths and two accidents, besides plenty of misery.

Must now leave off. I shall not be writing Friday as it will be Good Friday, but will drop a line Saturday while at business. Goodbye, and keep cheerful; am always thinking about you.

May.

May to David   Beckenham   30.3.18

My dear David,

This will be a short letter, as we are very busy, and only 5 girls have turned up this morning, one or two being queer and having to stay away. I hope it is not another outbreak of measles like last winter. Don't think so.

Percy Wraight's holiday was cancelled, but the folks at Huntingdon wired Ethel to go without him; she would not go at first, but afterwards did. We have not heard from her, but then the post had not arrived when I came away.

It is cold and showery. Yesterday morning kept bright, and I was able to do a little gardening but not much as it had rained during the night and the ground was rather sodden, Ern went out for a bike ride. He planted his tomato seeds in the afternoon, thus stealing a march on Ethel with her cucumbers. We sat over the fire in the afternoon and evening, and read, knitted and talked. Went to bed soon after 10.0. I had a p.c. from Mrs Taylor in the morning saying she was just off to Watford for Easter. I am very glad she has gone. She went to see Miss Massey on Wednesday and found her better.

My poor old cleaner Mrs Matthews is ill. I had a letter from her doctor this morning to say she was suffering from general debility and sickness, but that he hopes she will recover. It does not sound very grand, does it? I must go and see her next week. I wish I knew of a home to get her into.

I do hope a letter comes from you this weekend. It is almost 4 weeks since I had heard, though a p.c. came to Balham mentioning your letter of the 1st Feb, so I know it is on its way. Must not stop any longer, so Goodbye.

May

David to May   Holzminden   1. 4. 18.   Letter No.20

My Dearest,

Mum tells me that you paid for the books you sent me. It is good of you, but really you shouldn't & again she says that you gave her my photo enlarged & framed & told her it was from both of us. Now this was an awfully nice thought of yours & Mum seems to be particularly pleased & again you know that I had no hand in it. You seem to be constantly doing things like this. You are a dear. It is well over a week ago that I had your letter telling me about your argument with the G.M. & now of course I am most anxious to know the result of it & your following letter doesn't come. Altho' you cannot tell me the cause of it, I know that it must have been something touching the welfare of your girls & I am jolly glad you told him what you did, though I don't in the least like the confounded fellow bullying you. I don't for a moment expect he will accept your resignation, as he is no fool. As regards learning my work, I don't know if you would care to make a start at this, (whether you leave your present office or not). If you would, I should get Mitchell's Elementary Building Construction from my bookcase (the advanced book deals with Graphic Statics & Formulae generally & you won't want these yet, if at all) & work through it, drawing out the various parts as you go along, as this is by far the best means of getting the idea of things & will help you considerably too, to read drawings. Also in my room there should be a set of Mitchells Building Plates (in a sort of flat music case) & I should use these in conjunction with the book as they are practically the book sketches amplified. In the cupboard in Polly's room there is a collection of notes of mine on various subjects which may be of some use to you, but I fancy most of them may be somewhat too advanced to begin with. Mitchells plates may be with them. I believe there is a book of Quantities in my bookcase, but I wouldn't start this yet, as you must have a fair knowledge of Construction first & besides one can't learn Quantities from a book, it grows on you like corns, & when I get back I shall be able to teach you in a fraction of the time that you can dig it out of a book.

I am enclosing sketches of two houses, the result of part of my day dreams. Tell me what you think of them, and let me know if you like the idea of them and general appearance and which you think would be more suitable. Give me any alterations you think of and any ideas which strike you. I have lettered them A & B, and have copies of them so that you can refer to them. I haven't gone into the cost of either. Of course B is a good deal larger than A and would cost considerably more. I have marked the sizes of the various rooms. You will see that I have put cupboards and wash basins in each bed room. In A I have arranged that bedroom No. 4 could, if necessary, be divided into two small rooms by simply putting a partition across the centre. I think the external walls might be rough cast between the half timbering. In A the front elevations are not so attractive as the back, but I don't know that that would matter a great deal. What do you think?   In both I have put a door leading from the drawing roam into the garden, and I think you might have shutters over it to close and make things cosy in the evenings. Also the front door might have double doors, one solid and the inner one glazed so that the outer one could be thrown back during the day. Would you care to have a small serving hatch from the kitchen to dining room? You will notice that I have put the living rooms facing south, but I think the whole arrangement can be turned round to suit the aspect of the ground. If you think either would suit you, can you think of any scheme of internal decoration? I can't hit on any sort of satisfactory idea.

Thanks most muchly for seeing about Mum's business matters & seeing that you have been so successful as to reduce the amount I think you'll have to take this job on permanently in future. Thanks too for sending on that form to the Board of Education. I have all the books now, so please destroy the second form. Why must you work on Saturday & tire yourself out, without giving yourself a chance of recovering from the weeks work over the weekend? Today is quite an April day with brilliant sunshine & snow showers alternately & the hills & valleys round the camp are lovely. A cloud will come down & fill up one of the valleys with mist, until at this distance it looks as though the whole gap between the hills were filled with a huge smouldering fire, while at the same time the hills on both sides are perhaps all golden in the sun, with the woods higher up standing out with sharp, clear cut, black shadows. What would I have given to have been with you really at Maud's to have heard the Prelude & the Cradle piece? Do you remember the last time you played the Prelude to me? I wish you would play more than you do. You know you play infinitely better than most people & yet you are letting it drop. Please don't. All the same I would rather you lost some of the beauty of your music, than that that feeling you used to have should come back to you.
Goodbye.

David. I enclose Mum's letter.

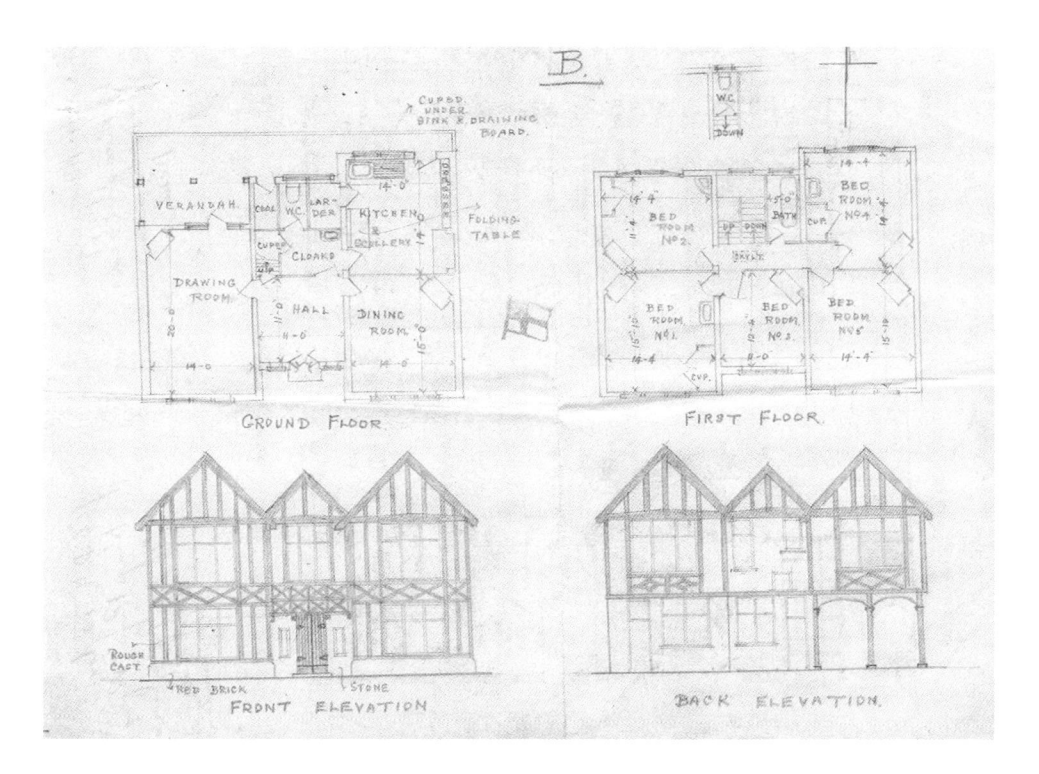

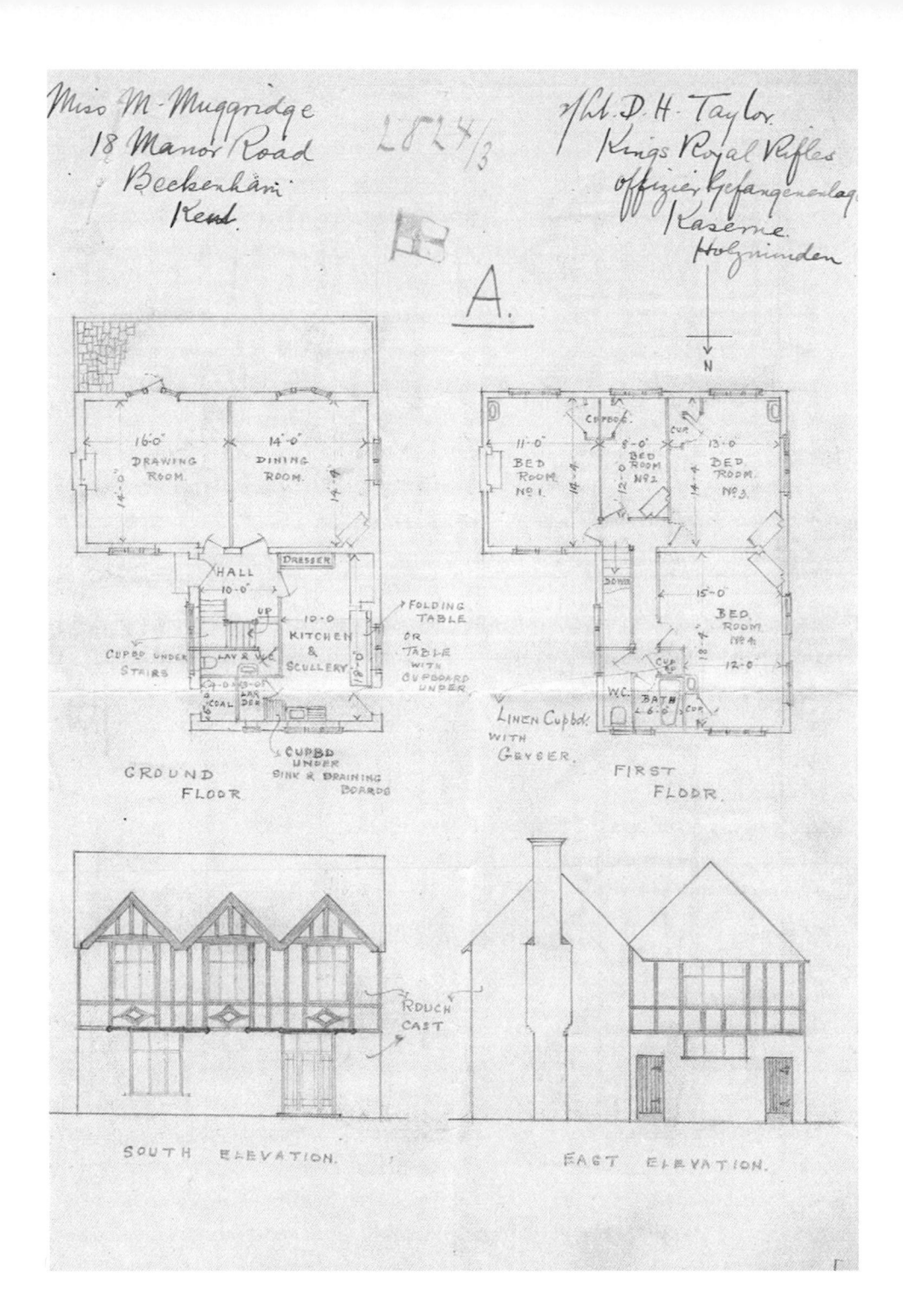
Miss M. Muggridge
18 Manor Road
Beckenham
Kent.
L824/3
Lt. D. H. Taylor
Kings Royal Rifles
Offizier Gefangenenlager
Kaserne
Holzminden
A.
N
16-0"
DRAWING ROOM.
14'-0"
DINING ROOM.
HALL
10-0"
DRESSER
UP
10-0
KITCHEN & SCULLERY
FOLDING TABLE OR TABLE WITH CUPBOARD UNDER
CUPBD UNDER STAIRS
LAV & W.C.
COAL
LARDER
CUPBD UNDER SINK & DRAINING BOARDS
GROUND FLOOR
11-0"
BED ROOM No 1.
CUPBOD.
8-0"
BED ROOM No 2
13-0
BED ROOM No 3.
DOWN
15-0
BED ROOM No 4.
12-0
W.C.
BATH
LINEN Cupbd. WITH GEYSER.
FIRST FLOOR.
ROUGH CAST
SOUTH ELEVATION.
EAST ELEVATION.

May to David   Beckenham   2.4.18

My dear David,

Easter is over, and it was not at all a bad one considering, but I guess next will be very very much better, as I fully expect you will be with me. I have had the feeling that you have not been over grand these last few days. Am I right?

Saturday was a busy day for us in the morning. In the afternoon I did some shopping and dropped a line to the old cleaner, Mrs Mathews to say I would go and see her one night this week. Mama is going to make up a basket of eatables for her. I had a letter from her doctor Saturday as follows: "With reference to my patient Mrs Matthews of 20 Granby St I may say that she is suffering from great general debility and has had a good deal of sickness. She is somewhat better today and I hope will gradually improve, though she requires careful dieting and nursing."

I am hoping to get her into a Convalescent Home, and think perhaps the Salvation Army have one. I will call at their headquarters this afternoon and see.

Saturday evening I finished my first stocking. Went to bed in good time.

Sunday was showery. Was very busy in the morning and planted mustard and cress seeds in the afternoon (and on Sunday too!) while in the evening I read The Mystery of a Hansom Cab. It is a very interesting book and I finished it in the train this morning.

Monday up early, and had a most strenuous day. We are asked to employ as little labour as possible, so as the workmen are coming to do three rooms on Wednesday, and the sweep today, we set to work and got the aforesaid rooms ready. I polished furniture on and off all day long and stacked it in the drawing room, and washed pictures and vases. Really it was enjoyable. We had three postcards from Ethel giving views of Huntingdon and Cambridge. She seems to have gone about s lot in spite of showers. Also had a letter from Mrs Taylor enclosing a postcard from you dated 5th March, mentioning you have no soap. She is at Watford where it was cold and wet. Apparently you do not get all the parcels from Harrods. I believe they send one each week, and a few days ago I wrote asking them to include a stick of shaving soap as I hear that it is very precious in Germany. By the bye, each time Mrs Taylor send you clothes she includes a piece of soap. There are some very interesting articles in one of our papers written by a man who has just returned from Germany and who has been there during the whole of the war. He mentioned that soap was unprocurable, and a good many other things too. It does read as though that country was in a bad way. We have not run out of anything, nor does it seem that we are likely to. We have been warned to be careful of one or two things but we are having a sufficiency of them. I thought Germany was supposed to be self-supporting, and that we were not. However, as heaps of oats and potatoes are being cultivated, and people are now allowed to keep pigs in their back gardens we reckon we can support ourselves. Statistics show that the poor children are better fed and clothed than they used to be in the past.

I must not stop any longer. Interviewed a new girl this morning and engaged her, but I have two away on holidays now and our busy time is just commencing.

Your letter has not yet arrived, the one dated 1 Feb containing the letter to Cox. Shall be glad to have it. Still, I do not worry, and shall not as long as the post cards come. Goodbye, and I do wish you were feeling as cheerful as I am – I know you are not.

May

May to David   Beckenham   4.3.18 [3 April]   Letter No 99

My dear David,
Ethel had an enjoyable time at Gt Stukely and learnt something of rural life. It must be alright for a holiday but I don't reckon I would like to live at that hole, chiefly on account of the water arrangements, or rather, the want of them as the portion of the village that Ethel stayed in depended on one pump for their water, and that went wrong some time back, so instead of getting it mended they use the water out of their water butts! Ethel said it made the tea taste smokey. Aren't some folks the limit. We must have water laid on at the bungalow. The Wraights who are now living at Purley have invited Ethel there for the day next Sunday and she says she must go as it was through them she had her holiday, and she has some messages for them. Nuisance. I wanted to spend the weekend at Balham; now I shall have to write to Mrs Taylor and put her off a week, and I know she wants me. She always does, bless her, and makes me so welcome. She is spoiling me wholesale which you will find out when you return, and which I expect will be before the summer is over.
Esther wrote to me the other day. David is expected to be sent abroad any day now, and she wants a cottage somewhere in the country, and do I know of one etc etc. Their furniture is still at Finchley Rd flat, but they have been living in Bucks, lately. Not being an encyclopedia like you I have told her to write to the town clerk of whatever provincial town she would like.
The workmen started yesterday, and moreover, turned up again this morning. We are in hopes of getting them out of the house by the end of the week. Guess I will have a busy Sunday.
I told you my old cleaner was taken queer. I now hear that she was so bad last Saturday that they had to take her to the Infirmary as she must have attention night and day. I wrote to her there telling her I would come and see her one day, and that I thought she was very wise to be taken there (she had told me some time back it would break her heart to go) seeing she would get hospital treatment and get well quicker that way, but she was too ill to write, and someone else replied for her. Poor soul, I guess her days are about up.
Do you remember I told you about one of our Acquired Companies that was not working satisfactorily and worrying chief into his grave? Well, they have fetched up from the Liverpool Office one of our men who is reckoned smart, and I was introduced to him. As far as I can make out he seems very shrewd but has no experience in the kind of work now before him, and has asked me, through the Accident Supt mostly, to help him. He is having a room to himself in this other Company, so I promised to run down to him every now and then and give him $\frac{1}{2}$ hour when I could spare it. He sees a decent sort, but there are not many men who can tackle girl clerks somehow. Isn't it strange?

We are fearfully busy and getting worse, so I must dry up. Your letter hasn't come yet, ie the one dated 1st Feb.

Goodbye.

May

MEMORANDUM

From **B. T. Batsford, Ltd**
BOOKSELLERS & PUBLISHERS
ARCHITECTURE
DECORATION
FINE ARTS
ENGINEERING
APPLIED SCIENCE
Telephone: Central 7693

94 High Holborn W.C.1

London 4th April, 1918

Dear Madam,

In reply to your letter of the 3rd inst., we regret we have not yet been able to obtain a copy of Watson's "In the Twinkling of an Eye" from the publishers, and have, therefore, not forwarded the books to Lieut. D. H. Taylor. Would you like us to send the other little book separately, as no definite date is promised for the delivery of the 'Watson'?

Yours faithfully,
B. T. BATSFORD. LTD.

PTO.

David to Ginger   Holzminden   April 5th 1918

Post Card No 8

Your birthday. Very many happy returns. I wish I could send you a present. Never mind I shall probably be able to next time. I have your letter of Jan 14th via Berne saying you are sending two pairs of socks. They however have not arrived. I am awfully sorry to hear about John's brother Mitchell. Could you manage to send me some belting to repair boots. I cannot get it from home & in consequence shall soon be walking on my hands upside down in order to save boot leather. Please also send some hob nails. Can you also send me occasionally The American Architect Brick Builder or Architectural Record or any other paper of this type. They should be able to come through the letter post. I have had some books sent from home, so am now able to do a little work which will probably be of some use later on. Hope you are all well. Haven't had a letter from the kiddies.

David

May to David   Beckenham   6.4.18   Letter No 100

My dear David,

When I reached home last night I found your letter of the 14th February waiting. Wasn't I glad! The previous letter containing the one to Cox has not yet come, but I expect it will within a day or two. They have come out of order before. I will reply to the letter next week as I am too busy just now.

It is a wet day for which I am glad as we are staying this afternoon till 4.30 to try to get up our back work a bit. This morning I posted on to Mrs Taylor your letter for her and one for C Webber; also a copy of most of mine. If I am not too tired tomorrow I shall be going over in the afternoon to stay the night. The workmen have finished and we are getting nice and straight. Put the larder and pantry right last night. I am not working too hard, so you need not worry. I am just enjoying myself immensely and feel I too am getting on with the war. One of our men came back from the front during the week. Of course he came straight in to the office, although it was only a few weeks ago that he was married. The office has great attractions for the men. I asked him if the war was going to last another 2 – 5 years as some folks liked saying. He emphatically said "No, of course not. No nation can stand losing hundreds of thousands of men a week. This is the end." Since then I have felt more cheerful about seeing you soon. I did not altogether like the idea of waiting another 5 years before I got a glimpse of you. Now, don't get a swelled head over that. I know I am not particularly given to flattering folks, am I?

Look here, you remember I told you about a dream I had respecting a beach hut or barn in which there was sleeping accommodation for about 4 folks. The more I think about that dream the more I like it and think it practicable. It ought to be turned to good account. When this wretched war is over practically all folks who are now in a state of single blessedness (what was that you said? Don't you know the proverb 'Where singleness is bliss 'tis folly to be wives'?) will be getting married, and then there will be shoals of children. They are expensive luxuries and accommodation at seaside places often not easy to get, as many boarding houses will not take them if young, and also some apartments, so small inexpensive huts near the beach fitted up a la board ship ought to let like wild fire. Will you think it over, and work out cost. It might pay us to erect a row in some place where there are sands.

Must stop now as it is 1.20 and I am about to work 3 hours and so earn 6/-. Goodbye.

May

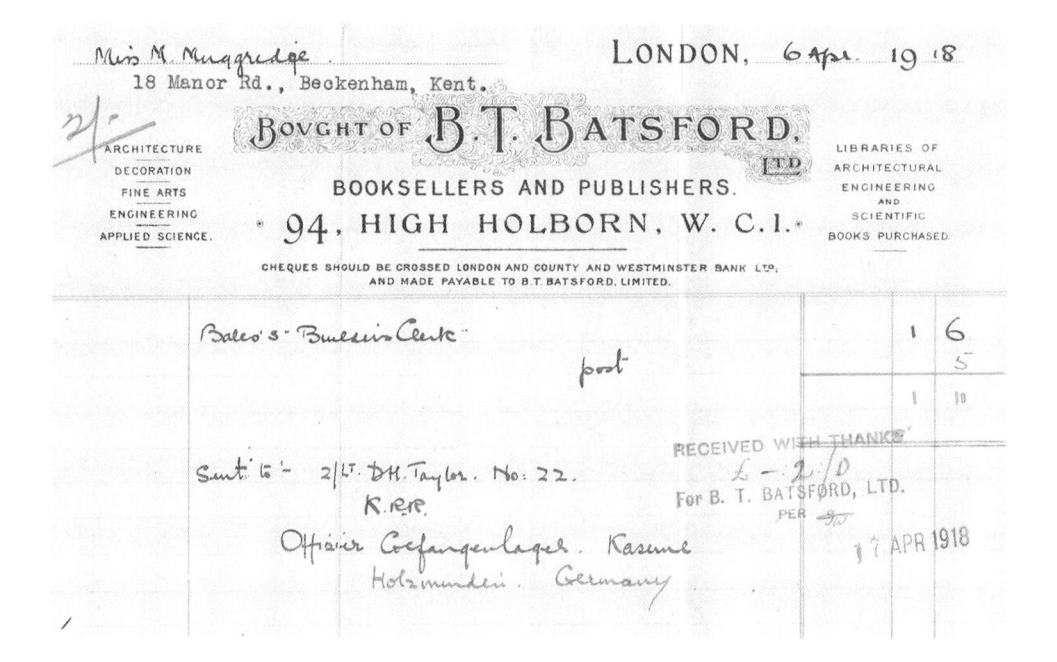

May to David   Beckenham   8.4.18   Letter No.101

My dear David,

On Saturday we worked till 4.30, at least I did while some of the others stayed till 5.30. In the evening I did some needlework and a little straightening and went to bed soon after 11.0. We have never had the spring cleaning done so quickly before. It was only the week before last we asked the landlord to have 3 rooms done up, and he asked when we would like the men to come. We said "Wednesday" (we had the sweep in Tuesday), and by the end of the week all was done! It does look nice.

Sunday morning your letter of 1st March No 18 arrived. No 16 is still missing. Perhaps the mail train was blown up. No 18 made me feel very much happier, as No 17 sounded as though you were fed up with everything. I am glad your waistcoat fits so well. It sounds as though I had taken measurements with my arms. Not that I would ever do such a thing, (much prefer your arm around me).

I am very much afraid I do not answer all the points in your letters. The fact is I answer them in thought while in the train in a compartment to ourselves, enjoying many arguments, and then when later on I have 10 minutes to write you I forget some of the points. That note to the Board of Education, for instance, I sent on, but I will enclose the second with a note to say they were asked for before but have not yet arrived. I am posting on Cox's letter. I do hope you are not running yourself too short.

After all I did not go to Balham on Sunday. The weather turned horrible, and it was pouring when it was time for me to start for the train, so I sat over the fire and finished reading a library book – The Man from Nowhere. An exciting book somewhat. The hero in the first chapter is penniless; in the last he has an income of £50,000 a year. In the intermediate chapters he gets shot at by the heroine, whom he marries in the end, also shot at by two ruffians, and almost has his head cut off by an axe. There are a few murders, a poisoning case, and an abduction case and a thrashing or two just to liven up things a bit. The hero too does his bit by smashing the faces of the two men in and then gets run in to Bow St on a murder charge, wrongly, but gets acquitted soon after. And all this happens within one week!

There now, the time is up and I have not yet answered your last two letters. Will have another try during the week. We are awfully busy, thank goodness.

Goodbye

May

May to David   Beckenham   10.4.18

My dear David,

The weather has turned out horrible again, for which I am not sorry as this week we are working till 6.30. We are being paid for the extra hour, 1/-, 1/6 and 2/- according to the standing of the clerk. I shall not stay Friday, as that is a busy day, and I am not going to overtire myself.

Helen came in yesterday to the office to say that she had heard from two soldiers who had seen Jack lying dead, and they buried him. He had been very badly wounded and had put his papers in a bottle beside him evidently with the idea of saving them better. She also told me that there is a man who works with her, or used to, named Hagell (I think that was the name) and he started to talk one day to her about you, thinking you had had bad luck.

Now for answering your last two letters.

Re bungalow. I don't want any brasswork in it – brass wants cleaning. Your cinder arrangement is great, but I do not think it would be worth the extra cost. There would not be many cinders, and the few there would be would not be any trouble to see to. As I particular want casement curtains, and so do away with venetial blinds and lace curtains which entail so much work. I should think door like windows would look best, but I would like some sort of ventilation above them in case it is too windy or cold to have the window open.

Regarding the metric system; I cannot find that question has been raised here for the last few years, but have written Batsfords about it, telling them you would want a book on it if is going to be adopted. I have not yet had their reply. Also I have written about the list of books not enclosed. I believe they have sent lists twice, but suppose they have not passed the censors yet.

About my birthday; it is awfully good of you to think of me like that, but I cannot think of anything I want, except perhaps you. (Don't stick your nose up so high, it might get frost bitten). Even if you were here I should not be able to see much of you, being so busy. We are expecting to have some more men called up from the Office, and consequently expect to be busier still.

Cousin Bert has married the girl he was originally engaged to. I don't believe the engagement was ever broken off, although we were told it had been.

That enlarged photo of you was the last you had taken, in your officer's uniform, nearly full faced. You will never have a better phot of yourself; it is excellent.

About vegetables; I mean to grow my own beans, potatoes, and a few other things, on principle. I don't know how much is saved, but home grown beans are infinitely nicer to eat than market ones, and cabbages are best left growing till the last moment.

Regarding washbasins fitted in the bungalow; what about the expense? I doubt whether it will be worth it, but then of course I don't know.

I have written to Ethel Barnett giving your message.

From your description of the walks you have had, Germany sounds rather a beautiful country. I hope you go for several more.

Cannot stop any longer. Goodbye.

May

PoW Book Scheme card to May   10.04.18

We sent the books out to 2/L DH Taylor and he ought to have received them before now. We received his request for them on 27 Dec 17; the books on bookkeeping and shorthand were sent to him first, and those on specification & civil engineering later on account of the difficulty in obtaining them.

Yrs truly A.J.D.

May to David   Beckenham   12.4.18

My dear David,

What do you think I found when I reached home Wednesday? A letter from Mrs Taylor containing £4 which she said were from you! It took my breath away. What am I to do with it all? I have written to tell her she must help me buy something, and the rest must go back into your account again. Really, you are a dear, but as I have told you before you are too good. Next month we shall be much slacker, and then Mrs Taylor and I are going to have a few days' flutter. You shall have particulars of what happens.

The weather today has turned out glorious, a nice change from the last week or so. I am now in hopes of the front garden drying sufficiently for me to do it up. The grass has not been cut yet, nor the beds dug up. I have trimmed the ferns, and the hedge looks alright. I have never been so late with the front before.

I do not think I shall have to stay later tomorrow afternoon. I am wanting to go to the Infirmary to see poor old Mrs Matthews, and then on to Balham for the weekend. I hope, too, we shall see Miss Massey on Sunday. As far as I know she is still in the Hospital.

The Prisoners Book Scheme folks have written me as under;-

 "We sent the books out to 2/Lt DH Taylor and he ought to have received them before now. We received his request for them on 27th Dec 1917. The books on bookkeeping and shorthand were sent him first, and those on specification and civil engineering later on account of the difficulty we had in obtaining them."

I say, if the war goes on much longer (though I do not think it can at the rate folks are being killed off at present) and you spend your time in studying, won't you be desperately clever? I shall feel an ignorant worm. Look here, instead of my reading novels like I do on the train now, had I better not study? And what had I better start on? You have heaps of books in your bookcase. Let me down lightly to start with, and chose simple things for me. I shall not be any use to you unless I have some idea of the work you do. I have never learnt bookkeeping, though I did all the bookkeeping at my previous place, and all the accounts, shipping and invoicing. I wanted to learn bookkeeping but Kidd said "No, you don't. If you learn scientifically you will then know how to cheat me." Wasn't he a darling? But still, before I went to him, the poor beggar had a proper bookkeeper who cheated him dreadfully, and he could not afford it in those days, as he was having uphill work, and had three babies to keep and some big doctor's bills to pay, so I felt sorry for him.

If I only wrote to you twice while I was at Littlehampton this should be letter No 103. How many of them have you had?

Your letter which ought to have been written at the end of January has not yet turned up. One of your early ones did not reach me though I had the envelope and other enclosures. The remainder I have had. Not so bad, is it?

I am reading the "Glory of Clementina Wing" by Wm Locke, and think it will be a good tale. Clementina is a character, and is as outspoken as your mother, bless her heart. I have just written to her to tell her to expect me for the weekend. I know she will be pleased. There is no accounting for taste.

I have not after all thanked you in this letter for your present, but I did last night and the night before. Goodbye.

May

From David to May   Holzminden   April 15th 1918   Letter No 21

My Dearest,

I have most of your letters up to March 1st. So you have been spending your money on me again – you naughty dear little girl. It is good of you to do it, but you shouldn't really. I haven't yet got "In the Twinkling of an Eye" or the other, but I expect they will come shortly. I am sorry you were queer with that cold, but I am awfully glad Mrs Muggridge would not let you go to the office. Of course the GM has climbed down, but he might have had the decency to apologise to you. Things here go on as usual. A small (but most select) number of us go out in the mornings and do Mullers jerks and other weird contortions much to the amusement and edification of the sentries. Then I go for a run round the enclosure. Truly life is strenuous – at all events for a quarter of an hour in the mornings. There is a physical jerks class, which usually contains three members, but like most other people I prefer to do my "ten minutes for health's sake" on my own, as I can get through about twice as much as they do and take less time over it and this is an item, as breakfast is always crying out to be got through before roll call. Have you settled which of those two houses you like or have you some better ideas? Since writing about them, I have altered the plan of the smaller one somewhat. I have knocked out the coal store and made it all larder. I did not like the coal store there, as it meant that the door to it would have to be in the front of the house. So I have now a coal store and general store in a lean-to addition outside the Kitchen and Dining Room fireplaces. Also upstairs I have reversed the positions of the Bathroom and cupboard with the Lavatory, so that now the Bathroom will have two small windows. The cupboard will also have a small window. I have added a Porch which should look rather well, I think, but it is rather difficult to sketch and I haven't been able to do it decently yet. It has two steps up of red bricks and then on one side, it has a dwarf wall of about 3'6" high of red bricks built herringbone pattern on a stone curb. Between the top of this wall and the roof is a balustrade, with turned balusters and the whole capped with a red tile roof hipped back against the corner of the main building. By having this Porch we could have a solid outer door on the outside of the Porch which could be open during the day, with a glazed door inside opening into the Hall. Have you though of any scheme of interior decoration? How do you think this would look for the hall. The ceiling and cornice white. The walls and woodwork to the stairs painted a fairly deep cream, (or a faint dull grey blue) and the skirting, (a very small skirting) doors and handrail to the stairs finished in a glossy black enamel. The floor stained and wax polished, with some sort of rug. I am not quite certain how the black doors would look. What do you think?

Mrs Muggridge seems to have got better again. By the way you say, "Mrs Taylor and I had port for dinner, then during the evening we sat around the fire and drank port, later we had supper and drank port (in tumblers this time). After supper we had a final warm before retiring and drank port and all talked and laughed at once, goodness knows what about, and then I noticed soon afterwards and that I was getting drowsey and that the others were asleep" (strange, very strange). "We woke up about 12.30 and rolled into bed about 12.40 I woke up several times during the night, but having taken the precaution to have a bottle under the bed – drank more port." Seems to me you must both have exceeded your ration slightly. Oh yes – and then "Got up in time to be 20 minutes late for chapel." Which is again very very surprising. The other evening we had a concert which was nothing very special, the best part being the preparation for it. Two of the men in my room were taking part and we assisted them to make up, a wonderful business. They had some grease paint and powder and we coated their faces with every colour in turn and once or twice decorated them in stripes and patches and we finally finished them off a charming terra cotta colour with the blackest of black eyes. They were gorgeous looking heather. There were several songs and one of two small sketches. Nothing very great, but still as good as one can expect here and the fellows who got it up went to a good deal of trouble to make it as good as possible. They painted some scenery etc but as the room is used as a dining room during the day and the stage is formed of the tables they are rather handicapped, but still they really turned the whole thing out surprisingly well. The other day we had another small exhibition of sketches by another many here but they weren't nearly so good as the first exhibition, although they were much about the same style. There were one or two landscapes, but nothing really good, but then this man is not in the same class as the other fellow and has only done sketching for advertisements I believe. I haven't the least objection to promising to be ill on all holidays in order than you can fuss me up, in fact I'll be ill every day and all day with the same inducement. I have been longing for a long time to have a bad attack. Goodbye.

David
I enclose letters to Mum and Uncle Alfred

May to David   Beckenham   15.4.18

My dear David,

We did not stay late at the office on Friday or Saturday; in fact we do not expect to again for some months. We have the work quite up to date, and the new girl has turned out well.

On Saturday I walked down to Bethnal Green Infirmary, and saw poor old Mrs Matthews. It took 3/4ths of an hour to get there, through a most interesting locality, though I admit I came back by bus. This Infirmary looks a most dismal hole. I found the old soul sitting on her bed. It was the first time she had got up after dinner. She was feeling dreadfully upset at having to go to an Infirmary, thinking apparently it was a shocking disgrace, but she bucked up and cried with gratitude. I pitched yarns as to how badly we were faring without her, and took messages from some of the men too. It cheered her greatly, and she said she would soon be back. I think she will, too. For two days she could not take anything at all, then four days she lived on milk, now she is eating a little. It appears that a chair fell on her head and that brought the crisis, which was really a good thing, as her breakdown later on might have been worse.

I left that dismal place at 3.15 and arrived at Balham at 4.30 and then had a cheerful weekend. We went to bed at 10.0 on Saty night, and it was 10.20 next morning when I started to get up. I had almost slept the round of the clock! By 12.0 I had finished breakfast, and we then went for a walk across Tooting Common which was looking very pretty. It was a cold day with a sharp north wind. We all three enjoyed ourselves, the third of course being Peter, who doubled me up with laughter. He felt awfully frisky, and fancied he was a pup again, and a small dog joined him in his antics. When this other dog was in the air going along quickly Peter would suddenly dive under him and toss him. The sensation must have been queer. They evidently both liked it as they kept up the game for many minutes. While there I went across to peep at Glenroy while Mrs Taylor sat on a seat. I told her afterwards that I should write to tell you I had been hanging around your lady-killing cousin's house in the hopes of catching him. She laughed heartily; but I have told you! After dinner we sat over the fire, and after tea went to chapel, which was again packed, every seat being taken. We stayed to a prayer meeting, and then went to Clapham Common with Peter, afterwards packing you a parcel of nicies; at least I did nothing but look on. Supper then bed. It was raining this morning & I did not want to come away. Mrs Day told me she has written to you 8 times.

In one of your letters to Mrs Taylor I read last night that you told her you had written to Cox's to pay her your balance less £25. Now that is the letter that never arrived here. The one I sent on to Cox's increased your payment to £15 a month.

The "Builder's Clerk" has at last left England. They do take a long time.

By the bye, there were two pieces of soap put in your parcel. How are you managing without soap? Do you use sandpaper, and are you growing a beard? I hear the Germans are using a soap substitute which is ruining their skins. We can get as much as we like, and the yellow soap has not even gone up in price. The last time I bought some toilet soap the girl said it would soon be going up $\frac{1}{2}$d, so I am being dreadfully careful.

No more to say now, so Goodbye.   May

From Rushbrooke to David   London   April 17 1918

Only a line, my dear David, to say how much sympathy I feel for you in your enforced inactivity, and how hopeful I am that, from what I heard from some other prisoners of war, you too are being well and kindly treated. Get a message from home sent me, if you can do no more. Be of good courage.
Yours affectionately

WG Rushbrooke
St Olave's, Tower Bridge SE1

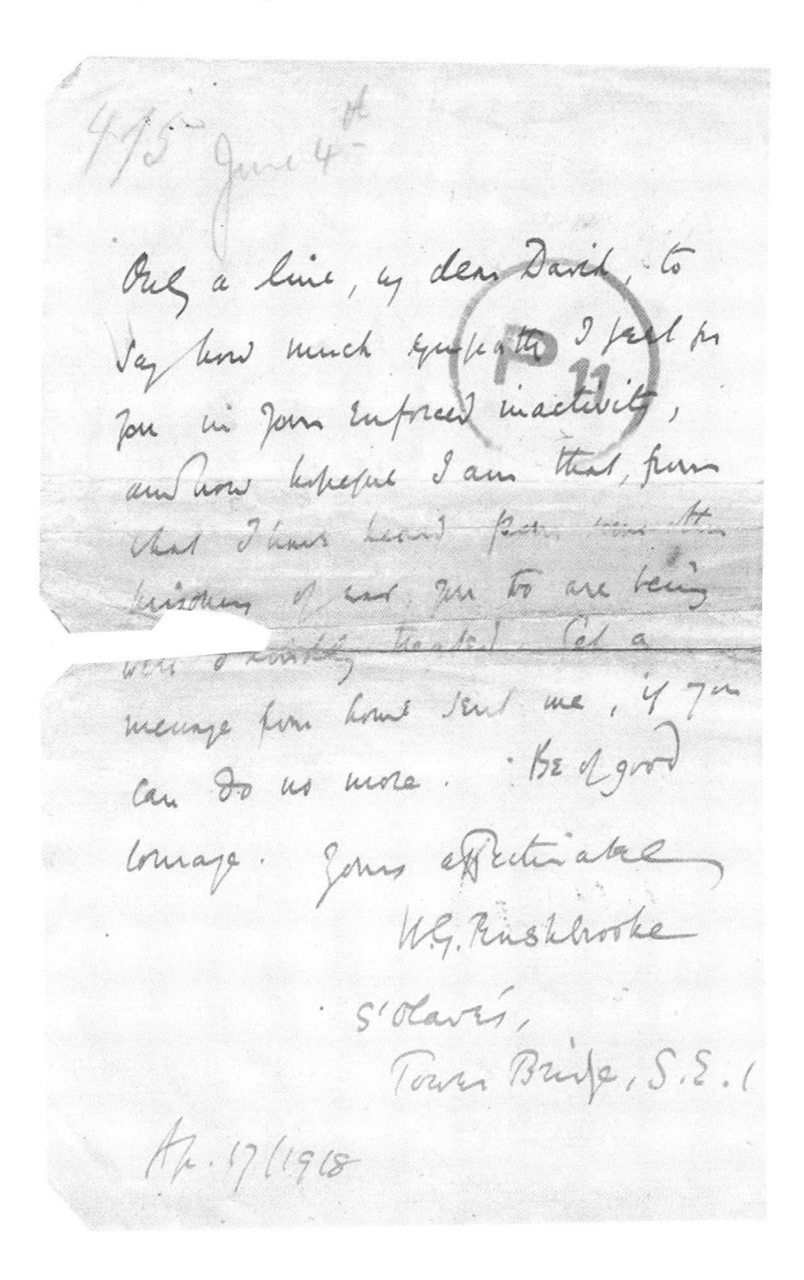

May to David   Beckenham   17.4.18

My dear David,

Talk about weather! When it isn't raining it is sleeting. It was like this last Monday and it hasn't ceased yet. I guess you have it cold and miserable too. Thank goodness you have your books and warm waistcoat. Just imagine I am with you too, and then you will be complete.

There is no news. Everything going on here as usual, and plenty of fighting on the continent. Both sides still winning. Really, men do strike me as being funny things. One side is "winning" by losing a colossal number of men, world's records I should think; while the other side is "winning" by losing ground. I am wondering if, when the men are tired of this upheaval, the men of all nations will say to the women of all nations "Ladies, we humbly crave your pardon for making such a hash of the world after trying in vain to run it for thousands of years. While you have been constructive we have been destructive. Millions of lives that you have been at pains to rear we have ruthlessly thrown away, and taxed our brains to the utmost in order to destroy them wholesale. Please forgive us, put the world right, and never give us a chance of spoiling it again. In future we will be your humble servants, as we feel you could not make a bigger mess of it than we have."

Somehow I cannot imagine any man talking like this, can you?

In the evening paper last night there were two paragraphs that were rather interesting. One was at a police court. A black man had to be sworn. The magistrate said to him "Are you a Christian?" to which the man respectfully replied "No, sar, we be quiet…folk."

The other piece was about a dirty old woman in a tram car. The girl sitting next her moved away when she could which made the old woman say "You needn't be so proud. You have only eighteen pence in your pocket", which turned out true. A gentleman opposite was amazed and asked how much he had with him, not knowing himself. She told him exactly, being something over £17, and how much of it was in notes etc. He then said "Perhaps you can tell when the war will be over, when she said "In April in a snowstorm." He asked for her address and promised to send on the £17 odd if her prediction came true.

I forgot to mention in my last letter that Mrs Taylor said I was to buy something in gold with the money you sent me, and she is coming with me to help choose. I wanted her to put some of it in your banking account, but she would not hear of it.

Must now get on with my work. We are up to date with it, and not working late now. Goodbye.

May

PS I dreamt of fire last night. On turning up your dream book I find it means that the dreamer's lover is well and happy and that happiness will continue. May it be true.

MEMORANDUM

From

B.T. Batsford, Ltd.
BOOKSELLERS & PUBLISHERS
ARCHITECTURE
DECORATION
FINE ARTS
ENGINEERING
APPLIED SCIENCE

Telephone: Central 7693.

94 High Holborn W.C.1

London   19th April, 1918

Dear Madam,

We are in receipt of your letter of the 9th inst., and are very glad to learn that the books have reached Mr. Taylor.

We are quite sure that the lists of "Everyman and Wayfarers" Libraries were included in the last parcel, and think there is no doubt they were extracted before the books were handed to him. We are, however, sending fresh copies, together with catalogues of Engineering books.

With regard to the Library List of Architectural books of the Surveyors Institution, this is only supplied to members of the Institution. A syllabus, price 1/6d net, can be obtained, but the

Institution prefers that the application be sent direct by the client interested. Doubtless, an application from you on behalf of Mr. Taylor would be sufficient.

A very practical little book for calculations in the metric system is Molesworth's "Metrical Tables," price 2/0d net. We shall be happy to forward same to Mr. Taylor if you think it would be useful to him.

Yours faithfully,
B. T. BATSFORD. LTD.

Miss M. Muggridge.

May to David   Beckenham   19.4.18

It is as cold now as it has been all the winter; too cold even to rain now. Occasionally it snows. Uncle Ken called in the other day to see Mama. I don't know whether he thought by grumbling about the two little boys' noise that Mama would sympathise with him and offer to take one to stay for a little time and so give him and Auntie some rest, but she didn't. In fact she told him what she thought of him and that was more forceful than polite. I rather fancy she called him a disagreeable old man who ought to be ashamed of himself and whose duty was to play with them and feel most thankful to have them in the house, etc etc. We do not expect him to call again in a hurry. Of course Auntie hasn't been since Ethel said "My Giddy Aunt" just before last Christmas. I am getting out at Penge tonight to pay the butcher's bills and Mama asked me if I wouldn't like to call and see Auntie who only lives a quarter of an hour's walk away from the butcher's. I said "Not particularly". I guess she feels that she has pitched into Uncle pretty hard. Mama has adopted a prisoner in Germany, a man named Bale who was in Bert's Company or something of that sort, and Ern has adopted one also. They cost £40 a year each. The money is sent to the Central Prisoners of War Committee, and they do the rest.

For some unknown reason I have been feeling so pleased during the last 2 days, and last night I had a lovely dream. I dreamt you were in England and had written to ask me to meet you at a certain station, which did not seem to be in London. I went and found you waiting behind several others for the tickets. You were in uniform. When you turned & saw me you were laughing to yourself and looking awfully cheeky. Eventually you told me your joke in these words. "Ethel's here in England and has been trying to make me give you up. I have invited her out today (we shall meet her soon), & I guess she will be wild at seeing you. Still more so when she finds out I want her as witness." On asking the reason for a witness you said "I am not going to wait any longer, and have made arrangements to marry you this morning a few stations down so as it will be quiet." I promptly objected, but you calmly went on smiling, saying you were going to have your way, when I woke up – just in time.

It is snowing. I hope you are keeping warm and well.

Tomorrow we are going to Maud's to tea! Don't you wish you were coming too? I shall be calling for Mrs Taylor. Expect to go home in the evening and spend Sunday night with Mrs Taylor.

No more now, so goodbye.

May

May to David   22.4.18   Letter No 107

Now for the recital of my weekend. Saturday morning I arrived at the office soon after 9.30, started the cherubs at work, and then took myself to the salubrious district of Bethnal Green. Arrived soon after 10.0 and found poor old Mrs Matthews in bed. She looked shocked at being discovered in bed by "My Lady" as she will call me. She had returned from the Infirmary on the Thursday and cried with joy to be back in her little top floor back, which she said struck her as being a palace after the Infirmary. The doctor says she is making wonderful progress, but she is very weak. Mama made her an isinglass blancmange, and I turned it out while talking to her. She gazed at it mystified, and asked whatever on earth it was. It certainly was a pretty shape and turned out perfectly; moreover, it smelt strongly of brandy. I told her it was an isinglass blancmange, and she immediately said, "But what is that, and what is it made of?" Poor old soul, I don't think she had seen such a thing before. After leaving a few more things and some more money I departed and reached the office again at 11.20 only to leave at 12.30 to go to Balham. As usual I arrived in time for a lovely dinner, and then we migrated in our best bib and tucker, to say nothing of our best manner, to Maud's to tea. Really, I had on my new dress for the first time, and Mrs Taylor approves of it. Poor Peter would have approved too, but wasn't allowed to. It wasn't at all bad at Maud's. She had had the place swept and garnished for the occasion. She sang several songs, and when she was not singing she was talking about business, still impressing upon us that she is really doing her best, though a fool at times. We did tease her. We even stayed to supper and did not leave till 10.30. Maud slept on till 10.30 next morning, but we were more respectable, having our "early" cup of tea in bed at 9.30, and getting up at 11.30 to breakfast, which we finished soon after 12.0. It was a pouring wet day, so we stayed in and talked (at least Mrs Taylor talked all day long, enjoying many recitations of past deeds, one being her wedding day) over the fire in the drawing room. In the evening we went to chapel which was again full in spite of the rain. We were in time, just! The minister was in very good spirits, like everyone else, more or less, smiling away, and talked so cheerfully. I could not help smiling when one hymn was given out. Mrs Taylor remarked in a stage whisper "That was my old Daddy's favourite hymn", and then when the organ played the first verse by itself, as usual, she whistled it, certainly rather quietly, all through! Then we came home and read through and counted all your postcards again. The only one missing is No 24, and that she might have got somewhere. The last one she had was No 25 which arrived Saturday morning. We wrote to Harrods telling them to only send 2 more, and then you will get parcels from the Stores which, by the bye, are cheaper, so you must not expect them to be quite so good, but the main thing is to get them delivered to you. Your missing letter to me has not yet turned up, and is evidently the one you wrote replying to mine about the Xmas holiday. It also evidently contained a letter to Cox's telling them to pay Mrs Taylor the balance all but £25, or something of that sort.

This morning I left Balham at 8.20, Mrs Taylor as usual seeing me into the tram, and arrived at the office by 9.30. The weather has now turned beautiful, and at last the sun is shining.

I think we both thoroughly enjoyed our weekend. I know I certainly did.

Goodbye.

May

PS By the bye there is a quicker method of shorthand than Pitman's which can be learnt in something like 3 weeks. I will make enquiries and if good send you a book on it. Pitmans is a bit slow.

May to David   Beckenham   24.4.18

My dear David,

Batsfords write me as follows:- "We are quite sure that the lists of 'Everyman & Wayfarers &c' were included in the last parcel. We are, however, sending fresh copies, together with the catalogue of Engineering books. With regard to the Library List of Architectural books of the Surveyors Institution, this is only supplied to members of the Institution. A syllabus, price 1/6 net can be obtained, but the Institution prefers that the application be sent direct by the client interested. Doubtless an application from you on behalf of Mr Taylor would be sufficient. A very practical little book for calculations in the metric system is Moleworth's 'Metrical Tables'. We shall be happy to forward same to Mr Taylor if you think it would be useful to him." I am ordering this, but what about the Architectural books catalogue? You see we cannot send any of the books &c from your stock at home; they must be fresh ones direct from Publishers.

I am worried about your feet. They will soon be bare, I am afraid. A few weeks back Mrs Taylor sent you a pair, but not your field boots. She was waiting to hear if you had received the others first, but considering how long parcels are taking I will ask her to despatch at once. She has sent, I believe, 10 pairs of socks, but it does not look as if you have had many of them. The other day the damp was showing through in my bedroom, so the next morning Ethel called at the landlord's office and told him. The same day the long ladder and a couple of men came and put it right. The landlord has turned over a new leaf recently, and is so prompt in sending his men to put the place right. Perhaps he is frightened in case we give notice to quit. Yesterday it rained all day again and looked very dismal. However, our Palmist called up in the evening and looked at my hand again and so livened things up. She said it had changed a good deal, but the black men were still there. Also I should be working amongst fresh faces for a while, and have a good rise for it. There was plenty of good luck coming to me, my worst time being over. You would be home within a few months. I can't think of anything else just now. Today it is fine with sunshine! But the wind is still north.

I hear Dutton's shorthand is catching on better than Pitman's now, owing to the fact that it can be learnt in 3 days, and speed obtained in a few weeks. I don't know whether it is any good. At any rate I am asking Batsfords to send you on a book with the one on the Metric system. It will help kill time, if nothing else.

We are still very busy, but not working late, although I suppose we ought.

Nothing more to say just now, so I will close.

By the bye I don't think you have been feeling well for the last few days, though I know you will declare you are quite "alright". At any rate I have been imagining you are not. Goodbye.

May

Dranoutre 1914-1918 — Maisons en ruines. Houses in ruins.

May to David   Beckenham   26.4.18

My dear David,

Yesterday the only thing to record was a big thunderstorm which lasted in London and suburbs from 3.0 till 8.0 and was a pretty bad one. Fields are under water. Alas my poor front garden! Just as it seemed likely to dry up a bit! It has not rained this morning so far, and now (1.0) the sun is coming out, so perhaps it will dry up and allow me to work tomorrow. In the afternoon I am going to see my old cleaner first and take some more nicies to her, and her last fortnight's money which I managed to get out of the housekeeper this morning with the aid of a little soft soap; and on Sunday I hope to go to Balham and stay the night.

This morning your letter of the 1st April came with the plans. They both look very enticing. I gazed at them and almost my train, and then got into the Main line train instead of the Mid Kent, and gazed again, all the way to Holborn. I wonder if our daydreams were alike. I must get that book of Construction out of your bookcase and start studying. I will willingly wait for you to teach me Quantities.

Now look here, you thank me far too much. The first parcel of books Mrs Taylor paid for. Also,

Mrs Taylor really looked after her own affairs. I practically did nothing. Moreover, a further charge on one lot of houses came in afterwards as they noticed the mistake in the tax charged; so after all the same amount was paid last year.

It seems that you did not get all my letters. I am writing generally three times a week, but they are all short letters and typed. I daresay you would rather see my writing, bad as it is, but I think of the Censors. Of all the hateful jobs, censoring must be about the worst. It must make them feel they are prying into other folks' affairs, and affairs they don't want to know anything about.

I cannot remember the last time I played that Prelude to you. In fact, I don't think I ever really played it in my life – but only stumbled at it.

I do like the description of the scenery around your camp. It sounds enticing but I don't think I'll risk being taken prisoner even for that, though I wouldn't mind, if you were there, & we could be together. In fact, I expect we should both enjoy ourselves somehow.

I will answer your letter about the plans of houses on Monday, too busy now.

Goodbye.

May

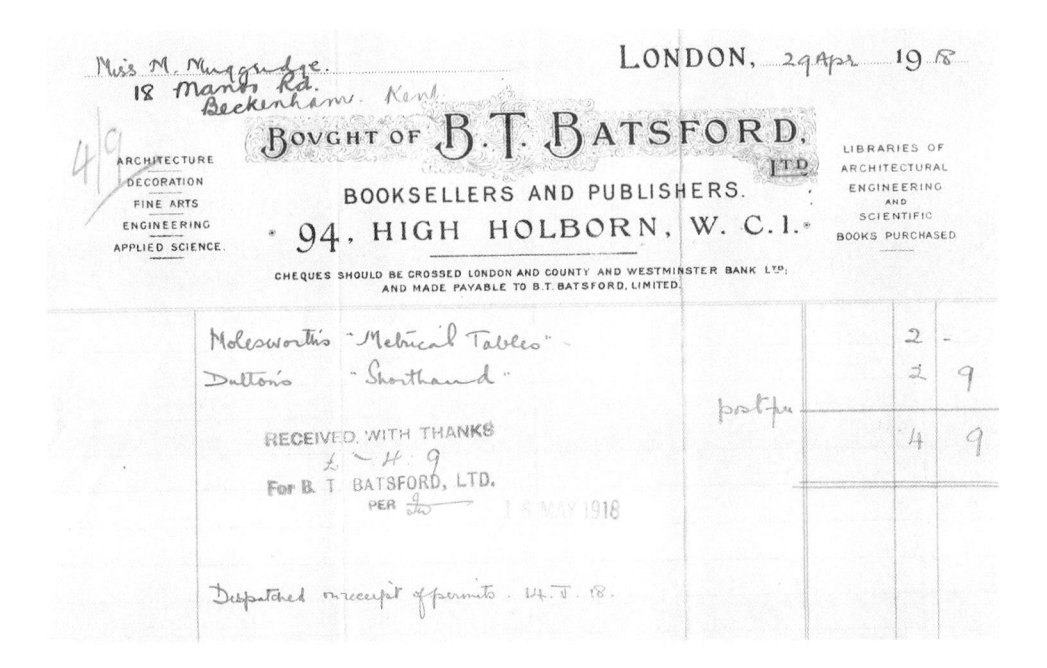

May to David   Beckenham   29.4.18   Letter No 110

My dear David,

Now for my weekend narrative.

Saturday turned out to be a glorious day. I left the office at 12.30 and walked to Bethnal Green to see my old cleaner, and take her a pudding &c. She had just gone out, for which I was really thankful, so I left the things in her room and went for a walk round. One turning looked very inviting. It was named Brick Lane, and had a row of stalls either side. It was packed. I walked down the middle of the road observing people. You could buy everything on these stalls. Outside the busy ones people instinctively formed queues (I suppose people got that idea from waiting outside cinemas), and the haggling was very interesting. If you wore a rusty black bonnet and a coat and looked as though you had a good opinion of yourself you were addressed as "Ma"; if a bonnet and shawl, then it was "Mother"; but if no bonnet then you were not addressed in any way. Of course those folks had shawls over their heads. I overheard two talking thus:- "'Ark, that's a hairyplane", "No, it ain't; its a siren," with a good accent on the "reen". I spoke one venerable looking old soul. She deliberately looked me up and down, and then, apparently approving of me, addressed me as "My dear"! I walked back to St Paul's Station, calling in at Lyons near the station, and imagined you were with me as usual. Caught the 2.16 home. Then at last I worked in the front garden and cut both plots of grass. I am still stiff. Went to bed early Saturday with a view to getting up early next morning. Soon asleep, and slept on till after 8.0! Of course I had to have 1½ hours daydreams before I got up. We discussed the houses you have planned. Owing to many interruptions we did not get much settled. However, we decided on plan A as I had not lived in a house anything like that before. All the walls are to be painted, the drawing room a delicate green, that being the most restful colour for the nerves; the dining room terra cotta, with pink tinted globes that will go with the walls – if we can get them. Green casement curtains, and green paint on the doors &c.

Cannot stop any longer now. Too busy.

Sunday was pouring with rain, so stayed in. Very sorry not to go to Balham, but I had not promised, so Mrs Taylor was not expecting me. How it poured! Had a letter from her this morning. I have written making an appointment to go to the Stores about your parcels. May you get them more regularly than you did Harrod's. I hope you are getting soap. A lot has been sent you.

I am going to study that book of yours on Construction so as to understand plans properly, and, I hope, draw some. Also, one one I am going to White Hill, Caterham, to look at some lovely bungalows that Ethel saw there a few Sundays back. As the Censors passed your plans they might mine, though I guess mine will look rather suspicious, to say the least of it. However, I will try. They might resemble houses!

Plan A would do well for a corner house. A lawn and fernery outside the dining & drawing room, and kitchen garden along the west side of the garden.

Cannot stop any longer, so Goodbye.

May

David to May   Holzminden   May 1st 1918   Letter No 22

My Dearest, Your birthday tomorrow and still I am not with you. It does seem an awful time since I left you. Never mind, next time I shall be able to wish you many happy returns in the only proper way. Your letter of March 18th was half cut away, which makes me say thanks each time I look at it. By the way I cannot write to more than one person each time now, so will you please explain to Mum.

It's awfully good of Muriel to think of sending books to me. Will you please give her my very best thanks and tell her I would write, but correspondence is so limited. "In the Twinkling of an Eye" hasn't come yet but it should be here soon. Could you send me the following:- (and please get the money from Mum or else how am I to ask you to send me further books) "The Market Garden", "Manures and Manuring", "War-Time Gardening", published by The Small-Holder, 16-18 Henrietta St, WC, at 1/- each I think.

Why couldn't the G.M. come direct to you with regard to the girls of that other company instead of doing the thing through the Accident Supt. They have got themselves into a mess and instead of coming to you in a decent way and asking you to get them out of it they must get all they can out of you in a round about fashion and then try to clear the matter up that way. Of course they will fail and then you are to have the job of managing the thing "for a while", or in other words "straightening out the tangle" for them. Though I'll bet two phennigs (you notice I gamble in German now) they won't dream of raising your salary to equal that of the manager of the concern, or even repay you in any way and will most probably take all the credit to themselves.

I am enclosing another sketch of the small house with the plans altered somewhat and the elevations worked in a different way. You will see that I have increased the size of the Hall, Kitchen and Larder. Instead of having the porch outside, I have now cut it off the Hall, so that it will form a recess under the Stairs, which can be used for hanging coats etc. In the Drawing Room I have put the fireplace in the corner, which will make that room more comfy, as it gives a much bigger space round the fire. I have also put the north window up the other end facing east, and you will see I have a built-in bookcase. I have put doors leading to the garden in the Dining and Drawing Rooms and these I think we should fit with rolling shutters. Instead of having two windows on the Stairs I have put one, which will go up two stories and which we can glaze with some sort of ornamental glass. Upstairs I have increased the size of bedroom 4 and have altered the position of the bathroom slightly. In bedroom No 1 I have put the fireplace in the corner and have put bay windows in Nos 1 and 3. Of course the elevations are entirely different. I think we might have them entirely in rough cast, with the woodwork stained dark oak. I have put a small canopy over the Entrance door, hung up to the wall with ornamental iron brackets and the frame of the window next to it, (the Hall and stairs window) will stand out from the wall slightly. On the back elevation the two bedroom windows will of course project over the ground floor and also the gables above, these being supported at the ends by ornamental wood brackets.

I have had a letter from Ethel dated February 1st which Mum apparently forwarded. Mum says she read one of Ethel's letters. I hope it wasn't this one, as Ethel seems to be tearing her hair rending her garments because Mum is sending me the parcels from Harrods now instead of she (Ethel) herself. Ethel is upset because she says "I enjoyed sending those packages, as it was the one bit I felt I was doing." There seems to have been a misunderstanding between them about a ham I asked for. Ethel's letters are sometimes awfully amusing, although perhaps she doesn't write them for that point of view.

I quite agree with Mrs Muggridge and I am glad she has taken you in hand and is now making you feed decently, instead of the scrappy way you used to. You ought to get some exercise though, especially as you are shut indoors all day. It was strange that you should dream of that bungalow as I have been sketching one, but I haven't yet drawn it so I cannot send it to you, but will do so next time.

We have two small pups in the camp, one of which seems to have fallen violently in love with me. They usually spend the greater part of their time fighting one another and at the moment are scrapping under my chair. One of them has found a mouse in a very high state of decomposition and they have both suddenly discovered that they cannot possibly live without that mouse. They are always finding things such as this and the more decayed the mouse is, the better they like it.

You mention Easter in your letter. Apparently Easter is a great time here as on the Monday evening I noticed several bonfires round about the camp, one, some distance off, was quite a large one and there was a crowd of lanterns or torches (I could not see which) flickering round about it as though some sort of a dance were going on. Your description of the Ladies Golf Corset picture is positively awful (the picture I mean). To what depths have our illustrated papers sunk, and what were you doing to be looking at such pictures, more especially as you say that the picture was "far more shocking to look at". I am surprised, not to say pained, and I think I shall go to the next church service in order to pray for you.

I think when I get back we must spend a month having train journeys together – no we won't though, because I expect we shall find lots of other things to do that will be much nicer even than that. Can't you think of some – I can.

Goodbye.

David

GROUND FLOOR

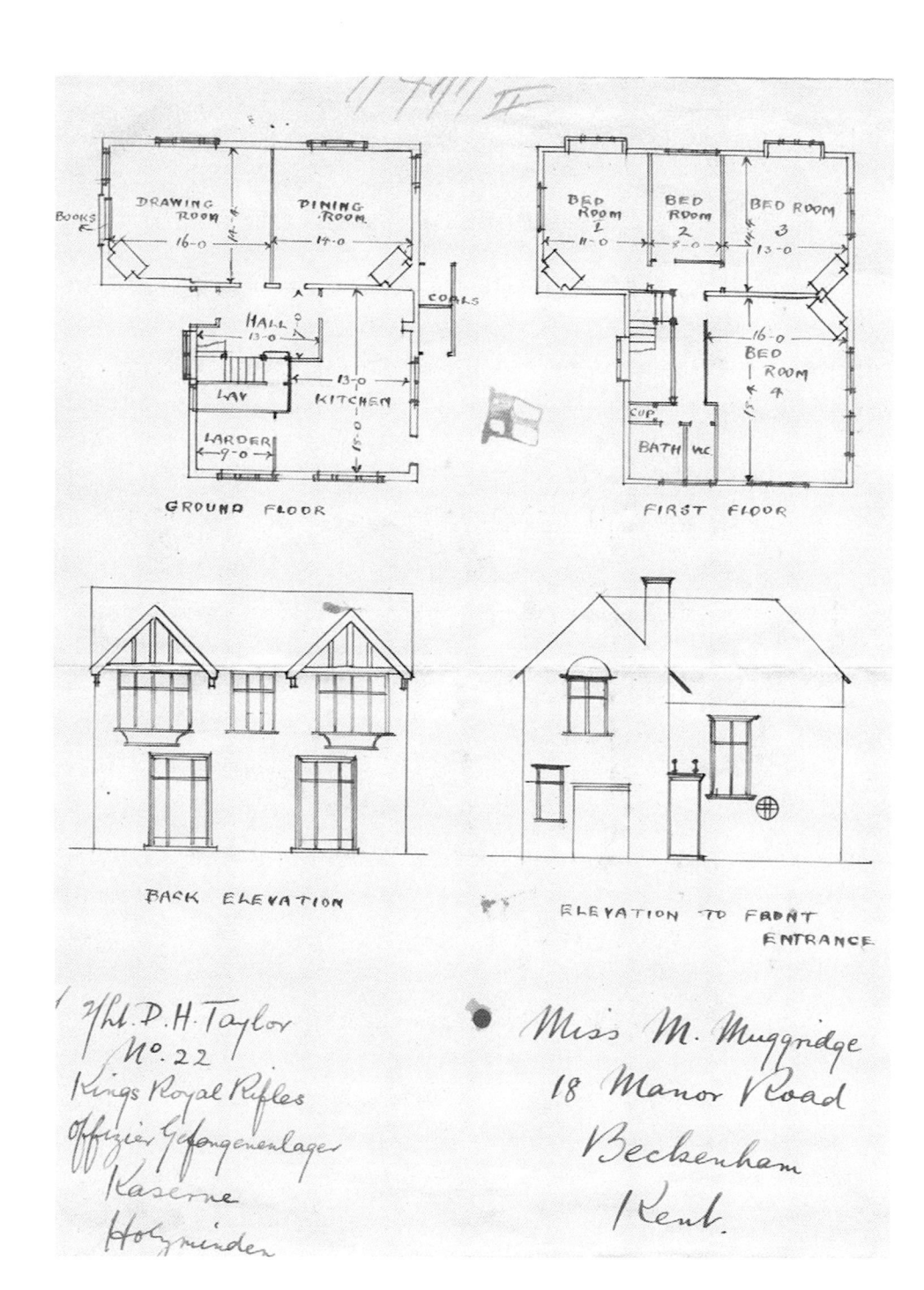

- BOOKS
- DRAWING ROOM 16-0
- DINING ROOM 14-0
- COALS
- HALL 13-0
- LAV
- KITCHEN 13-0 / 15-0
- LARDER 9-0

FIRST FLOOR

- BED ROOM 1 — 11-0
- BED ROOM 2 — 8-0
- BED ROOM 3 — 13-0
- BED ROOM 4 — 16-0
- CUP
- BATH WC

BACK ELEVATION

ELEVATION TO FRONT ENTRANCE

2/Lt. D. H. Taylor
No. 22
Kings Royal Rifles
Offizier Gefangenenlager
Kaserne
Holzminden

Miss M. Muggridge
18 Manor Road
Beckenham
Kent.

May to David   Beckenham   1 May 1918

My dear David,

I have just been reading your letter of 1 April again, the one that contains the plans of the two houses which you say are the result of part of your day dreams. I wonder if I can guess what some of the other day dreams are. Expect I can. Of course at home they think these houses are for the "bungalow", and naturally Mama thinks they are rather on the large size, so I told her I would study your business and try to draw something smaller, but she said she did not think I had any original ideas, and as to the decorations she is sure I have no idea. I shall take a fit of going over empty houses again with a view to getting some. I don't how you could work out the cost just now, as most things have gone up in price. I don't know about building material, but I do know I have to pay an increase of 4d a lb. on meat over pre war prices and 5d a pair on my stockings. I read about a gentleman who returned from Germany about a month ago, and was struck with our shops looking the same as in pre war days. It is quite true, they do look the same, and just as well stocked, but practically everything is a copper or two dearer. I had to pay 4/6 a yard for my last dress two or three months ago, whereas the stuff is not worth more than 3/11. Of course a man back from Germany, or anywhere else, would not know that.

I don't think I would like a hatch between the dining room and the kitchen. Don't you think it would look too businesslike? At any rate, it is somewhat like a boarding house; and we had one at school, I remember.

Mrs Taylor called in yesterday morning, and together we sojourned to the Stores and put in hand a standing order for you for a weekly parcel. Each parcel will contain a cake of soap. By the bye, there will be other things as well, including an occasional pot of honey in case you get a sore throat.

I am not sure whether I will have wash basins fitted in the bedrooms, as there may be a smell from the pipe. Don't you think so? I know I am fussy about health. I do like the idea of double doors to the hall, but could that be done to plan A? Apparently in this plan there will be an extra piece of ground on the eastern side. If that could only be on the west it would make a nice warm piece of kitchen garden, but of course it all depends on where the road comes. If on the east it had better be a flower bed, and then the kitchen garden would be north, worse luck. Oh dear, perhaps we had better wait till we get the ground first, and then do some twisting round.

This letter sounds a bit disconnected to say the least of it, but the fact is that it is the 21st birthday of one of the girls and everyone is excited for her; also we have presented another of the girls with her wedding present today (cut glass salad bowl). She and young Westland got married 3 weeks ago in a big hurry. They had their honeymoon in Devonshire, and have now parted company again, she back here & her hubby in the army again.

Too busy to say more, so Goodbye.

May

May to David   Beckenham   2 & 3 May 1918

My dear David,

This is my birthday, and I am enjoying it in spite of the fact that you are not really with me. Miss Willsher has left me an enlarged photo of myself, which I think is very flattering, but the girls at the office don't think so, so they say. At any rate I shall hand it over to you when you return, unless you don't want it. I shall have it framed the same as yours. Miss Willsher also wants me to go out with her to see some wonderful old mansion that Sir Arthur Lee has given to the nation as the country residence of the Prime Minister. It is a good way out on the G.W.R. I have promised to go. The girls have given me a fancy silver dish on ornamental legs, for holding sweets I think. It looks very handsome and I told them seemed suitable for a wedding present, when one cheeky beggar, Miss Daffarn, informed me she had looked up the meaning of my Christian name, and found it meant "Beloved" which they considered appropriate! What am I to say to such giddy kippers? And I am supposed to be strict with them. Muriel has written me a nice letter and in it mentions she has a £20 rise which she politely puts down to the early training I gave her! I have not spent your £4 but expect to soon with Mrs Taylor's aid. We had got behindhand with the work, so have been staying late this week. We have now got on very well, so perhaps the week after next I might start my holiday. I am saving for a fortnight for the early autumn, or late summer when I expect you will be back, especially as they are getting on so well with the war. I have also had given me by the girls a lottery ticket with their best wishes for a prize. I forgot to mention further back that Muriel has been too busy to write you lately for which she is sorry, but will do so as soon as possible. I have a lovely large bunch of pinkish tulips given me by the temporary girls, and roses to match. Last night on the way home I invested £14 and still have £10 at home to go on with. Everyone seems to be making money wholesale.

This is tomorrow. After leaving Office yesterday I went to St George's Hall and booked 22 seats for the staff girls for Saty aft 25th May. This is the first time I have been out for a year excepting going to Balham, and the other Saturday to Maud's.

Mrs Taylor has sent me some lovely handkerchiefs. I must write to her now. Tomorrow I shall be having off – I have much to do – and on Sunday I shall be going to Balham to stay the night.

I must not stop any longer as we are so busy. Goodbye.

May

PS Last night I dreamt I was wearing that ring. I wonder what that is a sign of?

David to Ginger   Holzminden   Post Card No 9   May 3rd 1918

I have just had your letter of Feb 21st. By the way if you send letters direct to me they come quicker. I am awfully sorry to hear that John has had to have another operation but Mum in her last letter said it had been successful & he was better. I hope he will get thoroughly well again now. I am sorry your arrangement with regard to the Harrods parcels got messed up. I told you some time ago that the Berne people had discontinued their bread since December. I am trying to do a little work now, having got some books on Civil Engineering & Building from home but it is somewhat difficult as one cannot get alone by oneself. Could you send me any of the American Building Journals such as the American Architect, Architectural Record or brick Building or papers like these. They should come through by letter post. Please write more often than you do. I hope the kiddies are alright & you yourself also.

David

Post Card No 9. May 3rd 1918.

I have just had your letter of Feb. 21. By the way, if you send letters direct to me they come quicker. I am awfully sorry to hear that John has had to have another operation, but Mum in her last letter said ~~he was~~ it had been successful & he was better. I hope he will get thoroughly well again now. I am sorry your arrangement with regard to the Harrods parcels got messed up. I told you some time ago that the Berne people had discontinued their bread since December. I am trying to do a little work now, having got some books on Civil Engineering & Building from home but it is somewhat difficult as one cannot get alone by ~~oneself~~ ones self. Could you send me any of the American Building journals such as the American Architect, Architectural Record or Brick Builder or papers like these. They should come through by letter post. Please write more often than you do. I hope the kiddies are alright & your yourself also. David.

May to David   Beckenham   Letter No 113   6.5.18

My dear David,

I had last Saturday off, as I said I would, and it turned out a glorious day. We could almost see the leaves growing on the lime trees! Had a very busy day pottering about. Planted four cucumber pips, and some cress. The cauliflowers and lettuces are coming up, but I have lost all the geraniums owing to frost. I shall have to buy plants for the cemetery, the first time for many years. My slug hatching season has commenced, and I managed to pick up 139 on Saturday – not a bad beginning. Wish I knew how to prevent them. That lime I put down, and which was supposed to kill, they simply love. Mama found one big slug sleeping in a cavity in a lump of lime, and as for soot, the black ones live on it, when they are not feeding on shoots, and then I cannot see them so well! Picking them up seems the only remedy. The fresh air made me sleep very soundly that night. I did not wake till 8.0, and of course stayed in bed till after 9.0. Sunday was drizzling up till about 6.0. I went to Balham as arranged, via Victoria on account of damp, and then to chapel in the evening, which we both enjoyed. The pastor is a fine man, and I have grown quite used to his enthusiastic manner and voice. The place was packed, people sitting on steps as usual. We were there 8 minutes too soon! Afterwards we went for a good walk with Peter to Wandsworth Common.

I showed Mrs Taylor the plans of houses, but she has not decided which rooms she will have yet. She is worrying yourself about your boots, the field ones, the only item you have asked for which she has not sent. The reason is that some relation said they would never reach you, so rather than upset her we talked about another pair of your brown ones with huge nails in and soles inches thick, which she is going to send off this week. She also says she has many other pairs of your boots partly worn which she would rather send you than your field boots to which she has evidently taken a great fancy, so I said I would ask you if others received their field boots alright, and if she should send off your remaining ordinary boots first with plenty of nails in. She now seems easier in her mind. She will not touch your money for any of your parcels. Apart from that little bit of worry she seems very well, and has had no trouble with any of the tenants. I did not have time to get out that book of Mitchell's, but if I am not over next weekend I shall be the one after, Whitsun, when I hope to do some gardening. Our garden looks lovely, but the one at No 56 does not appear too neat yet. Most likely at Whitsun I shall be starting a fortnight's holiday which I expect will be divided between No 18 & No 56. Mrs Taylor gave me the April number of the Artists this morning which I partly read in the tram. The Artists Rifles Regimental Association is getting on, and is a very good thing I should think; it has become affiliated to the British Empire Producers' Organization. It is another glorious day today, the same as Saturday. Must get on now with my work, so Goodbye for the time being.

May

PS You ought by now to have received a pair of brown boots, sent off in March. Mrs Taylor has a letter from Ethel which contains no grumbles whatsoever, but an account of her house decorations, so she is going to forward it to you.

May to David   Beckenham   8.5.18

My dear David,

Yesterday was pouring with rain all day, only leaving off a little in the evening to let me go out and pick up slugs by the handful (more or less). I lost count of them, but think there were close to 100 again.

Today is glorious, and I just feel as though I would like to go out for a lovely long walk in the country with someone. I mean somebody nice.

There is no news. I heard from Muriel yesterday; such a nice letter; thanking me for a photo of myself I sent her, the same as you have, and also saying she will be pleased to come to St George's Hall on 25th with us all.

The only other item is that I have had a lapse of my model behaviour, that new leaf of mine I turned over some time ago, and have once again acted the "little divvil". Everything has been so tame of late, that a diversion came in very nicely. The General Manager sent for me, and I found him in a totally different humour. He was acting the pleading one! He has discovered that I had kept my word most vigorously. I am referring to a difference of opinion we had some weeks ago, when I told him straight out that I was going to defy him. He actually had not believed I would keep my word. Doesn't know me like you do, does he? Well, he finished pleading with these words "If you defy me I cannot make any of the girls obey me," to which I replied "No, but I can make them obey you, and have done without a murmur from any of them, though they see every day I disobey you." As he looked so puzzled and hopeless I explained thus, "You see I did not repeat your message to them as you gave it to me. I was tactful and put it this way....". Then I got up to let him bite it well, as he prides himself on his tact, and really he hasn't got any. As a parting shot at the door I called out "If you don't approve of my behaviour the remedy is in your own hands" which made the poor man give me a most hopeless laugh. Honestly I think it is too bad of me, but I would sooner leave than give way, tho' it is such a small point, quite childish in fact. He told me during the conversation that I was not thinking of after the war, which made me smile, as I think of little else.

Nothing more to say now, so Goodbye.

May

May to David   Beckenham   9.5.18

My dear David,

A couple of letters back I told you I had dreamt I was wearing that ring. I have turned up our wonderful dream book, and by the way of a change find it is a lucky dream. According to this book my dreams usually mean I am going to be hanged, drawn, quartered, imprisoned, lose all my friends, and have bad luck generally. This dream, however, means I shall quickly be united with the object of my affections. Perhaps you will be exchanged with the next batch of prisoners. You are damaged, and have been a prisoner for almost a year now, so I am living in great hopes.

I had a letter this morning from Mrs Taylor asking me to go to Balham for the weekend. We had not arranged last weekend as she did not know whether she would be going to Watford. I have replied saying I would go, but wanted to work in the cemetery on Saturday afternoon. It must look deplorable. The frost got in the conservatory during the winter (Mama was studying war economy, and would not light up the oil stove, with disastrous results), so I am thinking of plants stocks. Some of them are supposed to bloom for 11 weeks, and ought to be a grand sight.

Will continue this letter tomorrow.

10.5.18

This morning I had a letter from Mrs Taylor enclosing a post card from you dated 18th March. I had your letter of 1 April about a fortnight ago, and generally the post cards are much quicker coming. I expect during my holiday Mrs T and I will go to Cox's with this post card in which you say they are to pay over the balance except £25. The letter you wrote them has never come to hand. Of it may yet. I saw in the paper a few days back that the post to Germany had got congested, but that things were now getting better.

Another glorious day. At lunch time we are going to settle holidays.

5.30 Here endeth another busy day. Just off now to pay the butcher's bills. Goodbye.

May

May to David   Beckenham   13.5.18

My dear David,

Last Friday I mowed the front grass plots and Ethel cut the hedges. The front garden now looks very nice.

On Saturday I left business early, had "dinner" at Lyons (I can almost see you scowl, but I did enjoy it – coffee and bread & butter and honey, my favourite) and then went to the cemetery. It was cold when I left home so I put on my winter coat and fur hat, but it turned out piping hot with a blazing sun. I was melted all the afternoon, and the ground was hard to dig up. It took me just two hours, and now I am not entirely satisfied. I left it with plenty of lime on. Reached home soon after 5.0, had a big tea, then a bath, and by the time I was dressed dinner was ready, roast beef & vegetables. Had a hearty dinner, and then went off to Balham. Walked out with Mrs Taylor & Peter, had supper and then off to bed early. How I slept! Sunday was wet, pouring first thing, so we stayed in bed and talked till after 11.0. Had breakfast at 12.0 when it turned out beautiful, so Peter took me out for a walk. Dinner at 2.30 which I enjoyed immensely. Mrs Taylor, bless her heart, had made me one of her custards. I made a pig of myself, as usual. In the afternoon, having no energy for walking, I finished my book, The Broad Highway, rather a nice tale by Farnol. After tea we walked on to Tooting Common which was a lovely sight. The May trees are now out, and the place smells simply lovely. Mrs Day is staying over till Tuesday at her daughter's, so I am going back to Mrs Taylor tonight. I must write a note to Mama to tell her, as she has no idea of it.

There was a very pressing invitation from Mrs Capel this morning for Mrs Taylor to spend Whitsun with her. I have tried to persuade her to go. Mrs Capel's daughters both have invitations for the holiday but don't want to leave their mother alone. I expect Mrs Taylor will go, and I expect she will enjoy herself.

Our overtime money has just come up, and I am richer by 16/-. What shall we do with it? Can't stop any longer, want to leave early if possible and spend some time in Balham. As it is a beastly wet day today I might practice, and look at your photo over the piano.

Goodbye,

May

May to David   Beckenham   14th May 1918

My dear David,

I am an idiot. Last week I meant to have wished you very many happier and still happier returns of your birthday, and now when you get this I expect your birthday will be over. Never mind, I guess your next birthday will be spent with me. I wonder what we shall be doing. Specks we shall manage to enjoy ourselves somehow.

Last night as promised I went to Balham, had supper, and then went up to practice while you gazed at me from your photo. I made any amount of mistakes, but you never so much as scowled at me; maybe pure indifference! While murdering some of those pieces out of the Star albums Mrs Day returned unexpectedly. Her son-in-law came back unexpectedly, so she came home, not knowing that I should be at Balham. During the evening your postcard of 8th April arrived saying you had received one boot. We are delighted, as by now you have no doubt received the fellow one. There was nothing else in the parcel beside the boot. There is still another pair on the way to you by now, so that you will be set up again.

I have taken that building book out of your bookcase and in the tram was looking it through. The diagrams made me think of Bert when he was at school boy glancing at his homework. It so often made him say "I'm sure I can't do this stuff unless I am sitting on your lap." He worked his sums out best with his right arm round my neck very frequently.

The work is slackening down alright now, so that I shall be able to start my fortnight's holiday at the end of this week. Mrs Taylor is writing today to Mrs Capel promising to go to her for Whitsun, and she says she might take me down there a fortnight later for a very long weekend. Miss Willsher called in this afternoon about our next Saturday's outing. The place is Little Kimble, Bucks, 45 miles away. Leave Paddington 1.0 return there 9.17. That day we will arrange an outing on our own for Whit Monday. Looks like having an enjoyable fortnight.

You ask for leather laces to be sent to you, but they are amongst the list of forbidden things. You have some mohair laces sent you.

15th May

Last night a letter came from Uncle for me and in it he said "Do you ever hear from David Taylor. The next time any of you write we shall be glad to know how he is doing."…"Glad you bazaar was such a success. You are as energetic in a good cause as ever, and you are apparently going to have your reward in this life. It is my heartfelt wish that you may live long in the country of unclad blacks before you have to die and leave them all behind." Isn't he cheeky – like you. You see I had told him about our Palmist. This morning Batsfords wrote to say that they had at last got the permit for the book on the Metric System and Dutton's shorthand, and that the 2 books had been despatched. Weather is much warmer today, but cloudy.

No more news, so Goodbye.

May

PS Of course you will have your present when you return.

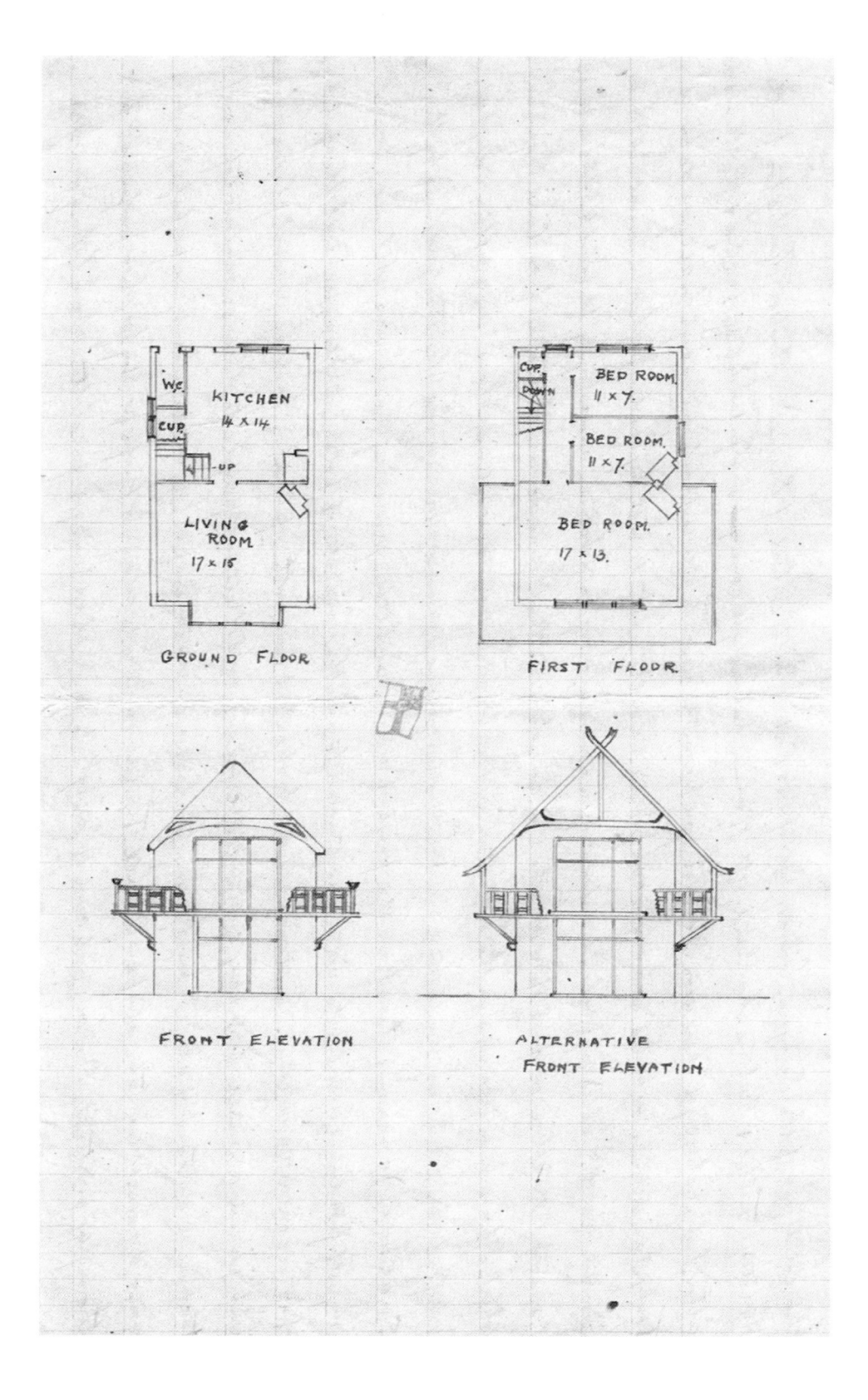

David to May   Holzminden   May 16th 1918

My Dearest,

Your letter of April 26th came yesterday and said you had had mine of April 1st. I thinks this is a record. Wasn't it good of the censors to let it come through so quickly, I haven't yet had several of your previous letters so I don't know yet if you have had my letter of February 1st and the two March letters. I am rather anxious about Cox's letter. I think the amount of the balance to be paid Mum should have been between £90 and £100. I hope Mum has seen Cox about it and explained that the letter had gone astray and so stopped any payment being made to anyone other than herself and that through her bank. If I don't hear from you in the meantime I shall write Cox next month. I am able to write 3 letter cards in place of 2 letters, so if you only receive 2 of these you will know that the third has gone to Cox. Will you please ask them to send me a statement every 3 months.

I like your idea for that beach bungalow very much indeed and I think it would be a good thing to put some up somewhere after the war is over, but don't you think that most people want to rent this type of hut rather than purchase it outright and I doubt if we shall have enough surplus capital to do it with, at all events for a year or so. However I will sketch some sort of a scheme for it and see what you think of it. I don't know if you saw the Shaw's bungalow at Shoreham. It was roofed over so that the central portion formed the Living Room and Kitchen with small sleeping rooms on each side. I am enclosing, as I promised in my last letter, a sketch of a bungalow, or course on a much more elaborate plan than the one you suggest, one which perhaps we might put up for ourselves someday. It is roughly on the lines we used to talk about you remember. We might have big folding doors opening out of the front of the Living Room and the same leading out of the front Bedroom on to the Verandah, which as you see, I have put round 3 sides so that any time one side will be sheltered from the wind. This Bedroom by the way could be, if necessary, divided, thus making 4 small bedrooms instead of 2 and one fairly large one. Let me know what you think of it all and give me any alterations you see.

Yesterday and today a perfect shower of books descended on me with nothing to say who they were from. They came through the Board of Education Book Scheme. I think they must be from you as there was a list of Batsfords and of Engineering books amongst the. Thanks ever so much for them. The books that have come are Belloc's "French Revolution", "Mohammedanism" by Prof Margolionth, Wosley's "Napoleon", Lockwoods Price book, Lamb's "Essay's of Elia", and Macaulays Essays (these last 3 you remember you have already sent, but they will be useful as I am passing them on). There were also catalogues of the Everyman Library, Batsford's list and Griffins list of Engineering book. Thanks too for the Metric Tables and Duttons Shorthand, both of which haven't yet come and "The Twinkling of an Eye" and the other book either, but I shall get them soon I expect. I'll never to be able to thank you enough for all you do for me. Truly I am well off for books now and you can picture me sitting outside with my head swathed in several wet towels, (ice not being obtainable) my forehead inches deep in wrinkles and my head between arms trying to read 6 books at once and surrounded with a rampart of a 100 others in case of need. Which reminds me, that apart from Civil Engineering which I have been reading in the hope that it may be useful to us sometime, I have been grabbing every book on gardening, (I asked you to send me "The Market Garden", "Manures & Manuring" and "War-Time Gardening" by the Small-Holder) and reading them from the point of view of profitable gardening, until now, at times, I catch myself pondering deeply, the vital question as to whether nitrate of potash will agree with the equilibrium of forces on a cantilever.

And now I have broken out in another place, in fact in several places and have just joined a small but very cultivated circle of architectural people to discuss various topics of technical interest and also I am having two lessons a week in poultry management, so perhaps part of your dreams may take shape after all. The fellow who is teaching us keeps poultry for show purposes and is thoroughly practical. In my post card of January 17th to you, I had got your letter about taking over Marine Insurance and I told you that the Insurance Institute, 11 Queens Street, holds classes in insurance subjects and have a very good library for which they only charge a small fee and that The London School of Law, Lincolns Inn, gives instruction by correspondence in various insurance subjects.

It makes me wild to hear that another man has been given the job of putting that Acquired Company right while you are really doing it yourself and getting no credit for it. They are a pretty mean crowd, the whole lot of them. I am very sorry to hear your old cleaner has broken down, I hope she will get over it.

As regards your thinking of my being ill, please don't. Because I asked for salts etc, I am not taking it. I asked for that stuff after that attack of pain in my side last year, in case of a recurrence, but I haven't needed anything of the sort. The other day I jumped on a letter thinking it was from you and then found it was only from Maud. She says "May is picking up again, but will have to take every care." This sounds as though you were worse than you told me about. Are you really alright again? Please thank Maud for her letter.

I wouldn't trouble about that Surveyors Institution Catalogue, as Batsford have sent their list, altho' even then they only sent a pamphlet and not their full catalogue, but still it will do I think. By the way I shall want to know all about the "shocking" book. If it is as shocking as all that, you oughtn't to be reading it. Talking about hats with wide brims – when I get back you'll have to wear brimless hats or no hat at all. The idea of the war lasting another 5 years and being away from you all that time gives me fits. I am envious of that 6/- of yours. I wish my time were as profitable and I do hope some of the things your palmist says come true. Goodbye.

David

May to David   Beckenham   16.5.18

My dear David,

The weather has turned out glorious, like mid-summer, and I am feeling most fearfully hot.

I do not suppose you will get so many letters from me during the next fortnight, on account of my holiday.

The other day I saw a fine sketch in a paper. A girl land worker, looking very pleased, a farmer looking simply awful, a pigstye with curtains daintily looped with sashes, and two beautiful pigs with bug flapper bows. The words were "It gave the landworker pleasure and the farmer apoplexy".

The General Manager has gone away for 10 days, which is a good thing as the weather has turned so hot, and no one feels like work. Strange to say there does not seem to be so much work to be done now.

Yesterday afternoon Mrs Taylor called in and took me away from my beloved business for an hour. We went to the GPO, and invested another £20 for you, and then on to Wallace's and she bought some calico. We also did a good deal of shop gazing, which we both enjoyed. She goes today to Watford for Whitsun, while I am going out with Miss Willsher to the Chequers at Little Kimble, the Country Residence of the Prime Ministers, tomorrow, and elsewhere with her on Monday. I think she wants to do some more of the Tower of London, and so do I, so expect we will go there. It is far too crowded for you to take me to such a place. As I mentioned before my fortnight's holiday will be commencing tomorrow, and I shall be dividing my time between No 18 and No 56. Very likely if the weather breaks up Mrs Taylor & I might go to a matinee at your expense. Guess we shall enjoy ourselves whatever we do.

There is a beautiful thunderstorm going on, and has been for the past hour. Do you remember those flying storms at Gidea Park? I see that according to the "Artists Magazine" a good deal of golf is being played on those links. I wonder if they are still using, or rather misusing, our particular bunkers. The men do not get leave now like they used to in your time, so some of the clerks who have left us and are now there tell me. You were lucky.

I am expecting a letter from you this weekend. That missing one never turned up. I wonder how you are, really. Are there many in your camp, and have you had that pain in your side again? What about your indigestion, and the noises in your head?

Cannot stop any longer, so Goodbye for the time being.

May

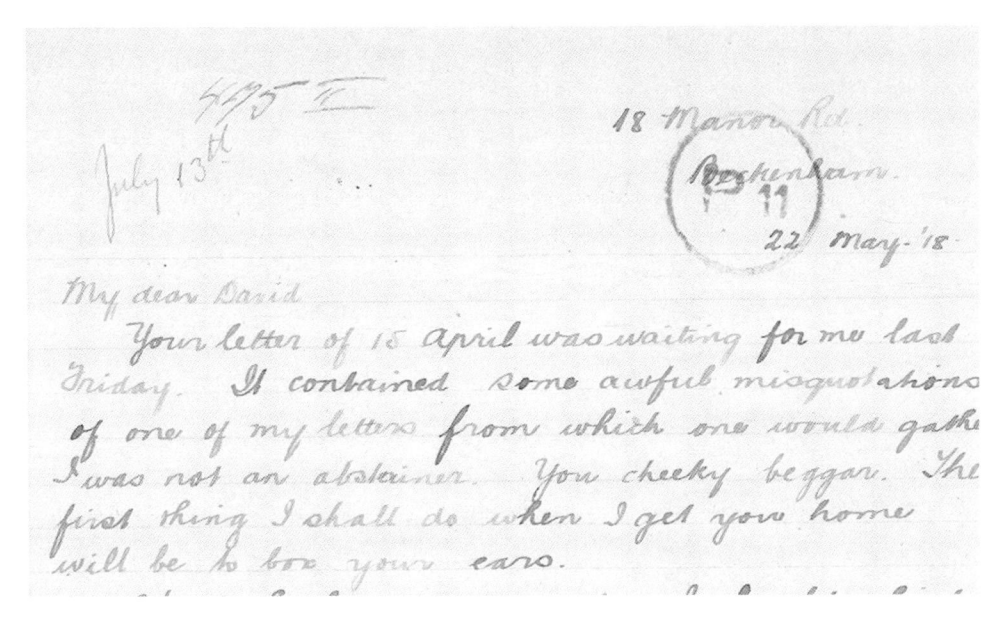

May to David   Beckenham   22 May '18

My dear David,

Your letter of 15 April was waiting for me last Friday. It contained some awful misquotations of one of my letters from which one would gather I was not an abstainer. You cheeky beggar. The first thing I shall do when I get you home will be to box your ears.

About the house decorations, I should think the white, blue-grey & black would look very striking, but striking things get rather tiring after a while, don't you think? Black shows the dust awfully. Have you ever seen dark green doors inside a house? I haven't. How do you think they would look? Green & oak combine well, but are very ordinary.

Last Saturday Miss Willsher & I went over that old mansion & park in Bucks, & I looked out for ideas. The whole place was lovely, & it was hard to believe there was a war on. Needless to say I didn't get any ideas, except one, viz a secret staircase by which we could avoid well intentioned clergymen & suchlike who call for donations, & also relations who wish to give advice. The walls were either panelled or covered with awful tapestry. I draw the line at tapestry. The weather is still perfection, blue sky, blazing sun, & lovely breeze. Sunday I stayed at home; Monday I went for a picnic with Miss Willsher. We inspected the white garden & rock garden adjoining Streatham Common. They looked lovely. I took a quart thermos flask of tea, which we soon emptied. I hear the river was packed, long queues waiting for the streamers. Yesterday I did some gardening, & cleaned my white coat. It does look nice. A letter came from Mrs Taylor asking me to go with her to Mrs Pratt from next Wednesday to Monday. I am going. Today I have been to see Auntie. She is a martyr. By the bye, I have never seen her otherwise. From what I saw of Bucks I should think it would be a good part for your business.

Cannot think of anything else to write about, so Goodbye.

May

May to David   Beckenham   28.5.18

My dear David,

Now for my weekly. Last Saturday afternoon I took my girls to St George's Hall. First I met Muriel who looks better than I ever saw her look, & who says if I don't marry you on your return after all you have been through she is going to kill me. I asked after Mr Williams, but she knows nothing beyond the fact that he joined up some time back. She added "I was mad when I thought I was in love with him. I've really fallen in love several times since, but they have each gone to the front & got killed." (It seems she is rather a fatal young lady.) Then we journeyed to the Hall & I received the remaining 20 girls on the steps. They were all in their best & full of smiles. The performance was splendid & I took them all to tea afterwards, & then left them, seeing Muriel back to Liverpool St. The weather was & is lovely. After that I went to Balham for the weekend. Nothing much happened. Went to bed early tired out & slept on till 8.30 next morning. Had breakfast about 11.30 – too late for chapel, so walked across Tooting Common with Peter & left a rate at Glenroy, but did not stop. Your cousin has been called up & passed A.1. As his work is of national importance his folks think he may be kept at it, but of course, don't know. I do hope they send him across. My girls told me Saty that the Actuary & General Manager are called up. I guess Lutt is chuckling.

Also some others are called, so I shall be busy next week seeing about more girls. I have 80 as it is. Something like a family!

Ern is going to be examined again on Thursday.

Tomorrow I join Mrs Taylor at the "Elephant" (outside, not in) at 2.30, & then we are off to Mrs Pratt's till next Monday.

I have been gardening & the garden looks lovely. It now contains :- lime trees, plenty of stones, ferns, grass, chickweed, slugs, potatoes, lettuces, snails, beans, beansticks, auricular, cauliflowers, dandelions, tomatoes, parsley, mint, cucumbers, mustard, cress, daisies, weedkiller, woodlice, roses, & today, I have sown some stock seed. Goodbye for the present.

May

PS I have been having lovely dreams about you.

May to David   15 King St Watford   31.5.18

My dear David,

You will see by above address that Mrs Taylor & I have kept our word & are spending a most enjoyable holiday together. I can quite understand Mrs & Mr Pratt being your favourite Aunt & Uncle. Last night Mrs Pratt made me laugh more than I had done since you left me, & it is certainly the most enjoyable holiday I have had since you left England. If we are not wandering across fields and such like we are in the garden, & Mrs Taylor told me this afternoon I was getting quite brown. It was not dirt as I had just washed my face.

I believe I have often told you you are a cheeky beggar. I now know where you get your saucy politeness from: - Mrs Pratt. What do you think she said last night? I was to write to you & she would censor the letter! Now I am wondering if she ever let anyone censor her letters to Mr Pratt before they were married. I have my doubts. And look here, I believe both Mr & Mrs Pratt could teach you lots in the art of fondling. When you return you might take a few lessons from them – they are just a couple of lovey-doveys still. (I wonder of our lady censor will box my ears for putting this.)

I have been hearing such nice things about you – of course when you were too young to know worse. It appears you were the sweetest, duckiest & prettiest baby that ever came in to the world. Isn't it strange how some people change as they grow up? (I didn't say I meant you.) Your Aunt was the first to take you out. She was only going in to the next road, & it took ten policemen to keep the people in orderly queues to have a peep at you. Just before the Lord Mayor & Aldermen drove up in the State Carriage & the tenants from Buckingham Palace Mrs Pratt thought you had been gazed at enough & so took you in. (What did you say just now? I am horrified! You never said such things when she used to take you out. Now I won't put anything more in this letter.)

Goodbye

Dear David,

Being of a generous disposition I've censored this letter free of charge. I am passing it as being quite harmless & unobjectionable. I had written thus far as a matter of form before reading the letter thinking from what I have seen of the writer, I might safely assume this much but I find I was altogether wrong as to my first adjective. It is understood you will disagree with my verdict, but this will only make something to squabble about when we meet. We are having perfect weather, & May thinks we are surrounded with most delightful Country. So glad to hear of your recovery. Mama is quite well, Goodbye

Aunty Sophia.

15 King Street
Watford. 31.5.18

My dear David

You will see by above address that Mrs Taylor & I have kept our word & are spending a most enjoyable holiday together. I can quite understand Mrs. & Mr. Pratt being your favourite Aunt & Uncle. Last night Mrs Pratt made me laugh more than I had done since you left me, & it is certainly the most enjoyable holiday I have had since you left England. If we are not wandering across fields & such like we are in the garden. Mrs Taylor told me this afternoon I was getting quite brown. It was not dirt as I had just washed my face.

I believe I have often told you you are a cheeky beggar. I now know where you get your saucy politeness from: — Mrs. Pratt. What do you think she said last night? I was to write to you & she would censor the letter! Now I am wondering if she ever let anyone censor her letters to Mr. Pratt before they were married. I have my doubts. And look here, I believe both Mr. & Mrs Pratt could teach you a lot in the art of fondling. When you return you might take a few lessons from them — they are just a couple of lovey-doveys still. (I wonder if our lady-censor will box my ears for putting this.)

93 II

I have been hearing such nice things about you — of course when you were too young to know worse. It appears you were the sweetest, duckiest & prettiest baby that ever came into the world. Isn't it strange how some people change as they grow up? (I didn't say I meant you.) Your Aunt was the first to take you out. She was only going into the next road, & it took ten policemen to keep the people in orderly queues to have a peep at you. Just before the Lord Mayor & Aldermen drove up in the State Carriage & the tenants from Buckingham Palace Mrs Pratt thought you had been gazed at enough & so took you in. (What did you say just now? I am horrified! You never said such things when she used to take you out. Now I won't put anything more in this letter)
Goodbye.

Dear David.

Being of a generous disposition I've censored this letter free of charge. I am passing it as being quite harmless & unobjectional, & ms I had written thus far as a matter of form before reading the letter, thinking from what I have seen of the writer, I might safely assume this much but find I was altogether wrong as to my first adjective. It is understood you will disagree with my verdict. But this will only make something to squabble about when we meet, we are having perfect weather, & May thinks we are surrounded with most delightful Country so glad to hear of your recovery. Mama is quite well, goodbye Aunty Sophy

Alfred Christmas

Sophia (Christmas) Pratt

Annie Capel

Harry Webber

Jack Linn

David to May   Holzminden   Letter No 23   June 1st 1918

My Dearest,

Your ideas with regard to the house are exactly the same as mine. I think plain painted walls are infinitely better than paper in every way. I had shown casement windows and I can arrange them so that they can be cleaned from the inside and as regards ventilation the upper portion can open like a fanlight and can be regulated so as to open to any required extent. You shall not have any brass, not even taps (which I know you dote on) as I think we can get these oxidized. As regards the wash basins, I should put a water sealed trap immediately below the basin, so that no smell could come up from the pipe and as regards cost, this would have to be set against wash stands etc but even then they would probably cost a pound or so extra, but I thought the saving of work would be worth it. The ideal piece of ground would be a piece (not necessarily more than 50' 0" wide) running north and south so that the house faced north and south, that is to say the Dining Room and Drawing Room would face due south and would look straight down the garden, the front garden being between the Larder and Kitchen and the road, on the north side. In this case the Hall, Kitchen, etc could be turned over to the other side without any alteration in the arrangements of the plan so that the extra piece of ground would be on the west side as you say, instead of the east, indeed I think this is altogether a much better arrangement from the point of view of the other rooms too. Got any ideas for the decoration and furnishing of the bedrooms? When I get back we'll go to the show rooms of the leading decorators – they have rooms decorated in different ways – and we may get some ideas from them.

I am writing to Cox (a post card) by the same post as this letter, similar to my letter of February 1st as follows:-

"Will you please pay the amount standing to my credit above the sum of £25 to Mrs F Taylor of 56 Ramsden Road. Please make the payment through the London County & Westminster Bank, Newington, as before." Please tell Mum this and ask her to find out from Cox if they receive this post card. She will of course have one post card less this month. I am enclosing a rough sketch of the beach hut. I don't know if it is anything like the one you thought of. You will see that it is for four as you suggested. I thought that each bed might have a drawer fitted under it, sufficiently large to take one's clothes etc, or the beds might be hinged, so as to fold up against the wall and so leave the whole of the room clear during the day. I have dotted the position of the beds. The Kitchen could have a portable range and the Living Room a store if necessary. There could also be a trap door into the loft under the roof for storing spare furniture etc. The front windows would have folding doors opening direct on to the beach. I have sketched two elevations, one of course being more expensive than the other. I cannot yet give you much idea as to cost, but it should not be very great.

I am awfully sorry to hear that Helen's husband has been killed. I thought there might be a chance of the news of him being better. The world certainly seems very small, Hagell was chief draughtsman to a firm of architects and used to be in and out of the office a good deal. He also used to do a fair amount of drawing for us from time to time and is also a member of the

Lodge, but I was never particularly struck with him. Funny that Helen should come in touch with him.

With regard to gardening I think we might grow the greater part, if not all, of our own vegetables. Could you keep some rough account of the amounts of the various different things you have, so that we know roughly how much we shall require and also how much to plant.

I have just read rather a good book, "Adventures in Contentment" by Davie Grayson. It is written by a man who gave up city life and bought a farm and describes the characters he meets while working on it, from a stiff man of millions who he gets to grease a cart wheel, to a mad tramp whom he invites to stay and live with him, but who disappears in the night.

Just lately altho' the weather has been lovely, there have been some fairly high winds and for some reason or other, several times there have been small whirl winds in the camp. One, the other day, started and was about 30 feet in diameter and 50 feet high, a column of whirling dust, which kept going for fully 2 or 3 minutes and then lifted off the ground and went about 100 feet up in the air, the cloud of dust and pieces of paper etc spinning round up there for quite a long time. It was really funny especially as it started amongst a dozen fellows who were sitting outside and who of course scattered in all directions on account of the dust. I went for a walk yesterday afternoon. There has been a tremendous change in the hills during the last few weeks. Some are now entirely covered with the glorious dark green of the woods, whilst others have their lower portions, cut into a patchwork of crops of various colours. It is not unlike the North Downs, (do you remember our walk over Leith Hill) but the whole country is shut in by hills with more hills stretching away behind, and they more wooded than the Downs.

Today they are having sports in the camp and at the moment there is a good deal of yelling going on outside, but I cannot say I am keenly interested, altho' perhaps I ought to be, anyhow I much prefer being here inside writing to you. I saw one race a little while ago, the boot race. The fellows had to take their boots off which were then piled together in a heap and well mixed. Then the race started, each man searching for his own boots. The one man would grab two boots and go off about ten yards or so and scramble in to them, suddenly find one of them did not belong to him, fling it away in disgust and rush off to find the missing one, which by this time was probably being worn by somebody else. It was not the sort of race that you could say who would win with any real degree of certainty.

I am glad you go to Mum so often, she mentions you in every letter. On one she says "I am looking for May to come to tea and stay on" and again "May is my only visitor". It is good of you. Of course I'll be delighted to have that big photo of you. I do hope it is really like you. I am glad you are having part of your holidays early and if the weather was like we had you should have had it beautifully fine. I hope you went away as I know you always need your holidays. I do wish I could have been with you, but as it is I can only dream and dream and that doesn't seem to make one any forrader.

Goodbye.

David

> 2/Lieut. D. H. Taylor,
> Kings Royal Rifles
> Offizier-Gefangenen-Lager
> Holzminden
>
> 9342π 5
>
> Miss M. Muggridge
> 18 Manor Road
> Beckenham
> Kent.
>
> + rush off to find the missing one, which by this time was probably being worn by somebody else. It was not the sort of race that you could say who would win with any real degree of certainty. I am glad you go to Mum so often, she mentions you in every letter. In one she says "I am looking for May to come to tea & stay on" & again "May is my only visitor." It is good of you. Of course I'll be delighted to have that big photo of you. I do hope it is really like you; I am glad you are having part of your holidays early & if the weather was like we had you should have had it beautifully fine. I hope you went away as I

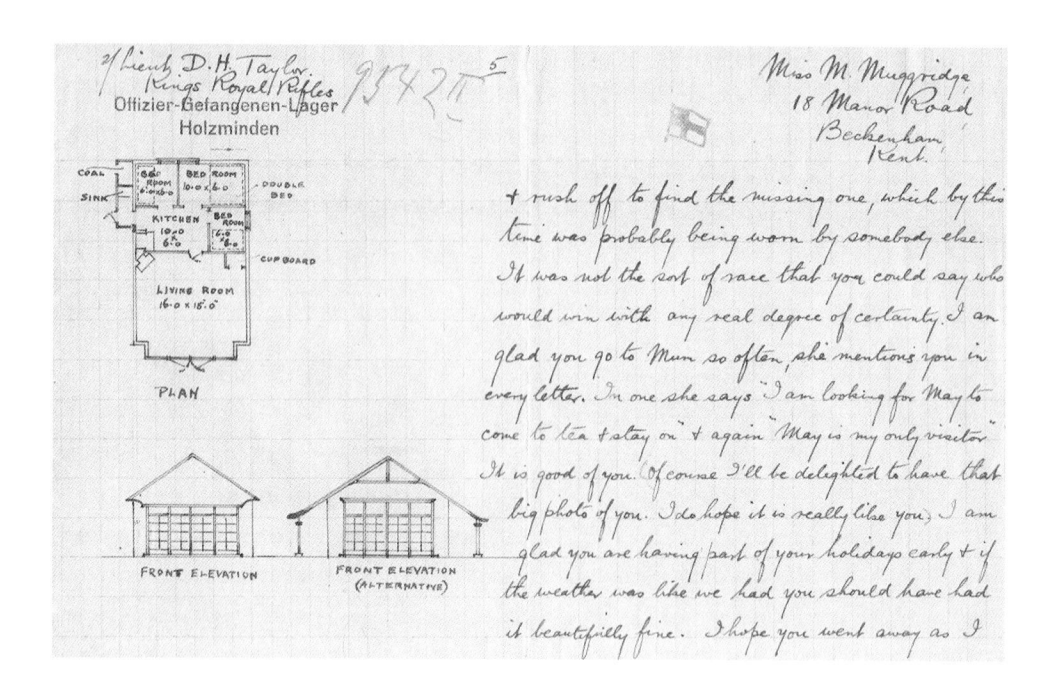

May to David   Beckenham   3.6.18

My holiday is over, worse luck, and I am back again in the land of work. I have had a grand time at Watford; went for long walks every day, and have worn out a pair of shoes. We were scarcely indoors at all, and went a fresh walk each time. One day we took our dinner; walked to Sandy Lodge, and I actually recognised the station as being the one we passed on the way to Chenies, where you told me you had once got out and walked to Watford. We then took the train to Rickmansworth, and walked back from there through Moor Park. Except when at Rickmansworth we scarcely saw a soul. The solitude I believe would even have met with your approval. We have hardly seen a cloud during the whole holiday.

One day we called on Mrs Capel for a short time. She reminded me of a Chinaman, her face being somewhat yellow and a bit thinner. I did not make any other calls. I don't think one could find many folks jollier than Mrs Pratt. We got only very well together, and so I did with Mr Pratt. It was he would made Mrs Pratt put in her postscript that I was not harmless, but he only doubled up with laughter and looked saucy when I tried to make him explain the reason. He never did explain. Another cheeky beggar. I took some music with me in case it turned wet. Being awfully hot Sunday afternoon, after dinner I amused myself on their little piano, and all but went through it. I tried the Prelude on it! Mr Pratt was the only one who had the pluck to stay in the room, the remainder being down the garden. After tea Mrs Pratt & I went to Marjoribanks on our own, Mrs Taylor having gone to Mrs Capel. On Saturday we had an early tea and walked alongside Rippingdell. On the way we met, by arrangement, Mr Wright and three Miss Pratts, at least I think they were; all very affable. Mr Pratt was surprised because Nellie would take possession of me, taking my arm on her own account. I was a bit surprised myself, as I thought she was rather an unsociable sort, so I had not taken much trouble to talk to her. However, she, too, was calling me May before my stay was over. They all say they want me down again. Strange taste. I was also introduced to other folks by Mrs Pratt as "My nephew's young lady" which took my breath away. Don't folks jump to conclusions? Mr Pratt I believe already looked upon me as a niece.

While I was away Mama wrote to say there was a letter from you, but she did not send it on, so now I am anxious to be home. I don't feel a bit like work today, and have practically done none. Had better leave off and try again.

Mr Pratt's brother-in-law, Mr Wright, by the way, is now a widower of a few weeks standing, but he made himself very interesting and sociable. He has been to Norway 20 times, Switzerland 3 times, and Palestine & round about there once. This last holiday cost him over £50. Edith Capel has given up working for Mr Pratt, and in a week's time starts a different career as assistant superintendant of a munition girls' hostel. Nellie Archer has joined the Land Workers' Army, and is waiting to be called up. Guess it will be a good thing for her. She will most likely be sent away on to a farm. She has signed on for six months. Mrs Pratt is pleased about it, though of course she will miss her, especially during thunderstorms which upset her. Must leave off now.

Goodbye.

May

May to David   Beckenham   4.6.18

My dear David,

I read your letter of 1st May last night, and as usual enjoyed it immensely. You seem extra near then.

So a piece had been cut off one of my letters which does not seem to have pleased you. I feel very amused, as my letters are always so full of twaddle, most of them being about "my constant companion" & me going in the train or out for walks. Needless to say the "constant companion" refers to thoughts of you. When alone I always image you are with me, but I suppose the censor began to think I mean some spy, and thereby have a double meaning to my innocent letters. Fancy me being so profound! It is quite complementary to think I might have so much brain. In future I will leave out reference to my constant companion, but you will know I think of you as much as ever.

That plan I think is excellent. I was studying it in the train this morning, and do not think it could possibly be improved upon. You mention rough cast. Is that white? White gets so dirty in London that I think I prefer that biscuit coloured wall with small pebbles in it. Mrs Pratt had some nice bead curtains. Do you like them? I am glad the drawing room is large. It is much better for music. What a bonny kitchen! Do you expect much cooking done?

About business; I have not heard anything more about going to that other Company to superintend the girls. I am pretty well kept going with my 80 odd as it is.

I cannot make Ethel out. America certainly does not agree with her, and I suppose having Mr

Linn ill made her extra nervy. Mrs Taylor could not send you a ham from here, and particularly wanted to, so said to me "I wonder if Ethel could". I said "Write and ask her". She told me what she put and it sounded very simple. However, Ethel evidently jumped to the conclusion that Mrs Taylor wanted to take orders away from her, which was entirely wrong, and wrote several insulting letters which upset Mrs T. If Ethel gives way to these tempers she will go off her head. I was surprised at her. I wrote Mrs Taylor last night and explained about your only being able to write one letter, and sent her a part of yours which I knew would interest her. I do not expect you to address all future letters to me now. Your letter to Cox's has never turned up, so I suppose you will send them a postcard if you wish them to pay over the balance to Mrs Taylor, minus £25. I expect they would do so from your p.c. referring to it, but they would probably want to keep the p.c. and I know Mrs Taylor would not like that. Mrs Taylor copies out the interesting parts of your letters & postcards and sends to Ethel. She really is awfully good to her, and could not do more, while Ethel seems to find fault with as much as she can; got an unhappy knack of reading things wrongly. Guess she did my letter as I never had a reply. I told her about your enclosure for her as it seemed from what I was hearing months ago that we might get bombed, and if we all get despatched to glory and you did not return Ethel might lose something.

Ern has got his discharge papers. He is now having a week's holiday, but unlike him has not gone away, but cycles each day.

5.6.18

Yesterday afternoon Mrs Taylor called in to see how I was after the holiday. She was "on her way" to Miss Massey's. She admits she likes calling at the office, and it certainly makes a nice diversion for me. She looks well, and so do I. I ordered those gardening books. My word, won't you come back learned? I am going over to No 56 on Sunday, and expect I shall stay the night. I shall most probably call, or rather, go home with Maud tonight to make out her income tax papers.

Weather still glorious. How are you? Goodbye.

May

> My dear David,
> I read your letter of 1st May last night, and as usual enjoyed it immensely. You seem extra near then.
> So a piece had been cut off one of my letters which does not seem to have pleased you. I feel very amused, as my letters are always so full of twaddle, most of them being about "my constant companion" & me going in the train or out for walks. Needless to say the "constant companion" refers to thoughts of you. When alone I always imagine you are with me, but I suppose the censor began to think I might mean some spy, and thereby have a double meaning to my innocent letters. Fancy me being so profound! It is quite complimentary to think I might have so much brain. In future I will leave out reference to my constant companion, but you will know I think of you as much as ever.
> That plan I think is excellent. I was studying it in the train this morning, and do not think it could possibly be improved upon. You mention ~~plaster-cast~~ rough cast. Is that white? White gets so dirty in London that I think I prefer that biscuit coloured wall with small pebbles in it. Mrs. Pratt had some nice bead curtains. Do you like them? I am glad the drawing room is large. It is much better for music. What a bonny kitchen! Do you expect much cooking done?
> About business; I have not heard anything more about going to

David to Ginger   Holzminden   Post Card no 10   June 5th 1918

I have your letters of Mar 5th, 17th & Apr 11th together with Uncle Charlie's letter enclosed. I am glad you sent this on to me as it gives a fuller account of Aunt Martha. I had heard of the ulcer & her fall downstairs but not the other details. John has had a bad time of it, but it is great good news to hear that he has got over the second operation & is able to be back at business again. You mention making socks. I don't make them I darn them, (most thoroughly in the other sense) in fact one or two of them consist of one big darn (in a variety of different coloured wools) with a bit of sock round it. The Berne bread stopped, as far as I was concerned last December & as Mum is sending bread from Copenhagen through the Red Cross, I don't think I can have it from both places. I have had two parcels from Harrods through Mr Charrington dated Mar 26th & Apr 5th. Thanks very much indeed for again continuing these parcels & also for trying to get the bread sent on. I hope John has got completely well again by this time & the kiddies & yourself are well.

David

May to David   Beckenham   7.6.18

My dear David,
This will be a short letter as it is late. Have tried to write all day, but been busy interviewing girls & such like.
The Datchelor school have a business training class and they wrote me. The two they sent were not proficient enough for me, but one I think will do for the Accounts Dept. That Dept wanted to take another of my girls and let me have a new one to train, so naturally I failed the girls who came for their test today. Really though, they were too slow, though I have taken on slower.
War-Time Gardening is now out of print, but I am sending on The Allotment Book in place of it. "Market Gardening" is reprinting.
Tomorrow I expect I shall be going up to the cemetery in the afternoon, and doing needlework in the evening. Sunday I am off to No 56.
Wednesday night I went to Maud's and did her income tax paper. Weather is hot and lovely. This morning Ethel read in the paper that in one part of Prussia the glass was below zero. We cannot imagine it here. It has been exceptionally hot the last week or two.
Cannot stop any longer, so Goodbye, hoping you are keeping well, but having my doubts about it.,

May

PS I have not even yet bought a present with the money I had from you. Am I not awful? I cannot make up my mind. What I want I can't have. Just like this world, isn't it?

May to David   Beckenham   Letter No 125   10.6.18

My dear David,

Now for my weekend narrative. I had a very busy and satisfactory one. On Saturday I left Office about 1.20, trained to Peckham Rye, bought a box of stocks and took them straight up to the cemetery and planted them. Some of the blooms are just showing, and I think the grave will look very nice. The ground was fearfully dry, and the weather fearfully hot. Walked home as far as Penge, and then caught a train. I did want my tea, and enjoyed it accordingly. After that I did a little needlework while I was resting, and then cut the front grass plots and edged them. After that I continued some lace edging I am making to put on a couple of towels to give to Miss Willsher for her bazaar which comes off on 13th June. I have not yet done three-quarters of the quantity yet, and have been a fortnight over the job already. Must work desperately hard tonight and tomorrow to get it finished in time. Personally I don't like crotchetwork lace on towels, as if you wipe on it by mistake it almost takes your skin off, but they sold well at our bazaar, so I thought I would do some for Miss Willsher. She always has a plant stall, but cannot get enough ferns this year, consequently she will sell anything she had given her. Went to bed soon after 10.30 tired, and slept like a top till 8.30 when I got up promptly. After breakfast I was off to the cemetery again as it looked like another baking day; lost my train going, so walked all the way. The plants are doing very well. After dinner I went to Balham where I stayed the night. Of course it rained during the afternoon! And again after tea as we were going to chapel. We had a very nice service and the minister made us laugh outright several times during the sermon! He is a sensible man. No wonder the building is always so packed. He is usually very cheerful, and was particularly so last night. I read a letter from Ethel which was addressed to Mrs Taylor. Such a different letter to what she had been writing for a long time past – quite domesticated. I really must tell you about it as it will amuse you. The children have the measles and she sat up one night with the boy while Mr Linn sat up with Erl. (Mr Linn has now gone away on business.) The charwoman has left and Ethel has now been doing washing! She has a machine which makes it much easier, but she has not grumbled about it!!! Moreover she did half the ironing and the nurse the other half. And she winds up saying she would not mind having another baby, only she does not want another Linn. Evidently she thinks her two take after the Linn family, and now if she has another boy I presume she would like it to take after her brother, or if a girl, her mother. Is it not complimentary? I pointed it out to Mrs Taylor but she only said "She's mad", which made me laugh; I couldn't help it.

After chapel we went with Peter for a walk, and then I had a practice and supper; then letter writing and bed. While at tea we discussed your amended plan of the smaller house which I carry about with me. That large bedroom Mrs Taylor says will take all the sitting room furniture she will require, and a bed, but in the winter she will move her bed, or have another, in a south bedroom, and use the large one for her sitting room only. I think this letter is long enough, so will close. Goodbye.

May

PS Your two gardening books were despatched last Friday. These people are much quicker than Batsfords.

May to David   Beckenham   12.6.18

My dear David,

This is your Birthday, and how I wish - . Never mind, I guess I shall have you next year. I really wanted to do some shopping this morning, but felt I must have a compartment to myself so purposely lost the early train. Consequently the shopping is not done.

Yesterday I had your letter of the 16th May which I did not expect till quite the end of the week. I think the censors must be putting in some overtime as letters are getting through quicker than they used. They have my best thanks.

Now for answering your letter.-

Your letter containing one to Cox has not turned up, and I have an idea it was destroyed with many others. I heard several trains and stations had been bombed, and it looks as though it might be true, though of course I do not believe all I hear. There are always plenty of rumours going about. Making up rumours is a favourite pastime with some folks, I believe. I have written to Cox telling them what has happened and that you would be writing them direct, and sent this letter on to Mrs Taylor for approval and signature. She has not said whether she has seen them. I don't fancy she has. I have also asked them to send you a statement every 3 months.

About that beach bungalow, my idea was that if it seemed popular we might have several and let them, i.e. if it would likely by a paying concern. I heard of someone who had a place at Shoreham. They had it for their own holidays, and let it other times, making 15% on their outlay. I like that plan immensely, and so does Mama. It gave me such lovely thoughts that I did not go to sleep last night for hours, and I am not at all tired this morning. When I did sleep I dreamt Ern had got married! I wish he would. We are going to have plenty of deck chairs in the bungalow. I like that verandah upstairs covered over very much. You are a genius at drawing plans.

Don't take any notice of Maud's idea of my health. She is suffering from an elephantine attempt at sentiment, the outcome of having been kept under too much and too long. Thinking of health is her specialite just now, especially her own health. She often tells me how much she is missing her mother. Now it seems to me if you really are missing anyone very much you feel too upset to speak of it. When I came back from my holiday everyone said how well I looked, and even brown – all except Maud who shook her head over me. I think she wishes to convey sympathy because you are behind the barbed wire. Now you know I am practical, and I fully realize that if you were not behind the wire you would be in the present terrible fighting which really would worry me. Although the wire separates us bodily it is having the opposite effect on our spirits, and that is the more important. If I get ill you may depend on Mrs Taylor telling you.

Regarding that shower of books: you remember Muriel asked to send you some, and wanted to know what sort you liked. I gave her a list of all you had asked for, and told her I had ordered them from Batsford, but with a certain few exceptions they had not reached you yet. She has a friend at the Board of Education to whom she passed on the list, and there you are.

I have copied out part of your letter which came yesterday, with certain alterations, for instance I did not mention any were duplicated, and sent on to her, and I thanked her on your behalf. Still, I know you will send her another message in reply to this.
I think this letter is long enough, and will therefore wish you all sorts of nice things and Goodbye.

May

PS I went down to that Acquired Co this afternoon, and am going to pay them a weekly visit. We are going to run that Co on the same lines as our own. When I came up again I found Mrs Taylor sitting in my room waiting for me. She did look so nice.

May to David   Beckenham   13.6.18

My dear David,
Rather a funny thing has happened. Some weeks back I was going home with Maud and she started to tell me about a family scandal. She commenced by saying that an aunt of her father's though wealthy was a very doubtful character. After her hubby died she made matters worse by marrying a man named Butler who was not respected by the community at large; she did not say why; and as a climax said in a most impressive tragic whisper "The clergyman does not call on her"! I put my foot in it by saying "Well, that's nothing against her", whereupon she dried up, and I did not hear any of the scandal. This morning one of the supers brought me up a note from Maud saying "I am so excited I cannot contain myself. Mrs Butler (Father's Aunt) has sent me a cheque for £100 to invest in War Loan." I wonder if she is respectable now.
I told you I was making a couple of towels for Miss Willsher's bazaar. We raffled them at the office and they fetched 8/6.
14.6.18
Yesterday evening I went to the Bazaar. It was in aid of the Aged Pilgrims, some of whom were there sitting on forms either side of the garden, while the lawn was covered by a big markee. The poor old souls were dressed in their best, and did not look as though they were particularly enjoying it. I bought two fancy pots of mixed plants, mostly of the cactus tribe. Fortunately it was a beautiful day. Reached home just before 9.0. Miss Rudge was at the Bazaar, and also a girl I had not seen for many years. Each time I see her she gives me most pressing invitations. She used to invite me to their annual party until they were tired of the refusals I suppose. They really are a nice family, but I am not keen on making friends.
I wrote you on your birthday. Did you get the letter, and did you like it? I mentioned that Acquired Company. Had a long confab the Branch man we put in charge. Naturally he is having a tough job, as all the men seem against him. He has got a new head girl in, and he wants me to "Northernise" her the same as he is "Northernising" the men. I had a talk with her; she is not quite our class, but I think with tact could be managed alright; and I have

promised to go down and see her once a week, every Monday. There are thirty odd girls in that firm, so now I have over 110 to keep an eye on.

It is doing a fine drizzle for which thank goodness. We have not had any rain for ages, and the ground does want it. It will save me a jaunt to the cemetery tomorrow afternoon. Mrs Taylor says I may have this weekend to myself, but I have promised to spend the following with her. It looks as if I shall have to put in some overtime. We cannot get even with the work, and next month is our busy time. Well, 2/- an hour sweetens overtime, and the work is easy for us as we are so used to it.

I must leave off now. I do not get a chance to say half of what I want to you. Never mind; we will make up for lost time one day.

Goodbye.

May

David to May   Holzminden   Letter No 24   June 15th 1918

My Dearest,

I don't like the idea of your having a holiday and not going away, but staying home – I know that sort of holiday. Still as I can't get at you I suppose its no use bullyragging you. Rather funny that you should have written asking what you should start reading, just about the time I wrote. Let me know how you get on and make any notes of any difficulties or write to me about them and do as much drawing as possible, even if it is only rough sketches. Of course take any books or other things of mine that you want.

As regards bookkeeping, you know more about that than I do, as I have never done any. Anyway I expect you'll have to look after that. And that reminds me – as I am not doing more than a dozen things now, I have just started lessons in horse management from one of the fellows here. So with this and poultry keeping etc I should think it highly possible that I may be able to get a job as a farm labourer some day, always provided, of course, that I study hard at various other things and wear a special costume on the lines of those land ladies you told me about. Your books have not come yet, but I expect they will be here soon, in the meantime I seem to have my time fairly fully employed, if not profitably as I would like.

I have altered the elevations of the house again and I am enclosing sketches, which of course are all out of drawing, but which will, perhaps, give a very rough idea of the alterations I have made. You will see that on the South elevation I have put a bay window to the drawing room and I have only one door leading out into the garden, that from the drawing room, the dining room having an ordinary window now only. I didn't think that a door from the dining room was needed, and the bedrooms above have no bays now as they would have been of little or no use and of course cost more than the flat windows. I altered this elevation because the whole thing seemed top heavy and ill balanced. With the North elevation I have lowered the roof slightly as this will cheapen things somewhat and I think gives a better appearance and I have put the two top windows in dormers which looks somewhat better I think. Also I have put the entrance to the Kitchen here and the Coal Store in a small projection round the corner on the West side. I have moved the chimney to the Drawing Room next to the Front Entrance, as this will help considerably with the fitted bookcase inside and also will go a long way with a fitted cupboard in the bedroom above.

I am not by any means pleased with any of it though, and am still trying to turn it into something better. Lordy me, how I do want to talk it all over with you. I have also tried to sketch the Hall but….Still it may give you a better idea of the whole thing than the bare plan. Now, pull it to pieces and let me know what you would like and give me any scheme of decoration you think would look well.

I have just got hold of a book on American houses from an architect here, which may possibly have a few useful things in it. That ash shoot was an American idea by the way, but if we have it I think I can improve on it by having a sieve in it too. I have got in touch with several architects and such like people in the camp, but I am afraid most of them will be going to Holland shortly, but still, perhaps I shall catch them up again later on. I think I told you that we have a small meeting once a week, when we discuss various lofty subjects, such as "Housing of the Working Class" etc. It is like brimstone and treacle – does you good, and moreover if you do happen to drop off to sleep, they don't wake you too violently.

I gave you in one of my previous letters an idea of decoration for the Hall. What do you think of it. Of course the same scheme would have to be carried for the first floor passage, but I don't think we would have the doors black up there, but the same colour as the other woodwork. I think we might have a hedge running down the road to the front corner of the North elevation, so as to shut off the kitchen etc completely from the front entrance. On the first of this month I wrote a post card to Cox direct, again telling them to pay Mum my balance less £25. Will you ask Mum to find out if they received the post card.

Did I tell you that I had a spring bed? It descended upon me, like the mantle of Elijah, from another man in my regiment who has gone to Holland and who bought it in the early days. It's really awfully comfy and we do enjoy ourselves. Naturally everybody covets it and I have been offered untold wealth for it – and abuse when I refuse. My only fear now is that I may wake up one night and find myself murdered by one of the others for the sake of the bed. I have changed my room and altho' at the time I didn't care about moving, I am glad now as I like both the men and the room better than the other.

If only that dream of yours about my meeting you at a railway station were true, but your ending, "when I woke up – just in time", is most unsatisfactory, but still I never have had my way – have I now.

I was rather amused at the idea of Ethel trying to separate us. Your dream too about the ring was splendid and the dream books translation of it too. I only wish I were home and then it would be actually time, wouldn't it.

Goodbye.

David

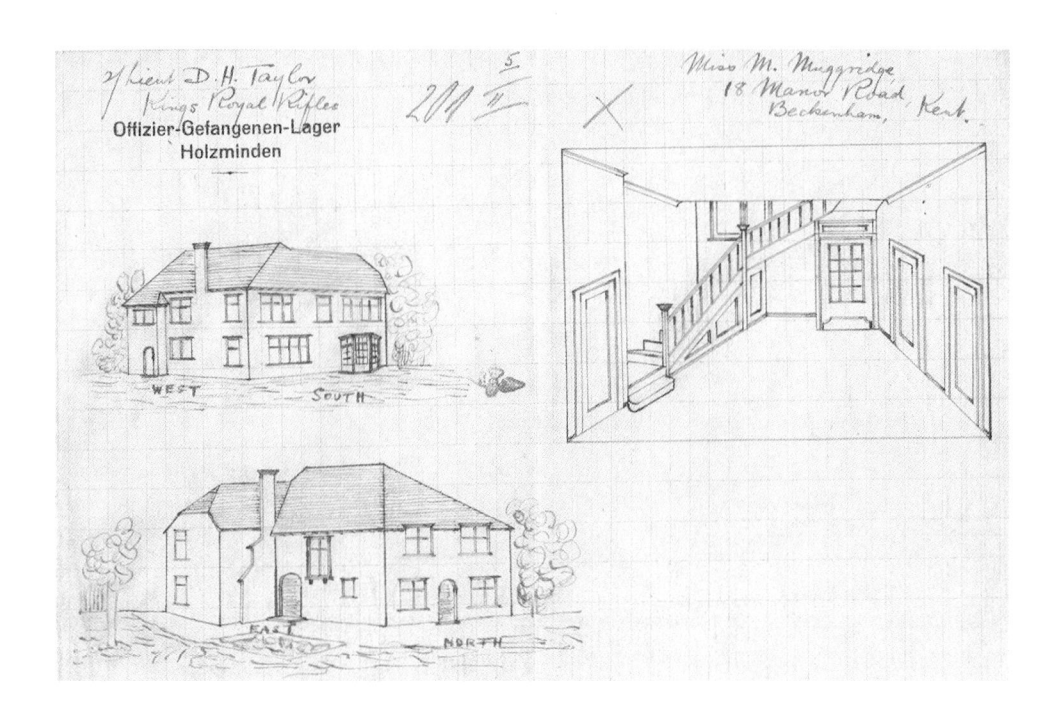

May to David   Beckenham   Letter No 128   17.6.18

My dear David,

Our glorious weather has broken up. It lasted a good long time. It rained all Friday afternoon and evening, and I arrived home wet. Saturday and Sunday we had a series of thunderstorms with bright intervals. I went to business on Saturday morning, and in the afternoon took my enlarged photo to Sydenham to have it framed exactly like yours. Also left my shower proof coat to be cleaned. I have not worn that for ages. Do you remember it? I took it with me to Switzerland, and you fastened the collar up and nearly choked me; at least I said so at the time. You were in a very playful mood that day I remember. I think it was the same day that Uncle tried to read me a lecture. Poor Uncle. He could not make me out. Thought I was too frivolous, and behaved in an empty headed way, and yet knew far too much. He did not actually say so, but I think that was what he meant. I remember I felt like a mother to him. That was not the lecture he read to me at midnight, after we danced so, and had Old Lang Syne at Geissbach. This was another occasion, when we two strolled on for a walk and left you and Auntie alone. I am afraid I pained the two poor souls at times. Uncle does not approve of women having worldly knowledge.

Saturday evening I mended stockings & did other needlework.

Sunday I was busy as usual in the morning, and in the afternoon and evening read "Simon the Jester" which I finished in the train this morning. The book is written by Wm Locke, but does not come up to Aristide Pujol. I did not wake up til 9.0 which was a nuisance as I had no time for daydreams. I believe I dreamt about you last night but cannot recollect what it was.

There is a good deal of talk in the papers about changing prisoners. It would be heavenly to have you back again, but if you come I do not want you to go off to the front again, but hope the army doctors will consider the wound in your head too bad. As I before said I would rather think of you as a prisoner than in the trenches.

I have been looking at the plans of the bungalow and house again. I carry them about with me, and it makes me feel that we are getting on towards settling down. I shall be staying late most likely each night, and the money will go towards the bungalow.

Goodbye.

May

PS Just had a £5 bonus given me. Another brick for the bungalow.

May to David   Beckenham   18.6.18

My dear David,

[several lines of letter cut out by censors]

I am now making socks again, and it is so nice to be on them. I have not yet finished the stockings I was making for myself. It is much nicer doing things for others. I believe there are still several pairs awaiting you at No 56.

I had your postcard about the Marine business; thanks very much. I attended one lecture, and that was all, except that I parted with two promising girls who are getting on very nicely in that department. I expect they will soon want a third.

Had a nice letter from Muriel today. Wants me to go over and see their roses, and also take with me the plans of houses and bungalow so as to talk decorations. She says –

"I'm so glad to hear Mr Taylor has received the books safely as it will help the time pass more quickly for him, and I'm only too pleased to have been able to help him in any way. I feel I owe him a very big debt for all his kindness to me that glorious day on the river and at Bexhill – but apart from this I am only too pleased to do anything to help the poor fellows. After all, I haven't done anything except write a 1d letter – what a magnificent piece of goodness!"

I haven't replied that you will take her out on the river one day for each book she sent.

19.6.18

Another letter from Muriel this morning. I am going to see her Saturday week, and I am to take with me all your photos.

Yesterday and Monday I worked till 7.0, another 6/- for the bungalow. Don't think I shall be working tonight.

It is weeks and weeks since I had my last rumpus with the Powers that be, so things were getting awfully tame. Therefore, it behoved me to make a slight stir in the working of the office. It is only Lutt I am up against, but I have spent the entire morning getting the other chiefs (except the General Manager) to agree with me. They have all agreed except one who can't on account of business, so now I expect the fun will commence. Poor Lutt, I do feel sorry for him; but somehow, the first time I saw him I domineered over him, and I really cannot stop myself even now he is my chief. He means well. Sometimes I wonder whether I do. Nothing more to say now, so Goodbye,

May

PS The chief has had to give in.

May to David   Beckenham   21.6.18

My dear David,

I added a hurried postscript to my last letter. The chief actually confessed in the end I was right. Considering I was backed up by all the chiefs and the temporary girls as well as my own, I should think it was rather obvious to him. Mrs Taylor looked in during the afternoon and brought me a lovely bunch of roses and two cakes. I am eating one now. It is a beauty. I believe you have a rival in your affections for me. I will not keep you in a terrible suspense but like a decent Christian will mention the name, and then you will be able to deal accordingly, in spite of the miles there are between us. I wonder if you have any idea who the rival is. I admit a very great liking on my part, but there is no need to tear your hair or grind your teeth, seeing that the aforesaid rival is none other than your (I ought really to put "To be continued in our next" here, or else the Censor ought to cut a piece off. As the chances are he has been in love himself he will have pity on you and pass the letter entire) Mother. What awful words are those you are muttering under your breath? You know it is wrong to swear.

There is no news. Everything going on alright.

22.6.18

Worked late last night. I shall be earning quite a lot in overtime. As it is mechanical work we do after hours (typing home fire policies which I could do in my sleep now) we are none the worse for it; and think of the bricks I am earning for the bungalow! If this goes on much longer I shall be able to build a town.

This morning I dreamt of you. You had returned home, appeared alright, but looked as if you wanted fussing and petting generally. I was just starting when I woke up hearing it strike 7.0. I did feel cross at waking just then. Had to get up then as I must be at the Office by 9.0. Fridays as it is payday.

Weather is much better again. Tomorrow I leave at 12.30, go to Balham for dinner and then we are off to Wimbledon where we shall have tea; back in time for supper. Shall stay till Monday morning.

Nothing more to say now, so Goodbye.

May

PS Did you get my letter about Read & Brigstock? I sent you all particulars, and it looks to me as if you are a certificate short. I asked if you would write to them direct. I have not full particulars with me as they are locked up in the Bank; but next Mrs Taylor goes I will ask her to look again for numbers of shares etc.

May to David   Beckenham   24.6.18

My dear David,

I have had such a lovely weekend. It was sea-side weather, plenty of wind and sun. On Saty I left the office at 12.30, reached Balham soon after 1.0; hot a hot dinner, gooseberries out of the garden, and then took trams to Wimbledon, and on to cemetery. We worked there about 2 hours almost, and left the grave looking very well. A small part of the saxifrage has died off, but as Mrs Taylor has some in the garden we will be taking it up next time, and planting it. Then we had tea on the Common at the Windmill, taking some lovely cakes Mrs Taylor had made with us. We were in very good company as a clergyman and curate were there with 2 dozen imps. Mrs Taylor quickly concluded they were choirboys. Had no experience of them myself, but as I hear you were once a choirboy no doubt Mrs Taylor is right. We sat on the Common until about 8.15, knitting, and then came home to supper. I almost finished a sock, when Mrs Taylor discovered I had got the wrong sized needles which accounted for the sock being rather tight. Had it shrunk it would have been uncomfortable. Sunday morning before breakfast I undid that sock. It didn't take long. After breakfast I took Peter for a run, and then Mrs Taylor and I went for a lovely walk across Tooting Common, along some allotments which were very fascinating, to Streatham Common. There I introduced Mrs Taylor to a new portion, the terraces, rock gardens and white garden, and old English garden. She had never seen them before and is in love with them. She and Mrs Day will on fine days take their needlework there. We took with us a book on Africa, or rather Mrs T took it, while I nicked some more of her cakes and stuffed my pockets full. I read to Mrs Taylor, while we both eat cakes and forgot the time, till it was after 4.0! We then took a tram and train back. Too late for dinner, so we had tea, went to chapel and heard Mr C Spurgeon speak. He was grand, and made us laugh ever so much more than Mr Brown does. He believes in the text "Be of good cheer" with a vengeance. After chapel (by the bye all the hymns were favourites of Mrs Taylor's, and other folks too I should think by the noise) we went for a walk round with Peter and then home to dinner. I played several pieces of music to your enlarged photo which is over the piano with that of Ethel, and the awful cat with the wink between, (Mrs Taylor's triplets), wrote a couple of letters and then to bed, feeling fresh air tired. It was a job to wake up this morning, but I managed to reach business in time.

In our garden we must grow perpetual spinach, potatoes, carrots, marrows, curly kale, mint, parsley and beans. Don't forget.

I was reading the Artists magazine in the train this morning. They are still full of interest. Wish I could send them to you.

Must not stop longer, so Goodbye.

May

May to David   Beckenham   26.6.18

My dear David,

I have not a scrap of news to tell you. Everything is going on alright. I am reading two books – The Morals of Marcus Ordeyne by Wm Locke, which I think will be rather funny, and Scarlet & Purple by Sidney Watson, the man who wrote In the Twinkling of an Eye, & the Mark of the Beast. I will ask another shop to send these three to you. The references are very interesting. The present war is prophesied and its result, the League of Nations which will lead to the Anti Christ and his Prophet and Armageddon.

I have been reading through some of your back letters, even those from Gidea Park. I thought I had destroyed all those from the camp, but I haven't, and can't either, -they are nice.

We are working till 7.0 each night, which means a few more bricks for the bungalow, though I suppose we ought to get the house first.

Had another interview with the chief this morning. We must have looked funny. We were arguing, as usual, I sitting on his table, he leaning forward, though standing, and our noses three inches apart. Can't you imagine it? He remembered our previous talk evidently, as he was very careful not to let me cut the ground away from his feet again. I hope I did not show my suppressed laughter. He was really very nice – for him.

Don't think I will stay late tonight after all; the front grass wants cutting badly. Goodbye.

May

May to David   Beckenham   Letter No 133   28th June 18

My dear David,

This is our payday, and I have also earned £1 in overtime, consequently am very well off and good tempered, in spite of the fact that one of my supers, the best, has given notice to go. She has a place at £3 a week, and we won't go beyond 55/-. I don't mind a bit. Shall get a junior in next, and they are more amenable.

Tomorrow I go to Muriel with the plans. In the small bungalow you have put rather a large kitchen. I am wondering if that could not be made into a living room, by partitioning off a part for cooking. Could you manage it?

Had a nice letter from Mrs Taylor this morning. She was going to let me off this week, but has written to say she would like me on Sunday. Bless her; guess I will go.

Did I tell you we have an extra quarter of an hour for lunch? We have had it all this week now, and we all like it. It took some time to get the chief to agree to it. Chiefs are silly things some times.

Of course there will not be a letter from you this weekend as Cox's will have it; so I have to content myself with re-reading some of the others.

Our palmist is going to give her services at a bazaar Muriel is going to on 24th July. She will read my palm again later on, but I must give it time to change a bit. I reminded her this morning that my greatest surprise had not come off yet. She firmly believes it will.

The quarter of an hour is now up, and I am desperately busy. Ought really to stay tonight, but want to pay the butcher's bills, and can't possibly do both.

Well, goodbye for a little while. Hope you are keeping A1, and not worrying about anything – there is nothing to worry about really.

May

PS Did I tell you Maud was away with the flu? Mr Bishop had it last week, and directly he came back Maud began to get queer, and now she is away with it, so I wrote her last night pointing out it was very foolish beside being wrong to kiss Mr Bishop. I wonder what she thinks of it?

David to May   Holzminden   Letter No 25   July 1st 1918

My Dearest,

I have not had a letter from you since I wrote to you last, and only one from Mum. Your last was No 116. I hope nothing is wrong. None of your books have arrived either but I expect they will shortly. In the meantime I still seem to feel to have a lot of work ahead of me. I have just started doing the quantities of the house, but of course it is all very indefinite simply because practically every item I come to I want to discuss with you. I have got hold of a book on American houses which is pretty good, but there are no really very new ideas in it, although of necessity their methods differ from ours on a number of points owing, more particularly, to the climate – still there are a number of things which we might easily adopt with advantage. For instance they apparently sometimes have a permanent pipe put through the house for connecting up to a vacuum cleaner from the street, so that the whole of the dirt is simply sucked straight outside which seems rather good. We ourselves must certainly have some sort of portable arrangement anyhow.

I have also been reading an American book on small holdings, but it is not very good. It talks a good deal about the enormous number of dollars that various people, including infants at school, had made out of pieces of land from the size of a postage stamp upwards, but beyond that it did not contain a great deal of information.

With regard to your beach hut, the material from the army huts which will be sold after the war do extremely well for that sort of thing, but I guess it will be used for a thousand and one other things too. Talking about the house, I know you see the local as well as the other papers sometimes. Will you look out for any land sales and make a note of the particulars and prices and send them to me, so that we can get some sort of rough idea of the cost of land per acre. If it is not too late, will you ask Mum to keep an account of the amount of fruit she gets from the gooseberry bushes.

In some of your letters you ask if I am growing a beard. I have not reached that stage yet, although some of the fellows here have, one of them in particular is a fearful looking object.

His beard has grown very bushy and in the wrong places. I have never seen anything quite like it, it is unique. He's an awful warning to the rest of us. Did I tell you I have had another letter from the Lodge. At their last meeting they apparently passed a resolution wishing the absent members a speedy return etc etc.

The last two or three parcels from home have been addressed by you. It is nice to think you helped to pack them. By the way, in that February letter I think I told you I had received the second copy of your photo. It was good of you to send two, so as to make sure of my getting it. I am very glad you are taking your girls out again this year and I am most anxious to get your letter describing the whole affair. Didn't the booking office people think you had rather a large family? But why don't you go about more, I wish you would. On the first of June I wrote a post card to Cox direct, telling them to pay any balance over £25 to Mum. Will you please ask her to see if they got this.

I have broken two teeth off my plate which is a nuisance to say the least of it, as I have now got a rough edge which makes my tongue sore.

I think something must have gone wrong with the works of the Board of Education, as they have sent me four books viz River and Canal Engineering, Maccauly's History of England, and The Clerk of Works, all of which of course you yourself have already sent through Batsfords, and you remember a few weeks ago they sent me a parcel with three of four of the other books, amongst others Lockwoods book; which you had already sent. I wonder how they got hold of the names of these. However they will not be wasted as I have passed them on to the library. I have finished my poultry course and have got some sort of a rough idea of things, but I must get a book to read it up, if we ever want to do anything in this way. And that reminds me, I have just taken up another subject which is Dutch. Truly in time I shall have a nodding acquaintance with a number of things and not know much of anything. So far have had one lesson, just sufficient to have hit up against the first big difficulty. I have found out that they pronounce their g as hg with a guttural sound, which is a regular tongue twister. I am learning Dutch from a South African who of course has only Cape Dutch, but still it is good enough for what I want. We are a most cosmopolitan crowd in the camp, drawn from all the ends of the earth. The other day I was talking to a man who was in Japan and came home to join up. I think he was in a shipping office. I sit at table at meals with a man from Buenos Ayres, and I sleep opposite a man who was clearing timber to make a farm on Prince Edward Island off the West Coast of British Columbia. At one time we had four of the Indian officers here, but of course they have gone to Holland.

I have had one copy of the "Architect" and one of "The Builder" both for May 17th. It is good to see these old papers again, even advertisements that somebody's asphalte is now being used by everyone and somebody else's paint is like nothing on earth, are most interesting. Please thank Mum very much for them. I have passed them on to three or four other fellows here.

In a few days I shall have done twelve month "time". It seems an age. A man today asked me, if when, I went to Holland, (the fact of seeing others going to Holland, you get into the way of looking forward to going yourself, although it is still a long way off) I was going to have my wife

over there, as he had heard that this might be possible. I said I hoped so. But still I don't want to go to Holland, I want to get home to you.
Goodbye

David.

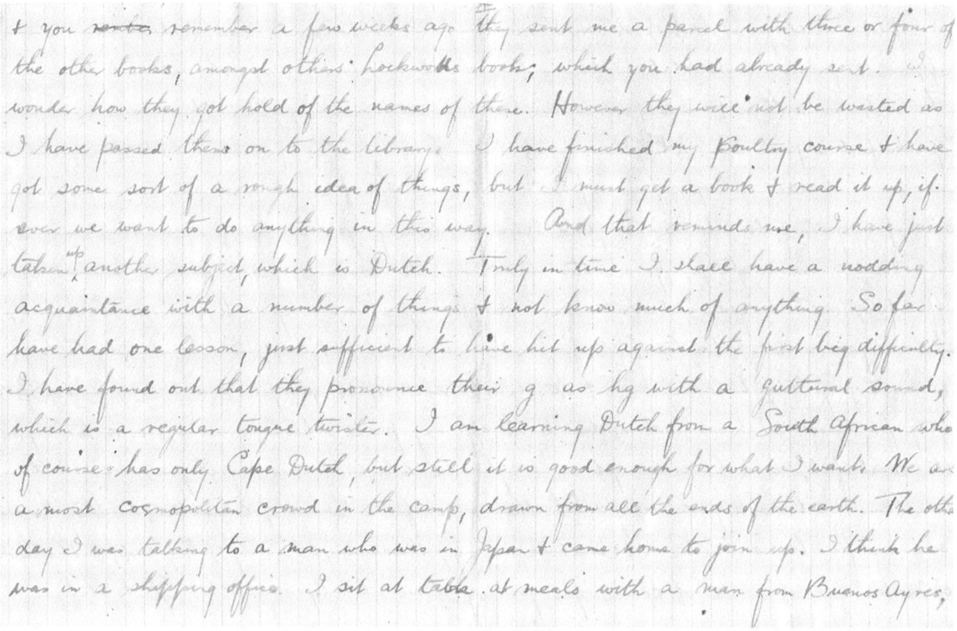

[handwritten letter]

May to David   Beckenham   1.7.18

My dear David,
Talk about being busy – I get worse and worse, but somehow I shall always find a few minutes for my darling three times a week.
Saturday the weather was lovely. I left the office 12.35 caught the 12.45 to Bush Hill Park. Mr Mac was waiting for me at the station. Had a most enjoyable afternoon and evening there. The place is a sight of roses. I took all your photos and told Muriel I would repeat all the extravagantly flattering remarks she said about you, only I have forgotten them. I think she began with "O, the sweet little pet!" They seem to enjoy gazing at your likenesses, then that lady came that came when we were last there, and she inquired about you, and remembered your name and knew you in the photos. Muriel has found out a way of making chocolate, and will not be happy till she has sent you some. I said she might. They have a bazaar for the local V.A.D. Hospital on the 24th of this month for which I am going to make some socks. Shall be working late at the office from now onwards, so will practically only be able to work on the train. Muriel was keen on the plans of houses, and said I must have a Mystery room. She changed her mind about it pretty frequently, but I think the last idea was black and silver decorations, with greeny blue dragons. However, I am to go again soon as they have not said

half they wanted, and Muriel will have fresh suggestions to make.

Sunday morning I walked up to the cemetery. The stocks have come on beautifully and the grave looked very well. Then I went round to Maud's to water that, and found it a sight of weeds in full bloom, and tufty grass, with the blighted remains of 3 beastly evergreens, four mouldy geraniums and 3 apologies of marguerites. Of course the evergreens have practically poisoned the ground, except for the weeds which were certainly bonny. I was going to give Maud a lecture today, but she is away again, poor girl. She came up Saturday feeling very shaky. I think she had the flu. We have had very hot weather with cutting winds; the result being that many folks have chills – I've got 6 away in my department alone! It comes of playing tennis mostly. As I don't, I am alright. Sunday was our hottest day this year, and in the afternoon I went over to Balham decked in my new voile dress which I had made last year but never wore. Mrs Taylor likes it very much. We went to chapel in the evening, and heard a grand sermon. I have no time to tell you about it or I would.

When I have finished five more pairs of socks I am going to make Muriel a sports coat, knitted, and the money for making is going to the Red Cross. I have done several things for them in this way, and enjoy it so much. Your mother said yesterday she was feeling so happy about you, so thinks you must be quite well.

Goodbye.

May

May to David   Beckenham   2.7.18

My dear David,

I forgot to mention in my last letter that Mrs Maconachie said she did not think I had altered in the least, and I think it was either 2 or 3 years ago when she last saw us. I thought I had aged lately, but perhaps I have not.

I have only just finished the pair of socks I started making a fortnight ago; must be quicker with the next lot. Mama helped me wind a pound of wool last night. This is for Mrs Maconachie's bazaar.

We are sending Mrs Matthews to Brighton for next week. She is very elated.

Two of the staff invalids have returned this morning, and Maud is back again. I have not seen her, though. I have a slight breaking out on my lip, so suppose I, too, have had a cold, though I was unaware of it. Couldn't have been very bad.

Worked until 7.0 last night, and shall be for many nights. Maud has just looked in. Her nerves have given way and the doctor says she must give up. She has been to Lutt who says she had better take her fortnight's holiday at once, and then they will keep her place open for another 2 weeks, without pay of course. After that, if she is not alright she must of course leave. So she has written down to Watchet to know if they can take her at once for a month. Her landlady has put up her rent 6d a week, and she has had a mishap with the water which has brought down a ceiling she will have to pay for that in part.

3.7.18

Saw Maud again this morning. She showed me her doctor's certificate. She is suffering from general debility, and the man adds that after a month's rest she ought to be fit for work again. Somehow, I don't think much of that doctor, and Maud is too fond of thinking of her health and so playing into the doctor's hands. She says it is all through the strenuous time she went through when her mother died, and through missing her mother. She is very fond of that last phrase, so I told her how her mother's grave looked. She looked dismayed and said she really could not look after it. I told her she need not, that I would do it myself.

I have no news. O yes I have. The Malayalam Co is going to pay 8%. Did you get my letter giving the no. of your shares? Ethel is going to see Mrs Bullock on Saturday, so I have written to Mrs Taylor asking if I shall go to her early Sunday morning, instead of Saty afternoon, to do her grave. It only wants a patch of saxifrage and some dirt put on one corner.

Weather lovely. We are longing for a letter from you, but don't expect one for a fortnight. Goodbye.

May

PS Mrs Taylor has just been in; brought your p.c. of 21st May, some lovely flowers, a cake for my tea, and a present for Mrs Maconachie's bazaar, a tea-pot cosy made by wounded soldier. Isn't she sweet?

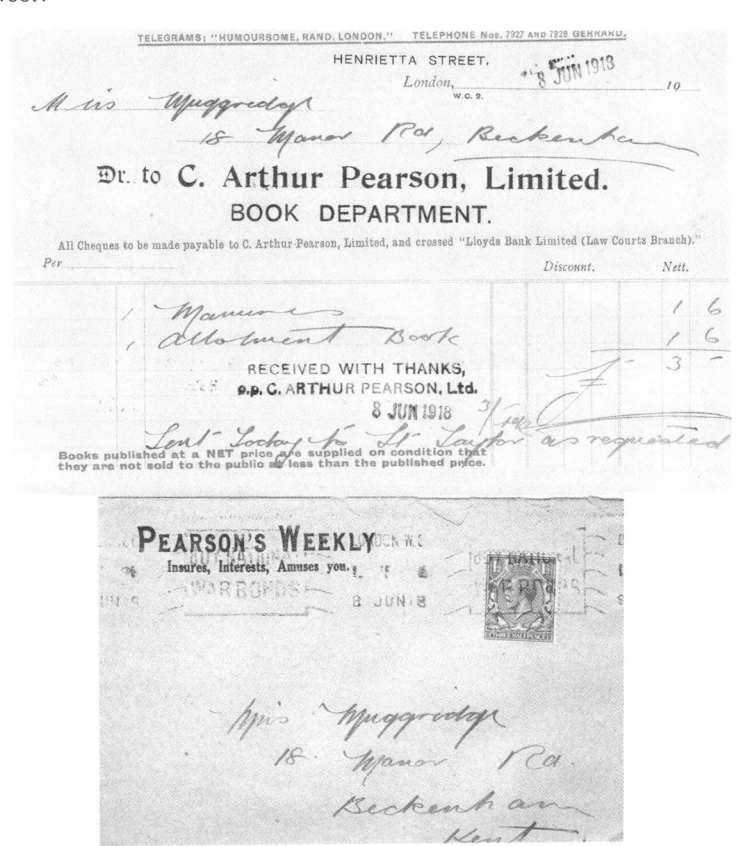

May to David   Beckenham   4.7.18

My dear David,

I forgot to tell you the other day that Miss Willsher called in at the Office and said they took £103 at their bazaar, and expect another £7 to be sent. This is record. They usually get £70. It is only a private affair which takes place in a back garden when fine and in doors when wet. She wants me to do some more outings with her, one to Hatfield on Saturday before August, but I am not able to make any promises yet. Don't know what Mrs Taylor is doing, or if Ethel is going out.

Our station is being done up very nicely, and smells beautifully of tar. It will be looking fit for peace celebrations! I have not heard any talk lately about when we are to expect peace. Everyone is talking about holidays instead, and the weather is keeping glorious. Devonshire seems a favoured spot this year as well as Bognor and round about there. How I wish I was on Exmoor with you. Shall have to do a little more imagining. Well, it is a pleasant occupation, and quite enjoyable.

I would like a peep at you. How do you cook your meals? Do you each cook your own? It does not seem to me that you have any dinner. Are you as thin as you were when you had your photo taken with your platoon? I forgot to take it with me last Saturday, so have handed it to Mr Maconachie to-day.

I am earning about 12/- a week overtime pay now. Don't worry, I am not overworking myself. I catch a train at 7.15 fast to Dulwich and Beckenham, and on down to Maidstone. It will all help towards the bungalow which I think we might call "Overtime Villa" instead of "Mayville" which Mama suggested.

5.7.18

Yesterday was a grand day in London. It was Independence Day, and the place was pretty full of Americans for the day. There were feasts and games and rejoicings generally. I would like to know how many people shouted themselves hoarse.

We are getting steadily behind with the work, but the weather is too glorious to worry over it. I am expecting two more invalids back next week which will make a big difference to us. Shall not be working late tonight, but will pay the bills on the way home instead. I would rather work late.

I want to do some knitting now for Mrs Maconachie's bazaar, so you won't mind my leaving off, will you? Just give me one more kiss. Thanks. Goodbye.

May

David to Ginger   Holzminden   Post Card No 11   July 8th 1918

I have had no letter or anything from you since my last post card at the beginning of last month. In two days time I shall have done twelve months "time" & am already looking forward to going to Holland, so much so that I have taken up Dutch. Its a lovely language, the first thing to learn being that g is pronounced hg with a guttural sound. Its lovely. Yesterday I had a small tinned cake sent me the first I have had since I left France which reminds me that your last Buzzard cake was delivered to me the day before I was taken, & I had only eaten one slice when it went aloft with the dugout & the remainder of my things. I have mourned that cake long & bitterly & even now, every time I think of it, I weep. I hope you are all alright especially the kiddies. I have not heard from them for months.

David

May to David   Beckenham   Letter No 137   8.7.18

My dear David,
I reckon 15 minutes after lunch on Mondays belong to you, i.e. for your letter, and the whole of that time has been taken up listening to complaints. I ought to be used to them by now. Well, I must take another quarter of an hour for you, or you will be complaining!
Friday night I left at proper time and paid the butcher's bills. I am honest sometimes, you will see. Saturday I left at 12.30, could not get to Holborn on account of the crowds seeing the King & Queen (we are having grand times) so went to St Paul's and on to Herne Hill and cemetery. Our grave looks lovely, at least the flowers do, but not the stone. Then watered Maud's, and walked home, calling for my enlarged photo. The frame matches yours exactly. After tea finished the first pair of socks for the bazaar. Sunday morning got up at 8.0 and caught the 10.40 to Balham. Took Peter to Common, where the young tinker took my character away. There were a lot of men being drilled by an officer. Of course Peter went to inspect their legs and boots generally. He pretended he did not know me just because I had my new dress on, but was busy looking for me amongst the soldiers, peering up into their faces as though asking them what they had done with me; or maybe he was looking for you. When he came to the bawling officer, and he was bawling too, his expression fairly said "What is the matter with you, sonny; don't you feel well?" When I did get him away I took him straight home. Dinner was ready and we did enjoy it. Afterwards we went to Wimbledon and Putney, when we did some more weeding, but Mrs Taylor would not take the piece of saxifrage from the garden, so we shall have to go again. We left home at 2.45 and got back at 8.45. We did sleep well that night. Maud starts to-day for Watchet. May it do her good! Just because I did not sympathise with her she told me she could see it was a crime in my sight to be ill in business. Guess I must look a dragon.
Must leave off now, so Goodbye once again.

May

May to David   Beckenham   10.7.18

My dear David,

I forgot to mention in my last letter that it looks as though your cousin will have to join up. I hope so. The Board he is working for say they do not think the work he is doing is of sufficient national importance to get him exemption! In spite of his many fancied ailments he has passed A1. It is funny.

Mrs Maconachie writes me as under –

"Thanks so much for letting us see of the photo of Mr Taylor with his platoon. We think it is very nice of him. He looks thin & must be longing for the day when he can have all the fondling he must expect will be given him"!

What about hiring a polar bear? I fancy they can do some hugging.

I have just written the following letter, and it reminds me of Gilbert & Sullivan:-

"We approve the recommendations of the Sub-Sub-Sub-Committee going forward to the Emergency Sub-Committee as the recommendations of the Emergency Sub-Sub-Committee." (The dictator is still at large).

This morning, wishful of doing some shopping, I caught the early mainline train, but did not like the journey at all as I could not get a compartment to myself. Am I not an island? I have missed the solitude all the morning. I won't be early again.

I have finished reading "The Morals of Marcus Ordeyne", a queer sort of book, but it does not come up to Aristide Pujol which seems to be Locke's best.

I think out station is finished, and now the roads are being done up. We shall be smart.

To-day it is raining for which I am pleased. We want rain badly. We have received a letter from Mrs Matthews at Brighton, and a very amusing letter it is. We have all had a go at understanding it, and have come to the conclusion that she has left out a lot, but that she is intensely happy and feeling a lady of the first water.

I am now working on my second pair of socks for the bazaar.

Ethel starts her fortnights holiday on Saturday, but so far is not going away except for the middle weekend when she will be staying with some folks in north London, so I have written to Mrs Taylor to tell her I am free this weekend.

Can't think of anything else to say. Still working late, and making my fortune. Just one more kiss. That will do. Thanks.

May

May to David   Beckenham   11.7.18

My dear David,

My income tax paper arrived this morning – so welcome -, and while hunting through some private papers for ideas for filling up I came across a copy letter I had written to Read & Brigstock, which gives me some particulars I wanted without troubling Mrs Taylor again. I have, therefore, written them the following letter, and will ask Mrs Taylor to sign it when I see her next time, which I expect will be Saturday:-

"On 30th April 1917 my son, &c., bought some Malayalam Rubber Shares. In May 17 he bought 10 more for which he sent a cheque for £19. He again wrote for 10 in June '17 but did not enclose the money. Shortly after that he was taken prisoner. I cancelled the third request for shares, and in due time received the certificate for the 10 bought in May 17. He is now writing from Germany asking if I have received the certificate for the first shares bought in April 1917. I have not received this certificate, and have asked him to write to you direct as I cannot tell you the number he bought or the price paid. Did you send it to him in France? If so, and you can give me date and particulars, I will take up the matter with the Post Office."

How will that do? It ought to get a reply of some sort.

The weather is dreadfully wet. Poor Maud!

It is years since I had a letter from you. I shall soon begin to feel a desolate widow.

12.7.18

A letter from you this morning. Horray. And a nice one too, though I know you are feeling fed up. You need not, as there are plenty of nice thoughts to have. The letter was dated 1st June, and contained a very nice plan of the hut on one floor. My ideas of furnishing are to save work as much as possible. The cutlery will be the same as Mrs Pratt's – no cleaning required. I like the idea of the drawer under the beds. You have made two of the small bedrooms 6' on one side. I thought they ought to be 6'6". Could that be arranged? I have shown the sketch to the elder girls at the office, and they are in love with it, want me to have it and let it to them. We might take your camp bed when we go, and put it in the living room. One of the elder girls here has an allotment, and she is getting on well with it, and gives me tips.

As regards weather, we have awful deluges, and beautiful intervals. I am glad you can get out for walks. That boot race sounds funny.

Mama seems to be looking at my big photo as though it belongs to her. Well, if she wants one I will get another, but I think the photographer has joined up now.

A post card came from Mrs Taylor last night saying she is looking forward to having me for the weekend. Also a letter card from Maud who is evidently black out with me as I said I hoped the Dr wasn't playing the fool with her. She writes "Dear May, Just a line to tell you I am comfortably settled here. The doctor's opinion here coincides exactly with Dr White's. We had a storm yesterday. The lightning was vivid. I am boating at all available opportunities. Norman is still very attentive, and I am finding several other people glad to see me. Love. Yours, M.A."

Isn't Maud funny when she tries to be dignified? She is the biggest baby I ever came across. I have replied enclosing her a smelling salts bottle full of powerful stuff, and a hope that she will not find it useful; also wished he many happy returns of her birthday (to-morrow); hoped she had taken with her suitable figleaves as the weather has turned so windy & wet, & suggested all she need wear is a ham frill & a shoulder strap. I wonder what she will reply.

Can't stop any longer, so say Goodbye to me. (You do want a shave badly.)

May

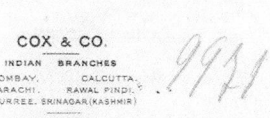

COX & CO.

INDIAN BRANCHES
BOMBAY. CALCUTTA.
KARACHI. RAWAL PINDI.
MURREE. SRINAGAR (KASHMIR)

AGENCY FOR
COX & CO (FRANCE) LTD
PARIS. ROUEN. HAVRE
BOULOGNE. MARSEILLES.
AMIENS. LYONS.

TELEGRAPHIC ADDRESSES.
"COXIA".

TELEPHONE GERRARD 7001.

16, CHARING CROSS,
LONDON, S.W.1.

12th July 1918

IN REPLY
PLEASE QUOTE REFERENCE A. 2.

Sir,

    In reply to your letter of the 1st ultimo, we beg to inform you that the balance standing to the credit of your account is £148 0.3. and of this we are remitting the sum of £123..0.0. to the London County, Westminster & Parr's Bank, Newington, for the credit of Mrs. Fanny Taylor, as desired.

    We are forwarding you a statement of account under separate cover, and this will be rendered at the end of each quarter in future.

We are, Sir,
Your obedient Servants,
COX & CO.

For the Manager.

D.H. Taylor, Esq.,
    King's Royal Rifles,
        Keserne,
           Holzminden. GERMANY.

May to David   Beckenham   15.7.18

My dear David,

This is St Swithin's Day, so of course it has rained. A week ago people were moaning about the dry weather. Now they are moaning about the wet.

Saturday I left early, at 12.30, and went to Balham, just in time for a lovely dinner. During dinner we discussed where we should go for the afternoon and finally decided in Streatham Common – then the rain came down in bucketfuls, so we sat in the drawing room and knitted instead, while Mrs Taylor told me how busy she had been during the week. Your bedroom is now prepared for you, walls rubbed down etc etc, and this week your study will be spring cleaned ready for your speedy return. It looks as if you might be back before long, and we are feeling cheerful accordingly. As the rain was not in a hurry to leave off we had tea, and by that time it had cleared off. On the way to Streatham Common we did some shop gazing, and more shop gazing, and still more shop gazing, with the result we did not get much further than the High Road. Finding it was getting on for 9.0 before we reached the Rly Station we turned back and took Peter out on to Clapham Common. Then we had supper and went to bed. How I slept! Ten hours straight off. Sunday it was raining again nearly all day. We took Peter out twice, went to Chapel once, wrote several letters, and did some reading and that was our day's work. No, I am forgetting I made a pig of myself over eating too much cream, with the awful result that I woke up this early this morning and thought of our journey in the North Sea during a gale, and that hurricane in the English Channel when Auntie & I shared a cabin. I was frightened to eat a hearty breakfast, so had a usual one. However, I did not starve as Mrs Taylor put in my case a large meat roll (enough for two dinners), five cakes, two being decidedly large, a lot of biscuits, two oranges and two lemons, and wanted to give me more! Mrs Taylor had your p card on Saturday dated 16th June. She was very pleased with it, and also your letter which she thought sounded cheerful. Of course I tried to make it sound cheerful, but it struck me you had the hump, and pretty badly too. Cheer up, my hearty. I wonder if you say to yourself each night, as I do, "Another day nearer to him." Eh? Now I didn't say you were the "him". O, you know it, do you? Who told you?

I must leave off now, as we are still desperately busy. Goodbye.

May

David to May   Holzminden   July 15th 1918

My Dearest,

I was awfully surprised and amused to get suddenly your letter describing "my young lady's" visit to Watford, for I had had none of your previous letters during your holiday and had no idea you were going there. But I am glad you went as I expect it did you a lot more good than staying at home, as I expect you would probably have spent the greater part of your time indoors and I thought you would be getting good weather as it was here altho' it has been pretty wet ever since. I am awfully glad it was fine all the time and that you were able to get about a fair amount. What did you do with yourself for the remainder of your holiday? I have your letter telling me of your two days with Miss Willsher, but what else did you do? I am glad you got on so well with Aunt Sophy and Uncle Pratt. I always used to stay with them when I was small and had a holiday in Watford. Thanks very much indeed for your birthday wishes. I do hope your prediction for next year will come true.

At last your books have arrived today, that is the Builders Clerk (which by the way from what I have seen of it, seems rather good and which you must read some time), Metrical Tables and Shorthand book and key. They also enclosed a list of the Everyman and Wayfarers Libraries. Thanks very much indeed for them all. It is good of you. The "Twinkling of an Eye" hasn't come along yet but is doubtless still at the censors. I don't know if you have received my letter of March 15th, you make no mention of it in any of yours so far. Talking about the Artists Magazine – there are crowds of Artists here, two besides myself in my room. I would give anything to get back to those bunkers again wouldn't you? I have also had a "Builders Journal" for May 29th. You don't know how good it is to get these trade papers again, except it makes one thirst to get back to it all again, and from that you wander off into great and glorious fantasies of what we too may perhaps do together. You read of meeting with several of the names of well known people mentioned and you begin to wonder whether we shall be competing some day with these same men and firms. I have asked Ethel to send me some of the American technical papers, but whether she will be allowed to or not remains to be seen, of course.

I see from the Builders Journal that there has just been formed an Architectural Assistance Welfare Committee drawn from the three chief Architectural Societies and I notice that one of the members is a lady. I think she is probably a member of the Architectural Association as I believe they have lady members, altho' I don't think the Institute of British Architects have adopted this yet. But this seems to be rather a step forward for a lady to be serving on a sort of joint committee. In one of your letters you ask if I have had the pain in my side again. I have had no trace of it since and in fact to look at me you would imagine I had been to the seaside, my face being its usual lobster hue, and my knees about mahogany colour, though this last fact not being altogether due to dirt, but that my usual costume at present consists of stockings (or rather darn, with a bit of stocking round it) a shirt, and shorts, and your waistcoat and that I keep outside as much as possible.

With regard to the building construction, you must be prepared for an extremely severe

examination in it as soon as I come back. By the way let me know of any difficulty you come across and I will try to explain. I am enclosing three sketches of the latest alterations from the house. You will see that I have knocked out the bay window to the drawing room on the back elevation and have put a small door in the corner of the room. I did this because it makes a better shape room and should make it warmer and also balance the elevation better. I have also altered the North elevation again, taking out both doors. The external entrance to the Kitchen is now round the corner on the East side and the Coal Store is there too, just beside the Kitchen door, so that it is as close as possible but still outside, so that no coal dust can get in. I have attempted to sketch the drawing room in order to give you some idea of it. The two book cases have fitted into the plan rather well and should together with the fireplace, give a sort of panel appearance to the two sides of the room at all events, without being quite so costly as panelling and at the same time being useful. I am getting on very well with the quantities, but as I said before it is all very much in the air as I want to discuss so much of it with you and of course I am tied down a good deal too, as if I were at home I could refer to all sorts of things in order to compare different methods of construction to see which would be the cheapest. However it will give us some sort of closer idea of the whole thing.
Goodbye

David

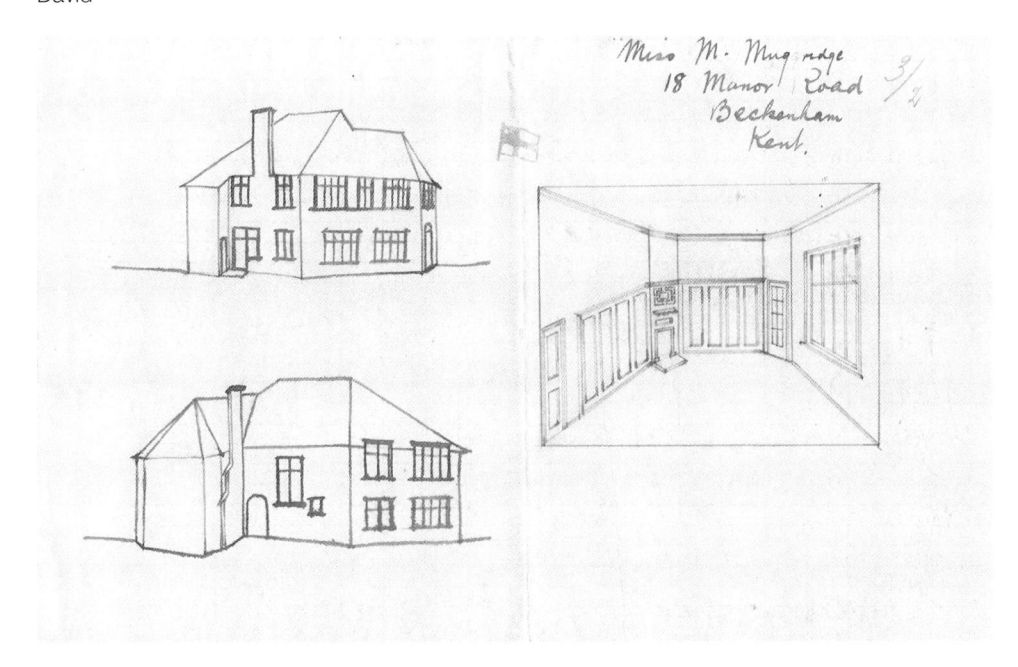

May to David   Beckenham   16.7.18 Tuesday

My dear David,

Just a line to say Mrs Taylor has come into the Office with Read & Brigstock's reply about your first share certificate. They write:-

"In reply to your letter received this morning we are holding the certificate for the 15 Malayalam Shares purchased on account of your son. Will you kindly let us know if you wish us to forward the same to you?"

To which we have replied Yes.

When you were taken prisoner Mrs Taylor put this matter into your cousin's hands, obtaining fro me copies of all you had written about the shares. She has vowed never to ask him anything again!

Fearfully busy, but all alright. Goodbye.

May

May to David   Beckenham   17.7.18

My dear David,

This morning one of my letters to you, dated last February, was returned to me, the envelope being marked "Not in Holland" against the word Holzminden. Well, considering I had also put "Hanover, Germany", it was rather obvious; but I had written it by hand, so presume my writing was not clear. Monday night we had a terrible storm. It did not last long, but the quality was alright. The thunder was one continuous roar and there were 60 flashes to the minute. I did not count them, but that was what the newspaper said, so it must be so.

I am very busy on my third pair of socks for Mrs Maconachie's bazaar.

I wrote the other day to say your first certificate for 15 shares of Malayalam were being sent to Mrs Taylor. Being shorthanded and having heaps to do I am going to ask you to excuse more just now. This is letter No 142. I would like to know how many have gone astray.

Goodbye.

May

PS Forgot to mention on Monday I had an acknowledgement from Maud of the present I sent her. Her nose is still out of joint. She is awfully funny when on her dignity. It is a great improvement, so I reckon I will keep her like that. She evidently doesn't like being called a "piece of machinery" which when going wrong is a nuisance. We are only machinery in business, the chief says so, and he ought to know.

Uncle Ken is retiring. Auntie is coming to see Mama Thursday, and then I will be able to write more fully about it.

I re-enclose the returned letter.

May to David   Beckenham   19.7.18

My dear David,

On the way home last Wednesday I was caught in a short but most select thunderstorm, and was held up for ¾ hour at Post Office Station. The road was like a river and the thunder overhead and incessant all the time. They also had it very bad at home, and the cellar was flooded.

We are still fairly busy and making our fortunes.

The only item of news I have is that Mrs Day's daughter wrote to say she was not well (I have my suspicions that there is another youngster on order), and Mrs Taylor packed Mrs Day off at once and told her to stay until her daughter could be left. Then Mama said Mrs Taylor must not be left alone at night, so I am packed off to Balham to sleep each night until further notice. Ethel is spending her holidays at home. Ern starts his to-morrow, but does not yet whether he will go to Margate or not. Nothing like driving things till the last moment.

Your certificate for the 15 shares of Malayalam has arrived.

It is raining most beautifully, and could not look more dismal, but everyone seems very cheerful and more or less excited.

I cannot think of anything else to say just now, so Goodbye.

May

PS One of my girls is staying not far from Maud, and she says the weather is simply awful and it is impossible to go out. Poor Maud. What a blessing people down there are "so kind" to her.

May to David   Beckenham   22.7.18

My dear David,

On Saturday I left early, went home, was busy all the afternoon, left soon after tea, and went back to Balham. Ethel was to have gone away for the weekend, but had a letter from her friends to say one was ill, so she stayed at home. Ern has started his holidays, but has not gone away yet – can't make up his mind.

Sunday seemed like a seaside day, - windy, bright, with passing showers. After breakfast I took Peter round the pond on Clapham Common. He did enjoy himself; then Mrs Taylor & I went to Streatham Extension, which we did not leave till 3.30. (we don't have any time on Sundays – have enough of that all the week). We had dinner after we got home, and then went off to chapel which we both enjoyed. It was hospital Sunday, and the collection came to £36. They do have tremendous collections at that place – Sunday after Sunday. There is a lot of money in the neighbourhood. After chapel we went for another walk, and off to bed at 10.0. How we both slept. We are still very busy. The girls stayed last Saty afternoon till 6.30. I shall stay till 7.30 to-night. Last week I made 18/- overtime – the others have made much more.

Last Saturday I had a letter from Esther – first for many months. A tale of woe as usual. She is in a small cottage just outside Huntingdon which place does not suit the children, and she herself has been ill. They have warehoused the furniture. Just as they were settled there alright (they have had two places there) David was ordered off to Cornwall. He apparently came up one weekend and made arrangements for them to pack up and be off there, when another letter came from him to say he was just being sent off somewhere else, but did not know where. It made her feel so awful that she sat down and wrote to me. She wants news of you, so as I have not anything else to tell you I will spend the rest of my lunch time condoling with her. It is really absurd trying to rush around with 3 babies after her hubby. I shall tell her to keep quiet and write to her hubby each day telling all the doings of the 3 little angels. By the bye, Mrs Taylor was told we were not to write you any war news, so that is why I do not. Do the others in your camp receive any news from England. I do wish I could tell you news. You would not feel so down as I know you do at times. You mentioned in one of your back letters that Mrs T had read one of your letters from Ethel. I can't say which one it was but I have an idea that it was one about me, and written in a bad temper – the outcome of my stupidity in telling her of all the letters I had received from you. The reason I think is that one Saturday when I went to Balham Mrs Taylor was very upset, and said it was caused by a letter from Ethel, and she would not tell me anything more; but during that weekend she murmured things like this = "I won't have him upset". "Nothing would wound him more than anyone saying things against May". "Look at what he is doing for us all". "She's a bad tempered, jealous, little beast." Etc etc, so if you receive a letter minus a portion, I reckon that was the one she read, as apparently she made up her mind to keep back a part for your sake. "It's for his sake" she murmured several times.

Goodbye.

May

May to David   Beckenham   24.7.18

My dear David,

I am making my fortune. That is to say, I am making 5/- per day extra, and I am not killing myself in the process. The work is easy and purely mechanical. I am leaving Balham a few minutes after 8.0 and returning at 8.30 to find a nice supper waiting for me. We go to bed at 10.0 and are soon asleep. I believe Mrs Taylor enjoys my living with her, and does not seem anxious to get Mrs Day back. There is a letter from Mrs Harris this morning to say her mother is getting on very nicely. I believe she has had the influenza, which she must have caught from her daughter.

There was also a cheerful letter from Ethel this morning. She has opened a bowling green. I expect she did look nice.

Did I tell you some weeks back that there was a notice in the paper about Royalty giving first and second class awards to hospital workers? There were not many firsts given, but shoals of seconds, and among the latter was Miss Friend. I reckon she was disappointed at not getting a first. I guess she had worked hard for it, being the kind of work she loves. Well, better luck for her next time.

Last Sunday I was practicing some of your songs – I mean the accompaniments, as you are coming back to us again one day, and I don't think it will be long either.

I cannot think of anything more to say. O yes I can. I notice those Submarine pictures that we saw at the Philharmonic are coming down to Balham next week, so I shall be taking Mrs Taylor. She says I might.

Goodbye.

May

May to David   Balham   26.7.18

My dear David,

Mrs Maconachie's bazaar was a great success. It was only a small affair but they cleared £250. Our "Palmist" was there, and was the hit of the evening. The clergyman was the first to visit her, and the next was the house surgeon. She talked incessantly from 3.0 till 9.0 and took £2.15/- in that time. She was only charging 1/-. Everyone seemed pleased with her. Muriel has made you some chocolate all by herself, so Mrs Taylor is making you up a parcel. I forget whether you have been told, but the Red Cross parcels will not be as good as they have been as they have discontinued making up the "Special" parcels, and only send ordinary ones now. Sorry you are put on the "ordinary" basis. You will no longer be able to fancy yourself a colonel. You are limited in meat, sugar and grease, and these are being sent you by the Red Cross, so that they cannot be included in the Stores parcel.

I have been expecting you to ask for some more books – technical ones.

We are still making our fortunes, and strange to say I am not at all tired with this overtime. Mrs

Taylor told me last night she thought I was even looking better than usual. I expect next week will finish our late work. Last week I made 18/-. This week it will be more.

Bother, I have run short of envelopes, and will have to "borrow" one from the office. You won't mind, will you?

To-morrow afternoon I am going home for an hour or two when I hope to find a letter from you. There is one due.

Must now get on with my work, Goodbye,

May.

May to David   Balham   29.07.18

My dear David,

I have just made up the overtime for the month of July, and I have taken £3.11.-. The rush is now over, and the work is slackening down very much. There will not be much, if any, overtime to do next month.

On Saturday I left at 1.0 & went home, leaving there at 7.30, and reaching Balham at 8.45. On Sunday after breakfast I took Peter for his scamper on Clapham Common, and then Mrs Taylor & I walked to Brockwell Park. It turned out a lovely day and we quite enjoyed ourselves. In the evening we went to chapel. To-day is hot and misty.

This morning Mrs Taylor had a letter from your Aunt Bessie, at least I think it was from her. Mrs Capel is getting worse, and Mrs Taylor wants to go and nurse her, but can't because Mrs Day is still away. I don't know whether I have put my foot in it, but I said it was a good thing she could not go as she would only get doing all the nursing etc and knock herself up, whereas Mrs C has two daughters living with her, and two sisters handy, who have an easier time than Mrs Taylor, and they ought to do all the work; but that Mrs T might go down for a day and come back the same night. She said she would lock up the house and stay at Mrs Capel's if she could only get rid of Peter for the time being, so I have not offered to take him home, thinking you would rather I did not let Mrs Taylor go away. She really is too good.

In this letter from Watford was a very nice sentence, viz that at the Pratts there was some war talk the other day, and it was thought that the war would be over in September this year. Since then the war news has been still better.

The regular pastor is away on holidays, and the man we had yesterday spoke quite ordinarily, and did not get excited; the result was that one man close by gave occasional snores, while Mrs Taylor nodded, and her eyes were closed. She afterwards informed me that she was not asleep, but has heard the sermon before, and as she knew it she closed her eyes.

Uncle Ken has retired from business, and is thinking of living at Solihull in Warwickshire. Auntie wanted Mama to take Helen & the children, but Mama declined with thanks as Helen goes to business. At present Uncle & Auntie have gone to Leatherhead for a fortnight, and Helen and the children with Vi and Harry have gone to Paignton.

In case the letter went astray I repeat that Mrs Taylor has received your first certificate for the Malayam shares.
I am staying till 7.0 to-night, but expect to leave at 5.0 to-morrow.
Goodbye.

May

May to David   Balham   Letter No 148   31.7.18

My dear David,
On Monday I left at 7.0 reaching Balham before 8.0, and took Peter for a scamper, and after that pottered about in the garden. The weather has again turned gorgeous.
Yesterday, Tuesday, I left the Office at 5.30, no, 5.20 and was home at 6.0. Seated in the drawing room window was your Aunt Maria. Isn't she the one of the aunts you wanted to raffle? I got on with her very well, at least I suppose I did. She was telling Mrs Taylor how she did not get to bed till 2.0 that morning on account of sitting up for her son-in-law who had left his key at home in mistake. I looked severely at her and said in my strictest manner "I don't believe you are respectable". She did look at me. (She had taken stock of me when I first went in, I suppose wondering if I was good enough to be her niece.) It is no good blaming me if I am cheeky, as you taught me, so it is all your fault. The Submarine Photography pictures were on at Balham, so I took both the ladies there. However, we arrived late, and those pictures we did see were somewhat disappointing as a tale had been made up – a regular sensational overdone tale suitable for picture palaces only. A diver went down to a wreck, and the villain tried to cut the air pipe, and then that black man, Buller, dived down without diver's clothes and did some rescuing. Of course the sharks were numerous, but they were not villains.
On coming out of the Palace your Aunt surprised me by taking my arm. At supper Mrs Taylor asked her if she would like some whiskey. She said No, she would have it on going to bed. I said "I am shocked at you. You evidently don't expect to be able to walk upstairs after taking your dose." Again she looked hard at me, but when I said goodnight, (I was the first to go to bed) she got up out of her chair, put her arm round me and kissed me!
This morning there was a letter from Mrs Pratt to say Mrs Capel was sinking and asking for Mrs Taylor, and would she go down and stay with Mrs Pratt for the weekend. It was a very nice letter but I think Mrs Taylor felt a bit upset about Mrs Capel, though she had been expecting to hear the news for some time past. Mrs Day is still away, but had written asking if she should come back Thursday or Friday, so I dropped her a post card this morning, saying "Mrs Taylor heard from Watford this morning that Mrs Capel is sinking and asking for her. Can you come back to-morrow. I will stay with you." I added the last sentence as Mrs Taylor was wondering if she would be well enough to go backwards and forwards to the Webbers each day. Now she need not, as I shall be there to sleep. I think Mrs Christmas will go down to Watford with Mrs Taylor tomorrow. I hope so; it will be company for her.
In my imagination I shall be spending my holiday with you, and will stay all the time in the

garden most probably. It does want some trimming. Everything is so prolific, especially the snails, and overgrown.

Can't stop any longer, so Goodbye.

May

PS Over a week ago Maud wrote to me saying she was better, but her heart was queer, so the local doctor said, but nothing what would get well again. I did not reply. However, she has written to one of the temporary girls to find out if I have received that letter, and she must have said a lot more, all her private affairs. I told the girl I had had it but that it did not require a reply. However, I did write her yesterday, and told her she had better give her heart away, and that was all the sympathy she got, I am afraid.

David to May   Holzminden   Letter No 27   August 1st 1918

My Dearest,

I have just had four of your letters altogether and so took them outside to thoroughly enjoy myself. I am awfully glad you do manage to "find a few minutes for your darling" as life would be pretty empty without your letters. I have received a parcel of three books containing "Mr Issacs", "The Barrier" and "The Simpkins Plot" and since then Mitchell's Building Construction. Did you send them? If you did it is good of you, but you shouldn't do it. D'you hear? Thanks too for ordering those gardening books for me. The Allotment Book sounds as though it ought to be better than the one I asked for. Of course they haven't come yet, but should turn up soon. "The Twinkling of an Eye" hasn't arrived either. Please thank Muriel very much indeed for the books she sent and tell her that three or four of them were on subjects upon which I had already had other books, so that they are particularly useful as they give me different points of view. Please tell her that I am most anxious for her to take the three of us up the river again. Her threat to kill you might possibly relieve her feelings, but wouldn't be any sort of satisfaction to me. Its awfully sad that her several love affairs have all ended so suddenly and tragically. I would write to her if I could, but she knows I can't at present. I don't know if you have read "Mr Issacs". It is an Indian tale with a marvellous man in it, who, altho' he doesn't claim to be anything out of the ordinary, yet does miraculous things such as being in two different places at the same time etc etc. "The Barrier" is a tale of Klondyke with the usual hero, heroine, and a sprinkling of villains, but both books are not at all bad. I haven't read "The Simpkins Plot", but I am told by another fellow who borrowed it, that it is funny.

You don't tell me much about what you did when you took your girls out. I want to know all about it. How they behaved themselves and how you misbehaved yourself and where you went to tea and what it felt like to steer a family of 22 into a theatre and down the middle of a tea shop. Thanks very much for writing to Cox. I rather expected they would do nothing without actually having a note from me, but they should, by this time, have had my post card of June 1st, and paid the balance to Mum. Look here I shall not send you any more plans of bungalows or other things, if you are going to keep awake at nights over them. Thanks very much for my birthday letter. I did like it, but I expect I would have liked that train journey better. By the way I have had a letter from Maud. There was nothing in it – I believe she mentioned that she missed her mother or brother and one or two things like that. Please thank her for me. I also had a letter this week from an old school fellow of mine. Harold Gordon, I think I told you about him. You remember I received a letter from his girl while I was in France. He writes from Princetown where apparently he has been doing "time" and although he does not say so, I think he wrote with the idea that I might be able to find a job for him. Of course I haven't his address here, but I believe it is in a small address book in one of my drawers. I wish you would ask Mum to write to him and explain that I cannot.

I have finished the Quantities of the house and have made some attempt at getting at a price for it, but from the result I seem to be all at sea with the prices. It works out at about £800 at present, so that I shall have to go through it again. But of course this pricing is of very little use under the present conditions, except that it gives me some rough idea of what each item will be likely to come to. While writing this an idea struck me. I think we might perhaps lower the Kitchen and Hall half of the house by about a foot and so save the cost of a foot of everything over that portion. I must see how it works. You remark on the Kitchen being on the large size. I thought you would like this, especially as it is Kitchen and Scullery combined, as you probably have noticed. I also have another idea which is to put an attic floor in the roof. There is plenty of room for it without any alteration besides windows. It should give three or four more rooms up there and this of course would add considerable to the value of the house if ever we wanted to sell it, altho' of course we should not need them ourselves. I have not gone into it yet, but I think in any case we might make a provision for this addition, so that it can be done easily if we wanted, even if we don't do it to start with. Fifteen per cent for that bungalow with the use of it thrown in, sounds attractive enough and seems quite feasible provided the spot is well chosen. The ideal place I should think would be within $1^1/_2$ to 2 hours of London and within easy reach of a town. In fact another Shoreham, but transported elsewhere. No more building papers have turned up, but I expect some more will come along soon. There are numbers of books I want to read, in fact the more I read the more books I want, but it isn't worth while asking you to send them as I already seem to have more than enough work ahead of me now to keep me very well employed for some considerable time yet. I haven't touched any bookkeeping yet. My Dutch progresses. I was doing so well at one time with their G, that I thought that in the course of a year or so and the aid of a bad cold in my throat, I might be able to pronounce it sufficiently well for a Dutchman to have a dim idea of what I was driving at, and then suddenly it turned up twice in one word! That did it! I turned my face to the wall and wept. I think I shall now have to teach them all French in order to talk at all or carry on as a dentist and I did once. We used to converse in the most fluent sentences compounded of French, German, Latin and English carefully compounded into a rich and intricate mixture. Esperanto was a fool to it.

I have not yet had your letter about Malayalans, but this is what happened. On April 30th 1917, I bought 15 shares on June 6th – 10 more and on June 25th 10 more making 35 in total. Mum cancelled the last order so that I should have 25, but still I don't think it is worth while writing about it now, as it has gone so long, it may as well go on a bit longer. You seem to be awfully busy most of your time. I do wish it wasn't necessary to stay late though and you are continually doing it now. I know what effect this sort of thing has on you. Can't you stop it?

Goodbye.

David

May to David　　Balham　　2.8.18

My dear David,

What do you think? Your highly respectable and much esteemed Aunt Maria deliberately winked at me the other day – last Wednesday evening it was, about 7.30. Shall I ever recover from the shock, I wonder? No small wonder that, later on in the evening when I was helping to put the supper, and Mrs Taylor said "You have not put the whiskey on the table" I replied "I did not think there was any left". Your Aunt pretended to look horrified at me then. O, these pious Aunts!

Yesterday Mrs Taylor & Mrs Christmas left about 4.30 for Watford, and I found Mrs Day in charge. She did not look so well as usual, and when I asked her she said she had a wretched cough that kept her awake at night time, so I asked her to try some ovaltine. It acted like magic. She has scarcely coughed since, and consequently had a good night. She looks all the better this morning. She has promised to take some more during the day. It is very soothing. Can I send you any? Or haven't you got a cough?

A post card came from you, dated about 23rd June, yesterday, and we were so glad to have it. To-morrow afternoon I shall pop home to see if there is anything from you awaiting me. Hope so.

We are opening our West End Branch on 23rd August, and I shall have to supply two girls, one a senior and the other a junior. We have engaged two new ones to take their places. More training to do. A lot more work has come in, so that I shall have to put in a little overtime next week, but I don't expect to stay later than 7.0 any night.

The weather has turned awful again. Thank goodness, as then no one minds staying late. I must not stop any longer, so Goodbye once again.

May

David to Ginger   Holzminden   Post Card No 12   Aug 4th 1918

I have your letters of April 16th & May 24th & 26th and lastly one from Erl with a vastly amused gentleman on the heading & a page full of kisses. Please thank her very much indeed & tell her I will write to her when I get to Holland later on. Mum tells me she has received the belting. Please thank John very much for getting it for me. I have now got my marching boots, so that for the moment I am well off in this way, but I shall be glad to have the belting too. Very glad my fellows got your socks & that you have had letters from some of them. The boy seems to be in fine form physically, judging by the gymnasium examinations. I was amused by his anxiety as to how he would look in the girls eyes, but not at all surprised, seeing that he is the son of his mother &, well.... It looks as though it is in the blood. Doesn't it? Here's to him! Hope you are alright & quite recovered from measles.

David

Kriegsgefangenensendung.

Mrs Ethel Linn
246 Aycrigg Avenue
Passaic,
New Jersey,
U.S.A.

Offizier-
Gefangenen-Lager
Holzminden.

Post Card No 12.   Aug. 4th 1918.

I have your letters of Apr. 16th & May 24th & 25th & lastly one from Eol with a vastly amused gentleman on the heading of a page full of kisses. Please thank her very much indeed & tell her I will write to her when I get to Holland later on. Mum tells me she has received the belting. Please thank John very much for getting it for me. I have now got my marching boots, so that for the moment I am well off in this way but I shall be glad to have the belting too. Very glad my fellows got your socks & that you have had letters from some of them. The boy seems to be in fine form physically, judging by the gymnasium examination. I was amused at his anxiety as to how he would look in the girls eyes but not at all surprised, seeing that he is the son of his mother &, well ---- It looks as though it's in the blood. Doesn't it? Here's to him! Hope you are all alright & quite recovered from measles
David

May to David   Beckenham   6 August 1918

My dear David,

On Friday I went back to Balham reaching there at 8.0, and Mrs Day & I retired at 9.30, both feeling ready for bed.

On Saturday I went home, after working from 9.0 til 2.0. It thundered in the afternoon. Caught the 6.0 train back to Balham, and found Mrs Taylor sitting in the drawing room. Very glad to see her back. She said she could not do anything at Watford; that Mrs Capel was in bed, but might last weeks yet, so that she might just as well come home and enjoy herself.

On Sunday morning the weather was lovely, and Mrs Day, Peter & I went on Clapham Common. Walking up the hill puffed Mrs Day a bit and she was glad to sit down on the common. She looks heaps better. While in bed on Sunday morning we heard Mrs D give a slight cough. Coughing seems to worry your mother. She said to me "Hark at that. I took on some trouble when I took her. I think I must have been a fool." I said "I think the Almighty made you take her, thinking you would be the best one He could trust Mrs Day's declining years to." She was very thoughtful after that, and since then each time she has spoken to Mrs Day she has finished up with the word "Dear", or "Duckie". Now I am wondering if I am an extra special big humbug. While we were on the Common Ern brought over your letter of 15th June with the plan of the Hall. We had that for dinner – and ever since. It was a nice letter. How we discussed the house! I don't remember what ideas we finally came to, but Mrs Taylor wants to know where her garage and motor are to go, and Mrs Day wishes to know which rooms are to be allocated to her. I said she should have a boudoir providing she had a boudoir costume to match the room to which she agreed. In the afternoon we read and dozed. In the evening, chapel, and after that Mrs T & I went on to Tooting Common. Monday it rained on and off all day. In the afternoon Mrs T & I started for Wimbledon, taking with us the saxifrage, but when we reached Merton there was such a tremendous queue waiting for the Wimbledon tram that we came home instead, finding Mrs Webber comfortably installed in your large chair. My word, she just fills it! She asked Mrs D to go back with her and be nursed. You should have heard Mrs D say "Thank you, but I am looked after here very well indeed. No one could do more for me, and you will not see me at Glenroy for a long time to come". She did look severe. You see she is black out with the Webbers because although they knew she was away queer at her daughter's no one went to see if Mrs Taylor were alone. She will never forgive them for that. I think Mrs W went away feeling a little bit uncomfortable. Hope so. She turned to me once for sympathy because her poor dear Harry would not eat any meat, bacon or eggs. I suppose because he is daily expecting his papers and will be parted from Widow Madge. I said "Don't worry about him. I've met that behaviour before. You can safely rely on his having plenty to eat in the City. He looks fat enough." In the evening Mrs T & I walked to Wandsworth Common. To-night I go home to sleep. We shall be working till 7.0 most probably, so I had better not stop to write any more just now. Goodbye.

May

May to David   Beckenham   7.8.18

My dear David,

This morning we had a compartment to ourselves for half the journey, and we discussed lots of things. At any rate, we started to discuss lots of things, but interruptions prevented decisions. We wondered if, as the drawing room according to the plan was a large one, we could have a grand piano. Of course they are very expensive but then they take up a lot of room and we should not require so much other furniture. We decided to have as little furniture as we could do with, but of course the place must not look too bare. We did not decide whether the hall was to be parquet floored or tiled. We were to have plenty of rugs about and cushions, and that was about all as far as I can remember.

I am so glad that you have that spring bed. No wonder I sleep so well!

I have started Muriel's coat, and it is going to take a long time. I am shocked to say I have not done any studying, and you must be shocked too. Yesterday I only put in $1\frac{1}{2}$ hours overtime. It was awfully funny yesterday. The General Manager sent for me to talk about our Westend branch. They want me to supply two girls. Well, I am letting Miss Daffarn only go. She is the G.M.'s girl, and I don't think he is too pleased at letting her go, but I recommended her, and she wants to go, so she is going. I happened to mention to him that I did not want her to go for a couple of weeks as we had not yet quite got over our strenuous time, which was accelerated by several girls having influenza, and that some of us had been getting to the Office at 8.0, and some working on till 8.30 for several weeks. The poor man almost jumped out of his skin, rang for Lutt and bullyragged him awfully. Now, it was not Lutt's fault at all. The G.M. takes girls away from me and tells Lutt to supply their places which he has not been able to do as the Government Offices want all the shorthand typists they can get hold of, consequently we have had harder work than ever. Lutt evidently was thinking I was complaining to G.M. about him, so I said "It is alright; I am not complaining. Mr G carries on like this periodically", and then they both laughed. Lutt said to the G.M. "I can't make bricks without straw" to which the G.M. replied "No, but you can refuse to build. Remember this dept is under your immediate supervision and if you let it down again I will give you a warm 5 minutes." Of course he did not realize it was all his own doing. I had a new girl in yesterday. To-day she did not turn up. There are two more coming. In the meantime we have started holidays in earnest, and the work is slackening very much. O, I did enjoy yesterday.

Time is up again, and I must leave off, so Goodbye.

May

PS I saw in last night's paper that 120,000 prisoners are to be exchanged, but I don't know any particulars.

1918
Sept 14th

18 Manor Road,
Beckenham.
7. 8. 18.

My dear David,

This morning we had a compartment to ourselves for half the journey, and we discussed lots of things. At any rate, we started to discuss lots of things, but interruptions prevented decisions. We wondered if, as the drawingroom according to the plan was a large one, we could have a grand piano. Of course they are very expensive but then they take up a lot of room and we should not require so much other furniture. We decided to have as little furniture as we could do with, but of course the place must not look too bare. We did not decide whether the hall was to be parquet floored or tiled. We were to have plenty of rugs about and cushions, and that was about all as far as I can remember.

I am so glad you have that spring bed. No wonder I sleep so well!

I have started Muriel's coat, and it is going to take a long time. I am shocked to say I have not done any studying, and you must be shocked too. Yesterday I only put in 1½ hours overtime.

It was awfully funny yesterday. The General Manager sent for me to talk about our Westend branch. They want me to supply two girls. Well, I am letting Miss Daffarn only go. She is the G.M's girl, and I don't think he is too pleased at letting her go, but I recommended her, and she wants to go, so she is going. I happened to mention to him that I did not want her to go for a couple of weeks as we had not yet quite got over our strenuous time, which was accelerated by several girls having had influenza, and that some of us had been getting to the Office at 8.0., and some working on till 8.30. for several weeks. The poor man almost jumped out of his skin, rang for Lutt and bullyragged him awfully. Now, it was not Lutt's fault at all. The G.M. takes girls away from me and tells Lutt to supply their places which he has not been able to do as the Government Offices want all the shorthand typists they can get hold of, consequently we have had harder work than ever. Lutt evidently was thinking I was complaining to G.M. about him, so I said "It is alright; I am not complaining. Mr. G. carries on like this periodically", and then they both laughed. Lutt said to the G.M. "I can't make bricks without straw" to which the G.M. replied "No, but you can refuse to build. Remember this dept. is under your immediate supervision and if you let it down again I will give you a warm 5 minutes." Of course he did not realize it was all his own doing. I had a new girl in yesterday. To-day she has not turned up. There are two more coming. In the meantime we have started holidays in earnest, and the work is slackening very much. O, I did enjoy yesterday.

Time is up again, and I must leave off, so Goodbye.

May.

P.S. I saw in last night's paper that 120,000 prisoners are to be exchanged, but I don't know any particulars.

May to David   Beckenham   9.8.18

My dear David,

Thursday morning another letter came from you – two in under a week. Your letter was dated 1st July, and contained the news that you had not heard from me for about a fortnight, I think. On two occasions I have had to wait 5 weeks for new from you. It did seem an age, as the p.c.s were kept back also. No doubt you have had a bundle of letters since.

What a nuisance you have broken two teeth. Were you fighting, or how did you manage it? Fancy taking up more studies. And Dutch too. I had an uncle who was a sailor, and he said Dutch was the most useful language he thought for a traveller to know. He learnt it.

So your year's imprisonment has seemed an age. Poor fellow, I feel very sorry for you. It has not seemed an age to me. We have so much to do. Now look here, if you were not where you are you would be fighting, and that would worry me dreadfully. I don't want more worry. Even if you were considered too disabled for that, I should not be seeing much of you, and your own business is at a standstill, so personally I prefer to think you are resting. I cannot leave business now while the war is on, and that reminds me, it seems to me we have now reached the clearing-up stage of the war. As an ignorant civilian I was feeling anxious a few weeks back, but now apparently the worst is over. At any rate, everyone seems most cheerful and satisfied.

When we get together again it will seem as though we had not parted for long.

We are still very busy, but I am not staying late to-night, so will leave off this letter and get on with the work. Will reply to your letter next Monday.

Goodbye.

May

May to David   Beckenham   Letter No 153   12.8.18

My dear David,

Friday I left business at 5.30 and called at the butcher's to pay the bills on the way home. In the evening we worked hard at the garden. Next day I was consequently stiff. Saturday I worked till 3.0. Tonight I shall be working till 7.0. I don't feel any the worse for the longer hours, and certainly look alright.

On Sunday we walked up to the cemetery, and then I went round to Maud's grave. Ours looks very lovely; the stocks are a blaze of colour and 2 feet high. By the way, I have not heard from Maud yet. She was due back at the office last week, I thought, but she has not turned up yet. I suppose I have upset her. I think I told you she had written me saying that her heart was queer, but that it would get alright again; she was only run down and that had made her heart weak. I wrote back and said "Don't worry about your heart. Give it away," and now I've put my foot in it, I suppose.

Ah well!

Sunday afternoon Uncle and Auntie came to tea and supper. They returned from Leatherhead the previous day. Uncle hasn't made up his mind whether he will take up any hobby, or where he shall move to, or if he will stay on in Sydenham. Auntie was very funny and made us laugh a good deal. She evidently enjoyed herself, as when departing she said "I shall come again soon". She is a character.

This morning there was a letter from Mrs Taylor saying Mrs Capel was dead. Honestly I think it is a blessing for everyone. I have written to Mrs T telling her if she want to go to the funeral I will stay with Mrs Day, as she ought not want to try to get back the same night. Mrs Day is getting on well.

Everyone seems very jolly. The war is getting on nicely, or I should say the "Clearing up is progressing favourably".

Your money has been paid in to Mrs T's account alright, and you have nothing whatever to worry about as regards matters over here, and your letters sound as though you are being treated alright, and that makes me feel happy.

Four new girls turned up this morning. That makes 87 of us! Haven't I got a big family?

Muriel is at Torquay. I had a p.c. from her Saturday. She is enjoying herself immensely. It looks a nice place – quite good enough for a honeymoon.

I must tell you this. Last week Mrs Taylor & Mrs Day were teasing me very much about the future. Presently I said "It is all very well for you two to take everything for granted, but no promises are made yet." Whereupon Mrs T suddenly said "If you don't marry my boy after all he has gone through I'll kill you". I told her she would have to be quick about it as Muriel has threatened the same thing. See how other folks are looking after your interests – or at any rate, think they are. I read an article yesterday which said that realization was never so nice by a long way as anticipation. Now, shall I have to pity you, or you me?

I am sorry that saccharine, or rather saxin, was taken out of your parcel. I am afraid I cannot get any more, but will try.

Helen & her children, with Vi & her hubby, are away at Paignton for 3 weeks. Georgie lays down the law to other children about leaving his ponds alone, while Bills says to George, "Never mind, let do and look for little dirls". Last year Georgie used to look for little girls, and one he was found kissing. He has evidently grown out of that now.

I am looking for land ales, but there is nothing much being done in that line now. Everyone has at last woke up to the fact a war is on, and all are helping by either doing war work or else cultivating allotments.

We must certainly have a vacuum cleaner in our home.

That man's beard you write about amuses me mightily. You say it grows in wrong places. Does it come out of his forehead.

No more room, so Goodbye.

May

May to David   Beckenham   14.8.18

My dear David,

I have just had 10 minutes' hindrance, and I only get quarter-of an hour for writing to you. Isn't it too bad?

Heard from Mrs Taylor this morning. The funeral is to-day at 3.30. Mrs Taylor is going and will stay the night. Mrs Day is staying at Glenroy, though I did offer to go to No 56 for the night. However, I am going there for the weekend.

The weather is simply glorious, and it is time I started to think about my second fortnight. Now, where shall we go?

Ethel is in high glee. She has won two bets from Ern – a couple of large boxes of chocolates. I helped her eat them, as a sisterly duty.

Did you know that your father used to speak of me to Mrs Taylor as "Our little daughter"? Just fancy!

This week will finish the late work. I am only staying till 7.0. When I reached home I water the garden and do a little knitting, and then it is too dark to see. I have started on Muriel's coat.

I have already explained about the Board of Education sending you those books. Muriel had them sent free (she has a friend in that place) because I said how slow Batsfords were, and how I thought some books were going astray entirely. I must look through my correspondence with that firm, and see if they have despatched all I have ordered. I believe they take the orders and then forget, tho' they declare it is because the permits take such a time to reach them. I feel I have neglected you lately over books, but it is because we have had so much to do.

Next year we shall be spending our holidays together.

Goodbye for the present.

May

David to May   Holzminden   Letter No 28   August 15th 1918

My Dearest,

Two gardening books have arrived, and I have read them. Both are quite good. Thanks very much indeed for sending them. Thanks too for thinking of sending me those other novels. It is good of you. I shall feel like a miniature Mr Mudie soon. Now I am going to bother you again. Could you please send "The Timber Merchant and Builders's Vade Mecum" by G Bonsfield, published by W Rider & Son Ltd, 8 Paternoster Row, EC, at 4/- and also "Reinforced Concrete" by F Rings, published by Batesford at 7/6. This last I asked for in my letter of March 15th, but as you have never mentioned it, the letter has probably gone astray. If of course you have already ordered it to be sent, please cross it out. I am putting these on a form to the Board of Education, so will you please forward it to them, as I think this is the quickest means of getting them and will also be less trouble for you. I have been reading an American book on modern farming, dealing more particularly with soil research. It's awfully interesting. The scientists of the American Agricultural Department seem to have brought forward an absolutely new theory with regard to the working of soils and the feeding of plants in direct opposition to all existing theories and from their experiments there would seem to be something in it, although everybody else, including our own people, seem to be opposed to it. The curious part of it all is, that although the old theory and the new theory are entirely different, yet the ordinary system of cultivation is correct.

Just as I was starting this letter I had an accident to my fountain pen, the one you gave me, and dropped it on the point, which naturally hadn't improved it. I have not yet had your letter telling me about the Malayalam particulars, although I have had the others in which you mention the matter. Its awfully good of you to go to Putney with Mum to look after the grave. I guess it wants some lime or manure, or some fresh mould. You see it is about five years ago since it was planted. I am very glad you get a longer break in the middle of the day, though I don't like you staying late as much as you do. Can't you possibly stop it? I have had a letter from Mrs Munro of Moorlands, Inverness, asking for news of her husband. I wish you would write to her for me, something like the following:- Dear Mrs Munro, I am sorry I am unable to write to you direct, but I have already used my allowance of letters this month. I am afraid I can give you very little further information. As you probably know, Mr Munro was in charge of the company at the time. I left him in our dugout with another officer and on my return some hours later, I found the whole place completely blown up, and although I questioned those of the men that I came in touch with after being captured, I was unable to find anyone who could give me any information of him, or who had seen him away from the dugout, so that I could only conclude that he was in the dugout when the shell exploded. I am extremely sorry I am unable to give you anything more definite. Thanking you very much indeed for your kind wishes. Yours very truly, DHT. I should have written to before had I had her address. I have also had another letter from that old school friend of mine, Harold Gordon. He, apparently, is now to be allowed to return to ordinary private life, and also he has managed to get married just lately.

With regard to your question as to the size of the Kitchen in the bungalow – I have been looking at the plan again and it would be quite an easy matter to make the front living room larger by moving the partition, or if you like, another smaller room could be put between the Living Room and the Kitchen which could be used as a second Living Room or an extra bedroom. It seems to me that a second Living Room is hardly needed. Of course in either case the Kitchen would be considerably smaller. I haven't done anything further with the House but that idea of mine of lowering the Kitchen portion by a foot, would work quite well and would I think be a distinct improvement, as it would lower the roof over that portion too, which at present seems rather heavy. It would mean that the Kitchen and Hall would be 8'6" high, the two Living Rooms being 9'6". As a matter of fact the difference wouldn't be noticed in the ordinary way I think, as the difference in the levels wouldn't, or course, show anywhere. Don't you wish it were built and we were in it. I do.
Goodbye.

David

May to David   Beckenham   16.8.18

My dear David,
I have just spent all my spare lunch time looking through your letters, and yours of March 15th and Feb 1st are missing, but your of the 15th July came just two days ago. That makes three letters from you within the last three weeks! Record. If the censors are anything like our temporary workers they will be asking for a rise. If these clerks can't think of anything else to ask for that is what they fall back on. The cheek of some of them is something awful.
From your letter of 15th July it appears that several of mine to you have not reached their destination. Guess they have been blown up. It is too bad: the folks might have taken out my letters first, but I suppose they did not think.
When not at Watford I was working hard at home, but I have forgotten what at now, except one day I washed my white woolly coat.
As advised previously "In the twinkling of an eye" is or was out of print, but I will try again now, and also for two others I want you to read, "Scarlet & Purple" and "The Mark of the Beast", all the same type of book.
The description of your present time dress makes me blush for you. I hope you won't want to dress like that in England.
As regards that Building book, you will be shocked to hear I have not yet started studying it, but will before long. We really have had rather a strenuous time the last few weeks. However, this week finishes it.
The plans make me feel quite excited. I am referring to the plans of the house you enclose. There is a house like it, I believe, in the Kings Hall Road, backing on to the railway, and I always look at it when I pass. There is a brick, red, terrace outside the dining and drawing rooms, with three steps down to the garden, and the effect is alright. Sha'n't we have a lot to

talk about next year? I can't stop any longer now as time is up, and I am paying the temporary girls. By the bye, you remember at Gidea Park I said I wanted to save £1000 before I left business. Well, I counted up this morning how much I had, and roughly speaking it is £900! Haven't I been quick? But everybody seems to be more or less rolling in wealth. We never were so flourishing, and heaps of folks seem to think that next Spring will finish the clearing up of the war. Hope so.

Goodbye.

May

May to David   Beckenham   Letter No 156   19.8.18

My dear David,

On Saturday it turned wet again, although the glass was above 30, which was scandalous. However, I left the Office at 12.30 reaching Balham about 1.15 to find a lovely hot dinner ready, which was not scandalous. The marrow was Mrs Taylor's own growing, and it was a beauty. Mrs Day looks much better, but she has not recovered her strength entirely yet. I would like to take her and Mrs Taylor away in September, but could not get any promises out of your mother. I thought she would be dismal after losing Mrs Capel, but she wasn't in the least. I heard an account of the funeral, and it seems to me nobody was upset, but all felt it was a relief to think Mrs C was at rest. I fancy Mrs Brunning expected more money to be left to her – she evidently read the will before her mother died, but for my own part I think everything ought to have been left to the two single girls, and so does Mrs Taylor think it. I don't know what the two girls are going to do yet. Edith had left Mr Pratt's at Whitsun and tried to work in a hostel near Birmingham, but left it after a month as it was too hard for her. Now she is a lady at large.

In the afternoon we all three sat up in the drawing room with the windows wide open knitting. After tea it left off raining and your mother and I walked about Tooting Common. We went to bed early and woke late.

Sunday was a lovely seaside day. Mrs Day and Peter and I went to Clapham Common in the morning and examined the allotments. We all three approved of them. There is one man who is a discharged soldier with one arm who has a plot, and who is very fond of talking. He manages alone, and is doing excellently. He knew nothing of gardening before he had this ground.

After an early dinner Mrs Taylor & I went over to Streatham Common, and sat down on the top amongst the bracken and blackberries. I had a book which Mrs Taylor told me to read to her while she lay down. It was called "The White Dove". I had lent it to Mrs Day and she enjoyed it. I am afraid the people are not too moral in this book. I read for an hour and then came to the conclusion that Mrs T was asleep, so read to myself after that. Suddenly she woke up saying "I have not been asleep, but we will now eat oranges. I heard all you were reading, and you have got as far as so-and-so" by which I knew she had fallen asleep long before I thought, in fact after I had read about 5 minutes!

We got back at 5.20, had tea, and then went to chapel and listened to a new preacher, who gave a very good sermon, which could be summed up as follows – If you worry then you know you are not putting enough trust in the Almighty, and there is not enough Salvation in you. I am putting it clumsily. I told Mrs Taylor if she worried any more about the cotton-bull stories her tenants tell her I should have a very poor opinion of her christianity, and she at times is rather fond of preaching to me, and I encourage her as I think it is good for her. She is still calling Mrs Day "Dear" and "Duckie", and they are consequently on the best of terms, which I know you will be pleased to hear.

Lunch time is up, so I must cease. To-day it is lovely, and I reached the Office at 9.0. Two more new girls here this morning. That makes 89 of us.

Goodbye.

May

PS On Wednesday I am going to meet Mrs T at her bank, when we are going to make an investment for you.

May to David   Beckenham   21.8.18

My dear David,

I expect you will be delighted to hear we are now leaving at 5.30 and have been forbidden by Mr Lutt to stay longer. Well, the weather is glorious, and it is lovely to be out.

On the way home yesterday (Tuesday) I called at Miss Rudge's. She is selling up her home and will be going into apartments close by. Miss Willsher went away to the country yesterday morning.

This morning I met Mrs Taylor at her Bank, and she invested £100 of your money in your name through the Bankers. The dividends will be paid into your account. You will be back before many divs are paid in. Then we went to the Stores and she ordered some more parcels for you.

After writing your letter Monday one of my most hopefuls came to me to say she had just given in her resignation, and then promptly started to cry. Later on she explained herself thus. – She has a good post offered her, only a small firm, but £2.10/- a week, with a promise of more. She argued that although it was nearly breaking her heart to leave here she felt the war would be over in a few months, and seemed quite positive that I would be leaving then, (why, I don't know, as I have not hinted at it) and she could not bear the place without me, and other places would then be harder to get, so she was taking her opportunity then. She has just this minute brought me in her photo, and has asked me for one of mine. When I got home that night, Ethel said to me "Let's go into the conservatory and do the darning". We did. We had no sooner sat down than Ethel confided in me that she had had a brain wave. (She does have brain waves sometimes, so she says, but they are quite harmless.) And this is almost word for word what she said. "I've been thinking, and have come to the conclusion that I shouldn't be at all surprised if David wants to marry you when he comes back. And you can't say No after all he has gone through. And those plans of bungalows he sends, he means to build one but it is to be your home. Of course Mama will carry on and say how absurd it is for you to marry him, and all that, but I will take the bull by the horns and talk her down. I'll stand up for him. I can manage Mama alright. I did think we would all three retire soon to Falmouth, but unless David settles down there as well we won't do it, as I should not like to be too far away from you. I think if you two have to live in London then we will retire to a place like Bognor. In fact you can have your bungalow there and Mama & I will live in it. We will pay you rent, and you can come down very frequently; then it won't be dull for me." I did not tell her how matters stood between us, as she is much happier thinking it is all her idea. Most folks like to feel they are clever. This morning before breakfast she went on "I have been sketching a bungalow for us to retire to, and I think you have better start making things for your bottom drawer at once". I said "Aren't you taking things for granted too much?" She said "Yes, I guess I am. O well, I'll start doing crochet work for you. You can choose your own designs. Mama won't think anything of seeing me do crochet work, as I'm always at it." I told her she could, as at any rate the things would do for us to use when we retire. I think it is awfully good of her, but you can't send her any message.

While out with Mrs Taylor this morning I tried to persuade her to come with me to Bognor for a fortnight and I think I shall succeed. At any rate I said I would spend this coming weekend with her, and will try again.

Cannot stop any longer, so Goodbye.

May

Picture post card to May   Bognor   23 Au 18

We're both having a lovely time & have forgotten about pols and premiums.
We're having a lazy time, doing nothing but reading. Hoping you're not too busy.
Yours [two initials: May's work 'girls']

Esplanade. West of Pier, Bognor.

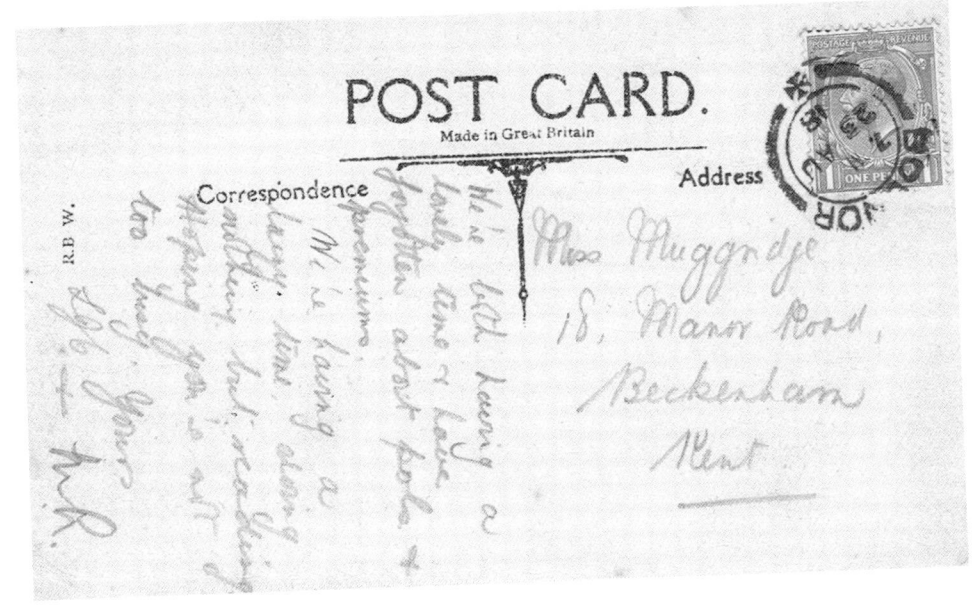

my dearest

May to David   Beckenham   23.8.18

My dear David,

I have not much to write about to-day.

The heat was terrific yesterday & the previous day, but it is cooler to-day. On the way home yesterday I called at the cemetery and watered our grave and Maud's. They were parched. The best of our blooms are now over.

Maud has written to the Office to say she will return on Monday. She has been away since 6th July. She has never written me since I told her to give her heart away. I think I have at last stopped her gushing "friendship" for me. I hope so.

Mrs Taylor called in this morning. She was on her way to the dentist and brought a couple of your post cards for me to see, dated 20th and 27th July.

Yesterday I wrote to two addresses in Bognor in the hope of going away with her there.

Ethel has started some crochet work lace to go on our sheets already. I said to her "I must really tell David you are commencing to make things for the bungalow", at which she smiled very much, so you may know that much officially. She said "I wish he would draw me a plan of a house to live in if I let him know some idea of what I want". So I will ask you later on. Look here, could you sketch me a beach hut that would sleep 6 people?

This is letter No 158.

I am going to Balham to-morrow for the weekend.

Cannot stop any longer, so Goodbye.

May

May to David   Beckenham   Letter No 159   26.8.18

My dear David,

On Friday it turned wet, and when I went to put my umbrella up I found I had broken it. I didn't get very wet though.

On Saturday morning there was a reply from Bognor. The earliest date I could go there would be 28th Sept. Mrs Taylor thinks that is too late. There ought to be another reply for me when I get home. I have also written to a boarding house this morning where Miss Carter is now staying.

Saturday afternoon we went to Putney and worked at the grave. There were some bonny dandelions to get up. We left the place looking very nice, but it took us 2 hours. Then we had tea at the Windmill to the strains of "The Maiden's Prayer" while we talked holidays. It was about 8.40 when we arrived home. It had been a lovely day. We went to bed at 10.0, and I for one slept tremendously, and so I did Sunday night.

Sunday was not nearly so nice. We all three went to chapel in the morning, thinking it might turn out better in the afternoon and evening, instead of which it turned out worse and poured with rain. To-day it is showery. In the afternoon I finished reading "The Whip Hand", a short book, well written, by Keble Howard. The one who has the whip hand is the one who has no fine feelings, and in this case it was the mother-in-law, but of course it turned out alright in the end. In the evening I practiced.

To-day Maud turned up. She looks awfully well and fat. It was rather funny. She came across to my desk and put a letter on it for me from herself. I went to speak to her, but she gave me such a shame-faced look and walked out. Later on I read the letter which was thus – "Just a line to thank you for giving me such a welcome surprise when I went up to Honor Oak yesterday to mother's grave. The flowers looked lovely and there was not a single weed. I appreciate your kindness and thoughtfulness so much." Poor Maud, I do feel sorry for her. She had evidently been nursing a grievance against me, and it has ended like this. Later on she came into the dressing room, and as no one was about she put her arms around my neck, nearly having my head off, and gave me several good smacking kisses, but she seems as though she can scarcely speak. Her Aunt, the one who is not a Christian, as the clergyman does not call on her, has given her another £100.

This morning I came across two "Christian" names – "Favoretta Walterina". The lady was married, so the names evidently didn't choke her sweetheart off. Thinking you might like a daughter with that name I let you know about this grand sounding combination.

Nothing more to say just now, so Goodbye once again.

May

May to David   Beckenham   28.8.18

My dear David,

I have not much to write about to-day. The weather has turned pretty awful, but as the newspapers continue to contain excellent news no one minds. Fancy no one grumbling at the weather!

Yesterday Mrs Day went to the East End and stayed the night, so I went home to Balham, just for the night. Mrs T was so pleased to see me, and was quite jolly. We talked about our proposed holiday, and this morning a letter came for me from a boarding house at Bognor, where two of my girls are staying. This boarding house can take us on 16th Sept for a fortnight. I have written accepting, at the same time asking if they cannot take us a week earlier, and sent the letter on for Mrs Taylor's approval. She would like the week earlier, but for my own part I don't mind which. I am going with the idea of seeing if the place is suitable for a bungalow.

Your friend Campbell is wounded. He is a major. I saw the news in the newspaper.

I have a picture postcard from Miss Willsher who is staying near Tunbridge Wells. She is going about each day to different parts, mostly walking. She is a wonder.

We have five cucumbers coming, and heaps of tomatoes. We have dug up several pounds of potatoes already.

I forget whether I told you Mrs Taylor only got about $2^{1}/_{4}$ lbs off her gooseberry bushes. She has had several marrows.

We are still behind with the work, so I will now stop and get on with it. There are several girls away on holidays, and they are all enjoying themselves immensely.

Goodbye,

May

W Rushbrooke to David   St Olave's Grammar School   Aug 28 1918

Just a line, my dear David, not so much because I have anything to tell you and because your mother has just sent me your address and this is the best acknowledgment I can give. I have just come from Victoria where I went to see one of my old boys 2/Lt like yourself off for France at 7.35 and stayed on to see two more trains steam off, full of officers and men for the front, all of them, I think, returning after leave. It was a moving sight, & one's head was full of pride & gratitude and hope - & confidence in the nearing issue which will convince our mighty for that there is something bigger than any mere nationalism & that the world is going to be safe for all countries little as well as big. (You heard that Gen Sir Wm Robertson came for our Prize Day) It is 3 years since you called last, I believe: at least 1915 Nov 18 is the date I have entered for your last visit. I hope it will not be nearly so long before .. you again safe back to help build up the new England, & the brighter world when Peace returns

I am ever most truly

WG Rushbrooke

May to David   Beckenham   30.08.18

My dear David,

Last night and the night before I worked till 8.30, then in my dreams you tried to be cross with me, so I promptly turned my back on you, only to be as promptly turned round again by you. And then we spent a lovely time making it up. You see I am starting my holidays in a fortnight's time. As I told you before, Mrs Taylor & I are going to a boarding house at Bognor. We go on Monday, 16th Sept for a fortnight, and I would like to leave the work up to date. We are getting on alright now. I made up the overtime list this morning, and during August I earned £2.19.-. So you see I have not done so much this month. Next month we shall not do any overtime. It is payday to-day, too, so we are all feeling very pleased with ourselves.

Ethel is going to stay with some friends of hers in north London this weekend, so I shall be at home – for a change. Guess I shall find plenty of odds and ends to do.

Nothing more to say, so Goodbye once again.

May

In this short letter the word "so" occurs five times! I must turn over a new leaf, and think what I am writing about. By the bye, I am using your attaché case. Yes, it is a cheek; but mine is a little too small for the knitting I am doing. You remember I am making a coat for Muriel. She is back from Devonshire, and doesn't like being back, so her father says. Another "so". O, my new leaf. I must tell you this. I have told you about our patriarch, Watkins. Well, he is going away on his holidays this afternoon, and he is wandering in and out of our room in a light knickerbocker suit! It is a good thing for him I am here.

David to Ginger   Holzminden   Post Card No.13   Sept 1st 1918

I haven't heard from you for well over a month. Mum tells me that you still have a particular longing to stop people bleeding by tying knots in them, as in the old days of the first aid classes. I shouldn't if I were you, as I guess the kiddies need you far more than the people in France. I wonder if you could get me the "Engineering News Record" for the weeks Mar 14th & 21st 1918. They have articles which I want to read. Please don't send them here, but keep them for me. I have been practicing war economy. Having worn out a couple of shirts & being in need of a sheet, I turned the one into the other. As you may guess, a shirt does not altogether lend itself to sheet making without a little cutting here & a little patching there. However, the completed design is certainly striking & out of the ordinary, the whole effect being greatly enhanced by the fact that one of the shirts was originally a khaki cotton one & the other, (which I bought from a Frenchman) in grey flanelette & that the sewing is elegantly done with brown wool which I unravelled from a worn out sock. I think the pattern might be nouveau art perhaps.

David.

David to May   Holzminden   Letter No 29   Sept 1st 1918

My Dearest,

It was good of you to go and stay with Mum while Polly was away, and please thank Mrs Muggridge very much indeed for packing you off as you call it. From certain of your letters I imagine everybody at home, as well as here, has been indulging in the so called Spanish plague. About eighty per cent of the camp got it I should think, in fact most people except me. (I certainly flopped about on my bed the greater part of one day, but that was not the plague I think.) All the others in my room had it except two of we old cronies, (the other fellow is a year older than me, but we are both several years older than the rest). However its quite gone now and everything is as usual again. I have been practicing war economy. Having worn out a couple of shirts and being in need of a sheet, I have turned the one into the other. As you may guess, a shirt does not altogether lend itself to sheet making without a little cutting here and a little patching there. However the completed design is certainly striking and distinctly out of the ordinary, the whole effect being greatly enhanced by the fact that one of the shirts was originally a khaki cotton one, and the other a grey flannelette, (one which I bought from a Frenchman when I was first captured) and that the sewing is elegantly done with brown wool, which I unravelled from a worn out sock. I think the pattern might possibly be considered to be after the nouveau art style, or futurist perhaps, I haven't quite settled which. Its almost like one of those special treasures that isn't made for use, but which is wrapped up in tissue paper and locked away in a drawer, only to be brought out at Christmas and on Saints Days.

Thanks ever so much for taking all the trouble you have over that Malaylam business. Of course I thought everything would be alright, but still it is satisfactory to know that you have all the papers now. In my last letter I asked if you would send "The Timber Merchant and Builders's Vade Mecum", by G Bonsfield, published by W Rider & Son Ltd, 8 Paternoster Row, and also "Reinforced Concrete" by F Rings, published by Batsford, and enclosed a form with them on to the Board of Education, as I think they come quicker that way. As regards your sending me news of people and things, you can send any general news you like and certainly would be glad to hear a little about things. I have had another letter from Uncle Charlie Webber telling me all about a house of his, or rather a quarrel with the man who owns the adjoining house to his, over a fence. His letters are awfully amusing, although perhaps he doesn't quite see the things he describes in that way. This is the second affair he has had with the same man, over the same fence, and each time it has nearly ended in a law suit.

I have been reading an account by a Swiss doctor of Barbed Wireitis, which is a particular form of madness said to inflict prisoners of war, and as usual with most people who have just read up a pet ailment, I find that I have all the symptoms, to say nothing of a few added ones, which the learned doctor doesn't even mention (strangely enough, he doesn't say anything about the longing to be back with you). I am afraid the rigmarole is a bit too long to describe, but anyhow, after reading his account, (and being a learned doctor, of course he must be correct) I am sure I am going very quickly on the down grade am already "pale and interesting" and in time shall be a "puffick shadder" of my former self.

With regard to the beach hut. The bedrooms could of course be easily made 6'6" one way as you suggest. It would only mean adding that much to the length of the hut. I should think it would be a job for Esther to follow David around, as of course he is liable to be sent about anywhere at a moment's notice. I rather wonder at him expecting her to do it. That letter of Ethel's to which you refer never reached me so obviously it must have been addressed to Mum herself and not to me. I wish to goodness Ethel would keep this sort of letter to herself, as it upsets Mum considerably and hasn't the least desired effect on me. Look here, I can't have Mrs Muggridge looking upon my photo of you as hers. It won't do at all. I am perfectly certain it belongs to me, so that unless you are wishful to be the direct cause of a riot when I get back you had better get another done "himmedgit", if not sooner. I don't remember feeling particularly thin when I had that platoon photo taken. Certainly I had been getting a large amount of exercise at that time, but still that was not unusual. About your question as to how we cook etc. We split up into small parties of two, three, or five, etc each one of course taking his turn at cooking. Personally being particularly hedgehoggy and unsociable, as you know, I cater for myself and in consequence have reduced my cooking to a fine art, or perhaps some people would suggest that it is laziness par excellence, in as far as I make one lot of cooking carry me over two, or perhaps even three days. For instance, I make enough porridge at once for four breakfasts, so that I only have to warm it up each morning instead of cooking it, and the other things in the same way. I find catering for myself suits me in many ways as I can just feed when and as I choose, which of course would not be so if some of the other fellows had a hand in it, although perhaps I might get a greater variety of dishes than I take the trouble with now. But still, when I get back you shall feed me just as you like.

Goodbye.

David

May to David   Beckenham   2.9.18 Monday

My dear David,

Last weekend I spent at home. In the afternoon, Saturday, I cut the front grass and trimmed the ferns. The front garden did want doing up and it now looks all the better for it.

Sunday was very windy and rather cold. I pottered about in the house during the morning, looking out the clothes I shall be taking away with me, etc, and in the afternoon and evening I finished reading the book "Blinds Down". Not a bad tale. It is about a couple of maiden ladies, very grand, and just like Mrs Anstey. They shut their eyes and ears to everything that is horrid. Strictly proper themselves and what people would call very harmless; but alas, those "harmless" folks are not so harmless, or so the Author points out. The tale is worth reading. Ethel came home about 10.0. Sunday morning I slept on till 9.0 much to my horror, and this morning it was 7.25 when I woke up. Don't know what has got me to sleep like that. Perhaps it is the cooler weather.

I told you last week that Mrs Taylor & I are going to Bognor in a fortnight's time for a fortnight. We are going to the same boarding house that 2 of the girls have been staying at. They returned to business this morning and look very fit and fatter.

This year I have earned £9.16.- in overtime, so I can afford a holiday, can't I? I am going down with the idea of seeing about a suitable place for a bungalow.

I do want another letter from you badly, and I missed my hour's dream of you yesterday morning.

Can't stop any longer, so Goodbye for a short time.

May

PS Yesterday I also read the newspapers to see if the war were over. It isn't, but at the present rate it cannot last much longer. How I do wish I could send you the papers!

18 Manor Road,
Beckenham.
4. 9. 18.
(Wednesday)

My dear David,

I have one small item of news for you this time. Yesterday the General Manager sent for me and spoke about the new girl he was to have, as his girl is off to our West End Branch, as I told you. Then he asked after my health! I never remember his doing such a thing before. I wondered why. Then it came out. He said "You have not finished your holidays yet?" "No". "When do you go?" "In a fortnight's time". (Less now). "Where?" "Bognor". He fairly jumped. "That is where Mrs. Gayford would like to take John. What address are you going to, as she can't get in anywhere?" I gave it, and he said "I'll write there at once". I said "It is only a small boarding house." "That'll do". "And it is the extreme end of the place". "That's alright". Now I wondering if they take her in what Mrs. Taylor will think of it. She is a very nice lady, far better than her hubby, I think.

In case my previous letters have been blown to atoms or anything else has happened to them I repeat the main points of my last few:-
Your mother has invested £100 through her bankers, the dividends from which will be paid into your account.
I have not had your letters of March 15th, or Feb. 1. and want them awfu' bad.
We go to Bognor on Sept. 16th for a fortnight.
Can you design a beach hut to accommodate 6 people?

My next holiday after going to Bognor will be next May when you are going to take me to Cornwall & south Devon.
Sometimes it looks as though you might be home for Christmas, but I am not building on that.
Yesterday was a lovely day, but this morning it has rained a bit, and it is much warmer again.
In the evenings I am getting on with Muriel's coat, but O, it is a slow job, or else I am getting slow.
We are not working late now. In fact, the work has not been so slack the whole of this year as it has been this week.
In the plan of the house you have sent me I would like the lower part of the kitchen windows to be coloured glass. I forget whether I told you. I like Mrs. Pratt's bead curtains very much, and also her stainless cutlery.
Goodbye.
May.

May to David   Beckenham   6.9.18

My dear David,

Yesterday morning, just as I was mentally giving away worlds to get a letter from you, one came – for nothing. It was dated 1st August. Those missing two I am afraid have gone for ever.

Now for answering the main points, though I have not much time.

I don't know who sent those books – "Mr Isaacs", "The Barrier" and "The Simpkins Plot", so have written to Muriel first. If she denies it I will write to Ethel Barnett. Failing her it must be Mrs Archie Webber. She has written several nice letters to Mrs Taylor, and seems to be the best of your relatives on that side. I read "Mr Isaacs" years ago, but will read it again with the other two which I have not heard of.

I expect you know the gardening books by heart now. I am trying to grow winter spinach, as I hear that it is prolific and hardy. Watkins has a border of it all round his garden.

You ask how the girls behaved themselves and I misbehaved myself on the day I took them out. I don't know what you mean, but I shall want an apology. I felt quite at home looking after a family of 22. My present family numbers 90, and another is expected Monday.

Since Maud has come back she has changed, and for the better. She won't talk about her health now, or moan over anything, and quite surprised me by saying she was not going to Watchet any more. I don't know why. I think her previous babyish behaviour was the outcome of having been kept under too much, and suddenly getting her freedom. Well, she is toning down now, and it is a great improvement. May it last.

I have written to Harold Gordon; quite civilly. I did not tell him what I thought of him.

Yesterday one of the girls showed me some post cards of Bognor, one being of the house we are going to stay at. I took them home, and Mama who always spoke against the place, tho' she has never been there, fell in love with it, and told Ethel she might like to live there when we retired, that is, if the place is really like the pictures of it!

About the plan of the house. – I don't mind if the kitchen & scullery is small really, as it won't be used much; practically only for cooking and keeping clean. It certainly would be a good idea to put an attic floor. You might like a billiard room at the top of the house; or someone else might if we sold the place.

I read out that piece about your Dutch, much to everyone's amusement. It sounds a sportive kind of language to speak. I suppose Dutchmen's throats are pretty tough.

I repeat that I have taken up with Read & Brigstock about your Malayalam Shares, and they have handed over the first certificate.

I guess the Censor thinks this letter is long enough, so I will close.

Goodbye.

May

PS I expect to go to Balham on Sunday and stay the night. Ethel will be out on Saturday till late.

May to David   Beckenham   Letter No 165   10.9.18 Tuesday

My dear David,

Last Friday on the way home I called at the butcher's and paid the bills, then I called for two pairs of shoes I had left the previous week to be mended, and found the blighters have put on rubber heels, instead of my favourite iron tips. Mama is delighted as she objects to the important noise I make when I walk. That noise is the only important thing about me.

Saturday morning I had off. I helped Mama get up the potatoes. It was a very nice day but the glass had gone back a good deal, so we thought we had better dig while we had the chance. As Sunday was a drencher we were glad. I weighed the potatoes, and they came to 61 lb 15 oz, the largest being $10^1/_2$ oz. We are feeling very pleased with ourselves, as we have only one bed to grow them on, and that is not very big.

Sunday I felt tired, and as though a cold were coming on, so did not go to Balham. I pottered about in the morning and read all the afternoon, and practiced in the evening.

Monday morning I woke up with the cold decidedly there. Thinks I "This is a nuisance as my colds usually last a fortnight, and to-day week I mean to go to Bognor; therefore I will be wise and stay in bed". Imagine me fancying myself a grand lady all day. I had a grand appetite which Mama appeased very well. When I was not eating or dozing I was thinking of my future home. O, I did enjoy myself. Strange to say I slept like a top when it came to bedtime, and did not wake up till 7.0 when I jumped out of bed and went for the dumbbells. I have almost worked, or slept, my cold away.

A letter came from Mrs Taylor this morning enclosing your post card of Aug 8th.

Yesterday Mrs Gayford telephoned through for me. She is going to our boarding house on next Saturday and will be having the bedroom next to ours. I have just written to Mrs Taylor and told her. Dear me, I am afraid I shall have to put on my very best behaviour. As you will not be there I might succeed. You cannot punish me for that cheek as you are too far away. Now I stand a chance of getting some of my own back.

This morning I had a nice letter from Muriel. I will give you the contents in my next letter. Goodbye.

May

May to David   Beckenham   11.9.18 Wednesday

My dear David,

This morning I called at London Bridge and inquired about trains to Bognor, and find there is one at 1.50 change at Barnham, the station before Bognor. I guess we will go by that. It gets down at 4.0. In my last letter I referred to one I had had from Muriel. I will now quote parts of it. I had sent her a copy – more or less – of your last letter to me as you referred to her.

"I was so pleased to have your letter and to hear the latest news of Mr Taylor. It is very good of you to let me see his letters, and needless to say we are all always most interested to have them. He seems wonderfully cheerful, doesn't he? I am so glad the books get to him safely. It must be a help in passing the long hours. He evidently means business about the bungalow, so it won't be any good your camouflaging any more when he comes back!!! It reminds me of a sort of siege – you have held our very gallantly, but I'm afraid the fall of the heart of the city cannot be prevented now. (I hope you like my little simile – please tell Mr T about it next time you write).

I am very glad to hear you are going for your holiday on Monday. I do hope you may be very lucky with the weather, and have a thoroughly nice rest. I know several friends who have stayed at Bognor and they are all very pleased with it, so I hope you and Mrs Taylor will be too.

In your letter while I was away you asked me about Babbacombe and whether I considered it a suitable place for a honeymoon. (Of course I have no doubt you are making the inquiry on behalf of some friend who is meditating marriage, not at all from a personal point of view, which I quite understand.) Well, my answer is a very emphatic Yes. I think it would be ideal, and I am bearing it in mind myself, if ever occasion offers! It is most charming. By staying there one can get delightful scenery, perfect solitude right away in the heart of the country, lovely bathing, picnics, walks, etc or by way of a change Torquay is within walking distance, and it is quite a nice town with concerts, theatres etc and is a charming place at the same time. Babbacombe abounds in quiet little nooks and delightful little glades and places. Now what more could be desired (except the right man, of course)? I feel ever so much better for my holiday. It was perfect in every way. The old farm where we stayed was charming, and the catering excellent, and all very clean and good cooking and attention. All for the modest sum of £2.2/- a week inclusive! I am ever so keen on bathing. I have never been allowed to bathe before so I made the most of it, you can imagine. Isn't the war news splendid just now. One can only hope it will last.

Mother asked me to send you her kind remembrances when I wrote. Hoping you will spend a very nice holiday, and with much love

Yours affectionately

Muriel

PS The dress I made has turned out quite well, and I'm quite pleased with it for a first attempt."
I have no news for you to-day, so Goodbye.

May

May to David   Beckenham   13.9.18

My dear David,

I have not much to say to-day, but expect my next letter will be more interesting as it will be written from Bognor.

This afternoon I want to leave a little early and do some shopping on the way home.

Also I want to leave early to-morrow as I am going to Balham for dinner.

This morning I had a letter from Mrs Taylor saying Mrs Day has a grandson.

Last night Mama sneezed, so Ern said "I have a bottle of Fine Old Jamaica Rum by me. I will open it and you must have some on going to bed." She did. He said I had better have some too in case my cold had not entirely gone. I said I would have it in milk in place of my ovaltine. I heated three quarters, or very nearly, of a breakfast cup of milk and then asked Ern to put the rum in, as I did not know the right quantity. He said he did not either, so I filled the cup up. It tasted awfully hot, so Ern had a taste of it and said "You had better drink it up quickly." I tried but could not as it took my breath away each time. When I had finished he said "Now get into bed as quickly as you can" which I did, and only just in time. I don't know now whether it was the bed that rocked or me. However, I seem to sleep heavily, and woke up this morning dreaming a huge bull was sitting on me. I felt better after a cup of tea, and have had a busy morning. I think if he wants me to have any to-night I shall say my cold has entirely disappeared. As a matter of fact I still have the sniffles, but I think Mama has a cold coming on.

Nothing more to relate.

Goodbye.

May

David to May   Holzminden   Letter No 30   September 15th 1918

My Dearest,

Yesterday was a great day with me, in as far as I received four letters from you all together. Of course at the time I like receiving them in batches but afterwards I would much rather they came singley, as I know there must be a blank when I shall get nothing. It was good of you to stay with Mum and to do all that you did while Polly was away. Mum mentions you in nearly all her letters, saying how much she likes having you with her. In one she says "Dear May came for the weekend and we had a nice time together (we always do), she is a great comfort to me and helps me in many ways." Thanks too for not encouraging her in the idea of not going to Watford to nurse Aunt Annie. So you have been introduced to another of the family curios. I mean Aunt Maria. I had almost forgotten her existence, as she only turns up at rare intervals. Please thank Muriel for making the chocolate. My mouth waters already and will continue to do so and it arrives and has been eaten and then of course will follow the regret for a good thing gone for ever. Thanks for sending on that letter of February 6th "Not in Holland". Just as though anybody ever accused me of being there. And that reminds me – your news of the exchange going forward sounds too good to be true. Let me know any further news you see or hear.

A letter to one of the fellows said that we are to have stripes for every year that we remain prisoners. With service stripes, wound stripes, prisoner stripes and a few more they will doubtless invent our arms will look like zebras legs. In my letter of August 15th I asked you to send me two books through the Board of Education, and later I sent a post card on which I asked you to add Mitchells Advanced Building Construction, the latest edition, published by Batsford. I wonder if you got that card in time.

I quite agree with the GM that you should not be allowed to work until seven or eight in the evening. There's no reason at all why your department should be understaffed in order to make up deficiencies elsewhere, and I am very glad that Lutt was bullyragged. If I were at home I would bullyrag you as well but as it is, I can't, but I think you are doing far too much. So there's for you.

It may possibly be somewhat of a surprise to you, but I have become a Sunday school teacher, thereby at least attaining the height of my ambition. Please tell Maud. This came about in this way. The other day I was buttonholed by two of the tame Architects in the camp (one of whom is taking a class in Building Construction) who said, "We wish you would take a class in Quantities, we should like to come to it and the men in the Building Construction class are anxious as well." So having put it that way, what could I do. The only times that a class could be arranged for was on Sunday afternoons and Wednesdays. So now behold me on my hind legs, holding forth on "How it should be done" to men (some of them) much older than myself and with about three times my experience, (though I says it as didn't oughter) and without having made a very big fool of myself so far. In giving these lessons I realize that this sort of thing requires some practice, as one is very apt to get off the point that one is talking about. You start explaining a thing and someone asks a question and in answering it you get right away from what you were talking about first. Then again you get so many degrees of knowledge with the different men. Some know absolutely nothing about things while others do, so that at times you have to go very minutely into very elementary things or otherwise you would be talking over the heads of some of them. And I have also found that these same Architects, like many others, are very well up from the artistic point of view of building, but from the practical constructive portion, there are many things which they don't know. Still it is most excellent experience for when I come to teach you, as difficulties crop up which I probably shouldn't notice in the ordinary way and which I shall be able to explain to you. That reminds me, I have just learnt, or rather am learning, (one of these same Architects is teaching me) perspective drawing, which I have never done before, so now, if you suddenly get a gorgeous art study of the house you'll know what's happened.

With regard to your suggestion as to parquet flooring in the Hall, - I don't think we can have it, as it is much too expensive and tiles always seem so cold. I think however I can get quite a good effect with an ordinary wood floor. We'll have the grand piano if, (I say if), we can afford it and the rugs and cushions by all means – lots of them. Can't you send some more snapshots of yourself. I was looking at some another man had today, and it set me longing. Goodbye.

David

May to David   'Sealands' Aldwick Rd Bognor   18.9.18 Wednesday

My dear David,
Here we are sitting on the shore, with the tide up & all!
I missed writing you Monday. I really had not the time. On Saty I went to Balham as arranged & decided where to meet Mrs Taylor on the Monday. Well, when I got home Saty night I found Mama wrapped up in 2 shawls looking bad. A few minutes later she went to bed – a feverish cold. She was light headed that night. Sunday she could scarcely get her head off the pillow, so I wrote & told Mrs Taylor, saying if she did not see me at London Bridge next day to go on without me. About tea time on Monday Mama suddenly got better, & at 10.0 on Tuesday she got up, so I did the shopping, packed up & caught the 12.4 from Beckenham, & the 1.36 from Victoria. The train filled up on the way down. Had to change at Barnham & take a short train to Bognor, arriving here to the minute – 4.7. Mrs Taylor was waiting for me at the station. The weather seems to have turned fine now I have come. We had tea immediately we got in. Mrs Gayford had introduced herself to Mrs T the same evening your mother arrived. After tea we all walked along the beach as far as the pier & back & John aged nearly 7 have me lessons in how to kick a football. The knowledge might come in useful later on. One never knows. After dinner Mrs G had to stay in, so I got Mrs T to myself & she took me out & lost me. My bump of locality & the moon saved the situation, & we arrived back by 8.30 after all. We were in bed at 9.0.
It is a nice boarding house, & so far I think Bognor would be better than Bexhill for the bungalow, but I have not seen much of the place yet. We are the extreme west end of the town.
Mrs Taylor says "Tell him the holiday is not complete without him." Guess you know this.
We have had breakfast & have succeeded in escaping to the beach without Mrs Gayford & John, but most probably not for long. We both slept well last night. With love from us both

May

May to David   Bognor   20.9.18 Friday

My dear David,

We are having April weather with March winds thrown in & these are blowing all the cobwebs off my brain. Yesterday morning we walked to Nyetimber & Pagham, two nice little villages – very small. Pagham boasts of a church & that is the biggest thing about the place. Nyetimber has a very small sort of barn containing a few forms, 2 small oil lamps & some texts, & is called the Wesleyan Chapel. One service each Sunday. Holds about 30 people providing they are not too fat. Pagham, the further place, is 3 miles away. We should never have walked so far had you been with us. At the back of our road is a bungalow colony. You must come & see it. It is a picture. I have been twice – the second time $\frac{1}{2}$ hour ago with Mrs Gayford, while her small son John hugged the hedges etc & made himself look generally awful. Yesterday afternoon a letter came from Mama saying she was alright. Her writing was not a bit shaky so she evidently is much better, & that in spite of the fact she had been drinking champagne. Excuse this dreadful writing, but the pen is a boarding house pen (& they as you know resemble post office pens), John having sharpened my pencil with his new knife & thereby rendering it past hope. The same post brought a letter for Mrs Taylor saying your Uncle Alfred Christmas had pneumonia. As he has diabetes it sounds bad, so this morning Mrs Taylor went off to Watford for the weekend. She will be back on Monday. In the meantime I am having lovely imaginations & quite enjoying them. Of course you don't figure in them! Eh? You cheeky beggar. Mr Gayford comes down tonight for the weekend. Guess I will make myself scarce. One of the kids in this house has just said "I am baby falling off Mummie's lap." The thumps are awful. The place will crack if she is not stopped.

Goodbye. Hope you are not being hard worked. Love

May

Oct 25th/1928

"Sealands"
Aldwick Rd. Bognor.
Monday. 23.9.18.

My dear David

In my last letter I told you Mrs. Taylor has just gone off to Watford because her brother Alfred was ill. I have had a letter from her to say the funeral takes place today & that she will return tomorrow. Her train gets in at 4.7. so of course I will be meeting her. I have missed her the last few days, & then, of course, I miss you too. I see Mrs. Gayford & her little boy each day & they are both very nice. The General Manager came down for the week end & they all 3 went to Worthing on Saty. to see the ex General Manager. Feeling a bit lonesome Saty. aft. I went to the theatre & saw 'Billeted'. The play was rather short but quite good & I enjoyed myself. Up in the gallery were some young-sters, quite young from 3 to 12 I should guess, & they took a most lively interest in the play. Their heroes were the colonel & captain whom they talked to & backed in their shrill piercing voices. The actors must have heard. The vicar they derided. Between the acts they climed up the bars, leant over as far as they could, & fought each other, but left off directly the curtain was raised. On Sunday I walked all round the back of Bognor & was just going in to dinner when I ran into Mr. Gayford. He told me to meet him on the pier in the afternoon which I did, & saw some diving. After that we all four walked to Felpham. I think I told you it was an awful hole. It looked worse this time as we had had some rain during the night. I said it was Eden, thinking of Martin Chuzzlewit, but Mr. G. said "No, it isn't; no Adam would stay here." Then we went over Felpham Church & down came the rain. I saw them again during the evening for a short time, & then a thunderstorm came on – a real one I mean, & I went in & read a book I had borrowed. It was an awful night, the worst for years I'm told, but I slept soundly. Six huts were washed away & the promenade is in places 6 inches deep in pebbles & seaweed. This morning was glorious; bright sun, huge waves & plenty of wind. This afternoon a bit showery. I have spent both morning & afternoon with Mrs. Gayford on the front. The tide was

May to David   Bognor   23.9.18 Monday

My dear David,

In my last letter I told you Mrs Taylor has just gone off to Watford because her brother Alfred was ill. I have had a letter from her to say the funeral takes place today & that she will return tomorrow. Her train gets in at 4.7 so of course I will be meeting her. I have missed her the last few days, & then, of course, I miss you too. I see Mrs Gayford & her little boy each day & they are both very nice. The General Manager came down for the week end & they all 3 went to Worthing on Saty to see the ex General Manager. Feeling a bit lonesome Saty aft I went to the theatre & saw "Billeted". The play was rather short but quite good & I enjoyed myself. Up in the gallery were some youngsters, quite young, from 3 to 12 I should guess, & they took a most lively interest in the play. Their heroes were the colonel & captain whom they talked to & backed in their shrill piercing voices. The actors must have heard. The vicar they derided. Between the acts they climbed up the bars, leant over as far as they could, & fought each other, but left off directly the curtain was raised. On Sunday I walked all round the back of Bognor & was just going in to dinner when I ran into Mr Gayford. He told me to meet him on the pier in the afternoon which I did, & saw some diving. After that we all four walked to Felpham. I think I told you it was an awful hole. It looked worse this time as we had had some rain during the night. I said it was Eden, thinking of Martin Chuzzlewit, but Mr G said "No, it isn't, no Adam would stay here." Then we went over Felpham Church and down came the rain. I saw them again during the evening for a short time, & then a thunderstorm came on – a real one I mean, & I went in & read a book I had borrowed. It was an awful night, the worst for years I'm told, but I slept soundly. Six huts were washed away & the promenade is in places 6 inches deep in pebbles & seaweed. This morning was glorious; bright sun, huge waves & plenty of wind. This afternoon a bit showery. I have spent both morning & afternoon with Mrs Gayford on the front. The tide was very high, the waves washing across the promenade, & the roadway to the gardens opposite. I am just off for an hour's sharp walk with you in imagination & then back to dinner. It is beautifully fine again, but we had a short thunderstorm tea time. Goodbye.

May

May to David   Bognor   25.9.18 Wednesday

My dear David,

Here we are sitting on a lovely beach (stones not padded though) with the sinking sun shining on our faces & scarcely a cloud to be seen. It is heavenly. It only wants you in the flesh to make it complete. (Am I growing poetical, or do I need see a doctor? My health is splendid, therefore it must be the former.)

I spent yesterday morning & afternoon with Mrs Gayford & John, who last week reached the advance age of 7. Later in the afternoon John & I went to the station to meet Mrs Taylor. She was full of talk & seem glad to be back again. We walked round Aldwick after tea & after dinner 2 folks, mother & daughter, in the house gave us a concert, which we enjoyed very much. I don't think I told you on Monday night I went with these 2 to the pictures, & saw a very good play – Admiral Creichtons by Barry.

This morning we went for a walk inland about five miles. There are some pretty houses around here. Feeling a bit tired this afternoon & having no beach to sit on, the tide being very high, we turned our attention to the theatre, & saw an American play, "Kick in", or, at any rate, saw part of it. Of all the silly sensational rubbish this took the biscuit. The slang was ridiculous, & the acting none of the best. It was about a thieving case, & there was a murder in it, & another was stabbed but even that did not induce us to stay to the end. Arrived home just in time for tea.

These 2 folks who gave us a concert last night want me to go to a palmist on the pier. They have both been & say he is good. I have not promised to go, but perhaps I will tomorrow. Nothing more to tell you just now, so Goodbye.

May

May to David   Bognor   27.9.18 Friday

My dear David,

Yesterday morning your letter of August 15th arrived, just as I was coming to the conclusion all sorts of things were happening to you. When your letters are overdue I do think silly things. Now i am skyhigh again. Your letter of March 15 is no doubt skyhigh also as it has never reached me. I promptly forwarded your request for the two books. When I get back I will try to send you on those novels of Watsons. They have been out of print. I could get copies elsewhere I believe, but they must be sent direct through firms with permits which seems to me silly, but I suppose it is alright. I have written to Mrs Munro, poor soul.

In the plan of the house you sent me, would you like a little sanctum sanctorum or study? If so, couldn't you take it off the kitchen? You see if you have a big kitchen you might expect big elaborate meals and I am no cook. There are all sorts of pretty houses & bungalows round here, & we go fresh walks each day with the future in view. I do wish you were here. Yesterday morning while on the pier I popped into that palmist. I was not struck with him. He seemed frightened to say anything about our future, no doubt in case I was a detective, & of course fortune telling is against the law. He said I should make a good draughtsman & decorator, & then asked me if I were a public singer.

Me!

I told him not quite. He said I really ought to be a manageress & organiser, that I would change my work & surroundings & be settled down in 2 years' time. Also said my future hubby was abroad, but not fighting & would be quite safe till his return; would have no scars etc on him. Specks he thought you would get them afterwards as he added "You mean well." He mentioned you were very very refined, & said he would like to see a photo of you. When parting he again said he would take it as a favour if I would show him a photo of you – seemed more interested in you than me. Guess he was really pitying you as he added "You have a master mind." I said "Don't worry, I won't let him know he is henpecked" & walked out. Went to a good concert in evening & heard the best of the singers sing "Little Grey Home". Didn't it make me long for the two years to be up? Shall have you long before that, though.

May

May to David   Bognor   29.9.18 Sunday

My dear David,

I don't expect I'll get much time to write you tomorrow, therefore am taking the opportunity today. The weather is awful today, the first bad day we have had on our holiday. It looked grey when we got up this morning. After breakfast we walked along the front to the extreme other end intending to come back to our end & then sit down and read. However, it started to rain just as we were turning back, & as we were by a shelter, we sat down and read. I bought a book yday called "The Canon in Residence" by Whitechurch, & found it highly interesting, especially so as it is evidently a take of Chichester, the place where we enjoyed ourselves yday. The morning flew rapidly, & we walked back thro' the rain to dinner. Since dinner it has poured & is still pouring, but we have been sitting over a huge fire, & I have just finished the book. You must read it. Mrs Taylor has been reading a paper Miss Massey has lent her on natural history. (Here comes the tea.)

Yesterday we caught the 10.50 to Chichester, & did that place thoroughly. It is picturesque & old-world. We went into the cathedral twice, the second time to hear the organist practice. It is a fine organ. When we got outside Mrs Taylor remarked "I prefer the outside of this building – blue sky & green fields"! It certainly was a beautiful day. After doing all the main streets we walked 2½ miles westward almost to Bosham where the Chichester Channel runs up, & at high water there are yachts to be seen. We caught the 5.38 back. Besides the Cathedral we went in to 7 other churches, and in some cases watched the festival decorating being done. We did not favour any of the Dissenting Churches with our presence – they were closed. Chichester contains 12,591 inhabitants but must be a wicked place to require so many churches. Of course we walked into the Bishop's private garden & looked at his gardeners working. I did not see the Bishop, or would have asked where his potato patch was. Everyone was asked to grow potatoes, & he ought to have set a good example. I am shocked! How I would like to tell him so!

On Friday night I went with a party to see some pictures, one being the WAA Co at work. They did look jolly over their bread making. Another picture was of Warwick Castle. I would like to go there. Another film was "The Ghost House", very well acted, not overdone; but the "Admirable Crichtons" were the best. Tomorrow we go home by the 2.25. We both look & feel the better for our change. This seems a more favourable spot for the bungalow, but I can't find the Golf Links. It is only a 7 hole course, & most probably in marshy ground. We have finished tea. The party besides Mrs Taylor & I, consisted of 5 old maids, 4 of them having white hair. They all look so extremely proper that I have a strong desire to get on with knitting the coat. Dare I? & so horrify them? Yes, I will. Nothing like setting a good example. Goodbye, I mustn't waste any more time.

May

David to May   Holzminden   Letter No 31   Oct 1st 1918

My Dearest,

Just had two lovely letters from you, Aug 9th & 21st. I am glad Ethel has guessed how things stood between us & its awfully good of her to offer to make things for you. By the result of Mum gooseberry bushes this year I guess I shall have to have quite a number of them & other fruit bushes. I like your idea of leaving strictly at 5.30 which you mention in one letter & in the next you say you stayed till 8.30. What do you mean by it? Still I do like the way we made it up after our quarrel over it. Hope you have a real good time at Bognor, wish I were going too. I hope you have better weather than we have had here as it has been none too fine. I have had another letter from Charles Webber. I was rather glad to get it as it gave me one or two particulars of the Bonds which I expect you are buying. I should like to have some further particulars of these sometime. Anyhow I shouldn't buy anything but short dated things. We cannot write letters anymore only these letter cards but you will get three of these a month instead of two letters. By the way if my idea of starting building does come about I begin to see a fair chance of getting work from the Assurance Company that I worked for before. You remember that I knew the chief of the department pretty well & also his two assistants who dealt with that type of work, one of whom I got on particularly well with. The other has just been killed, so Godwin tells me & he (Godwin) has been offered a job to fill the vacancy & also my delightful cousin maybe useful too, so that I think I should come off fairly well & it is the type of thing that pays particularly well. Talking about cooking (you mentioned it in one of your letters) sausages form one of the stable items of diet here (everybody, the Red Cross, Stores, everyone sends sausages) & as you know these things when frying are apt to burst & the fact of them being tinned seems to make them especially explosive, so that the elite here politely refer to them as "bangers". This is the sort of thing that happens – there will be a crowd round a stove & somebody in the middle cooking sausages. Suddenly there is a report as one of the "bangers" explodes blowing off a red hot piece into the next man's (usually a Major's) face or neck (in the nature of things it always lands on some uncovered part) who immediately yells, upsets his porridge, stew, or whatever he happens to be stirring, into the sausages & then calls down the Wrath of Heaven on the sausage owner & all his ancestors, describing them luridly & minutely. Will you please tell Mum that the last Red Cross parcel was worse than any before it had only a small tin of corned beef, an army ration which is nearly all vegetable (although quite good of its kind) & no milk nor "grease" of any kind nor sugar. (I am awfully glad you have at last started on the bottom drawer. It was certainly the best suggestion Ethel ever made).
Goodbye

David
Will you please ask Mum to include some flour in her own parcels.

Offizier-Gefangenenlager Holzminden a. d. Weser.

Camp. Nr.
Regiment: Kings Royal Rifles No. 22
Christian name: D. H.
Name: Taylor
Sender: Oct 1st 1918

Kriegsgefangenensendung.

Miss M. Muggridge
16 Manor Road
Beckenham
Kent
England

[Stamp: Kriegsgefangenensendung Postprüfstelle Offizier-Gefangenenlager Holzminden. Geprüft F. A.]

NOV 13 18

OPENED BY CENSOR.
P.W. 1326

my dearest 467

May to David   Beckenham   2.10.18

My dear David,

I think this is letter 174. My last was written on Sunday, teatime, while the rain was coming down. In the evening all the old maids in the boarding house, including myself, sat and knitted. We went to bed early. Next morning was lovely, and we walked to the Golf Links, a 9 hole course which did not look very exciting, passing on the way the Dome House, about 100 years old, where Princess Charlotte used to stay. After lunch we came home. For several miles the fields were under water more or less, which made me feel rather sad, as I am afraid it will be too damp for Mama to retire to after all. She and Ethel are disappointed to hear it. I had been sending them picture postcards galore, and they were getting quite excited about the thoughts of retiring there.

The trains were packed. There were 13 in our compartment, five being children. I read that more people than ever have been to the seaside this year; I suppose as everyone is so wealthy. O, we were never so flourishing. It was close on 7.0 when I got home.

I have not relied entirely to your last letter. I wrote a special letter about those Malayalam shares, but that letter must have gone to glory. I wrote to Read & Brigstock asking for the first certificate, and they said they had it, and should they send it on. Of course we said Yes, and it is now at the bank safely deposited. When you were first taken prisoner, and we did not know your fate, Mrs Taylor asked your business-like cousin, H Webber, to see about those shares, telling me to write down all I knew about the matter. Of course I did, and then he seemed to make a muddle of things generally. However, the affair is quite alright now. I can't think why he is not in khaki. I wish he was. He is an A1 man.

About those food parcels not being so good: I wrote you saying the Red Cross were giving up send the extra-goo-fit-for-Generals-and-such-like which you used to have, but you ought to be having your share of meat and sugar. I guess Mrs Taylor is taking that up with the Red Cross people.

In last night's newspaper there was a notice that a military gentleman of some good position (name was not given) has booked 6 seats at the Alhambra for Peace Night. It certainly seems according to the news we have been having for the last few weeks that you might be home for Christmas.

You don't say how you are in your letter. I don't believe you are feeling up to the mark. We are all feeling skyhigh.

Cannot stop any longer, so Goodbye.

May

May to David   Beckenham   4.10.18

My dear David,

We are all fearfully excited, so if this letter is disjointed you will know the reason. It is not the news in the papers that is doing it, though that is enough to make us all stand on our heads, including the highly respectable and much respected chiefs, but it is owing to the fact that we have had our war bonus doubled, and the extra is to start from the beginning of last July. Our bonus has been $12\tfrac{1}{2}\%$, in addition to having had our standard salary raised. Now we are to have 25% on the first £150, and 50% on the second £150. When I came back from my holiday last Monday I had over £22 waiting for my gracious acceptance, and now we get this news!

Your letter of 1st Sept, however, pleased me still more than the bonus as it sounded as though you were more cheerful than when you wrote the previous one. Now for answering it. I read your description of sheet making out to Mama & the others, and we all laughed heartily. When we are settled you will certainly have to look after the house linen. It will then be unique, to say the least of it.

I posted the form on to the Education people.

So I can send you general news. Very well. I will add a postscript to this letter, so that if the Censor considers I am saying too much he can cut it off.

I like your description of Barbed-Wireitis, and am sure you will want an extra lot of fussing up generally when you return, and I expect you will see that you get it, too. I wonder what you will look like when you become a "puffick shadder". I am not keeping you company, as, sad to relate, my last winter's clothes are somewhat tight on me; but I comfort myself with the thought that Maud is fatter than me. She looks awfully well.

I wish I could get another enlargement of me like the one we have, but the photographer has been and gone and got killed.

O, your cooking! Perhaps my own won't seem to you so awful after all. I can't understand those things, viz meat, sugar & butter, being left out of your parcels. The matter is being taken up with the Red Cross.

I shall not be going to Balham this weekend, as I must go to the cemetery, and I also want to call on Helen as she wants a little jersey I made one of her children last winter made a little larger. By the way last time I went to Putney I put some fresh mould on the grave, some I commandeered.

Cannot stop any longer, fearfully busy. Goodbye.

May

PS The general situation from our standpoint seems, to my ignorant civilian mind, to be excellent.

David to Ginger   Holzminden   Post Card No 14   Oct 5th 1918

I haven't had a letter from you since I dunno know when. By the way address everything to Braunschweig & not Hanover as we are just over the border & sometimes things get delayed by this. Mum tells me that you are again sending me parcels through Mr Charrington. Thanks very much indeed. Its jolly good of you. Letters & parcels are about all we live for or by here. On my last post card I asked if you could get me the American Engineering News Record for Mar 14th & 21st, but don't send them on. Please keep them for me. I have your letter of July 15th. Your letters or what's left of them are most interesting & contain more news than any others I get. With regard to your ball at the bowling green, going quite straight. This sounds very well but…Well having been missed so many times by sleepy pears, tomatoes & such like from you in my youth, I can scarcely credit. I'm sorry, but obviously you must have improved. Lets have some more snapshots when you can.

David

May to David   Beckenham   7.10.18

My dear David,
I had planned a busy weekend thus:- Saturday off; do up the front garden for the winter in morning; back garden in afternoon; knitting in evening. Sunday; cemetery in morning; dig up grave and leave loose for the frosts; see Helen about the Jersey I made Billy a year ago, to try to do it up for this winter.
What happened was this:- Saturday morning, wet; Saturday afternoon, wet; evening dismal. Sunday, glorious but wet under foot. Saturday morning a letter came from Mrs Taylor saying Mrs Day had gone to her daughter who had a bad cold, and that she would be pleased if I could go over Sunday. Instead of gardening I practiced being domesticated and did beeswaxing. Grand experience. The afternoon and evening were spent in darning holes I had made while walking round Bognor. I almost had to remake two pairs of stockings.
Sunday morning I went to Helen's. I am going to lengthen the jersey and mend it in places; also going to make gaiters to go with it, and Helen has some red flannel to make the little man some knickers. I have made him a cap. Georgie is staying until Xmas with some relations near Liverpool. He is very happy with them and does not want to go home. Uncle does not seem at all happy now he has retired.
Sunday afternoon I went off to Balham and will be staying there till Mrs Day comes back. Mrs T has been alone since last Wednesday. I don't think it is right. We went to chapel in the evening which was very lively, being an Anniversary or something. They are always having some special occasions there. I wonder whether it is to please the music conductor and exercise the lungs of the choir. Miss Massey is still in Hampshire. She returns on 14th inst.
I will add a postscript about our current news, so that if the Censor does not approve he can cut it off. Was my last p.c. cut off?

I must tell you this. I read it in the newspaper a little while back. When a Canadian soldier was told the Australians had entered Bethlehem he remarked "I reckon the shepherds are watching their flocks".

There are grand things going on in Trafalgar Square. Some soldiers have made the square look like a battle field, with trenches, no man's land, guns etc. In this remarkable place are banks where you can buy War Bonds, but I think if you purchase something like £20,000 worth you need not call, a gun converted to a bank will call on you. Unfortunately I have not sufficient to spare, in spite of my increase, to have a gun call on me. There was some talk about the aircraft guns going off to make it all the more realistic, but I have not heard them. I wonder if they are too rusty to fire.

It is now time I got on with my work. We are not working late.

Dreamt you were home last night. You soon will be.

May

---

18 Manor Road,
Beckenham,
7. 10. 18.

My dear David,

I had planned a busy weekend thus:- Saturday off; do up the front garden for the winter in morning; back garden in afternoon; knitting in evening. Sunday; cemetery in morning; dig up grave and leave loose for the frosts; see Helen about the Jersey I made Billy a year ago, to try to do it up for this winter.

What happened was this:- Saturday morning, wet; Saturday afternoon, wet; evening dismal. Sunday, glorious, but wet under foot. Saturday morning a letter came from Mrs. Taylor saying Mrs. Day had gone to her daughter who had a bad cold, and that she would be pleased if I could go over Sunday. Instead of gardening I practised being domesticated and did beeswaxing. Grand exercise. The afternoon and evening were spent in darning holes I had made while walking round Bognor. I almost had to remake two pairs of stockings.

Sunday morning I went to Helen's. I am going to lengthen the jersey and mend it in places; also going to make gaiters to go with it, and Helen has some red flannel to make the little man some knickers. I have made him a cap. Georgie is staying until Xmas with some relations near Liverpool. He is very happy with them and does not want to go home. Uncle does not seem at all happy now he has retired.

Sunday afternoon I went off to Balham and will be staying there till Mrs. Day comes back. Mrs. T. had been alone since last Wednesday. I don't think it is right. We went to chapel in the evening which was very lively, being an Anniversary or something. They are always having some special occasions there. I wonder whether it is to please the music conductor and exercise the lungs of the choir. Miss Massey is still in Hampshire. She returns on 14th inst.

I will add a postscript about current news, so that if the Censor does not approve he can cut it off. Was my last p.c. cut off?

I must tell you this. I read it in the newspaper a little while back. When a Canadian soldier was told the Australians had entered Bethlehem he remarked "I reckon the shepherds are watching their flocks".

There are grand things going on in Trafalgar Square. Some soldiers have made the square look like a battle field, with trenches, no man's land, guns &c. In this remarkable place are banks where you can buy War Bonds, but I think if you purchase something like £20,000 worth you need not call, a gun converted into a bank will call on you. Unfortunately I have not sufficient to spare, in spite of my increase, to have a gun call on me. There was some talk about the aircraft guns going off to make it all the more realistic, but I have not heard them. I wonder if they are too rusty to fire.

It is now time I got on with my work. We are not working late.

Dreamt you were home last night. You soon will be. May.

David to War Office   Holzminden   Oct 9th 1918

Sir, Will you kindly remit the value of the articles of kit mentioned below, which I lost when I was captured at Nieuport, Belgium, on July 10th 1917.

Pistol & Holster & Lanyard	£3.14.4
Ammunition Pouch	2.9
Prismatic Compass & Case	2.10.9
Field Glasses & Case	8. 8. 0
Protractor	2.9
Folding Pocket Dividers	7.6
French Coat	5.15.6
Electric Torch	7.6
Leather Gloves	9.6
Canvas Wash Basin	3.6
Leather Holdall containing "Auto-Strop")	
Safety Razor & Strop, Brush & Comb, Mirror)	2. 2. 0
Soap Dish)	
Suit of Underclothing	15.0
Shirt	10.6
3 Collars	3.0
3 Handkerchiefs	4.6
	£25.17.1

I am, Sir,
Your obedient Servant,

D H Taylor
2/Lieut
KRRC

From
Sec. Lieut. D. H. Taylor Offizier Gefangenenlager,
2nd Kings Royal Rifle Corps Holzminden
Home address:- Braunschweig,
 56 Ramsden Road, Germany.
  Balham,
   London, S.W.12

To — The Secretary, Oct. 9th 1918
   Department 72
    War Office
     London S.W.

Sir,

Will you kindly remit the value of the articles of kit mentioned below, which I lost when I was captured at Nieuport, Belgium, on July 10th 1917.

Pistol + Holster + Lanyard	£ 3 - 14 - 4
Ammunition Pouch	2 - 9
Prismatic Compass + Case	2 - 10 - 9
Field Glasses + Case	8 - 8 - 0
Protractor	2 - 9
Folding Pocket Dividers	7 - 6
Trench Coat	5 - 15 - 6
Electric Torch	7 - 6
Leather Gloves	9 - 6
Canvas Wash Basin	3 - 6
Leather Holdall containing "Auto-Strop" Safety Razor + Strop, Brush + Comb, Mirror, Soap Dish.	2 - 2 - 0
Suit of Underclothing	15 - 0
Shirt	10 - 6
3 Collars	3 - 0
3 Handkerchiefs	4 - 6
	£ 25 - 17 - 1

 I am, Sir,
  Your obedient Servant,

My to David   Beckenham   9.10.18

My dear David,

Lovely wet weather we are having, but no one minds, the news all round being so excellent that we can't see anything dismal.

Eleven weeks to Xmas, so I am told. I wonder if we shall have you back by then. It isn't long. Perhaps it will be the Spring, though. The betting that peace will be signed by the 31st March next is very high. By the bye, I don't know whether that is the right expression, but you know what I mean. Then we are off to Cornwall and Devon, aren't we?

Mrs Harris wrote this morning saying she was much better, but would like her mother to stay over the week end, so I shall be going off to Balham each night till then. On Saturday afternoon I have promised to call at Helen's with that jersey. I haven't finished it yet, but hope to to-night. Mrs Stanley called last night, and we all talked. She is fatter than ever, and looks so well.

I haven't any news. Ethel has written to Mrs Taylor to say she is now allowed to send letters to you direct and also parcels, for which I am very pleased.

I will add a postscript giving news in general, so that the Censor can cut it off if he does not approve.

Goodbye.

May

Forgot to mention further up that Mrs Stanley told us a lot of Datchelor girls were studying to be doctors. A scholarship is given, but I don't know any particulars.

One of my own girls has just asked me if she can have Friday & Saturday off as she wants to try and paint & paper her bedroom! I wished her luck. Never had such a request before. Seems to me that girls want to try their hand at everything.

PS In my last letter I mentioned that apparently the Central Powers were wanting peace, ar at any rate an armistice. [censored   ] As a result the fighting is as fierce as ever. My cousing Bert is in the thick of the fighting [censored   ]. He was alright up to a fortnight ago.

Nov. 21st

18 Manor Road,
Beckenham.
9.10.18.

My dear David,

    Lovely wet weather we are having, but no one minds, the news all round being so excellent that we can't see anything dismal.
    Eleven weeks to Xmas, so I am told. I wonder if we shall have you back by then. It isn't long. Perhaps it will be the Spring, though. The betting that peace will be signed by the 31st March next is very high. By the bye, I don't know whether that is the right expression, but you know what I mean. Then we are off to Cornwall and Devon, aren't we?
    Mrs. Harris wrote this morning saying she was much better, but would like her mother to stay over the week end, so I shall be going off to Balham each night till then. On Saturday afternoon I have promised to call at Helen's with that jersey. I haven't finished it yet, but hope to to-night. Mrs. Stanley called last night, and we all talked. She is fatter than ever, and looks so well.
    I haven't any news. Ethel has written to Mrs. Taylor to say she is now allowed to send letters to you direct and also parcels, for which I am very pleased.
    I will add a postscript giving news in general, so that the Censor can cut it off if he does not approve.
    Goodbye.   May.

    Forgot to mention further up that Mrs. Stanley told us a lot of Datchelor girls were studying to be doctors. A scholarship is given, but I don't know any particulars.
    One of my own girls has just asked me if she can have Friday & Saturday off as she wants to try and paint & paper her bedroom! I wished her luck. Never had such a request before. Seems to me that girls want to try their hand at everything.

<u>P.S.</u> In my last letter I mentioned that apparently the Central Powers were wanting peace, or at any rate an armistice.

    As a result the fighting is as fierce as ever.
    My cousin Bert is in the thick of the fighting
    He was alright up to a fortnight ago.

May to David   Beckenham   11.10.18

My dear David,

I am still staying at Balham, as Mrs Day will be away at her daughter's until next Tuesday. In the meantime Mrs T & I are having a quiet enjoyable time. We both knit in the evening and talk over the day's events, and the excellent news in the newspapers, trying to calculate how soon you will be home. The latest possible date we have thought of is 31st March – no extra special reason for that day.

Yesterday afternoon Mrs Taylor went to the Central Prisoner's Committee, and told them about your food shortage. They gave her lists of what have been sent off, which lists I meant to have copied out for you to-day, but left them behind. I will send them next week. Some of the articles have been lost en route as meat is sent you in each parcel, also butter or grease of some sort, and sugar.

This morning Ern brought up a letter from you dated 15th September. I will reply to it briefly as bring Friday I am very busy.

I don't believe Mrs Taylor has sent off your chocolate yet. She was just going to when Ethel wrote for some coupons to be sent to Mr Charrington, and then the Stores wanted some more. Food cannot be sent off without permits, and a certain number are sent each month. About the exchange of prisoners; I have not seen any more news of that sort. Believe everyone is far too busy fighting. Goodness, I am glad you are out of it; it seems worse than ever, though we have never got on so well and continuously as during the last few weeks.

I have not had your postcard asking for Mitchells Advanced Building Construction, but I expect Muriel will be able to get it through the Board of Education. I will try, as that is so much quicker than Batsfords. They are about a couple of months getting a permit!, and then you would be home before the book reached you.

We are not working late, and don't expect to. The Aircraft work has just about come to a standstill, and we had a lot of girls on that work, Maud amongst them. Bishop is getting her on to some other work. By the bye, he is not called up yet, neither are several other A1 men, including your cousin. Suppose they are not really wanted, especially with all these Americans pouring over each week.

I don't mind your wanting to bullyrag me. You would never get far. I shall be going part of my way home with Maud, and will read a portion of your letter out to her. Won't she be shocked? I would like to hear your lecture. Do you think you would get off the point when giving me lessons? I don't! I am expecting some "gorgeous art studies" from you, which I will have framed.

About the flooring in the Hall; I would like something I could beeswax, that being such grand exercise.

I will ask Ern to take some snapshots of me.

Cannot stop longer, so Goodbye.

May

May to David   Beckenham   Letter No 179   14.10.18 Monday

My dear David,

Friday evening while in the tram I read that part of your letter about Sunday School teaching to Maud. She was shocked. After a few minutes, however, she whispered tragically to me "You need not tell him but really I admire him." Then I was shocked.

Friday evening Mrs Taylor & I enjoyed ourselves. I read parts of your letter to her over and over again. Sunday afternoon at 3.0 we wondered if you had commenced your lecture. We shall expect you to come back an orator at least. I could not help smiling last night, as after we came home from Chapel Mrs Taylor told me she did not think so much of the sermon, although the man spoke as well as ever. In her estimation no one will come up to you.

Saturday morning, the General Manager did not turn up, and as I had plenty to do I thought I might leave a little early. I did, and caught the 11.20 from Holborn! I took the jersey round to Helen's. She had not returned, but I saw Auntie, who had on one of her fits of martyrdom. She suffers from them periodically. This was a very bad attack. I listened for about 10 minutes, and then burst out laughing. I couldn't stop. It did not improve her attack. Then I went home and read your letter to Mama and she enjoyed it very much. After that I did my week's mending etc and caught the 6.0 train back to Balham. Did more knitting in the evening, and a little writing for Mrs Taylor. That reminds me. You will have a fit when you see your accounts, but don't worry, you will be able to unravel the mystery from the pass book. The fact is Mrs Taylor has ideas of her own, and I won't upset her on any account. She has no confidence in herself when it comes to the point. She does not seem as though she can start anything, so I do. Then she pops in with her ideas which I carry out, telling her she is a fine business woman. Her health is keeping very good, but when you come back I guess she will pass everything on to you, and it will be time she did. Writing business letters seem to worry her a bit, so I say to her "I'll write that as I can see better than you. Shall I say this or that", and then she promptly knows what she wants said. Now don't worry and think you mother is at all queer. She is not, and has not been, either, but when you come back, as you will now very shortly, I don't want you to say she should have done anything differently. She worries in case you will not be pleased, and I keep on telling her you will be delighted with her management.

Sunday morning I enjoyed exceedingly. You seemed so near to me, in fact there was only one thing wanting. Peter and I went on to the Common, and afterwards Mrs T & I went to Streatham Common and Extension. In the afternoon Charles Webber came. He looked very well, and told us all the latest war news, which I will put in a postscript in case the censor objects to it, and that we can expect you home either just before Xmas, or in the Spring at the latest.

I expect Mrs Day will return to-morrow, so that I will be going to Balham to-night and will help pack a parcel for you, and return home to-morrow. By the bye I have written to Muriel asking her friend to forward that book on Construction direct from the Board of Education.

Mrs Taylor has not reduced the number of your parcels from the Stores. [censored]
Cannot stop any longer, so Goodbye.

May.

David to May   Holzminden   Oct 15th 1918

My Dearest,
I have written my third letter card this month to the War Office, claiming for the things I lost when I was captured, so that you mustn't expect another one. Its a nuisance, but I thought it better to get the claim in now. I do hope you had a good holiday & what you say about your next one...well, I'll tell you what I think of that when I get you to myself. By the way what's it feel like to be holiday making & on your best behaviour, for obviously the G.M. got his wife to go to the same place with the idea of looking after your behaviour or shall I say with the idea of restraining you somewhat. Will you tell Ethel "That officially I think its an excellent idea to get things for the bungalow as far forward as possible" & "That unofficially its awfully good of her to think of making lace for our things". I will sketch anything she wants, if she will only give me some details of the things she would like. With regard to your beach hut for 6 people, I have only just got your letter, but will send a sketch next time. I have had a letter from Maud. She says nothing except, "a look from May often expresses volumes". Naturally from now onwards I shall live in a state of jumpy nervousness of seeing this awesome, nerve shattering, soul destroying, never-to-be-forgotten-volume expressing LOOK.
In one of my previous letters I think I said I was feeding by myself. I have now joined a mess of six & I think it certainly is an improvement, although of course it hasn't been working long yet, but anyhow I have a good deal less to do, (we each have our special jobs which makes each ones work pretty light) & also I get a much greater variety of things to eat, as before I was much too lazy to prepare a number of things for myself & so went without. I have just dined from a dish which one of the fellows said was steak & kidney in theory, but in practice was tinned liver & bacon, kidney, army ration & baked beans mixed. Still it was pretty good. One man is a fairly good cook & strangely (& luckily for us) likes cooking, so of course we don't discourage him, & he does the greater part of it. The other night somebody in the room was wondering what it will be like to get back to a decently served meal, eaten from a decently laid table. Here, sitting at table its quite an ordinary question to be asked "where's our teaspoon", or somebody requests the loan of your knife, which, after you have carefully (more or less) scraped the stew on the side of your plate, you hand him, the scraping being necessary of course, because he wants the knife to spread butter with. From the news that one hears here it seems likely that I may be getting back to you soon. Heaven send that its not long. Can't you send me some more snapshots.
Goodbye.

David

May to David   Beckenham   16.10.18

My dear David,

I told you the other day Mrs Taylor went up to Thurloe Place about your parcels not containing all they should, and they gave her a list of what they sent. Each parcel weighs approximately 15 lbs when packed. Sometimes the contents of these parcels are slightly altered.

A Parcel
2 lb Beef
½ lb vegetables
1 lb tin rations
½ lb tea
1 lb tin milk
½ lb dripping or margarine
1 lb tin jam
1 ½ lb biscuits
1 pkt quaker oats, grape nuts or milk pudding
50 cigarettes
1 tin sardines
1 tablet soap
1 lb tin herrings
1 lb beans

¼ lb cocoa
½ lb bacon

C Parcel
1 lb beef
1 lb bacon
1 lb beans
¼ lb tea
1 lb tin milk
One ½ lb tin beef, ham or veal loaf
1 lb biscuits
1 lb rations
½ lb tin dripping or margarine
1 lb rice, sago or tapioca
1 lb tin jam, tinned fruit or dates
1 small potted meat
100 cigarettes
1 tablet soap

B Parcel
1½ lb biscuits
½ lb cocoa
1 lb milk
1 lb Lyles syrup
1 lb rice or dates
1 small potted meat
1 tablet soap
1 lb tin rations
1 lb tin sausages
1 lb sugar
1 lb suet pudding
½ lb chocolate
One 1lb tin veal, ham or beef loaf
1 pkt quaker oats, grape nuts or milk pudding
onions
2 oz tobacco
1 lb corned beef

D Parcel
1 lb tin rations
1 lb tin beef
1 lb tin Irish stew or haricot mutton
1 lb biscuits
1 lb tin jam
1 lb tin pork and beans
¼ lb tea
1 lb sugar
1 lb tin meat and potato pudding or tripe &
½ lb cheese
1 tin sardines
½ lb tin margarine
50 cigarettes
1 tablet soap
One ½ lb veal, ham or beef loaf
½ lb bacon

I have not a list of the Stores parcels.

my dearest   479

Last night I went back home again, and made the discovery that the coat I am making for Muriel is too wide. Am afraid the greater part of it will have to be undone. Fortunately it does not take long to undo – but there is the doing up.

You remember I told you Trafalgar Square was done up to represent a battle field, and that were dugouts where you could buy war loans. Well, several more millions of money were paid in than required. Everyone seems to be made of money.

I will add a postscript giving the news, so that the Censor can cut it off if he does not approve. Did you ever get the letter I wrote to you from Watford, which Mrs Pratt censored by means of adding something saucy at the end? She and Minnie Capel are now at Eastbourne, but are having bad weather.

No more now.

Goodbye.

May

PS It seems to me that the Allies won't allow armistices, but only unconditional surrenders. One country has surrendered thus, and apparently two others are considering it.

```
        A Parcel.                              B Parcel

2 lb. Beef                             1½ lb. biscuits
½ lb. vegetables                       ½ lb. cocoa
1 lb. tin rations                      1 lb. milk
½ lb. tea                              1 lb. Lyles syrup
1 lb. tin milk                         1 lb. rice or dates
½ lb. dripping or margarine            1 small potted meat
1 lb. tin jam                          1 tablet soap
1½ lb. biscuits                        1 lb. tin rations.
1 pkt. quaker oats, grape              1 lb. tin sausages
    nuts or milk pudding.              1 lb. sugar
50 cigarettes                          1 lb. suet pudding
1 tin sardines                         ½ lb. chocolate
1 tablet soap                          one 1 lb. tin veal, ham or beef loaf.
1 lb. tin herrings                     1 pkt. quaker oats, grape nuts or milk
1 lb. beans                                pudding
¼ lb. cocoa                            2 oz. tobacco
½ lb. bacon.                           1 lb. corned beef.

        C Parcel.                              D Parcel

1 lb. beef                             1 lb. tin rations
1 lb. bacon                            1 lb. tin beef
1 lb. beans                            1 lb. tin Irish stew or haricot mutton
¼ lb. tea                              1 lb. biscuits
1 lb. tin milk                         1 lb. tin jam.
One ½ lb. tin beef, ham or veal        1 lb. tin pork and beans
    loaf.                              ¼ lb. tea
1 lb. biscuits                         1 lb. sugar
1 lb. rations                          1 lb. tin meat and potato pudding or
½ lb. tin dripping or margarine            tripe & onions
1 lb. rice, sago or tapioca            ½ lb. cheese
1 lb. tin jam, tinned fruit or         1 tin sardines
    dates.                             ½ lb. tin margarine
1 small potted meat.                   50 cigarettes
100 cigarettes                         1 tablet soap
1 tablet soap.                         One ½ lb. veal, ham or beef loaf
```

May to David   Beckenham   18.10.18

My dear David,

Yesterday I had a letter from Muriel and this is what she says:-

"Thank you very much for your letter, which I should have answered before, but we had a friend spending the weekend with us, and also some people came in the last two evenings, so I did not get an opportunity.

I wrote off at once to my cousin with the name of the additional book for Mr Taylor. I am only too pleased to be able to help him in any way. I hope they will all get to him safely eventually. There is nothing to pay to the Book Scheme at all.

It was good of you to copy his letter for me. As you know we are always glad to hear news of him. Her certainly writes very cheerfully. The part about the "Sunday School" teaching amused us very much. I expect the men appreciate the lectures.

No, I don't know Bognor at all, but have heard many people sing its praises. As to the bungalow, it seems to me that the actual place does not matter so much as long as the right two people are in it. Perhaps this sounds very romantic, but I think it is the most essential fact and the house itslf is only the setting as it were. You tell Mr T what I say, and I am sure he will confirm it."

We are very busy, so I cannot stop to write any more.

I will add a postscript giving general news, so that the Censor can cut it off if he does not approve.

I am expecting to spend the weekend at home. The weather is lovely, so I am hoping to do gardening. The front grass has not been cut for quite a month!

Goodbye.

May

PS Last night's paper said the previous day was the best the Allies have ever had since the beginning of the war.

Northern France is clear, and so is Western Belgium.

Our Allies are also getting on beautifully everywhere else.

May to David   Beckenham   21.10.14

My dear David,

Friday night it turned wet again, thus spoiling all hope of gardening Saturday and Sunday. Saturday was bright, and I had a bright inspiration during the morning. It is astonishing how one's thoughts can run on while typing policies. I never know what I have typed. I have just consulted the girls about my inspiration, and they mostly agree; therefore I shall be going downstairs this afternoon to the chief with a paper as follows:-

<u>St Dunstan's Hostel for Blinded Soldiers & Sailors</u>
The Lady Clerks of the staff of the N.A.Co wish to send a cheque to the above Organization on 2nd December.
It is proposed to raise the money in the following ways:-

1. Collections.
2. Raffles. Will those who have articles they do not require, suitable for raffles, please hand them to the Typing Dept?
3. Sale of second-hand books. Will those who have books they do not require please hand them to the Typing Dept? Those unsold will be returned to the donors.
4. Sale of hand-knitted socks, scarves, bedsocks, and other woollen garments suitable for gentlemen in civil life as well as soldiers and sailors; also articles suitable for Xmas presents.

The above Sales to be held in the Board Room on 29th Nov after Office hours.

Last year a cheque for £162 was sent to St Dunstan's, when help was received from the Branches, "National Guarantee" and "Royal Scottish". Cannot the Head Office, Marine Dept and West End Branch send £100 this year?

Will every lady make as many articles as she can and get her friends to as well?
<u>Please do not forget the men lost their sight protecting US.</u>

I have set the above out to fill a page, and it looks quite businesslike. Those two Companies belong to us, and we have also acquired a few more.
Only five weeks! How we shall have to work! And I have several away with the flu.
Of course I don't expect to get £100. Shall be delighted if we get £20, but £100 looks well.
Saturday afternoon and evening I was busy with Muriel's coat, undoing parts of it.
Sunday it rained all day long. I was busy bustling about in the morning trying to think I was busy, and indulging in lovely day-dreams all the time. I wonder if you can guess what they were. In the afternoon and evening I sat over the fire and studied various newspapers. I will add the news in a postscript.
And that is all the news I have of a "domestic nature". How are your lectures getting on? Do your hearers keep awake? I don't mind cheeking you as you are at a safe distance, though

won't be much longer, I know.
Goodbye.

May

PS Northern Belgium, as well as Northern France, is cleared.
Good progress is being made all round.

May to David   Beckenham   23.10.18

My dear David,
I am feeling worried about you as I see in the papers the influenza is very bad in Germany. We certainly have a few cases here, but if we feed up we can ward it off, which we are doing; but you cannot feed up or take any precautions. O dear, how I wish etc etc etc.
Next Monday the winter session of the Insurance Institute commences. Mr Robertson, one of our joint General Managers, is President this time, and he will give the lecture Monday. He has sent us a message to say he hopes we shall all be there, but that we shall probably find his lecture unorthodox. That was not the word he used, but he meant that. I have been typing out pieces of his address.

Other lectures are:-
Nov 25th "The Romance of Insurance". (Comments and interrogations by the girls regarding this are amusing)
Dec 1th "Some Notes on Insurance Shares"
Jan 20th "The Land Problem in Scotland: its bearing upon Investments"
Feb 17th "Africa, and Developments there over the last thirty seven years"
Mar 17th "The Road" (Limelight Views)

The programme sounds interesting, and I hope to go to all.

The eldest boy Bullock is in the Army, and he has been for several months. He used to be a Scout, and is very keen on soldiering. He wrote a very good letter, giving descriptions of the places he has been to and the work he does, and wound up with these words "There is only one drawback to the Army. You have the knowledge that you cannot give a week's notice, and you know they won't give it to you." Rather descriptive of the British, isn't it?
I will add a short paragraph giving outline of current events.
Isn't it time I had another plan? I do like them. At the same time I want all the pages of writing too. I am now re-knitting that coat of Muriel's. I did want to jump on it last night, but I have hopes it will resemble a coat by the time I have finished with it. I was trying to iron it the way it should go yesterday.

We have not started work for the Sale yet. I don't think anyone has decided what to do. We all want to do small things as there won't be much time.

Goodbye for the present.

May

PS Good progress still being made all round.

May to David   Beckenham   25.10.18

My dear David,

There is not much to write about to-day.

I am having another new girl in next week. I don't want her, but Lutt says he would rather I had as many girls as I could, and then turn them adrift into other departments when I have got them into working order. It does not sound very complimentary to the men. They certainly don't shine in training them, and then apparently the girls rule the men – at least some of the older men are ruled, if not all.

Yesterday it was "Our Day", ie collection day for the Red Cross. £1,000,000 wanted. By 1.0 there was a notice put up at the Exchange, so I am told, saying that 1½ millions had already come in, and people were still anxious to give. We never were so flourishing before.

To-day I am giving each temporary girl as I pay her a leaflet we have stencilled asking for help for St Dunstan's. I copied out the wording for you two letters back. I have not asked Mr Gayford's permission yet, but I guess I ought, as we want to use the Board Room which is the Sanctum Sanctorum.

I am now getting back my influenza patients, and not having any fresh cases. I am feeling anxious about you. By the bye, isn't it your turn to be sent into Holland yet?

I will add a postscript giving current events.

I am going over to Balham on Sunday, hoping to do my gardening on Saturday, but it looks like turning out wet again.

Commencing the week after next, when our rush will be over, I am going to let the girls in my section get off at 4.30 once a week, providing they don't let the cat out of the bag. They have sworn secrecy.

Nothing more to say just now, except that I dreamt all my teeth dropped out, which is a dreadful sign, meaning I shall lose all my friends and that my sweetheart won't marry me! Goodbye.

May

PS News from the front still continues excellent.
[three lines removed by censor   ]
I saw a heading in the paper yesterday that women were to be allowed to sit in Parliament, but was too busy to read all about it.

May to David   Beckenham   28.10.18

My dear David,

Saturday the ground was too damp for gardening, so it will have to wait still another week. Sunday I was a perfect angel. I woke up with a headache and knew I had a cold coming on. It was drizzling with rain, so I stayed in bed till after tea. I was sorry to disappoint Mrs Taylor as I had promised to spend the afternoon and night with her, so Ern went over in the morning with the wool (she and Mrs Day are going to make socks for the sale, bless them), while I fancied myself a grand lady. I have been out with you with a cold much worse, before now, but as you are not here to scold me I feel I am on my honour, hence my taking care of myself. I won't do it when you return, though. Moreover, I feel I must keep well and strong to nurse you when you return, because you are going to be awful bad then. There are still cases of influenza about, though I have nearly all my invalids back now. We did enjoy ourselves on Sunday and discussed heaps of things, but I have no time to tell you as I am going off home now. If I stay till 5.30 they will expect me to go to the lecture to-night, and that would make me very late home which you would not approve of. Besides, I want to finish Muriel's coat this afternoon. I had a letter from Mrs Taylor morning enclosing your postcard of Sept 23, or thereabouts. So I only to have letter cards, and that means no more plans. Well, I shall hear from you more frequently and that will be a grand thing.
Goodbye.

May

May to David   Beckenham   30.10.18

My dear David,

This is payday and everyone is in a good temper, even myself. Muriel has just rung up to say they are making us up a parcel for our Sale, and the best of it is that I have not get the General Manager's consent. You see I have just the slightest cold, so dare not approach him till it is gone.

To-night I shall be finishing her coat. It looks alright, very fashionable, but too clumsy to suit my taste. It is awfully hot and heavy.

What do you think? You know that lovely old mansion, Langley Court, standing in Park Langley. Well, it is being filled with German prisoners. It is a job to know where to put them all, we have been taking so many for months past now. They will have a lovely Park for their recreation ground. We have well over 300,000 prisoners, but I don't think they are all in England. These men get 7 oz jam each week. Now we read in the papers that jam is running rather short, so that we shall have to be rationed. And our portion is to be $1/4$ lb each, while the prisoners will still be getting their 7 oz. Jam is not essential for adults, while it is for children. If I had any children shouldn't I be feeling furious?
I am adding a postscript.

We heard from cousin Bert the other day. He was having a "rest", but were all chafing to get to the fighting again. He wrote most cheerfully.

The weather has turned beautiful, like June.

Maud is away to-day, and so she was yesterday. I wonder if she has the flu. I have just written to her.

I hope it has not broken out in your camp again. I do feel anxious about you.

No more news just now, so Goodbye.

May

PS There is a rumour, but no confirmation, that the Emporer of Austria has retired from business as he has not a business to look after, the Austrian Empire having gone in for the popular craze and divided themselves up into allotments. What is true is that a note from Austria has arrived in London, which reads to me as though they will surrender unconditionally. Turkey is also parleying. British soldiers are pouring through Bulgaria into Roumania. And Germany stands alone, talking pluckily and fighting hard.

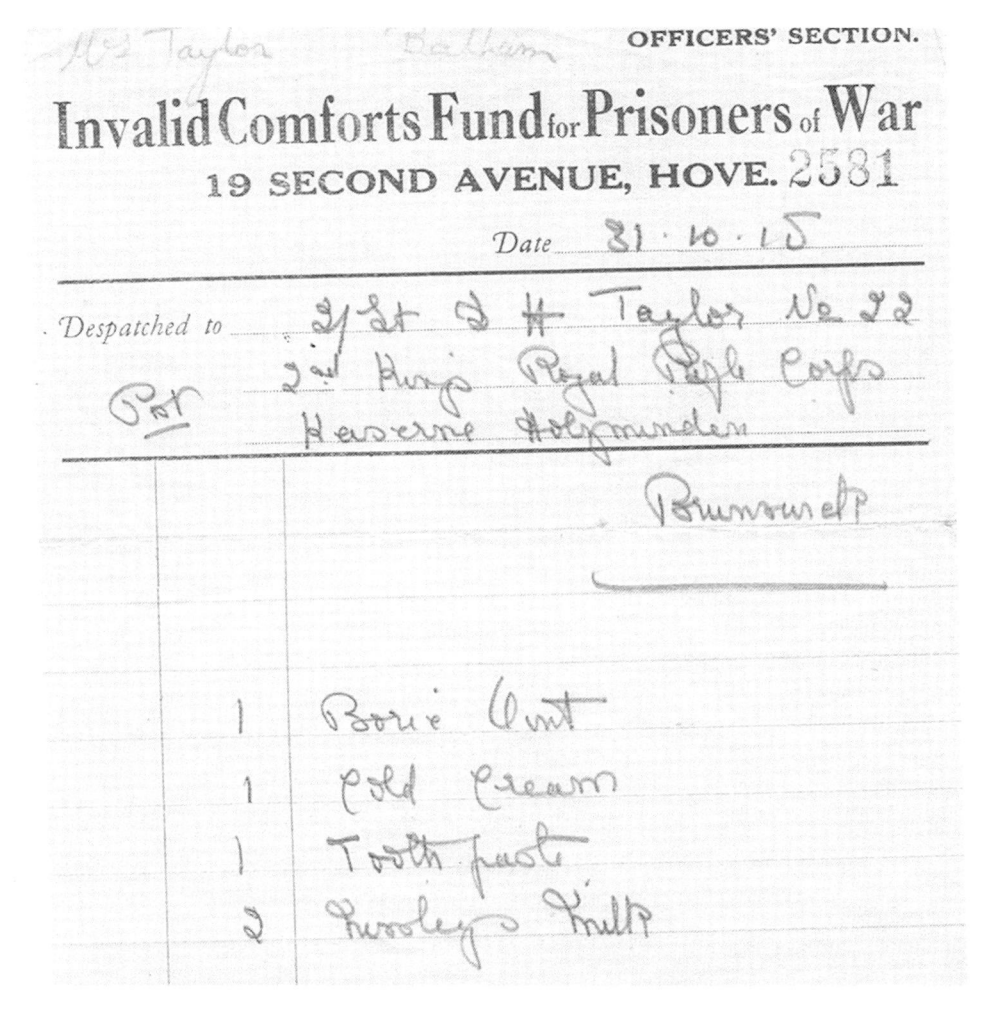

May to David   Beckenham   1.11.18

My dear David,

Last night I finished the coat! The next thing to be finished is the war. I hear someone on the Stock Exchange yesterday wanted to bet it would be over in a fortnight's time, but no one would take him on. One of the girls has just told me that in France a lot of folks are betting it will be over by Christmas, so that I might get you home for the holiday after all. I am not building on it in case of disappointment, but I feel convinced I shall have you home soon after. And then -. What? Maud is wondering what her next post will be. There is practically no aircraft work to do.

The influenza is dying out. We have only got about half a dozen cases. Do hope you are alright. We are very much behindhand with the Fire Policies, but are not staying late.

One of the girls has just brought me a strong looking piece of canvas, only it is not canvas but is made of paper. It has come from Germany, and people are making clothes of it, so she tells me. It must be very strong paper, but fancy making clothes of paper. You won't notice any difference in our shops here, and I think people are dressier than ever. I'm not, but then I am anxious to get that £1000. Not far short now. Am investing over £10 over month.

Tomorrow I shall have off, and on Sunday I am off to Balham.

I must now write to Mrs Maconachie, so Goodbye, but not for long.

May

David to May   Holzminden   Letter No 33   November 1st 1918

My Dearest,

It will be nearly Christmas again by the time you get this, so will you be a dear little girl and buy yourself a present for me. Some fellows here would have one believe there is a possibility of our getting home for Christmas, in which case of course I shall be able to buy you something myself. Will you also please ask Mum what she would like and buy it for her. Please get the money from her of course. I am glad Maud wrote to you about her mother's grave. Its about time she began to show you a little gratitude and be rather less self-satisfied. Its awfully good of you to go with Mum to see about my things. Perhaps I may be back again soon and be able to thank you really properly.

Below I am writing an order to Cox to pay Mum £40. This of course in addition to the monthly payments. Will you please let her have it. Will you please ask Mum on no account to stop sending me parcels, even if these peace arrangements that are in the air do come about, until she hears definitely from me to do so, as we may be here a considerable time after things are settled and if parcels stopped I would be stranded.

I have only had two of your letters while you were away, but your holiday doesn't seem to have been as good as I hoped it was going to be. Things did seem to work against you. I guess you won't be lonesome next time and we'll have the best holiday we ever had. From

your letter you seem to persevere very successfully with Ern's Fine Old Jamaica and talking about bulls sitting on you, I suppose you haven't seen any snakes have you? I haven't room to put your bungalow on this card but will try to next time. I am still going out for walks and the woods round the camp for the last week or so have been splendid again, one mass of greens, browns and yellows. I wished numbers of times that you could see them, or that I could transport them to make bits of our garden that is to be.
Goodbye.

David

David to Ginger   Holzminden   Post Card No 15   Nov 1st 1918

By the time this gets to you it will be Christmas again. I hope you have a very good time & the kiddies get all they want in their stockings. Thanks awfully much for thinking of sending me a Xmas pudding. It is good of you. Two days ago I received a parcel through the American Prisoners of War Committee, Berne. Amongst other things it contained a slab of toffee & chocolate, both very excellent & very much appreciated. It also had soap, a towel & some jolly good patent buttons etc. I can only think it came from you. I have also had two more parcels from Harrods through Mr Charrington both very good. Thanks very much indeed for them all. I have just had your letter of Aug 29th. You mention Frenchmen in the camp. That was at Karlsruhe – there are only British here, so that one doesn't get a chance of exchanging talk. You also mention Holland, but this is all off & some fellows here have one believe that we shall be home for Xmas. One never knows.

David

May to David   Beckenham   6.11.18

My dear David,

Beckenham is excited to say the least of it. It always did think itself a MOST IMPORTANT place, but imagine its feelings now that the new Lord Mayor is a Beckenham man, and of course he will be the Peace Lord Mayor. The tradesmen's boys are full of it. Our milk boy is a typical Beckenhamite. He was talking about the new Lord Mayor the other day to Mama, and said "I serve the Marshalls with milk. Of course you know Mr Marshall, don't you ma'am?" Mama was awful enough to say No. The boy almost fell backward, and finally gasped "But you must; he lives close by, and has a dozen and a half daughters, and keeps the chain up at the side door!" Alas, Mama only shook her head, keeping a straight countenance with difficulty. He doesn't deign speak to her now.

I almost finished Bill's gaiters last night, and will quite to-night. In the train this morning I started some lace to go on a couple of towels – not for the bottom drawer. Can't imagine you liking to wipe a nice tender skin on some scrubby crochetwork. These towels are for our sale. Ern gave half a dozen silver spoons he had won at shooting, and had them put in a case. I reckon they are worth £2.2/-. We raffled them, and thereby got £4.1/- for them. I did the drawing, and the spoons fell to Eccles. He is awfully pleased with them. I was quite honest in the drawing. Mr Maconachie promptly offered him 10/- for them and was very hurt because his offer was spurned! All the men are indignant that Eccles was the winner, saying "What does that crusty old bachelor want with spoons?" I tell them he is starting a bottom drawer on the quiet. Poor man, he will get teased before long.

I am no longer counting the months till your return, but weeks!

Goodbye for a little while.

May

PS The Lord Mayor's Show does not come by the Office this time. Really I am pleased. It is such a hindrance as I can't get much work done, and I have now got 93 girls to get excited!

Ginger Linn to David   Passaic New Jersey USA   Nov 9 1918

Dear Kid,

Today a year ago we were going to the hospital with John, he was first operated on on Nov 10. Last year was bitterly cold, with lots of ice on the rivers, this year is warm, & we have only had two or three morning frosts so far.

Today I am taking Erl to a specialist, as she still limps.

Later.

Erl has been examined & this doctor says that from what I have told him, he should judge Erl had had a very slight attack of infantile paralysis, but by immense good luck she was one of the very few children who came through it without having some serious defect. He says her thighs are stiff, but can find nothing else. Except for this limp, which is sometimes more marked than others, she seems particularly well.

Thursday was a tremendous day here. A report came through that the armistice had been signed, & the nation went wild. We were at lunch down-town, when suddenly factory whistles began to blow at no special working time, & kept on. We were waiting for the motor-car & still the whistles blew, & then we were told what it was. My first comment was, "Imagine being in this one horse town instead of being in London at such a time." Next I said to John "Wouldn't you like to be in New York?" & next "I shall take the children and get the 3.5 train to NY, & then I had the bright idea of his driving up in the car, as he was going up on business, & taking us. Cars & on the whistles blew, & in the end all factories were closed, & we drove to NY. All business there had ceased at 1 o'c, & then someone had the bright idea of throwing a waste-basket & its contents out of the window, & then up went many thousands of windows & all waste baskets were emptied out orders, letters, telephone books, & any old paper that would tear, were ... up & thrown out, the whole making impromptu confetti, & my word ! you should have seen the mess – right from the Bakery up to 45th St – that is miles of roadway. Flags and anything that would make a noise everywhere. Unfortunately before we got to New York we had found it was a false report, passed by a Navy Censor, & although it might be a matter of days or weeks, or months, we knew the result would at the end be as we wanted, the sudden disappointment put a damper on us, but still people went on rejoicing, & I was glad to have seen NY in such circumstances. Erl asked today if Uncle David would come straight to Passaic.

Happy New Year.

Yours as ever,

Ethel

David to May   Holzminden   Letter No 34   Nov 10th 1918

My Dearest,

I think I have all your letters while you were away. You seem to have done a good deal of walking while you were there. From the news one hears here there seems a possibility of my getting home by Christmas even now. Wouldn't it be glorious if it really came about? Everyone here seems anxious for the war to end & from what one hears it is the same everywhere. The original administrative authorities in the district have been replaced by a soldier's and workmans Council which is running everything now, the change having been made yesterday, I think. So far this has not affected us in any way & from accounts most things outside are as usual. With regard to the sanctum sanctorum which you suggest might be cut off the kitchen. I thought you might like one of the two rooms which I have put on the 3rd floor (& which by the way I haven't yet sent you a plan for) as your own particular room. I could be made especially comfy, and naturally, I should want to share it. We might have two arm chairs up there, or perhaps one would be sufficient. It will not be easy to take another room off the kitchen altho' I have an idea for cutting off a part to form the coal store instead of putting it outside, as at present. This would reduce the size of the kitchen, but would leave it still big enough I think, & would also save something in cost. Talking of Chichester I rode through there once on a bicycle, but about the only thing I remember is the old cross in the centre of town where the four main streets meet & I remember these streets were very narrow & the whole place very busy with traffic as there was a race meeting at Goodwood that day & a crowd of motors were going through the town on their way to the course. Subsequently I remember riding in company with a procession of motors along a never ending, very very hot, dusty road for about 5 miles reviling all motors & motorists past & future & most particularly those then present. I like the idea of "doing" 8 different churches including a cathedral. It sounds like a pilgrimage, or possible a penance for sins committed during your holiday, sins which presumably even the august presence of the GMs wife couldn't prevent. The picture of you leading the old maids at the boarding house astray in persuading them to knit on a Sunday appals me. I tremble to think to what lengths you would induced them to go, had it not been the end of your stay.
Goodbye.

David

Charrington to Ethel Linn   London   Nov 11th 1918 1pm

"The Day"

Dear Mrs Linn,
Only time to say thank God the fighting is over. Of course the devils would sign anything but they can't be trusted. The City has gone mad. Guns went off at 11 o'clock, everyone cheered, traffic stopped & it looks like 10 Lord Mayor Shows. I saw several American Navy boys opposite Cannon St Station dancing with girls who had made their hats out of Union Jack flags. At the Mansion House you see dense crowds & thousands of small hand flags. I saw a good sized dog running up & down Cannon St with a Union Jack tied to its tail the stick was no trouble at all & he seemed to enjoy the excitement as much as anyone.
Yours sincerely
E Charrington

Hope you brother will return soon.

May to David   Beckenham   11.11.18

My dear David,

I expect this will be the last letter I shall address to Holzminden, and I guess it will not reach you, as I hope you will be here before then.

Saturday was Lord Mayor Show Day, and a grand show it was. The day was glorious and cold, just the very day for new winter clothes, and there were plenty of them to see. I saw a good deal of the Show lined up Moorgate & Coleman Streets, London Wall etc. I left early, took Underground from Moorgate St to London Bridge, & caught the 12.43 to New Beckenham. We had the compartment to ourselves all the way. Then I went to Auntie's. Both Auntie and Helen gave me £1 towards our Sale for the Blind. I said I would buy something for them, but they don't want their money's worth!

In the afternoon I did some gardening, and in the evening I did my week's mending, like an angel.

Sunday was dull. In the morning I cleaned my bottom drawer contributions the girls had given me – silver spoons and tea knives. In the afternoon I went to Balham where I stayed the night. I practiced while over there, and what do you think I played? You will never guess, so I will tell you – the Wedding March and Home Sweet Home.

This is Monday – one of the most memorable days for Great Britain. Since 11.0 the noise has been deafening. We are letting half staff off this afternoon. Of course it is the news that the armistice has been signed, and we shall get our prisoners home at once. The thought makes me want to dance on my head. Guess I had better change the subject for fear of shocking the Censor.

When I told Mrs Taylor yesterday that it looked as if you might be home any day now she calmly said "Then I had better put a hot water bottle in his bed and air it well." I always thought I was practical and undemonstrative, but –

Goodbye for a few days. The other day I was counting the weeks till your return, so I told you in a letter; now I am counting the days. Isn't it grand?

May

David to May   Holzminden   Nov 20th 1918

My Dearest,

Until today I had not had a letter from you since I last wrote to you. Today two came uncensored, or rather uncensored on this side, although our people had had a go at them, so now I am in clover again. From them I imagine you have my letters of Sept 1st and 15th. Of course everything at present is delayed owing to transport difficulties. It is splendid new that you have your bonus doubled & also have it anitdated. Mum, in her last letter, said that she was sending me a parcel in which you had included a package. Now I am itching to get that parcel to see what it is. I am also anxious to get the book parcel from the Educational people. Thanks very much for sending them the form. I am awfully disappointed about that enlargement of your photo, but you will have to get one done by somebody else for I must have one. It is too good of you to stay with Mum each time Polly is away & she is left alone. I'll never be able to thank you enough, & from her letters Mum appreciates it just as much. Again as you are at present only doing twice as much work as you should be doing you must needs add to it by getting up another bazaar. I think its a great idea & I hope you get very much more than your proposed £100 but still I hope you won't overdo things & knock yourself up. As regards the "hearers" at my class, of course they keep away & indeed I find that they are very keen indeed & as regards your ckeeking me it doesn't seem to make any difference at all whether I am a safe distance or otherwise I get it all the same. Anyway by the time you get this I hope I shall be with you again & perhaps the distance won't be so safe then, for I'll be able to exact the strict & proper penalties. Don't you wish it may be so. I do, I am longing for you again more than ever. The last few days (since we heard that the thing had been finally signed) have seemed endless & now I am all ready to get up & walk out the moment the order comes. Nobody of course knows when we are going yet or how we are likely to go. May it be quickly.
Goodbye

David

David to May   Holzminden   Letter No 36   Dec 1st 1918

My Dearest,

And still I am here, though I haven't given up hope of being with you before this gets there. In the meantime we get no news as when we are likely to go, although of course there are innumerable wild & wonderful rumours continually floating around. I have heard from the Educational people that they have sent on one of the three books, but I haven't got it yet of course. Hope it comes before I leave here. Will you please thank Muriel for writing to them. There is a man in camp here who comes from Dublin, & I have been talking to him a good deal lately & some of his phrases etc are Mrs Sandy's exactly. You say you are possibly sending me some more snapshots. I do hope I get them. There is no need for you to worry about my getting influenza for I have not had the slightest tendency that way & then you have been bad yourself & been in bed. I am the one to worry, & I have wanted to nurse you, but still it was good of you to take care of yourself. Those lectures at the Insurance Institute sound most interesting & I would very much like to hear several of them myself. I know you must be up to your eyes with work between the bazaar & the office & I am just hoping you won't absolutely fag yourself out. I wonder if you reach £200 this time. Somehow I have an idea you will. Since we have known that at last the war is really over the days seem like weeks & one cannot settle down to read, work, or do anything else, with any sort of decent result. Then at one time you seem absolutely confident that you will be home for Christmas & another this hope fades away into a mere possibility. Naturally we hope to be amongst the first to go, but of course we are quite a minor detail compared with the numbers elsewhere & the tremendous numbers of other things all having to be done quickly. Still once I do get home everything will be different, only one wants things & wants them now.
Goodbye

David

David to Ginger   Holzminden   Post Card No 16   Dec 1st 1918

A day or so ago I suddenly got three letters from you dated Sept 13th, Oct 4th & 13th together with a picture from Erl. Please thank her very much indeed. I am awfully sorry the poor kiddie was so bad with rheumatism. I hope she is quite alright again now. I am hoping against hope that I may get your Christmas pudding before I leave here, but I rather think its doubtful, although we have had no news whatever of when we are likely to leave here or what route we are likely to take. Still I suppose we shall be going sometime & I sincerely hope soon, as the last three weeks have dragged no end & you cannot settle down to do anything with any decent result.

David

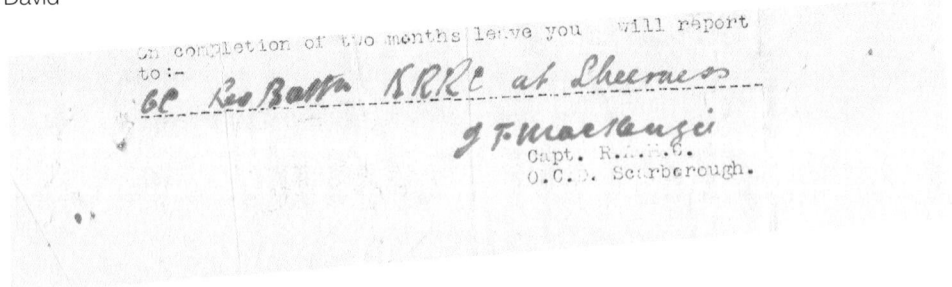

David to Ginger   56 Ramsden Rd Balham   Dec 24th 1918

Dear Ginger,

I am home again, as of course you know by this time by the cablegram, & naturally awfully glad to get home too.

We had a tremendous reception on landing, which was all the more wonderful seeing that of course we were not the first prisoners to get home by some thousands. It started in Holland, (we came via Rotterdam) as soon as we crossed the border there was a continuous string of small children & people along the railway & all tinkling tiny bells & yelling, as the train passed. Our boat anchored off the mouth of the Humber at night & at daybreak the next morning we moved up the river to the accompaniment of the hooting & screeching of sirens. Every boat, small and large, began to bellow & screech as we passed, even those that were moored permanently seemed to get up sufficient steam to scream for our benefit & they were all flying the signal "Welcome Home". We met a procession of Grimsby steam trawlers just moving out, all yelling for all they were worth, & one of two of their skippers made anxious enquiries of us such as "What shall we do with the Kaiser" or "Are we downhearted" etc etc & a bit further up there was a tramp moored which had an effigy of the Kaiser hanging to the yardarm & as we came up some humorist started him kicking & jerking his legs & arms.

On landing at Hull there was a message from the King read to us & a number of ladies handed round newspapers & chocolate etc etc & while waiting for the train we were taken off to a local club & given refreshments. Then we were taken to Scarborough. Here we were met by a brass band & taken in tram cars (altho' the distance was only 200 to 300 yards) to the hotel of the place there to be received by a brigadier & the mayor of the town & were generally made much of.

I had to stay one night at Scarborough to give certain particulars & receive orders etc, then got two months leave & started for home.

It all seems very wonderful.

Here in London people seem willing to do anything for you if you are in khaki.

For instance, I went to see Mr Charrington to thank him & as I was not sure of his number I was looking in a various doorways. When a man asked what name I wanted & as he couldn't direct me, took me up into his own office & looked up the address in the directory, all entirely without being asked, & this sort of feeling seems to be general.

I have not been specially well since I have been home, I think I had a slight touch of the "flu" & I seem rather off colour generally as I am cultivating boils & have sores on my face & hands. However its not very serious.

In one of your letters you say you are coming home as soon as the restrictions are removed. Can't you make them believe that its an absolute necessity for the good of the USA & the Allies generally that you should come home? Anyhow, stir them up & get home as soon as you can.

I have bought you a pewter bowl as a Christmas present but Heaven knows when you'll get it as there are all sorts of permits & licences to be got before one can send a parcel to you. In fact apparently you have to get a special Act of Parliament to sneeze in these days.

And now for my news. May & I are going to be married. When – depends on circumstances as I have got to find a job of some sort, & things dont seem very promising at present. Building has been stopped during the war & will not start again for some months to any extent.

I have ideas of starting contracting on my own account, or getting some sort of share in an existing business, the difficulty of course being the amount of capital required added to the fact that I am out of touch with things a good deal. In the meantime I am in the Army & it may take some time before I am allowed to leave.

Yours

David

---

56 Ramsden Road
Balham
London S.W.
Dec. 24th 1918

Dear Ginger,

I am home again, as of course you know by this time by the cablegram & naturally awfully glad to get home too.

We had a tremendous reception on landing, which was all the more wonderful seeing that of course we were not the first prisoners to get home by some thousands. It staked in Holland, (we came via Rotterdam) as soon as we crossed the border there was a continuous string small children & people along the railway & all tinkling tin bells & yelling as the train passed. Our boat anchored of the mouth of the Humber at night & at daybreak the next morning we moved up the river accompanied of the hooting & screeching of sirens. Every boat, small & large, began to bellow & screech as we passed even those that were moored permanently seemed to get up sufficient steam to scream for our benefit & they were all flying the signal "Welcome Home"

K.R.R.C.
3.

56 Ramsden Road
Balham S.W.12

Jan 2nd 1919

Sir,

Will you kindly send me the necessary forms for a claim for indemnification for loss viz:-
Army Form O.1784 in duplicate

Yours faithfully,
2/Lt D. H. Taylor

The Secretary.
War Office

Replacement of Revolver, Field Glasses, Saddlery, Compass or Blankets

Army Form O. 1784.

Claim for ~~Indemnification~~ Officers.

RETURN of Baggage, Camp equipage, or Horse Equipment lost on Service by

(rank)_____ (name)_____ (unit)_____

on (date)_____ at (place)_____

_____ under the following circumstances (give full details)

Total amount ... £					

The foregoing is a true and correct statement of my loss on the occasion referred to; and I hereby certify, upon my honour, that the actual cost of each article, and its true value at the time of loss are correctly stated according to the best of my judgment and belief; that I was not at the time deviating in any respect from the Orders of the General or other Officer Commanding; that I have neither received nor applied for indemnification on account of the above loss through any other channel than that in which the present claim is submitted, that indemnification is not obtainable from any other source, and that I have re-equipped myself for service with the articles in respect of which this claim is made.

(To be signed by the Officer making this claim)_____ Date_____

I hereby certify, that I have particularly examined and enquired into the facts and circumstances of the before-mentioned loss, and that I have every reason to believe the same to be correctly and justly stated

[P.T.O.

Adjutant,
5th Bn. K.R.R. Corps

Passed. This Officer is not on the strength of this Battalion.

J. Giddins

Sheerness,   Lieut.
10th Jan. 1919   A/Adjutant 6th Bn. KRRC

Lt D. H. Taylor
5b Ramsden Rd
Balham S.W. 12

Herewith 2
blank O.1784 as requested
The 6th KRRC is now disbanded.

A. L. Stokes 4/

Sheerness
12.1.19

Adjt
KRRC

To 2/Lieut. D. H. Taylor.
K.R.R.C.

Forwarded with the compliments of the Secretary of the War Office with reference to your letter dated January 2nd 1919. Your claim should be submitted to the General Officer Commanding in Chief, Eastern Command; 50, Pall Mall. S.W.1.

H.B. War Office

January 10th 1919

Army Form O. 1784.

Claim for Indemnification—Officers.

RETURN of Baggage, Camp equipage, or Horse Equipment lost on Service by (rank)_____ (name)_____ (unit)_____ on (date)_____ at (place)_____ _____ under the following circumstances (give full details)

1 Articles separately detailed for the loss of which compensation is claimed	2 Actual cost of each article	3 Actual value at the time of loss see Allowance Regulations, para. 554 (b)	4 Date of original purchase	5 Remarks
	£ s. d.	£ s. d.		
Total amount ... £				

The foregoing is a true and correct statement of my loss on the occasion referred to; and I hereby certify, upon my honour, that the actual cost of each article, and its true value at the time of loss are correctly stated according to the best

Instructions to Claimant.

1. This claim must be made out in duplicate *in your own handwriting*, and countersigned by the officer under whose command you are serving at the time of making this claim.

2. The particulars required overleaf must be carefully completed; receipted bills showing the original cost of the *lost* articles and date of purchase should be attached in support of claim, and in cases where abnormal charges are made will invariably be required as a condition of payment. Indemnification is only admissible in respect of the actual value of the lost articles at the time of loss (*see* para. 554, Allowance Regulations).

3. In stating the circumstances in which the loss took place it must be made clear on what service you were engaged, *especially when the loss occured in transit.*

4. You should not claim for more articles than you require in order to carry out the duties for which you are medically fit—see certificate below, which must be signed. Indemnification is only granted after re-equipment has become necessary, and *has been effected.* No compensation is admissible in respect of articles not included in the scale laid down or in excess of the number therein.

5. In case of losses in transit, articles not known to have been irretrievably lost should be so indicated, and a *full* statement of the efforts you have made to trace them should be given, together with any documentary evidence you may have from the unit with which you were serving, and a certificate from Messrs. Cox showing that they have no trace of the articles.

6. Claims for *revolvers, field glasses, compasses* and *blankets* should be submitted on a separate Army Form O. 1784 (the certificate of re-equipment being struck out), with a view to replacement from store, if admissible.

Certificates.

The following certificate to be signed by the claimant in all cases:—

I certify that I was passed on (date)   as fit for* { general / home / light duty } service, which necessitates reprovision of the articles for which indemnification is claimed.

*Cross out two of these.

Signature_____

The following additional certificate to be signed in cases where articles lost in transit are not known to be irretrievably lost:—

If any of the kit for which I am claiming is eventually recovered, I agree to accept (or refund if actually paid) half the amount which would have been admissible if the kit had never been found, or to return the recovered articles for which compensation has been paid to the nearest **Command Salvage Depot.**

David to May   Sheerness   [14th] Feb 1919 Friday

Darling,

I got here with very little trouble & so far have been fortunate.

First of all I went to report myself & while talking to the Adjutant (I could not see the Colonel) I asked him to get the Z15 form signed.

When I said this, another fellow in the room asked what I was & on my saying an Architect & Surveyor he replied that there was no need to fill in the form, but that he could fix things up for me. He turned out to be the demobilisation officer & took me along to his office & put me down on the list straight away.

The only thing that might upset things he said, was the fact that I did not join the Artists until February 1916 but he said he thought the fact that I was in the OTC in 1915 would put things right. He also said that if things went well I should get out in a week, that is if the Colonel gives his sanction, & this is quite possible, as there are more officers here than they know what to do with.

After that I went to look for a billet. I was given a list of six names & went to all the lot before I found one that could take me. However having got it I think it will be alright. I have a large room & a large bed with a sofa, arm chair etc etc, the only thing wanting is you.

But really I wouldn't care for you to stay here – Sheerness isn't nearly good enough for you.

I had to hang about for about an hour before seeing the Adjutant & walked along the sea wall to kill time.

There was a sea fog on & you couldn't see more than a quarter of a mile out so that it didn't look brilliant at all.

As far as I can tell there is not much doing here in the way of work.

There seemed to be nobody about this afternoon & everybody apparently had gone to a football match.

Having gone to all the trouble of brining my bed down here together with my valise of course I don't need it now, but you never can tell in the Army.

Everything is altered here, there are so many officers that they haven't room in the barracks & so have to put us into billets (which of course I infinitely prefer) & even the mess isn't large enough so we subalterns & such like small fry have a separate mess in what used to be a YMCA hut, but I like it better, as it is freer, there being no senior officers here to stand aside for.

I am scoring rather over my billet, for when I asked how much the room was to be, I was told 10/6 a week & as I shall get an allowance of 21/- I feel I have at last got something out of the Army & feel quite an old soldier.

Tomorrow I have to go to see the doctor.

I have been missing my ring all day.

You wont get this by the first post tomorrow as the last post leaves here at 7 o'clock & I could not catch it, but I know you wont mind.

Goodbye, just off to bed.

David

David to May   Sheerness   Saturday [15th] Feb 1919

Darling,

This morning I went & saw the doctor & that is the total amount of my day's work. Seem to be earning my money, don't I?

He said my heart was strained a little, but that was nothing very serious.

Just before going into breakfast I thought I would look at the letters in case there was one for me, & then I had a lovely surprise, because I really didn't expect one from you until tomorrow. You are a dear.

So Maud has been chattering again. I wonder if she described the ceremony in full, what you were dressed in, the presents & who were at the church etc etc.

She is a busybody if ever there was one.

From what I can hear I am attached to a Company having a crowd of officers & no men, with the consequence that there is nothing for us to do. I understand though, that some men are coming back on Monday so I suppose we may have something to do then, but it will only be in the mornings as nobody does anything in the afternoons.

This afternoon by way of "earning" some more money I studied "Allowance Regulations" to see what allowances I can claim but didn't find out very much.

Last night after posting your letter I ran into the demobilisation officer again & he told me that he had put in my name to headquarters here & so far it had gone alright, & now the latest news (I think it is in the papers, but I haven't seen it myself) is that no more officers are to be demobilised until further orders, in order to see how many are required for the army of occupation.

Its been a fine day here all day & I went for a walk along the sea front this morning after seeing the doctor, but I did want you, & the only thing I could do was to sit down & read your letter again.

Goodbye, I am waiting for your letter tomorrow now.

David

David to May   Sheerness   Sunday [16th] Feb 1919

Darling,

Got up a bit early this morning in order to get your letter sooner. Of course I was later than yesterday, but I mean early for Sunday.

It wasn't foggy here yesterday except at sea, but otherwise it was quite fine. I wish you had been here with me, except that this would be a wretched place for you to be in. Hope you didn't get delayed by that train smash. I'm glad Mrs Muggridge's cold is rather better. I hope she'll be rid of it quickly.

I like Maud's impudence in "demanding" to know why she was first to go. Apparently she is not only ungrateful for all you have done for her, but seems to imagine that you have done her some injury. I like to tell her what I think of her.

Of course I have earned my salary again today but doing nothing. There was only church parade this morning & as my Company has no men, we did not have to appear so after breakfast I went for a walk along the sea front. It's not a very pleasant day, misty & inclined to rain, so I didn't go far & came back in order to start my letter to you. I will add some more before I post it.

With your letter came one from Webber the Martyr (I enclose a copy of it & also one of my reply – I am keeping his original in case I have to write again).

The answering or advertisements which he refers to I imagine to be the Romford one, which you remember I mentioned to Pitt, & which Pitt has evidently told him about.

However he has effectively got me out of the difficulty of going back to him.

I have not yet needed the letter I am asking him for & possibly may not, but I may as well get it from him in case I do, as there is a notice down here, that officers having offers of employment in writing, should submit them to the demobilisation officer – I suppose in order to assist in case ones other qualifications are not sufficient. However I have not been asked for such a letter yet.

This afternoon I have been writing letters all the afternoon. I have written to Ethel in reply to her letter that I got the other day & I have also written to the T Square Lodge, sending on my subscription & telling them I want to remain on the non-dining members list for the present. I don't think it is worth while paying the full subscription while we are in this unsettled state & I can always transfer to the town members list when I want to.

It has been pouring with rain here the whole afternoon so it is just as well I had letters to write.

The post goes out at 5.30 today so I had better stop.

This morning I woke up before 7 & from that time until I got up we were very close to each other, but the imagining is not a bit like the real thing is it?

Goodbye

David.

The following information is required to support claims for allowances for an officer on sick leave from an Ex. Force:-

1. With which Ex. Force were you serving (British in France, Egyptian, Mesopotamian, Indian etc)? — *British in France*

2. Were you actually invalided home or did you proceed on ordinary leave? — *Leave granted as Prisoner of War.*

3. Is this the first occasion on which you have been invalided from an Ex. Force; if not give date of previous occasion. — —

4. When did you arrive in England? — *Dec. 14th 1918*

5. Have you been in hospital in England? Please state name, periods, and date of discharge — —

6. Have you been passed fit yet? If so render a copy of Battn. Orders showing date of joining for duty — *Joined for duty Feb. 14th 1919.*

7. Are you, or have you been in receipt of pay under Indian Regulations? — *No.*

Certified that during the period of the attached claim I was not maintained (a) in a military hospital (b) in a civil hospital administered as a (temporary) Military Hospital or (c) in a civil hospital to which payment is made from army funds that public quarters were not retained and that Lodging Allowance was not drawn under paras. 276, 285 and 286 Allowance Regulations and that I am not in receipt of pay at Indian Rates.

(Signature) *D. H. Taylor.*

Date: *Feb. 17th 1919.*

David to May   Sheerness   Monday [17th] Feb 1919

My Darling,

Another fearfully busy day. I went down this morning to see if there were anything to be done & was told that there was nothing, & would not be until tomorrow. I then went back to the mess & was told that an order had come that there was to be a lecture at the local cinema & that all officers were to go. This at 10.45. So naturally I went. The men had been marched there too. We waited some minutes & then they started showing us some pictures. The usual type of thing, the first was a wild west "comedy" with lots of cowboys racing on horses & showing of pistols etc etc.

Then the lights went up & there was a pause & the men began yelling for more. So they put on a film of recent events, which showed the King opening Parliament. This wasn't at all bad. Another pause, & more yelling from the men. They put on another "comedy" representing a drunken husband coming home in the early hours & his wife getting out of bed & shaking him. However they hadn't got far with this one, when the General turned up & introduced Sir Francis Younghusband who gave us a lecture on some of his experiences with the army on the Indian Frontier & also doing exploration work there. It was rather interesting & he had some very good slides showing the country, chiefly pictures of mountains of course.

Apparently some years ago the Russians had sent an officer to one of the tribes up there, with the idea of winning them over & also of finding a way across the mountains that Russian troops could cross into India. Younghusband was sent with 6 men to get there before him & do the same job. He found a possible road that might be used by the Russians & did not succeed in winning over the native chief & two years later they sent an expedition up there & cleared out the chief & put his brother in his place. Since then we have built roads & now the tribe is under our protection. He met the Russian officer while there, who calmly told him that all the Russians knew that they were going to invade India some time & all were anxious to do it.

Otherwise they were perfectly friendly.

Before today I hadn't met anyone that I knew. Today I ran in to two separate men within two minutes. Of the four of us who went to France together, two have been killed, one fairly early on & the other in the March push, the third is the man I met this afternoon.

He apparently went into hospital with some internal trouble & had an operation & has been home ever since. For the time being he is staying in the army & has a regular job here. He has been in Sheerness since last November & has his wife here.

The other man I met was at Holzminden & went to Holland about last April. He only came down here yesterday & also has his wife & kiddie here. As he is an old regular, promoted from the ranks, I think he will probably stop on too.

I haven't heard anything more yet about my demobilisation.

This afternoon, or part of it, I spent in filling up forms claiming various allowances in all amounting to something over £50. Of course I don't expect to get it, but still it may come off. You never can tell.

Its been a glorious afternoon, pouring with rain & a sea fog thrown in & a constant wailing coming over the sea from some lightship or buoy. I don't think we'll have our honeymoon in Sheerness.

After posting this I think I'll go back to my billet & drown my sorrows in a 7 novel.

I haven't yet written to Jean as you asked me to. I forgot it, but I will do so.

I want to be hugged awfully badly & hard.

Goodbye

David

PS I do hope you are not slaving away late in the evening & fagging yourself entirely.

Dave to May   Sheerness   Wed [19th] Feb 1919

My Darling,

I do hope you didn't get wet yesterday or caught cold. I am very glad the back work is better & that there is a possibility of getting level with it this week. I wish you hadn't to stay late. Never mind you won't next week, as I shall probably be there to stop you.

I suppose I ought to write to Ethel Barnett to thank for her offer to send me books, I believe I did from Germany didn't I?

Dont you think you manage me quite well enough as it is without anyone giving you hints, & in any case I don't think you would have cared to have taken hints from the lady on the film.

You have done it now. I have got "Theres a Land" on the brain. I expect when we are married you will wake up to find me asleep, but gently humming "Until" or some such thing into your ear.

If I can get back to London from Surbiton in time on Friday I may be able to meet you. I don't quite know yet what train I am to catch, or how long I am likely to be at Surbiton, but if I can manage to come along to you I will telephone first.

So far there doesn't seem to be any hitch in the leave arrangements here. Nearly everyone has gone except one or two, who like myself, have been kept back to do certain jobs & they are going when these jobs are done.

With regard to Saturday. I shall if possible catch the 9.35 which gets to London Bridge at 12.8, when I will come straight to you at the office & send my card up. Failing this I will catch the 10.20 getting to Holborn at 1.37 & I will then go to Slaters in Poultry where we usually go. Of course if they suddenly stop my leave I will wire to you.

In any case you will go to Balham this weekend won't you? I have written to Mum telling her I shall most likely be home, so she will expect you too, as I told her you would most likely come.

Today I think I have done more work than I have since I have been here. It amounts to nothing of course. I have only taken three parties of boys to school. Certainly I had to walk about a mile each time as they are in huts about $\frac{1}{2}$ mile away from the mess but still it does seem a lot of nonsense.

Last night they turned the search lights on all along the front. They have them every few hundred yards or so, so you may guess they make things pretty brilliant.

While I have been here the man at Holzminden – Lucas – offered to buy my valise when I got demobilised. Do you want to keep my camp bed & sleeping bag, or shall I sell the whole lot?

Later

This afternoon I took 30 or 40 men for a route march – a gentle walk for an hour. I am beginning to feel quite hard worked.

By the way Lucas invited me to go to tea on Sunday, but of course I told him I hoped to get away on leave.

The days wont go quickly enough. Never mind in two days now I ought to be with you. Goodbye Dear.

David

> Command Pay Office,
> Southern Command,
> SALISBURY.
> 4/3/1919.
>
> TO: 2/Lt D H Taylor
> 5th K.R.R.C.
>
> Your Lodging Claim for period 15/2 - 13/2 Sheerness is returned herewith. It is regretted that there is no Regulation which entitles an Officer Repatriated Prisoner of War to this Allce., unless the claim is accompanied by War Office Leave Certificate shewing that Leave was recommended on Medical Grounds.
>
> [signature] Actg., Paymr.,
> for Command Paymaster, Southern Command.

Dave to May   Sheerness   Wednesday [5th] March 1919

My Darling,

I am here & everything is upside down. The battalion is going to Cannock Chase tomorrow morning, but I am remaining here, together with a number of other officers.

I have found out that they have started demobilisation of officers again & six are going off tomorrow, so "the country looks better" as you said it would & I am beginning to hope again.

I am back in my old billet & got down here & did everything quite comfortably.

As all the men & everyone are going tomorrow it almost looks as though those of us who are left behind will have still less to do, but I cannot tell yet.

We are turned out of our hut as a mess & are all together, at the old place, a tremendous crowd, but I suppose there wont be so many tomorrow.

No time for any more as the post is going.

Goodbye, Darling. Give me one more.

David

David to May   Sheerness   Thursday [6th] March 1919

My Darling,

I got your letter this morning, you do write nice letters & just when I want them.

I am very sorry you have several girls away, as I know that means harder work for you.

Muriel does seem to be having a bad time doesn't she?

Today I have done nothing, that is to say in the way of work.

I got up, had breakfast & then walked along the front, found a quiet spot & then read your letter again & began to dream dreams of what we might do if.... After a time I woke up to the fact that I was cold & so walked on again until I came to what seemed the end of all things or rather I ended up in some fields which were under water & too wet to walk across so I came back.

The battalion in the meantime had gone off to Rugeley. I did not go to see them off as a good many did, as I am not interested in anyone in it.

I had to report to Headquarters at 12 o'clock but it was only to give in my name, what class I was in & whether I had volunteered for the Army of occupation. That consists of my days work.

I cannot get any sort of information as to what is happening with regard to the demobilisation business, or if I am likely to get away, or when.

While at Headquarters we had to give our names in to move out of our billets into the barracks, but I did not rush forward so that they filled all the rooms up before my turn came, so I am still in my billet which of course I prefer.

I have had a letter from Jones saying he will do what he can for me at Swansea.

I have also had one of my claims back stating that it cannot be allowed, as there is no regulation permitting it. It was for £6 for lodging money while I was on leave. I wonder if the other claim will go through.

Its a splendid day down here & as far as the weather goes I wish you were with me instead of being in the office at work. Sheerness would be infinitely better with you here with me.

What was it kept you awake last night? You must get as much sleep as possible. I can't have you lying awake like that.

Later

I went along this afternoon to see if I could get anything out of the demobilisation officer. He said that demobilisation has not yet started again. It stopped on Feb 15th, the day after my application went in, but he thinks it may begin again in the next few days. Apparently the men who went away today are discharged unfit & not demobilised as I thought. Isn't it sickening to be kept hanging about like this, not knowing what is going to happen. Still I suppose I am lucky in being here & not being sent off to Rugeley for at least there is a possibility of getting up to see you from here & there would be none from Rugeley.

Goodbye my Darling, I am looking forward to your letter tomorrow.

David

David to May   Sheerness   Monday [17th] March 1919

My Darling,

I got down here fairly comfortably, stopped at most stations but eventually arrived at 2.30. Went along & reported myself & then went straight to the demobilisation officer.

He said no orders had come through yet, but that they were waiting for a list of officers who had volunteered for Germany & had been approved to come from the War Office & as soon as that arrived a batch of us would be sent off that is demobilised. So Heaven knows when I shall get away now that the thing depends on the War Office.

However while I was with them I filled up four different forms, which presumably have to go with me, so that now I am all ready to go at a moments notice, at least, I hope I am.

There is also a list in the mess for officers who wish to be demobilised immediately orders come along, so of course I have put my name down on it.

So having done as much as that, I suppose I must now possess my soul with patience but it takes a big effort.

I am in a billet again, not my old one as the room was taken, so I had to look for another. This time I have a bedroom & a small sitting room opening off it.

It goes by the grand name of Sea View Terrace, the name being given to it because the back windows look upon the sea wall & over the sea wall is of course the sea.

However I am not satisfied with the place as it is not as clean as it might be, so I hope I shall not be here very long.

Later

I have just had tea & while there I got talking to another man who says that the Garrison Artillery here have restarted demobilising their officers today. So this certainly looks rather more hopeful, as of course we are in the same command & they may get round to us shortly. Let's hope so.

At tea I met a man who was captured with me & who I have not seen since. He looks pretty queer having been down with "flu" & only just got back from his leave after Germany.

Of course there is nothing to do down here & I believe several fellows went away on leave again today, so of course I may be given leave again shortly, but I want to stay here a day or so at least, to see if there is any possibility of getting out.

Goodbye, Darling, I wish I could write a more cheerful letter. Looking forward to yours tomorrow.

David

David to May   Sheerness   Tuesday [18th] March 1919

My Darling,
No letter from you today. I expect you didn't get time to write yesterday or else they are playing about with your letters in the post. I did want one too.
This morning I woke up pretty early & then lay & tried to imagine you were with me, but it couldn't be done. I wanted you yourself too badly for that.
If nothing happens between now & say Friday I think I shall try to get leave for the weekend, or I may possibly try Thursday but I will let you know.
I rather misjudged my billet yesterday. When I first looked at the bed the sheets looked dirty, but when I went back after dinner they had been changed & clean ones put on so that was alright. Also there was a fire burning which made things rather more comfortable & this morning the landlady brought me a cup of tea.
There is no news of course of demobilisation starting again. Everybody is waiting, doing nothing, & saying it may start at any moment, but the moment doesn't come. I suppose it will in the course of time.
Later
I have just been told that I have to take a party of men to Surbiton tomorrow (Wednesday) so I will run along & see you as I did last time. I will telephone to you sometime in the afternoon. This afternoon I went back to the billet & read up Fowey & dreamed dreams of what we will do when we are there. Dont you wish we were there now?
Goodbye, Dear, until tomorrow.

David

David to May   Sheerness   Thursday [20th] March 1919

My Darling,

I got back here just before 10 o'clock last night, looked in to the mess to see the orders for today, which practically consisted of nothing, & then went along to the billet.

Just after I got in, the landlady brought me up a cup of cocoa, so I sat down & ate your orange, (it was a beauty) & drank the cocoa, having quite a small feast.

Then I read your two letters through again, got into bed, cuddled you up close as I could & was soon asleep.

I have been thinking, - if the loyal & trusty railwaymen should strike again, I do hope you won't work late next week & also I should not go to Days, as you may have a big job to get home & the earlier you start for home the better. Better still I should go to Balham if you think you stand a better chance of getting there & take Ethel along there too.

In consequence of that crowd of officers being sent to Rugeley I have had orders to give up my billet & go into barracks, as of course there are a number of empty rooms there now. However the room is not so bad, might be a good deal worse.

If the railway people strike, of course there will be no leave & it was useless asking today as they don't know is likely to happen & headquarters here have been told to hold themselves in readiness in case of trouble. But seeing that there are only about one man & a boy here I don't see that we can do much.

However they will perhaps send a few men to the station although that wont be necessary as there are scarcely any railwaymen here.

In consequence of all this we were treated this morning to a lecture by the commanding officer on what we may do & what we may not do.

It seems to me that we are allowed to do anything we like, but if we do do anything at all, we get a court martial directly after.

We were told that we of course had to obey orders but if we did & things went wrong we of course would get hung etc etc etc.

Anyway what is most important of all is that it is going to stop my weekend as those officers who went away on leave during the week have been recalled.

This afternoon I took up my quarters in the barracks & spent partly in reading the guide book (this time Falmouth) & partly in sleeping.

Last night at Victoria I waved to you & thought you waved back & then I watched you until you got as far as the bookstall but I lost you then.

I have read both those lectures. Mr Robertsons is most interesting. I will return them when I see you so will you remind me.

Goodbye, Darling, give me a good big hug & now one more kiss. Thanks that's lovely.

David

David to May   Sheerness   Friday [21st] March 1919

My Darling,

There is no prospect of getting weekend leave as you have probably guessed by this time. However if nothing happens to prevent me I shall try to come up on Sunday & will come on to Beckenham in that case. Of course as usual I shall not know definitely until Sunday morning, so I cannot let you know in time.

If I do come I ought to get to Beckenham about one o'clock.

I do not think your guide book description of Sheerness describes the place really well. I could give it quite a number of much more expressive adjectives. By the way one name for it down here is Sheernastyness.

The latest tale down here is that we are all going to Rugeley some time next week but which day nobody knows. Lovely prospect isn't it?

Sheerness may be all sorts of things, but I imagine Rugeley is worse, at any rate I shall not be able to run up to see you which at present I can always look forward to.

Last night I went to bed fairly early as I have got a cold in my head & it has given me a headache. I slept pretty well except for waking up once or twice for a short time, but I did want you there really. I am alright today.

The commanding officer has just been into the mess & says he expects that the list of officers for the Army of Occupation will be here in a day or so, when those who are being demobilised will be allowed to go off. This sounds hopeful, but then this sort of thing has been said ever since they stopped it.

This afternoon having nothing to do as usual I sat in front of the fire & read "The Canon in Residence". I have got about two thirds of the way through it.

Its awfully cold down here & it was as much as I could do to keep warm, the fire being a very small one & the room a large one. However after a time I managed to get a good fire going, but one has to go carefully as the coal supplied is very limited & we are not allowed fires in our quarters until the afternoon.

Be careful with yourself & don't catch cold & don't work too hard.

Somehow or other in spite of the Rugeley rumour I have felt much less humpy today & have had a sort of feeling that I shall get some good news shortly. I do hope so, don't you?

Wont it be lovely to have you all to myself for a whole month & ever afterwards. I am longing & longing for the time to come. Goodbye, Dear, hope to see you on Sunday. I want another now. Thats lovely.

David

David to May   Sheerness   Monday [24th] March 1919

My Darling,

Its was a false alarm, or at least a semi false alarm. I got down here at 11.15 & went straight along to the Adjutant & asked him if there were any further news of getting away. He said "No, but the Brigade Major says we shall hear on Tuesday or Wednesday". So its the old old tale again. It seems that the Brigade Major came in on Saturday & said that the details had come through, but of course he was doing this unofficially, so of course it will take some time to get the thing through officially. I am awfully sorry that I came up with a tale like that and stirred you up for nothing, but you never can be in the least bit certain of anything in the army as you know. Still I am hoping & hoping for Tuesday or Wednesday now. I am afraid I said a lot of wicked words when I heard that the thing hadn't started & my only consolation was your letter which was waiting for me. You are a darling to write little bits to me like that all through the day, it makes me feel as though I am with you.

I wrote to Headquarters at Rugeley last night, asking them to put my name in for promotion. Hope it goes through alright as it will mean a little extra money for us.

That reminds me there is no further talk of us moving to Rugeley yet, apparently they wired here & said they had no accommodation for us, so thats some comfort.

Later

I have heard no further news this afternoon. This afternoon I went back to my room in the barracks, sat in front of the fire (& read that booklet on Falmouth at least I read a bit of it & fell asleep in the middle of it).

Before this I had started off for a walk, but is was so cold & blowing a gale that I turned back. It seems that it was just as well that we needed this week out of our reckoning, but Oh I do hope it will next week as we arranged.

Goodbye, perhaps I shall see you o Wednesday or before. Kiss me.

David.

my dearest

David to May   Sheerness   Tuesday [25th] March 1919

My Darling,

There is no further news yet, so I suppose we shall hear nothing again today. Isnt it maddening to have to wait around like this, while the set of idiots who have this thing in hand fool about day after day. I suppose they will start the thing again some day.

I got your letter this morning – you shouldn't worry about me. I am quite alright & my cold is much better.

I am glad you told Lutt that you might be going next week, it is just as well to let him know in case I do get out by any chance, & I still have hopes of it.

How is your job getting on? I do hope you are not working too hard & fagging yourself too much, as it will not help your indigestion a little bit. How are you now, have you been able to sleep at night & is the indigestion any better? You dont say anything about it in your letter.

I suppose you went to Days last night. I wanted to be there with you.

This morning after breakfast I went for a walk of about 6 or 7 miles viewing the lovely & picturesque scenery of the delightful Isle of Sheppey (the wording is the result of the Falmouth guide book) by way of killing a little time & removing a little of the impatience & hump.

Its a fine day but awfully windy, too windy to make walking pleasant & very dusty too. However it was better than sticking in Sheerness, or lounging about doing nothing in the mess.

I see that the strikes seem likely to be settled which is rather good, as it wont interfere with us if we do happen to get away next week.

Later

Nothing has happened during the day.

This afternoon I sat in front of the fire in my room dozing & day dreaming & wishing you were with me, as I always do as soon as I am alone.

Now I am going back to read "The Canon in Residence". Goodbye, Darling, I hope to have better news tomorrow.

David

David to May   Sheerness   Wednesday [26th] March 1919

My Darling,

Wednesday & still nothing more is heard of demobilisation. I do wonder how much longer they are going to hang about.

So you couldn't get Days to promise you your dress by Saturday. They seem to be taking their time over it. They have had it three weeks haven't they?

Is April the second the day that your big job has to be finished that Lutt is so keen for you to stay until then. That brings us up to Thursday. I do hope its no later than that don't you Darling, that is of course, always supposing I am out of the army & at present I can get no sort of hint as to anything doing in that line at all. I hardly know how to contain myself, sitting about down here & hearing nothing as to it getting any nearer.

So Maud has got a job & as you say is in heaven, at a small salary – very small I expect, but still, I suppose as she likes it its alright. As you say, she will be in her element to have the affairs of the parish under her thumb. She is funny in the way that she thinks people in business are desperately interested in her affairs.

This morning having nothing to do of course, I went for my usual walk & bought a book on the way "The Children of the Forest" by Marryat.

I have finished "The Canon in Residence" and think it quite good and as it isn't possible to get anything to read down here, I was forced to buy another book for myself.

I am down to be orderly officer tomorrow, so that should leave me clear for the weekend if I am still here.

I shall of course try to get leave for the weekend and if I can't shall come up on Sunday. May it not be necessary and may I be there for good.

Again you say nothing about yourself or how you are. Have you been able to sleep decently or only for a while each night.

6.30

I have just seen the demobilisation officer who told me that the details had gone to Rugeley, so they ought to send them back here soon, so I might get out this week after all.

A glean of hope as the papers would say about the strikes.

I have been for a walk this afternoon with a fellow who was at Holzminden with me and who gave me quite a lot of food when I was first there and had nothing. He has been in Holland and is only just back from his 2 months leave.

Now don't get working too hard and knock yourself up.

Goodbye Darling.

David

David to May   Sheerness   Thursday [27th] March 1919

My Darling,

I really have good news today.

Last night those details came through & naturally I thought I should be off to you today & went so far as to get my kit packed up & sent to the station.

Then I trotted off to get my papers, as I thought, from the demobilisation officer, but he said that everything was ready for us to go but he had to apply for vacancies at the dispersal camps.

He said that he ought to get these permits today & then we should go tomorrow or Saturday but that nothing was certain. I could have told him that, having a considerable amount of experience.

Still this has brought things very much nearer & I really think I shall get away this time, then it means going to the Crystal Palace. I don't know what they do there, whether they search up records or not or what, but according to the fellows down here the procedure can be got through in under an hour provided there is no crowd.

Isn't it lovely, Darling, I feel like doing back somersaults & kissing my hand to the C.O.

I am orderly officer today & early this morning I went to see the mens breakfasts which of course were alright.

At 10 o'clock I mounted the new guard.

It was a funny sort of guard, half the men having only just been discharged from hospital & their kit being at Rugeley they were not exactly all they should have been, but still what did that matter, if they had stood on their heads & waved their feet at me I should have looked the other way.

As it was I felt like doing a Highland Fling for their benefit, but restrained myself, in case they thought it somewhat out of the ordinary & not knowing the cause would of course misunderstand.

For goodness sake don't work too hard. I am awfully glad your indigestion has gone but do take care of yourself.

I am rather amused at your Aunt's visit, those poor kiddies must have a life of it.

However Georgie got one back at her over his gloves.

Later

So far I have heard nothing further as to going tomorrow.

My name with a list of others (there are 12 in all) has been put up in the mess to hold themselves in readiness for early demobilisation.

When tomorrow's orders are published this evening they may say that we are to go tomorrow, but of course they may never come round in time for me to let you know.

Of course if I do come up tomorrow I will either wire or telephone to you.

Goodbye, Darling,

David

From 2/Lieut D H Taylor.　　56 Ramsden Rd
　　　　5th K.R.R.C.　　　　　Balham
To.
　Command Paymaster　　　June 14th. 1919.
　　Southern Command
　　　Salisbury
　　Sir,
　　　On Feb 17th last I forwarded from Sheerness a claim for ration allowance covering the period 12/7/17 to 13/2/19

　　　As I have heard nothing further of this I shall be pleased if you will let me know if this has gone forward for payment.
　　　　　I am Sir,
　　　　　Yr obed Ser.
　　　　　D H Taylor.

W9572—GD1960 11,000 2/19 HWV(P896)   H8064

> Any further communication on this subject should be addressed to—
> The Secretary,
>   War Office,
>   London, S.W.1,
> and the above number quoted.

WAR OFFICE,

LONDON, S.W.1.

27 June 1919.

162661/4 A.G.3(P.W.)

The Secretary of the War Office presents his compliments to 2nd Lieutenant D. H. Taylor,

The King's Royal Rifle Corps.

and begs to state that he is commanded by the Army Council to inform him that his statement regarding the circumstances of his capture by the enemy having been investigated, the Council considers that no blame attaches to him in the matter.

The investigation was carried out by a Standing Committee of Enquiry composed as follows:—

Major-General L. A. E. PRICE-DAVIES, V.C., C.M.G., D.S.O.

Brigadier-General C. R. J. GRIFFITH, C.B., C.M.G., D.S.O.

Brevet-Lieut.-Col. E. L. CHALLENOR, C.B., C.M.G., D.S.O.

G.M.P. CIRCULAR NO: 5.   C.P.E. 2/3035 Indem.
                                                  C.R.E.C. 7/12847

Rank & Name. 2/Lieut D.F. Taylor, 2 KRRC.
Unit & Address. 56 Ramsden Rd, Balham, SW.12.

With reference to your claim for indemnification which was submitted to the Major General i/c Administration, Eastern Command, for consideration, the sum of £ 10:15:3 has been disallowed on grounds of inadmissibility and inadequate depreciation, vide paragraph 554 Allowance Regulations and Army Council Instruction 292 of 1918.

The sum of £ 9:8:— has been sent to your Agents for credit to your account.

                                                    for Colonel.
                                                    Command Paymaster.
                                                    Eastern Command.

Exhibition Road, S.W.7
Date. 6-8-1919.

The Major General i/c Administration, Eastern Command, approves of the free issue from store of

if and when you are ordered Overseas.
The demand on the Army Ordnance should be supported by this Authority in original.

                                                    for Colonel
                                                    Command Paymaster
                                                    Eastern Command

Exhibition Road, S.W.7
Date: _____ 1919.

Epilogue

David and May married in April 1919. They had one child, a daughter, born May 1920. They built their house in Beckenham and lived there for the rest of their lives. The house has remained the home of their descendants.

When David died aged $92\frac{1}{2}$ the house and contents passed, by deed of family arrangement, to David's and May's granddaughter. The house is now owned by the granddaughter and great-granddaughter.

All the original documents that appear in this book were found in the Beckenham house by their granddaughter, including those that had been posted to New Jersey, USA.

The houses at 18 Manor Road, Beckenham and 56 Ramsden Road, Balham still exist.

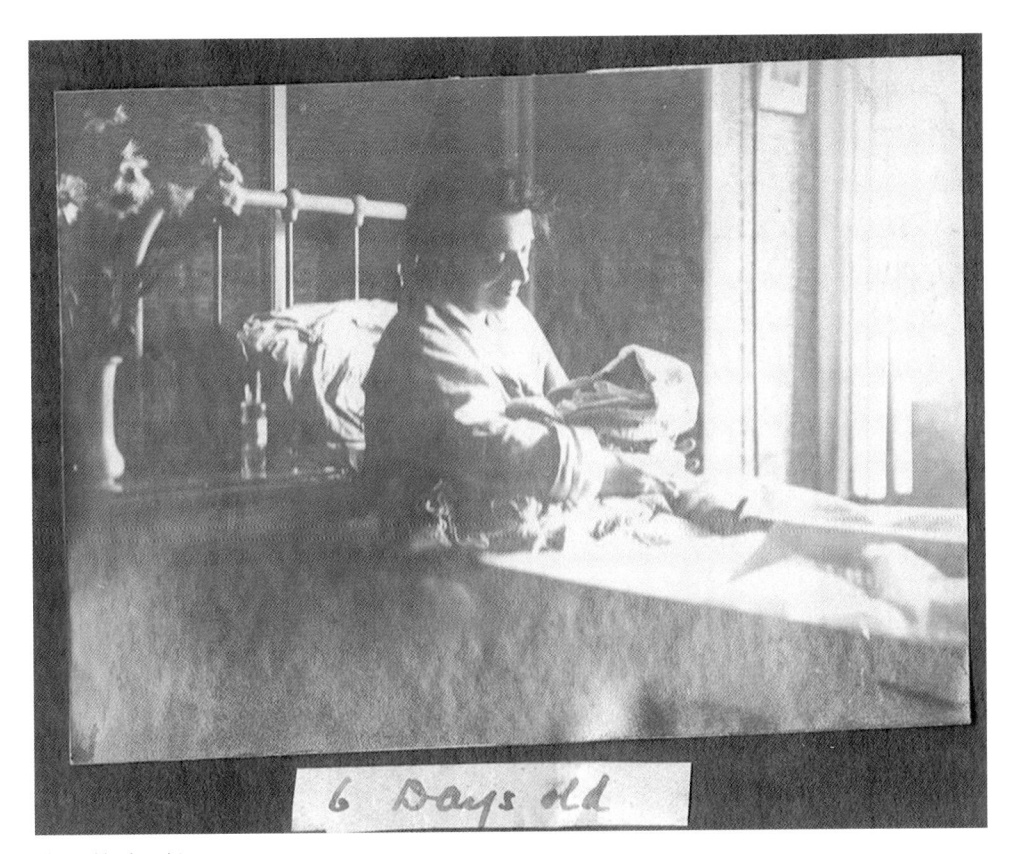

May with daughter

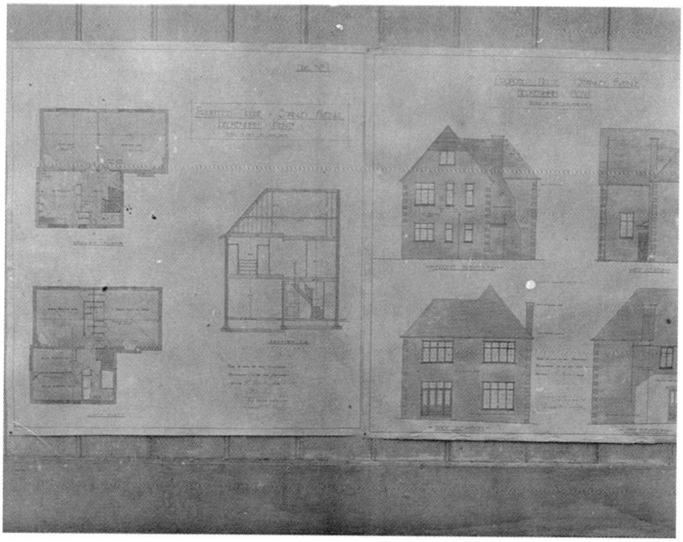

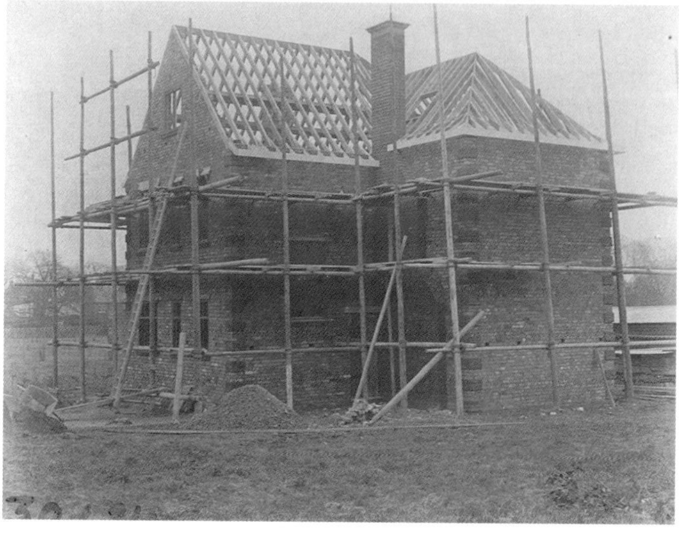

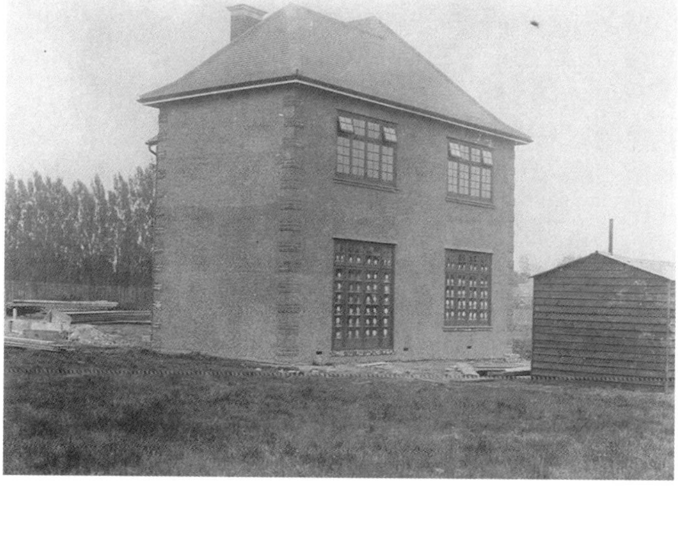